Lecture Notes in Computer Science 7162

Commenced Publication in 1973
Founding and Former Series Editors:
Gerhard Goos, Juris Hartmanis, and Jan van Leeuwen

D1725749

Edmund Clarke   Irina Virbitskaite
Andrei Voronkov (Eds.)

Perspectives of System Informatics

8th International Ershov Informatics Conference, PSI 2011
Novosibirsk, Russia, June 27 - July 1, 2011
Revised Selected Papers

 Springer

Volume Editors

Edmund Clarke
Carnegie Mellon University
5000 Forbes Avenue, Pittsburgh, PA 15213-3891 USA
E-mail: dcm@cs.cmu.edu

Irina Virbitskaite
A.P. Ershov Institute of Informatics Systems
6, Acad. Lavrentiev Ave., Novosibirsk, 630090 Russia
E-mail: virb@iis.nsk.su

Andrei Voronkov
The University of Manchester
Oxford Road
Manchester M13 9PL, UK
E-mail: andrei@voronkov.com

ISSN 0302-9743   e-ISSN 1611-3349
ISBN 978-3-642-29708-3   e-ISBN 978-3-642-29709-0
DOI 10.1007/978-3-642-29709-0
Springer Heidelberg Dordrecht London New York

Library of Congress Control Number: 2012935891

CR Subject Classification (1998): F.3, D.3, D.2, D.1, C.2

LNCS Sublibrary: SL 1 – Theoretical Computer Science and General Issues

Typesetting: Camera-ready by author, data conversion by Scientific Publishing Services, Chennai, India

Printed on acid-free paper

Springer is part of Springer Science+Business Media (www.springer.com)

Preface

PSI is a forum for academic and industrial researchers, developers and users working on topics relating to computer, software and information sciences. The conference serves to bridge the gaps between different communities whose research areas are covered by but not limited to foundations of program and system development and analysis, programming methodology and software engineering, and information technologies. Another aim of the conference is improvement of contacts and exchange of ideas between researchers from the East and the West.

The previous seven PSI conferences were held in 1991, 1996, 1999, 2001, 2003, 2006 and 2009, and proved to be significant international events. Traditionally, PSI offers a program of tutorials, invited lectures, presentations of contributed papers and workshops complemented by a social program reflecting the amazing diversity of the culture and history of Novosibirsk.

The PSI 2011 conference was dedicated to the 80th anniversary of a pioneer in theoretical and system programming research, academician Andrei Petrovich Ershov (1931–1988) and to the 100th anniversary of one of the founders of cybernetics, a member of the Soviet Academy of Sciences Aleksei Andreevich Lyapunov (1911–1973).

Aleksei Lyapunov was one of the early pioneers of computer science in Russia. He worked at the Steklov Institute of Mathematics in Moscow and Institute of Applied Mathemetics. In 1961 he moved to Novosibirsk where the Siberian Branch of the USSR Acadamy of Sciences had been founded. Initially, Aleksei Lyapunov worked at the Institute of Mathematics, then at the Institute of Hydrodynamics. He played an important role in the organization of the Physics and Mathematics School for talented children from all over Siberia, and was a professor at the Novosibirsk State University. In 1996 he posthumously received the IEEE Computer Society Computer Pioneer Award for his contribution to Soviet cybernetics and programming. There are many distinguished mathematicians among the students of Alexei Lyapunov, including Andrei Ershov.

Andrei Ershov graduated from Moscow State University in 1954. He began his scientific career under the guidance of professor Lyapunov, who was the supervisor of Andrei's PhD thesis. Andrei Ershov worked at the Institute of Precise Mechanics and Computing Machnery, and later headed the Theoretical Programming Department at the Computing Center of the USSR Academy of Sciences in Moscow. In 1958 the department was reorganized into the Institute of Mathematics of the Siberian Branch of the USSR Academy of Sciences, and by the initiative of the academician Sergei Sobolev Ershov was appointed the head of this department, which later became part of the Computing Center in Novosibirsk Akademgorodok. The first significant project of the department was aimed at developing the ALPHA system, an optimizing compiler for an extension of Algol 60 implemented on a Soviet computer M-20. Later the researchers of the department created the Algibr, Epsilon, Sigma, and Alpha-6 programming systems for the BESM-6 computers. The list of achievements also includes the first Soviet time-sharing system AIST-0, the multi-language system BETA, research projects in artificial intelligence and parallel programming, integrated tools for text processing and publishing, and many more. Andrei Ershov was a leader and participant of these projects. In 1974 he was nominated as a Distinguished Fellow of the British Computer Society. In 1981 he received the Silver Core Award for his services to IFIP. Andrei Ershov's brilliant speeches were always the focus of public attention. Especially notable was his lecture on "Aesthetic and Human Factor in Programming" presented at the AFIPS Spring Joint Computer Conference in 1972.

This edition of the conference attracted 60 submissions from 26 countries. We wish to thank all their authors for their interest in PSI 2011. Each submission was reviewed by four experts, at least three of them from the same or closely related discipline as the authors. The reviewers generally provided high-quality assessment of the papers and often gave extensive comments to the authors for the possible improvement of the contributions. As a result, the Program Committee selected 18 high-quality papers as regular talks and 10 papers as short talks for presentation at the conference. A range of hot topics in computer science and informatics was covered by a tutorial and five invited talks given by prominent computer scientists from various countries.

We are glad to express our gratitude to all the persons and organizations who contributed to the conference: the authors of all the papers for their effort in producing the material included here; the sponsors for their moral, financial and organizational support; the Steering Committee members for their coordination of the conference; the Program Committee members and the reviewers who did their best to review and select the papers; and the members of the Organizing Committee for their contribution to the success of this event and its great cultural program. Finally, we would like to mention the fruitful cooperation with Springer during the preparation of this volume.

The Program Committee work was done using the EasyChair conference management system.

November 2011

Andrei Voronkov
Irina Virbitskaite

Organization

Program Committee

Samson Abramsky	Oxford University, USA
Frederic Benhamou	Nantes Atlantic Universities, France
Leopoldo Bertossi	Carleton University, Canada
Eike Best	Universität Oldenburg, Germany
Kim Bruce	Pomona College, USA
Mikhail Bulyonkov	A.P. Ershov Institute of Informatics Systems, Russia
Gabriel Ciobanu	A.I.Cuza University, Romania
Edmund Clarke	Carnegie Mellon University, USA
Dieter Fensel	University of Innsbruck, Austria
Jean Claude Fernandez	VERIMAG/Université Joseph Fourier de Grenoble, France
Jan Friso Groote	Eindhoven University of Technology, The Netherlands
Heinrich Herre	University of Leipzig, Germany
Victor Kasyanov	A.P. Ershov Institute of Informatics Systems, Russia
Joost-Pieter Katoen	RWTH Aachen, Germany
Laura Kovacs	TU Vienna, Austria
Gregory Kucherov	LIFL/CNRS/INRIA, France
Kim Guldstrand Larsen	Aalborg University, Denmark
Johan Lilius	Åbo Akademi University, Finland
Pericles Loucopoulos	Loughborough University, UK
Andrea Maggiolo-Schettini	Università di Pisa, Italy
Klaus Meer	BTU Cottbus, Germany
Dominique Mery	LORIA, France
Hanspeter Moessenboeck	University of Linz, Austria
Torben Aegidius Mogensen	DIKU, Denmark
Peter Mosses	Swansea University, UK
Peter Mueller	ETH Zurich, Switzerland
Valery Nepomniaschy	A.P. Ershov Institute of Informatics Systems, Russia
Nikolaj Nikitchenko	National Taras Shevchenko University of Kiev, Ukraine
Jose Ramon Parama Gabia	University of A Coruna, Spain
Francesco Parisi-Presicce	Sapienza Università di Roma, Italy
Wojciech Penczek	Institute of Informatics Problems, Moscow and University of Podlasie, Russia
Peter Pepper	Technische Universität Berlin, Germany

Alexander Petrenko	Institute for System Programming, Moscow, Russia
Jaroslav Pokorny	Charles University of Prague, Czech Republic
Vladimir Polutin	Hewlett Packard Labs, Russia
Wolfgang Reisig	Humboldt-Universität zu Berlin, Germany
Donald Sannella	University of Edinburgh, UK
Klaus-Dieter Schewe	Johannes Kepler Universität, Linz, Austria
David Schmidt	Kansas State University, USA
Nikolay Shilov	A.P. Ershov Institute of Informatics Systems, Russia
Val Tannen	University of Pennsylvania, USA
Lothar Thiele	ETH Zurich, Switzerland
Mark Trakhtenbrot	Holon Institute of Technology, Israel
Irina Virbitskaite	A.P. Ershov Institute of Informatics Systems, Russia
Andrei Voronkov	University of Manchester, UK
Alexander Wolf	Imperial College London, UK
Tatyana Yakhno	DEU, Turkey
Wang Yi	Uppsala University, Sweden

Additional Reviewers

Agrigoroaiei, Oana	Höger, Christoph
Aman, Bogdan	Idrisov, Renat
Andriamiarina, Manamiary	Jacob, Marie
Anureev, Igor	Juhasz, Uri
Attiogb, Christian	Kassios, Ioannis
Bauereiß, Thomas	Keiren, Jeroen
Bochman, Alex	Knapik, Michał
Brihaye, Thomas	Kreinovich, Vladik
Ceberio, Martine	Lamarre, Philippe
Cranen, Sjoerd	Lampka, Kai
Danelutto, Marco	Lorenzen, Florian
Demin, Alexander	Lv, Mingsong
Dikovsky, Alexander	Ma, Hui
Ferrara, Pietro	Melatti, Igor
Fertin, Guillaume	Meski, Artur
Fleischhack, Hans	Mikučionis, Marius
Garanina, Natalia	Monahan, Rosemary
Gierds, Christian	Müller, Richard
Glück, Robert	Nguyen, Viet Yen
Gordeev, Dmitry	Niehren, Joachim
Gray, Robert M.	Niewiadomski, Artur
Gretz, Friedrich	Olesen, Mads Chr.
Guan, Nan	Olsen, Petur

Perathoner, Simon
Promsky, Alexey
Prüfer, Robert
Pyjov, Konstantin
Raffelsieper, Matthias
Rama, Aureliano
Rohloff, Judith
Ruskiewicz, Joseph
Schulte, Christian
Shkurko, Dmitry
Singh, Neeraj
Stasenko, Alexander
Stigge, Martin

Stoimenov, Nikolay
Stoyanovich, Julia
Szreter, Maciej
Tarasyuk, Igor
Thalhammer, Andreas
Tronci, Enrico
Von Styp, Sabrina
Wagner, Christoph
Wang, Qing
Willemse, Tim
Winkowski, Józef
Yang, Hoeseok
Zwirchmayr, Jakob

Table of Contents

Petri Net Distributability

Eike Best[1,*] and Philippe Darondeau[2]

[1] Parallel Systems, Department of Computing Science,
Carl von Ossietzky Universität Oldenburg, D-26111 Oldenburg, Germany
eike.best@informatik.uni-oldenburg.de
[2] INRIA, Centre Rennes - Bretagne Atlantique,
Campus de Beaulieu, F-35042 Rennes Cedex
Philippe.Darondeau@inria.fr

Abstract. A Petri net is distributed if, given an allocation of transitions to (geographical) locations, no two transitions at different locations share a common input place. A system is distributable if there is some distributed Petri net implementing it.

This paper addresses the question of which systems can be distributed, while respecting a given allocation. The paper states the problem formally and discusses several examples illuminating – to the best of the authors' knowledge – the current status of this work.

1 Introduction, and Historical Remarks

Petri nets [16] and related models such as process algebras [11,14,15] have frequently been used for the description and the analysis of concurrent and/or distributed systems. In this paper, we shall argue that a *concurrent system* is not necessarily also *distributed*, and may even not be *distributable* (while often, little distinction is made between these notions). More precisely, we shall raise the following question, which we consider to be important, but also slightly neglected by Petri net and related communities:

> *Can concurrency manifested in the (Petri net)* description *of some system actually be* realised *in a distributed way or not?*

To begin with, we reconsider three standard situations in Petri net theory, as shown in Figure 1. In the case of a conflict as on the left-hand side of the figure, one may ask: Can a_1 and a_2 be on two different locations A_1 and A_2? If so, information about the *start* of executing a_1 must travel in time 0 from A_1 to A_2. Otherwise, a_1 may have started to occur while a_2 can also start to occur during some small but nonzero lapse of time, contrary to the idea that a_1 and a_2 strictly exclude each other. Hence our answer is negative; we shall require transitions a_1 and a_2 to be on the *same* location, which is also the location of p.

In the case of a handshake synchronisation as in the middle of the figure, one may ask: Can p_1 and p_2 be on different locations P_1 and P_2? There seems to be no

* The first author gratefully acknowledges the support of Deutsche Forschungsgemeinschaft (DFG) under grant No 436 RUS 113/1002/01.

E. Clarke, I. Virbitskaite, and A. Voronkov (Eds.): PSI 2011, LNCS 7162, pp. 1–18, 2012.

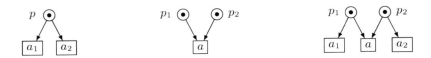

Fig. 1. Conflict, handshake, and confusion

a priori reason why such a distribution should not be possible. However, consider the handshake to be embedded in a more complex environment, such as on the right-hand side of the figure. In Petri net theory, this is called a *confusion*. In such a case, a_1 is in conflict with a, and a is in conflict with a_2. By the argument about conflicts, a_1 and a_2 are both required to be on the same location as a, that is, there can be no proper distribution of a_1, a_2 and a, and p_1, p_2 must be on the same location. (So, the answer to the question is: "it depends...".)

This phenomenon was discussed between the first author and Richard Hopkins in the context of Hoare's original paper on Communicating Sequential Processes (CSP [11]), and our Petri net based language $B(PN)^2$ [4]. In CSP, a so-called *rendezvous*

$$\underbrace{\cdots\ c_2!v\ \cdots}_{\text{Process } c_1 \text{ (sender)}} \quad \| \quad \underbrace{\cdots\ c_1?x\ \cdots}_{\text{Process } c_2 \text{ (receiver)}} \qquad\qquad c_1 : \boxed{x{:=}v} : c_2 \qquad (1)$$

was suggested, by which a sender process c_1 can send some value v into a variable x of a receiver process c_2. Sending the value v is defined to be simultaneous with receiving it in x, having the combined effect of an assignment $x{:=}v$. It is plausible that in terms of Petri nets, the rendezvous gives rise to a single two-input and two-output handshake synchronisation labelled by $x{:=}v$, as on the right-hand side of (1).

Again, c_1 and c_2 might be involved in a choice context with some local actions a_1 and a_2, such as in

$$\underbrace{(a_1 + c_2!v)}_{\text{Process } c_1} \quad \| \quad \underbrace{(c_1?x + a_2)}_{\text{Process } c_2} \qquad\qquad (2)$$

where $+$ denotes the nondeterministic choice operator. This is similar to the confused situation described earlier. Indeed, let us assume that we want to distribute c_1 and c_2 in (2) onto two different locations. Without loss of generality, assume that c_2 is the location of the assignment $x{:=}v$. What should c_1 do if it is ready for the rendezvous but c_2 is not? Should it be possible for c_1 to commit to it, thereby excluding a_1, even before c_2 is also ready to enter the rendezvous? Or should c_1 be allowed to poll the status of c_2, repeatedly testing whether it is ready, and be able to back up each time the test is found negative? These two possibilities are shown in terms of Petri nets, using so-called *silent transitions*, in Figure 2.

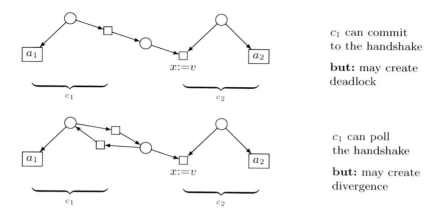

c_1 can commit
to the handshake

but: may create
deadlock

c_1 can poll
the handshake

but: may create
divergence

Fig. 2. Trying to distribute CSP's rendezvous

Both transformations are hardly acceptable, as they are stable only under the weakest possible equivalence. More precisely, the first transformation may introduce new deadlocks while the second transformation may introduce so-called *busy waiting* (also known as *divergence*). Most equivalence relations, other than language equivalence, do not tolerate one or the other, or either [10]. We know of no acceptable way of distributing the handshake in a confused circumstance. Indeed, the results of [17] seem to imply that no such distribution is possible.

The two transformations applied in Figure 2 are well-known in Petri net theory where it is customary to denote silent transitions by a label τ (see Figure 3). Either transformation can be used to show that the language of any Petri net is also the language of a free-choice Petri net. However, for the same reason as above, this insight is of rather limited helpfulness for behavioural Petri net analysis in general, i.e., when considering the effects of branching.

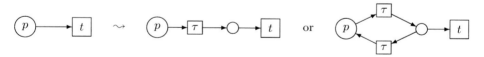

Fig. 3. Two transformations of a place-transition arc in a Petri net

A related problem surfaced in the language $B(PN)^2$ where inter-process communication can be effected by buffers of length $n \geq 0$. Buffers of length $n > 0$ correspond to first-in-first-out queues of capacity n. For reasons of uniformity, buffers of length $n = 0$ correspond to rendezvous. Obviously, bounded buffers of length > 0 can be implemented by a series of handshakes between intermediate processes, but there seems to be no direct converse implementation, for much the same reasons as before (i.e.: the unavoidability of new deadlocks or new divergences in certain contexts). Prompted by such considerations, Richard Hopkins discussed a classification of "favourable" restrictions, along with a definition of *distributability*, in [12]. Such a definition was deemed necessary in order to show formally that under certain conditions, busy waiting is avoidable.

Hopkins' definition of distributability was later re-examined and simplified by Benoît Caillaud in [1], and built into a tool SYNET [5] which is based on the theory of regions [2]. A basic implication is that if a place p resides at one location and if there is an arc from p to t, then t is necessarily required to reside at the same location as p. Tokens can thus always be seized and consumed in zero time. As a consequence, arcs from places p to transitions t (such as in Figure 3) ought to stay direct arcs and in any implementation, they are disallowed to be expanded as was done in the middle of the figure. By contrast, an arc from a transition t to a place p, as shown in Figure 4, does *not* prevent t and p to reside at different locations, since producing tokens in non-zero time does not compromise choices. As a consequence, such an arc is allowed to be prolonged indefinitely. Note that in contrast to the symmetric construction in the middle of Figure 3, adding τ-transitions as in Figure 4 does not create any new deadlocks, nor any new divergences.

Fig. 4. Prolongation of a transition-place arc in a Petri net

Based on Caillaud's notion of distributability, this paper discusses the question as to under which circumstances Petri net based transition systems are distributable and under which they are not. Our approach diverges totally from the approach taken in [8], where rules are proposed for splitting a net into distributed components that may perform joint steps (in each step, one master transition involves the synchronous firing of one or several slave transitions located in other components). Note that synchronous steps are just another form of rendezvous.

2 Coloured Petri Nets and Transition Systems

In this section the distribution problem is captured in more precise, formal terms. Let *COLOURS* be some globally defined, finite, and suitably large, set of colours.

2.1 Definitions, Intuition, and First Examples

Definition 1. COLOURED TRANSITION SYSTEMS AND PETRI NETS.

A *coloured transition system* is a 5-tuple $TS = (Q, A, \rightarrow, s_0, col)$ where Q is the set of states, A is the set of labels, $\rightarrow \subseteq Q \times A \times Q$ is the transition relation, s_0 is the initial state, and col is a colouring function $col: A \rightarrow COLOURS$.

Without loss of generality, we assume that all states are reachable from s_0. TS is called *deterministic* if $s \xrightarrow{a} s_1$ and $s \xrightarrow{a} s_2$ entail $s_1 = s_2$.

A *coloured Petri net*, in this paper, is a 5-tuple $N = (S, T, F, M_0, col)$ where S is a finite set of places, T is a finite set of transitions, F is the flow function $F: ((S \times T) \cup (T \times S)) \to \mathbb{N}$, M_0 is the initial marking, and col is a colouring function $col: T \to COLOURS$.   □ 1

The reachability graph $RG(N)$ of a net N is a deterministic transition system with label set $A = T$, and the colouring function of N is also a colouring function of $RG(N)$. The converse question:

> *Given a coloured transition system, is there a coloured Petri net implementing it?*

is much more difficult to answer. The idea behind colouring is that each colour specifies some *location*. If two transitions t_1, t_2 of a net satisfy $col(t_1) = col(t_2)$, then they are supposed to reside on the same location. By contrast, if $col(t_1) \neq col(t_2)$, then t_1 and t_2 are assumed to be on different locations. A bad case which we want to avoid is that two differently coloured transitions share a common input place. The next definition specifies the good cases.

Definition 2. DISTRIBUTED NETS (CAILLAUD).

A Petri net whose transitions T are coloured by $col: T \to COLOURS$ is called *distributed* if all t_1, t_2 with $col(t_1) \neq col(t_2)$ satisfy ${}^\bullet t_1 \cap {}^\bullet t_2 = \emptyset$, that is, the sets of pre-places of differently coloured transitions are disjoint.   □ 2

Once a net is distributed, the colouring function can be uniquely extended to places with at least one output transition. For a place p with $p^\bullet \neq \emptyset$, just pick any one of the output transitions $t \in p^\bullet$ and define the colour of p to be the same as $col(t)$. Since all transitions in $p^\bullet$ have the same colour by distributedness, this is unproblematic. Places without any output transition are uninteresting; they can be coloured with any suitable colour. Intuivtively, in a distributed net, every place, all of its output transitions, and all arcs between them, can reside at the same location.

Three simple examples are shown in Figure 5. In all of them, transitions a and b are supposed to be located on different sites. This is indicated by drawing a in a different "colour" (solid lines) than b (zigzag lines). Notice how this carries over to the reachability graphs of the three nets, given to the right of them.

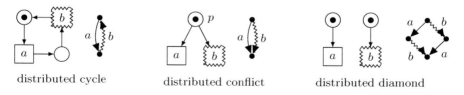

distributed cycle   distributed conflict   distributed diamond

Fig. 5. Distributed nets (l.h.s., r.h.s.) and a non-distributed net (middle)

The nets on the left-hand side and on the right-hand side are clearly distributed because there are no output-branching places. The net shown in the middle of Figure 5 is not distributed because place p has two output transitions of different colours. Moreover, there is a true conflict between these two transitions. In such a case, there is no chance whatsoever that a distributed Petri net can be found which implements the system. In terms of the transition system, this situation is captured by the existence of a state from which two arrows of different colours emanate but do not form a *distributed diamond*. Such a situation is called a *distributed conflict*. We will exclude distributed conflicts by the following definition. In the remainder of the paper, all transition systems will be assumed to be potentially distributable.

Definition 3. POTENTIAL DISTRIBUTABILITY.

A transition system is called *potentially distributable* if $s_1 \xrightarrow{a} s_2$ and $s_1 \xrightarrow{b} s_3$ and $col(a) \neq col(b)$ imply that there is a state s_4 such that $s_2 \xrightarrow{b} s_4$ and $s_3 \xrightarrow{a} s_4$.

$\square$ 3

2.2   Distributed Implementability

Consider some Petri net which is not distributed but whose reachability graph is potentially distributable. An example is shown in Figure 6. This net is not distributed, because transitions a and b are on different locations but share a common input place. Note that this place is non-redundant, i.e., omitting it alters the behaviour of the net. Nevertheless, the reachability graph of this net, shown on the right-hand side of the figure, is potentially distributable, because there is no state which enables both a and b at the same time. In such a case, there may exist another Petri net with the same reachability graph (or a very similar one) which *is* distributed. If this is the case (as it is indeed, as we will show), we call the Petri net and its reachability graph "distributable". It has been shown in [1] that any bounded and distributed Petri net can be translated to a branching bisimilar and divergence free system of communicating automata, with one automaton per location or colour, where sending or receiving asynchronous messages are considered as τ actions.

In the case of bounded Petri nets, the general theory of regions and the distributed net synthesis algorithms supplied by the tool SYNET [5] can be used to decide whether a net is strongly distributable (meaning that the reachability graph of the net is isomorphic to the reachability graph of some distributed Petri net) and to produce a distributed implementation. In this paper, we shall consider a more general concept of distributability, where the reachability graphs of a net and of its distributed implementation are similar but not necessarily isomorphic. We address in general the following questions: what is a "distributed implementation" and which methods can be used to achieve such an implementation?

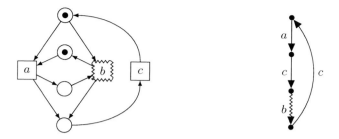

Fig. 6. A non-distributed Petri net with a distributable reachability graph

Informally, a coloured transition system TS shall be called *distributable* if there is some similar transition system TS' with an induced colouring such that TS' is the reachability graph of an actually distributed Petri net. Clearly, TS has to be potentially distributable in the first place, before one may think of actually distributing it. In the following, we describe four methods of distributing transition systems, of which we will reject one and accept three: *refinement*; *direct realisation*; *renaming*; and *unfolding*. All four methods determine relations of conformity between a transition system TS and its distributed implementation TS' which we shall denote by the generic name *conform*(TS, TS') although they are quite different.

2.3   Unacceptable Method: Refinement by τ-Transitions

It could be argued that every coloured Petri net can be distributed using τ-transitions. There are at least two techniques for doing so: arc refinement and transition refinement.

The first technique consists of replacing every place-transition arc by a busy wait loop involving two τ-transitions, as shown in Figure 3(r.h.s.). For a given place p, we may just pick one of its original output arcs and use the target transition's colour for all of the new τ-transitions emanating from p. If each τ-transition back to p inherits its colour from the original transition t which it is conflicting with (see r.h.s. of Figure 3), then this creates a distributed net. The construction has two drawbacks, however. The first problem, already discussed in Section 1, is that divergence may newly (and undesirably) be introduced. The second problem is that a τ-transition that emanates from an original place p after an arc from p to t has been refined may reside on a location different from the location of the transition t, which is unrealistic and counterintuitive.

The second technique consists of refining every transition t by a sequence $(\tau; t)$, giving some freedom for colouring the newly introduced τ-transitions. For instance, we might use a unique colour for all of them. Figure 7 shows the result of applying such τ-refinement to transitions a and b of the net shown in Figure 6. The new τ-transitions were coloured uniformly by the colour of b. Obviously,

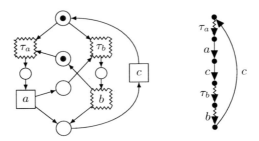

Fig. 7. Introducing some τ-refinements in Figure 6

the net is now distributed. However, this construction is again rather artificial. In general, it amounts to shifting *all* relevant choice resolutions (except ones that are already inside a location) onto only one fixed master location, which is not what we mean by "distributing" a net.

2.4   Acceptable Method: Isomorphism

This method consists of finding a distributed, coloured net with reachability graph TS. The relation $conform(TS, TS')$ here coincides with the relation of isomorphism. In the example depicted in Figure 6, a direct realisation exists, as shown on the left-hand side of Figure 8. This net is produced by SYNET [5] upon inputting the transition system TS with the two colours specified there. (Without colouring, the net in Figure 6 is produced.)

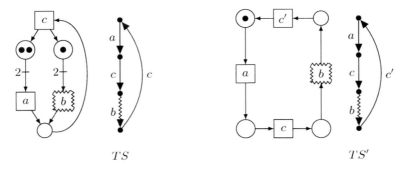

Fig. 8. Direct realisation (l.h.s.) and renaming (r.h.s.) of Figure 6

2.5   Acceptable Method: Renaming

A second approach for distributing the net shown in Figure 6 follows from the observation that the two transitions labelled c in its reachability graph could be considered as distinct, because they are not mutually involved in distributed diamonds. Given that they are distinct, we might as well actually distinguish the two transitions by renaming either one of them to c'. This is what happened in Figure 8 on the right-hand side. Once they are renamed, it is possible, in this simple case, to find a distributed Petri net realising the resulting transition system.[1]

So far, two ways of implementing a coloured transition system TS were identified (the first method is just a special case of the second):

(i) *Direct realisation*: Find a coloured net with reachability graph TS. The conformity relation $conform(TS, TS')$ is then just the "identity" (isomorphism) relation.

(ii) *Renaming*: Find a coloured transition system TS' which is the reachability graph of a distributed Petri net by renaming some transitions of TS suitably but leaving the set of states unchanged.[2] The conformity relation $conform(TS, TS')$ is then label refinement (some transitions with identical labels in TS have different labels in TS', whereas transitions with identical labels in TS' have identical labels in TS).

As an aside, it should be noted that renaming is not entirely innocuous, since it may transform a Petri net reachability graph into a transition system which is not a Petri net reachability graph (cf. Figure 9 where the transition system on the right-hand side cannot be produced by any Petri net).

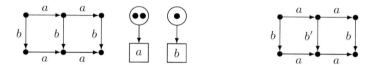

Fig. 9. Reachability graph (l.h.s.) and no reachability graph (r.h.s.)

2.6   Distributed and Non-distributed Diamonds

Renaming can also be useful in more involved circumstances. Recall the right-hand side of Figure 5 which shows a so-called *distributed diamond*. Such a diamond is characterised by the property that its opposite edges have the same colour and its consecutive edges have different colours. A distributed diamond is supposed to describe concurrency between transitions that are located at different sites, and we consider it, therefore, not to be allowed to rename any of them unless opposite edges are relabelled in the same way.

By contrast, consider the diamond formed by a and c in Figure 10. It is a so-called *local* or *non-distributed diamond*, as all four edges involved have the

---

[1] If a transition system is labelled injectively and if it has no distributed conflict, then it can be transformed into a distributed Petri net by just replacing every node by a place and every arc by an arc-transition-arc compound.

[2] In the region community, this operation is also known by the name of *splitting* [6], but we avoid this terminology in the present paper, in order to avoid confusion with transition refinement.

same colour. We argue that the problem of distributing a net is not changed if it is decided to rename locally the transitions of a non-distributed diamond. With this intuition, consider the renamed version shown on the right-hand side of Figure 10. Clearly, it coincides with the reachability graph of a distributed Petri net because it is injectively labelled.

Fig. 10. A coloured transition system (l.h.s.) and a renamed version (r.h.s.)

As a more complex example, consider the transition system shown on the left-hand side of Figure 11. It is indeed the reachability graph of a Petri net, namely the one depicted in Figure 12. However, this net is not distributed, since transition b shares an input place with f and d. When asked about this transition system, SYNET answers that no distributed net implementation exists for it. We check whether renaming can help. All b transitions in Figure 11 are involved in distributed diamonds. Hence it is not allowed to rename only one of the b transitions but not the other two. By contrast, the diamond formed by a and c, shown in the middle of the figure, is a local diamond. With the above intuition, it is permitted to rename this diamond partly, resulting in the transition system shown on the right-hand side of Figure 11. It so happens that the latter is distributable, and a distributed Petri net implementation is shown in Figure 13.

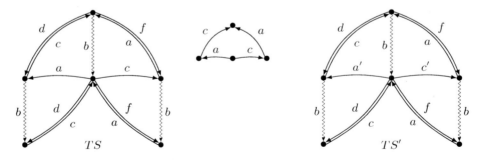

Fig. 11. A coloured transition system (l.h.s.) and an admissible renaming (r.h.s.)

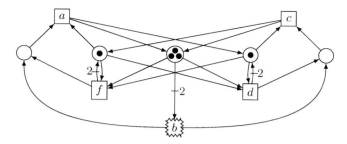

Fig. 12. A non-distributed net corresponding to Figure 11(l.h.s.)

2.7   Acceptable Method: Unfolding

Figure 10 can be modified in order to show that not all distribution problems can be solved by renaming alone. Suppose that the example is changed in such a way that the diamond is no longer local but distributed; this was done in Figure 14(l.h.s.) where two colours, rather than just one, are involved in the diamond. The transitions of this diamond may no longer be renamed. In particular, the previous solution is no longer admissible.

The modified transition system may be given the non-distributed Petri net implementation shown on the right-hand side of Figure 14. In this net, transitions b and d share a common input place, although there is no state in the transition system in which an alternative choice between b and d is actually offered. This situation is somewhat similar to the situation encountered in the example shown in Figure 6, except that in Figure 14(l.h.s.), contracting both a-labelled edges reveals some kind of "conflict" between b and d. By trial and error, or by invoking SYNET, it can be proved that *no* renaming whatsoever leads to a distributed Petri net implementation of this example.

Nevertheless, the distributed Petri net implementation problem specified in Figure 14 can be resolved by *unfolding* once the transition system, as shown on the left-hand side of Figure 15 where renaming has been used in combination with unfolding. The second copy of the original transition system produced by this one round unfolding has actually been provided with fresh names. After these two combined operations of unfolding and renaming, a reasonable distribution of the system can indeed be derived, as depicted on the right-hand side of Figure 15.

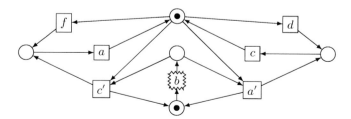

Fig. 13. A distributed net corresponding to Figure 11(r.h.s.)

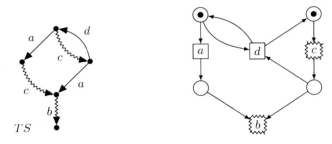

Fig. 14. A coloured TS (l.h.s.) and its non-distributed Petri net (r.h.s.)

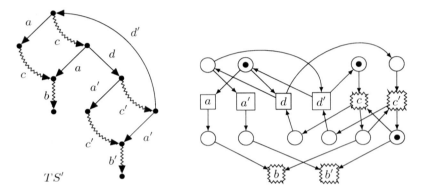

Fig. 15. An unfolded TS (l.h.s.) and its distributed Petri net (r.h.s.)

The considered example can be modified in an even nastier way. Consider Figure 16 which makes use of three instead of two colours. The third colour is indicated by dashed arrows. The diamond formed by the transitions labelled with a and c is still distributed. However, for this transition system, the distributed implementation problem cannot be solved using unfolding, or renaming, or any combination thereof. Worse, no distributed net implementation is possible after any finite or infinite unfolding, such as the one shown on the right-hand side of Figure 16 (even though one allows distributed Petri nets to be unbounded). If one wants to get in the end a finite (but possibly unbounded) Petri net, one cannot use any infinite set of labels. Therefore, in every case, there must exist in the unfolding some path $d^{(p)}c^{(p+1)}d^{(p+1)}\ldots d^{(p+q)}$ between two nodes n and n' that enable the same sequence $a^{(p)}b^{(p)}$ for some labels $a^{(p)}, b^{(p)}$ (where $x^{(p)}$ is an alias for x). Now, the node reached from the node n by the path $d^{(p)}c^{(p+1)}\ldots d^{(p+q-1)}$ enables $a^{(p)}$ but not $a^{(p)}b^{(p)}$. This means that the considered sequence of transitions consumes resources attached to the location of b, which is impossible (in any distributed net) since the locations of the c and the d differ from the location of the b.

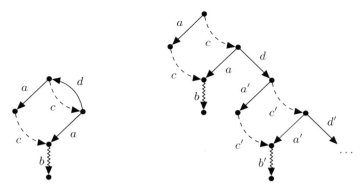

Fig. 16. A coloured TS (l.h.s.) and its infinite unfolding (r.h.s.)

Summarising the section, a third method of implementing a coloured transition system TS was identified (in addition to (i) direct realisation, and (ii) renaming):

(iii) *Unfolding*: Find a coloured transition system TS' by unfolding and renaming the given transition system TS suitably, and find a Petri net implementing TS'. Thus, $conform(TS, TS')$ means here that TS' is a renamed unfolding of TS.

3   Towards a Systematic Approach

In this section, patterns that may be obstructive for distributability are identified. The previous examples are briefly recapitulated in the light of these patterns.

3.1   Dangerous Non-distributed (Half-)Persistency

The pattern depicted in Figure 17 involves two transitions, a and d, of the same colour, which are forming three quarters of a diamond. This is called *half-persistency* because a persists over d, but d does not persist over a, and it is called *non-distributed*, because the edges are from the same colour. Suppose that a transition b of a different colour is enabled after a on the short path of this $\frac{3}{4}$-diamond while b is disabled after a on the long path, as depicted in the figure. Then, we call this a *dangerous* situation, because it signifies a kind of implicit conflict between d and b which may be revealed by contracting both a-edges. Such a pattern may require in any Petri net implementation the presence of some place which is an input place both of d and of b, making it non-distributed.

Observe that this pattern occurs in Figure 11 (check the central state with transitions f playing the role of d, a and b), and we consider that it is the decisive reason why one of the a transitions has to be renamed to a'. Symmetrically, one of the c transitions has to be renamed, yielding the solution to the distribution

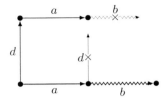

Fig. 17. Illustration of non-distributed half-persistency

problem. The same pattern also occurs in Figure 10 (check the state on the right with transitions d, and a and b). This can be mended immediately by renaming one of the a transitions, because the a-c diamond is non-distributed. The pattern also occurs in Figure 14, but can be mended there only after an unfolding step.

In case of dangerous non-distributed (half-)persistency, renaming or unfolding combined with renaming may suffice to remove the danger. Indeed, if one of the two a transitions in Figure 17 can be renamed, either in the transition system directly, or in an unfolding thereof, then the situation may change completely as regards distributed implementability. This is what happened with the renaming that led to Figures 11(r.h.s.) and 12, and also with the unfolding / renaming which led to Figure 13.

In general, one may encounter dangerous situations due to non-distributed (half-)persistency more involved than the simple situation shown in Figure 17. An exhaustive analysis of such situations has yet to be worked out.

3.2   Bad Cycles

Figure 18 depicts an even less desirable situation which we call *bad cycles* and which cannot be mended at all. The right-hand part of the figure implies that c should produce in some place p some tokens which are consumed by b (that is coloured differently). The middle part of the figure shows that the c transitions form a diamond with the transitions a, that are coloured differently, hence they cannot be renamed. The left part of the figure shows that one of the c-transitions forms a cycle with d. The cycle containing c does not contain any transition of the same colour as b. Therefore, in view of the token balance equation for cycles in Petri net reachability graphs, all tokens produced by c on the cycle must be consumed by d. Hence some tokens are taken from the place p and consumed both by b and by d. Altogether, the place p must be an input place both to b and to d which have different colours. A transition system with bad cycles can therefore not be distributed. For example, the system shown in Figure 16 has bad cycles, hence no distributed Petri net implementation is possible. In fact, bad cycles may be more intricate than suggested by Figure 16, but an exhaustive analysis of the induced situations is yet to be worked out.

So far, this section may be summarised as follows.

– It is difficult to give precise conditions characterizing the transition systems which may be implemented by distributed Petri nets.

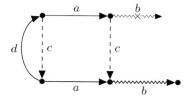

Fig. 18. Illustration of the bad cycle condition

- In case of dangerous non-distributed (half-)persistency, one may hope to get rid of it by renaming and/or unfolding.
- If bad cycles are present, there is no hope of getting a distributed implementation at all.

We do not know whether the absence of dangerous non-distributed (half-)persistency and of bad cycles already guarantees distributed implementability. Therefore, it seems sensible to check the distributable implementability of classes of transition systems which do not exhibit either of these patterns, in order to try to see whether all detrimental situations have been avoided thus, or whether there exist other nasty patterns.

3.3   A Class of Transition Systems

In this section, we consider Petri nets and their reachability graphs satisfying the following properties:

(a) They are bounded (i.e.: they have a finite reachability graph).
(b) They are persistent (i.e.: if a reachable marking enables a and b, and if $a \neq b$, then also ab and ba are enabled).
(c) They are reversible (i.e.: the initial marking can be reached from any reachable marking).
(d) All simple cycles in the reachability graph have the same Parikh vector (i.e.: all such cycles contain every transition equally often, and at least once).

Dangerous non-distributed half-persistency is prevented by Property (b), and bad cycles are excluded by Property (d).

Let us recall that a Petri net is *output-nonbranching* (ON, for short) if every place has at most one output transition, and that it is a *marked graph* [7,9,18] if every place has at most one input transition and at most one output transition. Clearly, ON nets (and *a fortiori* also marked graphs) are distributed for any colouring, by definition.

The class of nets satisfying (a)–(d) includes live marked graphs and plain, bounded, persistent, and reversible nets which are k-marked with $k \geq 2$ [3]. Another example is the net shown on the left-hand side of Figure 19, whose reachability graph is shown in the middle of the figure. The reader can easily verify that all cycles contain all labels an equal number of times, and if they are minimal, exactly once. This transition system does not represent the reachability graph of any marked graph, however,[3] nor of any k-marked persistent net with $k \geq 2$. The example proves that Properties (a)–(d) delineate a class of nets that is larger than live marked graphs and k-marked persistent nets with $k \geq 2$.

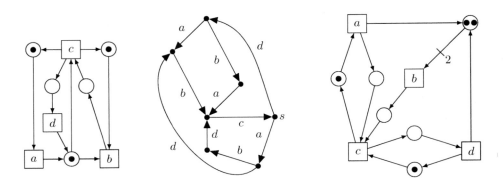

Fig. 19. A system satisfying (a)–(d) (l.h.s., middle), and an ON Petri net (r.h.s.)

Observe that the system shown on the left-hand side of Figure 19 can be realised as an output-nonbranched Petri net, shown on the right-hand side of the figure (which is not the one produced by standard region theory, nor the one returned by SYNET). At the time of writing, we suspect that this observation can be generalised and that all reachability graphs satisfying (a)–(d) correspond to ON Petri nets and are distributable. If so, this would mean that Method (i) identified above – namely, isomorphism-based direct distributability – is sufficient to treat this class of reachability graphs.

4   Concluding Remarks

This paper describes what the authors consider to be an open problem in the realm of Petri nets and related system models: Can a system described by some Petri net exhibiting concurrency actually be distributed? Many open subproblems can be identified:

- Prove the conjecture described in section 3.3.
- Collect and formalise necessary conditions for distributability.
- Collect and formalise sufficient conditions for distributability.

---

[3] This can be seen as follows: At state s, transition b is not enabled, but the sequences ab and db are enabled. Because ab is enabled and b is not, there must be some place p which is an output place of a and an input place of b and which does not carry enough tokens in s to enable b. If this place is not also an output place of d, then db cannot be enabled at s. Hence p is an output place of both a and d, and thus cannot belong to a marked graph.

- Solve the distributability problem, i.e.: find a *necessary and sufficient* condition for distributability.
- Explore the theory's practical applicability by finding decision procedures checking which nets can be distributed and which cannot.

It may also be reasonable to modify (and possibly simplify) the problem somewhat by considering transition-labelled Petri nets.

Moreover, there may be a connection to Lamport's notion of *arbitration-free synchronisation*. Informally, arbitration denotes the resolution of nondeterministic choices by some device called *arbiter*. The following is a quote from [13]:

> "*The impossibility of implementing arbitration in a bounded length of time seems to be a fundamental law of nature. Hence, what kind of synchronization can be achieved without arbitration should be a fundamental question in any theory of multiprocess synchronization. We know of no previous attempt to answer this question...*"

Intuitively, any arbitration-free class of systems should also be distributable. Indeed, as Lamport shows in [13], one of the arbitration-free classes of systems defined there is equivalent with marked graphs. Another class of systems defined in [13], called *or-waiting*, seems to correspond to Petri nets where local processes (of a single colour) do not obey special requirements while inter-process communication is achieved by places with arbitrarily many input transitions but only one output transition. Such a class of Petri nets is evidently also distributable. This connection could be explored in future work.

References

1. Badouel, É., Caillaud, B., Darondeau, P.: Distributing Finite Automata through Petri Net Synthesis. Journal on Formal Aspects of Computing 13, 447–470 (2002)
2. Badouel, É., Darondeau, P.: Theory of Regions. In: Reisig, W., Rozenberg, G. (eds.) APN 1998. LNCS, vol. 1491, pp. 529–586. Springer, Heidelberg (1998)
3. Best, E., Darondeau, P.: Separability in Persistent Petri Nets. In: Lilius, J., Penczek, W. (eds.) PETRI NETS 2010. LNCS, vol. 6128, pp. 246–266. Springer, Heidelberg (2010)
4. Best, E., Hopkins, R.P.: $B(PN)^2$ - a Basic Petri Net Programming Notation. In: Reeve, M., Bode, A., Wolf, G. (eds.) PARLE 1993. LNCS, vol. 694, pp. 379–390. Springer, Heidelberg (1993)
5. Caillaud, B.: http://www.irisa.fr/s4/tools/synet/
6. Carmona, J.: The label splitting problem. In: Desel, J., Yakovlev, A. (eds.) Proc. Applications of Region Theory 2011. CEUR Workshop Proceedings, vol. 725, pp. 22–35 (2011)
7. Commoner, F., Holt, A.W., Even, S., Pnueli, A.: Marked Directed Graphs. J. Comput. Syst. Sci. 5(5), 511–523 (1971)
8. Costa, A., Gomes, L.: Petri Net Partitioning Using Net Splitting Operation. In: 7th IEEE Int. Conf. on Industrial Informatics (INDIN), pp. 204–209 (2009)
9. Genrich, H.J., Lautenbach, K.: Synchronisationsgraphen. Acta Inf. 2, 143–161 (1973)

10. van Glabbeek, R.J.: The Linear Time – Branching Time Spectrum II. In: Best, E. (ed.) CONCUR 1993. LNCS, vol. 715, pp. 66–81. Springer, Heidelberg (1993)
11. Hoare, C.A.R.: Communicating Sequential Processes. Communications of the ACM 21(8) (1978)
12. Hopkins, R.P.: Distributable Nets. Applications and Theory of Petri Nets 1990. In: Rozenberg, G. (ed.) APN 1991. LNCS, vol. 524, pp. 161–187. Springer, Heidelberg (1991)
13. Lamport, L.: Arbiter-Free Synchronization. Distributed Computing 16(2/3), 219–237 (2003)
14. Lauer, P.E., Torrigiani, P.R., Shields, M.W.: COSY – a System Specification Language Based on Paths and Processes. Acta Informatica 12, 109–158 (1979)
15. Milner, R.: A Calculus of Communication Systems. LNCS, vol. 92, p. 171. Springer, Heidelberg (1980)
16. Reisig, W.: Petri Nets. EATCS Monographs on Theoretical Computer Science, vol. 4. Springer, Heidelberg (1985)
17. Schicke, J.-W., Peters, K., Goltz, U.: Synchrony vs. Causality in Asynchronous Petri Nets. In: Luttik, B., Valencia, F.D. (eds.) Proc. 18th Intl. Workshop on Expressiveness in Concurrency (EXPRESS 2011). EPTCS, vol. 64, pp. 119–131 (2011), doi:10.4204/EPTCS.64.9
18. Teruel, E., Chrząstowski-Wachtel, P., Colom, J.M., Silva, M.: On Weighted T-systems. In: Jensen, K. (ed.) ICATPN 1992. LNCS, vol. 616, pp. 348–367. Springer, Heidelberg (1992)

Connector Algebras, Petri Nets, and BIP*

Roberto Bruni[1], Hernán Melgratti[2], and Ugo Montanari[1]

[1] Dipartimento di Informatica, Università di Pisa, Italy
[2] Departamento de Computación,
Universidad de Buenos Aires - Conicet, Argentina

Abstract. In the area of component-based software architectures, the term *connector* has been coined to denote an entity (e.g. the communication network, middleware or infrastructure) that regulates the interaction of independent components. Hence, a rigorous mathematical foundation for connectors is crucial for the study of coordinated systems. In recent years, many different mathematical frameworks have been proposed to specify, design, analyse, compare, prototype and implement connectors rigorously. In this paper, we overview the main features of three notable frameworks and discuss their similarities, differences, mutual embedding and possible enhancements. First, we show that Sobocinski's nets with boundaries are as expressive as Sifakis et al.'s BI(P), the BIP component framework without priorities. Second, we provide a basic algebra of connectors for BI(P) by exploiting Montanari et al.'s tile model and a recent correspondence result with nets with boundaries. Finally, we exploit the tile model as a unifying framework to compare BI(P) with other models of connectors and to propose suitable enhancements of BI(P).

1 Introduction

Recent years have witnessed an increasing interest about a rigorous modelling of (different classes of) connectors. The term *connector*, as used here, has been coined within the area of component-based software architectures, to name entities that can regulate the interaction of a collection of components [27]. This has led to the development of different mathematical frameworks that are used to specify, design, analyse, compare, prototype and implement suitable connectors. As such connectors have been often designed by research groups with different background and having different aims in mind (e.g. efficient verification of embedded system, generality and extensibility, implementability over a distributed architecture), many existing proposals are built over specific features that on the one hand complicate a comparison in terms of expressiveness and on the other hand make it difficult to enhance one model with additional features coming from another model. Similarly, one were to enhance all models with the same

---

* Research supported by European FET-IST-257414 Integrated Project ASCENS, ANPCyT Project BID-PICT-2008-00319, and UBACyT 20020090300122. The travel expenses of Ugo Montanari for participating to PSI'11 have been supported by Formal Methods Europe.

E. Clarke, I. Virbitskaite, and A. Voronkov (Eds.): PSI 2011, LNCS 7162, pp. 19–38, 2012.

new feature, then different solutions would be required. As an example, no uniform agreement about how to define dynamically reconfigurable connectors has been set up yet.

In this paper, we overview our recent advancements towards a unifying theory of connectors by focussing on the comparison of three notable connector frameworks, namely the BIP component framework [6], Petri nets with boundaries [30] and the algebras of connectors [11,2] based on the tile model [20,9]. The main result establishes that BIP without priorities, written BI(P) in the following, is equally expressive to nets with boundaries. Thanks to the correspondence results in [30,12], we can define an algebra of connectors as expressive as BI(P), where a few basic connectors can be composed in series and parallel to generate any BI(P) system. The algebra is a suitable instance of the tile model, which we propose as unifying framework for the study of connectors. In fact, the generality of the tile model as a general semantic framework has been already witnessed in [26,14,18,16,24,21,13].

Connectors basics. Component-based design relies on the separation of concerns between coordination and computation. Component-based systems are built from sequential computational entities, the *components*, that should be loosely coupled w.r.t. the concurrent execution environments where they will be deployed. The component interfaces comprise the number, kind and peculiarities of communication ports. The communication media that make possible to interact are called *connectors*. They can be regarded as (suitably decorated) links between the ports of the components. Graphically, ports are represented as nodes and connectors as hyperarcs whose tentacles are attached to the ports they control. Several connectors can also be combined together by merging some of the ports their tentacles are attached to. Semantically, each connector can impose suitable constraints on the communications between the components it links together. For example, a connector may impose handshaking between a sender component and a receiver component (Milner's CCS synchronization). A different kind of connector may require global consensus on the next action to perform (Hoare's CSP synchronization) or it may trigger the broadcasting of a message sent from one component to all the other linked components. The evolution of a network of components and connectors (just *network* for brevity) can be seen as if played in rounds: At each round, the components try to interact through their ports and the connectors allow/disallow some of the interactions selectively. A connector is called *stateless* when the interaction constraints it imposes over its ports stay the same at each round; it is called *stateful* otherwise. To address composition and modularity of a system, networks are often decorated with input and output interfaces: in the simpler cases, they consist of ports through which a network can interact. For example, two networks can be composed by merging the ports (i.e. nodes) they have in common. Ports that are not in the interface are typically private to the network and cannot be used to attach additional connectors. The distinction between input and output ports indicates in which direction the data should flow, but feedback is also possible through short-circuit connectors.

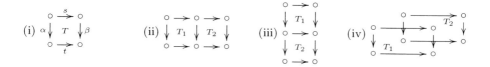

Fig. 1. Examples of tiles and their composition

The BIP component framework. BIP [6] is a component framework for constructing systems by superposing three layers of modelling: 1) Behaviour, the lower level, representing the sequential computation of individual components; 2) Interaction, the middle layer, defining the handshaking mechanisms between these components; and 3) Priority, the top level, assigning a partial order of privileges to the admissible synchronisations. The lower layer consists of a set of atomic components with ports, modelled as automata whose arcs are labelled by sets of ports. The sets of ports of any two different components are disjoint, i.e., each port is uniquely assigned to a component. The second layer consists of connectors that specify the allowed interactions between components. Roughly, connectors define suitable relations between ports. The third layer exploits priorities to enforce scheduling policies over allowed interactions, typically with the aim of reducing the size of the state space. One supported feature of BIP is the so-called *correctness by construction*, which allows the specification of architecture transformations preserving certain properties of the underlying behaviour. For instance it is possible to provide (sufficient) conditions for compositionality and composability which guarantee deadlock-freedom. The BIP component framework has been implemented in a language and a tool-set. In absence of priorities, the interaction layer of BIP admits the algebraic presentation given in [7].

The tile model. The Tile Model [20,9] offers a flexible and adequate semantic setting for concurrent systems [26,18,15] and also for defining the operational and abstract semantics of suitable classes of connectors.

A *tile* $T : s \xrightarrow[\beta]{\alpha} t$ is a rewrite rule stating that the *initial configuration* s can evolve to the *final configuration* t via α, producing the *effect* β; but the step is allowed only if the 'arguments' of s can contribute by producing α, which acts as the *trigger* of the rewrite. The name 'tile' is due to the graphical representation of such rules (see Fig. 1(i)). Triggers and effects are called *observations* and tile vertices are called *interfaces*.

Tiles can be composed horizontally, in parallel, or vertically to generate larger steps. Horizontal composition $T_1 ; T_2$ coordinates the evolution of the initial configuration of T_1 with that of T_2, yielding the 'synchronization' of the two rewrites (see Fig. 1(ii)). Horizontal composition is possible only if the initial configurations of T_1 and T_2 interact cooperatively: the effect of T_1 must provide the trigger for T_2. Vertical composition is sequential composition of computations (see Fig. 1(iii)). The parallel composition builds concurrent steps (see Fig. 1(iv)).

Roughly, the semantics of component-based systems can be expressed via tiles when: i) components and connectors are equipped with sequential composition $s; t$ (defined when the output interface of s matches the input interface of t) and with a monoidal tensor product $s \otimes t$ (associative, with unit and distributing over sequential composition); ii) observations have analogous structure $\alpha; \beta$ and $\alpha \otimes \beta$. Technically, we require that configurations and observations form two *monoidal categories* [25] with the same underlying set of objects.

Tiles express the reactive behaviour of connectors in terms of trigger/effect pairs of labels (α, β). In this context, the usual notion of bisimilarity over the derived Labelled Transition System is called *tile bisimilarity*. Tile bisimilarity is a congruence (w.r.t. composition in series and parallel) when a simple tile format is met by basic tiles [20].

The wire calculus. The wire calculus [29] shares strong similarities with the tile model, in the sense that it has sequential and parallel compositions and exploits trigger-effect pairs labels as observations. However it is presented as a process algebra instead of via monoidal categories and it exploits a different kind of vertical composition. Each process comes with an input/output arity typing, e.g., we write $\vdash P : (n, m)$ for P with n input ports and m output ports. The usual action prefixes $a.P$ of process algebras are extended in the wire calculus by the simultaneous input of a trigger a and output of an effect b, written $\frac{a}{b}.P$, where a (resp. b) is a string of actions, one for each input port (resp. output port) of the process.

In [30] a dialect of the wire calculus has been used to give an exact characterisation of a special class of (stateful) connectors that can be alternatively expressed in terms of so-called Petri nets with boundaries. Technically speaking, the contribution in [30] can be summarized as follows. Nets with boundaries are first introduced, taking inspiration from the open nets of [5]. Nets with boundaries can be composed in series and in parallel and come equipped with a labelled transition system that fixes their operational and bisimilarity semantics. Then, a suitable instance of the *wire calculus* from [29] is presented, called *Petri calculus*, that roughly models circuit diagrams with one-place buffers and interfaces. The first result enlightens a tight semantics correspondence: it is shown that a Petri calculus process can be defined for each net such that the translation preserves and reflects operational semantics (and thus also bisimilarity). The second result provides the converse translation, from Petri calculus to nets, which requires some technical ingenuity. The work in [30] has been recently improved in [12] by showing that if the tile model is used in place of the wire calculus then the translation from Petri calculus to nets becomes simpler and that the main results of [30] can be extended to P/T Petri nets with boundaries, where arcs are weighted and places can contain more than one token.

Structure of the paper. In § 2 we recall the main definition and notation for BIP and nets with boundaries. In § 3 we prove that BI(P) and nets with boundaries are equally expressive. In § 4 we exploit the results in § 3 and in [30,12] to define a suitable algebra of BI(P) systems and compare it with the work in [8]. We discuss related work in § 5. Some concluding remarks and open issues for future work are in § 6.

2   Background

2.1   The BIP Component Framework

This section reports on the formal definition of BIP as presented in [8]. Since we disregard priorities, we call BI(P) the framework presented here.

Definition 1 (Interaction). *Given a set of ports P, an* interaction *over P is a non-empty subset $a \subseteq P$.*

We write an interaction $\{p_1, p_2, \ldots, p_n\}$ as $p_1 p_2 \ldots p_n$ and $a \downarrow_{P_i}$ for the projection of an interaction $a \subseteq P$ over the set of ports $P_i \subseteq P$, i.e., $a \downarrow_{P_i} = a \cap P_i$. Projection extends to sets of interactions in the following way $\gamma \downarrow_P = \{a \downarrow_P \mid a \in \gamma \land a \downarrow_P \neq \varnothing\}$.

Definition 2 (Component). *A component $B = (Q, P, \to)$ is a transition system where Q is a set of states, P is a set of ports, and $\to \subseteq Q \times 2^P \times Q$ is the set of labelled transitions.*

As usual, we write $q \xrightarrow{a} q'$ to denote the transition $(q, a, q') \in \to$. We let $q \mathbin{\because} a \mathbin{\therefore} q'$ be the *name* of the transition $q \xrightarrow{a} q'$. Given a transition $t = q \mathbin{\because} a \mathbin{\therefore} q'$, we let $^\circ t$, t° and $\lambda(t)$ denote respectively its source q, its target q' and its label a. An interaction a is enabled in q, denoted $q \xrightarrow{a}$, iff there exists q' s.t. $q \xrightarrow{a} q'$. By abusing the notation, we will also write $q \xrightarrow{\varnothing} q$ for any q.

Definition 3 (BI(P) system). *A BI(P) system $B = \gamma(B_1, \ldots, B_n)$ is the composition of a finite set $\{B_i\}_{i=1}^n$ of transitions systems $B_i = (Q_i, P_i, \to_i)$ such that their sets of ports are pairwise disjoint, i.e., $P_i \cap P_j = \varnothing$ for $i \neq j$ parameterized by a set $\gamma \subset 2^P$ of interactions over the set of ports $P = \biguplus_{i=1}^n P_i$. We call P the underlying set of ports of B, written $\iota(B)$.*

The semantics of a BI(P) system $\gamma(B_1, \ldots, B_n)$ is given by the transition system $(Q, P, \to_\gamma)$, with $Q = \Pi_i Q_i$, $P = \biguplus_{i=1}^n P_i$ and $\to_\gamma \subseteq Q \times 2^P \times Q$ is the least set of transitions satisfying the following inference rule

$$\frac{a \in \gamma \qquad \forall i \in 1..n : q_i \xrightarrow{a \downarrow_{P_i}} q_i'}{(q_1, \ldots, q_n) \xrightarrow{a}_\gamma (q_1', \ldots, q_n')}$$

Example 1. Figure 2 shows a simple BIP system consisting of three transitions systems B_1, B_2, and B_3 and the synchronization $\gamma = \{ab, cd, d\}$.

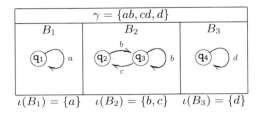

Fig. 2. A simple BIP system $B = \gamma(B_1, B_2, B_3)$

2.2   Nets with Boundaries

Petri nets [28] consist of *places* (i.e. resources types), which are repositories of *tokens* (i.e., resource instances), and *transitions* that remove and produce tokens.

Definition 4 (Net). *A net N is a 4-tuple $N = (S_N, T_N, {}^\circ{-}_N, {-}^\circ_N)$ where S_N is the (nonempty) set of places, $\mathsf{a}, \mathsf{a}', \ldots$, T_N is the set of transitions, $\mathsf{t}, \mathsf{t}', \ldots$ (with $S_N \cap T_N = \varnothing$), and the functions ${}^\circ{-}_N, {-}^\circ_N : T_N \to 2^{S_N}$ assign finite sets of places, called respectively source and target, to each transition.*

Transitions t, u are independent when ${}^\circ t \cap {}^\circ u = t^\circ \cap u^\circ = \varnothing$. This notion of independence allows so-called contact situations. Moreover, it also allows consume/produce loops, i.e., a place p can be both in ${}^\circ t$ and t°. A set U of transitions is mutually independent when, for all $t, u \in U$, if $t \neq u$ then t and u are independent. Given a set of transitions U let ${}^\circ U = \cup_{u \in U} {}^\circ u$ and $U^\circ = \cup_{u \in U} u^\circ$.

Definition 5 (Semantics). *Let $N = (P, T, {}^\circ{-}, {-}^\circ)$ be a net, $X, Y \subseteq P$ and $t \in T$. Write:*

$$(N, X) \to_{\{t\}} (N, Y) \stackrel{\text{def}}{=} {}^\circ t \subseteq X \wedge t^\circ \subseteq Y \wedge X \backslash {}^\circ t = Y \backslash t^\circ$$

For $U \subseteq T$ a set of mutually independent transitions, write:

$$(N, X) \to_U (N, Y) \stackrel{\text{def}}{=} {}^\circ U \subseteq X \wedge U^\circ \subseteq Y \wedge X \backslash {}^\circ U = Y \backslash U^\circ$$

Note that, for any $X \subseteq P$, $(N, X) \to_\varnothing (N, X)$. States of this transition system will be referred to as markings of N.

The remaining of this section recalls the composable nets proposed in [30]. In the following we let $\underline{k}$, $\underline{l}$, $\underline{m}$, $\underline{n}$ range over finite ordinals: $\underline{n} \stackrel{\text{def}}{=} \{0, 1, \ldots, n-1\}$.

Definition 6 (Nets with boundaries). *Let $m, n \in \mathbb{N}$. A net with boundaries $N : m \to n$ is a tuple $N = (S, T, {}^\circ{-}, {-}^\circ, {}^\bullet{-}, {-}^\bullet)$ where $(S, T, {}^\circ{-}, {-}^\circ)$ is a net and functions ${}^\bullet{-} : T \to 2^{\underline{m}}$ and ${-}^\bullet : T \to 2^{\underline{n}}$ assign transitions to the left and right boundaries of N, respectively.*

The representation of the left and right boundaries as ordinals is just a notational convenience. In particular, we remark that the left and the right boundaries of a net are always disjoint.

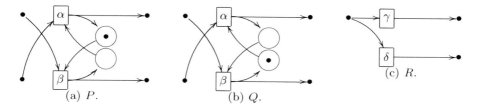

(a) P.   (b) Q.   (c) R.

Fig. 3. Three nets with boundaries

The notion of independence of transitions extends to nets with boundaries in the obvious way: $t, u \in T$ are said to be *independent* when

$$^\circ t \cap {}^\circ u = \varnothing \ \wedge \ t^\circ \cap u^\circ = \varnothing \ \wedge \ {}^\bullet t \cap {}^\bullet u = \varnothing \ \wedge \ t^\bullet \cap u^\bullet = \varnothing$$

The obvious notion of net homomorphism between nets with equal boundaries just requires that source, target, left and right boundaries are preserved, and a homomorphism is an isomorphism iff its two components (places and transitions) are bijections. We write $N \cong M$ when there is an isomorphism from N to M.

Example 2. Figure 3 shows two different nets with boundaries. Places are circles and a marking is represented by the presence or absence of tokens; rectangles are transitions and arcs stand for pre and postset relations. The left interface (right interface) is depicted by points situated on the left (respectively, on the right). Figure 3(a) shows the net $P : 2 \to 2$ containing two places, two transitions and one token. Net Q is similar to P, but has a different initial marking. Differently from P and Q, R has just one node in its left interface.

Nets with boundaries can be composed in parallel and in series. Given $N : m \to n$ and $M : k \to l$, their tensor product is the net $N \otimes M : m + k \to n + l$ whose sets of places and transitions are the disjoint union of the corresponding sets in N and M, whose maps $^\circ-, -^\circ, {}^\bullet-, -^\bullet$ are defined according to the maps in N and M and whose initial marking is $m_{0N} \oplus m_{0M}$. Intuitively, the tensor product corresponds to put the nets N and M side-by-side.

The sequential composition $N; M : m \to k$ of $N : m \to n$ and $M : n \to k$ is slightly more involved and relies on the following notion of synchronization: a pair (U, V) with $U \subseteq T_N$ and $V \subseteq T_M$ mutually independent sets of transitions such that: (1) $U \cup V \neq \varnothing$ and (2) $U^\bullet = {}^\bullet V$.

The set of synchronisations inherits an ordering from the subset relation, i.e. $(U, V) \subseteq (U', V')$ when $U \subseteq U'$ and $V \subseteq V'$. A synchronisation is said to be minimal when it is minimal with respect to this order. Let

$$T_{N;M} \stackrel{\text{def}}{=} \{(U, V) | U \subseteq T_N, V \subseteq T_M, (U, V) \text{ a minimal synchronisation}\}$$

Notice that any transition t in N (respectively t' in M) not connected to the shared boundary n defines a minimal synchronisation $(\{t\}, \varnothing)$ (respectively $(\varnothing, \{t'\}))$ in the above sense. The sequential composition of N and M is written

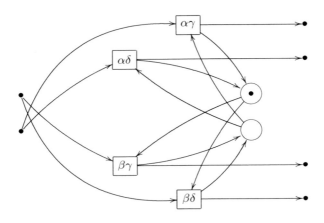

Fig. 4. Net $P; (R \oplus R)$

$N; M : m \to k$ and defined as $(S_N \uplus S_M, T_{N;M}, {}^{\circ}-_{N;M}, -{}^{\circ}_{N;M}, {}^{\bullet}-_{N;M}, -{}^{\bullet}_{N;M})$, where pre- and post-sets of synchronizations are defined as

- ${}^{\circ}(U, V)_{N;M} = {}^{\circ}(U)_N \uplus {}^{\circ}(V)_M$ and $(U, V)^{\circ}_{N;M} = (U)^{\circ}_N \uplus (V)^{\circ}_M$
- ${}^{\bullet}(U, V)_{N;M} = {}^{\bullet}(U)_N$ and $(U, V)^{\bullet}_{N;M} = (V)^{\bullet}_M$.

Intuitively, transitions attached to the left or right boundaries can be seen as transition fragments, that can be completed by attaching other complementary fragments to that boundary. When two transition fragments in N share a boundary node, then they are two mutually exclusive options for completing a fragment of M attached to the same boundary node. Thus, the idea is to combine the transitions of N with that of M when they share a common boundary, as if their firings were synchronized. As in general several combinations are possible, only minimal synchronizations are selected, because the other can be recovered as concurrent firings.

Sometimes we find convenient to write $N = (S, T, {}^{\circ}-, -{}^{\circ}, {}^{\bullet}-, -{}^{\bullet}, X)$ with $X \subseteq S$ for the net $(S, T, {}^{\circ}-, -{}^{\circ}, {}^{\bullet}-, -{}^{\bullet})$ with initial marking X and extend the sequential and parallel composition to nets with initial marking by taking the union of the initial markings.

Example 3. Consider the nets P and R in Figure 3. Then, the net $P; (R \otimes R)$ obtained as the composition of P and R is shown in Figure 4.

For any $k \in \mathbb{N}$, there is a bijection $\ulcorner\_\urcorner : 2^{\underline{k}} \to \{0, 1\}^k$ with

$$\ulcorner U \urcorner_i \overset{\mathsf{def}}{=} \begin{cases} 1 \text{ if } i \in U \\ 0 \text{ otherwise} \end{cases}$$

Definition 7 (Semantics). *Let $N : m \to n$ be a net and $X, Y \subseteq P_N$. Write:*

$$(N, X) \xrightarrow[\beta]{\alpha} (N, Y) \overset{\mathsf{def}}{=} \exists \text{ mutually independent } U \subseteq T_N \text{ s.t}$$

$$(N, X) \to_U (N, Y), \alpha = \ulcorner {}^{\bullet}U \urcorner, \text{ and } \beta = \ulcorner U^{\bullet} \urcorner$$

3   Encoding BIP into Nets

This section studies the correspondence between BI(P) systems and nets. We start by showing that any BI(P) system can be mapped into a bisimilar net (§3.1). Then, we introduce a notion of composition of BI(P) systems (§3.2) and then, by exploiting compositionality of nets with boundaries, we provide a compositional encoding of BI(P) systems into nets with boundaries (§3.3).

3.1   Monolithic Mapping

It is folklore that a BIP system can be seen as 1-safe Petri net with priorities. This section shows a concrete mapping of a BI(P) system into a net.

Definition 8. *Let* $B = \gamma(B_1, \ldots, B_n)$ *be a BI(P) system. The corresponding net is* $N_B = (P, T, {}^{\circ}{-}_N, -{}^{\circ}_N)$ *where* $P = \iota(B)$,

$$T = \{\langle q_1 \because a \downarrow_{P_1} \therefore q_1', \ldots, q_n \because a \downarrow_{P_n} \therefore q_n' \rangle \mid$$

$$a \in \gamma \ \wedge \ a = \uplus_i(a \downarrow_{P_i}) \wedge \ \forall i \in 1..n : (q_i \in Q_i \wedge q_i \xrightarrow{a \downarrow_{P_i}} q_i')\}$$

with ${}^{\circ}{-} : T \to 2^P$ *and* $-{}^{\circ} : T \to 2^P$ *s.t.*

$$\begin{aligned}
{}^{\circ}\langle q_1 \because a \downarrow_{P_1} \therefore q_1', \ldots, q_n \because a \downarrow_{P_n} \therefore q_n' \rangle &= \{q_i \mid a \downarrow_{P_i} \neq \varnothing\} \\
\langle q_1 \because a \downarrow_{P_1} \therefore q_1', \ldots, q_n \because a \downarrow_{P_n} \therefore q_n' \rangle^{\circ} &= \{q_i' \mid a \downarrow_{P_i} \neq \varnothing\}
\end{aligned}$$

Given a transition $t = \langle q_1 \because a \downarrow_{P_1} \therefore q_1', \ldots, q_n \because a \downarrow_{P_n} \therefore q_n' \rangle$, we let a be the label of t, i.e., $\lambda(t) = a$.

Intuitively, the places of the net N_B are in one-to-one correspondence with the states of the components, while the transitions of N_B represent the synchronized execution of transitions on the components.

Example 4. Consider the BI(P) system $B = \gamma(B_1, B_2, B_3)$ shown in Figure 2. The net N_B corresponding to the BI(P) system is shown in Figure 5. Note that the net contains as many transitions as the allowed synchronizations among components. For instance, the net has two different transitions that match the interaction ab, any of them describing one possible synchronization between components B_1 and B_2. In fact, interaction ab is possible when B_1 executes $q_1 \xrightarrow{a} q_1$ and B_2 does either $q_2 \xrightarrow{b} q_3$ or $q_3 \xrightarrow{b} q_3$.

Theorem 1 (Correspondence). *Let* $B = \gamma(B_1, \ldots, B_n)$ *be a BI(P) system. Then,* $(q_1, \ldots, q_n) \xrightarrow{a}_\gamma (q_1', \ldots, q_n')$ *iff* $(N_B, \{q_1, \ldots, q_n\}) \to_{\{t\}} (N_B, \{q_1', \ldots, q_n'\})$ *and* $\lambda(t) = a$.

Proof. The result straightforwardly follows by construction of the net. □

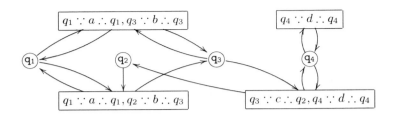

Fig. 5. Mapping of the BI(P) system $N_{\gamma(B_1, B_2, B_3)}$ into a net

3.2   Composite BI(P) Systems

In this section we introduce a notion of composition for BI(P) systems that allows to take BI(P) systems as components of larger systems. We start by introducing a notion of coherence between interactions that will be used for defining allowed compositions of BI(P) systems.

Definition 9 (Coherent interaction extension). *Given two sets of interactions γ and γ' we say that γ' is a coherent extension of γ over the set of ports P, written $\gamma \triangleright_P \gamma'$, iff $\gamma' \downarrow_P \subseteq \gamma$.*

The idea underlying coherent extension is that the extended set of interactions γ' does not allow more interactions between the ports in P than those specified by γ.

Definition 10 (Composite BI(P) system). *A composite BI(P) system is either a BI(P) system $C = \gamma(B_1, \ldots, B_n)$ or a composition $\gamma(C_1, \ldots, C_n)$ where $\{C_i = \gamma_i(C_{i,1}, \ldots, C_{i,n_i})\}_{i=1}^n$ is a family of composite BI(P) systems such that their sets of underlying ports are pairwise disjoint, i.e., $\iota(C_i) \cap \iota(C_j) = \varnothing$ for $i \neq j$, and γ a set of interactions over $\uplus_{i=1}^n \iota(C_i)$ s.t. $\gamma_i \triangleright_{\iota(C_i)} \gamma$.*

Note that the definition of composite BI(P) systems generalizes the notion of BI(P) systems. In fact, any transition system $B = (Q, P, \rightarrow)$ can be seen as a BI(P) system $2^P(B)$, i.e., a BI(P) system composed by exactly one transition system whose allowed interactions are all possible combination of ports (i.e., any possible label in 2^P is allowed by the interaction 2^P). It is straightforward to show that B and $2^P(B)$ have isomorphic transitions systems.

The semantics of composite BI(P) systems is defined analogously to that of BI(P) systems by viewing each subsystem as a component.

Next result states that any BI(P) system can be seen as a composite BI(P) system of exactly two components. We will use this property when defining the compositional encoding of BI(P) systems.

Lemma 1. *Let $B = \gamma(B_1, \ldots, B_n)$ be a BI(P) system. Then, for any $i < n$, B is bisimilar to the composite BI(P) system $C = \gamma(\gamma \downarrow_{P_{1..i}} (B_1, \ldots, B_i), \gamma \downarrow_{P \setminus P_{1..i}} (B_{i-1}, \ldots, B_n))$ where $P = \iota(B)$ and $P_{1..i} = \uplus_{j \leq i} \iota(B_j)$.*

Proof. The proof follows by straightforward coinduction.   □

(a) Transition System.

(b) Corresponding Net with boundaries.

Fig. 6. Encoding of a transition system with ports $\{a, b\}$

3.3   Structural Mapping

In this section we present a structural encoding of BI(P) systems into nets with boundaries. We start by introducing the encoding of a transition system as a net with boundaries.

Given a finite set S with $k = \#S$, we use w_S to denote an injective function $w_S : S \to \underline{k}$ that orders elements of S. By abusing notation, we write also w_S to denote its expected extension $w_S : 2^S \to 2^{\underline{k}}$.

Definition 11. *Let $B = (Q, P, \to)$ be a transition system. The corresponding net with boundaries $[\![B]\!] : \underline{0} \to \#P$ is $[\![B]\!] = (S, T, {}^\circ-, -{}^\circ, {}^\bullet-, -{}^\bullet)$ where:*

- $S = Q$
- $T = \{q \because a \therefore q' \mid q \xrightarrow{a} q'\}$.
- ${}^\circ(q \because a \therefore q') = \{q\}$ *and* $(q \because a \therefore q'){}^\circ = \{q'\}$.
- ${}^\bullet(q \because a \therefore q') = \varnothing$ *and* $(q \because a \therefore q'){}^\bullet = w_P(a)$.

Example 5. Consider the transition system depicted in Figure 6(a). The corresponding net with boundaries is in Figure 6(b).

Lemma 2. *Let $B = (Q, P, \to)$ be a transition system. Then, $q \xrightarrow{a} q'$ if and only if $([\![B]\!], \{q\}) \xrightarrow[\ulcorner w_P(a)\urcorner]{} ([\![B]\!], \{q'\})$.*

Next definition introduces the encoding of a set of synchronizations glueing components as a marked net with boundaries.

Definition 12. *Let γ be a set of synchronizations over P. The corresponding marked net with boundaries $[\![\gamma]\!]_P : \#P \to \#P$ is $(\{P_\gamma\}, \gamma, {}^\circ-, -{}^\circ, {}^\bullet-, -{}^\bullet, \{P_\gamma\})$ with*

- ${}^\circ a = a^\circ = \{P_\gamma\}$.
- ${}^\bullet a = a^\bullet = w_P(a)$.

Note that the place P_γ guarantees that all interactions are mutually exclusive.

Example 6. Consider the set of interactions $\gamma = \{ac, bd\}$ and assume $w_{\{a,b,c,d\}}$ coincides with alphabetical order. Then, the corresponding net is shown in Figure 7(a).

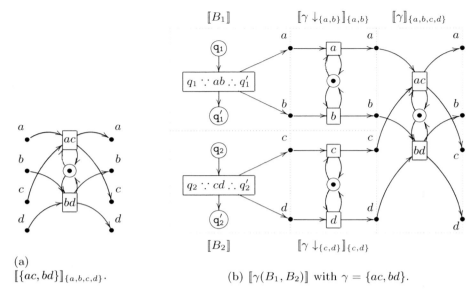

(a)
$\llbracket \{ac, bd\} \rrbracket_{\{a,b,c,d\}}.$

(b) $\llbracket \gamma(B_1, B_2) \rrbracket$ with $\gamma = \{ac, bd\}$.

Fig. 7. Compositional encoding

Lemma 3. *Let γ be a set of interactions over P. Then, $\llbracket \gamma \rrbracket_P \xrightarrow[\ulcorner w_P(a) \urcorner]{\ulcorner w_P(a) \urcorner} \llbracket \gamma \rrbracket_P$ iff $a \in \gamma$.*

Proof. It follows from the definition of $\llbracket \gamma \rrbracket_P$. □

Next definition introduces the compositional encoding of BI(P) systems.

Definition 13. *Let $B = \gamma(B_1, \dots, B_n)$ be a composite BI(P) system. The corresponding net with boundaries $\llbracket B \rrbracket : \underline{0} \to \#P$ with $P = \iota(B)$ is recursively defined as* [1]

$$\llbracket \gamma(B_1) \rrbracket = \llbracket B_1 \rrbracket; \llbracket \gamma \rrbracket_P$$
$$\llbracket \gamma(B_1, \dots, B_n) \rrbracket = (\gamma \downarrow_{P_1} \llbracket B_1 \rrbracket \otimes \llbracket \gamma \downarrow_{P \backslash P_1} (B_2, \dots, B_n) \rrbracket); \llbracket \gamma \rrbracket_P$$
$$\text{with } P_1 = \iota(B_1)$$

Example 7. Consider the BI(P) system $B = \{ac, bd\}(B_1, B_2)$ where B_1 has just one transition $q_1 \xrightarrow{ab} q_1'$ and B_2 has only $q_2 \xrightarrow{cd} q_2'$. The encoded net is in Figure 7(b). Note the necessity of considering all transitions in the encoding of $\{ac, bd\}$ to be mutual exclusive. Otherwise, the encoded form will also allow

---

[1] For technical convenience we define the encoding of $\gamma(B_1, \dots, B_n)$ in terms of a particular partition of the system: one subsystem containing just one component, i.e. B_1, and the other formed by the remaining components $B_2, \dots, B_n$. We remark that the results in this paper can be formulated by considering any possible partition of the system.

behaviours like $(\llbracket B \rrbracket, \{q_1, q_2\}) \xrightarrow[\ulcorner abcd \urcorner]{} (\llbracket B \rrbracket, \{q_1', q_2'\})$, i.e., will allow the synchronization $abcd$ that is not in $\{ac, bd\}$.

Theorem 2 (Correspondence). *Let $C = \gamma(C_1, \ldots, C_n)$ be a composite BI(P) system. Then, $(q_1, \ldots, q_n) \xrightarrow{a}_\gamma (q_1', \ldots, q_n')$ if and only if $(\llbracket C \rrbracket, \{q_1, \ldots, q_n\}) \xrightarrow[\ulcorner w_P(a) \urcorner]{} (\llbracket C \rrbracket, \{q_1', \ldots, q_n'\})$ with $P = \iota(C)$.*

Proof. By induction on the structure of the system C. Base case ($C = \gamma(C_1)$). There are two cases. (1) C is a basic composite BI(P) system, i.e., a BI(P) system, and C_1 is a transition system. Then, the proof is completed by using Lemmata 2 and 3. (ii) C is a composite system $C_1 = \gamma_1(C_1')$ with $\gamma_1 \triangleright_{\iota(C_1)} \gamma$. Note that $\iota(C) = \iota(C_1)$, hence $\gamma_1 \triangleright_{\iota(C_1)} \gamma$ implies $\gamma \downarrow_{\iota(C_1)} = \gamma \subseteq \gamma_1$. Then, the proof follows by using inductive hypothesis on $\gamma_1(C_1')$ and Lemma 3. Inductive step follows by inductive hypothesis on both subsystems and Lemma 3. □

3.4   Encoding Nets with Boundaries into BI(P)

This section shows that any net with boundaries without left interface can be seen as a BI(P) system consisting on just one component. The correspondence is stated by showing that there exists a straightforward encoding that maps states and transitions of the net to states and transitions of the transition system of the unique component.

Definition 14. *Let $N : \underline{0} \to \underline{n}$ with $N = (S, T, {}^\circ\!-, -^\circ, {}^\bullet\!-, -^\bullet)$ be a net with boundaries. Then, the corresponding BI(P) system $B_N = \gamma(B)$ is defined as follows:*

- $\gamma = 2^{\underline{n}}$
- $B = (2^S, 2^{\underline{n}}, \to)$ *with*

$$\to = \{q \xrightarrow{a} q' \mid q, q' \in Q \ \wedge \ U \subseteq T \ \wedge \ (N, q) \xrightarrow[\ulcorner a \urcorner]{} (N, q')\}$$

Note that the encoding of a net with right interface $\underline{n}$ is mapped to a component that has $2^{\underline{n}}$ ports, i.e., one port for any possible combination of the ports on the interface. We remark that the proposed encoding introduces the port named $\varnothing$ which makes internal movements of a component observable. We need such a port to be able to map any net movement of the form $(N, X) \xrightarrow[0^n]{} (N, X)$ with some movement of the BI(P) system.

Theorem 3 (Correspondence). *Let $N : \underline{0} \to \underline{n}$ be a net with boundaries and B_N the corresponding BI(P) system. Then, $(N, X) \xrightarrow{\alpha} (N, Y)$ iff $X \xrightarrow{\beta}_{B_N} Y$ where $\alpha = \ulcorner \beta \urcorner$.*

Proof. The result follows by construction of the BI(P) system. □

$$R ::= \bigcirc \mid \odot \mid I \mid \mathsf{X} \mid \nabla \mid \Delta \mid \perp \mid \top \mid \wedge \mid \vee \mid \downarrow \mid \uparrow \mid R \otimes R \mid R; R$$

Fig. 8. Petri calculus grammar

$$\frac{R : (k, l) \quad R' : (m, n)}{R \otimes R' : (k + m, l + n)} \qquad \frac{R : (k, n) \quad R' : (n, l)}{R; R' : (k, l)}$$

Fig. 9. Sort inference rules

$$\overline{\bigcirc \xrightarrow[0]{1} \odot} \quad \overline{\odot \xrightarrow[1]{0} \bigcirc} \quad \overline{\odot \xrightarrow[1]{1} \odot} \quad \overline{I \xrightarrow[1]{1} I} \quad \overline{\nabla \xrightarrow[11]{1} \nabla} \quad \overline{\Delta \xrightarrow[1]{11} \Delta} \quad \overline{\perp \xrightarrow[]{1} \perp} \quad \overline{\top \xrightarrow[1]{} \top}$$

$$\overline{\mathsf{X} \xrightarrow[yx]{xy} \mathsf{X}} \quad \overline{\wedge \xrightarrow[x\overline{x}]{1} \wedge} \quad \overline{\vee \xrightarrow[1]{x\overline{x}} \vee} \quad \frac{R_1 \xrightarrow[\sigma]{\alpha} R_2 \quad R'_1 \xrightarrow[\beta]{\sigma} R'_2}{R_1; R'_1 \xrightarrow[\beta]{\alpha} R_2; R'_2} \quad \frac{R_1 \xrightarrow[\beta]{\alpha} R_2 \quad R'_1 \xrightarrow[\sigma]{\rho} R'_2}{R_1 \otimes R'_1 \xrightarrow[\beta\rho]{\alpha\sigma} R_2 \otimes R'_2} \quad \frac{R : (m, n)}{R \xrightarrow[0^n]{0^m} R}$$

Fig. 10. Operational semantics for the Petri Calculus

4   The BIP Algebra of Connectors

Thanks to the result in § 3, we are now ready to provide a finite algebra for generating all BI(P) systems. The algebra we propose is the algebra of stateless connectors from [11], enriched with one-place buffers along [2,30,12]. We call it *Petri calculus* after [30]. Terms of the Petri Calculus are defined by the grammar in Fig. 8. It consists of the following constants plus parallel and sequential composition: the empty place $\bigcirc$, the full place $\odot$, the identity wire I, the twist (also swap, or symmetry) X, the duplicator (also sync) ∇ and its dual Δ, the mutex (also choice) $\wedge$ and its dual $\vee$, the hiding (also bang) $\perp$ and its dual $\top$, the inaction $\downarrow$ and its dual $\uparrow$.

Any term has a unique associated *sort* (also called *type*) (k, l) with $k, l \in \mathbb{N}$, that fixes the size k of the left (input) interface and the size l of the right (output) interface of P. The type of constants are as follows: $\bigcirc$, $\odot$, and I have type $(1, 1)$, $\mathsf{X} : (2, 2)$, ∇ and $\wedge$ have type $(1, 2)$ and their duals Δ and $\vee$ have type $(2, 1)$, $\perp$ and $\downarrow$ have type $(1, 0)$ and their duals $\top$ and $\uparrow$ have type $(0, 1)$. The sort inference rules for composed processes are in Fig. 9.

The operational semantics is defined by the rules in Fig. 10, where $x, y \in \{0, 1\}$ and we let $\overline{x} = 1 - x$. The labels $\alpha, \beta, \rho, \sigma$ of transitions are binary strings, all transitions are sort-preserving, and if $R \xrightarrow[\beta]{\alpha} R'$ with $R, R' : (n, m)$, then $|\alpha| = n$ and $|\beta| = m$. Notably, bisimilarity induced by such a transition system is a congruence.

Example 8. For example, let $R_1 \stackrel{\text{def}}{=} (\nabla \otimes \nabla); (\odot \otimes \mathsf{X} \otimes \bigcirc); (\Delta \otimes \Delta); \mathsf{X}$ and $R_2 \stackrel{\text{def}}{=}$ $(\nabla \otimes \nabla); (\bigcirc \otimes \mathsf{X} \otimes \odot); (\Delta \otimes \Delta); \mathsf{X}$. It is immediate to check that both R_1 and R_2 have sort $(2, 2)$, in fact we have: $\nabla \otimes \nabla : (2, 4)$, $\odot \otimes \mathsf{X} \otimes \bigcirc : (4, 4)$, $\bigcirc \otimes \mathsf{X} \otimes \odot :$ $(4, 4)$, $\Delta \otimes \Delta : (4, 2)$, and of course $\mathsf{X} : (2, 2)$. The only moves for R_1 are $R_1 \xrightarrow[00]{00} R_1$ and $R_1 \xrightarrow[10]{01} R_2$ while the only moves for R_2 are $R_2 \xrightarrow[00]{00} R_2$ and $R_2 \xrightarrow[01]{10} R_1$. It is immediate to note that R_1 and R_2 are terms analogous to the nets in Fig. 3 and that R_1 is bisimilar to $\mathsf{X}; R_2; \mathsf{X}$.

A close correspondence between nets with boundaries and Petri calculus terms is established in [30], by providing mutual encodings with tight semantics correspondence. First, it is shown that any net $N : m \to n$ with initial marking X can be associated with a term $T_{N,X} : (m, n)$ that preserves and reflects the semantics of N. Conversely, for any term $T : (m, n)$ of the Petri calculus there exists a bisimilar net $N_T : m \to n$. Due to space limitation we omit details here and refer the interested reader to [30].

Corollary 1. *The Petri calculus and BI(P) have the same expressive power.*

Proof. We know from [30,12] that the Petri calculus is as expressive as nets with boundaries, in the sense that given a net with boundaries we can find a bisimilar Petri calculus process and vice versa. The results in Section 3 show the analogous correspondence between nets with boundaries and BI(P) systems. Then, the thesis just follows by transitivity. □

It is interesting to compare the Petri calculus with the *algebra of causal interaction trees* from [8], generated by the grammar:

$$t ::= a \mid a \to t \mid t \oplus t$$

where a is an interaction. As a matter of notation, we can write $t \to t'$ meaning:

$$t \to t' = \begin{cases} a \to (t_1 \oplus t') & \text{if } t = a \to t_1 \\ (t_1 \to t') \oplus (t_2 \to t') & \text{if } t = t_1 \oplus t_2 \end{cases}$$

Intuitively, the causality operator $\to$ imposes a as a trigger of t in $a \to t$ (so that t can take part in a global interaction only if a does so), while the (associative and commutative) parallel composition operator $\oplus$ compose possible alternatives. Without loss of generality, we shall assume that in $t \oplus t'$ and $t \to t'$ the ports in t and t' are disjoint.

Example 9. Classical examples (taken from [8]) of interaction policies represented by the algebra of causal interaction trees over ports a, b, c and d are: the rendezvous $abcd$; the broadcast $a \to (b \oplus c \oplus d)$ corresponding to the set $\{a, ab, ac, ad, abc, abd, acd, abcd\}$; the atomic broadcast $a \to bcd$ corresponding to the set $\{a, abcd\}$; and the causal chain $a \to b \to c \to d$ corresponding to the set $\{a, ab, abc, abcd\}$.

The algebra of causal interaction trees has the advantage of distinguishing broadcast from a set of rendezvous by allowing to render the causal dependency relation between ports in an explicit way. Moreover, it allows to simplify exponentially complex models that cannot be a basis for efficient implementation and it induces a semantic equivalence that is also a congruence.

We can provide a direct translation from this algebra to the Petri calculus. To this aim, we fix some usual notation from the literature, that generalizes the simple connector constants to larger interfaces. Let $k > 0$, then we define $I_k : (k, k)$, $X_k : (1 + k, 1 + k)$, and $\wedge_k : (k, 2k)$ as below:

$$\begin{aligned}
I_1 &= I & I_{k+1} &= I \otimes I_k \\
X_1 &= X & X_{k+1} &= (X \otimes I_k); (I \otimes X_k) \\
\wedge_1 &= \wedge & \wedge_{k+1} &= (\wedge \otimes \wedge_k); (I \otimes X_k \otimes I_k)
\end{aligned}$$

Intuitively, I_k is the identity wiring, X_k swap the first port with the other $k - 1$ ports, and $\wedge_k : (k, 2k)$ splits a series of k ports.

Moreover, for $\alpha \in \{0, 1\}^k$ a binary string of length $k > 0$, we let $R^\alpha : (k, 1)$ denote the process inductively defined by:

$$R^0 = \downarrow; \top \qquad R^1 = I \qquad R^{x\alpha} = (R^x \otimes R^\alpha); \Delta$$

Intuitively, the term R^α synchronizes the ports associated to the positions of α that are set to 1.

We are now ready to encode causal interaction trees to Petri calculus processes. Let P be a set of ports, $n = \#P$ and t a causal interaction tree over P. We define the Petri calculus process $[\![t]\!]_P : (n, 1)$ by structural induction as below.

$$\begin{aligned}
[\![a]\!]_P &= R^{\ulcorner w_P(a) \urcorner} \\
[\![t \oplus t']\!]_P &= \wedge_n; ([\![t]\!]_P \otimes [\![t']\!]_P); (\wedge \otimes \wedge); (I \otimes \Delta \otimes I); (\vee \otimes I); \vee \\
[\![t \to t']\!]_P &= \wedge_n; ([\![t]\!]_P \otimes [\![t']\!]_P); (\wedge \otimes I); (I \otimes \Delta); \vee
\end{aligned}$$

The encodings $[\![a]\!]_P$ is straightforward. The encoding $[\![t \oplus t']\!]_P$ is obtained by first evaluating t and t' over the same input interface (see the sub-process $\wedge_n; ([\![t]\!]_P \otimes [\![t']\!]_P)$), then by requiring that either t and t' synchronize or that one of them executes alone. The encoding $[\![t \to t']\!]_P$ is analogous, but now either t and t' synchronize, or t executes alone.

Lemma 4. *The process $[\![t]\!]_P$ is stateless for any t, i.e., whenever $[\![t]\!]_P \xrightarrow[\beta]{\alpha} R'$ then $R' = [\![t]\!]_P$.*

Proof. The thesis follows simply by noting that $[\![t]\!]_P$ is composed out of stateless connectors, i.e., the encoding does not exploit the constants $\bigcirc, \odot$. $\square$

At the semantic level, the correspondence between t and $[\![t]\!]_P : (n, 1)$ can be stated as follows.

Proposition 1. *Let t be a causal interaction tree, let $\mathcal{I}(t)$ denote the set of interactions allowed by t and let $R = [\![t]\!]_P$. Then, $a \in \mathcal{I}(t)$ iff $R \xrightarrow[1]{\ulcorner w_P(a) \urcorner} R$.*

Proof. The proof is by structural induction on t. □

5   Related Work

In [11], an algebra of stateless connectors was presented that was inspired by previous work on simpler algebraic structures [10,31]. It consists of five kinds of basic connectors (plus their duals), namely symmetry, synchronization, mutual exclusion, hiding and inaction. The connectors can be composed in series or in parallel. The operational, observational and denotational semantics of connectors are first formalised separately and then shown to coincide. Moreover, a complete normal-form axiomatisation is available for them. These networks are quite expressive: for instance it is shown [11] that they can model all the (stateless) connectors of the architectural design language CommUnity [19]. The encoding shown in § 4 states that it is as expressive as the algebra of causal interaction trees. The algebra of stateless connectors in [11] can be regarded as a peculiar kind of tile model where all basic tiles have identical initial and final connectors, i.e. they are of the form $s \xrightarrow{a} s$. In terms of the wire calculus, this means that only recursive processes of the form $\mathbf{rec}\,X.\frac{a}{b}.X$ are considered for composing larger networks of connectors. The comparison in [11] is of particular interest, because it reconciles the algebraic and categorical approaches to system modelling, of which the algebra of stateless connectors and CommUnity are suitable representatives. The algebraic approach models systems as terms in a suitable algebra. Operational and abstract semantics are then usually based on inductively defined labelled transition systems. The categorical approach models systems as objects in a category, with morphisms defining relations such as subsystem or refinement. Complex software architectures can be modelled as diagrams in the category, with universal constructions, such as colimit, building an object in the same category that behaves as the whole system and that is uniquely determined up to isomorphisms. While in the algebraic approach equivalence classes are usually abstract entities, having a normal form gives a concrete representation that matches a nice feature of the categorical approach, namely that the colimit of a diagram is its best concrete representative.

Reo [1] is an exogenous coordination model for software components. Reo is based on channel-like connectors that mediate the flow of data and signals among components. Notably, a small set of point-to-point primitive connectors is sufficient to express a large variety of interesting constraints over the behaviour of connected components, including various forms of mutual exclusion, synchronization, alternation, and context-dependency. Typical primitive connectors are the synchronous/asynchronous/lossy channels and the asynchronous one-place buffer. They are attached to ports called Reo nodes. Components and primitive connectors can be composed into larger Reo circuits by disjoint union up-to the merging of shared Reo nodes. The semantics of Reo has been formalized in several ways, exploiting co-algebraic techniques [3], constraint-automata [4], coloring tables [17], and the tile model [2]. Differently from the stateless connectors of [11], Reo connectors are stateful (in particular due to the asynchronous one-place buffer connector). Nevertheless, it has been shown in [2] that the 2-colour semantics of Reo connectors can be recovered into the setting of the basic algebra of connectors and in the tile approach by adding a connector and a tile for the one-state buffer. It is worth mentioning that, in addition, the tile semantics of Reo connectors provides a description for full computations instead of just single steps (as considered in the original 2-colour semantics) and makes evident the evolution of the connector state (particularly, whether buffers get full or become empty).

The problem of interpreting BIP interaction models (i.e., the second layer of BIP) in terms of connectors has been addressed for the first time in [7], where BIP interaction is described as a structured combination of two basic synchronization primitives between ports: rendezvous and broadcast. In this approach, connectors are described as sets of possible interactions among involved ports. In particular, broadcasts are described by the set of all possible interactions among participating ports and thus the distinction between rendezvous and broadcast becomes blurred. The main drawback of this approach is that it induces an equivalence that is not a congruence. The paper [8] defines a causal semantics that does not reduce broadcast into a set of rendezvous and tracks the causal dependency relation between ports. In particular, the semantics based on causal interaction trees allows to simplify exponentially complex models that cannot be a basis for efficient implementation.

The Petri calculus approach [30] takes inspiration from the tile model and from the so-called Span(Graph) model [22,23]. The paper [30] is particularly interesting in our opinion because it relates for the first time process calculi and Petri nets via a finite set of basic connectors.

6   Conclusion

One of the main limitations of the state-of-the-art theories of connectors is the lack of a reference paradigm for describing and analysing the information flow to be imposed over components for proper coordination. Such a paradigm would allow designers, analysts and programmers to rely on well-founded and standard concepts instead of using all kinds of heterogeneous mechanisms, like semaphores, monitors, message passing primitives, event notification, remote call, etc. Moreover, the reference paradigm would facilitate the comparison and evaluation of otherwise unrelated architectural approaches as well as the development of code libraries for distributed connectors. To some extent, the reference paradigm could thus play the role of a unifying semantic framework for connectors.

We conjecture that the algebraic properties of the tile model can help relating formal frameworks that are otherwise very different in style and nature (CommUnity, Reo, Petri nets with boundaries, wire calculus). For instance, while compositionality needs often ad hoc proofs when other approaches are considered, in the case of the tile model, it can be expressed in terms of the congruence result for tile bisimilarity and it can be guaranteed by the format in which basic tiles are presented.

The most interesting and challenging research avenue for future work is the representation of priorities in approaches such as the Petri calculus and the tile model.

References

1. Arbab, F.: Reo: a channel-based coordination model for component composition. Mathematical Structures in Computer Science 14(3), 329–366 (2004)
2. Arbab, F., Bruni, R., Clarke, D., Lanese, I., Montanari, U.: Tiles for Reo. In: Corradini, A., Montanari, U. (eds.) WADT 2008. LNCS, vol. 5486, pp. 37–55. Springer, Heidelberg (2009)
3. Arbab, F., Rutten, J.J.M.M.: A Coinductive Calculus of Component Connectors. In: Wirsing, M., Pattinson, D., Hennicker, R. (eds.) WADT 2003. LNCS, vol. 2755, pp. 34–55. Springer, Heidelberg (2003)
4. Baier, C., Sirjani, M., Arbab, F., Rutten, J.J.M.M.: Modeling component connectors in Reo by constraint automata. Sci. Comput. Program 61(2), 75–113 (2006)
5. Baldan, P., Corradini, A., Ehrig, H., Heckel, R.: Compositional semantics for open Petri nets based on deterministic processes. Mathematical Structures in Computer Science 15(1), 1–35 (2005)
6. Basu, A., Bozga, M., Sifakis, J.: Modeling heterogeneous real-time components in BIP. In: Fourth IEEE International Conference on Software Engineering and Formal Methods (SEFM 2006), pp. 3–12. IEEE Computer Society (2006)
7. Bliudze, S., Sifakis, J.: The algebra of connectors - structuring interaction in BIP. IEEE Trans. Computers 57(10), 1315–1330 (2008)
8. Bliudze, S., Sifakis, J.: Causal semantics for the algebra of connectors. Formal Methods in System Design 36(2), 167–194 (2010)
9. Bruni, R.: Tile Logic for Synchronized Rewriting of Concurrent Systems. PhD thesis, Computer Science Department, University of Pisa, Published as Technical Report TD-1/99 (1999)
10. Bruni, R., Gadducci, F., Montanari, U.: Normal forms for algebras of connection. Theor. Comput. Sci. 286(2), 247–292 (2002)
11. Bruni, R., Lanese, I., Montanari, U.: A basic algebra of stateless connectors. Theor. Comput. Sci. 366(1-2), 98–120 (2006)
12. Bruni, R., Melgratti, H., Montanari, U.: A Connector Algebra for P/T Nets Interactions. In: Katoen, J.-P., König, B. (eds.) CONCUR 2011 – Concurrency Theory. LNCS, vol. 6901, pp. 312–326. Springer, Heidelberg (2011)
13. Bruni, R., Meseguer, J., Montanari, U.: Symmetric monoidal and cartesian double categories as a semantic framework for tile logic. Mathematical Structures in Computer Science 12(1), 53–90 (2002)
14. Bruni, R., Montanari, U.: Cartesian closed double categories, their lambda-notation, and the pi-calculus. In: LICS, pp. 246–265 (1999)
15. Bruni, R., Montanari, U.: Dynamic connectors for concurrency. Theor. Comput. Sci. 281(1-2), 131–176 (2002)
16. Bruni, R., Montanari, U., Rossi, F.: An interactive semantics of logic programming. TPLP 1(6), 647–690 (2001)

17. Clarke, D., Costa, D., Arbab, F.: Connector colouring I: Synchronisation and context dependency. Sci. Comput. Program 66(3), 205–225 (2007)
18. Ferrari, G.L., Montanari, U.: Tile formats for located and mobile systems. Inf. Comput. 156(1-2), 173–235 (2000)
19. Fiadeiro, J.L., Maibaum, T.S.E.: Categorical semantics of parallel program design. Sci. Comput. Program 28(2-3), 111–138 (1997)
20. Gadducci, F., Montanari, U.: The tile model. In: Plotkin, G.D., Stirling, C., Tofte, M. (eds.) Proof, Language, and Interaction, pp. 133–166. The MIT Press (2000)
21. Gadducci, F., Montanari, U.: Comparing logics for rewriting: rewriting logic, action calculi and tile logic. Theor. Comput. Sci. 285(2), 319–358 (2002)
22. Katis, P., Sabadini, N., Walters, R.F.C.: Representing Place/Transition Nets in Span(Graph). In: Johnson, M. (ed.) AMAST 1997. LNCS, vol. 1349, pp. 322–336. Springer, Heidelberg (1997)
23. Katis, P., Sabadini, N., Walters, R.F.C.: Span(Graph): A Categorial Algebra of Transition Systems. In: Johnson, M. (ed.) AMAST 1997. LNCS, vol. 1349, pp. 307–321. Springer, Heidelberg (1997)
24. König, B., Montanari, U.: Observational Equivalence for Synchronized Graph Rewriting with Mobility. In: Kobayashi, N., Babu, C. S. (eds.) TACS 2001. LNCS, vol. 2215, pp. 145–164. Springer, Heidelberg (2001)
25. MacLane, S.: Categories for the Working Mathematician, 2nd edn. Springer, Heidelberg (1998)
26. Montanari, U., Rossi, F.: Graph rewriting, constraint solving and tiles for coordinating distributed systems. Applied Categorical Structures 7(4), 333–370 (1999)
27. Perry, D.E., Wolf, E.L.: Foundations for the study of software architecture. ACM SIGSOFT Software Engineering Notes 17, 40–52 (1992)
28. Petri, C.: Kommunikation mit Automaten. PhD thesis, Institut für Instrumentelle Mathematik, Bonn (1962)
29. Sobocinski, P.: A non-interleaving process calculus for multi-party synchronisation. In: Bonchi, F., Grohmann, D., Spoletini, P., Tuosto, E. (eds.) ICE. EPTCS, vol. 12, pp. 87–98 (2009)
30. Sobociński, P.: Representations of Petri Net Interactions. In: Gastin, P., Laroussinie, F. (eds.) CONCUR 2010. LNCS, vol. 6269, pp. 554–568. Springer, Heidelberg (2010)
31. Stefanescu, G.: Reaction and control I. mixing additive and multiplicative network algebras. Logic Journal of the IGPL 6(2), 348–369 (1998)

Models of Provenance
(Abstract)

Peter Buneman

LFCS, School of Informatics,
Crichton Street Edinburgh EH8 9LE

As more and more information is available to us on the Web, the understanding of its provenance – its source and derivation – is essential to the trust we place in that information. Provenance has become especially important to scientific research, which now relies on information that has been repeatedly copied, transformed and annotated.

Provenance is also emerging as a topic of interest to many branches of computer science including probabilistic databases, data integration, file synchronization, program debugging and security. Efforts by computer scientists have resulted in a somewhat bewildering variety of models of provenance which, although they have the same general purpose, have very little in common.

In this talk, I will attempt to survey these models, to describe why they were developed and to indicate how they can be connected. There has been a particularly rich effort in describing the provenance of data that results from database queries. There are also emerging models for the description of provenance associated with workflows. Can they, or should they, be reconciled? I shall also talk about some of the practical issues involved in the recording and maintenance of provenance data.

E. Clarke, I. Virbitskaite, and A. Voronkov (Eds.): PSI 2011, LNCS 7162, p. 39, 2012.

End-to-End Guarantees
in Embedded Control Systems
(Abstract)

Rupak Majumdar

Max Planck Institute for Software Systems,
Kaiserslautern, Germany

Software implementations of controllers for physical subsystems form the core of many modern safety-critical systems such as aircraft flight control and automotive engine control. In the model-based approach to the design and implementation of these systems, the control designer starts with a mathematical model of the system and argues that key properties – such as stability and performance – are met for the model. Then, the model is compiled into code, where extensive simulations are used to informally justify that the implementation faithfully captures the model.

We present a methodology and a tool to perform automated static analysis of control system models together with embedded controller code. Our methodology relates properties, such as stability, proved at the design level with properties of the code. Our methodology is based on the following separation of concerns. First, we analyze the controller mathematical models to derive bounds on the implementation errors that can be tolerated while still guaranteeing the required performance. Second, we automatically analyze the controller software to check if the maximal implementation error is within the tolerance bound computed in the first step.

We present two examples of this methodology: first, in verifying bounds on the stability of control systems in the presence of errors arising from the use of fixed-point arithmetic, and second, in generating flexible schedulers for control systems sharing common resources.

E. Clarke, I. Virbitskaite, and A. Voronkov (Eds.): PSI 2011, LNCS 7162, p. 40, 2012.
© Springer-Verlag Berlin Heidelberg 2012

Mining Precise Specifications
(Abstract)

Andreas Zeller

Saarland University, Germany
zeller@cs.uni-saarland.de

Recent advances in software validation and verification make it possible to widely automate the check whether a specification is satisfied. This progress is hampered, though, by the persistent difficulty of writing specifications. Are we facing a "specification crisis"? By mining specifications from existing systems, we can alleviate this burden, reusing and extending the knowledge of 60 years of programming, and bridging the gap between formal methods and real-world software. But mining specifications has its challenges: We need good usage examples to learn expected behavior; we need to cope with the approximations of static and dynamic analysis; and we need specifications that are readable and relevant to users. In this talk, I present the state of the art in specification mining, its challenges, and its potential, up to a vision of seamless integration of specification and programming.

E. Clarke, I. Virbitskaite, and A. Voronkov (Eds.): PSI 2011, LNCS 7162, p. 41, 2012.

Detecting Entry Points in Java Libraries*

Thomas Baar and Philipp Kumar

akquinet tech @ spree GmbH,
Bülowstraße 66, D-10783 Berlin, Germany
{thomas.baar,philipp.kumar}@akquinet.de

Abstract. When writing a Java library, it is very difficult to hide functionality that is intended not to be used by clients. The visibility concept of Java often forces the developer to expose implementation details. Consequently, we find a high number of public classes and methods in many Java libraries. Thus, client programmers must rely on documentation in order to identify the *entry points* of the library, i.e. the methods originally intended to be used by clients.

In this paper, we introduce a new metric, called the *Method Weight*, that assists in detecting entry points. Applying this metric on some well-known open-source Java libraries considerably supported the process of identifying their entry points. Furthermore, the metric provides a classification criterion to distinguish libraries with focused functionality from plain collections of utility classes.

1 Motivation

Developing a Java library to be used by others is difficult. Moreover, writing it in a way that it is intuitively usable and open for future changes, without breaking existing client code, is extremely hard [8]. Joshua Bloch, a key contributor to the Java Standard Library and author of the influential book "Effective Java", encourages programmers to hide as many implementation details as possible. Every piece of software should be developed as if it were a library, i.e. its public methods must be carefully designed because they can potentially be used by clients [3]. As our empirical results in Section 4 show, even libraries from well-known programmers suffer from a high number of public classes and methods.

Why is the proper design and implementation of a Java library such a difficult task? Besides finding descriptive, intuitive names for classes and methods, the main problem lies in the elegant realization of information hiding. In Java, only classes and methods declared as public are visible to clients. There is, however, a strong incentive to also declare internal library elements as public, although these are intended to be used only within the library. The source for this incentive is the very restricted accessibility of non-public elements. Such elements can only be accessed from other classes of the same package or from subclasses. In other

---

* This work was supported by *Bundesministerium für Bildung und Forschung*, research framework *Unternehmen Region*, project *BIZWARE*.

E. Clarke, I. Virbitskaite, and A. Voronkov (Eds.): PSI 2011, LNCS 7162, pp. 42–54, 2012.

words, Java lacks a visibility concept that would allow packages within a library to access each other while being hidden to the library's client at the same time.

Granting access to too many elements of the library has several negative consequences. First, all contracts of exposed methods must be obeyed in future versions of the library, as client code might depend on them. Once made public, a method is no longer an implementation detail and therefore can not be easily changed by the library's author. Second, a high number of public methods obscures the intent and purpose of the library. The programmer of client code has to rely on documentation and tutorial examples in order to understand how the library is to be used.

In order to alleviate the second negative consequence, we propose a metric-based technique to determine *entry points*. In this context, an entry point is a method that is intended by the library author to be used by client code. A first attempt to identify entry points could be to select all public methods that are not used by other methods within the library. Speaking in terms of metrics, candidates for entry points would be all methods m that are public and have an *Afferent Coupling (CA)* of zero ($CA(m) = 0$). But, as shown in Section 4, this metric is insufficient in order to reliably identify entry points.

Better results are obtained by applying a new metric, which we call *Method Weight (MW)*. Basically, the Method Weight of method m is the code size of m and all its reimplementations in subclasses plus the Method Weight of all methods directly or transitively called by m. The Method Weight represents the size of the overall method implementation, taking – due to dynamic binding – variants (reimplementations in subclasses) and directly or transitively called methods together with their variants into account. Note that Method Weight is defined recursively:

$$MW(m) = size(m) + \Sigma_i\ MW(m_i)$$

where m_i is a reimplementation of or called by m. In case of a cycle in the relationships of m and m_i, the Method Weight MW(m) is defined as the least fixpoint satisfying the equation.

When computing the Method Weight of methods of existing open-source Java libraries, we recognized different kinds of libraries. For some libraries, such as *jarAnalyzer* [11], the majority of methods have a comparatively low weight. The few remaining high-weight methods are most likely entry points. In other libraries, such as *Apache Commons IO* [2], the method weight is equally distributed. This hints at a library consisting of utility classes rather than a library focusing on a single functionality.

The paper is organized as follows: In Section 2, we briefly revisit Java's visibility flags and show, using a well-known example, how they can be elegantly used to achieve information hiding. In addition, we present ongoing attempts to make Java libraries more modular. Section 3 defines the metric *Method Weight (MW)* and discusses its limitations and tool support. Section 4 describes the experiments we conducted in order to identify entry points of some well-known open-source libraries. While Section 5 gives an overview on related work, Section 6 concludes the paper.

2   Information Hiding in Java

One of the holy grails of the object-oriented paradigm is the support for data encapsulation and information hiding: A software entity can impose access restrictions to the internal state or state structure [16]. Thus, it allows programmers to hide implementation details of the class from other classes to keep them changeable in the future. Access restrictions are imposed by visibility flags that can be attached to classes, methods, and attributes.

In the following, we briefly revisit Java's visibility flags and present a well-known example how they can be utilized to achieve information hiding. Despite the elegant examples found in the Java Standard Library, there is an established consensus that Java's visibility modifiers are not fine grained enough, resulting in numerous attempts to introduce a modularization concept to Java. This trend will be discussed in Subsection 2.2.

2.1   Java Visibilities

Class members such as methods and attributes have one of the following visibility flags assigned: *public*, *private*, *protected*, *package* (being the default visibility). Access is granted from all classes, from the same class only, from subclasses, and from classes of the same package, respectively. Furthermore, the same visibility flags also apply to classes [6].

Often, Java's visibility flags are too coarse-grained and prevent programmers from hiding implementation details. For example, programmers are forced to declare a method C.m() as public as soon as this method is supposed to be called from another class C1 which neither resides in the same package as C nor is a subclass of C. Once made public, however, the method C.m() is exposed to any client, not only to classes within the same library. Thus, C.m() becomes a potential entry point for the library, although the intent of the programmer is to hide C.m() from outside the library.

Though Java's visibility flags are often insufficient in order to hide implementation details of a library, there are, nevertheless, examples of highly elegant usage of visibilities. For instance, we refer to the Java Collections Framework which is part of the Java Standard Library (see Fig. 1). The utility class java.util.Collections contains a number of public static methods, which transform the respective argument (a collection) into a new collection with certain properties. One of these methods is Collection synchronizedCollection(Collection c), which returns a new Collection object. This object is synchronized (i.e. thread-safe) while containing the same elements as the original collection.

What makes this piece of software so elegant is the fact that class SynchronizedCollection, which the returned object is an instance of, is completely hidden from the client and implemented as an inner class of class Collections. Note that the return value of method synchronizedCollection() is of type Collection and not of the more concrete type SynchronizedCollection.

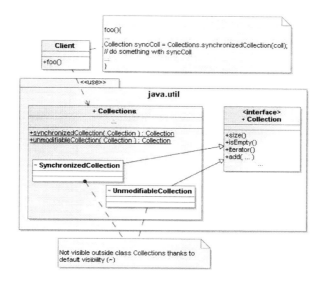

Fig. 1. Information hiding in the Java Collections Framework

Consequently, the inner class `SynchronizedCollection`, on whose services surely thousands of other applications rely, can be removed safely in future versions of the Java Standard Library.

2.2 Java Modularization Attempts

Currently, a Java package is the most coarse-grained software entity that can be attributed with a visibility flag. It is not possible to declare a visibility with respect to a group of packages, like a library.

To overcome this limitation, there are several efforts to introduce support for modular programming to the Java language. The most prominent specification request within the Java Community Process Program, JSR 294 [9], proposes a super-package concept capable of encapsulating multiple packages and hiding packages that are not explicitly exported. The most current effort, project Jigsaw [14], has been created within the OpenJDK Community and aims at modularizing the JDK. The introduced capabilities, such as a new *module* keyword, are also utilizable by developers to introduce modules to their systems.

A modularization technology already in widespread use is OSGi. The OSGi Alliance, formerly known as the Open Services Gateway Initiative, was founded in March 1999. It specified and actively maintains the OSGi standard. Originally intended to make development and dynamic deployment of applications for small-memory devices easier, the specification has grown and now defines a framework capable of service-oriented interactions and dynamic deployment of software components.

The OSGi Service Platform [15] introduces a module system for Java that allows to specify an interface for a software component. Such a component, called a *bundle*, can consist of multiple Java packages. It is commonly implemented as a JAR file, but with added meta information that describes the set of interfaces that the bundle uses (imports) as well as the part of the bundle's functionality that is offered to other bundles (exports). This effectively provides the means to define classes that are private to the bundle.

Thus, OSGi can reduce the number of entry points for a component, because it forces the developer to explicitly define the component's API, effectively encapsulating all other functionality. But, for the same reason, it can be difficult to adopt OSGi in existing systems that were not designed in a modular fashion. While avoiding malpractices such as cyclic dependencies, OSGi's strictness may necessitate a major restructuring of systems, especially legacy ones, before a partitioning into OSGi bundles becomes possible.

3   Metric: Method Weight

Metrics such as the well-known *Chidamber-and-Kemerer-* [4], *Halstead-* [7] or *McCabe*-metrics [13] are used to measure certain aspects of implementation code, such as code complexity, code size, or coupling and responsibility of classes. The measured values can point the programmer to smells and other anomalies of a software system.

Metrics seem to be also a good tool for the detection of entry points of a library. A promising candidate is the well-known metric *Afferent Coupling* [4] applied on methods $(CA(m))$. This metric counts the number of invocations of method m within the library. If $CA(m)$ is very low, then chances are good that method m was designed to be called by client code.

As our experiments with some open-source libraries show (cmp. Section 4), the metric Afferent Coupling is not sufficient for the detection of entry points. Therefore, we define below the metric *Method Weight (MW)*, which proved to be very useful for entry point detection (cmp. Section 4). Besides defining the metric MW, we also explore its limitations and inform about existing tool support for applying the metric on real-world examples.

3.1   Definition

The metric *Method Weight (MW)* is defined as follows.

Definition 1 (Method Weight). *Let m be a method of class C in library L. The* method weight of m *(MW(m)) is the* code size *for the* full implementation *of m within L. The full implementation is the overall code to implement*

- *m itself,*
- *all re-implementations of m in subclasses of C within L, and*
- *all methods m' within L that might be directly or transitively called by m and all reimplementations of m'.*

The code size *of a method is the size of byte code created by the compiler to execute the method. This includes byte code for manipulating datastructures, such as attributes of objects.*

Note that $MW(m)$ takes only the code size of m within library L into account, in which m is defined. If m calls a method defined in another library, the size of the called method does not contribute to the weight of m.

The decision to measure the *code size* in terms of byte code size is not mandatory. The measurement of code size could also have been based on the Lines of Source Code (LOC) metric, for which many variants exist. Our preference for byte code is motivated by already existing tool support (Sect. 3.3) for computing Method Weight. Note that - at least for the detection of entry points - we are not interested in absolute numbers for Method Weight, but rather in an ordering of methods wrt. their weight.

The following example illustrates the definition of Method Weight. We assume that library L consists of classes C and SubC.

Listing 1.1. Illustration of metric Method Weight (MW)

```
public class C {
    protected int a11, a12, a21, a22 = 0;

    public int m1() {
        m11(); m12();
        return a11 + a12;}

    public int m2() {
        m21(); m22();
        return a21 + a22;}

    private void m11() { a11++; }

    protected void m12() { a12++;}

    private void m21() { a21++;}

    private void m22() { a22++;}
}


public class SubC extends C {
    //redefinition of m2()
    public int m2() {
        ...
    }

    //redefinition of m12()
    protected int m12() {
        ...
    }
}
```

```
           C
#a11 : int
#a12 : int
#a21 : int
#a22 : int

+m1()
+m2()
-m11()
#m12()
-m21()
-m22()
```

```
          SubC

+m2()
#m12()
```

Class C has two public methods: m1() and m2(). The implementation of C.m1() calls the methods C.m11() and C.m12(), whereas the latter is overridden in class SubC. Thus, metric $MW(\text{C.m1}())$ is computed by summarizing

- the code size of C.m1() itself,
- the code size of called methods C.m11(), C.m12(),
- the code size of reimplementations of called methods, i.e. SubC.m12().

In this example, the implementation of C.m2() is defined analogously to C.m1(). However, since C.m2() is overridden, metric $MW(\texttt{C.m2()})$ is computed by summarizing the code size of C.m2(), C.m21(), C.m22(), and SubC.m2().

3.2 Limitations

It is important to note that metric *Method Weight (MW)* can be computed effectively only as long as all called methods (also transitively called methods) can be determined at compile-time. This is not the case as soon as the implementation of method m or one of its called methods use reflection facilities provided by Java. Consequently, the metric MW and our approach to detect entry points can only be applied safely on libraries that do not use reflection. All static analysis methods and metric computations suffer from this restriction and lose precision when applied on libraries relying on reflection. If reflection is used, it is possible that a library has methods with low weight although they are entry points. Consequently, our approach can miss some entry points in this case.

While this limitation is indeed a severe restriction for many libraries due to their usage of reflection, it does not have any influence on the results for the libraries we have chosen for our experiments in Section 4.

3.3 Tool-Support for Computing MW

The tool *ProGuard* [12], developed by Eric Lafortune, is able to compute metric *Method Weight MW*. ProGuard's main purpose is the shrinking and obfuscation of JAR files. Especially when programming Java applications for mobile devices, it is still of paramount importance to keep the memory footprint of the application as low as possible. The memory footprint of an application is the size of the application's JAR file plus the size of all required libraries.

In the past, programmers, who had to develop Java applications with minimal footprint, had to carefully decide if they wanted to base the application code on a new library. If the library is large but only very few functions are needed by the application, programmers started to look for alternatives in order to keep the application's footprint low. Thanks to ProGuard, programmers can now *shrink* the library to those elements that are actually needed when calling a method m. Instead of adding the original large library to their application, they can now add a shrunken, much smaller version of it. This shrunken version is generated by ProGuard and is semantically equivalent to the original library wrt. the execution of m.

The size of the shrunken JAR file is the weight of method m. We will in our experiments, however, not use the absolute size of the shrunken JAR file, but the quotient of size of shrunken JAR file to the size of the original JAR file. If this quotient is multiplied by 100, the resulting number is the percentage of the orginal JAR file that is necessary to execute method m.

4   Experiments

In this section, experimental results are presented, which we obtained when applying our approach to three open-source Java libraries. For each of the libraries, we briefly summarize its purpose and present the most important metric-values to characterize the size of the library, such as the number of classes and number of public methods. These basic metric-values have been obtained by applying Apache BCEL [1].

As the main step of the experiment, we measured then the metrics Afferent Coupling (CA) and Method Weight (MW) in order to detect entry points. We measured these metrics only on potential entry points. A method is a potential entry point if it is exposed, i.e. has public visibility and is owned by a public class, and if it is not a *getter* or *setter*[1].

The results of the metric computation are shown in Figure 2 - 4. On the X-axis of the diagram, each potential entry point method is represented by a number. The diagram shows two curves. The Y-values for the Afferent Coupling (CA) curve are the number of invocations of the respective methods. The Y-values for the Method Weight (MW) curve are scaled to the maximum value of 10. The value of 10 corresponds to a weight of 100 percent.

The methods are ordered in such a way that the CA-values are monotonically increasing. Recall that the value $CA(m)$ is the number of invocations of method m from a location within the library. Methods having an Afferent Coupling of 0 are not called at all from within the library.

4.1   ckjm - Spinellis' Implementation of Chidamber and Kemerer Metrics for Java

The library *ckjm* [17], written by Diomidis Spinellis, is a small library to compute the Chidamber and Kemerer metrics for a given JAR file. It is based on Apache Byte Code Engineering Library (BCEL) [1], used for parsing JAR files. Basically, ckjm computes the metrics by implementing visitors for the parsed syntax tree. It consists of 7 classes and has a size of 10 KB. All public classes together exhibit 36 public methods, from which 21 methods are neither getters nor setters.

As shown in Figure 2, among the 21 potential entry points there are 4 methods having an Afferent Coupling of 0 (CA(m) = 0).

The metric Method Weight (MW) divides the potential entry points into 3 groups: Two methods have a weight higher than 8, which is considerably higher than the weight of all other methods. The second group consists of 7 methods with a weight of about 6. The third group comprises the remaining methods with a weight lower than 2.

---

[1] A getter / setter is a method whose name starts with *get* / *set*. By convention, such methods are restricted to return or manipulate an attribute of an object. According to that convention, such methods do not call other methods and are never entry points for that reason.

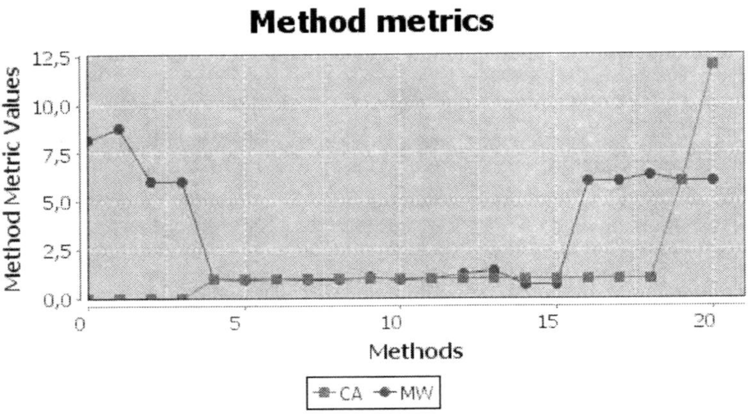

Method metrics

Fig. 2. Comparing metrics CA and MW for ckjm

The two methods with the highest MW-values are `MetricsFilter.run` `Metrics()` and `MetricsFilter.main()`. These methods are – according to the author's comments on these methods – indeed intended to be entry points.

The methods of the second group are all visitor methods which implement the traversal of a parsed syntax tree (see [5] for details on the Visitor pattern). Though two of them have an Afferent Coupling of 0, they are no dead code. These visitor methods are called by the BCEL-library because they implement an interface declared in BCEL.

4.2 jarAnalyzer

The library *jarAnalyzer* [11], authored by Kirk Knoernschild, is a library to analyze JAR files. It is based on BCEL as well. The library has a size of 24 KB and contains 24 classes. All public classes together exhibit 122 public methods, from which 67 methods are neither getters nor setters.

As shown in Figure 3, among the 67 potential entry points there are 15 methods having an Afferent Coupling of 0 (CA(m) = 0).

The metric Method Weight (MW) divides the potential entry points into roughly 2 groups: 9 methods have a weight higher than 5, while all the other methods have a weight below 1 (with one exception, method 35, which, however, can be ignored here).

The methods with the high weight are all contained in two classes: `XMLUISummary` and `DOTSummary`. Both classes have a method `main`, which has an Afferent Coupling of 0. They are represented in the diagram by the numbers 11 and 14 (X-axis) and are clearly the entry points. The implementation of these two methods delegate to methods with numbers 44, 45 and 47, 48. This explains the high weight of the called methods and their Afferent Coupling of 1.

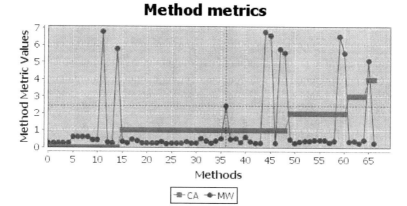

Fig. 3. Comparing metrics CA and MW for jarAnalyzer

4.3 Apache Commons IO

The library *Apache Commons IO* [2] is the standard library of the Apache Foundation for handling input/output-tasks. It has a size of 125 KB and contains 104 classes. The public classes together have 693 public methods, from which 616 are neither getters nor setters.

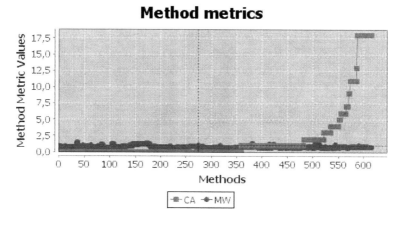

Fig. 4. Comparing metrics CA and MW for Apache Commons IO

As shown in Figure 4, among the 616 potential entry points there are 360 methods having an Afferent Coupling of 0 ($CA(m) = 0$). There are 28 methods having an Afferent Coupling of 18; these are all methods named `accept`, what indicates their role within a Visitor [5].

For all public methods, the value of metric Method Weight (MW) is basically the same (around 1). There are no significant differences that would allow one to classify any of the methods as entry points.

4.4   Discussion

We conducted our experiments on two relatively small libraries and one larger library. All libraries were written by well-known programmers, so the code is generally well-structured, understandable and well-documented.

The two small libraries have entry points, which can be clearly identified when reading the code. The metric Afferent Coupling (CA) was not able to detect these entry points. A method that is not called from within the library is not necessarily an entry point because there are several technical reasons to have such methods. In contrast to Afferent Coupling, the metric Method Weight (MW) was able to detect all entry points that were intended as such by the library authors. In case of jarAnalyzer, the metric also detected some non entry points, which are, however, called directly by an entry point and in which the main part of the implementation is realized. Note, however, that these methods that are "almost" entry points have an Afferent Coupling of 1. Consequently, the metrics Method Weight and Afferent Coupling applied together reliably detect entry points.

The library Apache Commons IO does not have clearly identifiable entry points. The metric Method Weight does not detect any method as entry point since all methods have a very low weight. Furthermore, more than half of the potential entry points have an Afferent Coupling of 0. We conclude that Apache Commons IO is a library that does not focus on few functionalities (as the two small libraries do) but provides a wide range of utilities. For these utilities, the metric Afferent Coupling is a far better detector than Method Weight.

5   Related Work

Software metrics for measuring certain properties of software systems has been standardized in the *IEEE Standard for a Software Quality Metrics Methodology 1061*, first published in 1992. The oldest metric that found wide adoption is lines of code (LOC). Though the metric looks very simple at the first glance, there had been many problems to be solved before software industry could agree on a standardized method to measure LOC. Some of these problems were related to handling of blank lines, comment lines, dead-code, multiple lines per statement, multiple statements per line.

To the best of our knowledge, LOC-metrics for methods always count the lines of code of a single method implementation only. They do not take the size of re-implementations of the method within subclasses into account, nor the size of methods, that are called by the method implementation. For this reason, we introduced the metric Method Weight (MW) in this paper.

The challenges when designing a library together with guidelines and best practices are described in recent textbooks, such as [3], [18], [10]. In [3], Bloch describes the *conceptional weight* of classes. It is defined as the number of all public members of a class. It is a metric for the maintainability of the library, because all public members have to be preserved (also semantically) in future versions of the library. A high conceptional weight increases the difficulty to find the entry points. This is a very practical problem, for which our approach is of help.

6 Conclusions

In this paper, we report on experiments we conducted on applying the metric Method Weight (MW) on public methods (that are neither getter nor setter methods) for some published open-source libraries. The original motivation was to investigate whether the metric Method Weight (MW) is suitable for the detection of entry points for those libraries. We also compared the metric value of Method Weight with that of Afferent Coupling.

The experiments uncovered results that we did not expect. First, we were astonished about the relatively high numbers of public methods. The conclusion we draw is that library authors do not use the visibilities offered by Java to clearly separate entry points from methods intended for internal use. There are also many technical reasons to make a method public. Second, the high number of methods with an Afferent Coupling of zero is very surprising. Again, there are several technical reasons to have public methods that are not used inside the library, e.g. Visitor methods.

The metric Method Weight can identify entry points more accurately. If only a few methods have a very high weight, then these methods are clearly intended as entry points. But there are also libraries – Apache Commons IO is an example – that lack methods with high MW values but rather have many methods with moderate MW values. Such a result indicates that a library is designed to be a collection of tools (i.e. many different methods for certain tasks like copying a file) rather than a library with a focused purpose.

So far, our approach has only been applied to the analysis of Java libraries. One direction of future work is to apply the same technique for other programming or even modeling languages, such as UML/OCL.

References

1. Apache Foundation: Byte Code Engineering Library (BCEL) 5.2, http://jakarta.apache.org/bcel/
2. Apache Foundation: Commons IO Library 2.0.1, http://commons.apache.org/io/
3. Bloch, J.: Effective Java, 2nd edn. Addison-Wesley (2008)
4. Chidamber, S.R., Kemerer, C.F.: A metrics suite for object oriented design. IEEE Trans. Softw. Eng. 20, 476–493 (1994), http://portal.acm.org/citation.cfm?id=630808.631131
5. Gamma, E., Helm, R., Johnson, R., Vlissides, J.: Design Patterns: Elements of Reusable Object-Oriented Software. Addison-Wesley, Reading/MA (1995)

6. Gosling, J., Joy, B., Steele, G.L., Bracha, G.: Java Language Specification, 3rd edn. Addison-Wesley (2005)
7. Halstead, M.H.: Elements of software science. Elsevier (1977)
8. Henning, M.: API Design Matters. Communications of the ACM (CACM) 52(5), 46–56 (2009)
9. Java Community Process: Java Specification Request (JSR)-294, http://jcp.org/en/jsr/detail?id=294
10. Kerievsky, J.: Refactoring to Patterns. Addison-Wesley (2005)
11. Knoernschild, K.: JarAnalyzer 1.2, http://www.kirkk.com/main/main/jaranalyzer
12. Lafortune, E.: ProGuard 4.6, http://proguard.sourceforge.net/
13. McCabe, T.J.: A complexity measure. IEEE Transactions on Software Engineering 2(4), 308–320 (1976)
14. OpenJDK: Project jigsaw, http://openjdk.java.net/projects/jigsaw/
15. OSGi Alliance: OSGi Service Platform Release 4.2 (2010), http://www.osgi.org/Download/Release4V42
16. Parnas, D.L.: On the criteria to be used in decomposing systems into modules. Commun. ACM 15, 1053–1058 (1972), http://doi.acm.org/10.1145/361598.361623
17. Spinellis, D.D.: ckjm 1.9 — an implementation of the Chidamber and Kemerer metrics for Java, http://www.spinellis.gr/sw/ckjm/
18. Tulach, J.: Practical API Design: Confessions of a Java Framework Architect. APress (2008)

Static Analysis of Run-Time Modes in Synchronous Process Network

Michael Beyer and Sabine Glesner

Chair Software Engineering for Embedded Systems Group,
Technische Universität Berlin,
Ernst-Reuter-Platz 7, 10587 Berlin, Germany
http://www.pes.tu-berlin.de

Abstract. For modeling modern streaming-oriented applications, Process Networks (PNs) are used to describe systems with changing behavior, which must be mapped on a concurrent architecture to meet the performance and energy constraints of embedded devices. Finding an optimal mapping of Process Networks to the constrained architecture presumes that the behavior of the Process Network is statically known. In this paper we present a static analysis for synchronous PNs that extracts different run-time modes by using polyhedral abstraction. The result is a Mealy machine whose states describe different run-time modes and the edges among them represent transitions. This machine can be used to guide optimizing backend mappings from PNs to concurrent architectures.

Keywords: static analysis, program modes, synchronous process networks, optimization, polyhedral abstraction.

1 Introduction

Modern embedded systems are getting increasingly dynamic to satisfy the users' requirements. Portable devices and digital audio/video equipment are enhanced with new functionalities and are combined to all-round devices like for instance next generation mobile phones. In many systems, not all of these functionalities run at the same time but instead the system operates in a specific mode in which only a selection of the available functionalities is active.

We address the problem of detecting such modes in embedded applications with the goal to map them more efficiently to existing hardware architectures like for instance reconfigurable Field Programmable Gate Arrays (rFPGAs). We want to statically analyze as much information as possible from a given concurrent program in order to shift runtime overhead to compile time. As in classical compilation flow, the analysis results are usable for new static optimizations. For example, *dead code elimination* could be carried over to concurrent programs. Moreover, we want the analysis to be proven correct to assure that applied optimizations preserve a program's semantics. The analysis separates control from data in a manner such that the computation and communication behavior is

E. Clarke, I. Virbitskaite, and A. Voronkov (Eds.): PSI 2011, LNCS 7162, pp. 55–67, 2012.

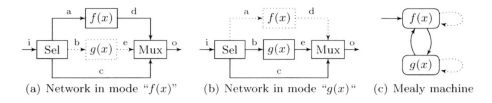

(a) Network in mode "$f(x)$"   (b) Network in mode "$g(x)$"   (c) Mealy machine

Fig. 1. Analysis result for a "two mode" application

known in a certain system-mode and can be used to guide backends in compilers mapping to the new upcoming parallel architectures.

In this paper, we present a novel approach to statically analyze run-time modes in synchronous PNs. These networks consist of a set of processes which communicate synchronously. Processes are written as sequential programs which have arbitrary granularities ranging from small functional descriptions as in Digital Signal Processor (DSP) applications to coarse grained structures like in Message Passing Interface (MPI) programs. Hence, our approach can be used to a broad range of applications.

A program mode is the repeated execution of a sequence of instructions. If we explore the system with an operational semantics, we get a state transition graph where a back edge indicates a repeatedly executed path. Each path begins in a certain state given by the control-flow and an assignment of values to variables which must satisfy the corresponding path precondition. While executing the path, tokens are read from or written to channels. These tokens are either internally produced or externally provided as input data. The tokens are consumed by other processes or are considered as output data. Due to the data transforming assignments and read tokens, the state at the end of the path is again the entry state of the loop or an entry state from another repeatedly executed path.

If we explore the full program, the states and transitions create a Mealy machine. Its nodes describe the program modes and its edges represent changes in the program execution behavior, which is captured in the different modes. Instead of using a concrete semantics enumerating all possible assignments of values for input tokens (which might statically not even be possible), we over-approximate concrete values by polyhedra. Within a process, a read token can be combined and assigned to local variables which are also elements of the polyhedral system. Depending on the conditions, different paths are taken partitioning the polyhedron in subsets which must be explored. If a process communicates with another process, a token will be produced which is also an element of the polyhedral system and will be consumed by assigning it to the local variables of the other process. The result is a connection between both processes formulated as a linear relation in the polyhedral system. From a programmer's point of view, linear relations among processes are in most cases sufficient for synchronization.

Fig. 1 depicts an application with two runtime modes. In Fig. 1a, all input data are routed over process "$f(x)$" in which "$g(x)$" is unused. If process "Sel" gets a special input token, its behavior changes to mode "$g(x)$" depicted in Fig. 1b and all data are transferred through process "$g(x)$". In this mode it is also possible to change back to "$f(x)$". Hence, we get the Mealy machine depicted in Fig. 1c which describes the runtime behavior of the application.

This paper is structured as follows: In Section 2, we introduce our PN representation. In Section 3, we show how the modes for a single process can be extracted and discuss how the Mealy machine for an entire PN can be built. Our implementation of this mode extraction and an analyzed example is described in Section 4. We discuss related work in Section 5 and conclude in Section 6.

2   Representation of Process Networks

In our approach we use synchronous PNs to describe concurrent applications. The PN consists of a set of processes **Prc** connected by a set of unidirectional channels **Chan**. The behavior of a process is implemented in a sequential host language extended by the communication primitives **read** and **write**. A process communicates with another process by sending a token $t \in$ **Token**, over the corresponding channel, where **Token** is an infinite set of tokens. In synchronous PNs, reading and writing a token are conjoined. This means that the writer blocks until the reader is ready and vice versa. We use the following while language with the syntactic categories: $x \in$ **Var** variables, $a \in$ **AExp** arithmetic expressions, $b, not(b) \in$ **BExp** Boolean expressions, $B \in$ **Block** atomic blocks labelled with $\ell, \ell' \in$ **Lab**, $S, S_1, S_2 \in$ **Stmt** statements, and $ch \in$ **Chan** channels. The abstract syntax of atomic blocks and statements is defined as follows:

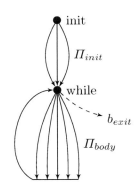

Fig. 2. Structure of a process

$$B ::= [x := a]^\ell \mid [cond(b)]^\ell \mid [skip]^\ell \mid [ch.\text{write}(a)]^\ell \mid [x := \text{read}(ch)]^\ell$$
$$S ::= B \mid S_1; S_2 \mid \text{if } (b) \; \{[cond(b)]^\ell; S_1\} \text{ else } \{[cond(not(b))]^{\ell'}; S_2\} \mid$$
$$\text{while } (b) \; \{[cond(b)]^\ell; S\}; [cond(not(b))]^{\ell'}$$

The atomic block $[cond(b)]^\ell$ asserts that the condition b is true when executing the block. It is used in the *if-then-else* construct to express the corresponding branch condition. Without loss of generality, we presume that processes contain only one while loop. Processes with more or hierarchical while loops can be flattened to this representation by introducing and adapting further path conditions. Fig. 2 depicts the structure of a process according to our representation.

Definition 1 (Process). *A process is a tuple* $(\Pi_{init}, \Pi_{body}, b_{exit}, \beta)$.

– *The finite set* $\Pi_{init} \subseteq$ **Lab*** *contains all paths from process start to the while entry point.*

- $\Pi_{body} \subseteq \mathbf{Lab}^{\star}$ *represents all paths through the while body from entry to entry.*
- *In case of leaving the loop, the exit condition* $b_{exit} \in \mathbf{BExp}$ *must hold.*
- *The function* $\beta : \mathbf{Lab} \rightarrow \mathbf{Block}$ *maps a label to the corresponding atomic block.*

Each channel is connected with at most one input and one output process. Channels that are not fully internally connected represent the in- and output channels of the network.

Definition 2 (Synchronous Process Network). *The synchronous Process Network is a tuple* $(\mathbf{Prc}, C, I, O)$, *where* $\mathbf{Prc}$ *is a set of processes, and* $C, I, O \subseteq \mathbf{Chan}$ *are sets of internal, input and output channels, respectively.*

During execution of a process or a whole network, tokens are consumed and produced on the channels. This is captured by communication signatures.

Definition 3 (Communication signature). *A communication signature is a function* $\gamma : Ch \rightarrow \mathbf{Token}^{\star}$ *that maps a general set of channels* $Ch \subseteq \mathbf{Chan}$ *to a string over tokens. For convenience, we use* $Sign^{Ch}$ *instead of* $Ch \rightarrow \mathbf{Token}^{\star}$.

If a process writes an arithmetic expression to a channel by $[ch.\mathrm{write}(a)]$, then a new token representing the evaluation of the expression is enqueued to the communication signature.

Definition 4. *For a given signature* γ, *the function enq enqueues a token* $t \in \mathbf{Token}$ *to channel* $ch \in \mathbf{Chan}$ *and returns the resulting signature.*

$$enq(\gamma, ch, t) = \gamma[ch \mapsto t \cdot \gamma(ch)]$$

In contrast, if a process reads a token $[x := \mathrm{read}(ch)]$, then, if a token is present, it is dequeued from the channel and assigned to the variable x.

Definition 5. *For a given signature* γ *and a channel* $ch \in \mathbf{Chan}$, *the function deq dequeues a token* $t \in \mathbf{Token}$ *and returns the resulting signature.*

$$deq(\gamma, ch) = \begin{cases} (t, \gamma[ch \mapsto s]) & \text{if } \gamma(ch) = st \text{ where } s \in \mathbf{Token}^{\star} \\ \text{undefined} & \text{if } \gamma(ch) = \epsilon \end{cases}$$

In the following, these definitions are used for the extraction of Mealy machines.

3   Extraction of Mealy Machines

In our approach we use Mealy machines to describe different runtime modes of synchronous PNs. In general a Mealy machine is a finite-state machine where the output depends on the input as well as on the current state. In our specific case, a state of the Mealy machine describes a mode in which a certain sequence of instructions is repeatedly applicable, hence, a state where only a fraction of the process code is executable. Consumed tokens of the process represent the input and produced tokens the output of the machine. We describe the extraction of a Mealy machine for an individual process and discuss the composition of all individual machines to an overall Mealy machine for the entire PN.

3.1   Abstraction of Paths and Their Execution

A mode of an individual process is defined as a process state in which a certain sequence of instructions is repeatedly applicable. In our PN representation, the paths through the while body are potential candidates. Each path $[\ell_0, \ldots, \ell_n] \in$ **Lab*** can be seen as a transition $pre \xrightarrow[{[\ell_0, \ldots, \ell_n]}]{\gamma_{in}/\gamma_{out} \; - \; rel} post$ from a process state pre to a process state $post$. The applicability of transitions does not only depend on the process state pre before the execution but also on the consumed tokens along the path. Hence, the edge is annotated with the input signature γ_{in} of type $Sign^I$ to describe consumed tokens, with the output signature γ_{out} of type $Sign^O$ for produced tokens, and with a relation rel among the consumed and produced tokens. The input and output signatures can be easily determined by considering the read and write statements along the path.

Definition 6 (Input/output signature). *The functions* $in :$ **Lab*** $\to Sign^I$ *and* $out :$ **Lab*** $\to Sign^O$ *take a path and return the corresponding input/output signature. Beginning with an empty signature, for every* read/write *on the path we generate a relating token on the corresponding channel.*

$$in(\epsilon) = \lambda ch.\epsilon$$
$$in(\mathcal{L}\ell) = \begin{cases} enq(in(\mathcal{L}), ch, t) & \text{if } \beta(\ell) = [x := read(ch)]^\ell \\ in(\mathcal{L}) & \text{otherwise} \end{cases}$$

where $t \in$ **Token** *is a new unused token. The function* out *is analogously defined. Instead of* $[x := read(ch)]^\ell$ *the atomic block* $[ch.write(a)]^\ell$ *is used.*

We describe the process states pre before execution and $post$ after execution as well as the relation rel among the input and output tokens by convex polyhedra. For this purpose, we abstract from concrete values by the use of convex polyhedra defined by linear constraints among process variables and tokens to describe linear relations among them and the corresponding state spaces [1]. From a programmer's point of view, linear constraints are in most cases sufficient for synchronization.

Definition 7 (Polyhedron). *A polyhedron* $p \in$ **Poly** *is the set of solutions to a constraint system. By using matrix notation, we have*

$$p = \{\boldsymbol{x} \in \mathbb{R}^n \mid \mathbf{C_1} \cdot \boldsymbol{x} = \boldsymbol{d_1}, \mathbf{C_2} \cdot \boldsymbol{x} \geq \boldsymbol{d_2}, \mathbf{C_3} \cdot \boldsymbol{x} > \boldsymbol{d_3}\}$$

where, for all $i \in \{1, 2, 3\}$, $C_i \in \mathbb{R}^{m_i} \times \mathbb{R}^n$ *and* $d_i \in \mathbb{R}^{m_i}$, *and* $m_1, m_2, m_3 \in \mathbb{N}$ *are the number of equalities, the number of non-strict inequalities, and the number of strict inequalities, respectively.*

In the following, we describe the function $poly :$ **Lab*** $\to$ **Poly** which abstracts a given path by a convex polyhedron. This polyhedron over-approximates all information needed to describe the execution of a path. At first we consider the execution of one atomic block as depicted in Fig. 3. We have a process state pre which describes valid assignments to the process variables on the atomic block's

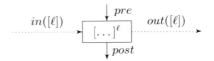

Fig. 3. Execution of an atomic block

entry and a process state *post* for the exit of the atomic block. Furthermore, tokens can be read or written by an atomic block and are given by the input signature $in([\ell])$ or the output signature $out([\ell])$, respectively. The polyhedron $p \in \mathbf{Poly}$ is described in a vector space with dimensions for each process variable at the entry as well as at the exit and for each token produced or consumed by the atomic block. The semantics of the atomic block is abstracted by linear relations among the process variables and the tokens of the signatures.

There are two kinds of atomic blocks. On one hand, we have assignments of the form $[x := a]$, $[ch.\mathrm{write}(a)]$ or $[x := \mathrm{read}(ch)]$, which transform the vector space. On the other hand, we have conditions $[\mathrm{cond}(b)]$ that further constrain the convex polyhedron. We presume the arithmetic expressions to be linear combinations. If they are not in a linear relation, we over-approximate them by a linear convex hull. Without loss of generality, we only consider Boolean expressions that are relations over arithmetic expressions. Indeed the syntax of our simple while language as introduced in Section 2 uses negation if an *if*-condition in the corresponding program path has been evaluated to *false*. We dissolve this by inverting the relation or, in case of inequality, by considering the relations "$<$" and "$>$" separately. The Boolean operators $b_1 \parallel b_2$ and $b_1 \ \&\& \ b_2$ within Boolean expressions can be replaced by nested *if*-statements.

To define an operational semantics based on polyhedral representations, we need to define how a state space, represented by a polyhedron, is modified when an atomic block is executed [2, 6]. In the following, Definitions 8 and 9 define this modification for each possible atomic block. The semantics for an entire path is defined by their functional composition, cf. Definition 10.

Definition 8 (Assignment function). *An assignment $[x := a]$ defines a transfer function $f_{x:=a} : \mathbf{Poly} \to \mathbf{Poly}$, which transforms a given polyhedron according to the assignment.*

At first we extend the given polyhedron by one dimension t and add the equality $t = x$. Secondly, the new assignment is added as the equality $x = a[t/x]$, where all occurrences of x in a are replaced by t, the old value of x. Finally, the new dimension t is removed, respectively the polyhedron is projected to the remaining dimensions.

Definition 9 (Polyhedron for conditions). *We define the polyhedron $P_b \in$* **Poly***, which corresponds to the condition $[\mathrm{cond}(b)]$, where $b \equiv \mathbf{c} \cdot \mathbf{x} \geq d$ is a relation over linear arithmetic expressions.*

By means of the assignment function $[x := a]$ and the polyhedron P_b for a condition b, we can define the abstraction function *path*.

Definition 10 (Path abstraction). *The function poly* : $\mathbf{Lab}^\star \to \mathbf{Poly}$ *abstracts a given path by a polyhedron, which describes the transition from one process state to another. The function is defined by an auxiliary function pl.*

$$poly(\pi) = pl(\pi, in(\pi), out(\pi))$$

The auxiliary function pl : $\mathbf{Lab}^\star \times Sign^I \times Sign^O \to \mathbf{Poly}$ *additionally gets the corresponding input and output signature of the given path and composes the abstract semantics of each atomic block.*

$$pl(\epsilon, \lambda ch.\epsilon, \lambda ch.\epsilon) = pre \equiv post \qquad \text{// empty path}$$

$$pl(\mathcal{L}\ell, \sigma, \omega) = \qquad\qquad \text{// non-empty path, different cases:}$$
$$\begin{cases} f_{x:=a}(pl(\mathcal{L}, \sigma, \omega)) & \text{if } \beta(\ell) = [x := a]^\ell \\ pl(\mathcal{L}, \sigma, \omega) \sqcap P_b & \text{if } \beta(\ell) = [cond(b)]^\ell \\ f_{x:=t}(pl(\mathcal{L}, \sigma', \omega)) & \text{if } \beta(\ell) = [x := read(ch)]^\ell \wedge deq(\sigma, ch) = (t, \sigma') \\ f_{t:=a}(pl(\mathcal{L}, \sigma, \omega')) & \text{if } \beta(\ell) = [ch.write(a)]^\ell \wedge deq(\omega, ch) = (t, \omega') \\ pl(\mathcal{L}, \sigma, \omega) & \text{otherwise} \end{cases}$$

The auxiliary function pl recursively iterates over the path. In case of an empty path ϵ, $pre \equiv post$ ensures that the process variables at the entry are equal to the process variables at the exit. In case of at least one atomic block, its semantics is applied to the process variables at the exit. Hence, we compose the transformations of each atomic block along the path. If a token is consumed or produced, the function deq dequeues tokens from the input and output signature and the assignment function from Definition 8 relates them to local variables.

The precondition, postcondition, and the relation between produced and consumed tokens can be uncoupled by projecting the polyhedron to a vector space where only the process variables $\mathbf{Poly}^{\mathbf{Var}}$ or the used tokens $\mathbf{Poly}^{\mathbf{Token}}$ remain.

Definition 11 (Selector functions). *The selector functions pre and post* : $\mathbf{Poly} \to \mathbf{Poly}^{\mathbf{Var}}$ *project a polyhedron to a vector space, where only the variables on the entry or respectively on the exit remain. In analogy, the selector function* $token : \mathbf{Poly} \to \mathbf{Poly}^{\mathbf{Token}}$ *projects a polyhedron to a vector space, where only the tokens remain.*

In this subsection, we have defined the function $path : \mathbf{Lab}^\star \to \mathbf{Poly}$ that abstracts a given path to a polyhedron. This polyhedron contains the precondition, postcondition, and relation between consumed and produced tokens. Furthermore, we have provided selector functions which can be directly composed, e.g., with $pre \circ poly : \mathbf{Lab}^\star \to \mathbf{Poly}^{\mathbf{Var}}$, we obtain the precondition of a given path. The consumed and produced tokens are related to the tokens of the input signature $in : \mathbf{Lab}^\star \to Sign^I$ and output signature $out : \mathbf{Lab}^\star \to Sign^O$, respectively. In the following subsections, we use this abstraction to extract a Mealy machine for an individual process.

3.2   Identification of States

A state of the Mealy machine describes a potential mode of a process. We define modes of a process as states in which a certain sequence of instructions is repeatedly applicable. In our PN representation, the paths through the while body are the only potential candidates. An initialization path is only executed once at the beginning. Each path has a precondition which ensures its applicability and describes a transition to another state in which the postcondition must hold.

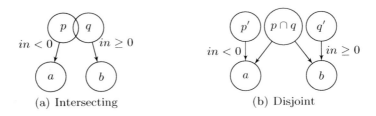

(a) Intersecting   (b) Disjoint

Fig. 4. Preconditions

At first sight, the states of the Mealy machine are given by the precondition. But these are not necessarily disjoint since two or more paths may have intersecting preconditions. In these cases, the taken path depends also on the consumed tokens along the path as it is depicted in Fig. 4. In state $p \cap q$, the next state depends on whether the input token is less than or greater equal zero. To obtain unambiguous states for the Mealy machine, it is necessary to separate the path preconditions. Therefore the function $disjointSet$ returns the set of disjoint polyhedra for a set of intersecting polyhedra. The states P of our machine are given by:

$$P = disjointSet \left(\bigcup_{\pi \in \Pi_{body}} \{pre \circ poly(\pi)\} \right) \cup \{p_0, p_0'\}$$

where p_0 is the initial state and describes the whole vector space and p_0' is the corresponding polyhedron from the exit condition b_{exit}.

3.3   Determination of Edges and Tags

The edges between the states of the Mealy machine are given by the path abstractions. A path describes the transition from one state to another. Therefore the state of the source of the edge must fulfill the precondition and the state of the target of the edge must fulfill the postcondition. The edge is annotated with the input and output signature of the path and the linear relation among the consumed and produced tokens.

An edge $(p \to p') \in \mathbf{Poly}^{\mathbf{Var}} \times \mathbf{Poly}^{\mathbf{Var}}$ from *init* to *while entry* exists if the following condition holds:

$$(p = p_0) \wedge (p' \in P \setminus \{p_0\}) \wedge (\exists \pi \in \Pi_{init}) : \qquad post \circ poly(\pi) \cap p' \neq \emptyset$$

In the intial state the precondition always holds because p_0 initially describes the whole vector space. We only need to check that the postcondition holds in any *while entry* state. In this case the post condition intersects with a *while entry* state. An edge $(p \to p')$ from *while entry* to *while entry* exists if the following conditions holds:

$$(p \in P \setminus \{p_0, p_0'\}) \wedge (p' \in P \setminus \{p_0\}) \wedge (\exists \pi \in \Pi_{body}) :$$
$$(p \sqsubseteq pre \circ poly(\pi)) \wedge (post \circ constrPre(p) \circ poly(\pi) \cap p' \neq \emptyset)$$

In contrast to initial edges, we additionally check, which *while entry* state intersects with the precondition. Due to partitioning, the polyhedron of the *while entry* state is always smaller than or equal to the path precondition. In case of a strictly smaller relation, the preconditions is constrained, which can also result in a strengthened postcondition. The functional $constrPre : \mathbf{Poly}^{\mathbf{Var}} \to \mathbf{Poly} \to \mathbf{Poly}$ constrains the precondition for a given polyhedron.

3.4 Mealy Machine of an Individual Process and the Whole Network

Based on the path abstraction, the identified states and edges, we define the Mealy machine as follows:

Definition 12 (Mealy machine). *The Mealy machine of a process or network is a tuple $(P, p_0, \Gamma^I, \Gamma^O, T, G, R, L)$ consisting of a:*

- *set of internal states $P \in \mathbf{Poly}^{\mathbf{Var}}$, which abstract value assignments to variables by polyhedra and an initial state $p_0 \in P$*
- *set of input signatures $\Gamma^I \subseteq Sign^I$ and output signatures $\Gamma^O \subseteq Sign^O$*
- *transition function $T : \mathbf{Poly}^{\mathbf{Var}} \times Sign^I \to \mathbf{Poly}^{\mathbf{Var}}$ describing edges from the current state p' to the next state p according to the input signature*

and similar to the transition function, we have the edge tagging functions:

- *output signature G maps to $Sign^O$*
- *relation function R maps to $\mathbf{Poly}^{\mathbf{Token}}$ a polyhedral system, which describes the linear relations between in- and output tokens*
- *path function L maps to $\mathbf{Lab}^\star$ the executed path.*

The Mealy machine of an individual process is given by the set of disjoint internal states P and the initial state p_0 from Section 3.2, the transition function $T(p', in(\pi)) = p$ determined in Section 3.3, the output signature $G(p', in(\pi)) = out(\pi)$, the relation function

$$R(p', in(\pi)) = token \circ constrPre(p) \circ constrPost(p') \circ poly(\pi)$$

and the path function $L(p', in(\pi)) = \pi$.

To summarize, in this section we have defined how to extract a Mealy machine from an individual process that represents its modes. Therefore, we have abstracted all paths given of our PN representation by a polyhedron. Furthermore, we have identified the states of the Mealy machine by the disjoint sets over the preconditions of all paths. Moreover, we have constructed the edges between them that represent the transitions between the various modes. The states together with the edges define the resulting Mealy machine for an individual process. The overall Mealy machine of the entire network can be constructed by the composition of all individual machines using the usual automata-theoretic composition of Mealy machines, thereby over-approximating the composition of polyhedra.

4   Implementation and Case Study

We have implemented our analysis in Java. The abstract syntax in Section 2 is extended by structural elements to describe the whole Process Network. We have used JavaCC to generate a parser which parses any arbitrary PN written in our language to an internal representation. We extract a Mealy machine for each individual process on this representation. Therefore, we have implemented an abstract semantics based on polyhedral abstraction. We have used the Parma Polyhedra Library (PPL) [1] which provides a representation of polyhedra and the corresponding operations. Based on the abstract semantics we can abstract whole paths and generate the Mealy machine for an individual process. In a second phase, we pairwisely compose all Mealy machine to an overall machine. The resulting Mealy machine is given by an annotated graph and is seen as an analysis result that offers information about the existing runtime modes of the program.

In the following we consider the process code in Fig. 5 of the given network in Fig. 1 and the resulting Mealy machine. The process "Sel" consists of two states $m \geq 0$ and $m < 0$. Depending on the state the consumed token will be either transferred to the output channel a or b. Simultaneously a token representing the state will be produced on channel c. If the process reads a *zero* on input i, the following token sets the new state of the process. The process "Mux" is connected to "$f(x)$" by d and to "$g(x)$" by e. Depending on the input token c, either the token from d or e will be transmitted to the output. The processes "$f(x)$" and "$g(x)$" consume a token, then correspondingly the function $f(x)$ or $g(x)$ will be applied and the result is sent by producing a token on the output.

After transforming each individual process into a Mealy machine and creating the overall composition, we get the resulting Mealy machine depicted in Fig. 6. The machine consists of an initial state annotated with *true* and two run-time modes annotated with "$m \geq 0$" and "$m < 0$". From the initial state, the program starts in mode "$m \geq 0$". In this mode either data are processed through

```
process  Sel(i)(a,b,c)  {
   [m:=1]¹;
   while  ([true]²) {
      [t:=i.read()]³;
      if  ([t==0]⁴)  [m:=i.read()]⁵;
      else  {
         [c.write(m)]⁶
         if  ([m>=0]⁷)  [a.write(t)]⁸;
         else  [b.write(t)]⁹;
} } }
```

```
process  Mux(d,e,c)(o)  {
   while  ([true]¹) {
      [m:=c.read()]²;
      if  ([m>=0])³ {
         [s:=d.read()]⁴
      } else  {
         [s:=e.read()]⁵;
      }
      [o.write(s)]⁶
} }
```

```
process  F(a)(d)  {
   while  ([true]¹ {[x:=a.read()]²;[d.write(f(x))]³;}
}
```

```
process  G(b)(e)  {
   while  ([true]¹ {[x:=b.read()]²;[e.write(g(x))]³;}
}
```

Fig. 5. Process code of the "two mode" application

process "$f(x)$" or the mode can be switched to the mode "$m < 0$" or to the present mode "$m \geq 0$". Similar to mode "$m \geq 0$", in mode "$m < 0$" either data are processed through process "$g(x)$" or the mode can be switched. The transitions are annotated with communication signatures (γ_{in}/γ_{out}), a linear relation *rel* among produced and consumed tokens and a path execution vector overall processes in the order Sel, F, G and Mux, which describes the executed atomic blocks. The Mealy machine exactly represents the possible run-time behavior of the given program.

5   Related Work

Some approaches exist that take advantage of the knowledge of run-time modes. In [4], a scenario-based design methodology for dynamic embedded systems is presented. Each individual scenario of the system is optimized at design-time. In contrast to our approach, the scenarios are a-priori known. Furthermore, predicting the current scenario and switching between scenarios is only very abstractly described.

To gain information about the expected behavior at run-time, one could also try to utilize simulation environments, e.g. YAPI [9] and SystemC [7]. They could be used to profile the network behavior. In contrast to our approach, the gained results would only represent imprecise and averaged behaviors. The idea of polyhedral analysis for automatic discovery of linear restraints between program variables has been presented in [2, 6]. We have based our analysis also on this idea and have adapted it to the analysis of run-time modes in PNs.

Besides synchronous PNs, a range of other models exists which try to separate dynamic from static aspects. We discuss a selection of them briefly: The

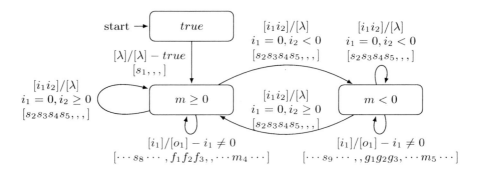

Fig. 6. Mealy machine of the "two mode" example

Scenario-Aware Dataflow (SADF) [10] model is a scenario-aware generalisation of the Synchronous Dataflow (SDF) model using a stochastic approach to model the order in which scenarios occur. In [5], the interaction of Finite State Machines (FSMs) with concurrency models is explored. FunState [11] (functions driven by state machines) distinctly separates control and data and enables methods for design and evaluation of schedules. In [3], Reactive Process Networks (RPNs) and their operational semantics are described. The behavior of a process is reconfigured by external events. Reconfiguration is only allowed in quiescent states. All of these approaches do not try to extract modes as we have done in our approach. They only model the behavior of systems.

In our approach we consider a given synchronous PN which changes its behavior by external events. In contrast to the discussed related approaches, we do not perform time consuming profiling or expect the programmer to separate dynamic from static aspects. Instead we perform a static analysis to identify run-time modes and their transitions by extracting Mealy machines. To the best of our knowledge, no approaches exist that analyze PNs for run-time modes.

6   Conclusion and Future Work

In this paper, we have presented a static analysis to detect run-time modes in Process Networks (PNs). Thereby we have extracted Mealy machines from PNs. The inputs and outputs of the machine correspond to the consumed and produced tokens. A state of the Mealy machine describes a mode in which a certain sequence of instructions is repeatedly executable. We have constructed the Mealy machines by using an abstract semantics in which states are described by convex polyhedra. In most practical situations such linear relations among processes are sufficient.

In future work we want to extend our approach to asynchronous PNs, similar to Kahn Process Networks (KPNs) introduced in [8]. Our analysis results could be used to optimize the network or to guide compiler backends. If we considered frequently used modes more specifically, static optimizations with respect to the most frequently used mode could be applied to reduce execution time. Moreover, optimizations over all processes can be developed, for instance a *dead code elimination* removing program fragments which will never be used in any mode. Targeting optimizations can use the analysis results to merge and split processes to meet a certain number of processing elements. Another use case is the guidance of backends. Quasi-static scheduling can be applied to reduce runtime overhead and for coarse-grained rFPGAs, the results can guide the partitioning of applications into synthesizable configurations.

References

1. Bagnara, R., Hill, P.M., Zaffanella, E.: The Parma Polyhedra Library: Toward a complete set of numerical abstractions for the analysis and verification of hardware and software systems. Science of Computer Programming 72(1–2), 3–21 (2008)
2. Cousot, P., Halbwachs, N.: Automatic discovery of linear restraints among variables of a program. In: POPL '78: Proceedings of the 5th ACM SIGACT-SIGPLAN symposium on Principles of Programming Languages. pp. 84–96. ACM, New York, NY, USA (1978)
3. Geilen, M., Basten, T.: Reactive process networks. In: EMSOFT '04: Proceedings of the 4th ACM international conference on Embedded software. pp. 137–146. ACM, New York, NY, USA (2004)
4. Gheorghita, S.V., Palkovic, M., Hamers, J., Vandecappelle, A., Mamagkakis, S., Basten, T., Eeckhout, L., Corporaal, H., Catthoor, F., Vandeputte, F., Bosschere, K.D.: System-scenario-based design of dynamic embedded systems. ACM Transactions on Design Automation of Electronic Systems 14(1), 1–45 (2009)
5. Girault, A., Lee, B., Lee, E.: Hierarchical finite state machines with multiple concurrency models. IEEE Transactions on Computer-Aided Design of Integrated Circuits and Systems 18(6), 742–760 (June 1999)
6. Halbwachs, N., Proy, Y.E., Roumanoff, P.: Verification of real-time systems using linear relation analysis. Formal Methods in System Design 11(2), 157–185 (1997)
7. IEEE Standard Association: IEEE Std. 1666-2005, Open SystemC language reference manual (2006), www.systemc.org
8. Kahn, G.: The semantics of simple language for parallel programming. In: IFIP Congress. pp. 471–475. North Holland Publishing Company, Stockholm, Sweden (August 1974)
9. de Kock, E., Essink, G., Smits, W., van der Wolf, R., Brunei, J.Y., Kruijtzer, W., Lieverse, P., Vissers, K.: YAPI: Application modeling for signal processing systems. In: DAC '00: 37th Design Automation Conference. pp. 402–405. Los Angeles, CA (June 2000)
10. Theelen, B., Geilen, M., Basten, T., Voeten, J., Gheorghita, S., Stuijk, S.: A scenario-aware data flow model for combined long-run average and worst-case performance analysis. In: MEMOCODE '06: Proceedings of the Fourth ACM and IEEE International Conference on Formal Methods and Models for Co-Design. pp. 185–194. Napa Valley, California (July 2006)
11. Thiele, L., Strehl, K., Ziegenbein, D., Ernst, R., Teich, J.: FunState—An internal design representation for codesign. In: ICCAD '99: Proceedings of the 1999 IEEE/ACM international conference on Computer-aided design. pp. 558–565. IEEE Press, Piscataway, NJ, USA (1999)

Compositional Methods in Characterization of Timed Event Structures*

Elena Bozhenkova

A.P. Ershov Institute of Informatics Systems SB RAS,
Novosibirsk, Russia
bozhenko@iis.nsk.su

Abstract. A logic characteristic formulas up to the timed testing preorders are constructed for model of timed event structures with discrete internal actions. Such logic formulas can be used for deciding a problem of recognizing timed testing relations. Timed event structures can be considered as a composition of their parts. And to simplify construction of characteristic formula we can try to use characteristic formulas of parts. In the paper we use compositional methods for construction of the characteristic formulas in a model of timed event structures with discrete internal actions.

Keywords: Timed event structures, testing relations, logical characterization.

1 Introduction

Complex systems are not trivial for analysis. One of useful tools for that is the notion of equivalence. As a matter of fact, equivalences are used in specification and verification both to compare two distinct systems and to reduce the structure of a system.

Among the variety of equivalences are testing ones presented in [9]. These equivalences have been considered for synchronous and asynchronous formal system models without time delays [1,6,7,9,10] and for models with discrete [8,11] and dense [3,4] time.

In paper [3], a framework for testing preorders and equivalences in the setting of timed event structures has been developed. In that model, a time interval associated with an event means the interval, during which the event can occur. Occurrence of the event does not take any time. The alternative characterization of the timed testing relations is given. In [5], the problem of decidability of timed *must*-equivalences is reduced to the model-checking one. As a basic logic, we take the timed logic L_ν[12], which has been used for construction of a characteristic formula for a timed automaton up to the timed bisimilarity and, as a consequence, for reduction of the timed bisimilarity decidability problem to

---

* This work is supported in part by the grant DFG-RFBR (N 436 RFBR 113/1002/01 and 09-01-91334).

E. Clarke, I. Virbitskaite, and A. Voronkov (Eds.): PSI 2011, LNCS 7162, pp. 68–76, 2012.

the model-checking one. In [5], a characteristic formula up to the timed testing preorders is constructed. We do it for timed event structures with discrete internal actions. The characteristic formula consists of formulas for each class of the class graph. Each subformula is modeling a possible transition from the class and contain conditions on the formula clocks.

Usually, complex systems consist of subsystems. In the case when events of different subsystems are in the same relation — partial order, conflict or concurrency — we say that the system is a composition of subsystems.

So, it is interesting to construct characteristic formulas for the whole system using only similar formulas for subsystems. In such way we can avoid construction of region and class graphs, algorithms for which are exponential. According to a usual structure of the characteristic formula, we construct its subformulas using the formulas for classes of substructures.

The rest of the paper is organized as follows. In Section 2, we remind the basic notions concerned with timed event structures and timed testing. In Section 3, we obtain a class graph from the state-space. In Section 4, we construct a formula which characterizes a timed event structure up to the timed testing preorders. In Section 5, the characteristic formula for a timed event structure is constructed on the basis of the formulas for its substructures. Conclusion is given in Section 6.

2 Timed Event Structures

In this section, we remind a model of timed event structures.

Let Act be a finite set of visible actions and τ be an internal action. Then $Act_\tau = Act \cup \{\tau\}$. A *(labelled) event structure* over Act_τ is a 4-tuple $S = (E, \leq, \#, l)$, where E is a countable set of events; $\leq \subseteq E \times E$ is a partial order (the *causality relation*); $\# \subseteq E \times E$ is a symmetric and irreflexive relation (the *conflict relation*); $l : E \to Act_\tau$ is a labelling function. It is supposed that the *causality relation* satisfies the *principle of finite causes*, i.e. $\forall e \in E$. $\{e' \in E \mid e' \leq e\}$ is finite, and the *conflict relation* satisfies the *principle of conflict heredity*, i.e. $\forall e, e', e'' \in E$. $e \# e' \leq e'' \Rightarrow e \# e''$. In the following, we will suppose that sets of events are finite.

For pairs of events are neither in causality nor in conflict relations, we define the *concurrency relation* as $\smile = (E \times E) \setminus (\leq \cup \geq \cup \#)$.

Let $C \subseteq E$. Then C is *left-closed* iff $\forall e, e' \in E$. $e \in C \land e' \leq e \Rightarrow e' \in C$; C is *conflict-free* iff $\forall e, e' \in C$. $\neg(e \# e')$; C is a *configuration* of S iff C is left-closed and conflict-free. Let $Conf(S)$ denote the set of all configurations of S. For $C \in Conf(S)$, we define the set of events enabled in C as $En(C) = \{e \in E \mid C \cup \{e\} \in Conf(S)\}$.

We propose some usual notations: $\mathbf{N}_0$ be the set of natural numbers with zero, $\mathbf{R}^+$ be the set of positive real numbers, and $\mathbf{R}_0^+$ be the set of nonnegative real numbers. For any $d \in \mathbf{R}_0^+$, $\{d\}$ denotes its fractional part, $\lfloor d \rfloor$ and $\lceil d \rceil$ — its smallest and largest integer parts, respectively.

Define the set $Interv(\mathbf{R}_0^+) = \{[d_1, d_2] \subset \mathbf{R}_0^+ \mid d_1, d_2 \in \mathbf{N}_0\}$.

We are now ready to introduce the concept of timed event structures.

Definition 1. *A* (labelled) timed event structure *over Act_τ is a pair $TS = (S, D)$, where $S = (E, \leq, \#, l)$ is a (labelled) event structure over Act_τ; $D : E \to Interv(\mathbf{R}_0^+)$ is a timing function such that $D(e) = [d, d]$ for some $d \in \mathbf{N}_0$ for all e with $l(e) = \tau$.*

In that model, a time interval associated with an event can occur during interval associated with it. Occurrence of the event does not take any time. An example of timed event structure is shown in Fig. 1.

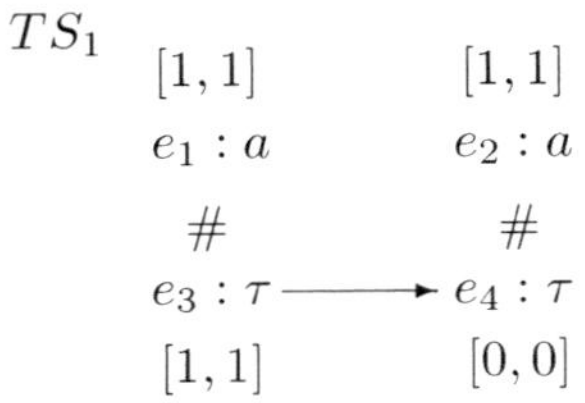

$$TS_1$$

$$[1,1] \qquad\qquad [1,1]$$

$$e_1 : a \qquad\qquad e_2 : a$$

$$\# \qquad\qquad\quad \#$$

$$e_3 : \tau \longrightarrow e_4 : \tau$$

$$[1,1] \qquad\qquad [0,0]$$

Fig. 1. An example of timed event structure

Let $\mathcal{E}_\tau$ denote the set of all labelled timed event structures over Act_τ. For convenience, we fix timed event structures $TS = (S = (E, \leq, \#, l), D)$, $TS' = (S' = (E', \leq', \#', l'), D')$ from the class $\mathcal{E}_\tau$ and work with them further.

TS is called *conflict-free*, if E is conflict-free. TS' is called *a substructure* of TS, if $E' \subset E$, $\leq' \subseteq \leq|_{E'}$, $\#' \subseteq \# |_{E'}$, $l' = l |_{E'}$, $D' = D |_{E'}$.

A *state* of TS is a pair $M = (C, \delta)$, where $C \in Conf(S)$ and $\delta : E \to \mathbf{R}_0^+$. The *initial state* of TS is $M_{TS} = (C_0, \delta_0) = (\emptyset, 0)$. Let $ST(TS)$ denote the set of all states of TS. A timed event structure progresses through a sequence of states in one of two ways given below. Let $M_1 = (C_1, \delta_1), M_2 = (C_2, \delta_2) \in ST(TS)$ such that $En(C_1) \neq \emptyset$.

The occurrence of e in M_1 *leads to* M_2 (denoted as $M_1 \xrightarrow{a} M_2$, if $l(e) = a$), if $\delta_1(e) \in D(e)$ and $\forall e' \in En(C_1) \exists d \in \mathbf{R}_0^+ . \delta_1(e') + d \in D(e)$, $C_2 = C_1 \cup \{e\}$ and $\delta_2(e') = 0$, if $e' \in En(C_2) \setminus En(C_1)$, or $\delta_2(e') = \delta_1(e')$, otherwise.

The passage of d in M_1 *leads to* M_2 (denoted as $M_1 \xrightarrow{d} M_2$), if $\forall e \in En(C_1) \exists d' \in \mathbf{R}_0^+ (d' \geq d) . \delta_1(e) + d' \in D(e)$, $C_2 = C_1$ and $\delta_2(e) = \delta_1(e) + d$ for all $e \in E$.

The *weak leading relation* $\Rightarrow$ on the states of TS is the largest relation defined by: $\xrightarrow{\epsilon} \Longleftrightarrow \xrightarrow{\tau}{}^*$ and $\xrightarrow{x} \Longleftrightarrow \xrightarrow{\epsilon}\xrightarrow{x}\xrightarrow{\epsilon}$, where $\xrightarrow{\tau}{}^*$ is the reflexive and transitive closure of $\xrightarrow{\tau}$ and $x \in Act \cup \mathbf{R}^+$. We consider the relation $\xrightarrow{d}$ as possessing the time continuity property.

From now on, we will use the following notions and notations. Let $Act(\mathbf{R}_0^+) = \{a(d) \mid a \in Act \wedge d \in \mathbf{R}_0^+\}$ be the set of *timed actions* of Act over $\mathbf{R}_0^+$, $(Act(\mathbf{R}_0^+))^*$ be the set of finite *timed words* over $Act(\mathbf{R}_0^+)$. The function $\triangle : (Act(\mathbf{R}_0^+))^* \to \mathbf{R}_0^+$ measuring the *duration* of a timed word is defined by: $\triangle(\epsilon) = 0$, $\triangle(w.a(d)) = \triangle(w) + d$. The domain for real-time languages is denoted by

$Dom(Act, \mathbf{R}_0^+) = \{\langle w, d\rangle \mid w \in (Act(\mathbf{R}_0^+))^*, d \in \mathbf{R}_0^+, d \geq \triangle(w)\}$. In natural way the weak leading relation $\Rightarrow$ is extended to timed words from $(Act(\mathbf{R}_0^+))^*$ and $Dom(Act, \mathbf{R}_0^+)$. We write here some rules: if $M \overset{d'}{\Rightarrow}\overset{a}{\Rightarrow} M'$, then $M \overset{a(d')}{\Rightarrow} M'$; if $M \overset{w}{\Rightarrow} M'$, then $M \overset{\langle w, \triangle(w)\rangle}{\Longrightarrow} M'$.

The set $L(TS) = \{\langle w, d\rangle \in Dom(Act, \mathbf{R}_0^+) \mid M_{TS} \overset{\langle w, d\rangle}{\Longrightarrow}\}$ is the *language* of TS. For instance, for the timed event structure TS_1 in Fig. 1, we have $L(TS_1) = \{\langle \epsilon, d\rangle, \langle a(1), 1\rangle, \langle a(1)a(0), 1\rangle \mid 0 \leq d \leq 1\}$.

We define the timed testing relations in terms of an alternative characterization [3]. For *must*-preoder to exist, inclusion of sets of enabled visible actions and the possibility of time passing in states of two timed event structures reachable by the same timed word are necessary. The formal definition relies on the following notations. Let $M \in ST(TS)$ and $\langle w, d\rangle \in Dom(Act, \mathbf{R}_0^+)$. Then $S(M) = \{x \in Act_\tau \cup \mathbf{R}^+ \mid M \overset{x}{\rightarrow}\}$ and $Acc(TS, \langle w, d\rangle) = \{S(M') \mid M_{TS} \overset{\langle \overline{w}, d\rangle}{\Longrightarrow} M', M' \overset{\tau}{\not\rightarrow}\}$ (timed acceptance set). Let $N, N' \subset 2^{Act \cup \mathbf{R}^+}$. Then $N \subset\subset N' \iff \forall S \in N \exists S' \in N' . [(S' \mid_{Act} \subseteq S \mid_{Act}) \wedge (S \mid_{\mathbf{R}^+} = \emptyset \Rightarrow S' \mid_{\mathbf{R}^+} = \emptyset)]; N \equiv N' \iff N \subset\subset N' \wedge N' \subset\subset N$.

Definition 2. $TS \leq_{must} TS' \iff \forall\langle w, d\rangle \in Dom(Act, \mathbf{R}_0^+) . Acc(TS', \langle w, d\rangle) \subset\subset Acc(TS, \langle w, d\rangle); TS \simeq_{must} TS' \iff TS \leq_{must} TS'$ and $TS' \leq_{must} TS$.

The timed event structures TS_2 and TS_2' shown in Fig. 2 are not timed *must*-equivalent, because, for example, for the timed word $\langle w, d\rangle = \langle a(0.5), 1.5\rangle \in L(TS_2) \cap L(TS_2')$ it is not true $(Acc(TS_2', \langle w, d\rangle) \subset\subset Acc(TS_2, \langle w, d\rangle))$.

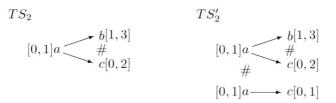

Fig. 2. An example of non-timed *must*-equivalent timed event structures

3   From State-Space to Class Graph

For the purpose of constructing a characteristic formula, the infinite state-space is transformed to a finite representation in such a way that states reachable by the same timed word be collected together in one class. We will briefly consider the transformation through this section. As usual, in order to get a discrete representation of the state-space of a timed event structure, the concept of regions (equivalence classes of states) [2] is used. To get a deterministic representation, classes are used.

In the definition of a region, we will use the notion of common states. A subset $\mu \subseteq ST(TS)$ is called a *common state* of TS. The *initial* common state of TS is $\mu_0 = \{M_{TS}\}$. Sometimes μ is denoted as $(M_1, \ldots, M_n)$ or $(\langle \mathbf{C} \rangle^n, \langle \delta \rangle^n)$, where $M_i = (C_i, \delta_i) \in \mu$ $(1 \leq i \leq n)$, $\langle \mathbf{C} \rangle^n = (C_1, \ldots, C_n)$, $\langle \delta \rangle^n = (\delta_1, \ldots, \delta_n)$.

Let $n^+ = \{1, \ldots, n\}$. Renaming $\pi(n) : n^+ \to n^+$ is extended to $\langle \mathbf{C} \rangle^n$ as $\pi(n)(\langle \mathbf{C} \rangle^n) = (C_{\pi(n)(1)}, \ldots, C_{\pi(n)(n)})$, in a similar way $\pi(n)(\langle \delta \rangle^n)$ is defined and $\pi(n)(\mu) = (\pi(n)(\langle \mathbf{C} \rangle^n), \pi(n)(\langle \delta \rangle^n))$.

A visible action and time can be executed in a common state only if an internal action is not enabled. So, the relation $\xrightarrow{z}$ is defined on common states as follows: $\mu \xrightarrow{\tau} \mu'$ iff $\mu \neq \mu'$ and $\mu' = \{(C', \delta') \mid \exists (C, \delta) \in \mu \ . \ (C, \delta) \xrightarrow{\tau} (C', \delta')\} \cup \mu$; $\mu \xrightarrow{z} \mu'$ iff $\mu \not\xrightarrow{\tau}$ and $\mu' = \{(C', \delta') \mid \exists (C, \delta) \in \mu \ . \ (C, \delta) \xrightarrow{z} (C', \delta')\}$ $(z \in Act \cup \mathbf{R}^+)$.

$STC(TS)$ denotes the set of all common states reachable from μ_0. Below we will consider common states only from $STC(TS)$. The leading relation on common states of $STC(TS)$ is extended to timed words from $Dom(Act, \mathbf{R}_0^+)$ just as on the states of $ST(TS)$.

Let $\mu = (C_1, \ldots, C_n, \delta_1, \ldots, \delta_n) \neq \mu' = (C_1', \ldots, C_n', \delta_1', \ldots, \delta_n')$. Then $\mu \simeq \mu'$ iff $(C_1, \ldots, C_n) = (C_1', \ldots, C_n')$ and $\forall 1 \leq i \leq m \ . \ \lfloor |\delta_1| \ldots |\delta_n(i)| \rfloor = \lfloor |\delta_1'| \ldots |\delta_n'(i)| \rfloor$; $\forall 1 \leq i, j \leq m \ \{|\delta_1| \ldots |\delta_n(i)|\} \leq \{|\delta_1| \ldots |\delta_n(j)|\} \iff \{|\delta_1'| \ldots |\delta_n'(i)|\} \leq \{|\delta_1'| \ldots |\delta_n'(j)|\}$, and $\{|\delta_1| \ldots |\delta_n(i)|\} = 0 \iff \{|\delta_1'| \ldots |\delta_n'(i)|\} = 0$, where $\delta_1| \ldots |\delta_n$ is the concatenation of vectors $\bar{\delta}_i$ $(1 \leq i \leq n)$ and $m = \sum_{1 \leq i \leq n} |C_i|$.

A set $R = [\mu] = \{\mu' \mid \exists \pi(n) \ \mu \simeq \pi(n)(\mu')\}$ is called a *region* of TS. We define $R_0 = [\mu_0]$. The leading relation on regions and the stable partition into regions are defined in usual way.

A *region graph* of TS is a tuple $RG(TS) = (V_{RG}, E_{RG}, l_{RG})$, where the set of vertices V_{RG} is the stable partition of $STC(TS)$, the set of edges E_{RG} is the leading relation on regions of V_{RG} and the labelling function $l_{RG} : E_{RG} \longrightarrow Act_\tau \cup \{\chi\}$ is defined as $l((R, R')) = z \iff R \xrightarrow{z} R'$.

An example of region graph is shown in Fig. 3. Let us consider common states included in some regions of $RG(TS_1)$. The region R_0 consists of the common state $\mu_0 = \{(\emptyset, \bar{0})\}$, $R_4 = [\mu_4]$, where $\mu_4 = \{(\emptyset, \bar{1}), (\{e_3\}, (1, 1, 1, 0)), (\{e_3, e_4\}, (1, 1, 1, 0)\}$, $R_5 = [\mu_5]$, where $\mu_5 = \{(\{e_1\}, \bar{1}), (\{e_2\}, \bar{1}), (\{e_2, e_3\}, (1, 1, 1, 0))\}$.

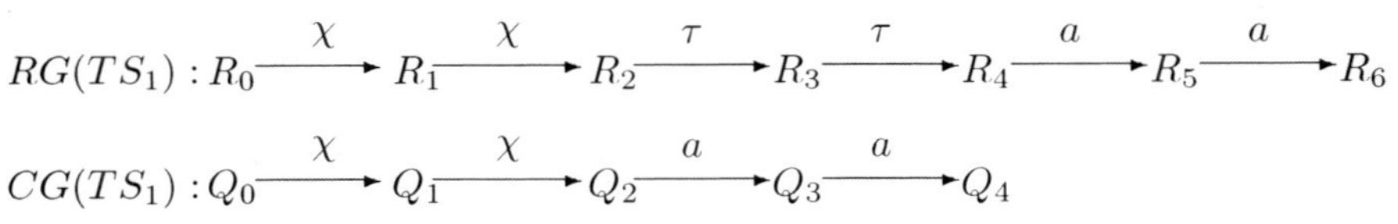

$$RG(TS_1) : R_0 \xrightarrow{\chi} R_1 \xrightarrow{\chi} R_2 \xrightarrow{\tau} R_3 \xrightarrow{\tau} R_4 \xrightarrow{a} R_5 \xrightarrow{a} R_6$$

$$CG(TS_1) : Q_0 \xrightarrow{\chi} Q_1 \xrightarrow{\chi} Q_2 \xrightarrow{a} Q_3 \xrightarrow{a} Q_4$$

Fig. 3. An example of region and class graphs

Each region R_i is associated with its own counter x_i from a countable set of counters X. $RC(R_i)$ denotes the set of counters used in predecessors of region R_i, x_i is included into $RC(R_i)$ if some event becomes enabled in states of region.

To eliminate τ-transitions, the notion of a class [3] as the τ-closure of regions is used. Let $Q \subseteq V_{RG}$. A set $Q^\tau = \{R' \in V_{RG} \mid \exists R \in Q \ . \ R \xRightarrow{\epsilon} R'\}$ is called a *class* of TS. Define $Q_0 = \{R_0\}^\tau$, and $Der(Q, z) = \bigcup_{R \in Q}\{R' \mid R \overset{z}{\rightarrow} R'\}$. For classes Q, Q_1 and $z \in Act \cup \{\chi\}$, the *leading relation on classes* is given by: $Q \overset{z}{\rightarrow} Q_1$, if $Q_1 = (Der(Q, z))^\tau$. In the following we will use notations: $S(Q) = \{z \in Act \cup \{\chi\} \mid Q \overset{z}{\rightarrow}\}$, $QC(Q) = \bigcup_{R \in Q} RC(R)$.

A *class graph* of TS is the labelled directed graph $CG(TS) = (V_{CG}, E_{CG}, l_{CG})$. The set of vertices V_{CG} is the set of reachable classes of TS, E_{CG} is the leading relation on the classes of V_{CG} and the labelling function $l_{CG} : E_{CG} \longrightarrow (Act \cup \{\chi\})$.

An example of class graph is shown in Fig. 3. Consider some classes of $CG(TS_1)$: Q_0 consists of region R_0, $Q_2 = \{R_2, R_3, R_4\}$.

4   Formula Construction

As a basic logic, we take the timed logic L_ν[12]. The characteristic formula of TS consists of the formulas of classes. In the formula, we use the notations Q_a and Q_χ, if $Q \overset{a}{\rightarrow} Q_a$ and $Q \overset{\chi}{\rightarrow} Q_\chi$, and we write its optional parts between $\langle\!\langle$ and $\rangle\!\rangle$. The clocks $\hat{x}_i$ correspond to counters $x_i \in QC(Q)$, and the clock $\hat{x}$ is used additionally. For each class Q, a formula F_Q is constructed as follows: $F_Q = \mathbb{W}\beta(Q) \Rightarrow \psi_Q; \psi_Q = \bigwedge_{a \notin S(Q)|_{Act}} [a]\mathit{ff} \wedge \bigwedge_{a \in S(Q)|_{Act}} [a](\langle\!\langle XQ_a \; in \rangle\!\rangle \; F_{Q_a}) \wedge \langle\!\langle F_\chi \rangle\!\rangle \wedge \langle\!\langle F_{Q_\chi} \rangle\!\rangle \wedge (ACC(Q) \vee \langle\tau\rangle\mathit{tt})$;
Informally, ψ_Q can be written as:

$$\psi_Q = \begin{bmatrix} \text{a part for actions which} \\ \text{can't be run in } Q \end{bmatrix} \wedge \begin{bmatrix} \text{a part for actions which} \\ \text{can be run } Q \end{bmatrix} \wedge$$
$$\langle\!\langle \; Q_\chi \text{ doesn't exist} \rangle\!\rangle \wedge \langle\!\langle \; Q_\chi \text{ exists} \rangle\!\rangle \wedge [\text{ a simulation of } Acc(TS, \langle w, d \rangle)].$$

The conditions $\beta(Q)$ hold for the time assignment of states only from $R \in Q s.t. R \overset{\chi}{\nrightarrow}$. $XQ_a = \{\hat{x} \mid x \in QC(Q_a) \setminus QC(Q)\}$ (the set of reset clocks) is added, if it is not empty; $F_\chi = \hat{x} \; in \; (\mathbb{W}\hat{x} > 0 \Rightarrow \bigwedge_{a \in Act_\tau} [a]\mathit{ff})$ is added into ψ_Q, if the class Q_χ does not exist; F_{Q_χ} charaterizes the existing class Q_χ; $ACC(Q)$ is simulating sets $Acc(TS, \langle w, d \rangle)$ for timed words connected with class Q;

For a timed event structure TS, a *characteristic must-formula* is defined as $F_{TS}^{must} = \hat{x}_0 \; in \; F_{Q_0}$.

Theorem 3. *[5]* $TS \leq_{must} TS' \iff TS' \models_D F_{TS}^{must}$, *where D corresponds to the definition of F_Q for each Q from $V_{CG(TS)}$.*

Let us consider characteristic *must*-formula for TS_1 and part of identifiers. Let $Act = \{a\}$. Then $F_{TS_1}^{must} = \hat{x}_0 \; in \; \left(\mathbb{W} \; \hat{x}_0 = 0 \Rightarrow \left[F_{Q_1} \wedge [a]\mathit{ff} \wedge (ACC_{(}Q_0) \vee \langle\tau\rangle\mathit{tt})\right]\right)$, $F_{Q_1} = \mathbb{W} \; 0 < \hat{x}_0 < 0 \Rightarrow \left[F_{Q_2} \wedge [a]\mathit{ff} \wedge (ACC(Q_1) \vee \langle\tau\rangle\mathit{tt})\right]$, $F_{Q_2} = \mathbb{W} \; \hat{x}_0 = 1 \Rightarrow \left[\hat{x} \; in \; (\mathbb{W} \; \hat{x} > 0 \Rightarrow [a]\mathit{ff}) \wedge [a]F_{Q_3} \wedge [a]\mathit{ff} \wedge (ACC(Q_2) \vee \langle\tau\rangle\mathit{tt})\right]$, $ACC(Q_0) = [a]\mathit{tt} \wedge \hat{x} \; in \; (\mathbb{W} \; \hat{x} > 0 \Rightarrow (\langle a \rangle\mathit{tt} \vee \langle\tau\rangle\mathit{tt}))$, $ACC(Q_2) = [a]\mathit{tt}$.

5   Compositional Methods

Let us consider timed event structures TS_1 and TS_2 from $\mathcal{E}_\tau$ and their characteristic *must*-formulas $F_{TS_1}^{must}$, $F_{TS_2}^{must}$. Suppose that their event sets do not intersect.

Let TS_1 and TS_2 be substructures of TS such that the event set of TS is a union of their event sets. We say TS is constructed from TS_1 and TS_2 using the operator $\|$ (; or #) if the events of TS_1 and TS_2 are in the pairwise $\smile$-relation ($\leq$-relation or #-relation, respectively). In the case of the operator ;, TS_1 must be conflict free. Our aim is to construct the characteristic *must*-formula for TS using characteristic *must*-formulas of its substructures without constructing the region and class graphs of TS.

Suppose $TS = TS_1 \alpha TS_2$, where $\alpha \in \{;, \#, \|\}$.

Let K_1 and K_2 be non-intersecting sets of clocks and Id_1 and Id_2 be non-intersecting sets of identifiers used in the characteristic *must*-formulas $F_{TS_1}^{must}$ and $F_{TS_2}^{must}$, and their meanings are specified by the declarations $\mathcal{D}_1$ and $\mathcal{D}_2$.

By definition, $F_{TS_1}^{must} = x_0^1$ *in* F_0^1 and $F_{TS_2}^{must} = x_0^2$ *in* F_0^2.

Composition with operator ;. Suppose $TS = TS_1; TS_2$, where TS_1 is a conflict free structure.

In the formula $F_{TS_1}^{must}$, there are subformulas for classes which are leaves in the class graph. Denote the set of such identifiers as $LIST(TS_1)$. By construction, $F_0^2 = \mathbb{W}\beta(F_0^2) \Rightarrow \psi(F_0^2)$ and F^1 from $LIST(TS_1)$ are of the form $F^1 = \mathbb{W}\beta(F^1) \Rightarrow \psi(F^1)$.

Let $K = K_1 \cup K_2$ be the set of clocks and $Id = Id_1 \cup Id_2$ be the set of identifiers. Then the declaration $\mathcal{D}$ of Id coincides with $\mathcal{D}_1$ and $\mathcal{D}_2$ on all identifiers except those from $LISTS(TS_1)$. For F^1 from $LIST(TS_1)$, we define $\mathcal{D}(F^1) = x_0^2$ *in* $\mathbb{W}\beta(F^1) \Rightarrow \psi(F_0^2)$, i.e. we combine time conditions of the leaves vertices of the class graph of TS_1 with the ψ-part of the formulas of the initial class of TS_2. Then $F = x_0^1$ *in* F_0^1.

Theorem 4. *F is the characteristic must-formula of TS.*

Composition with operator #. Suppose $TS = TS_1 \# TS_2$. Let K be the set of clocks and Id be the set of identifiers, which do not intersect with $K_1 \cup K_2$ and $Id_1 \cup Id_2$.

To connect clocks and identifiers from substructures formulas with those from the structure formula, we will use the synchronizing functions. The main idea of construction of the characteristic *must*-formula for TS is sequential consideration of formulas for classes of TS_1 and TS_2 and composition of parts of these formulas.

Let F, $F_0 \in Id$, $\hat{x}_0 \in K$, define $F = \hat{x}_0$ *in* F_0.

Base. Beginning from F_0, we construct identifiers from Id. Construct F_0 as a composition $F_0^1 \# F_0^2$, where $F_0^1 \in Id_1$, $F_0^2 \in Id_2$. By definition, the formula for the class F_0 is of the form $\mathbb{W}\beta(F_0) \Rightarrow \psi_{F_0}$. Define $\beta(F_0) = (\hat{x}_0 = 0)$ and construct ψ_{F_0} as a composition $\psi_{F_0^1} \# \psi_{F_0^2}$. Synchronize clocks $\hat{x}_0^1, \hat{x}_0^2$ and $\hat{x}_0$.

Step. Let F_m be the current identifier which we construct. We suppose that $\beta(F_m)$ has been defined already on previous step and ψ_{F_m} must be constructed as $\psi_{F^1} \# \psi_{F^2}$ for some identifiers F^1, F^2 from Id_1, Id_2, respectively.

Using the form of the characteristic formulas, define $\psi_{F_m} = \bigwedge_{a \in \overline{S^1} \cap \overline{S^2}} [a] \textit{ff} \wedge \bigwedge_{a \in S^1 \cup S^2} [a](\langle\!\langle X_a \; in \rangle\!\rangle \; F_a) \wedge \langle\!\langle F_\chi \rangle\!\rangle \wedge \langle\!\langle F_{Q_\chi} \rangle\!\rangle \wedge (ACC \vee \langle \tau \rangle tt)$.

Let us consider how to define parts of ψ_{F_m}. The acceptance set is modeled as $ACC = ACC^1 \vee ACC^2$.

If the action $a \in Act$ can be executed in both substructures, then F_a will be found as a composition of subformulas of the substructures formulas $F_a^1 \# F_a^2$. We construct the condition $\beta(F_a)$ such that it includes the corresponding conditions of the substructures formulas and additional conditions for clocks, for which only one synchronized clock exists K_1 or K_2, namely, if we add a new counter which is synchronized only with the counter from one substructure, we include the relation of the new counter with counters from another substructure. And we will keep similar relations on next steps. Define ψ_{F_a} as a composition $\psi_{F_a^1} \# \psi_{F_a^2}$.

If the action $a \in Act$ can be executed only in the substructure TS_1 (TS_2), then F_a is obtained from F_a^1 (F_a^2), by replacing synchronized clocks and identifiers.

If there is no $F_{Q_\chi}^1$ and $F_{Q_\chi}^2$, then F_χ is included. If there is only $F_{Q_\chi}^1$ (or $F_{Q_\chi}^2$), then F_{Q_χ} is obtained from $F_{Q_\chi}^1$ ($F_{Q_\chi}^2$) by replacing synchronized clocks and identifiers. Suppose $F_{Q_\chi}^1$ and $F_{Q_\chi}^2$ both exist. If clocks, corresponding to the relations $\xrightarrow{\chi}$ on classes in both substructures, are synchronized, then define $\psi_{F_{Q_\chi}}$ as a composition $\psi_{F_{Q_\chi}^1} \# \psi_{F_{Q_\chi}^2}$. Otherwise, we can order clocks from substructures formulas and decide which of $F_{Q_\chi}^i$ ($i = 1, 2$) to prefer. And then $\psi_{F_{Q_\chi}}$ is defined as a composition $\psi_{F_{Q_\chi}^i} \# \psi_{F^j}$ ($i \neq j \in \{1, 2\}$). $F_{Q_\chi}^j$ will be considered on next step.

Theorem 5. *The formula F is the must-characteristic formula of TS.*

Composition with operator $||$. Suppose $TS = TS_1 || TS_2$. Under assumptions on the sets of clocks, identifiers and synchronizing functions of the previous paragraph we construct *must*-characteristic formula of TS. Let $F', F_0 \in Id$, $\hat{x}_0 \in K$, define $F' = \hat{x}_0$ in F_0.

Base. Beginning from F_0, we construct identifiers from Id. Construct F_0 as a composition $F_0^1 || F_0^2$, where $F_0^1 \in Id_1$, $F_0^2 \in Id_2$. By definition, the formula for the class F_0 is of the form $\mathbb{W}\beta(F_0) \Rightarrow \psi_{F_0}$. Define $\beta(F_0) = (\hat{x}_0 = 0)$ and construct ψ_{F_0} as a composition $\psi_{F_0^1} || \psi_{F_0^2}$. Synchronize clocks $\hat{x}_0^1, \hat{x}_0^2$ and $\hat{x}_0$.

Step. Let F_m be the current identifier which we construct. We suppose that $\beta(F_m)$ has been defined already on previous step and ψ_{F_m} must be constructed as $\psi_{F^1} || \psi_{F^2}$ for some identifiers F^1, F^2 from Id_1, Id_2, respectively. Definition of parts of ψ_{F_m} is similar to the case for the operation $\#$. Note distinguishing feature, $\psi(F_a)$ is defined as a composition $((\psi_{F_a^1} || \psi_{F^2}) || (\psi_{F^1} || \psi_{F_a^2}))$.

Theorem 6. *The formula F' is the must-characteristic formula of TS.*

6   Conclusion

The characteristic formula allows us to decide the problem of recognizing the timed *must*-equivalence by reducing it to the model-checking one. This article is concentrated on constructing a characteristic formula for timed event structures which can be represented as a composition of its substructures. We develop the methods of composition of the characteristic *must*-formulas of substructures for operators of causality, concurrency and conflict. It is obvious that identifiers and declarations defined here could be easily used for constructing the characteristic *may*-formulas for all these operators.

References

1. Aceto, L., De Nicola, R., Fantechi, A.: Testing Equivalences for Event Structures. In: Venturini Zilli, M. (ed.) Mathematical Models for the Semantics of Parallelism. LNCS, vol. 280, pp. 1–20. Springer, Heidelberg (1987)
2. Alur, R., Courcoubetis, C., Dill, D.: Model checking in dense real time. Inform. and Comput. 104, 2–34 (1993)
3. Andreeva, M.V., Bozhenkova, E.N., Virbitskaite, I.B.: Analysis of timed concurrent models based on testing equivalence. Fundamenta Informaticae 43, 1–20 (2000)
4. Bihler, E., Vogler, W.: Timed Petri Nets: Efficiency of Asynchronous Systems. In: Bernardo, M., Corradini, F. (eds.) SFM-RT 2004. LNCS, vol. 3185, pp. 25–58. Springer, Heidelberg (2004)
5. Bozhenkova, E.N.: Testing equivalences for reak-time event structures. Journal of Computational Technologies 15(3), 52–68 (2010) (in Russian)
6. Castellani, I., Hennessy, M.: Testing Theories for Asynchronous Languages. In: Arvind, V., Sarukkai, S. (eds.) FST TCS 1998. LNCS, vol. 1530, pp. 90–102. Springer, Heidelberg (1998)
7. Cleaveland, R., Hennessy, M.: Testing Equivalence as a Bisimulation Equivalence. In: Sifakis, J. (ed.) CAV 1989. LNCS, vol. 407, pp. 11–23. Springer, Heidelberg (1990)
8. Cleaveland, R., Zwarico, A.E.: A theory of testing for real-time. In: Proc. 6th IEEE Symp. on Logic in Comput. Sci., LICS 1991, Amsterdam, The Netherlands, pp. 110–119 (1991)
9. De Nicola, R., Hennessy, M.: Testing equivalence for processes. Theoretical Comput. Sci. 34, 83–133 (1984)
10. Goltz, U., Wehrheim, H.: Causal Testing. In: Penczek, W., Szałas, A. (eds.) MFCS 1996. LNCS, vol. 1113, pp. 394–406. Springer, Heidelberg (1996)
11. Hennessy, M., Regan, T.: A process algebra for timed systems. Inform. and Comput. 117, 221–239 (1995)
12. Laroussinie, F., Larsen, K.L., Weise, C.: From timed automata to logic — and back. — Århus (1995) (Tech. Rep. / BRICS, Dept. Comput. Sci., Univ. of Århus; N RS-95-2)
13. Nielsen, B., Skou, A.: Automated Test Generation from Timed Automata. In: Margaria, T., Yi, W. (eds.) TACAS 2001. LNCS, vol. 2031, pp. 343–357. Springer, Heidelberg (2001)

Algorithmic Debugging of SQL Views[*]

Rafael Caballero, Yolanda García-Ruiz, and Fernando Sáenz-Pérez

Departamento de Sistemas Informáticos y Computación,
Universidad Complutense de Madrid, Spain
{rafa,fernan}@sip.ucm.es, ygarciar@fdi.ucm.es

Abstract. We present a general framework for debugging systems of correlated SQL views. The debugger locates an erroneous view by navigating a suitable computation tree. This tree contains the computed answer associated with every intermediate relation, asking the user whether this answer is expected or not. The correctness and completeness of the technique is proven formally, using a general definition of SQL operational semantics. The theoretical ideas have been implemented in an available tool which includes the possibility of employing trusted specifications for reducing the number of questions asked to the user.

1 Introduction

SQL [12] is the *de facto* standard language for querying and updating relational databases. Its declarative nature and its high-abstraction level allows the user to easily define complex operations that could require hundreds of lines programmed in a general purpose language. In the case of relational queries, the language introduces the possibility of querying the database directly using a *select* statement. However, in realistic applications, queries can become too complex to be coded in a single statement and are generally defined using *views*. Views can be considered in essence as virtual tables. They are defined by a *select* statement that can rely on the database tables as well as in other previously defined views. Thus, views become the basic components of SQL queries.

As in other programming paradigms, views can have bugs which produce unexpected results. However, we cannot infer that a view is buggy only because it returns an unexpected result. Maybe it is correct but receives erroneous input data from the other views or tables it depends on. There are very few tools for helping the user to detect the cause of these errors; so, debugging becomes a labor-intensive and time-consuming task in the case of queries defined by means of several intermediate views. The main reason for this lack of tools is that the usual *trace* debuggers used in other paradigms are not available here due to the high abstraction level of the language. A *select* statement is internally translated into a sequence of low level operations that constitute the *execution plan* of the

---

[*] This work has been partially supported by the Spanish projects STAMP (TIN2008-06622-C03-01), Prometidos-CM (S2009TIC-1465) and GPD (UCM-BSCH-GR35/10-A-910502).

E. Clarke, I. Virbitskaite, and A. Voronkov (Eds.): PSI 2011, LNCS 7162, pp. 77–85, 2012.

query. Relating these operations to the original query is very hard, and debugging the execution plan step by step will be of little help. In this paper, we propose a theoretical framework for debugging SQL views based on *declarative debugging*, also known as *algorithmic debugging* [11]. This technique has been employed successfully in (constraint) logic programming [11], functional programming [9], functional-logic programming [2], and in deductive database languages [1]. The overall idea of declarative debugging [7] can be explained briefly as follows:

- The process starts with an initial error symptom, which in our case corresponds to the unexpected result of a user-defined view.
- The debugger automatically builds a tree representing the computation. Each node of the tree corresponds to an intermediate computation with its result. The children of a node are those nodes obtained from the subcomputations needed for obtaining the parent result. In our case, nodes will represent the computation of a relation R together with its answer. Children correspond to the computation of views and tables occurring in R if it is a view.
- The tree is *navigated*. An external oracle, usually the user, compares the computed result in each node with the *intended* interpretation of the associated relation. When a node contains the expected result, it is marked as *valid*, otherwise it is marked as *nonvalid*.
- The navigation phase ends when a nonvalid node with valid children is found. Such node is called a *buggy node*, and corresponds to an incorrect piece of code. In our case, the debugger will end pointing out either an erroneously defined view, or a table containing a nonvalid instance.

Our goal is to present a declarative debugging framework for SQL views, showing that it can be implemented in a realistic, scalable debugging tool.

We have implemented our debugging proposal in the Datalog Educational System (DES [10]), which makes it possible for Datalog and SQL to coexist as query languages for the same database. The current implementation of our proposal for debugging SQL views and instructions to use it can be downloaded from https://gpd.sip.ucm.es/trac/gpd/wiki/GpdSystems/Des.

2   SQL Semantics

The first formal semantics for relational databases based on the concept of set (e.g., relational algebra, tuple calculus [3]) were incomplete with respect to the treatment of non-relational features such as repeated rows and aggregates, which are part of practical languages such as SQL. Therefore, other semantics, most of them based on multisets [4], have been proposed. In our framework we will use the *Extended Relational Algebra* [6,5]. We start by defining the concepts of database schemas and instances.

A *table schema* is of the form $T(A_1, \ldots, A_n)$, with T being the table name and A_i the attribute names for $i = 1 \ldots n$. We will refer to a particular attribute A by using the notation $T.A$. Each attribute A has an associated type (*integer*, *string*, ...). An *instance* of a table schema $T(A_1, \ldots, A_n)$ is determined by its particular

	Pet	
code	name	species
100	Wilma	dog
101	Kitty	cat
102	Wilma	cat
103	Lucky	dog
104	Rocky	dog
105	Oreo	cat
106	Cecile	turtle
107	Chelsea	dog

PetOwner	
id	code
1	100
1	101
2	102
2	103
3	104
3	105
4	106
4	107

Owner	
id	name
1	Mark Costas
2	Helen Kaye
3	Robin Scott
4	Tom Cohen

Fig. 1. All Pets Club database instance

rows. Each row contains values of the correct type for each attribute in the table schema. *Views* can be thought of as new tables created dynamically from existing ones by using a SQL query. The general syntax of a SQL view is: **create view** $V(A_1, \ldots, A_n)$ **as** Q, with Q a SQL *select* statement, and $V.A_1, \ldots, V.A_n$ the names of the view attributes. In general, we will use the name *relation* to refer to either a table or a view (observe that the mathematical concept of relation is defined over sets, but in our setting we define relations among multisets). A *database schema* D is a tuple $(\mathcal{T}, \mathcal{V})$, where $\mathcal{T}$ is a finite set of table schemas and $\mathcal{V}$ a finite set of view definitions. Although database schemas also include constraints such as primary keys, they are not relevant to our setting.

A *database instance* d of a database schema is a set of table instances, one for each table in $\mathcal{T}$. To represent the instance of a table T in d we will use the notation $d(T)$.

The syntax of SQL queries can be found in [12]. The *dependency tree* of any view V in the schema is a tree with V labeling the root, and its children the dependency trees of the relations occurring in its query. The next example defines a particular database schema that will be used in the rest of the paper as a running example.

Example 1. The *Dog and Cat Club* annual dinner is going to take place in a few weeks, and the organizing committee is preparing the guest list. Each year they browse the database of the *All Pets Club* looking for people that own at least one cat and one dog. Owners come to the dinner with all their cats and dogs. However, two additional constraints have been introduced this year:

- People owning more than 5 animals are not allowed (the dinner would become too noisy).
- No animals sharing the same name are allowed at the party. This means that if two different people have a cat or dog sharing the same name neither of them will be invited. This severe restriction follows after last year's incident, when someone cried *Tiger* and dozens of pets started running without control.

Figure 1 shows the *All Pets Club* database instance. It consists of three tables: *Owner*, *Pet*, and *PetOwner* which relates each owner with its pets. Primary keys are shown underlined. Figure 2 contains the views for selecting the

```
create or replace view AnimalOwner(id ,aname,species) as
  select O.id , P.name, P.species
  from Owner O, Pet P, PetOwner PO
  where O.id = PO.id and P.code = PO.code;

create or replace view LessThan6(id) as
  select id from AnimalOwner
  where species='cat' or species='dog'
  group by id having count(*)<6;

create or replace view CatsAndDogsOwner(id ,aname) as
  select AO1.id ,AO1.aname
  from AnimalOwner AO1, AnimalOwner AO2
  where AO1.id = AO2.id and AO1.species='dog'
        and AO2.species='cat';

create or replace view NoCommonName(id) as
  select id from CatsAndDogsOwner
  except
  select B.id from CatsAndDogsOwner A, CatsAndDogsOwner B
                where A.id <> B.id
                and A.aname = B.aname;

create or replace view Guest(id ,name) as
  select id , name
  from Owner natural inner join NoCommonName
             natural inner join LessThan6;
```

Fig. 2. Views for selecting dinner guests

dinner guests. The first view is *AnimalOwner*, which obtains all the tuples
(*id,aname,species*) such that *id* is the owner of an animal of name *aname* of
species *species*. *LessThan6* returns the identifiers of the owners with less than
six cats and dogs. *CatsAndDogsOwner* returns pairs (*id,aname*) where *id* is the
identifier of the owner of either a cat or a dog with name *aname*, such that
id owns both cats and dogs. *NoCommonName* is defined by removing owners
sharing pet names from the total list of cats and dog owners. Finally, the main
view is *Guest*, which selects those owners that share no pet name with another
owner (view *NoCommonName*) and that have less than six cats and dogs (view
LessThan6). However, these views contain a bug that will become apparent in
the next sections.

The Extended Relational Algebra (ERA from now on) [6] is an operational SQL
Semantics allowing aggregates, views and most of the common features of SQL
queries. The main characteristics of ERA are:

1. The table instances and the result of evaluating queries/views are multisets, (it is also possible to consider *lists* instead of multisets if we consider relevant the order among rows in a query result).
2. ERA expressions define new relations by combining previously defined relations using multiset operators (see [5] for a formal definition of each operator).
3. We use Φ_R to represent a SQL query or view R as an ERA expression, as explained in [5]. Since a query/view depends on previously defined relations, sometimes it will be useful to write $\Phi_R(R_1, \ldots, R_n)$ indicating that R depends on $R_1, \ldots, R_n$. If $M_1, \ldots, M_n$ are multisets we use the notation $\Phi_R(M_1, \ldots, M_n)$ to indicate that the expression Φ_R is evaluated after substituting $R_1, \ldots, R_n$ by $M_1, \ldots, M_n$.
4. Tables are denoted by their names, that is, $\Phi_T = T$ if T is a table.
5. The computed answer of Φ_R with respect to some schema instance d will be denoted by $\| \Phi_R \|_d$, where
   - If R is a database table, $\| \Phi_R \|_d = d(R)$.
   - If R is a database view or a query and $R_1, \ldots, R_n$ the relations defined in R then $\| \Phi_R \|_d = \Phi_R(\| \Phi_{R_1} \|_d, \ldots, \| \Phi_{R_n} \|_d)$.

Observe that $\| \Phi_R \|_d$ is well defined since mutually recursive view definitions are not allowed[1]. We assume that $\| \Phi_R \|_d$ actually corresponds to the answer obtained by a correct SQL implementation, i.e., that the available SQL systems implement ERA. In fact our proposal is valid for any semantics that associate a formula Φ_R to any relation R and allow the recursive definition of computed answer of item 5 above.

3   Declarative Debugging Framework

In this section, we assume a set of SQL views $\mathcal{V} = \{V_1, \ldots, V_n\}$ such that for some $1 \leq i \leq n$, and for some database instance d, V_i has produced an unexpected result in some SQL system. We also assume that this SQL system implements the ERA operational semantics of previous section. Our debugging technique will be based on the comparison between the answers by a SQL system implementing the ERA semantics, and the oracle intended answers. Next, we define the concept of intended answer for schema relations.

Definition 1. Intended Answers for Schema Relations
Let D be a database schema, d an instance of D, and R a relation defined in D. The intended answer for R w.r.t. d, is a multiset denoted as $\mathcal{I}(R, d)$ containing the answer that the user expects for the query select * from R; *in the instance d.*

The intended answer depends not only on the view semantics but also on the contents of the tables in the instance d. This concept corresponds to the idea of *intended interpretations* employed usually in algorithmic debugging. Figure 3

---

[1] Recursive views are allowed in the SQL:1999 standard but they are not supported in all the systems, and they are not considered here.

Fig. 3. Intended answer for the views in Example 1

contains the intended answer for each view defined in Figure 2. For instance, it is expected that *AnimalOwner* will identify each owner *id* with the names and species of his pets. It is also expected than *LessThan6* will contain the *id* of all four owners, since all of them have less than six cats and dogs. The intended answer for view *CatsAndDogsOwner* contains the *id* and *name* attributes of those entries in *AnimalOwner* corresponding to owners with at least one dog and one cat, and removing pets different from cats and dogs. View *NoCommonName* is expected to contain only one row for owner with identifier 3. The reason is that both owners 1 and 2 share a pet name (*Wilma*). Finally, the only expected *Guest* will be the owner with identifier 3, *Robin Scott*. If now we try the query select * from Guest; in a SQL system, we obtain a computed answer representing the multiset $\{|(1, Mark\ Costas),\ (2, Helen\ Kaye),\ (3, Robin\ Scott)|\}$. This computed answer is different from the intended answer for *Guest*, and indicates that there is some error. However, we cannot ensure that the error is in the query for *Guest*, because the error can come from any of the relations in its *from* clause. And also from the relations used by these relations, and so on. In order to define the key concept of erroneous relation it will be useful to define the auxiliary concept of *inferred answer*.

Definition 2. Inferred Answers
Let D be a database schema, d an instance of D, and R a relation in D. The inferred answer for R, with respect to d, $\mathcal{E}(R, d)$, is defined as

1. *If R is a table, $\mathcal{E}(R, d) = d(R)$.*
2. *If R is a view, $\mathcal{E}(R, d) = \Phi_R(\mathcal{I}(R_1, d), \dots, \mathcal{I}(R_n, d))$ with $R_1, \dots, R_n$ the relations occurring in R.*

Thus, in the case of tables, the inferred answer is just its table instance. In the case of a view V, the inferred answer corresponds to the computed result that would be obtained assuming that all the relations R_i occurring in the definition of V contain the intended answers. For instance, consider Example 1 and the instance d of Figure 1. Assume that all the tables contain the intended answers, i.e., for every table T, $\mathcal{I}(T, d) = d(T)$. Then the inferred answer for view *CatsAndDogsOwner* is the same as its computed answer

$\| CatsAndDogsOwner \|_d$:

$$\mathcal{E}(CatsAndDogsOwner, d) = \Phi_{CatsAndDogsOwner}(\mathcal{I}(AnimalOwner, d)) = \\ \{| (1, Wilma), (2, Lucky), (3, Rocky)|\}$$

However, this result is different from the intended answer for this view (Fig. 3). A discrepancy between $\mathcal{I}(R, d)$ and $\mathcal{E}(R, d)$ shows that R does not compute its intended answer, even assuming that all the relations it depends on contain their intended answers. Such relation is erroneous:

Definition 3. Erroneous Relation
Let D be a database schema, d an instance of D, an R a relation defined in D. We say that R is an erroneous relation when $\mathcal{I}(R, d) \neq \mathcal{E}(R, d)$.

Definition 3 clarifies the fundamental concept of erroneous relation. However, it cannot be used directly for defining a practical debugging tool, because in order to point out a view V as erroneous, it would require comparing $\mathcal{I}(V, d)$ and $\mathcal{E}(V, d)$. By Definition 2, to obtain $\mathcal{E}(V, d)$, the tool will need the intended answer $\mathcal{I}(R, d)$ for every R occurring in the query defining V. But $\mathcal{I}(R, d)$ is only known by the user, who should provide this information during the debugging process. Obviously, a technique requiring such amount of information would be rejected by most of the users. Instead, we will require from the oracle only to answer questions of the form *'Is the computed answer (...) the intended answer for view V?'* Thus, the declarative debugger will compare the computed answer –obtained from the SQL system– and the intended answer –known by the oracle– In a first phase, the debugger builds a *computation tree* for the main view. The definition of this structure is the following:

Definition 4. Computation Trees
Let D be a database schema with views $\mathcal{V}$, d an instance of D, and R a relation defined in D. The computation tree $CT(R, d)$ associated with R w.r.t. d is defined as follows:

- *The root of $CT(R, d)$ is $(R \mapsto \| \Phi_R \|_d)$.*
- *For any node $N = (R' \mapsto \| \Phi_{R'} \|_d)$ in $CT(R, d)$:*
  - *If R' is a table, then N has no children.*
  - *If R' is a view, the children of N will correspond to the CTs for the relations occurring in the query associated with R'.*

In practice, the nodes in the computation tree correspond to the syntactic dependency tree of the main SQL view, with the children at each node corresponding to the relations occurring in the definition of the corresponding view. After building the computation tree, the debugger will *navigate* the tree, asking the oracle about the validity of some nodes:

Definition 5. Valid, Nonvalid and Buggy Nodes
Let $T = CT(R, d)$ be a computation tree, and $N = (R' \mapsto \| \Phi_{R'} \|_d)$ a node in T. We say that N is valid when $\| \Phi_{R'} \|_d = \mathcal{I}(R', d)$, nonvalid when $\| \Phi_{R'} \|_d \neq \mathcal{I}(R', d)$, and buggy when N is nonvalid and all its children in T are valid.

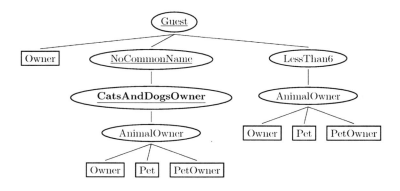

Fig. 4. Computation tree for view Guest

The goal of the debugger will be to locate buggy nodes. The next theorem shows that a computation tree with a nonvalid root always contains a buggy node, and that every buggy node corresponds to an erroneous relation.

Theorem 1. *Let d be an instance of a database schema D, V a view defined in D, and T a computation tree for V w.r.t. d. If the root of T is nonvalid then:*

– *Completeness. T contains a buggy node.*
– *Soundness. Every buggy node in T corresponds to an erroneous relation.*

The debugging process starts when the user finds a view *V* returning an unexpected result. The debugger builds the computation tree for *V*, which has a nonvalid root as required by the theorem. Figure 4 shows the computation tree for our running example (after removing the repeated children). Nonvalid nodes are underlined, and the only buggy node (in bold face) corresponds to view *CatsAndDogsOwner*.

4   Conclusions

In this paper, we propose using algorithmic debugging for finding errors in systems involving several SQL views. To the best of our knowledge, it is the first time that a debugging tool of these characteristics has been proposed. The debugger is based on the navigation of a suitable computation tree corresponding to some view returning some unexpected result. The validity of the nodes in the tree is determined by an external oracle, which can be either the user, or a trusted specification containing a correct version of part of the views in the system. The debugger ends when a buggy node, i.e., a nonvalid node with valid children, is found. We prove formally that every buggy node corresponds to an erroneous relation, and that every computation tree with a nonvalid root contains some buggy node. Although the results are established in the context of the Extended Relational Algebra, they can be easily extended to other possible SQL semantics, such as the Extended Three Valued Predicate Calculus [8].

The technique is easy to implement, obtaining an efficient, platform-independent and scalable debugger without much effort. The tool is very intuitive, because it automates what usually is done when an unexpected answer is found in a system with several views: check the relations in the *from* clause, and if some of them return an unexpected answer, repeat the process. Automating this process is of great help, especially when the tool includes additional features as advanced navigation strategies, or the possibility of using trusted specifications. We have successfully implemented our proposal in the existing, widely-used DES system.

As future work, we plan the development of a graphical interface, which can be very helpful for inspecting the computation tree providing information about the node validity. It will also be useful to consider individual wrong tuples in the unexpected results and study its provenance[13], for a fine-grain error detection.

References

1. Caballero, R., García-Ruiz, Y., Sáenz-Pérez, F.: A Theoretical Framework for the Declarative Debugging of Datalog Programs. In: Schewe, K.-D., Thalheim, B. (eds.) SDKB 2008. LNCS, vol. 4925, pp. 143–159. Springer, Heidelberg (2008)
2. Caballero, R., López-Fraguas, F., Rodríguez-Artalejo, M.: Theoretical Foundations for the Declarative Debugging of Lazy Functional Logic Programs. In: Kuchen, H., Ueda, K. (eds.) FLOPS 2001. LNCS, vol. 2024, pp. 170–184. Springer, Heidelberg (2001)
3. Codd, E.: Relational Completeness of Data Base Sublanguages. In: Rustin (ed.) Data Base Systems. Courant Computer Science Symposia Series, vol. 6. Prentice-Hall, Englewood Cliffs (1972)
4. Dayal, U., Goodman, N., Katz, R.H.: An extended relational algebra with control over duplicate elimination. In: PODS 1982: Proceedings of the 1st ACM SIGACT-SIGMOD Symposium on Principles of Database Systems, pp. 117–123. ACM, New York (1982)
5. Garcia-Molina, H., Ullman, J.D., Widom, J.: Database Systems: The Complete Book. Prentice Hall PTR, Upper Saddle River (2008)
6. Grefen, P.W.P.J., de By, R.A.: A multi-set extended relational algebra: a formal approach to a practical issue. In: 10th International Conference on Data Engineering, pp. 80–88. IEEE (1994)
7. Naish, L.: A Declarative Debugging Scheme. Journal of Functional and Logic Programming 3 (1997)
8. Negri, M., Pelagatti, G., Sbattella, L.: Formal semantics of SQL queries. ACM Trans. Database Syst. 16(3), 513–534 (1991)
9. Nilsson, H.: How to look busy while being lazy as ever: The implementation of a lazy functional debugger. Journal of Functional Programming 11(6), 629–671 (2001)
10. Sáenz-Pérez, F.: DES: A Deductive Database System. In: Spanish Conference on Programming and Computer Languages (September 2010) (in Press)
11. Shapiro, E.: Algorithmic Program Debugging. In: ACM Distiguished Dissertation. MIT Press (1982)
12. SQL, ISO/IEC 9075:1992, third edition (1992)
13. Vansummeren, S., Cheney, J.: Recording provenance for sql queries and updates. IEEE Data Eng. Bull. 30(4), 29–37 (2007)

Timed Transition Systems with Independence and Marked Scott Domains: An Adjunction*

Roman Dubtsov

Institute of Informatics System SB RAS,
6, Acad. Lavrentiev av., 630090, Novosibirsk, Russia
dubtsov@iis.nsk.su

Abstract. The intention of this paper is to introduce a timed extension of transition systems with independence, and to study its categorical interrelations with other timed "true-concurrent" models. In particular, we show the existence of a chain of coreflections leading from a category of the model of timed transition systems with independence to a category of a specially defined model of marked Scott domains. As an intermediate semantics we use a model of timed event structures, able to properly capture the dependencies and conflict among events which arise in the presence of time delays of the events.

1 Introduction

The behaviour of concurrent systems is often specified extensionally by describing their "state-transitions" and the observable behaviours that such transitions produce. The simplest formal model of computation able to express naturally this idea is that of labelled transition systems, where the labels on the transitions represent the observable part of system's behaviour. However, transition systems are an interleaving model of concurrency, which means that they do not allow one to draw a natural distinction between interleaved and concurrent executions of system's actions. Two most popular "true concurrent" extensions of transition systems, aiming to overcome the limitation of interleaving approach, are asynchronous transition systems, introduced independently by Bednarczyk [2] and Shields [7], and transitions systems with independence, proposed by Winskel and Nielsen [10].

Category theory [5] has been used to structure the seemingly confusing world of models for concurrency. Within this framework, objects of categories represent processes and morphisms correspond to behavioural relations between the processes, i.e. to simulations. This approach allows for natural formalization of the fact that one model is more expressive than another in terms of an "embedding", most often taking the form of a coreflection, i.e. an adjunction in which the unit is an isomorphism. For example, Hildenbrandt and Sassone [4] have constructed a full subcategory of a category of asynchronous transition systems

---

* This work is supported in part by DFG-RFBR (grant No 436 RUS 113/1002/01, grant No 09-01-91334).

E. Clarke, I. Virbitskaite, and A. Voronkov (Eds.): PSI 2011, LNCS 7162, pp. 86–94, 2012.

and have shown the existence of a coreflection between the subcategory and a category of transition systems with independence. In this paper we focus on the latter model due to its simplicity.

It is generally acknowledged that time plays an important role in many concurrent and distributed systems. This has motivated the lifting of the theory of untimed systems to real-time setting. Timed extensions of interleaving models have been studied thoroughly within the two last decades (see [1,3] among others), while real-time "true concurrent" models have hitherto received scant attention.

The intention of this paper is to introduce a timed extension of transition systems with independence, and to study its categorical interrelations with other timed "true-concurrent" models. In particular, we show the existence of a chain of coreflections leading from a category of the model of timed transition systems with independence to a category of a specially defined model of marked Scott domains. As an intermediate semantics we use a model of timed event structures, able to properly capture the dependencies and conflict among events which arise in the presence of time delays of the events.

The paper is organized as follows. In Section 2, the notions and notations concerning the structure and behaviour of timed transition systems with independence are described. In section 3, an unfolding mapping from timed transition systems with independence to timed occurrence transition systems with independence is constructed, and it is shown that together with the inclusion functor the unfolding functor defines a coreflection. Section 4 establishes the interrelations in terms of the existence of a coreflection between timed occurrence transition systems with independence and timed event structures. In Section 5, using the equivalence of the categories of timed event structures and marked Scott domains, stated in [8], functors between the categories of timed transition systems with independence and marked Scott domains are constructed to constitute a coreflection.

2   Timed Transition Systems with Independence

In this section, we describe the basic notions and notations concerning the structure and behaviour of timed transition systems with independence.

We start with untimed case. A *transition system with independence* is a tuple $TI = (S, s^I, L, Tran, I)$, where S is a countable set of *states*, $s^I \in S$ is the *initial state*, L is a countable set of *labels*, $Tran \subseteq S \times L \times S$ is the *transition relation*, and $I \subseteq Tran \times Tran$ is the irreflexive, symmetric *independence relation*, such that, using $\prec$ to denote the following relation on transitions $(s, a, s') \prec (s'', a, u) \iff \exists (s, b, s''), (s', b, u) \in Tran$ s.t. $(s, a, s') \ I \ (s, b, s'') \land (s, a, s') \ I \ (s', b, u) \land (s, b, s'') \ I \ (s'', a, u)$, and $\sim$ for the least equivalence relation containing $\prec$, we have:

1. $(s, a, s') \sim (s, a, s'') \Rightarrow s = s''$,
2. $(s, a, s') \ I \ (s, b, s'') \Rightarrow \exists (s', b, u), (s'', a, u) \in Tran \, . \, (s, a, s') \ I \ (s', b, u) \land (s, b, s'') \ I \ (s'', a, u)$,

3. $(s, a, s') \ I \ (s', b, u) \Rightarrow \exists (s, b, s''), (s'', a, u) \in Tran$. $(s, a, s') \ I \ (s, b, s'') \wedge (s, b, s'') \ I \ (s'', a, u)$,

4. $(s, a, s') \sim (s'', a, u) \ I \ (w, b, w') \Rightarrow (s, a, s') \ I \ (w, b, w')$.

Let $\mathrm{Diam}_{a,b}(s, s', s'', u) \iff \exists (s, a, s'), (s, b, s''), (s', b, u), (s'', a, u) \in Tran$. $(s, a, s') \ I \ (s, b, s'') \wedge (s, a, s') \ I \ (s', b, u) \wedge (s, b, s'') \ I \ (s'', a, u)$. We say that the transitions above form an *independence diamond*, and denote the $\sim$-equivalence class of a transition $t \in Tran$ as $[t]$.

A transition system with independence functions by executing transitions from one state to another. A sequence of transitions $\pi = t_0, \ldots, t_n$ such that $t_i = (s_i, a_i, s_{i+1}) \in Tran \ (0 \leq i < n)$ and $s_0 = s^I$ is called a *computation*. Let $\simeq \subseteq \mathrm{Comp}(TI) \times \mathrm{Comp}(TI)$ be the least equivalence relation such that $\pi_s (s, a, s')(s', b, u)\pi_v \simeq \pi_s (s, b, s'')(s'', a, u)\pi_v \iff \mathrm{Diam}_{a,b}(s, s', s'', u)$, and let $[\pi]$ stand for the $\simeq$-equivalence class of a computation π. A transition t is said to be *reachable*, if there exists a computation $\pi \in \mathrm{Comp}(TI)$ such that t appears in π. From now on, we consider only those transition systems with independence in which all transitions are reachable.

We now incorporate time into the model of transition systems with independence. By analogy with the paper [3], we assume a global, fictitious clock, whose actions advance time by nonuniform amounts and whose value is set to zero at the beginning of system's functioning. All transitions are associated with timing constraints represented as minimal and maximal time delays, and happen "instantaneously", while timing constraints restrict the times at which transitions may be executed. Unlike the paper [3], in our timed model the time domain is changed to the integers, and the maximal delays associated with transitions are always equal to ∞, therefore they are not specified explicitly. Also, it is worth saying that our timed model with the empty independence relation is a discrete-timed automata [1] with one clock which is never reset and with the only comparison operation $\geq$ appearing in the timing constraints of the clock.

Let $\mathbb{N}$ be the set of non-negative integers.

Definition 1. *A* timed transition system with independence *is a tuple* $TTI = (S, s^I, L, Tran, I, \delta)$, *where* $[\![TTI]\!] = (S, s^I, L, Tran, I)$ *is the underlying transition system with independence, and* $\delta : Tran \to \mathbb{N}$ *is the* delay function *such that* $\delta(t) = \delta(t')$ *for any* $t, t' \in Tran$ *such that* $t \sim t'$.

A *timed computation* is a sequence of pairs $\Pi = (t_0, d_0), \ldots, (t_n, d_n)$, where each pair is an element of $Tran \times \mathbb{N}$, such that:

1. $[\![\Pi]\!] = t_0, \ldots, t_n, \ldots \in \mathrm{Comp}([\![TTI]\!])$,
2. $i \leq j \Rightarrow d_i \leq d_j$, for all $0 \leq i, j \leq n$,
3. $\delta(t_i) \leq d_i$ for all $0 \leq i \leq n$.

The rationale behind the definition above is simple. Item 1 guarantees that any timed computation is well-defined from the untimed point of view. Item 2 asserts that in a timed computation the time moments at which the transitions are executed agree with the order of the transitions. Item 3 says that each execution of a transition respects the associated delay. We will denote the empty timed computation as ϵ and the set of all timed computations of TTI as $\mathrm{TComp}(TTI)$. Let $\Pi \simeq \Pi' \overset{def}{\Longleftrightarrow} [\![\Pi]\!] \simeq [\![\Pi']\!]$. It is easy to see that $\simeq$ is an equivalence relation; the $\simeq$-class of a timed computation Π is denoted as $[\Pi]$.

For timed transition systems with independence $TTI = (S, s^I, L, Tran, I, \delta)$ and $TTI' = (S', s'^I, L', Tran', I', \delta')$, a *morphism* $h : TTI \to TTI'$ is a pair of mappings $h = (\sigma : S \to S', \lambda : L \to^* L')^1$ such that

1. if $\Pi \in \mathrm{TComp}(TTI)$, then $h(\Pi) \in \mathrm{TComp}(TTI')$ and $\mathrm{cod}^2(h(\Pi)) = \sigma(\mathrm{cod}(\Pi))$, where $h(\Pi)$ is inductively defined as follows: $h(\epsilon) = \epsilon$, $h\big(\Pi((s,a,s'),d)\big) = h(\Pi)\big((\sigma(s),\lambda(a),\sigma(s')),d\big)$, if $a \in \mathrm{dom}\,\lambda$, and $h\big(\Pi((s,a,s'),d)\big) = h(\Pi)$, otherwise,
2. if $\Pi \simeq \Pi'$, then $h(\Pi) \simeq h(\Pi')$.

Timed transition systems with independence and morphisms between them form a category **TTSI** with unit morphisms $\mathbf{1}_{TTI} = (1_S, 1_L) : TTI \to TTI$ for any $TTI = (S, s^I, L, Tran, I, \delta)$, and with composition defined in a componentwise manner.

3   Unfolding of Timed Transition Systems with Independence

The aim of this section is to study unfolding of timed transition systems with independence. To that end, we first define a subclass of timed transition systems with independence that serves as a target of unfolding. After that, we construct an unfolding mapping and show that together with the inclusion functor it defines a coreflection.

A *timed occurrence transition system with independence* $ToTI = (S, s_0, L, Tran, I, \delta)$ is an acyclic timed transition system with independence such that $(s'', a, u) \neq (s', b, u) \in Tran \Rightarrow \exists s \in S$ s.t. $\mathrm{Diam}_{a,b}(s, s', s'', u)$ for all $t \in Tran$. Let **ToTSI** $\subset$ **TTSI** be the full subcategory of timed occurrence transition systems with independence.

Define an unfolding mapping $ttsi.totsi : \mathbf{TTSI} \to \mathbf{ToTSI}$ as follows. For each timed transition system with independence $TTI = (S, s^I, L, Tran, I, \delta)$, let $ttsi.totsi(TTI)$ be $(S_\simeq, [\epsilon], L, Tran_\simeq, I_\simeq, \delta_\simeq)$, where

- $S_\simeq = \{[\Pi] \mid \Pi \in \mathrm{TComp}(TTI)\}$,
- $([\Pi], a, [\Pi']) \in Tran_\simeq \iff \exists t = (s, a, s') \in Tran, \exists d \in \mathbb{N} \,.\, \Pi' \simeq \Pi(t, d)$,
- $([\Pi], a, [\Pi(t, d)]) I_\simeq ([\bar{\Pi}], b, [\bar{\Pi}(\bar{t}, \bar{d})]) \iff t I \bar{t}$,
- $\delta_\simeq([\Pi], a, [\Pi(t, d)]) = \delta(t)$.

Lemma 1. *Given a timed transition system with independence TTI, $ttsi.totsi(TTI)$ is a timed occurrence transition system with independence.*

---

[1] A partial mapping from a set A into a set B is denoted as $\theta : A \to^* B$. Let $\mathrm{dom}\,\theta = \{a \in A \mid \theta(a) \text{ is defined}\}$. For a subset $A' \subseteq A$, define $\theta A' = \{\theta(a') \mid a' \in A' \cap \mathrm{dom}\,\theta\}$.
[2] $\mathrm{cod}(\Pi)$ denotes the ending point of a timed computation Π.

In order to demonstrate that the mapping *ttsi.totsi* is adjoint to the inclusion functor **ToTSI** $\hookrightarrow$ **TTSI**, we define the following morphism and prove that it is the unit of this adjunction. For a transition system with independence TTI, let $\varepsilon_{TTI} = (\sigma_\varepsilon, 1_L) : ttsi.totsi(TTI) \to TTI$, where $\sigma_\varepsilon([\Pi]) = \text{cod}(\Pi)$ for any $[\Pi] \in Tran_{ttsi.totsi(TTI)}$. It is easy to see that ε_{TTI} is a morphism in **TTSI**.

Lemma 2 (ε_{TTI} is universal). *For any timed transition system with independence TTI, any timed occurrence transition system with independence $ToTI$ and any morphism $h : ToTI \to TTI$, there exists a unique $h' : ToTI \to ttsi.totsi(TTI)$ such that $h = \varepsilon_{TTI} \circ h'$.*

The next theorem presents a categorical characterization of the unfolding.

Theorem 1 ($\hookrightarrow \dashv ttsi.totsi$). *The unfolding mapping ttsi.totsi extends to a functor from **TTSI** $\to$ **ToTSI** which is right adjoint to the functor $\hookrightarrow$: **ToTSI** $\to$ **TTSI**. Moreover, this adjunction is a coreflection.*

4   Relating Timed Occurrence Transition Systems with Independence and Timed Event Structures

In this section we relate timed occurrence transition systems with independence and timed event structures, establishing the close relationships between the categories of the models.

We start with the definition of an untimed variant of event structures. An *event structure* is a triple $\mathcal{E} = (E, \leq, \#)$, where E is a countable set of *events*; $\leq \subseteq E \times E$ is a partial order (*the causality relation*) such that $\downarrow e = \{e' \in E \mid e' \leq e\}$ is a finite set for each $e \in E$, $\# \subseteq E \times E$ is the symmetric irreflexive *conflict relation* such that $e \# e' \leq e'' \Rightarrow e \# e''$. A set of events $C \subseteq E$ is said to be a *configuration* of an event structure $\mathcal{E}$ if $\forall e \in C$. $\downarrow e \subseteq C$, and $\forall e, e' \in C$. $\neg(e \# e')$. We say that events $e, e' \in E$ are *concurrent* and write $e \smile e'$ if $\neg(e \leq e' \wedge e' \leq e' \wedge e \# e')$. Introduce the concept of a *reflexive conflict* as follows: $e \mathbb{W} e' \iff e \# e' \vee e = e'$.

We recall the definition of timed event structures from [8].

Definition 2. *A timed event structure is a tuple $\mathcal{TE} = (E, \leq, \#, \Delta)$, where $(E, \leq, \#)$ is an event structure and $\Delta : E \to \mathbb{N}$ is the delay function such that $e' \leq e \Rightarrow \Delta(e') \leq \Delta(e)$.*

A *timed configuration* of $\mathcal{TE}$ is a pair (C, t), where C is a configuration of $(E, \leq, \#)$ and $t \in \mathbb{N} \cup \{\infty\}$ such that $\Delta(e) \leq t$ for each $e \in C$. The set of all (finite) timed configurations of a timed event structure $\mathcal{TE}$ is denoted as $\text{TConf}(\mathcal{TE})$ ($\text{TConf}^0(\mathcal{TE})$). We define a transition relation $\longrightarrow$ on the set $\text{TConf}(\mathcal{TE})$ as follows: $(C, t) \longrightarrow (C', t')$ if $C \subseteq C'$ and $t \leq t'$. Clearly, the relation $\longrightarrow$ specifies a partial order on the set $\text{TConf}(\mathcal{TE})$.

Let $\mathcal{TE} = (E, \leq, \#, \Delta)$ and $\mathcal{TE}' = (E', \leq', \#', \Delta')$ be timed event structures. A partial mapping $\theta : E \to^* E'$ is a *morphism* if $\downarrow \theta(e) \subseteq \theta \downarrow e$; $\theta(e) \mathbb{W} \theta(e') \Rightarrow e \mathbb{W} e'$, for all $e, e' \in \text{dom}\,\theta$; $\Delta'(\theta(e)) \leq \Delta(e)$, for all $e \in \text{dom}\,\theta$. Timed event structures with their morphisms define a category **TES** with unit morphisms $1_{TS} = 1_E : TS \to TS$ for all $TS = (E, \leq, \#, \Delta)$ and the composition being a usual composition of partial functions.

We now establish the categorical relationships between timed event structures and timed occurrence transition systems with independence. For this purpose, we first define a mapping $tpes.totsi : \mathbf{TPES} \to \mathbf{ToTSI}$ extending the mapping $pes.otsi$ from [6] to the timed case. For a timed event structure $\mathcal{TE} = (E, \leq, \#, \Delta)$, define $tpes.totsi(\mathcal{TE})$ to be $(S, s^I, L, Tran, I, \delta)$, where

- $S = \mathrm{Conf}(E, \leq, \#)$,
- $s^I = \varnothing$,
- $L = E$,
- $(C, e, C') \in Tran \iff C' \setminus C = \{e\}$,
- $(C, e, C') I(\bar{C}, \bar{e}, \bar{C}') \iff e \smile \bar{e}$,
- $\delta(C, e, C') = \Delta(e)$.

It is easy to see that the above definition is correct, i.e. $tpes.totsi$ maps timed event structures to timed occurrence transition systems with independence.

Next, we construct a mapping $totsi.tpes : \mathbf{ToTSI} \to \mathbf{TPES}$ which is an extension of the functor $otsi.pes$ from [6], transforming timed occurrence transition systems with independence into timed event structures. For a timed occurrence transition system with independence $ToTI = (S, s^I, L, Tran, I, \delta)$, let $totsi.tpes(ToTI)$ be $(Tran_\sim, \leq, \#, \Delta)$, where

- $Tran_\sim = \{[t] \mid t \in Tran\}$,
- $[t] < [t'] \iff$
  $\forall \pi \in \mathrm{Comp}(\llbracket ToTI \rrbracket) \, . \, \bar{t}' \sim t' \Rightarrow (\exists \bar{t} \in \pi \, . \, \bar{t} \sim t); \leq = (<)^*$,
- $[t] \# [t'] \iff$
  $\forall \pi \in \mathrm{Comp}(\llbracket ToTI \rrbracket), \forall \bar{t} \in [t], \forall \bar{t}' \in [t'] \, . \, \bar{t} \in \pi \Rightarrow \bar{t}' \notin \pi$,
- $\Delta([t]) = \max\{\delta(t') \mid [t'] \leq [t]\}$.

On morphisms $h = (\sigma, \lambda) : ToTI \to ToTI'$ in **ToTSI**, the mapping $totsi.tpes$ acts as follows: $totsi.tpes(h) = \theta$, where $\theta([[(s, a, s')]]) = [(\sigma(s), \lambda(a), \sigma(s'))]$, if $a \in \mathrm{dom}\,\lambda$, and $\theta([[(s, a, s')]])$ is undefined, otherwise.

Proposition 1. $totsi.tpes : \mathbf{ToTSI} \to \mathbf{TPES}$ *is a functor.*

Finally, we define the unit of the adjunction. For a timed event structure $\mathcal{TE}$, let $\eta_{\mathcal{TE}} : E_{\mathcal{TE}} \to E_{totsi.tpes \circ tpes.totsi(\mathcal{TE})}$ be a mapping such that $\eta_{\mathcal{TE}}(e) = [(C, \Delta(C)), e, (C \cup \{e\}, \Delta(C \cup \{e\}))]$. It is straightforward to show that $\eta_{\mathcal{TE}}$ is an isomorphism in **TPES**. In order to show the existence of the adjunction, we need to check that $\eta_{\mathcal{TE}}$ is indeed a unit, i.e. it is universal.

Lemma 3 ($\eta_{\mathcal{TE}}$ is universal).
For any timed event structure $\mathcal{TE}$, any timed occurrence transition system $ToTI$, and any morphism $\theta : \mathcal{TE} \to totsi.tpes(ToTI)$, there exists a unique morphism $h : tpes.totsi(\mathcal{TE}) \to ToTI$ such that $\theta = totsi.tpes(h) \circ \eta_{\mathcal{TE}}$.

The next theorem establishes the existence of a coreflection between the categories of timed event structures and timed occurrence transition systems with independence.

Theorem 2 (*tpes.totsi ⊣ totsi.tpes*). *The map tpes.totsi can be extended to a functor tpes.totsi* : **TPES** → **ToTSI**, *which is left adjoint to the functor totsi.tpes. Moreover, this adjunction is a coreflection.*

5   Marked Scott Domains

We conclude the paper by extending the established chain of coreflections to marked Scott domains. To that end, we first recall related notions and notations.

Let $(D, \sqsubseteq)$ be a partial order, $d \in D$ and $X \subseteq D$. Then, $\uparrow d = \{d' \in D \mid d \sqsubseteq d'\}$ is an *upper cone of element* d, $\downarrow d = \{d' \in D \mid d' \sqsubseteq d\}$ is a *lower cone of element* d. X is downward (upward) closed if $\downarrow d \subseteq X$ ($\uparrow d \subseteq X$) for every $d \in X$. X is a *compatible set* (denoted as $X\uparrow$), if the following assertion is true: $\exists d \in D \forall x \in X$. $x \sqsubseteq d$, i.e., X has an upper bound. If $X = \{x, y\}$, we write $x \uparrow y$ instead of $\{x, y\}\uparrow$. The least upper bound of the set X is denoted as $\bigsqcup X$ (if exists), and the greatest lower bound — as $\bigsqcap X$ (if exists). The least upper bound of two elements x and y is denoted as $x \sqcup y$, and the greatest lower bound — as $x \sqcap y$. X is a *finitely compatible set* if any finite subset of it $X' \subseteq X$ is compatible. X is a *(upper) directed set* if any finite subset $X' \subseteq X$ has an upper bound belonging to the set X (thus, X is a finitely compatible and nonempty set).

$(D, \sqsubseteq)$ is a *directed-complete partial order (dcpo for short)* if every directed subset $X \subseteq D$ has $\bigsqcup X$. d is a *finite (compact) element* of a dcpo $(D, \sqsubseteq)$ if, for any directed subset $X \subseteq D$, the following assertion is true: $d \sqsubseteq \bigsqcup X \Rightarrow \exists x \in X$. $d \sqsubseteq x$. The set of finite elements is denoted as $C(D)$.

A dcpo $(D, \sqsubseteq)$ is said to be *algebraic* if, for any $d \in D$, $d = \bigsqcup\{e \sqsubseteq d \mid e \in C(D)\}$. It is said to be *ω-algebraic* if $C(D)$ is countable. $(D, \sqsubseteq)$ is a *consistently complete partial order* (ccpo) if any finitely compatible subset $X \subseteq D$ has $\bigsqcup X$. Clearly, a ccpo has the least element $\bot = \bigsqcup \emptyset$, and is also a dcpo. An *ω-algebraic ccpo* is called a *Scott domain*. A Scott domain $(D, \sqsubseteq)$ is said to be *finitary* if $\downarrow d$ is finite for every $d \in C(D)$. An element p of a Scott domain $(D, \sqsubseteq)$ is said to be *prime* if, for any compatible subset $X \subseteq D$. $p \sqsubseteq \bigsqcup X \Rightarrow \exists x \in X$. $p \sqsubseteq x$. The set of the prime elements is denoted as $P(D)$. A Scott domain $(D, \sqsubseteq)$ is called *prime algebraic* if, for any $d \in D$, $d = \bigsqcup\{p \sqsubseteq d \mid p \in P(D)\}$; *coherent* if all subsets $X \subseteq D$ satisfying the condition $\forall d', d'' \in X$. $d' \uparrow d''$ have $\bigsqcup X$.

Let $(D, \sqsubseteq)$ be a Scott domain and $\prec = \sqsubseteq \setminus \sqsubseteq^2$ be a *covering relation*. For elements $d, d' \in D$ such that $d \prec d'$, the pair $[d, d']$ is called a *prime interval*. The set of all prime intervals is denoted as $I(D)$. We write $[c, c'] \leq [d, d']$ iff $c = c' \sqcup d \wedge d' = c' \sqcup d$. The relation $\sim$ is defined to be a transitive symmetric closure of the relation $\leq$. Note that $\sim$-equivalent prime intervals model the same action. Let $[d, d']_\sim$ denote the $\sim$-equivalence class of the prime interval $[d, d']$.

We are now ready to define marked Scott domains. Informally, a marked Scott domain is meant to be a prime algebraic, finitary, and coherent Scott domain with the prime intervals modeling two (instantaneous and delayed) types of system actions. The former actions do not require time and are marked by zero, and the latter ones take one unit of time and are marked by one. It is natural to require that the $\sim$-equivalent prime intervals corresponding to one and the same system action are marked identically.

Definition 3. *A* marked Scott domain *is a triple* $(D, \sqsubseteq, m)$, *where* $(D, \sqsubseteq)$ *is a prime algebraic, finitary, and coherent Scott domain and* $m : I(D) \longrightarrow \{0, 1\}$ *is the* marking function *such that* $[c, c'] \sim [d, d'] \Rightarrow m([c, c']) = m([d, d'])$.

Introduce auxiliary notions and notations. For $d, d' \in D$ and $i \in \{0, 1\}$, we write $d \prec^i d'$, if $d \prec d' \wedge m([d, d']) = i$, and $d \preceq^i d'$, if $d \prec^i d' \vee d = d'$; $\sqsubseteq^i = (\prec^i)^*$; $\downarrow^i d = \{d' \mid d' \sqsubseteq^i d\}$, and $\uparrow^i d = \{d' \mid d \sqsubseteq^i d'\}$; $P^i(D) = \{p \in P(D) \mid \exists d \in D \, . \, m([d, p]) = i\}$. For a finite element $d \in D$ and a covering chain σ having the form $\bot = d_0 \prec^{k_1} d_1 \cdots d_{n-1} \prec^{k_n} d_n = d$ (this chain is finite since $(D, \sqsubseteq)$ is finitary), define the *norm of* d *along* σ by $\|d\|_\sigma = \sum_{i=1}^n k_i$. Since $(D, \sqsubseteq)$ is prime algebraic and m respects $\sim$, the value of $\|d\|_\sigma$ does not depend on σ. Therefore, we shall use $\|d\|$ to denote the norm of a finite element d. The concept of the norm is extended to other elements $d \in D$ as follows: $\|d\| = sup\{\|d'\| \mid d' \in \downarrow d \cap C(D)\}$. A marked domain $(D, \sqsubseteq, m)$ is said to be *linear* if for any $d \in D$ such that $\|d\| < \infty$, $(\uparrow^1 d, \sqsubseteq^1) \cong (\mathbb{N}, \leq)$; *regular* if for any $d, d' \in D$, $d \uparrow d' \Rightarrow \forall d_1 \in \uparrow^1 d, \forall d_1' \in \uparrow^1 d' \, . \, (d_1 \uparrow d_1')$.

It is not difficult to see that linear regular marked domains, together with the additive stable mappings [9] preserving $\preceq^0$ and $\prec^1$, form the category **MDom**.

As shown in [8], marked Scott domains are related with timed event structures via a pair of functors *tpes.mdom* : **TPES** $\rightarrow$ **MDom** and *mdom.tpes* : **MDom** $\rightarrow$ **TPES** defined as follows[3].

For a timed event structure $TE = (E, \leq, \#, \Delta)$, let *tpes.mdom*$(TE)$ be $(\mathrm{TConf}(TE), \longrightarrow, m_{TE})$, where

$$m([(C, t), (C', t')]) = \begin{cases} 0, \text{ if } C' \setminus C = \{e\} \wedge d' = d, \\ 1, \text{ if } C' = C \wedge d' = d + 1. \end{cases}$$

For a marked Scott domain $MD = (D, \sqsubseteq, m) \in$ **MDom**, define *mdom.tpes*(MD) to be $(E, \leq, \#, \Delta)$, where $E = P^0(D)$, $p \leq p' \iff p \sqsubseteq p$, $p \# p' \iff p \not\uparrow p'$, and $\Delta(p) = \|p\|$.

Theorem 3. *[8]. The functors tpes.mdom and mdom.tpes constitute an equivalence between the categories* **TPES** *and* **MDom**.

Theorems 1, 2 and 3 yields the following corollary fact.

Theorem 4. *The functor* $\hookrightarrow \circ tpes.totsi \circ mdom.tpes :$ **MDom** $\rightarrow$ **TTSI** *is left adjoint to the functor tpes.mdom $\circ$ totsi.tpes $\circ$ ttsi.totsi :* **TTSI** $\rightarrow$ **MDom**. *Moreover, this adjunction is a coreflection.*

---

[3] We do not specify how *tpes.mdom* and *mdom.tpes* act on morphisms since it is not essential to this paper.

References

1. Alur, R., Dill, D.L.: A theory of timed automat. Theoretical Computer Science 126(2), 183–235 (1994)
2. Bednarczyk, M.A.: Categories of asynchronous systems. PhD thesis, University of Sussex, UK (1987)
3. Henzinger, T., Manna, Z., Pnueli, A.: Timed Transition Systems. In: Huizing, C., de Bakker, J.W., Rozenberg, G., de Roever, W.-P. (eds.) REX 1991. LNCS, vol. 600, pp. 226–251. Springer, Heidelberg (1992)
4. Hildebrandt, T.T., Sassone, V.: Comparing Transition Systems with Independence and Asynchronous Transition Systems. In: International Conference on Concurrency Theory, pp. 84–97 (1996)
5. McLane, S.: Categories for the working mathematician. Graduate Texts in Mathematics. Springer, Berlin (1971)
6. Sassone, V., Nielsen, M., Winskel, G.: Models for concurrency: towards a classification. Theoretical Computer Science 170(1-2), 297–348 (1996)
7. Shields, M.W.: Concurrent Machines. The Computer Journal 28(5), 449–465 (1985)
8. Virbitskaite, I.B., Dubtsov, R.S.: Semantic domains of timed event structures. Programming and Computer Software 34(3), 125–137 (2008)
9. Winskel, G.: Event Structures. In: Brauer, W., Reisig, W., Rozenberg, G. (eds.) APN 1986. LNCS, vol. 255, pp. 325–392. Springer, Heidelberg (1987)
10. Winskel, G., Nielsen, M.: Models for concurrency. Handbook of Logic in Computer Science 4, 1–148 (1995)

An Extensible System for Enhancing Social Conference Experience

Michael A.H. Fried[1], Anna Fensel[1],
Federico Michele Facca[2], and Dieter Fensel[1]

[1] Semantic Technology Institute, Innsbruck, Austria
{michael.fried,anna.fensel,dieter.fensel}@sti2.at
[2] CREATE-NET, Trento, Italy
federico.facca@create-net.org

Abstract. We combine Auto-ID and Web technologies in an extensible on-site event support system for enhancing experience of conference organizers as well as participants. Our system enables users to authenticate themselves using RFID badges and to access interactive Web-based services via a touchscreen terminal. The developed services aim at supporting social interactions of participants, and thus validate the promising usage directions of the combination of offline social networks and the online social Web. Technically, we have investigated employment of Web 2.0 technologies in social, sensor and mobile technologies enabled systems at conferences and events. This paper gives an overview of the overall system and its evaluation via a user survey and usage log data collected during the Extended Semantic Web Conference (ESWC) 2010 and similar international conferences, altogether with several hundred participants.

Keywords: RFID, conference support system, social networking activities, touch enabled terminal/kiosk.

1 Introduction

Social networking is a major aspect of conferences most participants benefit from. This includes the interest in (scientific) self comparison and the necessity to connect with other conference participants in order to gain new insights on various topics. Empowered by becoming more and more affordable devices and sensors, ranging from regular TV sets, touchscreen-enabled kiosks to tablet PCs designated for the mass consumer market, the ubiquitous RFID (Radio-Frequency IDentification) and smart phones, social networking is becoming supported by modern technology in a physical, on-site and location-aware manner, thus not only virtually as till the recent times.

While actively co-organizing several annual conferences on "Semantic Technologies and Future Internet", we are convinced that innovative IT systems have a potential to substantially support conference participants' networking activities on-site. For this purpose, we have developed and are offering easily accessible services to enhance the social experience during such events.

E. Clarke, I. Virbitskaite, and A. Voronkov (Eds.): PSI 2011, LNCS 7162, pp. 95–110, 2012.

The services are encapsulated in an extensible system utilizing Web 2.0 technologies as well as sensors, which rely on automatic identification and data capture (Auto-ID) techniques, such as for example RFID and bar codes (2 dimensional QR codes) for authentication of users. These Auto-ID techniques are nowadays mostly used in supply chain management [11] and the logistics sector for tracking of assets and inventory purposes, but are emerging as foundation of the Internet of Things [6,16] and are starting to become ubiquitous in our everyday lives.

Our system and services have been deployed and partly evaluated in particular at the following conferences:

– European Semantic Web Conference (ESWC) 2009
– European Semantic Technology Conference (ESTC) 2009
– Extended Semantic Web Conference (ESWC) 2010
– Future Internet Symposium (FIS) 2010.

During the ESWC 2010 and FIS 2010 all user interactions were logged to evaluate the system's overall performance and the performance of different services. Additionally over 30 people participated in a survey containing questions about the system's usability, service usefulness and user acceptance of different Auto-ID techniques. The collected data provides deep insights into the success of the project and indicates directions for the future.

The overall outcomes and contributions of the project include the evaluation of acceptance and usefulness of the services, identifying the social practices and types of services people prefer, Auto-ID/RFID acceptance, as well as techniques for promoting such a system during a conference and optimization of the interface and its adaptation to the requirements of a touchscreen or mobile device.

The next section of this paper discusses the overall architecture of the system, followed by a description of the developed showcase services in Section 3. Section 4 describes the project's history. Results form a detailed evaluation based on usage data collected during the ESWC 2010 can be found in Section 5. An outlook on related and future work as well as conclusions in Sections 6-8 finalize the paper.

2   System Architecture and Implementation

Our conference support system centers around a piece of software that enables conference organizers to deploy different services and conference participants to access them through traditional browsers and mobile clients. The authentication may potentially occur through different devices and technologies, such as Near field Communication (NFC), bar codes, and RFID tags. Moreover the user interface is designed to be intuitive and easy to use without requiring explicit instructions.

Figure 1 presents the architecture of our system for on-site conference services. At the core of the architecture, there is a flexible authentication mechanism that allows users to authenticate themselves by using an RFID tag. Devices (e.g. such

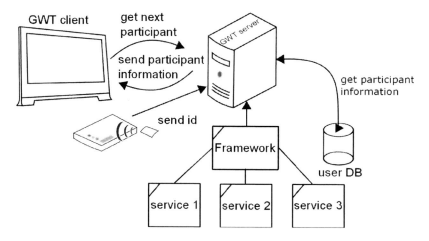

Fig. 1. Architectural overview

and RFID reader or mobile phones) send the authentication token to the server which looks up the user information in the underlying database. On successful login, users are provided with an overview page (Figure 2) showing all available services.

Recently the user database has been integrated with the STI International Community[1] website. This new platform aims at becoming a social network for STI members and the Semantic Web community. Core features include browsing the community, accessing the latest news from members on their projects and events, seeing showcases of semantic technologies, accessing public resources about semantic technologies and semantic data and view related media created by STI and its members. Conference registrees are being registered automatically to the community pages. They can change their profile information and access the different Community subsystems: Agora (blogs), Emporium (marketplace), Kudos (challenges) and Minerva (wiki). Moreover these profiles also play a key role in the future Facebook integration of our conference support solution. More details on this topics follow in Section 7.

To achieve the basic requirement of flexibility, the system is implemented using the Google Web Toolkit (GWT), a development toolkit for building complex Web 2.0 applications. GWT code is written in Java and later compiled to client side JavaScript that runs within a modern browser. Compatibility issues between different browsers as well as client server communication via GWT/RPC are handled automatically.

Services do not have to be necessarily created with GWT. The framework can integrate services written in any language or technology, such as PHP or Adobe's Flash, that is able to be executed within a browser. GWT based services will be added as modules, whereas others can be added with little programming effort

---

[1] http://community.sti2.org/

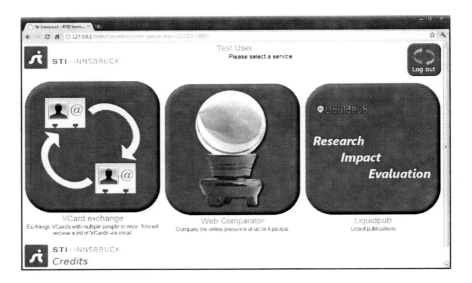

Fig. 2. Service overview page

(e.g. as a simple HTML page, external websites via i-frame HTML tag, a HTML page with Flash embedded etc.).

To enable interaction with the services by means of different devices, we adopted the Model-View-Controller pattern: the conference GWT server exposes the system to the clients and handles the authentication mechanism. Each service exposes and accesses data through either a RESTful or GWT-RPC interface. The client (browser) requests data either directly from the conference framework server, external websites using JSON with padding or external websites using the conference server as proxy (due to browser's same origin policy). The retrieved data is then rendered on the client according to the defined service view. All user interactions are logged centrally on the server.

At the moment we mostly concentrated our efforts on the touchscreen kiosk based version of the system and implemented a prototye using RFID for authentication, but first concepts have been tested also for mobile devices (see http://iot.sti2.at). Section 7 discusses our plans for mobile devices support.

3   Conference Services

Conference participants have several typical social needs, such as contact information exchange, people and publication comparison, learning new relevant things, etc. Alongside the framework, as a proof of concept and to showcase the on-site conference support system, various service ideas have been developed. The presented infrastructure and services aim to address the different social needs of conference participants. Not all of these services have been deployed at each conference. Table 1^2 gives an overview of which services have been deployed where. The emphasis of this paper is mainly to evaluate the usefulness and acceptance of the kiosk system itself and RFID technology. The service performance was evaluated, but these findings are secondary, since implemented services so far are only meant to be a proof of concept for the implemented Web based conference support system.

VCard Exchange service is inspired by a real world practice of business card exchange. The VCard application enables multiple people to exchange their contact information at once. When logged in, the participants who want to exchange VCards can achieve this by simply wiping their RFID tags over the reader. The user information, which has been provided at the registration for the conference, is serialized to a VCard 2.1 [8,4] compliant format. This method for exchanging contacts was chosen, because it is very compact and compatible with most modern email clients and phones. On confirmation, VCards of all participating people are exchanged via email.

Example VCard

```
BEGIN:VCARD
  VERSION:2.1
  FN:Michael Fried
  N:Fried;Michael;;;
  ADR:;;Technikerstrasse;Innsbruck;;A-6020;AUSTRIA
  TEL;WORK:0043987654321
  TEL;FAX:004398765432100
  EMAIL;INTERNET:michael.fried@sti2.at
  TITLE:Researcher
  ORG:STI Innsbruck
  URL:http://www.sti2.at
END:VCARD
```

Web Comparator showcases the boundaries of the current Web. It uses the names of up to four participants to look-up personal and professional information on the Web and present the result to the participants. In particular we distinct three different sources of information: Web pages (Google, Yahoo), images (Google Images, Yahoo Images, Flickr) as well as scientific publications (Google Scholar, CiteseerX).

In this way participants jointly authenticated on the system can compare their respective presence on the Web. In the first versions of the system the comparison was summarized through an index, called "Web points", that vaguely related to the number of results found. The missing transparency of how this index was calculated led to confusion amongst some users. Many of them did not intuitively realize the correlation between number of results and "Web Points" and were asking about their meaning. This flaw was eliminated by substituting them with the actual number of results found.

---

² Some values in the Table are approximations due to missing or corrupted data.

The service shows that in the current Web it is either very easy or very hard to retrieve meaningful information with just having a person's name. People with common names often tend to disappear in the "white noise" of results. On the other hand people who have more exotic names and are actively present on the Web in social networks and such, are easy to find and sometimes very detailed personal profiles could be generated with just one simple search. Most computer scientists should be well aware of their online presence and footprints they leave. This makes the service less interesting for people in the field, as it can be mainly seen as a fun application for people who do not know which variety of personal information is publicly available on the Web.

In future versions the Web Comparator will experiment with the use of semantic technologies (e.g. semantic search, consideration of Linked Open Data and inclusion of such into results, FOAF profiles, etc.) to reduce search result noise and compare traditional search results with semantically enhanced ones.

Research Impact Evaluation is an outcome of the LiquidPub[3] project. The project proposes a paradigm shift in the way scientific knowledge is created, disseminated, evaluated and maintained. The shift is enabled by the notion of liquid publications, which are evolutionary, collaborative, and composable scientific contributions. In our terminal we integrate the ResEval [12] tool for evaluating research contributions and people by using citation-based metrics. The application uses data of Google Scholar for calculating the metrics and is accessible via an online search form or RESTful Web service.

Currently the information available contains H-index [7], G-index [5], N (number of publications) and C (number of citations) of an author and a list of all the author's publications. Furthermore, for contributions the citation count can be accessed. We plan to extend this service by including further functionality offered by the LiquidPub project, such as Research Network Comparison and Research Community Comparison.

My Talks service enables participants to look at the schedule of the conference, decide which talks they want to attend and access their personal schedule on the terminal.

4   History of the Project

Started in spring of 2009, as a small demo for the ESWC 2009, the application evolved and has since been deployed at the following events:

1. ESWC 2009
   The first version of the system consisted only of the Web Comparator service presented on a non interactive TV screen. Back then the underlying active RFID infrastructure for our system was supplied by the LSS [15] experiment, which also took place at conference. LSS supports and guides social networking activities between researchers at conferences and similar events by integrating data and technologies from the Semantic Web, online social

---

[3] http://liquidpub.org/

networks and an RFID tracking platform. Participants were supplied with active RFID tags and their movements and interactions tracked on-site. Face to face interactions and social interaction graphs were visible on some screens within the conference area. According to the statistical information provided in [15], 305 people attended the conference, out of which 187 collected an RFID badge. 139 of the participants created an account on the LSS application site and were therefore able to use our system as well. We used an active tag placed below the TV to recognize people near the device (1 to 5 meters) and start the Web Comparator service automatically.

Due to the static presentation and the fact that the system often picked up signals from too many adjacent participants to guarantee proper authentication, the first experiment was not received exceptionally well by the audience.

2. ESTC 2009

Considering lessons learned from the first deployment, the system was upgraded to feature an interactive touchscreen and an authentication mechanism based on passive RFID technology, which is a cheaper solution and suits the requirement of our scenario better due to a more limited range. Instead of being recognized when approaching the terminal, participants had to wipe their uniquely numbered tag over a reader within a distance of 20 centimeters. The ESTC is a 2 days conference attended by around 100 people, with a stronger focus on business audience rather than researchers.

At this conference we realized that the system's promotion could be improved to draw more attention to the kiosk and its functionality.

3. ESWC 2010

After implementing new services, we decided to monitor activities on the terminal and to conduct a user survey for evaluating the system and service acceptance. Due to the size of the conference we expected to collect comprehensive data in order to further improve the experience and get new ideas for future development. The data received from the system logs as well as the survey will be evaluated in Section 5 of this paper.

The findings helped us to find weak spots in the services and define a future direction for the project.

4. FIS 2010

No new services were introduced for the conference. The focus was to fix minor issues that were pointed out in course of the ESWC 2010.

5   Evaluation

The data analyzed in this section was collected during ESWC 2010. We wanted to identify how frequently people use the system and which services are popular. In 2010, 312 people were registered for the ESWC out of which 83% were male. RFID tags were produced for all of them, but some participants who registered on-site did not pick up their tags. In total 120 people used the system which is approximately 38% of all attendees.

Table 1. Experiments overview

	ESWC 2009	ESTC 2009	ESWC 2010	FIS 2010
Participants	approx. 300	approx. 100	312 (53 female)	112 (16 female)
Countries	approx. 40	approx. 10	46	20
Users	approx. 80	approx. 20	120	11
Services	Web Comparator	Web Comparator	Web Comparator	Web Comparator
		VCard Exchange	VCard Exchange	VCard Exchange
		My Talks	Res. Impact Eval.	Res. Impact Eval.

The audience was international, yet 89% came form Europe, 21% from Germany, 12% from the UK and 7% from Austria. Remote usage logging from the client side was implemented by sending log messages to the server when a person either logged onto the system, chose a service or was added to one. The information contains the kind of interaction, unique ID of the user, as well as a time stamp. Participants had to agree that their personal data could be used, via a check box integrated in the online conference registration form, in order to receive an RFID tag. Only geographic data as well as gender information were kept for performing various statistical analysis. Names, e-mail addresses and all other personal information was deleted after the conference. The anonymization of data guarantees that a particular data set cannot be tracked back to one single participant. The system was promoted during the welcome speech and by an explanatory poster behind the terminal, which was prominently placed next to the conference registration desk, which was the single spot where every participant passed by at least once in order to receive a conference badge. Additionally one person was present most of the time in order to explain the system and answer questions risen by users.

In addition to the collection of usage logs, a feedback questionnaire was placed next to the terminal. Thirty-seven attendees participated in the survey, i.e. about 11% of the conference participants and over 30% of the people who actually used the system.

5.1   Results

Collected over the course of five full days, the logs unveil a large variety of facts. With a total of 587 logged interactions, Figure 3 indicates that most people used the terminal up to five times. One participant had 39 interactions, but all users that interacted with the system over 12 times can be considered statistical outliers. Over half of the people used the kiosk on exactly one out of the five days, whereas three registrees only logged in without selecting a service. May 31st was the busiest day, June 3rd the weakest. Male as well as well as female usage show a peak on the second day. A correlation between terminal usage and general attendance level cannot be proven, but our observations of the conference venue during the deployment indicate that more people were present on the second day

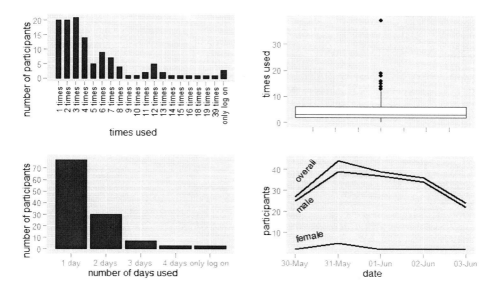

Fig. 3. Terminal usage statistics. Overview of how many times/on which days users accessed the terminal.

than on the last. Results shown in Figure 4 provide insight on how frequently people used the different services:

- Research Impact Evaluation drew the least user attraction (slightly over 60 users), but had fairly many interactions. This means that everyone using the service used it three times on average.
- VCard Exchange had the smallest number of interactions as well as reuse ratio. On average each of the service's users exchanged a VCard twice.
- Web Comparator was the most popular service by user base (90 users) as well as interactions (over 200).

This distribution unveils that there is a clear gap between the two, very similar, comparison services (Res. Impact Eval. and Web Comparator). Despite the assumption that IT people are well aware of their online presence, the Web Comparator drew the biggest attraction on the conference. Surprisingly the VCard Exchange service did not perform as well as expected. This could result from the fact that some people rather distribute traditional business cards than electronic ones. Another theory is that in a closed and comparably small community like the one represented in ESWC[4] most people simply know each other already.

If we compare our deployment to the results from the IntelliBadge project [3], we see various commonalities in the data. Out of the 2188 IEEE Supercomputing 2002 (SC 2002) registrees 872 people could be tracked as using the system. This

---

[4] Many European core researchers within the Semantic Web community frequently attend a limited number of annual conferences.

results show a similar user/conference participants ratio to our experiment. Also the usage declined after a peak on the first day. The IntelliBadge kiosks were accessed 1771 times on-site and 1370 times remotely. Every participant used the system about 4 times on average. Also the results of the LSS experiment [15] show a similar picture. Out of the 305 participants 187 people received an RFID tag and 139 used the system.

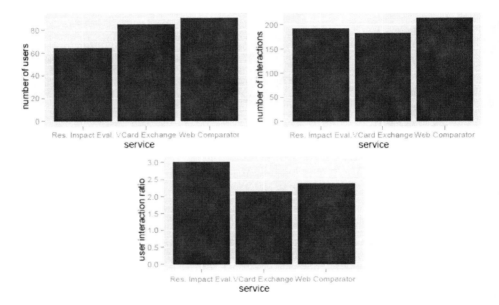

Fig. 4. Service usage statistics. Overall number of service users and service interactions.

When taking a look at the survey feedback evaluation, the results provide deeper insight into service and RFID acceptance. The questionnaire contained certain terminal specific questions which are depicted in Figure 6. Answers could range from 1 to 7 (where 1 marks the best grade and 7 the worst). Additionally Figure 5 contains an overview of RFID specific questions.

Two free text fields offered the possibility to provide "General notes/issues" and comment on the question "What services would you like to see in the future?". Some frequent answers hint at requirements desired by participants:

1. Integration with social networks
2. Bulletin board service
3. List of conference participants with photos to allow identification
4. Recommendations based on relations
5. One kiosk is not enough
6. Access services over mobile phones.

The social needs addressed by the services include the interest in self comparison and the necessity to connect with other conference participants. Results collected with the usage logs and survey indicate that the services performed well and met the users' demands. An interesting fact is the gap between the grading and usage of the Web Comparator and VCard Exchange service that can be seen in Figure 6. Whereas the latter had scored the best grade in the survey and has been elected the most useful service, it has not been used the most. The Web Comparator was graded least but turned out to be the most popular service.

Reasons for this usage distribution can result from various factors like service responsiveness, attractiveness, the fun factor, etc. This paper does not focus on explaining reasons for the discovered distributions, but rather provides an overview of general usage which has to be investigated further in future setups by adapting the feedback survey and trying different designs and service layouts.

Although most of the people came in contact with RFID before the conference, there is still skepticism towards RFID technology and users tend to prefer bar codes. We will address these concerns in future deployments of the system (e.g. information that no tracking is performed, introduction of bar codes, etc.). Nevertheless, the use of sensor systems for authentication has proven so far to be a secure and easy to use solution.

The survey shows that there are still improvements to make regarding terminal usability, interface design and overall experience. Yet, all in all, the use of RFID at conferences to offer services has been graded useful by the majority of participants.

6   Related Work

As a real world application, the proposed system touches multiple different fields of research: Web Engineering (exposing the system via a browser), Auto-ID Systems (use of RFID or QR Code for authentication) and Social Sciences (usability and acceptance studies).

The core idea of the project, i.e. to add value to conferences through technology means, has been occurring in research. For example the adoption of RFID for authentication is quite established in literature [2]. In their work, J. Bravo et al. focus on touch less interaction with a static kiosk. In comparison, our solution emphasizes haptic user interaction via a touchscreen and provides an interactive and simple way to expose and access services. Our services promote social networking and interaction among conference participants.

Ubiquitous community assistance (UbiCoAssist) and POLYPHONET [13] address as well the notion of services for social networking during conferences. These tools were showcased during UbiComp2005 and UbiComp2006 and contain a set of specialized services to point out social network relations between conference participants.

During the first demonstration of our system at ESWC 2009, we strongly interwove it with the ESWC Live Social Semantic (LSS) experiment [15], which was first described in [1]. LSS tracked conference participants using active RFID technology and we built on top of their infrastructure to support identification at our kiosk. A similar approach for tracking participants was experimented by the

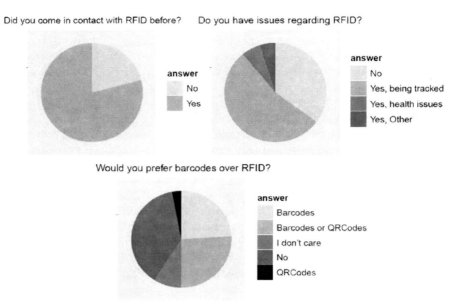

Fig. 5. Overview and results of RFID specific survey questions

IntelliBadge [3] project at the IEEE Supercomputing conference in 2002. Data collected by IntelliBadge and LSS provides us reference values for evaluating the performance of our system as discussed in Section 5.1.

Some commercial solutions have been developed as well, such as Spotme.[5] During conferences every participant receives a proprietary hand-held device that enables them to access services and exchange data with other people on-site. Spotme integrates social networking, audience response, and participant management tools. In comparison to such systems, our solution adopts standard Web technologies that make our system usable on different devices and simplify its development and integration: it is comparatively easy to develop new services and integrate existing ones.

The adoption of RFID for authentication grants a certain degree of security, since tags cannot be faked or reproduced trivially. RFID is slowly becoming ubiquitous in our every day life and several privacy thread and issues [10] (e.g. the ability to track people) have been raised on this technology. Inspired by existing research [9] we dedicated a part of our survey to the users' acceptance of Auto-ID systems.

7   Future Work

A key finding of the evaluation is that a significant amount of people, over one third of all participants, used the system, but the provided infrastructure

---

[5] http://www.spotme.com/

is not sufficient for large conference setups, i.e. one touchscreen terminal is not enough, since it is often occupied and conference venues can be very large, which means that participants could have to walk an ample distance in order to simply exchange a VCard for example. So spatial constraints, even if the touchscreen is placed in a highly visible spot, could discourage people from using the system.

Ultimately a shift to mobile devices appears to be necessary. This mobile integration will be the next big step in the evolution of the project.

There are strong indications that mobile RFID via NFC will be featured in many future phones, as Google has already integrated the technology in it's Nexus S branded phone and as Apple is allegedly looking into this technology for future versions of the iPhone. But currently QRCodes are still the state-of-the-art mobile Auto-ID technology which is supported by most modern phones and is planned to be used for authentication in upcoming installments of our system.

Further, we are planning on implementing a special version for mobile devices and focus on deeper integration of social networks. Some experiments based on QRCodes and Google's Android smart phone OS platform are already ongoing.

After migrating the user database to the STI Community website, integration of social networks within the STI Community user pages provides a strong social notion for future service development. Apart from the user and community management integration, semantic technologies will play a key role in the following components and approaches:

- A user will be able to connect a Facebook account to our system and use Facebook's functionality by means of different future services (e.g. people recommendation based on friends, automatic posting to the Facebook wall when using a service, adding people as friends when exchanging information, etc.).
- All user interactions will be stored in a semantic log, within an RDF triple store, according to the interactions ontology shown in Figure 7. This information can then be reused by new services (e.g. Terminal Interaction Graph service, people recommendation, evaluation). The log unveils social connections established by using the terminal and enables on-the-fly usage statistics. The interaction ontology was kept simple and generic in order to guarantee flexibility for new services.
- Data used within implemented and planned services originates from various sources such as the Google Search REST API and the Linked Open Data (e.g. FOAF profiles, DBLP publications, information from DBPedia, etc.) cloud. Also on the other side, services of the system could potentially serve as generators of semantic annotations.

Another important point is the implementation of new services and improving existing ones based upon comments collected in the user survey. Ideas for future services include the following:

Terminal Interaction Graph service visualizes the user interactions in a graph form using data provided by the semantic log. The graph shows the strength of connections (number of joined activities) between users and, when

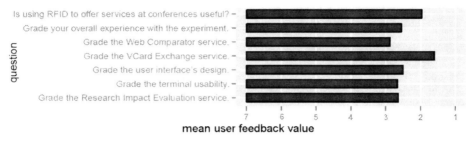

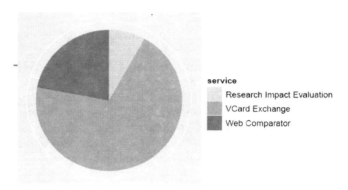

Fig. 6. Overview and results of terminal specific survey questions

applicable, the Facebook profile picture to facilitate identification. A participant can review all previous interactions and send a Facebook friend request to people whom he or she has been jointly logged on with. Additionally publication data retrieved via DBLP is shown.

Semantic Games is an entertainment service that can be used to create semantic content, a process which often cannot be solved automatically but

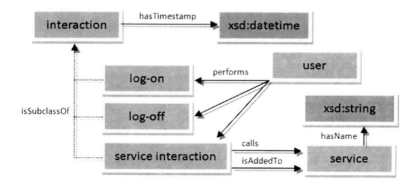

Fig. 7. Semantic interaction ontology

requires certain human effort [14]. Programmed in Flash and accessible within the browser, it is very easy to integrate them into the terminal. The first one to be playable is SeaFish (SEmantic Annotation FISHing), a single or two player game used for image annotation. The game shows a reference image to its players who have to "catch" related images floating around on the screen.

8 Conclusions

Extending conventional offline social networking activities, the presented system has been generally well received at the conferences. Existing services within the system have proven a valid and meaningful integration of very heterogeneous technologies, including RFID and Web 2.0. Future services will continue the idea of supporting ubiquitous social interaction of conference participants and foster integration of Mobile, Semantic and Social Web into the system. The system is designed to be easily extended with multi-purpose services, not only addressing the (computer) science community, but a far more general audience.

One of the aims of the project has been to test and evaluate the use and acceptance of Auto-ID technology in conference scenarios. Here a key finding is that relatively many people have concerns with the use of RFID technology that need to be carefully addressed when designing and deploying such a kind of systems.

As the evaluation shows, even more social, recommendation and dissemination features are desired, and new services such as talks/agenda recommendation and social network integration are important for the future success of the project. Altogether the system's ultimate goal is to grow into a social interaction hub for conferences and similar venues, especially the ones with a large number of participants, where it has been most demanded.

Acknowledgments. The work presented in this publication was partly done in the project PlanetData, funded by the European Community's Seventh Framework Programme FP7/2007-2013.

References

1. Alani, H., Szomszor, M., Cattuto, C., Van den Broeck, W., Correndo, G., Barrat, A.: Live Social Semantics. In: Bernstein, A., Karger, D.R., Heath, T., Feigenbaum, L., Maynard, D., Motta, E., Thirunarayan, K. (eds.) ISWC 2009. LNCS, vol. 5823, pp. 698–714. Springer, Heidelberg (2009)
2. Bravo, J., Hervás, R., Sánchez, I., Chavira, G., Nava, S.: Visualization Services in a Conference Context: An Approach by RFID Technology. Journal of Universal Computer Science 12(3), 270–283 (2006)
3. Cox, D., Kindratenko, V., Pointer, D.: IntelliBadge. In: Dey, A.K., Schmidt, A., McCarthy, J.F. (eds.) UbiComp 2003. LNCS, vol. 2864, pp. 264–280. Springer, Heidelberg (2003)
4. Dawson, F., Howes, T.: vCard MIME Directory Profile (1998), http://www.rfc-editor.org/info/rfc2426

5. Egghe, L.: An improvement of the h-index: The g-index. ISSI Newsletter 2(1), 8–9 (2006)
6. Gershenfeld, N., Krikorian, R., Cohen, D.: The Internet of Things. Scientific American (291), 76–81 (2004)
7. Hirsch, J.E.: An index to quantify an individual's scientific research output. Proceedings of the National Academy of Sciences of the United States of America 102(46) (2005)
8. Howes, T., Smith, M., Dawson, F.: A MIME Content-Type for Directory Information (1998), http://www.rfc-editor.org/info/rfc2425
9. Juels, A.: RFID security and privacy: a research survey. IEEE Journal on Selected Areas in Communications 24(2), 381–394 (2006)
10. Lee, H., Kim, J.: Privacy threats and issues in mobile RFID. In: Proceedings of the First International Conference on Availability, Reliability and Security (ARES), p. 5 (2006)
11. McFarlan, D., Sarma, S., Chirn, J.L., Wong, C.Y., Ashton, K.: Auto ID systems and intelligent manufacturing control. Engineering Applications of Artificial Intelligence 16(4), 365–376 (2003)
12. Muhammad, I., Marchese, M., Ragone, A., Birukou, A., Casati, F., Jara, L., Juan, J.: ResEval: An Open and Resource-oriented Research Impact Evaluation tool. Ingegneria e Scienza dell'Informazione, University of Trento, Technical Report. DISI-10-016 (2010)
13. Nishimura, T., Matsuo, Y., Hope, T., Hamasaki, M., et al.: Casual Interfaces for Ubiquitous Community Assistance. In: CSCW 2006 Workshop, Collaborating over Paper and Digital Documents, Banff (2006)
14. Siorpaes, K., Hepp, M.: Games with a Purpose for the Semantic Web. IEEE Intelligent Systems 23(3), 50–60 (2008)
15. Szomszor, M., Cattuto, C., Van den Broeck, W., Barrat, A., Alani, H.: Semantics, Sensors, and the Social Web: The Live Social Semantics Experiments. In: Aroyo, L., Antoniou, G., Hyvönen, E., ten Teije, A., Stuckenschmidt, H., Cabral, L., Tudorache, T. (eds.) ESWC 2010. LNCS, vol. 6089, pp. 196–210. Springer, Heidelberg (2010)
16. Welbourne, E., Battle, L., Cole, G., Gould, K., Rector, K., Raymer, S., Balazinska, M., Borriello, G.: Building the Internet of Things Using RFID: The RFID Ecosystem Experience. IEEE Internet Computing 13(3), 48–55 (2009)

Exponential Acceleration of Model Checking
for Perfect Recall Systems*

Natalia O. Garanina

A.P. Ershov Institute of Informatics Systems, Russian Academy of Science
6, Lavrentiev Ave., 630090, Novosibirsk, Russia
garanina@iis.nsk.su

Abstract. We revise the model checking algorithm for combination of Computation Tree Logic and Propositional Logic of Knowledge in finite multiagent systems with a perfect recall synchronous semantics. A new approach is based on data structures that are exponentially smaller than the structures used in the previous versions of the model checking algorithm. It reduces the time complexity of the algorithm exponentially.

1 Introduction

Combinations of traditional program logics [13,6,18] with logics of knowledge [7,17] are a well-known formalism for reasoning about multi-agent systems [10]. A focus of a number of researches is the development of model checking techniques for multi-agent systems specified by means of combined logics [2,5,11,14,15].

We investigate the model checking problem in trace-based synchronous perfect recall multiagent systems for various combinations of logics of knowledge with logics of time and actions. In such systems agents have a memory: their knowledge depends on states passed and on the previous actions. We can describe this kind of agents because semantics of knowledge is defined on traces, i.e. finite sequences of states and actions, and every agent can distinguish traces with different sequences of information available for it. Each element of a trace represents a state of the system at some moment of time.

The problem was under study in [9], [19], [20]. It has been demonstrated in [9] that the model checking problem in the class of finitely-generated trace-based synchronous systems with perfect recall is undecidable for logics Act-CTL-C$_n$, μPLK$_n$, and μPLC$_n$ (where $n > 1$), but is decidable for Act-CTL-K$_n$ (with a non-elementary lower bound). The paper [19] presents a direct (update+abstraction)-algorithm for model checking Act-CTL-K$_n$ in perfect recall synchronous environments. This algorithm checks formulas in a special model $TR_k(E)$ whose elements are "knowledge" trees. This model and the trees have the non-elementarily exponential size. In the paper [20] we demonstrate that the model $TR_k(E)$ provided with a special sub-tree partial order forms a

---

* The research has been supported by Russian Foundation for Basic Research (grant 10-01-00532-a) and by Siberian Branch of Russian Academy of Science (Integration Grant n.2/12).

E. Clarke, I. Virbitskaite, and A. Voronkov (Eds.): PSI 2011, LNCS 7162, pp. 111–124, 2012.

well-structured labeled transition system [1,8], where every property expressible in the μ-Calculus could be characterized by a finite computable set of maximal trees that enjoy the property. This feature of a tree model allow us to decrease the time upper bound of the algorithm, but it is still huge.

But there is another way to reduce the size of model states and the size of a tree model itself. In the present paper we suggest a new form of knowledge trees — cut trees that correspond to a formula structure. These cut trees are exponentially smaller than standard knowledge trees. We prove that semantics of every formula of combined logic Act-CTL-K_n in a tree model is equivalent to semantics of the formula in the corresponding cut-tree model. Moreover, we show that a cut-tree model is a well-structured model also.

2   Background Logics and Models

First, we would like to recall definitions of a combined Propositional Logic of Knowledge and Branching Time Act-CTL-K_n from [20] briefly. This logic is a fusion of Propositional Logic of Knowledge (PLK) [7] and Computational Tree Logic (CTL) [6,3,4] extended by action symbols. Semantics of Act-CTL-K_n is defined in terms of a satisfiability relation $\models$ in environments that are a special kind of labeled transition systems.

Let $\{true, false\}$ be Boolean constants, Prp and Act be disjoint finite alphabets of propositional variables and action symbols, and a finite set of natural numbers $[1..n]$ represents names of agents ($n \in \mathbb{N}$).

Definition 1. *(of an environment)*
An environment is a tuple $E = (D, \overset{1}{\sim}, \ldots, \overset{n}{\sim}, I, V)$, *where*

- the domain D is a non-empty set of states (or worlds);
- for every agent $i \in [1..n]$ the indistinguishability relation $\overset{i}{\sim}$ is an equivalence relation on $D \sim: [1..n] \to 2^{D \times D}$;
- the interpretation of actions I is a total mapping $I : Act \to 2^{D \times D}$;
- the valuation V is a total mapping $V : Prp \to 2^{D}$.

For every $a \in Act$ an a-run is a maximal sequence of states $ws = s_1 \ldots s_j s_{j+1} \ldots$ such that $(s_j, s_{j+1}) \in I(a)$ for all $j > 0$.

Every indistinguishability relation that is not an equality expresses the fact that an agent has incomplete information about system states.

For the illustration of some notions and definitions of this paper let us consider a toy example called a Meeting. Let Alice from Amsterdam, Berta from Berlin and Carl from Copenhagen try to appoint a date in Paris at some evening. They have to agree on a place (the Eiffel Tower or Montmartre) and on a time (6 or 7 p.m.). Let $Place = \{E, M\}$ and $Time = \{6, 7\}$ be sets of places and points in time.

For this example let the environment be $E_M = (D_M, \overset{A}{\sim}, \overset{B}{\sim}, \overset{C}{\sim}, I_M, V_M)$. The domain is $D_M = \{(p, t, a, b, c) \mid p \in Place, t \in Time, a, b, c \in \{0, 1\}\}$, where boolean variables a, b and c mean that Alice, Berta and Carl have or have not been talked, respectively. Let us denote a set of model states in which Alice has not been talked yet by $A_0 = \{d \in D \mid a = 0\}$, and a set of model states in which Alice has been talked by $A_1 = \{d \in D \mid a = 1\}$. The sets B_0, B_1, C_0, and C_1 are defined in the same manner.

Indistinguishability relations are based on the fact that an agent does not distinguish places and times iff the one had no talks. For the agent Alice these relations could be described as

- $d \overset{A}{\sim} d'$ iff $d, d' \in A_0$;
- $(p, t, 1, b, c) \overset{A}{\sim} (p, t, 1, b', c')$, where $p \in Place, t \in Time, b, c, b', c' \in \{0, 1\}$.

Indistinguishability relations for Berta and Carl are defined in the same manner.

In the system the agents could talk about a place p and a time t as follows. Let the set of action consist of the talks for Alice and Berta — $AB(p, t)$, for Alice and Carl — $AC(p, t)$, and for Berta and Carl — $BC(p, t)$, where $p \in Place, t \in Time$. Besides, the set of action includes the action $talk$ which is a non-determined choice from all possible talks: $talk = \bigcup_{p \in Place, t \in Time} AB(p, t) \cup AC(p, t) \cup BC(p, t)$. In particulary, the system action $AB(p, t)$ maps every state of the system to the set $(p, t, 1, 1, c)$, where $c \in \{0, 1\}$. This means that Alice and Berta had talk about the place p and the time t, and Carl could have or have not talks. Formally, $I_M(AB(p, t)) = \{(d, (p, t, 1, 1, c)) \mid d \in D_M, p \in Place, t \in Time, c \in \{0, 1\}\}$. Talks $AC(p, t)$ and $BC(p, t)$ are defined in the same way.

Let the set of propositionals be $\{p_M, t_7\}$. The propositional variable $p_M = \{d \in D \mid p = M\}$ means that a place of an appointment is Montmartre, and the propositional variable $t_7 = \{d \in D \mid t = 7\}$ means that a time of an appointment is 7 p.m.

Definition 2. *(of Act-CTL-K_n syntax)*
Syntax of *Act*-CTL-K_n consists of formulas that are constructed from Boolean constants, propositional variables, connectives $\neg$, $\wedge$, $\vee$, and the following modalities. Let $i \in [1..n]$, $a \in Act$, φ and ψ be formulas. Then formulas with the modalities are

- knowledge modalities: $K_i\varphi$ and $S_i\varphi$ (they are read as 'an agent i knows' and 'an agent i supposes');
- action modalities: $\mathbf{AX}^a\varphi$, $\mathbf{EX}^a\varphi$, $\mathbf{AG}^a\varphi$, $\mathbf{EG}^a\varphi$, $\mathbf{AF}^a\varphi$, $\mathbf{EF}^a\varphi$, $\mathbf{A}\varphi\mathbf{U}^a\psi$, and $\mathbf{E}\varphi\mathbf{U}^a\psi$ ($\mathbf{A}$ is read as 'for all futures', $\mathbf{E}$ – 'for some futures', $\mathbf{X}$ – 'next time', $\mathbf{G}$ – 'always', $\mathbf{F}$ – 'sometime', $\mathbf{U}$ – 'until', and a sup-index ^{a} – 'in a-run(s)').

Syntax of *Act*-CTL-K_n combines modalities of PLK [7] and CTL [6,3,4] with action symbols. Semantics of *Act*-CTL-K_n follows semantics of these logics.

Definition 3. *(of Act-CTL-K_n semantics)*
A satisfiability relation $\models$ between models, worlds, and formulas is defined inductively with respect to a structure of formulas. For Boolean constants, propositional variables, and connectives a satisfiability relation is standard. For the action modalities semantics is almost the same as for the standard CTL-modalities,

but sets for a-runs. For the knowledge modalities we define the semantics as follows. Let $w \in D$, $i \in [1..n]$, φ be a formula, then

- $w \models_E (K_i\varphi)$ iff for every w': $w \overset{i}{\sim} w'$ implies $w' \models_E \varphi$;
- $w \models_E (S_i\varphi)$ iff for some w': $w \overset{i}{\sim} w'$ and $w' \models_E \varphi$.

Semantics of a formula φ in an environment E is the set of all worlds of E that satisfies this formula φ: $E(\varphi) = \{w \mid w \models_E \varphi\}$.

Further we consider just Act-CTL-K_n normal formulas in which negation is used in literals only. Every Act-CTL-K_n formula is equivalent to some normal formula due to "De Morgan" laws.

For our Meeting example we would like to check the following statement which could be expressed by Act-CTL-K_n formula. It is possible that sometime the following fact will hold: Alice knows that Berta knows that they meet at Montmartre, and that Carl supposes that the meeting time is 7 p.m., while Berta supposes that Alice knows that they meet at 7 p.m. at Montmartre, and that Carl supposes that the meeting place is Montmartre. This statement could easily be expressed by the following Act-CTL-K_n formula:

$$\phi_M = \mathbf{EF}^{talk}\big(K_A(K_B p_M \wedge S_C t_7)\big) \wedge \big(K_B(K_A(p_M \wedge t_7) \wedge S_C p_M)\big).$$

Note, that in the given system this formula is not satisfiable because every agent is never sure that the other agents know the same time and place.

We investigate trace-based perfect recall synchronous (PRS) environments generated from background finite environments. In PRS environments (1) states are sequences of worlds of initial environments with a history of generating actions; (2) an agent does not distinguish such sequences if the background system performs the same sequence of actions, and the agent can not distinguish the sequences world by world; (3) there are transitions from a sequence to another one with an action a by extending the sequence with a state reachable by a from the last state of the sequence; (4) propositionals are evaluated at the last state of sequences with respect to their evaluations in the background environment.

Definition 4. *(of a PRS-environment)*

Let E be an environment $(D, \overset{1}{\sim}, \ldots, \overset{n}{\sim}, I, V)$. A trace-based *Perfect Recall Synchronous environment* generated by E is another environment $(D_{PRS(E)}, \overset{1}{\underset{prs}{\sim}}, \ldots, \overset{n}{\underset{prs}{\sim}}, I_{PRS(E)}, V_{PRS(E)})$:[1]

(1) $D_{PRS(E)}$ is the set of all pairs (ws, as), where non-empty $ws \in D^*$, $as \in Act^*$, $|ws| = |as| + 1$, and $(ws_j, ws_{j+1}) \in I(as_j)$ for every $j \in [1..|as|]$;

let $(ws, as), (ws', as') \in D_{PRS(E)}$:

(2) for every $i \in [1..n]$: $(ws, as) \overset{i}{\underset{prs}{\sim}} (ws', as')$ iff

$$as = as' \text{ and } ws_j \overset{i}{\sim} ws'_j \text{ for every } j \in [1..|ws|];$$

---

[1] In the definition, for every set S let S^* be the set of all finite sequences over S and the operation $^\wedge$ stand for the concatenation of finite words.

(3) for every $a \in Act$: $((ws, as), (ws', as')) \in I_{PRS(E)}(a)$ iff
$$as' = as^\wedge a, \; ws' = ws^\wedge w', \text{ and } (w_{|ws|}, w') \in I(a);$$
(4) for every $p \in Prp$: $(ws, as) \in V_{PRS(E)}(p)$ iff $ws_{|ws|} \in V(p)$.

In PRS-environments agents have some kind of a memory because an awareness expressed by an indistinguishability relation depends on a history of a system evolution.

We examine the model checking problem for Act-CTL-K_n in perfect recall synchronous environments generated from finite environments [19].

Definition 5. *(of the model checking problem for Act-CTL-K_n)*
The model checking problem for Act-CTL-K_n in perfect recall synchronous environments is to validate or refute $(ws, as) \models_{PRS(E)} \varphi$, where E is a finite environment, $(ws, as) \in D_{PRS(E)}$, φ is a formula of Act-CTL-K_n.

3   Model Checking of Cut-Trees

Special data structures, knowledge trees, for model checking of Act-CTL-K_n in PRS-environments were suggested in [16]. But the number of vertices in the trees is exponential on the number of agents in the system. Our new approach to the problem is based on pruning "unnecessary" branches of trees in accordance with a structure of knowledge in a checking formula of Act-CTL-K_n. In this section we give a definition of a new tree model based on cut trees and prove that semantics of Act-CTL-K_n formulas are equivalent in PRS-model and cut-tree model. In the following we assume we are given an environment E and $k, n \geq 0$.

Definition 6. *(of the knowledge depth)*
The *knowledge depth* of a formula is the maximal nesting of knowledge modalities in this formula. For every $k \geq 0$ let Act-CTL-K_n^k be sublogic of Act-CTL-K_n with knowledge depth bounded by k.

It is obvious that Act-CTL-$K_n = \bigcup_{k \geq 0} Act$-CTL-$K_n^k$.

Definition 7. *(of a cut tree)*
A k^{cut}-*tree* is a finite tree of height $k > 0$ whose vertices are labeled by worlds of the environment E and edges are labeled by agents. Two vertices w and w' are connected with an edge labeled i iff $w \overset{i}{\sim} w'$ for some $i \in [1..n]$.

Formally, a k^{cut}-tree tr has the form $(w, U_1, \ldots, U_n)$, $w \in D$. Let $i \in [1..n]$, then

- the world $w = root(tr)$ is a root of tr;
- U_i is a set of $(k-1)^{cut}$-trees (could be empty);
- if $U_i \neq \emptyset$ then for every $tr_i \in U_i$ holds $root(tr_i) \overset{i}{\sim} w$;
- 0^{cut}-tree has the form (w).

A subtree $tr_i \in U_i$ is an *inherent subtree* of the tr.
A k^{cut}-tree tr is a *complete tree* iff for every $i \in [1..n]$ $roots_i = \{root(tr) | tr \in U_i\} = \{w' \in D | w \overset{i}{\sim} w'\}$ and all inherent subtrees are complete trees.
A set of k^{cut}-*trees (or cut-trees) over E is denoted as $\mathcal{T}_{k^{cut}}$.

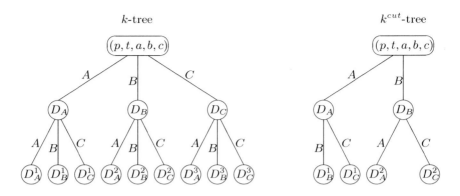

Fig. 1. k-tree and k^{cut}-tree for the formula ϕ_M

In other words, the root of cut-tree w represents the actual state of the universe, and for each $i \in [1..n]$ the set U_i represents knowledge of the agent i.

A standard k-tree $tr = (w, U_1, \ldots, U_n)$ from [16,19,20] has almost the same definition, but for every $i \in [1..n]$ the set U_i is not empty. The following definitions used for k^{cut}-trees are actual for standard k-trees.

Knowledge trees for the Meeting example are represented at picture 1 symbolically. A standard tree tr for some formula of knowledge depth 2 is placed on the left at the picture. A cut-tree tr^{ϕ_M} for the formula ϕ_M from our example is placed on the right at this picture. Roots of the trees are some model states $(p, t, a, b, c) \in D_M$. Adjacent symbolic vertices represent sets of states indistinguishable by agents labelling the connecting symbolic edges. The number of symbolic edges of the tr is equal to $\frac{3^3-1}{3-1} = 13$ because tr is 3-ary tree of height 3. The number of symbolic edges of the tr^{ϕ_M} is equal to the number of a knowledge modalities of the formula, i.e. 6.

Update functions $G^a_{k^{cut}}$ generate k^{cut}-trees obtained from some k^{cut}-tree after action a taking into account knowledge of agents included in the tree only.

Definition 8. *(of update functions)*
For every number $k \geq 0$ and $a \in Act$, *update functions* $G^a_{k^{cut}} : \mathcal{T}_{k^{cut}} \to 2^{\mathcal{T}_{k^{cut}}}$ is defined as: $tr' \in G^a_{k^{cut}}(tr)$ iff for every inherent j-subtrees tr'_j of tr' there exists an inherent j-subtree tr_j of tr that $(root(tr_j), root(tr'_j)) \in I(a)$, $j \in [0..k]$.

Update functions for k-trees are denoted as G^a_k [16,19,20].

Let us illustrate update functions for cut trees. We use our Meeting example again. Let us consider some initial state of the environment in which nobody had not talks yet. At this initial state Alice appoints a date to Berta at 7 p.m. at Montmartre. In this case the action $AB(M, 7)$ is performed. Hence an initial tree is transformed to the next tree by the update function $G^{AB(M,7)}_{2^{cut}}$. We compute the next tree from the root to leaves. The next state of every vertex and the next state of its successors are indistinguishable by the corresponding agents. At picture 2 some sets of states are represented symbolically because an exact presentation is

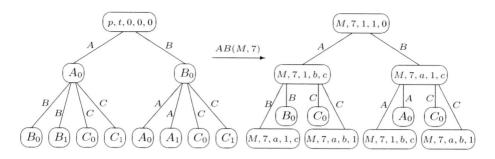

Fig. 2. The transition $AB(M,7)$ from an initial cut tree to the next cut tree for the Meeting example

too huge for the picture. The presentation $(M,7,1,b,c) = \{(M,7,1,b,c) \mid b,c \in \{0,1\}\}$ codes the states in which the meeting place is Montmartre, the meeting time is 7 p.m., Alice had a talk, and the other agents could or could not have a talk. The other similar symbolic vertices represent sets of states in the same manner. Let us recall that the sets X_0 ($X \in \{A, B, C\}$) denote states in which an agent X did not talk yet, and the X_1 — states in which the agent talked.

The following *cut-tree model* could be associated with the synchronous environment with perfect recall $PRS(E)$.

Definition 9. *(of a model $T_{k^{cut}}^E$)*
For every $k \geq 0$ let $T_{k^{cut}}^E$ be the following model $(D_{T_{k^{cut}}^E}, I_{T_{k^{cut}}^E}, V_{T_{k^{cut}}^E})$:

- $D_{T_{k^{cut}}^E}$ is the set of all 0-, ..., k^{cut}-trees over E for n agents;
- Let $tr, tr' \in D_{T_{k^{cut}}^E}$ and $tr = (w, U_1, \ldots, U_n)$ for some $w \in D_E$.
  for $i \in [1..n]$: $I_{T_{k^{cut}}^E}(i) = \{(tr, tr') \mid tr' \in U_i\}$;
  for $a \in Act$: $I_{T_{k^{cut}}^E}(a) = \{(tr, tr') \mid tr' \in G_j^a(tr)$ for some $j \in [0..k] \}$;
- $V_{T_{k^{cut}}^E}(p) = \{tr \mid root(tr) \in V(p)\}$ for $p \in Prp$.

For every $a \in Act$ an *a-cut-tree-run* is a maximal sequence of cut-trees $trs = tr_1 \ldots tr_j tr_{j+1} \ldots$ such that $(tr_j, tr_{j+1}) \in I_{T_{k^{cut}}^E}(a)$ for all $j > 0$.

We denote a model for k-trees from [16,19,20] as T_k^E here.
Let us define semantics of *Act-CTL-K$_n$* formulas in k^{cut}-tree models.

Definition 10. *(of Act-CTL-K$_n$ semantics in cut-tree models.)*
Let $tr = (w, U_1, \ldots, U_n)$, $p \in Prp$, $\varphi, \varphi_1, \varphi_2 \in Act\text{-}CTL\text{-}K_n$.

- $tr \models_{T_{k^{cut}}^E} p$ iff $w \in V(p)$;
- $tr \models_{T_{k^{cut}}^E} K_i\varphi$ iff there exists $tr_i : (tr, tr_i) \in I_{T_{k^{cut}}^E}(i)$ and $tr_i \models_{T_{k^{cut}}^E} \varphi$;
- $tr \models_{T_{k^{cut}}^E} \mathbf{EX}^a\varphi$ iff there exists $tr_a : (tr, tr_a) \in I_{T_{k^{cut}}^E}(a)$ and $tr_a \models_{T_{k^{cut}}^E} \varphi$;
- $tr \models_{T_{k^{cut}}^E} \mathbf{EG}^a\varphi$ iff $tr_j \models_{T_{k^{cut}}^E} \varphi$ for some a-cut-tree-run trs with $trs_1 = tr$
  and every $1 \leq j \leq |trs|$;

$-\ tr \models_{T^E_{k^{cut}}} \mathbf{EF}^a \varphi$ iff $tr_j \models_{T^E_{k^{cut}}} \varphi$ for some a-cut-tree-run trs with $trs_1 = tr$
and some $1 \le j \le |trs|$;

$-\ tr \models_{T^E_{k^{cut}}} \mathbf{E}(\varphi_1 \mathbf{U}^a \varphi_2)$ iff there exists a-cut-tree-run trs with $trs_1 = tr$,
$tr_j \models_{T^E_{k^{cut}}} \varphi_1$ for every $j \in [1..m)$, and $tr_m \models_{T^E_{k^{cut}}} \varphi_2$ for some $m \in [1..|trs|]$.

Semantics of other constructors is defined in a usual manner.

Let φ be a formula of Act-CTL-K_n. A correspondence cut^φ between k-trees and k^{cut}-trees $cut^\varphi : tr \mapsto tr^\varphi$ is defined by the structure of the formula φ.

Definition 11. *(of a cut correspondence)*
Let $tr = (w, U_1, \ldots, U_n)$ be k-tree and $tr^\varphi = cut^\varphi(tr)$.

- $\varphi = p$, $p \in Prp \Rightarrow tr^\varphi = (w)$;
- $\varphi = \mathbf{K}\psi$, $\mathbf{K} \in \{K_i, S_i\} \Rightarrow tr^\varphi = (w, \emptyset \ldots, \emptyset, U_i, \emptyset, \ldots, \emptyset)$;
- $\varphi = \mathbf{T}\psi$, $\mathbf{T} \in \{\mathbf{AX}^a, \mathbf{EX}^a, \mathbf{AG}^a, \mathbf{EG}^a, \mathbf{AF}^a, \mathbf{EF}^a\} \Rightarrow tr^\varphi = tr^\psi$;
- $\varphi = \varphi_1 \mathbf{D}\varphi_2$, $\mathbf{D} \in \{\wedge, \vee, \mathbf{AU}^a, \mathbf{EU}^a\} \Rightarrow tr^\varphi = (w, U_{11} \cup U_{12}, \ldots, U_{n1} \cup U_{n2})$,
  where $tr^{\varphi_1} = (w, U_{11}, \ldots, U_{n1})$ and $tr^{\varphi_2} = (w, U_{12}, \ldots, U_{n2})$.

For a set of k-trees Tr let $cut^\varphi(Tr) = \bigcup_{tr \in Tr} cut^\varphi(tr)$.

Let us estimate the sizes of some k-tree and the corresponding k^{cut}-tree. Let $exp(a, b)$ be the following function: (1) $exp(a, b) = a$, if $b = 0$, (2) $exp(a, b) = a \times 2^{exp(a, b-1)}$, otherwise. In the paper [19] was proved the following proposition about the size of k-tree model.

Proposition 1. *Let $k \ge 0$ be an integer and E be a finite environment for n agents with d states. Then*

- *the number of k-trees over E C_k is less than or equal to $\frac{exp(n \times d, k)}{n}$.*
- *if $n < d$ then the number of nodes in a $(k+1)$-tree over E is less than C_k^2.*

It is obvious that the size of a cut-tree is exponentially smaller than the size of the corresponding k-tree if a formula does not include (almost) all knowledge modalities for every agent at every nesting level. For example, let a formula be of knowledge depth k and include two knowledge modalities at every nesting level[2], and we consider the environment E from the above proposition. Then the number of vertices in the corresponding cut-tree is less than $(\frac{exp(2 \times d, k-1)}{n})^2$. It is very difficult to estimate exactly decrease of the number of tree vertices after pruning because it depends on the number of the states in an environment, on the structure of indistinguishability relations, and on the number of knowledge modalities used in a checking formula. However the following proposition allows to estimate a degree of decrease of an agents' knowledge representation.

Proposition 2. *For Act-CTL-K_n formula of depth k the number of vertices in a k^{cut}-tree is exponentially less than the number of vertices in the corresponding k-tree iff the number of knowledge modalities used in the formula is exponentially less then the number of vertices in n-ary tree of height $k + 1$.*

---

[2] Note, that the size of the formula is exponential on knowledge depth.

Sketch of the proof. Let us consider n highly informed agents whose indistinguishability relations are equalities. In this case a standard knowledge tree for some formula of depth k is a complete n-ary tree of height k with the number of vertices $\frac{n^{k+1}}{n-1}$. A cut knowledge tree for these agents includes the number of vertices is equal to the number of knowledge modalities of the formula plus one. If indistinguishability relations are not equalities then the number of vertices in a knowledge tree and in the corresponding cut-tree increases proportionally to the sizes of indistinguishability relations.   ∎

The next proposition states that transitions in tree models correspond to transitions in cut-tree models.

Proposition 3. *For every integer $k \geq 0$ and $n \geq 1$ and every environment E, for every formula φ of Act-CTL-K_n with knowledge depth k at most there exists correspondence $cut^\varphi : D_{T_k^E} \to D_{T_{k^{cut}}^E}$ that*

$$cut^\varphi(G_k^a(tr)) = G_{k^{cut}}^a(cut^\varphi(tr)).$$

Sketch of the proof.[3] The following two observations imply the proof immediately. First, the next state of every vertex at every distance from the root and the next state of its successors are indistinguishable by the corresponding agents. This fact holds for standard trees and cut trees due to definitions of update functions for standard and cut trees. Second, at every distance from the root of a standard tree a correspondence cut^φ retains only edges labeled by agents whose knowledge modalities are at the corresponding nesting level of the formula φ. This fact follows from the definition of a cut correspondence. Hence, the result of $cut^\varphi(G_k^a(tr))$ and $G_{k^{cut}}^a(cut^\varphi(tr))$ is the same set of cut trees.   ∎

The following proposition states equivalence of semantics of formulas Act-CTL-K_n in a tree model and a cut-tree model.

Proposition 4. *For every integer $k \geq 0$ and $n \geq 1$ and every environment E, for every formula φ of Act-CTL-K_n with knowledge depth k at most there exists correspondence $cut^\varphi : D_{T_k^E} \to D_{T_{k^{cut}}^E}$ that*

$$tr \models_{T_k^E} \varphi \ iff \ cut^\varphi(tr) \models_{T_{k^{cut}}^E} \varphi.$$

Sketch of the proof. We use induction on the structure of normal formulas. We prove some base cases only. The proof for the other cases could be done in the similar way. Let $tr = (w, U_1, \ldots, U_n)$, $cut^\varphi(tr) = tr^\varphi = (w, V_1, \ldots, V_n)$.
(1)$\varphi = p$, $p \in Prp$: $tr \models_{T_k^E} p$ iff $w \in V(p)$ iff $tr^\varphi \models_{T_{k^{cut}}^E} p$;
(2)$\varphi = K_i\psi$: $tr \models_{T_k^E} K_i\psi$ iff there exists $tr_i \in U_i$ such that $tr_i \models_{T_k^E} \psi$ iff
there exists $tr_i^\psi \in V_i$ such that $tr_i^\psi \models_{T_{k^{cut}}^E} \psi$ iff $tr^\varphi \models_{T_{k^{cut}}^E} K_i\psi$;

---

[3] This proposition follows also from the compatibility property of a standard tree based model T_k^E provided with a subtree order. This property is proved in [20] as a part of theorem 1.

$(3)\varphi = \psi_1\mathbf{EU}^a\psi_2$: $tr \models_{T_k^E} \mathbf{E}(\psi_1\mathbf{U}^a\psi_2)$ iff
there exists a-tree-run trs with $trs_1 = tr$, $tr_j \models_{T_k^E} \psi_1$ and $tr_m \models_{T_k^E} \psi_2$ for
some $1 \leq m \leq |trs|$ and every $1 \leq j < m$ iff (by ind. hyp. and prop. 3) there
exists a-cut-tree-run trs^φ: $trs_1^\varphi = tr^\varphi$, $tr_j^\varphi \models_{T_{k^{cut}}^E} \psi_1$ and $tr_m^\varphi \models_{T_{k^{cut}}^E} \psi_2$ for some
$1 \leq m \leq |trs^\varphi|$ and every $1 \leq j < m$ iff $tr^\varphi \models_{T_{k^{cut}}^E} \mathbf{E}(\psi_1\mathbf{U}^a\psi_2)$. ∎

The next theorem follows from proposition 1 in [20] and the previous proposition
immediately.

Theorem 1. *For every integer $k \geq 0$ and $n \geq 1$, and every environment E, for
every formula φ of Act-CTL-K_n with knowledge depth k at most, there exists a
bijective correspondence $tree_k : D_{PRS(E)} \to D_{T_k^E}$ and a correspondence $cut^\varphi :
D_{T_k^E} \to D_{T_{k^{cut}}^E}$ that*

$$(ws, as) \models_{PRS(E)} \varphi \ \ iff \ \ cut^\varphi(tree_k(ws, as)) \models_{T_{k^{cut}}^E} \varphi.$$

The following model checking algorithm is based on theorem 1 above:

1. Input a formula φ of *Act*-CTL-K_n and count its knowledge depth k;
2. input a finite environment E and construct the finite model $T_{k^{cut}}^E$;
3. input a trace (ws, as) and construct the corresponding k^{cut}-tree tr^φ;
4. model check φ on tr^φ in $T_{k^{cut}}^E$.

At the last step of the algorithm we could use any model checking algorithm
for CTL. The time complexity of the above algorithm is exponentially smaller
than the complexity of the model checking algorithm from [19] due to the size
of model trees becomes exponentially smaller. But the complexity is still huge,
therefore we try to decrease it at the next section.

4   Well-Structured Cut-Trees

The size of tree models and their elements is finite but huge as follows from
proposition 1. Hence it is reasonable to use an infinite-state model checking
technique [1,8] of well-structured transition systems. The essence of the technique
is that we could check formulas in some representative sets of model states, not in
all space. The standard tree model T_k^E is an ideal-based well-structured model
as shown in the paper [20]. In this paper we demonstrate that the formalism
of well-structured systems could be used for cut-trees also. Let us recall base
definitions from [20].

Definition 12. *(of a well-preordered transition system)*
Let D be a set. A *well-preorder* is a reflexive and transitive binary relation R on
D, where every infinite sequence $d_1, \ldots d_i, \ldots$ of elements of D contains a pair of
elements d_m and d_n so that $m < n$ and $d_m(R)d_n$. Let (D, R) be a *well-preordered
set* with a well-preorder R. An *ideal* (synonym: *cone*) is an upward closed subset
of D, i.e. a set $\{C \subseteq D \mid \forall d', d'' \in D : d'(R)d'' \wedge d' \in C \Rightarrow d'' \in C\}$. Every $d \in D$
generates *a cone* $(\uparrow d) \equiv \{e \in D \mid d(R)e\}$. For every subset $S \subseteq D$, a *basis* of

S is a subset $\{B \subseteq S \mid \forall s \in S \; \exists b \in B : b(R)s\}$. A *well-preordered transition system (WPTS)* is a triple (D, R, I) such that (D, R) is a well-preordered set and (D, I) is a Kripke frame.

We are mostly interested in well-preordered transition systems in which a well-preorder and an interpretation are decidable and compatible. The standard decidability condition for the well-preorder is straightforward: a relation $R \subseteq D \times D$ is decidable.

Definition 13. *(of an ideal-based model)*
Let (D, R, I) be a WPTS.

- *Decidability (tractable past) condition*: there exists a computable total function $BasPre : D \times Act \to 2^D$ such that for every $w \in D$, for every $a \in Act$, $BasPre(w, a)$ is a finite basis of $\{u \in D \mid (u, v) \in I(a) \text{ and } w(R)v\}$.
- *Compatibility condition*: the preorder R is compatible with the interpretation $I(a)$ of every action symbol $a \in Act$, i.e.
$$\forall s_1, s_2, s_1' \; \exists s_2' \; : \; s_1 \xrightarrow{I(a)} s_1' \wedge s_1(R)s_2 \; \Rightarrow \; s_2 \xrightarrow{I(a)} s_2' \wedge s_1'(R)s_2'.$$

An *ideal-based model* is a labeled transition system $\mathcal{I} = (D, R, I, V)$ with the decidable preorder R, $\mathcal{I}$ meets tractable past and compatibility conditions, and V interprets every propositional variable $p \in Prp$ by a cone.

Definition 14. *(of a cut-subtree order)*
Let us define a *binary relation* $\succ$ on $D_{T_{k^{cut}}^E}$. For all trees of equal height $tr = (w, U_1, \ldots, U_n)$ and $tr' = (w', U_1', \ldots, U_n')$ in $D_{T_{k^{cut}}^E}$, let us write $tr \succ tr'$ (and say that tr has a subtree tr') iff $w = w'$ and for every $i \in [1..n]$, if $U_i \neq \emptyset$ and $U_i' \neq \emptyset$ then for every $st' \in U_i'$ there exists $st \in U_i$ that $st \succ st'$.

Theorem 2. *A binary relation $\succ$ is a partial order on k^{cut}-trees such that a model $T_{k^{cut}}^E$ provided with this partial order becomes an ideal-based model, where semantics of every formula of Act-CTL-K_n is a cone with a computable finite basis.*

Sketch of the proof. The proof is rather technical. Hence let us present the basic ideas of the proof.

First, $\succ$ is a partial order. It is also a well-preorder since $T_{k^{cut}}^E$ is finite. It is a decidable relation due to finiteness of trees.

Second, $\succ$ enjoys tractable past because we could find a preimage of every tree for every 'action' transition and for every 'knowledge' transition (defined by $I_{T_{k^{cut}}^E}(a)$ and $I_{T_{k^{cut}}^E}(i)$, respectively for $a \in Act$ and $i \in [1..n]$, in def. 9) by scanning all states of $T_{k^{cut}}^E$. But there is more effective technique to find preimages based on an action decomposition on elementary bijective actions, and on using complete trees.

Third, $\succ$ is compatible with all 'action' transitions and all 'knowledge' transitions. For every action $a \in Act$, and for every pair of trees $tr \succ tr'$ there exists some sup-tree tr that is a-image of the greater tree tr and this sup-tree includes

a-image of the smaller tree tr' because a-images are computed recursively by processing each vertex of trees (def. 8). For every 'knowledge' action $i \in [1..n]$, and for every pair of trees $tr \succ tr'$ there exists some sup-tree tr that is i-image of the greater tree tr and this sup-tree includes i-image of the smaller tree tr' because computing of i-images of some tree is based on a transition to subtrees of this tree (def. 9).

Fourth, $T^E_{k^{cut}}$ is an ideal-based model. It is obvious that a valuation of every propositional variable forms a cone with a basis consisting of complete trees with roots that are states where this propositional variable holds. Note, that a negation of a propositional variable is a cone also.

Finally, we prove that semantics of every formula of Act-CTL-K_n is a cone with a computable finite basis by induction on the structure of normal formulas. Basis of disjunction of formulas is union of bases of these formulas. Basis of conjunction of formulas consists of maximal trees that are subtrees of trees from bases of these formulas simultaneously. Bases of $\mathbf{AX}^a$, $\mathbf{EX}^a$, K_i and S_i formulas are computable cones due to properties of tractable past and compatibility. Roughly speaking, all other path action modalities are combinations of disjunctions and conjunctions which are finite due finiteness of a cut-tree model. ∎

Theorem 2 could easily be generalized to the μ-Calculus [12].

5   Conclusion

In this paper we have shown that semantics of formulas of Act-CTL-K_n with knowledge depth k in a tree model T^E_k is equivalent to semantics of the formulas in the corresponding cut-tree model $T^E_{k^{cut}}$. This fact makes possible a model checking of Act-CTL-K_n formulas with perfect recall semantics in the corresponding cut-tree model. Then we have demonstrate that a cut-tree model $T^E_{k^{cut}}$ provided with the sub-tree partial order forms a well-structured labeled transition system where every property expressible in Act-CTL-K_n can be characterized by a finite computable set of maximal trees that enjoy the property. The latter fact accelerates the new model checking algorithm considerably. An experimental model checker based on this approach is in a process of implementation now.

A related approach to speed up the model checking for combination of logic of knowledge and time in perfect recall systems that exploits a formula structure is presented in [5]. The authors consider the complexity of the model checking problem for the logic of knowledge and past time in synchronous systems with perfect recall. It was shown that the upper bound for positive (respectively, negative) formulas is polynomial (respectively, exponential) in the size of the system irrespective of the nesting depth. An automata approach to the model checking problem is used in the paper.

Acknowledgements. I would like to thank Dr. N.V. Shilov for discussions.

References

1. Abdulla, P.A., Cerans, K., Jonsson, B., Tsay, Y.-K.: Algorithmic analysis of programs with well quasi-ordered domains. Information and Computation 160(1-2), 109–127 (2000)
2. Bordini, R.H., Fisher, M., Visser, W., Wooldridge, M.: Verifying Multi-agent Programs by Model Checking. Autonomous Agents and Multi-Agent Systems 12(2), 239–256 (2006)
3. Burch, J.R., Clarke, E.M., McMillan, K.L., Dill, D.L., Hwang, L.J.: Symbolic Model Checking: 10^{20} states and beyond. Information and Computation 98(2), 142–170 (1992)
4. Clarke, E.M., Grumberg, O., Peled, D.: Model Checking. MIT Press (1999)
5. Cohen, M., Lomuscio, A.: Non-elementary speed up for model checking synchronous perfect recall. In: Proceeding of the 2010 Conference on ECAI 2010, pp. 1077–1078. IOS Press, Amsterdam (2010)
6. Emerson, E.A.: Temporal and Modal Logic. In: Handbook of Theoretical Computer Science, vol. B, pp. 995–1072. Elsevier and MIT Press (1990)
7. Fagin, R., Halpern, J.Y., Moses, Y., Vardi, M.Y.: Reasoning about Knowledge. MIT Press (1995)
8. Finkel, A., Schnoebelen, P.: Well-structured transition systems everywhere! Theor. Comp. Sci. 256(1-2), 63–92 (2001)
9. Garanina, N.O., Kalinina, N.A., Shilov, N.V.: Model checking knowledge, actions and fixpoints. In: Proc. of Concurrency, Specification and Programming Workshop CS&P 2004, Germany. Humboldt Universitat, Berlin (2004); Informatik-Bericht Nr. 170(2), 351–357
10. Halpern, J.Y., van der Meyden, R., Vardi, M.Y.: Complete Axiomatizations for Reasoning About Knowledge and Time. SIAM J. Comp. 33(3), 674–703 (2004)
11. Huang, X., van der Meyden, R.: The Complexity of Epistemic Model Checking: Clock Semantics and Branching Time. In: Proc. of 19th ECAI, Lisbon, Portugal, August 16-20. Frontiers in Artificial Intelligence and Applications, vol. 215, pp. 549–554. IOS Press (2010)
12. Kozen, D.: Results on the Propositional Mu-Calculus. Theoretical Computer Science 27(3), 333–354 (1983)
13. Kozen, D., Tiuryn, J.: Logics of Programs. In: Handbook of Theoretical Computer Science, vol. B, pp. 789–840. Elsevier and MIT Press (1990)
14. Kwiatkowska, M.Z., Lomuscio, A., Qu, H.: Parallel Model Checking for Temporal Epistemic Logic. In: Proc. of 19th ECAI, Lisbon, Portugal, August 16-20. Frontiers in Artificial Intelligence and Applications, vol. 215, pp. 543–548. IOS Press (2010)
15. Lomuscio, A., Penczek, W., Qu, H.: Partial order reductions for model checking temporal epistemic logics over interleaved multi-agent systems. In: Proc. of 9th AAMAS, Toronto, Canada, May 10-14. IFAAMAS, vol. 1, pp. 659–666 (2010)
16. van der Meyden, R., Shilov, N.V.: Model Checking Knowledge and Time in Systems with Perfect Recall. In: Pandu Rangan, C., Raman, V., Sarukkai, S. (eds.) FST TCS 1999. LNCS, vol. 1738, pp. 432–445. Springer, Heidelberg (1999)
17. Rescher, N.: Epistemic Logic. A Survey of the Logic of Knowledge. University of Pittsburgh Press (2005)
18. Shilov, N.V., Yi, K.: How to find a coin: propositional program logics made easy. In: Current Trends in Theoretical Computer Science, vol. 2, pp. 181–213. World Scientific (2004)

19. Shilov, N.V., Garanina, N.O., Choe, K.-M.: Update and Abstraction in Model Checking of Knowledge and Branching Time. Fundameta Informaticae 72(1-3), 347–361 (2006)
20. Shilov, N.V., Garanina, N.O.: Well-Structured Model Checking of Multiagent Systems. In: Virbitskaite, I., Voronkov, A. (eds.) PSI 2006. LNCS, vol. 4378, pp. 363–376. Springer, Heidelberg (2007)

Bootstrapping Compiler Generators
from Partial Evaluators

Robert Glück

DIKU, Dept. of Computer Science, University of Copenhagen, Denmark

Abstract. This paper shows that bootstrapping of compiler generators from program specializers is a viable alternative to the third Futamura projection. To practically validate the technique, a novel partial evaluation-based compiler generator was designed and implemented for a recursive flowchart language. Three-step bootstrapping was found to be faster and to produce the same compiler generator that Gomard and Jones produced two decades ago by double self-application. Compiler-generator bootstrapping has distinct properties that are not present in the classic three Futamura projections, such as the ability to turn a specializer into a compiler generator in one step without self-application. Up to now, the approach of hand-writing compiler generators has only been used to avoid difficulties when specializing strongly-typed languages, not as a first step towards compiler-generator bootstrapping.

1 Introduction

This paper studies a technique for bootstrapping a compiler generator from a program specializer by means of an existing compiler generator. *Bootstrapping* is familiar from the area of compiler construction where it has been used since the late 1950's to compile compilers [22]. The technique is powerful and intriguing because it applies the methods of computing science to its major tools: to produce programs by means of programs.

The technique explored in this paper differs from compiler bootstrapping in that *compiler generators* are bootstrapped from *program specializers*. An investigation of the distinct properties of this technique has only recently been attempted [11].

In the 1970's Ershov introduced the concept of a *generating extension of a program* to emphasize the features common to a variety of program generators such as parser generators and compilers applied in system programming ("All processes which are more or less directly connected with an adaptation of universal components to predetermined parameters [...]" [6]). Compiler generators based on partial evaluation principles [18] play a key role in this context because they can automatically turn programs into generating extensions.

The bootstrapping technique investigated in this paper exploits the often disregarded fact that compiler generators *themselves* are generating extensions [11]. As a consequence, the *same* techniques that apply to the generation of ordinary

E. Clarke, I. Virbitskaite, and A. Voronkov (Eds.): PSI 2011, LNCS 7162, pp. 125–141, 2012.

generating extensions potentially also apply to the generation of compiler generators. This is the key to a "strange loop": a compiler generator can turn a specializer into a compiler generator, which, again, can turn a specializer into a compiler generator, and so forth.

In previous work, we explored the bootstrapping of compiler generators conceptually [11] based on an insight by Klimov and Romanenko [20, p. 6-7] and found that partial evaluation-based compiler generators are strong enough to carry out the initial step of bootstrapping [12]. To our knowledge, the results in this paper are the first to confirm that full *three-step compiler-generator bootstrapping* can be carried out in practice and that it is a viable and practical alternative to the third Futamura projection. As an independent benchmark, we demonstrate that three-step bootstrapping is *faster* than the third Futamura projection and produces the *same* compiler generator that Gomard and Jones [16] produced two decades ago by double self-application using Futamura's technique [9].

Getting started presents the chicken-and-egg problem familiar from compiler construction: one needs a compiler to bootstrap a compiler, and bootstrapping compiler generators is no exception. To this end, we designed and implemented a novel *partial-evaluation-based compiler generator* for a recursive flowchart language. The compiler generator has no binding-time analysis. Instead, the staging information is propagated in parallel with the generation of the generating extension ('online') and the generating extensions perform Bulyonkov's polyvariant specialization [3] recursively without the traditional pending list. Amongst other things, this allows our compiler generator to automatically turn a straightforward implementation of the Ackermann function into an efficient generating extension that produces the same residual programs as the manual specialization method described by Ershov [7].

Partial evaluation for flowchart languages is very well documented in the literature (*e.g.* [3, 4, 14, 16, 17]), which should make our results easily comparable and accessible. Throughout this paper, we assume that readers are familiar with the basics of partial evaluation, *e.g.*, as presented by Jones *et al.* [18, Part II].

2   How to Bootstrap Compiler Generators

We discuss how compiler generators can be bootstrapped (see also [11]) after briefly reviewing the basic notions of a specializer and compiler generator [18]. Unless stated otherwise, we assume for simplicity that all involved source, implementation and residual languages are identical and omit the language indices.

Staging Programs. Suppose p is a program with two inputs x and y. Computation of p in *one stage* is described by

$$\text{out} = [\![p]\!](x, y). \tag{1}$$

A *specializer* s is a program that takes p and x and produces a *residual program* r:

$$r = [\![s]\!](p, x). \tag{2}$$

Computation of p in two stages using s is described by

$$[[s] (p, x)] y = [p] (x, y).$$ (3)

A program cog, which we call a *compiler generator* for historical reasons [9, 18], takes p as input and yields a *generating extension* g *of* p:

$$g = [cog] p.$$ (4)

The generating extension g of p takes x as input and produces a *residual program*:

$$[[g] x] y = [p] (x, y).$$ (5)

Computation of p can now be carried out in three stages:

$$[[[cog] p] x] y = [p] (x, y).$$ (6)

This is the criterion of correctness for a compiler generator. A generating extension g of p can produce residual programs faster than a specializer s because g is customized with respect to p, while s can specialize any program. Often g speeds up residual-program generation by a factor of three to ten compared to s [18]. The staging of p above is performed with respect to a fixed division of the inputs: x is known before y. Input x is said to be *static* and y *dynamic*. Compiler generators and program specializers based on partial evaluation techniques have been built for languages including C, ML, Prolog and Scheme (*e.g.* [5, 15, 21, 25, 26]).

Full Bootstrapping. An intriguing feature of a compiler generator cog is that it can turn a *specializer* s into a new *compiler generator* cog′ in one step:

$$cog' = [cog] s.$$ (7)

By instantiating (5) accordingly, we obtain

$$[[cog'] p] x = [s] (p, x).$$ (8)

That cog′ is indeed a compiler generator can be seen by combining the equations:

$$[[[cog'] p] x] y \overset{(8)}{=} [[s] (p, x)] y \overset{(3)}{=} [p] (x, y).$$ (9)

The transformation (7) is the steppingstone to the *three-step bootstrapping* technique that we investigate in this paper. Repeating the transformation three times with s as the argument establishes a series of three transformation steps,

$$1. \quad cog' = [cog] s,$$ (10)
$$2. \quad cog'' = [cog'] s,$$ (11)
$$3. \quad cog''' = [cog''] s,$$ (12)

which ends with *self-generation* when carried out a fourth time [11]:

$$4. \quad cog''' = [cog'''] s.$$ (13)

Instantiating the characteristic equation (6) uncovers a remarkable equality:

$$\underbrace{[\![[\![[\![\text{cog}]\!]\,s]\!]\,s]\!]\,s}_{\substack{\textit{three-step}\\\textit{bootstrapping}}} \quad = \quad \underbrace{[\![s]\!]\,(s,s)}_{\substack{\textit{double}\\\textit{self-application}}}. \tag{14}$$

The expression on the right hand side is the *third Futamura projection*! The compiler generator produced by three-step bootstrapping (10-12) on the left-hand side is thus *textually identical* to the one produced by the third Futamura projection. The equality confirms that the functionality and efficiency of the final cog''' does not depend on the initial cog, only on s. The time required to perform the bootstrapping is the *sum* of the times required by each step and is dependent on cog. The time required for the double self-application is the *product* of the computational overhead of each layer of self-application of s, which is similar to the overhead of multiple layers of interpretation and is independent of cog.

Self-generation (13) can serve as a final *partial test of the correctness* of three-step bootstrapping. If we assume that the initial cog is well tested and correct, then s *must* contain an error if cog''' does *not* self-generate. The opposite is not true: even if cog''' self-generates, s may contain an error. The time needed to perform the self-generation also provides an indication of the efficiency of cog'''. Futamura noticed that a compiler generator produced by his third projection is self-generating [9], but not that a compiler generator can bootstrap *new* compiler generators. Self-generation is also known for other programming tools [13, 28].

Double self-application of a specializer (14) was first successfully carried out in 1984 by an *offline partial evaluator* [19], which was specifically invented to be able to perform all three Futamura projections. Complete three-step bootstrapping of a compiler generator has never been attempted. This paper explores the bootstrapping technique using specializers of the online and offline variety and a hand-written compiler generator, and compares the results to Futamura's technique.

Partial Bootstrapping. There are properties of bootstrapping which distinguish it significantly from Futamura's self-application technique.

The first potentially important property is that cog'' and cog''', which we obtain in the second and third step (11, 12), are *functionally equivalent*:

$$[\![\text{cog}'']\!] = [\![\text{cog}''']\!]. \tag{15}$$

The functional equivalence follows by simple substitutions from

$$[\![[\![[\![\text{cog}]\!]\,s]\!]\,s]\!]\,p \overset{(6)}{=} [\![s]\!]\,(s,p) \overset{(3)}{=} [\![[\![s]\!]\,(s,s)]\!]\,p \overset{(6)}{=} [\![[\![[\![[\![\text{cog}]\!]\,s]\!]\,s]\!]\,s]\!]\,p. \tag{16}$$

This means that *two* bootstrapping steps suffice to produce a compiler generator that has the exact same functionality as the one produced by the third Futamura projection, only their implementation may differ. If the initial compiler generator cog is strong enough, then cog″ may already be "good enough" for practical use and we need not perform all three bootstrapping steps.

We already know a second important property (8), namely that a generating extension of p produced by cog′, which we obtain in the first bootstrapping step (10), is functionally equivalent to s specializing p. In fact, the three compiler generators produce generating extensions that are all functionally equivalent:

$$[\![\,[\![\text{cog}']\!]\,p]\!] \;=\; [\![\,[\![\text{cog}'']\!]\,p]\!] \;=\; [\![\,[\![\text{cog}''']\!]\,p]\!]\,. \tag{17}$$

The functional equivalence on the right follows from (15) and on the left from

$$[\![\,[\![\,[\![\text{cog}]\!]\,s]\!]\,p]\!]\,x \overset{(6)}{=} [\![s]\!]\,(p,x) \overset{(3)}{=} [\![\,[\![s]\!]\,(s,p)\,]\!]\,x \overset{(6)}{=} [\![\,[\![\,[\![\,[\![\text{cog}]\!]\,s]\!]\,s]\!]\,p]\!]\,x. \tag{18}$$

Note that the three compiler generators produce at most two different implementations of the generating extension of p because cog″ and cog‴ are functionally equivalent. The cog′ produced in the first step may already have practical value, in particular when the initial cog is a mature compiler generator that can turn s into an efficient compiler generator in *one* step. For good results with one-step bootstrapping it is only necessary to "binding-time improve" s for cog. This is usually an easier task than to make s work effectively in the third Futamura projection, $[\![s]\!]\,(s,s)$, where s appears in three different roles at the same time: as the program to be run and specialized, and as the static input data.

General Bootstrapping. Generally speaking, bootstrapping involves three different specializers s_1, s_2, and s_3 and an initial compiler generator cog [11]:

$$1. \quad \text{cog}_1 = [\![\text{cog}]\!]\,s_1, \tag{19}$$
$$2. \quad \text{cog}_{12} = [\![\text{cog}_1]\!]\,s_2, \tag{20}$$
$$3. \quad \text{cog}_{123} = [\![\text{cog}_{12}]\!]\,s_3, \tag{21}$$

As long as new specializers are supplied, this series of bootstrapping steps does *not* end in self-generation:

$$4. \quad \text{cog}_{234} = [\![\text{cog}_{123}]\!]\,s_4. \tag{22}$$

Applying cog_{123} to a program p yields a generating extension g_{23} that is characterized by the following two equalities (23, 24). They tell us that g_{23} produces the same residual programs as s_3 applied to p and that g_{23} is textually identical to the generating extension produced by specializing s_3 by s_2 with respect to p:

$$[\![\text{cog}_{123}]\!]\,p = g_{23} = [\![s_2]\!]\,(s_3,p), \tag{23}$$
$$[\![g_{23}]\!]\,x = r_3 = [\![s_3]\!]\,(p,x). \tag{24}$$

3   An Online Compiler Generator for Recursive Flowchart

Flowchart is a simple imperative language used by Gomard and Jones in their work on offline partial evaluation [16]. A program consists of a sequence of labeled basic blocks with assignments and jumps. As is customary, the sets of values and labels contain integers, symbols and lists. Expressions include the usual arithmetic and relational operators, operators on lists and quoted constants (`'`). Programs are written in a list representation.

As an example of a program, consider the Ackermann function implemented in Flowchart (Fig. 1). The program is defined recursively, takes non-negative integers m and n as input, and starts execution at block ack.

The operational semantics of the language is identical to the one formalized and published by Hatcliff [17], except that we added a simple command for calling blocks [14]. We refer to the extended language as *Flowchart*. The call command, x := call l, executes the block l in a copy of the current store and assigns the returned value to x in the original store. For the sake of readability, we annotate each call with the variables that are live on entry to l. In (call ack m n) the m and n are thus not arguments, rather the variables live at block ack.

An Ackermann Generating Extension. The complete generating extension produced by our compiler generator from the Ackermann program is shown in Fig. 2 (m static, n dynamic). No post-optimization was performed. The only changes involved the use of shorter labels, and the reordering of blocks for readability. Given a value for m, the generating extension produces a residual program such as the one for m = 2 in Fig. 3. It is interesting to note that the generating extension yields the same residual programs as Ershov's manual specialization method [7].

The generating extension consists of three block generators, 1-0, 1-1 and 1-2, an implementation of the Ackermann function at block 5-0 (used to precompute constants for the residual version of block ack0) and a main block 0-0 that initializes the residual program with a new program header. The generating extension performs polyvariant block specialization [3]: *i.e.* several specialized versions of a subject block can be added to the residual program (*cf.* Fig. 3). To avoid generating the same residual block twice, a block generator produces a block only if it does not yet exist in the residual program. The general scheme of a *polyvariant block generator* for a subject block l is as follows (in pseudocode):

> **procedure** polygen-l :: $x_1 \times ... \times x_n \times code \to code$
> **if** no residual block labeled $(l, x_1, ..., x_n)$ exists in $code$
>   **then** $code$:= $code \cup$ generate residual block for l using $x_1, ..., x_n$;
> **return** $code$

A residual block labeled $(l, x_1, ..., x_n)$ is the code generated for the commands in subject block l using the values of the static variables $x_1, ..., x_n$. A block generator may recursively call block generators. Commands of the subject program that only depend on static variables $(x_1, ..., x_n)$ are executed when the generating extension runs, and commands are placed into the residual program in all other cases. For example, the static conditional (if (= m 0) ...) is executed in block 4-0 of the generating extension (the test depends only on static variable m). A residual conditional is generated for the dynamic conditional (if (= n 0) ...) at the end of block 4-2 (the test depends on dynamic variable n) and the two block generators 1-1 and 1-2 are called to generate the then- and else-block. The residual program code is single-threaded through the block generator calls.

```
((m n) (ack)
 ((ack  (if (= m 0) done next))
  (next (if (= n 0) ack0 ack1))
  (done (return (+ n 1)))
  (ack0 (n := 1)
        (goto ack2))
  (ack1 (n := (- n 1))
        (n := (call ack m n))
        (goto ack2))
  (ack2 (m := (- m 1))
        (n := (call ack m n))
        (return n)) ))
```

$$A(m,n) = \begin{cases} n+1 & \text{if } m = 0 \\ A(m-1,1) & \text{if } n = 0 \\ A(m-1, A(m,n-1)) & \text{otherwise} \end{cases}$$

Fig. 1. An implementation of the Ackermann function in Flowchart

```
((m) (0-0)
 ((0-0 (code := (newheader '(n) (list 'ack m))) (goto 1-0))      ; residual header
  (2-0 (return code))

  (1-0 (if (done? (list 'ack m) code) 2-0 3-0))                  ; block generator ack
  (3-0 (code := (newblock code (list 'ack m))) (goto 4-0))
  (4-0 (if (= m 0) 4-1 4-2))
  (4-1 (return (o code '(return (+ n 1)))))
  (4-2 (code := (call 1-1 m code))
       (code := (call 1-2 m code))
       (return (o code (list 'if '(= n 0) (list 'ack0 m) (list 'ack1 m)))))

  (1-1 (if (done? (list 'ack0 m) code) 2-0 3-1))                 ; block generator ack0
  (3-1 (code := (newblock code (list 'ack0 m))) (goto 4-3))
  (4-3 (n := 1)
       (m := (- m 1))
       (n := (call 5-0 m n))
       (return (o code (list 'return (lift n)))))

  (1-2 (if (done? (list 'ack1 m) code) 2-0 3-2))                 ; block generator ack1
  (3-2 (code := (newblock code (list 'ack1 m))) (goto 4-4))
  (4-4 (code := (o code '(n := (- n 1))))
       (code := (call 1-0 m code))
       (code := (o code (list 'n ':= (list 'call (list 'ack m) 'n))))
       (m := (- m 1))
       (code := (call 1-0 m code))
       (code := (o code (list 'n ':= (list 'call (list 'ack m) 'n))))
       (return (o code '(return n))))

  (5-0 (if (= m 0) 5-1 5-2))                                     ; precomputation of A(m,n)
  (5-1 (return (+ n 1)))
  (5-2 (if (= n 0) 5-3 5-4))
  (5-3 (n := 1) (goto 5-5))
  (5-4 (n := (- n 1)) (n := (call 5-0 m n)) (goto 5-5))
  (5-5 (m := (- m 1)) (n := (call 5-0 m n)) (return n)) ))
```

Fig. 2. Generating extension of the Ackermann program in Fig. 1 produced by $\mathbf{cog}_{dcb}$

```
((n) (ack-2)                            (ack-1  (if (= n 0) ack0-1 ack1-1))
 ((ack-2  (if (= n 0) ack0-2 ack1-2))    (ack0-1 (return 2))   ; A(0,1) = 2
  (ack0-2 (return 3))  ; A(1,1) = 3      (ack1-1 (n := (- n 1))
  (ack1-2 (n := (- n 1))                         (n := (call ack-1 n))
          (n := (call ack-2 n))                  (n := (call ack-0 n))
          (n := (call ack-1 n))                  (return n))
          (return n))                    (ack-0  (return (+ n 1))) ))
```

Fig. 3. Residual program produced by the generating extension in Fig. 2 (m = 2)

To keep the generating extensions simple and readable, we assume a number of useful operators for code generation. Operator done? checks whether a residual block labeled $(l, x_1, ..., x_n)$ exists in the current residual program code. Operator newblock adds a new empty block to code and operator o adds a new residual command to the current residual block in code.[1] A value is turned into a program constant by (lift v) = 'v.

The Ackermann generating extension already reveals the principles of turning a program into a generating extension: commands of the program that depend only on static variables are *copied* into the generating extension; all other commands are *converted* into code-generating commands. For example, m := (- m 1) was copied into block 4-4, while n := (- n 1) at the beginning of the same block was replaced by a command adding it to code by operator o. The principles of converting a program into a generating extension were described by Ershov [6], with the exception of the polyvariant control of program generation.

The Initial Compiler Generator. The compiler generator for Flowchart, which we call cog_{dcb}, is formalized as big-step operational semantics (Fig. 4), which reflects the recursive structure of the actual implementation. Given a subject program p and a division δ of the input parameters of p into static and dynamic, p is converted into a generating extension, such as the one in Fig. 3. The main task of the online compiler generator is to determine which of p's computations are static and which are dynamic, and to build an efficient generating extension.

The propagation of δ is performed by the compiler generator during the generation of the generating extension. There is no separate binding-time analysis and no program annotation. The division is represented by a set that contains the names of the static variables. The staging decisions are then based on a simple membership test: $x \in \delta$ implies x is static and $x \notin \delta$ implies x is dynamic.

An assignment x := e is static if all variables that occur in e are static, *i.e.* $vars(e) \subseteq \delta$; otherwise it is dynamic. Similarly for x := call l except that the variables live at block l determine whether the call is static, *i.e.* $live(l) \subseteq \delta$. The more accurate the information about the live variables, the more static calls can be discovered. A conditional if e l_1 l_2 is static if e is static; otherwise it is dynamic. A goto is unfolded and a return is treated as dynamic. For readability, we omit the parameter Γ containing the subject program from the rules in Fig. 4.

A static assignment is copied directly from the program into the generating extension k. In the event of a static call, x := call l, all blocks reachable from l are copied into k by $\vdash_{copyblocks}$ but relabeled to avoid name clashes. A static conditional is added to the generating extension with new jumps to blocks $4 \cdot l_1 \cdot \delta$ and $4 \cdot l_2 \cdot \delta$ which will generate code for the corresponding branch when the generating extension runs. Function · maps its arguments into a new label (*e.g.*, $4 \cdot l \cdot \delta$). Adding prefixes $(0, 1, ..., 5)$ to all labels is a simple way to avoid name clashes.

---

[1] Part of code is used as a stack: new blocks are pushed and new commands are appended to the topmost block; a finished block is popped and added to the res. prog.

Assignments

$$\frac{\text{vars}(e) \subseteq \delta}{\vdash_{asg} \langle x \; := \; e; \; a^*, \delta, k \rangle \Rightarrow \langle a^*, \delta \cup \{x\}, k \circ [x \; := \; e] \rangle}$$

$$\frac{\text{vars}(e) \not\subseteq \delta \quad e' = e{\uparrow}\delta}{\vdash_{asg} \langle x \; := \; e; \; a^*, \delta, k \rangle \Rightarrow \langle a^*, \delta \setminus \{x\}, k \circ [\text{code} \; := \; (\text{o code} \; \underline{x \; := \; e'})] \rangle}$$

$$\frac{\text{live}(l) \subseteq \delta \quad k \vdash_{copyblocks} l \Rightarrow k'}{\vdash_{asg} \langle x \; := \; \text{call} \; l; \; a^*, \delta, k \rangle \Rightarrow \langle a^*, \delta \cup \{x\}, k' \circ [x \; := \; \text{call} \; 5{\cdot}l] \rangle}$$

$$\frac{\text{live}(l) \not\subseteq \delta \quad k \vdash_{poly} [l, \delta] \Rightarrow k' \quad l' = l{\uparrow}\delta}{\vdash_{asg} \langle x \; := \; \text{call} \; l; \; a^*, \delta, k \rangle \Rightarrow \langle a^*, \delta \setminus \{x\}, k' \circ \begin{bmatrix} \text{code} \; := \; \text{call} \; 1{\cdot}l{\cdot}\delta \\ \text{code} \; := \; (\text{o code} \; \underline{x \; := \; \text{call} \; l'}) \end{bmatrix} \rangle}$$

Jumps

$$\frac{\text{vars}(e) \subseteq \delta \quad k \vdash_{block} [l_1, \delta] \Rightarrow k' \quad k' \vdash_{block} [l_2, \delta] \Rightarrow k''}{k \vdash_{jmp} [\text{if} \; e \; l_1 \; l_2, \delta] \Rightarrow k'' \circ [\text{if} \; e \; 4{\cdot}l_1{\cdot}\delta \; 4{\cdot}l_2{\cdot}\delta]}$$

$$\frac{\begin{array}{c} k \vdash_{poly} [l_1, \delta] \Rightarrow k' \quad l'_1 = l_1{\uparrow}\delta \\ \text{vars}(e) \not\subseteq \delta \quad k' \vdash_{poly} [l_2, \delta] \Rightarrow k'' \quad l'_2 = l_2{\uparrow}\delta \quad e' = e{\uparrow}\delta \end{array}}{k \vdash_{jmp} [\text{if} \; e \; l_1 \; l_2, \delta] \Rightarrow k'' \circ \begin{bmatrix} \text{code} \; := \; \text{call} \; 1{\cdot}l_1{\cdot}\delta \\ \text{code} \; := \; \text{call} \; 1{\cdot}l_2{\cdot}\delta \\ \text{return} \; (\text{o code} \; \underline{\text{if} \; e' \; l'_1 \; l'_2}) \end{bmatrix}}$$

$$\frac{e' = e{\uparrow}\delta}{k \vdash_{jmp} [\text{return} \; e, \delta] \Rightarrow k \circ [\text{return} \; (\text{o code} \; \underline{\text{return} \; e'})]}$$

$$\frac{k \vdash_{body} [\Gamma(l), \delta] \Rightarrow k'}{k \vdash_{jmp} [\text{goto} \; l, \delta] \Rightarrow k'}$$

Blocks

$$\frac{\vdash_{asg} \langle a^*, \delta, k \rangle \Rightarrow^* \langle \epsilon, \delta', k' \rangle \quad k' \vdash_{jmp} [j, \delta'] \Rightarrow k''}{k \vdash_{body} [a^* \; j, \delta] \Rightarrow k''}$$

$$\frac{4{\cdot}l{\cdot}\delta \notin k \quad k \circ [4{\cdot}l{\cdot}\delta :] \vdash_{body} [\Gamma(l), \delta] \Rightarrow k'}{k \vdash_{block} [l, \delta] \Rightarrow k'} \qquad \frac{4{\cdot}l{\cdot}\delta \in k}{k \vdash_{block} [l, \delta] \Rightarrow k} \qquad \frac{1{\cdot}l{\cdot}\delta \in k}{k \vdash_{poly} [l, \delta] \Rightarrow k}$$

$$\frac{1{\cdot}l{\cdot}\delta \notin k \quad k \vdash_{block} [l, \delta] \Rightarrow k' \quad l' = l{\uparrow}\delta}{k \vdash_{poly} [l, \delta] \Rightarrow k' \circ \begin{bmatrix} 1{\cdot}l{\cdot}\delta : \text{if} \; (\text{done?} \; l' \; \text{code}) \; 2 \; 3{\cdot}l{\cdot}\delta \\ 3{\cdot}l{\cdot}\delta : \text{code} \; := \; (\text{newblock} \; \text{code} \; l'); \; \text{goto} \; 4{\cdot}l{\cdot}\delta \end{bmatrix}}$$

Fig. 4. Compiler generator cog_{dcb} for Flowchart

Command-generating expressions:	Conversion of expressions and labels:

$$\underline{x := e} \quad = (\texttt{list } 'x \; ':= e)$$

$$\underline{x := \text{call } l} = (\texttt{list } 'x \; ':= (\texttt{list } '\text{call } l))$$

$$\underline{\text{if } e \; l_1 \; l_2} = (\texttt{list } '\text{if } e \; l_1 \; l_2)$$

$$\underline{\text{return } e} \quad = (\texttt{list } '\text{return } e)$$

$$v{\uparrow}\delta = 'v$$

$$x{\uparrow}\delta = \begin{cases} 'x & \text{if } x \notin \delta \\ (\texttt{list } '\text{quote } x) & \text{if } x \in \delta \end{cases}$$

$$(o \; e_1 \dots e_n){\uparrow}\delta = (\texttt{list } 'o \; e_1{\uparrow}\delta \dots e_n{\uparrow}\delta)$$

$$l{\uparrow}\{x_1, \dots, x_n\} = (\texttt{list } 'l \; x_1 \dots x_n)$$

Fig. 5. Conversion of Flowchart constructs into code-generating expressions

Dynamic commands are replaced by command-generating commands, *i.e.* commands that add new commands to the residual program when the generating extension runs.[2] Underlined commands are a short-hand for the command-generating expressions in Fig. 5. A dynamic expression e is converted under δ into an expression-generating expression $e{\uparrow}\delta$ as recursively defined in Fig. 5. Similarly, a label l is replaced by an expression $l{\uparrow}\delta$ that creates a residual label, *i.e.* a list containing l and the values of the static variables $x_1, \dots, x_n$. A block l reached with δ from a dynamic conditional or a dynamic call is turned into a polyvariant block generator labeled $1 \cdot l \cdot \delta$ in the generating extension.[3]

Definition 1 (Compiler generator cog_{dcb}). *Let* p *be a well-formed Flowchart program with initial label l, let division $\delta = \{s_1, \dots, s_m\}$ be the static parameters and $\{d_1, \dots, d_n\}$ be the dynamic parameters of* p. *Let the initial label of the new generating extension be $l' = 0 \cdot l \cdot \delta$. Define the compiler generator for Flowchart by*

$$[\![\text{p}]\!]_{\text{cog}_{dcb}} \; \delta \;=\; k \circ \begin{bmatrix} l' : \texttt{code} := (\texttt{newheader } '(d_1 \dots d_n) \; l{\uparrow}\delta); \; \texttt{goto } 1 \cdot l \cdot \delta \\ 2 : \texttt{return code} \end{bmatrix}$$

$$\textit{where } ((s_1 \dots s_m)(l')) \vdash_{poly} [l, \delta] \Rightarrow k.$$

The conversion of a program p into a generating extension always terminates because the number of labels and divisions is finite for any given p. No interpretive overhead is introduced in a generating extension (all static assignments are executed natively in a generating extension). This makes our compiler generator well-suited to the *incremental generation* of multi-level generating extensions [15]. Incremental generation stages a generating extension again when it has several parameters that are available at different times. The generating extensions yield the same residual programs as a typical online partial evaluator for Flowchart [14, 17], but do so faster. Note the relative simplicity of a compiler generator that produces good results (*e.g.*, the Ackermann

---

[2] If the name code already occurs in the subject program, another name is used.

[3] Block specialization is performed with respect to the static variables live at the entry of a block to reduce the risk of duplicating blocks in the residual program [16]. This technique is used in the implementation, but omitted from Fig. 4 for readability. In a slight abuse of our notation, we write $l \in k$ to denote that a residual block labeled l exists in residual program k.

generating extension). Written in Flowchart, the compiler generator cog_{dcb} is only 136 commands long (Tab. 3).

We characterize the compiler generator as follows. We imagine that the generating extensions that it produces are identical to those of a hypothetical specializer s_b specialized by a hypothetical specializer s_c with respect to p, that is $\text{g}_{cb} = [\![\text{s}_c]\!](\text{s}_b, \text{p})$, and that the compiler generator itself is the product of a hypothetical specializer s_d. This explains the index of cog_{dcb} (*cf.* general bootstrapping in Sect. 2). We omit δ and assume that all programs to which we apply cog_{dcb} have two arguments where the first is static and the second is dynamic.

4   Experimental Assessment

Full Bootstrapping. The purpose of the first series of experiments is to compare the bootstrapping technique directly with the third Futamura projection and to verify experimentally that full bootstrapping does produce identical results to Futamura's technique. We performed three full bootstraps, two of which use cog_{dcb} as the initial compiler generator and one which uses cog_{000}, which is itself a compiler generator that we bootstrapped with cog_{dcb}. We use two specializers in our experiments, and these represent typical offline and online partial evaluators for flowchart languages [14, 16–18].[4]

1. For an independent comparison, we use the classic *offline partial evaluator* mix by Gomard and Jones [16]. The bootstrapping starting with cog_{dcb} as initial compiler generator reproduced the mix-compiler generator cog_{111} and was about *twice as fast*. The total time consumed by the full bootstrap was 82.5 ms *vs.* 171.3 ms by the third Futamura projection (Tab. 1). That bootstrapping is faster is remarkable because two decades ago mix was not designed for bootstrapping, but for self-application. The initial cog_{dcb} was entirely factored out during the transformation process as predicted.
2. Likewise, bootstrapping the compiler generator of the *online partial evaluator* onmix [14] produced the same compiler generator cog_{000} as the third Futamura projection, but *2.5 times faster* (161 *vs.* 406 ms) (Tab. 2).
3. The third experiment used the onmix-compiler generator to bootstrap the mix-compiler generator. The full bootstrap of cog_{111} starting with cog_{000} as initial compiler generator instead of cog_{dcb} was slightly slower (94.1 *vs.* 82.5 ms), but still nearly twice as fast as the third Futamura projection (Tab. 1).

All the full bootstraps that we performed were faster than the third Futamura projection and produced identical results. Starting from a hand-written compiler generator was fastest (cog_{dcb}), but our results also demonstrate that even an

---

[4] Flowchart was implemented by an interpreter written in Scheme R5RS. All running times (Time) are the CPU time in ms incl. garbage collection (GC) using Petite Chez Scheme 7.4d (nonthreaded) on an Apple MacBook Pro (2.2 GHz Intel Core 2 Duo), Mac OS X 10.6. Typically, GC is less than 1% of Time. All times are the average of ten successive runs. The figures are subject to the usual uncertainties assoc. with CPU measurements. The program size is given as the number of commands (Cmd).

Table 1. Two full bootstraps of the Gomard-Jones mix-compiler generator [16]

Run		Time	Ratio
$\mathrm{cog}_{111} = [\![\mathrm{mix}]\!]\,(\mathrm{mix},\mathrm{mix})$		171.3	
$= [\![[\![[\![\mathrm{cog}_{dcb}]\!]\,\mathrm{mix}]\!]\,\mathrm{mix}]\!]\,\mathrm{mix}$		82.5	**2.1**
1. $\mathrm{cog}_{cb1} = [\![\mathrm{cog}_{dcb}]\!]\,\mathrm{mix}$		29.4	
2. $\mathrm{cog}_{b11} = [\![\mathrm{cog}_{cb1}]\!]\,\mathrm{mix}$		19.3	
3. $\mathrm{cog}_{111} = [\![\mathrm{cog}_{b11}]\!]\,\mathrm{mix}$		33.8	**5.1**
4. $\phantom{\mathrm{cog}_{111}} = [\![\mathrm{cog}_{111}]\!]\,\mathrm{mix}$		33.8	**5.1**

Run		Time	Ratio
$\mathrm{cog}_{111} = [\![\mathrm{mix}]\!]\,(\mathrm{mix},\mathrm{mix})$		171.3	
$= [\![[\![[\![\mathrm{cog}_{000}]\!]\,\mathrm{mix}]\!]\,\mathrm{mix}]\!]\,\mathrm{mix}$		94.1	**1.8**
1. $\mathrm{cog}_{001} = [\![\mathrm{cog}_{000}]\!]\,\mathrm{mix}$		35.9	
2. $\mathrm{cog}_{011} = [\![\mathrm{cog}_{001}]\!]\,\mathrm{mix}$		24.4	
3. $\mathrm{cog}_{111} = [\![\mathrm{cog}_{011}]\!]\,\mathrm{mix}$		33.8	**5.1**
4. $\phantom{\mathrm{cog}_{111}} = [\![\mathrm{cog}_{111}]\!]\,\mathrm{mix}$		33.8	**5.1**

Table 2. A full bootstrap of the onmix-compiler generator [14]

Run		Time	Ratio
$\mathrm{cog}_{000} = [\![\mathrm{onmix}]\!]\,(\mathrm{onmix},\mathrm{onmix})$		406.2	
$= [\![[\![[\![\mathrm{cog}_{dcb}]\!]\,\mathrm{onmix}]\!]\,\mathrm{onmix}]\!]\,\mathrm{onmix}$		161.2	**2.5**
1. $\mathrm{cog}_{cb0} = [\![\mathrm{cog}_{dcb}]\!]\,\mathrm{onmix}$		48.4	
2. $\mathrm{cog}_{b00} = [\![\mathrm{cog}_{cb0}]\!]\,\mathrm{onmix}$		50.2	
3. $\mathrm{cog}_{000} = [\![\mathrm{cog}_{b00}]\!]\,\mathrm{onmix}$		62.6	**6.5**
4. $\phantom{\mathrm{cog}_{000}} = [\![\mathrm{cog}_{000}]\!]\,\mathrm{onmix}$		62.6	**6.5**

automatically produced compiler generator (cog_{000}) can beat the third Futamura projection.[5] This can be compared to the reduction of multiple layers of interpretation by partial evaluation which yields substantial efficiency gains [18].

Self-generation that is more than three times as fast as the third Futamura projection indicates that a compiler generator is efficient and that bootstrapping new compiler generators may pay off. Given that the self-generation speedup ratios of offline compiler generators reported in the literature range between 1.6 [19] and 17.8 [24], we expect that many of them can be used for rapid bootstrapping. The self-generation speedup ratio of cog_{000} is 6.5 (Tab. 2). Clearly, the actual run times and speedup ratios depend on many factors including the optimizations performed by the compiler generators, the efficiency of the generating extensions and the underlying language implementation.

---

[5] The Gomard-Jones mix-compiler generator cog_{111} [16] accepts only non-recursive programs as input and can therefore not be applied to the recursive program onmix to bootstrap its compiler generator cog_{000}. A self-applicable offline partial evaluator that we wrote for recursive programs allowed a full bootstrap of cog_{000} from onmix.

Two-Step Compiler Generators. An important theoretical property discussed in Sect. 2 is that the compiler generators produced by the second and third bootstrapping step are *functionally equivalent*; see (15). We now examine whether compiler generators produced by the second bootstrapping step are already efficient for practical use.

1. Consider the two-step bootstrap from cog_{dcb} to cog_{b00} (Tab. 2). We find that cog_{b00} and cog_{000} not only have the same number of commands (Tab. 3), but are textually identical modulo renaming (*i.e.* disregarding block order and renaming of labels). This is because onmix and cog_{dcb}'s generating extensions have the same specialization strength (both use online partial evaluation techniques). This is accidental, but shows that two-step bootstrapping can produce the *same* compiler generator as the third Futamura projection, but about 4 times faster (about 99 ms *vs.* 406 ms).

2. Now consider the two-step bootstraps from cog_{dcb} to cog_{b11} and from cog_{000} to cog_{011} (Tab. 1). The two compiler generators cog_{b11} and cog_{011} are textually identical (modulo renaming) for the reason just discussed. However, if two initial constants in mix [16, App. I, block 0] are not dynamized to prevent the one-time unrolling of its main loop, then their size grows to 250 instead of 129 commands. Because that size is still relatively modest and does not affect their running time the two-step compiler generators may be considered as "good enough". In any event, the two-step bootstraps are about 2.9 and 3.5 times faster than the third Futamura projection (about 60 ms resp. 49 ms *vs.* 171 ms).

We conclude that two-step compiler generators can be useful. Unlike three-step compiler generators, their implementation depends on the strength of the initial compiler generator which produces the one-step compiler generator that generates them. For example, if the initial compiler generator performs a trivial staging then the two-step compiler generator is a trivial specialization of the given specializer with respect to a copy of itself and no speedup is achieved (a trivial specialization just "freezes" the value of a static argument by adding a constant assignment to the beginning of the original program).

One-Step Compiler Generators. Tables 1 and 2 show that the compiler generators cog_{cb0} and cog_{cb1} that we obtain after the first bootstrapping step are quite efficient raising the question of whether one always needs two or three bootstrapping steps to obtain a useful compiler generator. We know that the generating extensions that cog_{cb0} and cog_{cb1} produce are functionally equivalent to the ones produced by cog_{000} and cog_{111} respectively; see (17). Thus with respect to the generating extensions there is no loss of specialization strength. They produce the same residual programs; only their implementation may differ.

The efficiency of the two compiler generators can be seen from the time they take to stage specializers: cog_{cb0} is faster than cog_{000} when applied to onmix, and cog_{cb1} is faster than *any* of the other eight compiler generators that we obtained in our experiments when applied to mix. A reason for their efficiency is

Table 3. Sizes of the partial evaluators and compiler generators

Pgm	Cmd	Ratio	Pgm	Cmd	Ratio	Pgm	Cmd	Ratio	Pgm	Cmd	Ratio
cog_{dcb}	136		onmix	108		mix	67		mix	67	
			cog_{cb0}	186	**1.72**	cog_{cb1}	100	**1.49**	cog_{b01}	120	**1.79**
			cog_{b00}	216	**2**	cog_{b11}	129	**1.93**	cog_{001}	120	**1.79**
			cog_{000}	216	**2**	cog_{111}	129	**1.93**	cog_{011}	129	**1.93**

that no interpretive overhead was introduced by cog_{dcb} in cog_{cb0} and cog_{cb1} (*cf.* the Ackermann generating extension produced by cog_{dcb} in Fig. 2 and the one produced by onmix [14, Appdx. B]). Classic benchmarks of partial evaluation such as converting interpreters into compilers (Turing machine, MP language) [18] confirm their efficiency. Note that they are also the smallest compiler generators that we obtained from onmix and mix respectively (Tab. 3).

This indicates that if we start with a mature compiler generator, one-step bootstrapping may be sufficient to produce good results. This has the important advantage that the specializer to which the initial compiler generator is applied need not be self-applicable. This can be very useful when dealing with specializers where the source and implementation language differ, *i.e.* they *cannot* be self-applied, because the source language may not be well suited as an implementation language, such as a domain-specific language or a reversible programming language [29]. For good results, however, it is an advantage to binding-time improve the specializers for the initial compiler generator, here cog_{dcb}.

General Bootstrapping. For the sake of completeness, we generated all nine compiler generators and performed all the bootstraps that are possible with the two partial evaluators, mix and onmix, and our initial compiler generator, cog_{dcb}.

The bootstraps are illustrated in the diagram. Nodes are labeled with a compiler generator index and arrows with a specializer index (0 = onmix, 1 = mix). As an example, the step $[\![\mathrm{cog}_{dcb}]\!]\,\mathrm{onmix} = \mathrm{cog}_{cb0}$ leads in the diagram from node dcb to node $cb0$ along edge 0. All program sizes are recorded in Tab. 3; all generation times in Tabs. 1, 2 and $b00 \xrightarrow{1} 001$ (35.9 ms), $cb0 \xrightarrow{1} b01$ (30.3 ms) and $b01 \xrightarrow{1} 011$ (24.4 ms).

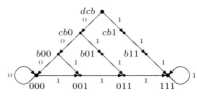

All that remains is the case of general bootstrapping. Starting with cog_{dcb} as the initial compiler generator, we performed two general bootstraps: $dcb \xrightarrow{0} cb0 \xrightarrow{0} b00 \xrightarrow{1} 001$ and $dcb \xrightarrow{0} cb0 \xrightarrow{1} b01 \xrightarrow{1} 011$. They reproduced compiler generators textually identical to those that we obtained before plus a new intermediate one, cog_{b01}, which follows from the theoretical considerations in Sect. 2. The two bootstraps were about 1.6 and 1.8 times faster than the two corresponding quasi self-applications $\mathrm{cog}_{001} = [\![\mathrm{onmix}]\!]\,(\mathrm{onmix}, \mathrm{mix})$ and $\mathrm{cog}_{011} = [\![\mathrm{onmix}]\!]\,(\mathrm{mix}, \mathrm{mix})$ respectively. Note that they do not end in self-generation.

5   Related Work

The first hand-written compiler generator based on partial evaluation principles was, in all probability, RedCompile for Lisp [2]. Few compiler generators based on online partial evaluation have been developed since then (an exception being [25]) and, it would appear, none that propagates binding-time information in parallel with the generation of the generating extension such as cog_{dcb} (Sect. 3). A compiler generator produced by the third Futamura projection was observed to contain a straightforward function for converting binding-time-annotated programs into generating extensions [23]. The present work is also part of our investigation into the foundations of metacomputation including [1, 4, 11–15, 29].

6   Conclusion

We conclude that bootstrapping compiler generators is a viable alternative to double self-application by the third Futamura projection. Until now, the third Futamura projection has been the only technique used to transform partial evaluators into compiler generators. Much attention in the area of partial evaluation was devoted to the problem of self-application in order to make use of Futamura's technique [8]. The present work shows that, once a compiler generator exists, partial evaluation can be liberated from the problem of self-application because double self-application is no longer required to turn specializers into compiler generators. It may also be helpful in mastering double self-application because one can inspect each intermediate compiler generator in a full bootstrap, which is not possible with the third Futamura projection.

The compiler generator presented in this paper is original and produces generating extensions that perform recursive polyvariant specialization and are as powerful as online partial evaluators for flowchart languages [14, 17]. Furthermore, the compiler generator is well suited to the incremental generation of multi-level generating extensions [15], making it possible to go beyond Ershov's two-level generating extensions.

Bootstrapping is not magic. Providing the same specializer three times yields, after three bootstrapping steps, the exact same compiler generator as the third Futamura projection. But bootstrapping can be faster and produce compiler generators of practical value after just one or two steps. By contrast, the third Futamura projection is an "all-or-nothing" approach: unless double self-application is successful, we obtain no useful compiler generator. Our results suggest that bootstrapping is a suitable subject for further research involving compiler generators for other programming languages and different specialization methods (*e.g.* [10, 27]). This seems worthwhile because bootstrapping has a number of potentially interesting applications including producing compiler generators for cross-compilers and domain-specific languages [11, 12].

Viewing old problems from a new angle may also provide fresh insights into the generation and construction principles of generating extensions, both of the two- and higher-level variety, and lead to stronger generating extensions than are currently familiar from partial evaluation.

Acknowledgements. This work benefited greatly from discussions at the Second International Valentin Turchin Memorial Workshop on Metacomputation in Russia 2010. The author would like to thank Sergei M. Abramov, Neil D. Jones, Andrei V. Klimov, Ilya Klyuchnikov, Julia Lawall, Simon Peyton Jones and Peter Sestoft for their comments. It is a great pleasure to thank Akihiko Takano for providing the author with excellent working conditions at the National Institute of Informatics, Tokyo.

References

1. Abramov, S.M., Glück, R.: Principles of inverse computation and the universal resolving algorithm. In: Mogensen, T.Æ., Schmidt, D.A., Sudborough, I.H. (eds.) The Essence of Computation. LNCS, vol. 2566, pp. 269–295. Springer, Heidelberg (2002)
2. Beckman, L., Haraldson, A., Oskarsson, Ö., Sandewall, E.: A partial evaluator and its use as a programming tool. Artificial Intelligence 7, 319–357 (1976)
3. Bulyonkov, M.A.: Polyvariant mixed computation for analyzer programs. Acta Informatica 21(5), 473–484 (1984)
4. Christensen, N.H., Glück, R.: Offline partial evaluation can be as accurate as online partial evaluation. ACM TOPLAS 26(1), 191–220 (2004)
5. Consel, C., Lawall, J.L., Le Meur, A.F.: A tour of Tempo: a program specializer for the C language. Science of Computer Programming 52(1-3), 341–370 (2004)
6. Ershov, A.P.: On the partial computation principle. Information Processing Letters 6(2), 38–41 (1977)
7. Ershov, A.P.: Mixed computation in the class of recursive program schemata. Acta Cybernetica 4(1), 19–23 (1978)
8. Futamura, Y.: Partial evaluation of computing process – an approach to a compiler-compiler. Systems, Computers, Controls 2(5), 45–50 (1971)
9. Futamura, Y.: Partial computation of programs. In: Goto, E., Furukawa, K., Nakajima, R., Nakata, I., Yonezawa, A. (eds.) RIMS Symposia on Software Science and Engineering. Proceedings. LNCS, vol. 147, pp. 1–35. Springer, Heidelberg (1983)
10. Futamura, Y., Konishi, Z., Glück, R.: Program transformation system based on generalized partial computation. New Generation Computing 20(1), 75–99 (2001)
11. Glück, R.: Is there a fourth Futamura projection? In: Partial Evaluation and Program Manipulation. Proceedings, pp. 51–60. ACM Press (2009)
12. Glück, R.: An experiment with the fourth Futamura projection. In: Pnueli, A., Virbitskaite, I., Voronkov, A. (eds.) PSI 2009. LNCS, vol. 5947, pp. 135–150. Springer, Heidelberg (2010)
13. Glück, R.: Self-generating program specializers. Information Processing Letters 110(17), 787–793 (2010)
14. Glück, R.: A self-applicable online partial evaluator for recursive flowchart languages. Software – Practice and Experience (to appear, 2012)
15. Glück, R., Jørgensen, J.: An automatic program generator for multi-level specialization. Lisp and Symbolic Computation 10(2), 113–158 (1997)
16. Gomard, C.K., Jones, N.D.: Compiler generation by partial evaluation: a case study. Structured Programming 12(3), 123–144 (1991)
17. Hatcliff, J.: An Introduction to Online and Offline Partial Evaluation Using a Simple Flowchart Language. In: Hatcliff, J., Mogensen, T.Æ., Thiemann, P. (eds.) Partial Evaluation. Practice and Theory. LNCS, vol. 1706, pp. 20–82. Springer, Heidelberg (1999)

18. Jones, N.D., Gomard, C.K., Sestoft, P.: Partial Evaluation and Automatic Program Generation. Prentice-Hall (1993)
19. Jones, N.D., Sestoft, P., Søndergaard, H.: An experiment in partial evaluation: the generation of a compiler generator. In: Jouannaud, J.-P. (ed.) RTA 1985. LNCS, vol. 202, pp. 124–140. Springer, Heidelberg (1985)
20. Klimov, A.V., Romanenko, S.A.: Metavychislitel' dlja jazyka Refal. Osnovnye ponjatija i primery. (A metaevaluator for the language Refal. Basic concepts and examples). Preprint 71, Keldysh Institute of Applied Mathematics, Academy of Sciences of the USSR, Moscow (1987) (in Russian)
21. Leuschel, M., Jørgensen, J.: Efficient specialisation in Prolog using the handwritten compiler generator LOGEN. Electronic Notes in Theoretical Computer Science 30(2), 157–162 (2000)
22. Masterson Jr., K.S.: Compilation for two computers with NELIAC. Communications of the ACM 3(11), 607–611 (1960)
23. Romanenko, S.A.: A compiler generator produced by a self-applicable specializer can have a surprisingly natural and understandable structure. In: Bjørner, D., Ershov, A.P., Jones, N.D. (eds.) Partial Evaluation and Mixed Computation, pp. 445–463. North-Holland (1988)
24. Sestoft, P.: The structure of a self-applicable partial evaluator. Tech. Rep. 85/11, DIKU, University of Copenhagen, Denmark (1985), extended version of a paper with the same title in LNCS, vol. 217, pp. 236–256 (1986)
25. Sumii, E., Kobayashi, N.: A hybrid approach to online and offline partial evaluation. Higher-Order and Symbolic Computation 14(2-3), 101–142 (2001)
26. Thiemann, P.: Cogen in six lines. In: ACM International Conference on Functional Programming, pp. 180–189. ACM Press (1996)
27. Turchin, V.F.: Metacomputation: metasystem transitions plus supercompilation. In: Danvy, O., Thiemann, P., Glück, R. (eds.) Partial Evaluation 1996. LNCS, vol. 1110, pp. 481–509. Springer, Heidelberg (1996)
28. Wilkes, M.V.: An experiment with a self-compiling compiler for a simple list-processing language. Annual Review in Automatic Programming 4, 1–48 (1964)
29. Yokoyama, T., Glück, R.: A reversible programming language and its invertible self-interpreter. In: Partial Evaluation and Program Manipulation. Proceedings, pp. 144–153. ACM Press (2007)

A Logic Characteristic for Timed Extensions of Partial Order Based Equivalences[*]

Natalya S. Gribovskaya

A.P. Ershov Institute of Informatics Systems, SB RAS
6, Acad. Lavrentiev Avenue, 630090, Novosibirsk, Russia
moskalyova@iis.nsk.su

Abstract. The intention of the paper is to provide a uniform logic characteristic for timed extensions of partial order based equivalences (pomset trace equivalence, history preserving bisimulation and hereditary history preserving bisimulation) in the setting of timed event structures. For this purpose, we use open maps based characterizations of the equivalences, provided in [10], and the logics of path assertions from [6].

Keywords: Timed event structures, timed partial order equivalences, logic characteristic, category theory.

1   Introduction

Category theory has been widely used for the specification, analysis and verification of concurrent systems, and for understanding the particular issues that can arise when concurrency is present. Two category-theoretic approaches were initiated by Joyal, Nielsen, and Winskel in [6] where they have proposed abstract ways of capturing the notion of behavioral equivalences through open maps based bisimilarity and its logical counterpart — path bisimilarity. In the open maps based approach, a category $\mathbb{M}$ of models is identified, and then a subcategory $\mathbb{P}$ of path objects corresponding to executions of the models is chosen relative to which open maps are defined. Two models are $\mathbb{P}$-bisimilar if and only if there exists a span of open maps between the models. Path bisimilarity is defined as a relation over paths which are morphisms of $\mathbb{M}$ from the objects of $\mathbb{P}$. As shown in [6], one can characterize this bisimilarity by an associated logic language of path assertions, which is a modal logic, where modalities are indexed by morphisms of $\mathbb{P}$. These category-theoretic approaches have been well studied in the context of a wide range of models for concurrency (see [2,6,8,9] among others). The situation is less settled in the case of real-time models, only few examples are known. In [4] and [10], it has been provided an open maps based characterization of bisimulation on timed transition systems and of partial order based equivalences on timed event structures, respectively. The categorical framework of open maps has been used in [3] to prove that timed delay equivalence is indeed

---

[*] This work is supported in part by DFG-RFBR (grant No 436 RUS 113/1002/01, grant No 09-01-91334).

E. Clarke, I. Virbitskaite, and A. Voronkov (Eds.): PSI 2011, LNCS 7162, pp. 142–152, 2012.

an equivalence relation in the setting of timed transition systems with invariants. In [11] it has been shown how several categorical (open maps, path-bisimilarity and coalgebraic) approaches to an abstract characterization of bisimulation relate to each other and to the numerous behavioural equivalences in the setting of timed transition systems.

The intention of the paper is to provide a uniform logic characteristic for timed extensions of partial order based equivalences (pomset trace equivalence, history preserving bisimulation and hereditary history preserving bisimulation) in the setting of timed event structures. For this purpose, we use open maps based characterizations of the equivalences, provided in [10], and the logics of path assertions from [6].

The rest of the paper is organized as follows. Basic notions and notations concerning timed event structures are introduced in Section 2. The timed behavioural equivalences — timed pomset trace equivalence, timed history preserving bisimulation and timed hereditary history preserving bisimulation — are developed in Section 3. In the next section, we recall open maps based characterizations of the equivalences under consideration, provided in the paper [10]. In Section 5, we treat the logics of path assertions from [6] to show that these logics are characteristic for the timed behavioural equivalences.

2   Timed Event Structures

In this section some basic notions and notations concerning timed event structures are introduced.

First, we recall a classical notion of prime event structures [12] which constitute a major branch of partial order models. Let L be a finite set of actions. A *(labelled) event structure* over L is 4-tuple $S = (E, \leq, \#, l)$, where E is a set of events; $\leq \subseteq E \times E$ is a partial order (the *causality relation*), satisfying the *principle of finite causes*: $\forall e \in E \circ \{e' \in E \mid e' \leq e\}$ is finite; $\# \subseteq E \times E$ is a symmetric and irreflexive relation (the *conflict relation*), satisfying the *principle of conflict heredity*: $\forall e, e', e'' \in E \circ e \# e' \leq e'' \Rightarrow e \# e''$; $l : E \to L$ is a labelling function. For an event structure $S = (E, \leq, \#, l)$, we define $\smile = (E \times E) \setminus (\leq \cup \leq^{-1} \cup \#)$ (the *concurrency relation*). For $C \subseteq E$, the *restriction* of S to C, denoted $S \lceil C$, is defined as $(C, \leq \cap (C \times C), \# \cap (C \times C), l \mid_C)$. Let $C \subseteq E$. Then C is *left-closed* iff $\forall e, e' \in E \circ e \in C \wedge e' \leq e \Rightarrow e' \in C$; C is *conflict-free* iff $\forall e, e' \in C \circ \neg(e \# e')$; C is a *configuration* of S iff C is left-closed and conflict-free. Let $\mathcal{C}(S)$ denote the set of all finite configurations of S.

We are now ready to present a dense time extension of event structures, called *timed event structures* [10]. In the model, time constraints are added to event structures by associating their events with a set of earliest and latest times, w.r.t. a global clock, at which the events can occur. The occurrences of enabled events themselves take no time but they can be suspended for a certain time (between their earliest and latest times) from the start of the system. Let $\mathbf{R}$ be the set of nonnegative real numbers.

Definition 1. *A* (labelled) timed event structure *over L is a triple $TS = (S, Eot, Lot)$, where $S = (E, \leq, \#, l)$ is a (labelled) event structure over L; Eot, $Lot : E \to \mathbf{R}$ are functions of the earliest and latest occurrence times of events, satisfying $Eot(e) \leq Lot(e)$ for all $e \in E$.*

A timed event structure $TS = (S = (E, \leq, \#, l), Eot, Lot)$ is said to *have a valid timing*, if $e' \leq e$ then $Eot(e') \leq Eot(e)$, and $Lot(e') \leq Lot(e)$, for all $e, e' \in E$. In the following, we will consider only timed event structures having a valid timing and call them simply timed event structures.

For depicting timed event structures, we use the following conventions. The action labels and time constraints associated with events are drawn near the events. If no confusion arises, we will often use action labels rather event identities to denote events. The $<$-relation is depicted by arcs (omitting those derivable by transitivity), and conflicts are also drawn (omitting those derivable by conflict heredity). To make our examples easier to understand, we will sometimes give for them algebraic expressions (see [1]) over actions with the time intervals of the corresponding events. The algebraic syntax includes the primitive constructs: sequential composition (;), parallel composition ($\|$), and sum ($+$). The operation ; ($\|$, $+$, respectively) may be easily 'interpreted' by indicating that all events in one component are in the $<$-relation ($\smile$-relation, $\#$-relation, respectively) with all events in the other.

Example 1. Contemplate the timed event structure TS shown in Fig. 1. We can see that TS consists of three events e_1, e_2 and e_3 labelled by actions a, b and c, respectively. The events have time constraints. For example, the earliest and the latest times of e_1 are 0 and 1, respectively. Moreover, e_1 causally precedes e_2, and e_3 conflicts with e_2.

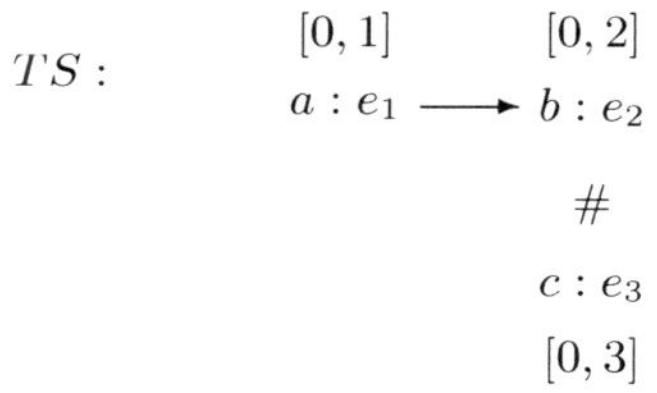

$$TS: \qquad \begin{array}{cc} [0,1] & [0,2] \\ a : e_1 \longrightarrow & b : e_2 \\ & \# \\ & c : e_3 \\ & [0,3] \end{array}$$

Fig. 1. A trivial example of a labelled timed event structure

Timed event structures $TS = (E, \leq, \#, l, Eot, Lot)$ and $TS' = (E', \leq', \#', l', Eot', Lot')$ are *isomorphic*, denoted as $TS \simeq TS'$, if there exists a bijection $\varphi : E \to E'$ such that $e \leq e'$ iff $\varphi(e) \leq' \varphi(e')$, $e \# e'$ iff $\varphi(e) \#' \varphi(e')$, $l(e) = l'(\varphi(e))$, $Eot(e) = Eot'(\varphi(e))$ and $Lot(e) = Lot'(\varphi(e))$, for all $e, e' \in E$.

An execution of a timed event structure is a *timed configuration* which consists of a configuration and a timing function recording global time moments at which events occur, and satisfies some additional requirements. Let $TS = (S, Eot, Lot)$ be a timed event structure, $C \in \mathcal{C}(S)$, and $T : C \to \mathbf{R}$. Then $TC = (C, T)$ is a *timed configuration* of TS iff $\forall\, e \in C \;\circ\; Eot(e) \leq T(e) \leq Lot(e)$ and

$\forall\, e, e' \in C \,\circ\, e \leq_{TS} e' \Rightarrow T(e) \leq T(e')$. Informally speaking, the first condition expresses that an event can occur at a time when its timing constraints are met; and the second condition says that for all two events e and e' occurred if e causally precedes e' then e should temporally precede e'. The *initial timed configuration* of TS is $TC_{TS} = (\emptyset, \emptyset)$. We use $\mathcal{TC}(TS)$ to denote the set of timed configurations of TS.

The semantics of timed event structures is defined by means of timed pomsets. A *timed pomset* is a timed event structure $TP = (E_{TP}, \leq_{TP}, \#_{TP}, l_{TP}, Eot_{TP}, Lot_{TP})$ with $\#_{TP} = \emptyset$ and $Eot_{TP}(e) = Lot_{TP}(e)$ for all $e \in E_{TP}$. We use $\mathcal{TP}om_L$ to indicate the set of timed finite pomsets labelled over L and $\mathcal{O}$ to denote the empty timed pomset $(\emptyset, \emptyset, \emptyset, \emptyset)$.

Let TS be a timed event structure and $TC = (C, T), TC' = (C', T') \in \mathcal{TC}(TS)$. The *restriction* of TS to TC, denoted $TS\lceil TC$, is defined as $(S\lceil C, T)$. Thus, a timed configuration TC of TS can be regarded as a timed pomset $TS\lceil TC$. We shall write $TC \to TC'$ iff $C \subseteq C'$ and $T'|_C = T$.

3   Observational Equivalences

In this section, we recall some notions and notations concerning timed extensions of partial order based equivalences (pomset trace equivalence, history preserving bisimulation and hereditary history preserving bisimulation) from the paper [10].

First, introduce the some auxiliary notations. Let $TP' = (E', \leq', l', Eot')$ and $TP = (E, \leq, l, Eot)$ be timed pomsets. Then TP' is an *augment* of TP, if there exists a bijection $\phi : E' \to E$ such that $e \leq' e'$ if $\phi(e) \leq \phi(e')$, $l'(e) = l(\phi(e))$, $Eot'(e) = Eot(\phi(e))$, for all $e, e' \in E'$. For a timed event structure TS, $L_{tp}(TS) = \{TP \in \mathcal{TP}om_L \mid TP$ is an augment of $TS\lceil TC$ for some $TC \in \mathcal{TC}(TS)\}$ is the *timed pomset language* of TS.

Definition 2. *Two timed event structures TS and TS' are* timed pomset trace equivalent (*tp-equivalent*) *iff $L_{tp}(TS) = L_{tp}(TS')$.*

Example 2. First, consider the timed event structures $TS^1 = a[0, 1]\ ;\ b[0, 2]$ and $TS^2 = (a[0, 1]\ ;\ b[0, 2]) + (a[0, 1]\ ;\ c[0, 2])$. Clearly, TS^1 and TS^2 are not *tp*-equivalent because, for example, the timed pomset $a[1, 1]\ ;\ c[2, 2]$ belongs to $L_{tp}(TS^2)$ but does not to $L_{tp}(TS^1)$.

Next, the timed event structure TS^2 and the timed event structure $TS^3 = a[0, 1]\ ;\ (b[0, 2] + c[0, 2])$ are tp-equivalent.

We now present the definitions of timed history preserving bisimulation and timed hereditary history preserving bisimulation from the paper [10].

Definition 3. *Let TS and TS' be timed event structures.*

- Timed history preserving bisimulation (*thp-bisimulation*) *between TS and TS' is a relation $\mathcal{B}$ consisting of triples (TC, f, TC'), where TC is a timed configuration of TS, TC' is a timed configuration of TS', and $f : TS\lceil TC \to TS'\lceil TC'$ is an isomorphism, such that $((\emptyset, \emptyset), \emptyset, (\emptyset, \emptyset)) \in \mathcal{B}$ and for all $(TC, f, TC') \in \mathcal{B}$ it holds:*

- **if** $TC \to TC_1$ **in** TS, **then** $TC' \to TC'_1$ **in** TS' **and** $(TC_1, f_1, TC'_1) \in \mathcal{B}$
  with $f \subseteq f_1$, **for some** $TC'_1 \in \mathcal{TC}(TS')$ **and** f_1,
- **if** $TC' \to TC'_1$ **in** TS', **then** $TC \to TC_1$ **in** TS **and** $(TC_1, f_1, TC'_1) \in \mathcal{B}$
  with $f \subseteq f_1$, **for some** $TC_1 \in \mathcal{TC}(TS)$ **and** f_1,
- *Thp-bisimulation* $\mathcal{B}$ *between* TS *and* TS' *is called* timed hereditary history
  preserving bisimulation *(thhp-bisimulation)* *if for all* $(TC, f, TC') \in \mathcal{B}$ *it
  holds:*
  - **if** $TC_1 \to TC$ **in** TS, **then** $TC'_1 \to TC'$ **in** TS' **and** $(TC_1, f_1, TC'_1) \in \mathcal{B}$
    with $f_1 \subseteq f$, **for some** $TC'_1 \in \mathcal{TC}(TS')$,
  - **if** $TC'_1 \to TC'$ **in** TS', **then** $TC_1 \to TC$ **in** TS **and** $(TC_1, TC'_1) \in \mathcal{B}$ **with**
    $f_1 \subseteq f$, **for some** $TC_1 \in \mathcal{TC}(TS)$,
- *TS and TS' are thp*-bisimilar *(thhp-bisimilar) iff there exists thp*-bisimulation
  (thhp-bisimulation) between TS *and* TS'.

Example 3. First, contemplate the timed event structures TS^2 and TS^3 from
Example 2. They are not *thp*-bisimilar, because, for instance, in TS^3 there exists
a timed configuration obtained by an execution of the action a at time 0, which
can be extended by a further execution of either the action b or the action c at
time 1 but it is not the case in TS^2.

Second, deal with the timed event structures $TS^4 = (a[0, 2] \parallel (b[0, 2] + c[0, 2]))$
$+ (b[0, 2] \parallel (a[0, 2] + c[0, 2]))$ and $TS^5 = ((a[0, 2] \parallel (b[0, 2] + c[0, 2]))+(a[0, 2]$
$\parallel b[0, 2]) + (b[0, 2] \parallel (a[0, 2] + c[0, 2]))$. It is easy to see that they are *thp*-
bisimilar. On the other hand, TS^4 and TS^5 are not *thhp*-bisimilar. For example,
the timed configuration obtained by an execution of the action a at time 1 in
the central part of TS^5 can be related only to the timed configuration obtained
by an execution of the action a at time 1 in the right part of TS^4. Hence, the
timed configurations further obtained by an execution of the action b at time 1
in the corresponding parts of TS^5 and TS^4 must be related. However, moving
back by an execution of the action a at time 1 we get the timed configurations,
which can not be related, because in TS^4 an execution of the action c at time 2
is further possible, but it is not the case in TS^5.

Finally, consider the timed event structures $TS^6 = \big(a[0, 1] \; ; \; (b[0, 2] + b[0, 2])\big)$
$+ c[0, 4]$ and $TS^7 = (a[0, 1] \; ; \; b[0, 2]) + c[0, 4] + c[0, 4]$. It is easy to see that they
are *thhp*-bisimilar.

4   Open Maps Bisimulation

4.1   Preliminaries

The concept of open map (open morphism) appears in work of Joyal and Moerdijk [5] where a concept of a subcategory of open maps of a (pre)topos is
defined. As reported in [6,8], the open map approach provides general concepts
of bisimilarity for any categorical model of computations.

First, a category $\mathbb{M}$ whose objects represent models has to be identified. A
morphism $m : X \longrightarrow Y$ in $\mathbb{M}$ should intuitively be thought of as a simulation
of the object X in the object Y. Then, inside the category $\mathbb{M}$, a subcategory

of 'path objects' and 'path extension' morphisms between these objects is to be chosen. The *subcategory of path objects* is denoted by $\mathbb{P}$. Given a path object P in $\mathbb{P}$ and a model object X in $\mathbb{M}$, a *path* is a morphism $p : P \longrightarrow X$ in $\mathbb{M}$. We think of p as representing a particular way of realizing P in X.

Second, we have to identify morphisms $m : X \longrightarrow Y$ which have the property that whenever a computation path of X can be extended via m in Y then that extension can be matched by an extension of the computation path in X. A morphism $m : X \to Y$ in $\mathbb{M}$ is called $\mathbb{P}$-*open* if whenever $f : P_1 \to P_2$ in $\mathbb{P}$, $p : P_1 \to X$ and $q : P_2 \to Y$ in $\mathbb{M}$, and $m \circ p = q \circ f$, there exists a morphism $h : P_2 \to X$ in $\mathbb{M}$ such that $p = h \circ f$ and $q = m \circ h$.

Third, an abstract notion of bisimilarity has to be introduced. The definition is given in terms of spans of open maps. Two objects X and Y in $\mathbb{M}$ are said to be $\mathbb{P}$-*bisimilar* if there exists a span $X \xleftarrow{m} Z \xrightarrow{m'} Y$ with a common object Z of $\mathbb{P}$-open morphisms.

4.2   Category $\mathcal{CTS}_L$

First, we recall the definitions of the category $\mathcal{CTS}_L$ of timed event structures and its two subcategories of timed pomsets from the paper [10].

Definition 4. *Let $TS = (E, \leq, \#, l, Eot, Lot)$ and $TS' = (E', \leq', \#', l', Eot',$ $Lot')$ be timed event structures. A mapping $\mu : TS \to TS'$ is called* morphism, *if $\mu : E \to E'$ is a function satisfying the following conditions: $l' \circ \mu = l$ and for all $TC = (C, T) \in \mathcal{TC}(TS)$ it holds:*

- *$\mu(TC) \in \mathcal{TC}(TS')$, where $\mu(TC) = (\{\mu(e) \mid e \in C\}, T')$ with $T' \circ \mu = T$,*
- *$\forall e, e' \in C \diamond \mu(e) = \mu(e') \Rightarrow e = e'$.*

Informally speaking, for any timed configuration TC of TS a morphism $\mu : TS \to TS'$ specifies the timed configuration $\mu(TC)$ such that $TS\lceil TC$ is an augment of $TS'\lceil \mu(TC)$. Hence, morphisms from Definition 4 represent some notions of simulation.

Timed event structures (labelled over L) with morphisms between them form a category of timed event structures $\mathcal{CTS}_L$ in which the composition of two morphisms defined as the usual composition of functions and the identity morphism is the identity function.

With respect to a set of actions L, let $\mathcal{TP}_L$ denote the full subcategory of the category $\mathcal{CTS}_L$ with objects of $\mathcal{TPom}_L$, and $\mathcal{TP}_L^0$ stand for the subcategory of the category $\mathcal{TP}_L$, whose morphisms are the identity functions and morphisms of $\mathcal{TP}_L$ with the empty timed pomset as domain.

The following theorem from [10] establishes that *tp*-equivalence and *thhp*-bisimulation coincide with $\mathcal{TP}_L^0$-bisimilarity and $\mathcal{TP}_L$-bisimilarity, respectively.

Theorem 1. *Let TS_1 and TS_2 be timed event structures of $\mathcal{CTS}_L$. Then,*

(i) TS_1 and TS_2 are tp-equivalent iff they are $\mathcal{TP}_L^0$-bisimular,
(ii) TS_1 and TS_2 are thhp-bisimilar iff they are $\mathcal{TP}_L$-bisimular.

The natural question is now: Do the timed partial order equivalences have logic characterizations in the spirit of e.g. the logic characterization of (strong) history-preserving bisimulation provided in the paper [6] in the setting of event structures? The question is answered positively in the next section.

5   Path Bisimulation

To obtain a logic characteristic of bisimilarity induced by a span of open maps, Joyal, Nielsen, and Winskel [6] have proposed its relation based generalization called path bisimilarity.

Let $\mathbb{M}$ be a category of models, let $\mathbb{P}$ be a small category of path objects, where $\mathbb{P}$ is a subcategory of $\mathbb{M}$, let I be a common initial object[1] of $\mathbb{P}$ and $\mathbb{M}$.

Definition 5. *A* path-$\mathbb{P}$-bisimulation *between objects X_1 and X_2 of $\mathbb{M}$ is a set $\mathcal{R}$ of pairs of paths (p_1, p_2) with common domain P, so $p_1 : P \to X_1$ is a path in X_1 and $p_2 : P \to X_2$ is a path in X_2, such that:*

(o) $(i_1, i_2) \in \mathcal{R}$, *where $i_1 : I \to X_1$ and $i_2 : I \to X_2$ are the unique paths starting in the initial object, and for all $(p_1, p_2) \in \mathcal{R}$ and for all $m : P \to Q$, where m is a morphism of $\mathbb{P}$, holds*

(i) *if there exists $q_1 : Q \to X_1$ with $q_1 \circ m = p_1$ then there exists $q_2 : Q \to X_2$ with $q_2 \circ m = p_2$ and $(q_1, q_2) \in \mathcal{R}$ and*

(ii) *if there exists $q_2 : Q \to X_2$ with $q_2 \circ m = p_2$ then there exists $q_1 : Q \to X_1$ with $q_1 \circ m = p_1$ and $(q_1, q_2) \in \mathcal{R}$.*

A path-$\mathbb{P}$-bisimulation *is called a* strong *path-$\mathbb{P}$-bisimulation if it holds*

(iii) *if $(q_1, q_2) \in \mathcal{R}$, with $q_1 : Q \to X_1$ and $q_2 : Q \to X_2$ and $m : P \to Q$, where m is a morphism of $\mathbb{P}$, then $(q_1 \circ m, q_2 \circ m) \in \mathcal{R}$.*

Two objects X_1 and X_2 are (strong) path-$\mathbb{P}$-bisimilar *iff there is a (strong) path-$\mathbb{P}$-bisimulation between them.*

It is easy to see that strong path-$\mathcal{TP}_L^0$-bisimilarity coincides with path-$\mathcal{TP}_L^0$-bisimilarity, since the morphisms of $\mathcal{TP}_L^0$ are either the identity functions or the morphisms of $\mathcal{TP}_L$ with the empty timed pomset as domain.

Recall the definition of path-$\mathbb{P}$-assertions A from [6]: $A := \bigwedge_{j \in J} A_j \mid \neg A \mid$ $\langle m \rangle A \mid \overline{\langle m \rangle} A$, where J is an indexing set, possibly empty or infinite, and m is a morphism of $\mathbb{P}$. The modality $\langle m \rangle$ is a 'forwards' modality, while $\overline{\langle m \rangle}$ is a 'backwards' modality. The empty conjunction (when the indexing set J is empty) stands for true.

For the semantics of path-$\mathbb{P}$-assertions, it is needed to specify when a path $p : P \to X$ satisfies a path-$\mathbb{P}$-assertion. For this purpose, the satisfaction relation $\models$ is defined by structural induction on assertions:

---

[1] In the case when $\mathbb{M}$ is $\mathcal{CTS}_L$ and $\mathbb{P}$ is $\mathcal{TP}_L^0$ or $\mathcal{TP}_L$, the initial object I is the empty timed event structure $\mathcal{O}$.

- $p \models \bigwedge_{j \in J} A_j$ iff $p \models A_j$ for all $j \in J$.
- $p \models \neg A$ iff $p \not\models A$,
- $p \models \langle m \rangle A$ for $m : P \to P'$ iff there is a path $p' : P' \to X$ for which $p' \models A$ and $p = p' \circ m$,
- $p \models \overline{\langle m \rangle} A$ for $m : P' \to P$ iff there is a path $p' : P' \to X$ for which $p' \models A$ and $p' = p \circ m$,

Intuitively, the formulas have the following meaning: the formula $p \models \bigwedge_{j \in J} A_j$ says that p satisfies A_j for all $j \in J$; the formula $p \models \neg A$ implies that p does not satisfy A; for any morphism $m : P \to P'$ of $\mathbb{P}$ the formula $p \models \langle m \rangle A$ denotes that there exists a path $p' : P' \to X$ such that p' satisfies A and p' is an extension of p via m; and for any morphism $m : P' \to P$ of $\mathbb{P}$ the formula $p \models \overline{\langle m \rangle} A$ means that there exists a path $p' : P' \to X$ such that p' satisfies A and p is an extension of p' via m. We call *forward path-$\mathbb{P}$-assertions* those built without backwards modalities.

Consider the following logic characteristics for path-$\mathcal{TP}_L^0$-bisimilarity and (strong) path-$\mathcal{TP}_L$-bisimilarity.

Theorem 2. *Let TS_1 and TS_2 be timed event structures of $\mathcal{CTS}_L$. Then,*

(i) *TS_1 and TS_2 are (strong) path-$\mathcal{TP}_L^0$-bisimilar iff the two initial paths $p_1^0 : \mathcal{O} \to TS_1$ and $p_2^0 : \mathcal{O} \to TS_2$ satisfy the same path-$\mathcal{TP}_L^0$-assertions;*

(ii) *TS_1 and TS_2 are path-$\mathcal{TP}_L$-bisimilar iff the two initial paths $p_1^0 : \mathcal{O} \to TS_1$ and $p_2^0 : \mathcal{O} \to TS_2$ satisfy the same forwards path-$\mathcal{TP}_L$-assertions;*

(iii) *TS_1 and TS_2 are strong path-$\mathcal{TP}_L$-bisimilar iff the two initial paths $p_1^0 : \mathcal{O} \to TS_1$ and $p_2^0 : \mathcal{O} \to TS_2$ satisfy the same path-$\mathcal{TP}_L$-assertions.*

Sketch proof: Immediately follows from Theorem 15 in the paper [6]. $\diamond$

We are now ready to present the main result of this work, establishing that the timed partial order equivalences can be characterized as relations over paths.

Theorem 3. *Let TS_1 and TS_2 be timed event structures of $\mathcal{CTS}_L$. Then,*

(i) *TS_1 and TS_2 are tp-equivalent iff they are (strong) path-$\mathcal{TP}_L^0$-bisimilar,*

(ii) *TS_1 and TS_2 are thp-bisimilar iff they are path-$\mathcal{TP}_L$-bisimilar,*

(iii) *TS_1 and TS_2 are thhp-bisimilar iff they are strong path-$\mathcal{TP}_L$-bisimilar.*

Sketch proof

(i) According to Theorem 1(i), *tp*-equivalence coincides with $\mathcal{TP}_L^0$-bisimilarity. The fact that $\mathcal{TP}_L^0$-bisimilarity implies (strong) path-$\mathcal{TP}_L^0$-bisimilarity follows from Lemma 16 [6]. Hence, it is sufficient to show that if two timed event structures TS_1 and TS_2 are path-$\mathcal{TP}_L^0$-bisimilar then they are *tp*-equivalent. Suppose that $\mathcal{R}$ is a path-$\mathcal{TP}_L^0$-bisimulation between $TS_1 = (E_1, \leq_1, \#_1, l_1, Eot_1, Lot_1)$ and $TS_2 = (E_2, \leq_2, \#_2, l_2, Eot_2, Lot_2)$. We only prove that $L_{tp}(TS_1) \subseteq L_{tp}(TS_2)$ (the proof of the reverse inclusion is similar). Take an arbitrary $TP = (E_{TP}, \leq_{TP}, l_{TP}, Eot_{TP}) \in L_{tp}(TS_1)$. This implies that TP is an augment of $TS_1 \lceil TC_1$ for some $TC_1 = (C_1, T_1) \in \mathcal{TC}(TS_1)$. Hence, there is a bijection $p_1 : E_{TP} \to C_1$ such that $e \leq_{TP} e'$ if $p_1(e) \leq_1 p_1(e')$, $l_{TP}(e) = l_1(p_1(e))$, $Eot_{TP}(e) = T_1(p_1(e))$, for all $e, e' \in E_{TP}$. Obviously, p_1 is a morphism from TP to TS_1 of the category $\mathcal{CTS}_L$. Let $i_1 : \mathcal{O} \to TS_1$ and $i_2 : \mathcal{O} \to TS_2$ be the initial paths. Clearly, $(i_1, i_2) \in \mathcal{R}$ and there is a morphism $m : \mathcal{O} \to TP$ in $\mathcal{TP}_L^0$ such that $p_1 \circ m = i_1$. Due to $\mathcal{R}$ being a path-$\mathcal{TP}_L^0$-bisimulation there exists $p_2 : TP \to TS_2$ such that $(p_1, p_2) \in \mathcal{R}$ and $p_2 \circ m = i_2$. Define TC as a pair (E_{TP}, Eot_{TP}). Since the timed pomset TP is a timed event structure with a valid timing, TC is a timed configuration of TP. According to p_2 being a morphism of $\mathcal{CTS}_L$, we have $p_2(TC) \in \mathcal{TC}(TS_2)$ and TP is an augment of $TS_2 \lceil p_2(TC)$. Hence, $TP \in L_{tp}(TS_2)$.

(ii) We first prove the "if" part (i.e. *thp*-bisimulation implies path-$\mathcal{TP}_L$-bisimilarity). Let $\mathcal{B}$ be a *thp*-bisimulation between timed event structures TS_1 and TS_2. For a triple $(TC_1, f, TC_2) \in \mathcal{B}$, specify morphisms $p_1^f : TS_1 \lceil TC_1 \to TS_1$ and $p_2^f : TS_2 \lceil TC_2 \to TS_2$ as the inclusions. Define a relation $\mathcal{R} = \{(p_1^f \circ m, p_2^f \circ f \circ m) \mid m : TP \to TS_1 \lceil TC_1$ is a morphism of $\mathcal{TP}_L$ and $(TC_1, f, TC_2) \in \mathcal{B}\}$. The properties of the relation $\mathcal{R}$, required of path-$\mathcal{TP}_L$-bisimulation, are inherited from those of $\mathcal{B}$.

We now prove the "only if" part, i.e. path-$\mathcal{TP}_L$-bisimilarity implies *thp*-bisimulation. Assume that $\mathcal{R}$ is a path-$\mathcal{TP}_L$-bisimulation between TS_1 and TS_2. Let $TP = (E_{TP}, \leq_{TP}, l_{TP}, Eot_{TP})$ be a timed pomset from $\mathcal{TPom}_L$ and let $TC = (E_{TP}, Eot_{TP})$. It is easy to see that TC is a timed configuration of TP, because the timed pomset TP has a valid timing. For a path $p_i : TP \to TS_i$ $(i = 1, 2)$, let TC^{p_i} denote the timed configuration $p_i(TC)$ of TS_i. Define a relation $\mathcal{B}$ as the set $\{(TS_1 \lceil TC^{p_1}, p_2 \circ p_1^{-1}, TS_2 \lceil TC^{p_2}) \mid (p_1, p_2) \in \mathcal{R}$, for all $i = 1, 2$ $p_i : TP \to TS_i$ is an isomorphism between TP and $TS_i \lceil TC^{p_i}\}$. Since $\mathcal{R}$ is a path-$\mathcal{TP}_L$-bisimulation, it is easy to check that for all $(p_1, p_2) \in \mathcal{R}$ p_1 is an isomorphism between TP and $TS_1 \lceil TC^{p_1}$ iff p_2 is an isomorphism between TP and $TS_2 \lceil TC^{p_2}$. Hence, the relation $\mathcal{B}$ inherits the properties required by the definition of *thp*-bisimulation from those of $\mathcal{R}$.

(iii) Due to Theorem 1(ii) *thhp*-bisimulation and $\mathcal{TP}_L$-bisimilarity coincide. According to Lemma 16 [6], $\mathcal{TP}_L$-bisimilarity implies strong path-$\mathcal{TP}_L$-bisimilarity. The proof of that strong path-$\mathcal{TP}_L$-bisimilarity implies *thhp*-bisimulation is similar to the proof of the "only if" part of item (ii). $\Diamond$

Example 4. First, consider the non-*tp*-equivalent timed event structures TS^1 and TS^2 from Example 2. According to Theorem 3, they are non-path-$\mathcal{TP}_L$-bisimilar. Hence, there exists a path-$\mathcal{TP}_L^0$-assertion which distinguishes TS^1 and TS^2, by Theorem 2. Really, the initial path $p_2^0 : \mathcal{O} \to TS^2$ satisfies the path-$\mathcal{TP}_L^0$-assertion $\langle m \rangle \bigwedge_{j \in J = \emptyset}$, where $m : \mathcal{O} \to a[1,1]$; $c[2,2]$ is a morphism of $\mathcal{TP}_L^0$, but the initial path $p_1^0 : \mathcal{O} \to TS^1$ does not.

Second, contemplate the timed event structures TS^2 and TS^3 from Example 2. Due to Example 3, TS^2 and TS^3 are non-thp-bisimilar. Hence, they are non-path-$\mathcal{TP}_L$-bisimilar, by Theorem 3. Then, there exists a path-$\mathcal{TP}_L$-assertion without backwards modalities, which distinguishes these timed event structures, according to Theorem 2. Let us verify the fact. Contemplate the following morphisms of $\mathcal{TP}_L$: $\mu_0 : \mathcal{O} \to a[1,1]$, $\mu_1 : a[1,1] \to a[1,1]$; $b[1,1]$, and $\mu_2 : a[1,1] \to a[1,1]$; $c[1,1]$. It is clear that the initial path $p_3^0 : \mathcal{O} \to TS^3$ satisfies the path-$\mathcal{TP}_L$-assertion $\langle \mu_0 \rangle \left[(\langle \mu_1 \rangle \bigwedge_{j \in J = \emptyset}) \bigwedge (\langle \mu_2 \rangle \bigwedge_{j \in J = \emptyset}) \right]$ but the initial path $p_2^0 : \mathcal{O} \to TS^2$ does not.

Finally, deal with the non-$thhp$-bisimilar timed event structures TS^4 and TS^5 from Example 3. Due to Theorem 3, they are non-strong path-$\mathcal{TP}_L$-bisimilar. This implies the existence of a path-$\mathcal{TP}_L$-assertion with backwards modalities which discriminates TS^4 and TS^5, by Theorem 2. Check the statement. Consider the following morphisms of $\mathcal{TP}_L$: $m_0 : \mathcal{O} \to a[1,1] \parallel b[1,1]$, $m_1 : a[1,1] \to a[1,1] \parallel b[1,1]$, $m_2 : b[1,1] \to a[1,1] \parallel b[1,1]$, $m_3 : a[1,1] \to a[1,1] \parallel c[1,1]$, and $m_4 : b[1,1] \to b[1,1] \parallel c[1,1]$. It is easy to see that the initial path $p_5^0 : \mathcal{O} \to TS^5$ satisfies the path-$\mathcal{TP}_L$-assertion $\langle m_0 \rangle \left[(\overline{\langle m_1 \rangle} \neg \langle m_3 \rangle \bigwedge_{j \in J = \emptyset}) \bigwedge (\overline{\langle m_2 \rangle} \neg \langle m_4 \rangle \bigwedge_{j \in J = \emptyset}) \right]$ but the initial path $p_4^0 : \mathcal{O} \to TS^4$ does not.

References

1. Boudol, G., Castellani, I.: Concurrency and atomicity. Theoretical Computer Science 59, 25–84 (1989)
2. Cattani, G.L., Sassone, V.: Higher dimentional transition systems. In: 11th Annual IEEE Symp. on Logic in Computer Science, pp. 55–62. IEEE Comp. Soc. Press, Washington (1996)
3. Gribovskaya, N.S., Virbitskaite, I.B.: Timed Delay Bisimulation is an Equivalence Relation for Timed Transition Systems. Fundamenta Informaticae 93(1-3), 127–142 (2009)
4. Hune, T., Nielsen, M.: Bisimulation and open maps for timed transition systems. Fundamenta Informaticae 38, 61–77 (1999)
5. Joyal, A., Moerdijk, I.: A completeness theorem for open maps. Annual Pure Applied Logic 70, 51–86 (1997)
6. Joyal, A., Nielsen, M., Winskel, G.: Bisimulation from open maps. Information and Computation 127(2), 164–185 (1996)
7. Katoen, J.-P., Langerak, R., Latella, D., Brinksma, E.: On Specifying Real-time Systems in a Causality-based Setting. In: Jonsson, B., Parrow, J. (eds.) FTRTFT 1996. LNCS, vol. 1135, pp. 385–404. Springer, Heidelberg (1996)
8. Nielsen, M., Cheng, A.: Observing Behaviour Categorically. In: Thiagarajan, P.S. (ed.) FSTTCS 1995. LNCS, vol. 1026, pp. 263–278. Springer, Heidelberg (1995)
9. Oshevskaya, E.S.: Open Maps Bisimulations for Higher Dimensional Automata Models. In: Kutyłowski, M., Charatonik, W., Gębala, M. (eds.) FCT 2009. LNCS, vol. 5699, pp. 274–286. Springer, Heidelberg (2009)
10. Virbitskaite, I.B., Gribovskaya, N.S.: Open maps and observational equivalences for timed partial order models. Fundamenta Informaticae 60(1-4), 383–399 (2004)

11. Virbitskaite, I.B., Gribovskaya, N.S., Best, E.: A Categorical View of Timed Behaviours. Fundamenta Informaticae 102(1), 129–143 (2010)
12. Winskel, G.: An Introduction to Event Structures. In: de Bakker, J.W., de Roever, W.-P., Rozenberg, G. (eds.) Linear Time, Branching Time and Partial Order in Logics and Models for Concurrency, School/Workshop. LNCS, vol. 354, pp. 364–397. Springer, Heidelberg (1989)

Proving the Correctness of Unfold/Fold Program Transformations Using Bisimulation

Geoff W. Hamilton[1] and Neil D. Jones[2]

[1] School of Computing, Dublin City University,
Dublin 9, Ireland
`hamilton@computing.dcu.ie`
[2] Computer Science Department, University of Copenhagen,
2100 Copenhagen, Denmark
`neil@diku.dk`

Abstract. This paper shows that a bisimulation approach can be used to prove the correctness of unfold/fold program transformation algorithms. As an illustration, we show how our approach can be use to prove the correctness of positive supercompilation (due to Sørensen et al). Traditional program equivalence proofs show the original and transformed programs are contextually equivalent, i.e., have the same termination behaviour in all closed contexts. Contextual equivalence can, however, be difficult to establish directly.

Gordon and Howe use an alternative approach: to represent a program's behaviour by a labelled transition system whose bisimilarity relation is a congruence that coincides with contextual equivalence. Labelled transition systems are well-suited to represent global program behaviour.

On the other hand, unfold/fold program transformations use generalization and folding, and neither is easy to describe contextually, due to use of non-local information. We show that weak bisimulation on labelled transition systems gives an elegant framework to prove contextual equivalence of original and transformed programs. One reason is that folds can be seen in the context of corresponding unfolds.

1 Introduction

Unfold/fold program transformation techniques were first presented by Burstall and Darlington [3], and are used in many program transformation systems such as partial evaluation [9], deforestation [18] and supercompilation [17,16]. Each of these program transformations apply (in some order) a sequence of meaning preserving rules, so the problem of proving that the transformations produce equivalent programs would appear to be trivial, but this is greatly complicated by the presence of folding. As a simple example: if function f is defined by $f = e$, then occurrences of the expression e can be replaced by calls to the function f in a folding step. However, if the occurrence of the expression e in this definition itself is folded, we obtain the non-terminating definition $f = f$. Thus unsupervised application of folding in any context may produce a program that is not equivalent to the original.

E. Clarke, I. Virbitskaite, and A. Voronkov (Eds.): PSI 2011, LNCS 7162, pp. 153–169, 2012.

To avoid this problem we express transformation by semantics-preserving manipulation of labelled transition systems. Within our framework, folding is only done with respect to proper ancestors in the transition system, thus avoiding the problem of folding $f = e$ into $f = f$. We eliminate intermediate data or function calls by removing silent transitions ($\xrightarrow{\tau}$) from the labelled transition system. We therefore use weak bisimulation for correctness proofs, based on a theorem that weak bisimulation is equivalent to contextual equivalence. This approach makes it easier to prove the correctness of unfold/fold transformations, as folds are seen in the context of corresponding unfolds. Further, correctness is decoupled from efficiency concerns, in contrast to Sands' theory of local improvement [14].

Plan: In Section 2 we define our higher-order functional language, and define a reduction semantics and contextual equivalence. In Section 3 we define labelled transition systems in general; a particular one for semantic analysis; and show that its weak bisimulation relation is equivalent to contextual equivalence. In Section 4 we use this framework to describe the positive supercompilation algorithm and show that it satisfies the correctness property. This requires an extended form of labelled transition system, one also equipped with fold transitions that rename program variables. In Section 5 we discuss related work and conclude. Appendices A, B and C define our own particular instances of homeomorphic embedding, expression generalization, and residualization which are used to define positive supercompilation within our framework.

2   Language

Definition 1 (Language Syntax). The simple higher-order functional language as shown in Fig. 1 is used throughout this paper.

A program in the language is an expression, which can be a variable, constructor application, function call, λ-abstraction, **case**, or **where**. Local functions are defined using **where**; it is assumed that these local definitions cannot contain any free variables. λ-abstracted variables and **case** expression pattern variables are *bound*; all other variables are *free*. We use $fv(e)$ and $bv(e)$ to denote the free

$$
\begin{array}{lll}
e ::= & x & \text{Variable} \\
& |\ c\ e_1 \ldots e_k & \text{Constructor Application} \\
& |\ f & \text{Function Call} \\
& |\ \lambda x.e & \lambda\text{-Abstraction} \\
& |\ e_0\ e_1 & \text{Application} \\
& |\ \textbf{case}\ e_0\ \textbf{of}\ p_1 \Rightarrow e_1\ |\cdots|\ p_k \Rightarrow e_k & \text{Case Expression} \\
& |\ e_0\ \textbf{where}\ f_1 = e_1 \ldots f_n = e_n & \text{Local Function Definition} \\
\\
p ::= & c\ x_1 \ldots x_k & \text{Pattern}
\end{array}
$$

Fig. 1. Language Grammar

and bound variables respectively of expression e. We write $e_1 \equiv e_2$ if e_1 and e_2 differ only in the names of bound variables. We also write $e_1 \equiv e_2$ (MVR) if e_1 and e_2 are equivalent modulo variable renaming.

Each constructor has a fixed arity; for example Nil has arity 0 and $Cons$ has arity 2. In an expression $c\ e_1 \ldots e_k$, k must equal the arity of c. Within the expression **case** e_0 **of** $p_1 \Rightarrow e_1 \mid \cdots \mid p_k \Rightarrow e_k$, e_0 is called the *selector*, and $e_1 \ldots e_k$ are called the *branches*. The patterns in **case** expressions may not be nested. No variable may appear more than once within a pattern. We assume that the patterns in a **case** expression are non-overlapping and exhaustive.

Function environment Δ. Without loss of generality, we can assume that a program contains only one **where** clause, at the outermost level. For notational convenience we sometimes assume these have been collected into a function environment, denoted by $\Delta = \{f_1 = e_1, \ldots, f_n = e_n\}$.

Example 1. An example program to calculate the sum of the squares of a list of numbers xs is shown in Fig. 2. We employ the usual notation $[]$ for Nil and $x : xs$ for $Cons\ x\ xs$. The functions *plus* and *square* in this program are assumed to be defined in an initial program environment.

$$
\begin{array}{ll}
sum\ (squares\ xs) \\
\textbf{where} \\
sum\ \ \ = \lambda xs.sum'\ xs\ Zero \\
sum'\ \ = \lambda xs.\lambda a.\,\textbf{case}\ xs\ \textbf{of} \\
\qquad\qquad\quad [] \qquad \Rightarrow a \\
\qquad\qquad\mid x' : xs' \Rightarrow sum'\ xs'\ (plus\ a\ x') \\
squares = \lambda xs.\,\textbf{case}\ xs\ \textbf{of} \\
\qquad\qquad\quad [] \qquad \Rightarrow [] \\
\qquad\qquad\mid x' : xs' \Rightarrow (square\ x') : (squares\ xs')
\end{array}
$$

Fig. 2. Example Program: Sum of Squares

The operational semantics of the language is normal order reduction. Erroneous terms such as $(c\ e_1 \ldots e_k)\ e$ and **case** $(\lambda x.e)$ **of** $p_1 \Rightarrow e_1 \mid \cdots \mid p_k \Rightarrow e_k$ are assumed not to occur.

Definition 2 (Substitution). We use the notation $\{x_1 := e_1, \ldots, x_n := e_n\}$ to denote a *substitution*. If e is an expression, then $e\{x_1 := e_1, \ldots, x_n := e_n\}$ is the result of simultaneously substituting the expressions $e_1, \ldots, e_n$ for the corresponding variables $x_1, \ldots, x_n$, respectively, in the expression e while ensuring that bound variables are renamed appropriately to avoid name capture.

Definition 3 (Context). A context C is an expression with a "hole" $[]$ in the place of one sub-expression (though not within a **where** clause). $C[e]$ is the expression obtained by replacing the hole in context C with the expression e. The free variables within e may become bound within $C[e]$; if $C[e]$ is closed then we call it a *closing context* for e.

The call-by-name operational semantics of our language is standard: define an evaluation relation $\Downarrow$ between closed expressions and *values*, where values are expressions in *weak head normal form* (i.e. constructor applications or λ-abstractions). We define a one-step reduction relation $\overset{r}{\rightsquigarrow}$ inductively as shown in Fig. 3, where the reduction r can be β (β-substitution), $=f$ (unfolding of function f) or κ (constructor elimination). We assume that the function definitions which are currently in scope are held in the environment Δ.

$$\frac{(f = e) \in \Delta}{f \overset{=f}{\rightsquigarrow} e} \qquad\qquad ((\lambda x.e_0)\ e_1) \overset{\beta}{\rightsquigarrow} (e_0\{x := e_1\}) \qquad\qquad \frac{e_0 \overset{r}{\rightsquigarrow} e_0'}{(e_0\ e_1) \overset{r}{\rightsquigarrow} (e_0'\ e_1)}$$

$$\frac{p_i = c\ x_1 \ldots x_n}{(\textbf{case } (c\ e_1 \ldots e_n)\textbf{ of } p_1 : e_1' | \ldots | p_k : e_k') \overset{\kappa}{\rightsquigarrow} (e_i\{x_1 := e_1, \ldots, x_n := e_n\})}$$

$$\frac{e_0 \overset{r}{\rightsquigarrow} e_0'}{(\textbf{case } e_0 \textbf{ of } p_1 : e_1 | \ldots p_k : e_k) \overset{r}{\rightsquigarrow} (\textbf{case } e_0' \textbf{ of } p_1 : e_1 | \ldots p_k : e_k)}$$

Fig. 3. One-Step Reduction Relation

We use the notation $e \overset{r}{\rightsquigarrow}$ if the expression e reduces, $e \Uparrow$ if e diverges, $e \Downarrow$ if e converges and $e \Downarrow v$ if e evaluates to the value v. These are defined as follows, where $\overset{r}{\rightsquigarrow}^*$ denotes the reflexive transitive closure of $\overset{r}{\rightsquigarrow}$:

$$e \overset{r}{\rightsquigarrow}, \text{ iff } \exists e'.e \overset{r}{\rightsquigarrow} e' \qquad\qquad e \Downarrow, \text{ iff } \exists v.e \Downarrow v$$
$$e \Downarrow v, \text{ iff } e \overset{r}{\rightsquigarrow}^* v \wedge \neg(v \overset{r}{\rightsquigarrow}) \qquad\qquad e \Uparrow, \text{ iff } \forall e'.e \overset{r}{\rightsquigarrow}^* e' \Rightarrow e' \overset{r}{\rightsquigarrow}$$

Definition 4 (Contextual Equivalence). Contextual equivalence, denoted by $\simeq$, equates two expressions if and only if they exhibit the same termination behaviour in all closing contexts i.e. $e_1 \simeq e_2$ iff $\forall C$. $C[e_1] \Downarrow$ iff $C[e_2] \Downarrow$.

3   Bisimulation

We first give standard definitions of *labelled transition system* and *weak bisimulation*, and then show how they can be used to describe runtime states of a functional program.

Definition 5 (Labelled Transition System). A labelled transition system (LTS for short) is a tuple $\Sigma = (\mathcal{S}, s_{init}, \delta, Act)$ where:

- $\mathcal{S}$ is the set of *states*.
- $s_{init} \in \mathcal{S}$ is the start state.
- the set of *actions* $\alpha \in Act$ include the *silent transition* τ.
- *transition relation* $\delta \subseteq \mathcal{S} \times Act \times \mathcal{S}$ relates pairs of states by actions.
- Notation: as usual, write $s \xrightarrow{\alpha} s'$ in place of $(s, \alpha, s') \in \delta$. We denote the set of *all* non-silent transitions from state s by $s \to (\alpha_1, s_1) \ldots (\alpha_n, s_n)$ (a simpler notation than the multilevel $\{s \xrightarrow{\alpha_1} s_1, \ldots, s \xrightarrow{\alpha_n} s_n\}$ or highly-parenthesized $\{(s, \alpha_1, s_1), \ldots, (s, \alpha_n, s_n))\}$.)

We write $s \Rightarrow s'$ iff there is a (possibly empty) sequence of silent transitions leading from s to s'. For each action α, we write $s_1 \xRightarrow{\alpha} s_2$ iff there are s'_1 and s'_2 such that $s_1 \Rightarrow s'_1 \xrightarrow{\alpha} s'_2 \Rightarrow s_2$.

Definition 6 (Weak Simulation). A binary relation $\mathcal{R} \subseteq \mathcal{S}_1 \times \mathcal{S}_2$ is a *weak simulation* of labelled transition system $\Sigma_1 = (\mathcal{S}_1, s_{init_1}, \delta_1, Act_1)$ by $\Sigma_2 = (\mathcal{S}_2, s_{init_2}, \delta_2, Act_2)$ if $(s_{init_1}, s_{init_2}) \in \mathcal{R}$, and for every pair $(s_1, s_2) \in \mathcal{R}$:

$$\forall \alpha \in Act_1, s'_1 \in \mathcal{S}_1. \text{ if } (s_1 \xRightarrow{\alpha} s'_1) \in \delta_1 \text{ then } \exists s'_2 \in \mathcal{S}_2 \, . \, (s_2 \xRightarrow{\alpha} s'_2) \in \delta_2 \wedge (s'_1, s'_2) \in \mathcal{R}$$

Definition 7 (Weak Bisimulation). A *weak bisimulation* is a binary relation $\mathcal{R}$, where both $\mathcal{R}$ and its inverse $\mathcal{R}^{-1}$ are weak simulations.

Definition 8 (Weak Bisimilarity). If there exists any weak bisimulation $\mathcal{R}$ between labelled transition systems Σ_1 and Σ_2, then there exists a unique maximal one, henceforth denoted by $\sim$. A notation: we also write $s_1 \sim s_2$ in place of $(s_1, s_2) \in \sim$.

In the spirit of Gordon [5] we now define a particular labelled transition system that characterises the immediate observations that can be made on expressions to determine their observational equivalence. We extend [5] by allowing free variables in expressions and thus also in actions. Observational equivalence will therefore require that the free variables in actions match up (bound variables must also match up, but this can be done by renaming).

Definition 9 (Driven LTS). Fig. 4 defines $\mathcal{D}[\![e]\!] = (\mathcal{S}, e_0, \to, Act_e)$ to be the *driven LTS* associated with program e_0. Here,

- Act_e is a set of actions with possible forms: v, c, @, λv, #i, **case**, p and τ.

  An action may be: x, a variable; c, a constructor; @, a function application; #i, the ith argument in an application; λx, an abstraction over variable x; **case**, a case selector; or p, a case branch pattern. Bound variables may have been renamed to avoid name clashes.

- $\mathcal{S} \subseteq (Exp \cup \{\mathbf{0}\})$ and $\to \subseteq Exp \times Act_e \times (Exp \cup \{\mathbf{0}\})$ are the smallest sets such that $e_0 \in \mathcal{S}$ and $\to$ satisfies Fig. 4. (Note that $e \xrightarrow{\alpha} e'$ means $(e, \alpha, e') \in \to$. When convenient we use the compact transition notation of Definition 5.)

1. Root and branch growth: $e_0 \in \mathcal{S}$. If $e \in \mathcal{S}$ and $e \xrightarrow{\alpha} e'$ then $e' \in \mathcal{S}$.

2. Functions: If $f \in \mathcal{S}$ and $(f = e) \in \Delta$ then $f \xrightarrow{\tau} e$

3. Applications:
   (a) If $e = x \, e_1 \ldots e_n \in \mathcal{S}$ then $e \to (x, \mathbf{0})(\#1, e_1) \ldots (\#n, e_n)$
   (b) If $e = c \, e_1 \ldots e_n \in \mathcal{S}$ then $e \to (c, \mathbf{0})(\#1, e_1) \ldots (\#n, e_n)$
   (c) If $e = (\lambda x.e_0) \, e_1 \in \mathcal{S}$ then $e \xrightarrow{\tau} e_0\{x := e_1\}$
   (d) If $e = e_0 \, e_1 \in \mathcal{S}$ and $e_0 \to (\mathbf{case}, e_0')(p_1', e_1') \ldots (p_n', e_n')$ then
       $e \to (\mathbf{case}, e_0')(p_1', e_1' \, e_1) \ldots (p_n', e_n' \, e_1)$
   (e) Otherwise, if $e = e_0 \, e_1 \in \mathcal{S}$ and $e_0 \xrightarrow{\tau} e_0'$ then $e_0 \, e_1 \xrightarrow{\tau} e_0' \, e_1$

4. **case**: If $\mathcal{S} \ni e = (\mathbf{case} \, e_0 \, \mathbf{of} \, p_1 \Rightarrow e_1' \mid \cdots \mid p_k \Rightarrow e_k')$ then

   (a) If $e_0 = x \, e_1 \ldots e_n$ and $e_i' = e_i''\{x' := e_0\}$ then
       $$e \to (\mathbf{case}, e_0)(p_1, e_1''\{x' := p_1\}) \ldots (p_k, e_k''\{x' := p_k\})$$
   (b) If $e_0 = c \, e_1 \ldots e_n$ and $p_i = c \, x_1 \ldots x_n$ then $e \xrightarrow{\tau} e_i'\{x_1 := e_1, \ldots, x_n := e_n\}$
   (c) If $e_0 \to (\mathbf{case}, e_0')(p_1', e_1') \ldots (p_n', e_n')$ then
       $$e \to (\mathbf{case}, e_0')(p_1', \mathbf{case} \, e_1' \, \mathbf{of} \, p_1 \Rightarrow e_1 \mid \ldots \mid p_k \Rightarrow e_k)$$
       $$\ldots (p_n', \mathbf{case} \, e_n' \, \mathbf{of} \, p_1 \Rightarrow e_1 \mid \ldots \mid p_k \Rightarrow e_k)$$
   (d) Otherwise, if $e_0 \xrightarrow{\tau} e_0'$ then $e \xrightarrow{\tau} (\mathbf{case} \, e_0' \, \mathbf{of} \, p_1 \Rightarrow e_1' \mid \cdots \mid p_k \Rightarrow e_k')$

5. λ-abstraction: If $\lambda x.e \in \mathcal{S}$ then $\lambda x.e \xrightarrow{\lambda x} e$

Fig. 4. The Driven Labelled Transition System $\mathcal{D}[\![e]\!]$

$\mathbf{0}$ corresponds to a state from which there are no transitions; transitions labelled with a variable or a constructor will lead into this state.

Note on rules 2, 3c, 4b: function unfolding, β-reduction and constructor elimination are not relevant to the observational equivalence of original and transformed programs. Thus they are represented by the silent transition τ, and weak bisimulation is appropriate for comparing program behaviour. All function applications are removed by driving, so no @ actions will appear in the driven LTS; these actions are only introduced as a result of generalization, described later.

Example 2. A portion of the driven LTS $\mathcal{D}[\![e]\!]$ constructed for the program in Fig. 2 is shown in Fig. 5. Functions *plus* and *square* are treated as free variables.

A central property: the weak bisimilarity relation $\sim$ between $\mathcal{D}[\![e]\!]$ and $\mathcal{D}[\![e']\!]$ is a congruence, and coincides with contextual equivalence.

Theorem 1 (Congruence). $\forall C \, . \, e \sim e' \Rightarrow C[e] \sim C[e']$

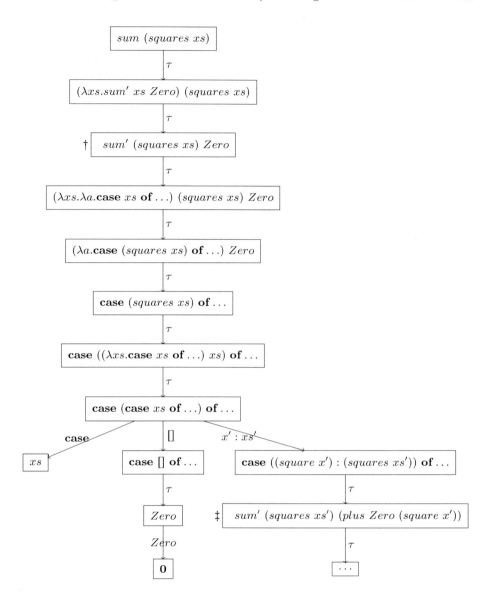

Fig. 5. Portion of the infinite LTS $\mathcal{D}[\![e]\!]$ resulting from Driving $sum\ (squares\ xs)$

Proof. Similar to that of Howe [8]; not given here due to space constraints.

Theorem 2 (Operational Extensionality). $\simeq\ =\ \sim$

Proof. The proof that $\sim\ \subseteq\ \simeq$ follows from the congruence of $\sim$. The reverse inclusion follows by co-induction after showing that $\simeq$ is a bisimulation on $\mathcal{D}[\![e]\!]$.

4   Positive Supercompilation

The positive supercompilation algorithm computes $\mathcal{T}[\![e]\!] = \mathcal{F}[\![\mathcal{G}[\![\mathcal{D}[\![e]\!]]\!]]\!]$. We show correctness of the more powerful distillation algorithm [6] in a future paper.

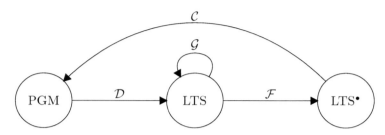

Given a program $e \in \text{PGM}$, the driving rules $\mathcal{D}$ of **Fig.** 4 are applied, beginning with the root e, to construct the labelled transition system $\mathcal{D}[\![e]\!]$. Although $\mathcal{D}[\![e]\!]$ can be infinite in general, our unfold/fold program transformer will traverse only finite portions by working lazily from the root. If a *danger of infinite unfolding* is detected ("the whistle is blown"), then generalization rules $\mathcal{G}$ are applied to transform the current labelled transition system into a new version without local danger of infinite unfolding. Overall, the effect is to transform $\mathcal{D}[\![e]\!]$ into an LTS $\mathcal{G}[\![\mathcal{D}[\![e]\!]]\!]$ that has only *a finite number of different expressions on any path* from its root (MVR, i.e., modulo variable renaming).

Finally, folding rules $\mathcal{F}$ are applied to this generalized LTS to produce a *folded labelled transition system* (a so-called LTS•) that contains *only a finite number of states*. A residual program can be constructed from this finite folded labelled transition system using the $\mathcal{C}$ rules defined in Section C. Its syntax and efficiency may be substantially different from those of the original program.

4.1   Generalization

A suitable *homeomorphic embedding* relation $\lesssim$ is defined in Appendix A, analogous to Sørensen's [16] but adapted to our language. Its essential property:

Lemma 1. *There exists a computable partial order $\lesssim$ on Exp such that in any infinite sequence of expressions $e_0, e_1, \ldots$ there exists some $i < j$ where $e_i \lesssim e_j$.*

By Lemma 1, if the set of paths from the root of $\mathcal{D}[\![e]\!]$ is infinite, an instance of homeomorphic embedding will occur, and can be computably detected while constructing $\mathcal{D}[\![e]\!]$. Generalization is performed while traversing $\mathcal{D}[\![e]\!]$ from its root. If "the whistle blows," a state that is a homeomorphic embedding of one of its ancestors will be generalized.

The first transformation step is to build from $\mathcal{D}[\![e]\!]$ a computationally equivalent new LTS with generalizations added by the insertion of @ transitions, representing the application of a generalized expression to the sub-terms which have been extracted from it. This generalization is sufficient to ensure that the only homeomorphic embeddings that remain are also renamings. Generalization by the insertion of @ transitions is performed by the *abstract* operation, defined in Appendix B. Adequacy is expressed by the following result:

Lemma 2 (Abstraction Lemma). *If* $e' \lesssim e$ *and* $e' \not\equiv e$ *(MVR), then there exists an expression* $e'' = abstract(e, e') = (\lambda x_1 \ldots x_n.e_0) \, e_1 \ldots e_n$ *such that* $e'' \overset{\beta}{\rightsquigarrow} e$ *and, for* $i = 0, 1, \ldots, n$, $e \not\lesssim e_i$.

This is equivalent to replacing e by **let** $x_1 = e_1, \ldots, x_n = e_n$ **in** e_0 (an idea from Turchin [17]). The node e in the LTS is therefore replaced by the following:

$$e'' \rightarrow (@, \lambda x_1 \ldots x_n.e_0)(\#1, e_1) \ldots (\#n, e_n)$$

Such generalized expressions are not further reduced by driving; driving is applied only to their sub-expressions e_i. Replacements (such as e by e'') are repeated until the LTS converges to a version in which the only homeomorphic embeddings along any path from the root of $\mathcal{D}[\![e']\!]$ are also renamings. This process terminates since each e_i is smaller than e. By König's Lemma, once it does terminate, the resulting LTS will have a finite set of nodes.

We will prove Lemma 1 and Lemma 2 in Appendices A and B, so these transformations are correct within the bisimulation framework.

Example 3. We generalize the labelled transition system in Fig. 5. Consider

$$e_\dagger = sum' \, (squares \, xs) \, Zero$$

(the expression at node †). Now $e_\dagger$ is homeomorphically embedded in expression

$$e_\ddagger = sum' \, (squares \, xs') \, (plus \, Zero \, (square \, x'))$$

at node ‡, i.e., $e_\dagger \lesssim e_\ddagger$. Thus we generalize $e_\ddagger$ with respect to $e_\dagger$ to give:

$$e'' = (\lambda v.sum' \, (squares \, xs') \, v) \, (plus \, Zero \, (square \, x'))$$

Edges $e'' \rightarrow (@, \lambda v.sum' \, (squares \, xs') \, v)(\#1, plus \, Zero \, (square \, x'))$ are added; and these subexpression are then further driven and generalized. The portion of the resulting LTS rooted at e'' is shown in Fig. 6.

Definition 10 (Generalization Algorithm). *Here* e, s *range over expressions.*

$$\mathcal{G}[\![e]\!] = \mathcal{G}'[\![e]\!]\{\}$$

If $e \overset{\tau}{\rightarrow} e'$ then

$$\mathcal{G}'[\![e]\!] \, \rho = \begin{cases} e \overset{\tau}{\rightarrow} e', & \text{if } \exists e'' \in \rho \, . \, e'' \equiv e \text{ (MVR)} \\[2mm] (e_0 \, e_1 \ldots e_n) \rightarrow (@, e_0')(\#1, e_1') \ldots (\#n, e_n'), \text{ if } \exists e'' \in \rho \, . \, e'' \lesssim e \\ \text{where } e_0 \, e_1 \ldots e_n = abstract(e, e'') \\ \quad \forall i \in \{0 \ldots n\} \, . \, e_i' = \mathcal{G}'[\![\mathcal{D}[\![e_i]\!]]\!] \, \rho \\[2mm] e \overset{\tau}{\rightarrow} \mathcal{G}'[\![e']\!] \, (\rho \cup \{e\}), & \text{otherwise} \end{cases}$$

If $e \rightarrow (\alpha_1, e_1) \ldots (\alpha_n, e_n)$ then
$$\mathcal{G}'[\![e]\!] \, \rho = e \rightarrow (\alpha_1, \mathcal{G}'[\![e_1]\!] \, \rho) \ldots (\alpha_n, \mathcal{G}'[\![e_n]\!] \, \rho)$$

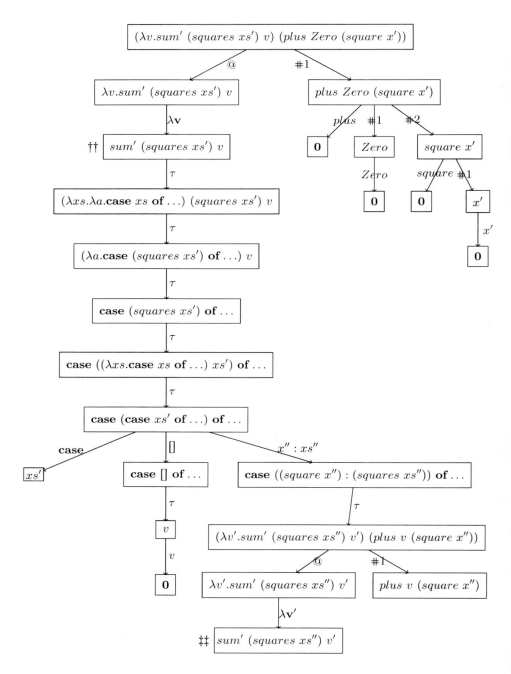

Fig. 6. Portion of LTS $\mathcal{G}[\![\mathcal{D}[\![e]\!]]\!]$ resulting from Generalizing $\mathcal{D}[\![e]\!]$

Style explanation in **Definition** 10:

- $\mathcal{G}, \mathcal{G}'$ each transform a rooted input LTS into a rooted output LTS.
- The algorithm constructs the transitions in the output LTS.
- Starting at the root e of the input LTS, $\mathcal{G}'$ inspects the transitions from e.
- When $\mathcal{G}'$ calls itself recursively, the output LTS includes the union of the output LTS's resulting from the recursive calls.

Content explanation in **Definition** 10:

- Transformation of the labelled transition system $\mathcal{D}[\![e]\!]$ begins at the root e.
- The set ρ is always a "history": the set of expressions from which silent transitions have been taken since traversing the root.
- To start, $\mathcal{G}[\![e]\!]$ calls $\mathcal{G}'[\![e]\!]$ with an empty history.
- For any expression e from which a silent transition issues:

  - $\mathcal{G}$ terminates if the source expression has already been seen (MVR)
  - if some ancestor e' is embedded in e then generalization is done; and the resulting expression components are driven and generalized further

- otherwise, $\mathcal{G}$ recursively processes all the children of expression e
- It suffices to do the embedding check only at silent transitions, since any infinite transition sequence would contain infinitely many silent transitions.

4.2   Folding

Let $\Sigma = \mathcal{G}[\![\mathcal{D}[\![e]\!]]\!]$ be the labelled transition system resulting from driving and generalization. The next step is to construct a bisimilar LTS $\Sigma^{\bullet}$ that has only a finite number of states in all. (Relatively easy to do, after generalization has done the hard work!) We adapt the classical folding technique to labelled transition systems. First, extend the definition of LTS by allowing *fold transitions* of the form $e \xrightarrow{\theta} e'$. Here e is an expression, e' is one of its ancestors in Σ, and θ is a renaming such that $e \equiv e' \, \theta$.

Definition 11 (Folded LTS). *A folded LTS has form* $\Sigma^{\bullet} = (\mathcal{S}, e_{init}, \rightarrow^{\bullet}, Act^{\bullet})$ *where*

$$Act^{\bullet} = Act_e \cup \{ \, \theta \mid \theta \text{ is a renaming} \, \}$$

A folded transition $e \xrightarrow{\theta} e'$ will generate a call to a residual function in the program output that supercompilation produces, see Appendix C.

4.3   The Folding Transformation

Definition 12 (Folding Algorithm). *This takes Σ into $\Sigma^{\bullet}$. The structure is similar to $\mathcal{G}$ (but simpler). We write $\rightarrow$ for both input and output transitions.*

$$\mathcal{F}[\![e]\!] = \mathcal{F}'[\![e]\!]\{\}$$

If $e \xrightarrow{\tau} e'$ then

$$\mathcal{F}'[\![e]\!] \, \rho = \begin{cases} e \xrightarrow{\theta} e'', & \text{if } \exists e'' \in \rho \, . \, e'' \equiv e \text{ (MVR)} \wedge e'' \equiv e\theta \\ e \xrightarrow{\tau} \mathcal{F}'[\![e']\!] \, (\rho \cup \{e\}), & \text{otherwise} \end{cases}$$

If $e \to (\alpha_1, e_1) \ldots (\alpha_n, e_n)$ then
$$\mathcal{F}'[\![e]\!] \, \rho = e \to (\alpha_1, \mathcal{F}'[\![e_1]\!] \, \rho) \ldots (\alpha_n, \mathcal{F}'[\![e_n]\!] \, \rho)$$

Within these rules, ρ is the set of previously encountered expressions. If an expression is encountered that is a renaming of one of them, then folding is performed. Since any infinite transition sequence has infinitely many silent transitions, the renaming check is only done at silent transitions.

The result of the above steps will be a labelled transition system $\Sigma^\bullet$ with folding. We need to show that the LTS for the original program is equivalent to the labelled transformation system with folding resulting from its transformation. First, a couple of definitions are needed.

Definition 13 (Folded Weak Simulation). Binary relation $\mathcal{R} \subseteq Exp \times Exp$ is a *folded weak simulation* of folded LTS $\Sigma_1 = (Exp, e_{init_1}, \delta_1, Act^\bullet)$ by folded LTS $\Sigma_2 = (Exp, e_{init_2}, \delta_2, Act^\bullet)$ if $(e_{init_1}, e_{init_2}) \in \mathcal{R}$, and for every $(e_1, e_2) \in \mathcal{R}$:
(a) $\forall e_1' \in Exp, \alpha \in Act_e$. if $(e_1 \xrightarrow{\alpha} e_1') \in \delta_1$ then $\exists (e_2 \xRightarrow{\alpha} e_2') \in \delta_2$. $(e_1', e_2') \in \mathcal{R}$
(b) $\forall e_1' \in Exp, \theta$. if $(e_1 \xrightarrow{\theta} e_1') \in \delta_1$ then $(e_1', e_2\theta) \in \mathcal{R}$.

Definition 14 (Folded Weak Bisimulation). A *folded weak bisimulation* is a binary relation $\mathcal{R}$, where both $\mathcal{R}$ and its inverse $\mathcal{R}^{-1}$ are folded weak simulations.

Theorem 3 (Correctness of Folding). *There is a folded weak bisimulation $\mathcal{R}$ between Σ and $\mathcal{F}[\![\Sigma]\!]$.*

Proof. Proof is by induction on length of paths from the roots of Σ and $\mathcal{F}[\![\Sigma]\!]$.

Example 4. Applying the folding pass to the labelled transition system in Fig. 6, the expression at node $\ddagger\ddagger$ is a renaming of the expression at node $\dagger\dagger$. The expression at node $\ddagger\ddagger$ (sum' ($squares$ xs'') v') is therefore folded into node $\dagger\dagger$, with the renaming $\{xs' := xs'', v := v'\}$.

The program of Fig. 7 is constructed from this labelled transition system with folding, using the rules shown in Appendix C.

```
case xs of
    []       ⇒ Zero
  | x' : xs' ⇒ f xs' (plus Zero (square x'))
where
f = λxs'.λv. case xs' of
    []        ⇒ v
  | x'' : xs'' ⇒ f xs'' (plus v (square x''))
```

Fig. 7. Supercompiled Example Program: Sum of Squares

5   Conclusion and Related Work

In this paper, we have described a new approach to proving the correctness of unfold/fold transformations. We have defined a labelled transition system semantics for programs to represent their behaviour and a weak bisimulation relation between these LTSs to show their observational equivalence. We then proved that this weak bisimulation implies contextual equivalence. We argue that this approach makes it easier to prove the correctness of unfold/fold transformations as folds can be seen in the context of corresponding unfolds, and correctness is also decoupled from efficiency concerns.

The seminal work in the area of proving the correctness of unfold/fold program transformations is Sands' theory of *local improvement* [14]. Using this approach, the correctness of program transformations is linked to showing the improvement in efficiency of local transformations. However, this is complicated by the use of folding, which causes a loss of efficiency locally, but not globally if it is always done in conjunction with a corresponding unfold. Also, tying the correctness of transformations to an improvement in efficiency restricts this approach to particular program semantics and transformation techniques.

Bisimilarity has been applied to functional programming languages before, notably by Abramsky in his study of applicative bisimulation and the lazy λ-calculus [1], and by Howe who developed a powerful method for showing that bisimilarity is a congruence [8]. Both showed that their definitions of bisimilarity are equal to contextual equivalence (operational extensionality). A labelled transition system semantics was first defined directly for a functional language by Gordon [5]. This simplified the definition of bisimulation and allowed a lot of the techniques used for process algebras to be applied to functional languages. We have extended Gordon's LTS semantics to incorporate additional language constructs and also to allow terms that contain free variables. Bisimulation has previously been used to prove the correctness of program transformations for imperative languages, which lend themselves more naturally to a labelled transition system semantics [11]. The focus of all the previous work on applying bisimulation techniques to functional programs was not on proving the correctness of program transformations. In this paper, we show how a slight modification to the definition of bisimulation allows it to be applied to the results of unfold/fold program transformations, thus giving us a straightforward technique for proving their correctness.

Acknowledgements. This work was supported, in part, by Science Foundation Ireland grant 03/CE2/I303_1 to Lero - the Irish Software Engineering Research Centre (www.lero.ie), and by the School of Computing, Dublin City University.

References

1. Abramsky, S.: The lazy lambda calculus. In: Research Topics in Functional Programming, pp. 65–116. Addison-Wesley (1990)

2. Bol, R.: Loop Checking in Partial Deduction. Journal of Logic Programming 16(1-2), 25–46 (1993)
3. Burstall, R., Darlington, J.: A transformation system for developing recursive programs. Journal of the ACM 24(1), 44–67 (1977)
4. Dershowitz, N., Jouannaud, J.P.: Rewrite Systems. In: van Leeuwen, J. (ed.) Handbook of Theoretical Computer Science, pp. 243–320. Elsevier, MIT Press (1990)
5. Gordon, A.D.: Bisimilarity as a theory of functional programming. Theoretical Computer Science 228(1-2), 5–47 (1999)
6. Hamilton, G.: Distillation: Extracting the Essence of Programs. In: Proceedings of the ACM SIGPLAN Symposium on Partial Evaluation and Semantics-Based Program Manipulation, pp. 61–70 (2007)
7. Higman, G.: Ordering by Divisibility in Abstract Algebras. Proceedings of the London Mathematical Society 2, 326–336 (1952)
8. Howe, D.J.: Proving congruence of bisimulation in functional programming languages. Information and Computation 124(2), 103–112 (1996)
9. Jones, N., Gomard, C., Sestoft, P.: Partial Evaluation and Automatic Program Generation. Prentice Hall (1993)
10. Kruskal, J.: Well-Quasi Ordering, the Tree Theorem, and Vazsonyi's Conjecture. Transactions of the American Mathematical Society 95, 210–225 (1960)
11. Lacey, D., Jones, N.D., Wyk, E.V., Frederiksen, C.C.: Compiler optimization correctness by temporal logic. Higher-Order and Symbolic Computation 17(3), 173–206 (2004)
12. Leuschel, M.: On the Power of Homeomorphic Embedding for Online Termination. In: Proceedings of the International Static Analysis Symposium, Pisa, Italy, pp. 230–245 (1998)
13. Marlet, R.: Vers une Formalisation de l'Évaluation Partielle. Ph.D. thesis, Université de Nice - Sophia Antipolis (1994)
14. Sands, D.: Proving the Correctness of Recursion-Based Automatic Program Transformations. Theoretical Computer Science 167(1-2), 193–233 (1996)
15. Sørensen, M.H., Glück, R.: An Algorithm of Generalization in Positive Supercompilation. In: Tison, S. (ed.) CAAP 1994. LNCS, vol. 787, pp. 335–351. Springer, Heidelberg (1994)
16. Sørensen, M.H., Glück, R., Jones, N.: A Positive Supercompiler. Journal of Functional Programming 6(6), 811–838 (1996)
17. Turchin, V.: Program Transformation by Supercompilation. In: Ganzinger, H., Jones, N.D. (eds.) Programs as Data Objects. LNCS, vol. 217, pp. 257–281. Springer, Heidelberg (1986)
18. Wadler, P.: Deforestation: Transforming Programs to Eliminate Trees. In: Ganzinger, H. (ed.) ESOP 1988. LNCS, vol. 300, pp. 344–358. Springer, Heidelberg (1988)

A   Homeomorphic Embedding for Supercompilation

Generalization is performed when an expression is encountered that is an *embedding* of a previously encountered one. This is done by *homeomorphic embedding*, which we denote using $\lesssim$. The homeomorphic embedding relation was derived from results by Higman [7] and Kruskal [10] and was defined within term rewriting systems [4] for detecting the possible divergence of the term rewriting process. Variants of this relation have been used to ensure termination within positive supercompilation [15], partial evaluation [13] and partial deduction [2,12].

Definition 15 (Well-Quasi Order). A well-quasi order on a set S is a reflexive, transitive relation $\lesssim$ such that for any infinite sequence $s_1, s_2, \ldots$ of elements from S there are numbers i, j with $i < j$ and $s_i \lesssim s_j$.

This ensures that in any infinite sequence of expressions $e_0, e_1, \ldots$ there definitely exists some $i < j$ where $e_i \lesssim e_j$, so an embedding must eventually be encountered and transformation will not continue indefinitely.

Definition 16 (Embedding of Expressions). To define our homeomorphic embedding relation on expressions $\lesssim$, we first define a relation $\trianglelefteq$, where $e_1 \trianglelefteq e_2$ if all of the free variables within e_1 and e_2 match up and $FV = fv(e_1)$.

$$\frac{e_1 \bowtie e_2}{e_1 \trianglelefteq e_2} \qquad\qquad \frac{e_1 \triangleleft e_2 \quad fv(e_1) \subseteq FV}{e_1 \trianglelefteq e_2}$$

$$v \bowtie v \qquad\qquad\qquad f \bowtie f$$

$$\frac{\forall i \in \{1 \ldots n\}.e_i \trianglelefteq e_i'}{(c\ e_1 \ldots e_n) \bowtie (c\ e_1' \ldots e_n')} \qquad\qquad \frac{\exists i \in \{1 \ldots n\}.e \trianglelefteq e_i}{e \triangleleft (c\ e_1 \ldots e_n)}$$

$$\frac{e \trianglelefteq (e'\{x' := x\})}{\lambda x.e \bowtie \lambda x'.e'} \qquad\qquad \frac{e \trianglelefteq e'}{e \triangleleft \lambda x.e'}$$

$$\frac{e_0 \bowtie e_0' \quad e_1 \trianglelefteq e_1'}{(e_0\ e_1) \bowtie (e_0'\ e_1')} \qquad\qquad \frac{\exists i \in \{0, 1\}.e \trianglelefteq e_i}{e \triangleleft (e_0\ e_1')}$$

$$\frac{e_0 \trianglelefteq e_0' \quad \forall i \in \{1 \ldots n\}.\exists \theta_i.p_i \equiv (p_i'\ \theta_i) \wedge e_i \trianglelefteq (e_i'\ \theta_i)}{(\mathbf{case}\ e_0\ \mathbf{of}\ p_1 : e_1 | \ldots | p_n : e_n) \bowtie (\mathbf{case}\ e_0'\ \mathbf{of}\ p_1' : e_1' | \ldots | p_n' : e_n')}$$

$$\frac{\exists i \in \{0 \ldots n\}.e \trianglelefteq e_i}{e \triangleleft (\mathbf{case}\ e_0\ \mathbf{of}\ p_1 : e_1 | \ldots | p_n : e_n)}$$

An expression is embedded within another by this relation if either *diving* (denoted by $\triangleleft$) or *coupling* (denoted by $\bowtie$) can be performed. Diving occurs when an expression is embedded in a sub-expression of another expression, and coupling occurs when two expressions have the same top-level construct and all the corresponding sub-expressions of the two constructs are embedded. Our version of this embedding relation extends previous versions to handle λ-abstractions and **case** expressions that contain bound variables. In these instances, the bound variables within the two expressions must also match up. Diving cannot be applied if the embedded expression contains any bound variables without their corresponding binders; this avoids the possibility of extracting these variables outside of their binders. The homeomorphic embedding relation $\lesssim$ can now be defined as follows:

$$e_1 \lesssim e_2 \text{ iff } \exists e.e_1 \equiv e(MVR) \wedge e \bowtie e_2$$

A technical point: within this relation, the two expressions must be coupled, but there is no longer a requirement that all of the free variables within the two expressions match up. Generalizing only when two expressions are coupled ensures that the result is not a variable, and there is no need for a *split* operation as used in [15]. It can be shown that the homeomorphic embedding relation is a well-quasi-order.

Lemma 1

Proof. This is very similar to the proof of [4].

B   Generalization Algorithm for Supercompilation

Definition 17 (Generalization of Expressions). The *generalization* of two expressions e_1 and e_2 is a triple $(e_g, \theta_1, \theta_2)$ where θ_1 and θ_2 are substitutions such that $e_g\theta_1 \equiv e_1$ and $e_g\theta_2 \equiv e_2$. This generalization is defined as follows:

$$(x\ e_1 \ldots e_n) \sqcap (x\ e_1' \ldots e_n') = (x\ e_1^g \ldots e_n^g, \bigcup_{i=1}^n \theta_i, \bigcup_{i=1}^n \theta_i')$$
$$\text{where}$$
$$\forall i \in \{1 \ldots n\}.(e_i^g, \theta_i, \theta_i') = e_i \sqcap e_i'$$

$$(c\ e_1 \ldots e_n) \sqcap (c\ e_1' \ldots e_n') = (c\ e_1^g \ldots e_n^g, \bigcup_{i=1}^n \theta_i, \bigcup_{i=1}^n \theta_i')$$
$$\text{where}$$
$$\forall i \in \{1 \ldots n\}.(e_i^g, \theta_i, \theta_i') = e_i \sqcap e_i'$$

$$(f\ e_1 \ldots e_n) \sqcap (f\ e_1' \ldots e_n') = (f\ e_1^g \ldots e_n^g, \bigcup_{i=1}^n \theta_i, \bigcup_{i=1}^n \theta_i')$$
$$\text{where}$$
$$\forall i \in \{1 \ldots n\}.(e_i^g, \theta_i, \theta_i') = e_i \sqcap e_i'$$

$$((\lambda x.e_0)\ e_1 \ldots e_n) \sqcap ((\lambda x'.e_0')\ e_1' \ldots e_n') = ((\lambda x.e_0^g)\ e_1^g \ldots e_n^g, \bigcup_{i=0}^n \theta_i, \bigcup_{i=0}^n \theta_i')$$
$$\text{where}$$
$$(e_0^g, \theta_0, \theta_0') = e_0 \sqcap (e_0'\{x' := x\})$$
$$\forall i \in \{1 \ldots n\}.(e_i^g, \theta_i, \theta_i') = e_i \sqcap e_i'$$

$$((\textbf{case}\ e_0\ \textbf{of}\ p_1 : e_1 | \ldots | p_k : e_k)\ e_{k+1} \ldots e_n) \sqcap ((\textbf{case}\ e_0'\ \textbf{of}\ p_1' : e_1' | \ldots | p_k' : e_k')\ e_{k+1}' \ldots e_n')$$
$$= ((\textbf{case}\ e_0^g\ \textbf{of}\ p_1 : e_1^g | \ldots | p_k : e_k^g)\ e_{k+1}^g \ldots e_n^g, \bigcup_{i=0}^n \theta_i, \bigcup_{i=0}^n \theta_i')$$
$$\text{where}$$
$$\forall i \in \{0, k+1 \ldots n\}.(e_i^g, \theta_i, \theta_i') = e_i \sqcap e_i'$$
$$\forall i \in \{1 \ldots k\}.\exists \theta_i.p_i \equiv (p_i'\ \theta_i) \wedge (e_i^g, \theta_i, \theta_i') = e_i \sqcap (e_i'\ \theta_i)$$
$$e \sqcap e' = (x, \{x := e\}, \{x := e'\}) \qquad \text{in all other cases.}$$

Within these rules, all forms of expression are represented as applications to a set of arguments (possibly the empty set). If both expressions have the same top-level construct, this is made the top-level construct of the resulting generalized expression, and the corresponding sub-expressions within the construct are then generalized. Otherwise, both expressions are replaced by the same fresh variable. It is assumed that the new variables introduced are all different and distinct from the original program variables. The following rewrite rule is exhaustively applied to the triple resulting from generalization to minimize the substitutions by identifying common substitutions that were previously given different names:

$$(e, \theta \cup \{x := e', x' := e'\}, \theta' \cup \{x := e'', x' := e''\})$$
$$\Downarrow$$
$$(e\{x := x'\}, \theta \cup \{x' := e'\}, \theta \cup \{x' := e''\})$$

We define an abstraction operation on expressions that extracts the sub-terms resulting from generalization.

Definition 18 (Abstraction Operation)

$$abstract(e, e') = (\lambda x_1 \ldots x_n.e_0) \; e_1 \ldots e_n$$
$$\text{where } e \sqcap e' = (e_0, \{x_1 := e_1, \ldots, x_n := e_n\}, \theta)$$

The correctness of this transformation can be proved locally at each point where generalization takes place by proving the following.

Theorem 4 (Correctness of Generalization)

$$\forall e, e'.abstract(e, e') \overset{\beta}{\leadsto} e.$$

Proof. Trivial. Proof of the "abstraction Lemma 2" is immediate from this.

C   Residualization

Definition 19 (Residual Program Construction). A residual program can be constructed from a labelled transition system with folding using the rules $\mathcal{C}$ as shown in Figure 8. Here ε is a "function environment", containing the definitions of the functions that appear in the residual program.

$\mathcal{C}[\![e]\!] = \mathcal{C}'[\![e]\!] \; \{\}$

If $e \to (x, \mathbf{0})(\#1, e_1) \ldots (\#n, e_n)$ then $\mathcal{C}'[\![e]\!] \; \varepsilon = x \; (\mathcal{C}'[\![e_1]\!] \; \varepsilon) \ldots (\mathcal{C}'[\![e_n]\!] \; \varepsilon)$
If $e \to (c, \mathbf{0})(\#1, e_1) \ldots (\#n, e_n)$ then $\mathcal{C}'[\![e]\!] \; \varepsilon = c \; (\mathcal{C}'[\![e_1]\!] \; \varepsilon) \ldots (\mathcal{C}'[\![e_n]\!] \; \varepsilon)$
If $e \to (\lambda x, e')$ then $\mathcal{C}'[\![e]\!] \; \varepsilon = \lambda x.(\mathcal{C}'[\![e']\!] \; \varepsilon)$
If $e \to (\mathbf{case}, e_0)(p_1, e_1) \ldots (p_n, e_n)$ then
$\qquad \mathcal{C}'[\![e]\!] \; \varepsilon = \mathbf{case} \; (\mathcal{C}'[\![e_0]\!] \; \varepsilon) \; \mathbf{of} \; p_1 \Rightarrow (\mathcal{C}'[\![e_1]\!] \; \varepsilon) \; | \cdots | \; p_n \Rightarrow (\mathcal{C}'[\![e_n]\!] \; \varepsilon)$
If $e \to (@, \lambda x_1 \ldots x_n.e_0)(\#1, e_1) \ldots (\#n, e_n)$ then
$\qquad \mathcal{C}'[\![e]\!] \; \varepsilon = (\mathcal{C}'[\![e_0]\!] \; \varepsilon)\{x_1 := (\mathcal{C}'[\![e_1]\!] \; \varepsilon), \ldots, x_n := (\mathcal{C}'[\![e_n]\!] \; \varepsilon)\}$
If $e \overset{\theta}{\to} e'$ then $\mathcal{C}'[\![e]\!] \; \varepsilon = (f \; x_1 \ldots x_n) \; \theta$, if $(f \; x_1 \ldots x_n = e') \in \varepsilon$
If $e \overset{\tau}{\to} e'$ then $\mathcal{C}'[\![e]\!] \; \varepsilon = \begin{cases} f \; x_1 \ldots x_n \; \mathbf{where} \; f = \lambda x_1 \ldots x_n.(\mathcal{C}'[\![e']\!] \; (\varepsilon \cup \{f \; x_1 \ldots x_n = e\})), \\ \qquad \text{if } \exists e''.e'' \overset{\theta}{\to} e \wedge \{x_1 \ldots x_n\} = fv(e) \\ \mathcal{C}'[\![e']\!] \; \varepsilon, \text{otherwise} \end{cases}$

Fig. 8. Rules For Constructing Residual Programs

Within these rules, the parameter ε contains the set of new function calls which have been created, and associates them with the expressions they replace. On encountering a renaming of one of these associated expressions, it is also replaced by an appropriate call of the corresponding function.

Secure Multi-execution in Haskell

Mauro Jaskelioff[1] and Alejandro Russo[2]

[1] CIFASIS-CONICET/Universidad Nacional de Rosario
[2] Dept. of Computer Science and Engineering, Chalmers University of Technology

Abstract. Language-based information-flow security has emerged as a promising technology to guarantee confidentiality in on-line systems, where enforcement mechanisms are typically presented as run-time monitors, code transformations, or type-systems. Recently, an alternative technique, called *secure multi-execution*, has been proposed. The main idea behind this novel approach consists on running a program multiple times, once for each security level, using special rules for I/O operations. Compared to run-time monitors and type-systems, secure multi-execution does not require to inspect the full code of the application (only its I/O actions). In this paper, we propose the core of a library to provide *non-interference* through secure-multi execution. We present the code of the library as well as a running example for Haskell. To the best of our knowledge, this paper is the first work to consider secure-multi execution in a functional setting and provide this technology as a library.

1 Introduction

Over the past years, there has been a significant increase in the number of online activities. Users can do almost everything using a web browser. Even though web applications are probably among the most used pieces of software, they suffer from vulnerabilities that permit attackers to steal confidential data, break the integrity of systems, and affect the availability of services. Web-based vulnerabilities have already outplaced those of all other platforms [1] and there are no reasons to think that this situation is going to change [9].

In this work, we focus on preserving confidentiality of data through the security policy known as non-interference [3, 10] (i.e. not leaking secrets into public channels). Confidentiality policies are getting more and more relevant for widely open connected systems as the web, where compromised confidential data can be used to impersonate users in Facebook, Twitter, Flickr, and other social networks.

Language-based information-flow security [27] has developed approaches to analyze applications' code, leading to special-purpose languages, interpreters or compilers [19, 24] that guarantee security policies like non-interference. Rather than producing new languages from scratch, security can also be provided by libraries [14]. The potential of this approach has been shown across a range of programming languages and security policies [32, 25, 23, 4, 15, 6].

Traditionally, information-flow analysis on a program is done statically (e.g. using a type-system), dynamically (e.g. using an execution monitor), or with a combination of both. Recently, authors in [7] devised an alternative approach, called *secure multi-execution*, based on the idea of executing the same program several times, once for

E. Clarke, I. Virbitskaite, and A. Voronkov (Eds.): PSI 2011, LNCS 7162, pp. 170–178, 2012.

each security level. As opposed to previous enforcement mechanisms, this novel approach does not demand to design type-systems or deploy heavy-weight monitoring of programs; it only requires modifying the semantics of I/O operations.

In this paper, we present the main ideas of a library based on monads [17, 16] to provide *non-interference* through secure-multi execution. The ideas can be easily applied to any pure language and are illustrated with an implementation for the programming language Haskell. To the best of our knowledge, this paper is the first one to consider secure-multi execution as library in a pure functional setting.

2   Secure Multi-execution

Devriese and Piessens [7] propose the novel approach of secure multi-execution to enforce non-interference. We organize security levels in a security lattice $\mathcal{L}$, where security levels are ordered by a partial order $\sqsubseteq$, with the intention to only allow leaks from data at level ℓ_1 to data at level ℓ_2 when $\ell_1 \sqsubseteq \ell_2$. Secure multi-execution runs a program multiple times, once for each security level. In order to enforce security, the I/O operations of those multiple copies of the program are interpreted differently. Outputs on a given channel at security level ℓ is performed only in the execution of the program linked to that security level. Inputs coming from a channel at security level ℓ are replaced by a default value if the execution of the program is linked to a security level ℓ_e such that $\ell \not\sqsubseteq \ell_e$. In that manner, the execution of the program linked to level ℓ_e never obtains information higher than its security level. In the case that $\ell_e = \ell$, the input operation is performed normally. Finally, if $\ell \sqsubseteq \ell_e$, the execution of the program linked to level ℓ_e reuses the inputs obtained by the execution linked to level ℓ.

Devriese and Piessens show that secure multi-execution is *sound* and *precise*. Soundness states that each execution linked to a given level cannot get any information from higher levels and consequently, all of its output will have to be generated from information at its level or below, guaranteeing non-interference. Precision establishes that if a program satisfies non-interference under normal execution, then its behavior is the same as the one obtained by secure multi-execution on terminating runs.

3   Secure Multi-execution in Haskell

In most pure functional programming languages, computations with side-effects such as inputs and outputs can be distinguished by its type. For instance, in Haskell every computation performing side-effects must be encoded as a value of the monad (or abstract data type) *IO* [22]. Specifically, a value of type *IO* a is an action (i.e., a computation which may have side-effects) which produces a value of type a when executed. This manner in which monads identify computations with side-effects fits particularly well with the idea of secure multi-execution of giving different interpretations to I/O operations as specified by the execution level.

For simplicity, we consider a two-point security lattice with elements L and H, where $L \sqsubseteq H$ and $H \not\sqsubseteq L$. Levels L and H represent public and secret confidentiality levels, respectively. The implementation shown here, however, works for an arbitrary finite security lattice. In Fig. 1 we show the implementation of the lattice as elements of the datatype *Level* and define the order relationship $\sqsubseteq$ and the non-reflexive $\sqsubset$.

data $Level = L \mid H$ **deriving** $(Eq, Enum)$

$\cdot \sqsubseteq \cdot, \cdot \sqsubset \cdot :: Level \rightarrow Level \rightarrow Bool$

$H \sqsubseteq L = False$

$\_ \sqsubseteq \_ = True$

$p \sqsubset q = p \sqsubseteq q \wedge p \not\equiv q$

Fig. 1. Security lattice

We propose a library that works by replacing I/O actions (i.e., values of the IO monad) by a pure description of them [31]. Haskell programs which perform some I/O actions have type $a \rightarrow IO\ b$. That is, given some argument of type a, the program performs some I/O actions and then returns a value of type b as the result. In secure multi-execution, the I/O actions performed by such program must be interpreted differently depending on the security level linked to a given execution (see Section 2). Hence, programs to be run under secure multi-execution do not return I/O actions, but rather a pure description of them. With this in mind, secure programs have the type $a \rightarrow ME\ b$, where monad ME describes the side-effects produced during the computation. When the program is executed, those I/O descriptions are interpreted according to the specification of secure multi-execution. For security levels L and H, the program is run twice, where the I/O actions are interpreted differently on the execution linked at level L, and on the one linked at level H. Figure 2 summarizes the ideas behind our library. Function run executes and links the program to the security level given as argument. Observe that function run is also responsible for the interpretation of the I/O actions described in the monad ME.

For simplicity, we only consider reading and writing files as the possible I/O actions. It is easy to generalize our approach to consider other I/O operations. Function $level :: FilePath \rightarrow Level$ assigns security levels to files indicating the confidentiality of their contents. We assume that, when

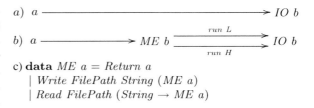

a) $a \xrightarrow{\hspace{4cm}} IO\ b$

b) $a \xrightarrow{\hspace{2cm}} ME\ b \xrightarrow[run\ H]{run\ L} IO\ b$

c) **data** $ME\ a = Return\ a$
   $\mid Write\ FilePath\ String\ (ME\ a)$
   $\mid Read\ FilePath\ (String \rightarrow ME\ a)$

Fig. 2. Type for a typical program with side-effects (a) and a secure multi-execution program (b), and definition of ME (c)

a file is read, its access time gets updated as a side-effect of the operation. An attacker, or public observer, is able to learn the content of public files as well as their access time.

Monad ME describes the I/O actions performed by programs and is defined in Fig. 2(c). Constructors $Return$, $Write$, and $Read$ model programs performing different actions. Program $Return\ x$ simply returns value x without performing any I/O operations. Program $Write\ file\ x\ p$ models a program that writes string x into file $file$ and then behaves as program p. Program $Read\ file\ g$ models a program that reads the contents x of file $file$ and then behaves as program $g\ x$. Technically, ME is an intermediate monad that provides a pure model of the reading and writing of files in the IO monad.

Users of the library do not write programs using the constructors of ME directly. Instead, they use the interface provided by the monad: $return :: a \rightarrow ME\ a$ and $(\ggg) :: ME\ a \rightarrow (a \rightarrow ME\ b) \rightarrow ME\ b$. The $return$ function lifts a pure value into the ME monad. The operator $\ggg$, called $bind$, is used to sequence computations. A bind expression $(m \ggg f)$ takes a computation m and function f which will be applied to the *value* produced by m and yields the resulting computation. These are the only primitive operations for monad *ME*, and consequently, programmers must sequence individual computations explicitly using the bind operator. Fig. 3 shows the implementation of *return* and $\gg\!\!=$. The expression *return* x builds a trivial computation, i.e., a computation which does not perform any *Write/Read* actions and just returns x.

Values in *ME* are introduced with *Return*, so this is the only case where f is applied. In the other two cases, the *Write/Read* operations are preserved and bind with f ($\gg\!\!=f$) is recursively applied. Besides *return* and ($\gg\!\!=$), the monad *ME* has operations to denote I/O actions on files. These oper-

instance *Monad ME* **where**
$$
\begin{aligned}
return\ x &= Return\ x \\
(Return\ x)\ &\gg\!\!= f &= f\ x \\
(Write\ file\ s\ p)\ &\gg\!\!= f = Write\ file\ s\ (p \gg\!\!= f) \\
(Read\ file\ g)\ &\gg\!\!= f &= Read\ file\ (\lambda i \rightarrow g\ i \gg\!\!= f)
\end{aligned}
$$

Fig. 3. Definitions for *return* and $\gg\!\!=$

ations model the equivalent operations on the *IO* monad and are given by the following functions.

$$
\begin{aligned}
&writeFile :: FilePath \rightarrow String \rightarrow ME\ () &&readFile :: FilePath \rightarrow ME\ String \\
&writeFile\ file\ s = Write\ file\ s\ (return\ ()) &&readFile\ file = Read\ file\ return
\end{aligned}
$$

4   An Interpreter for the Monad *ME*

$run :: Level \rightarrow ChanMatrix \rightarrow ME\ a \rightarrow IO\ a$
$run\ l\ \_\ (Return\ a) = return\ a$
$run\ l\ c\ (Write\ file\ o\ t)$
 | $level\ file \equiv l$ $= \mathbf{do}\ IO.writeFile\ file\ o$
            $run\ l\ c\ t$
 | $otherwise$ $= run\ l\ c\ t$
$run\ l\ c\ (Read\ file\ f)$
 | $level\ file \equiv l$ $= \mathbf{do}\ x \leftarrow IO.readFile\ file$
            $broadcast\ c\ l\ file\ x$
            $run\ l\ c\ (f\ x)$
 | $level\ file \sqsubset l$ $= \mathbf{do}\ x \leftarrow reuseInput\ c\ l\ file$
            $run\ l\ c\ (f\ x)$
 | $otherwise$ $= run\ l\ c\ (f\ (defvalue\ file))$

Fig. 4. Interpreter for monad *ME*

Fig. 4 shows the interpreter for programs of type *ME a*. Intuitively, *run l c p* executes *p* and links the execution to security level *l*. Argument *c* is used when inputs from executions linked to lower levels need to be reused (explained below). The implementation is pleasantly close to the informal description of secure multi-execution in Section 2. Outputs are only performed (*IO.writeFile file o*) when the confidentiality level of the output file is the same as the security level linked to the execution (*level file* $\equiv l$). Inputs are obtained (*IO.readFile file*) when files' confidentiality level is the same as the security level linked to the execution (*level file* $\equiv l$). Data from those inputs is broadcasted to executions linked to higher security levels in order to be properly reused when needed (*broadcast c l file x*). If the current execution level is higher than the file's confidentiality level (*level file* $\sqsubset l$), the content of the file is obtained from the execution linked to the same security level as the file (*reuseInput c l file*). Otherwise, the input data is replaced by a default value. Function *defvalue* :: *FilePath* → *String* sets default values for different files. Unlike [7], and to avoid introducing runtime errors, we adopt a default value for each file (i.e., input point) in the program. Observe that inputs can be used differently inside programs. For instance, the contents of some files could be parsed as numbers, while others as plain strings. Therefore, choosing a constant default value, e.g. the empty string, could trigger runtime errors when trying to parse a number out of it.

An execution linked to security level ℓ reuses inputs obtained in executions linked to lower levels. Hence, we implement communication channels between executions, from a security level ℓ' to a security level ℓ, if $\ell' \sqsubset \ell$. In the interpreter, the argument of type *ChanMatrix* consists of a matrix of communication channels indexed by security levels. An element $c_{\ell',\ell}$ of the matrix denotes a communication channel from security level ℓ' to ℓ where $\ell' \sqsubset \ell$; otherwise $c_{\ell',\ell}$ is undefined. In this manner, execution linked at level ℓ' can send its inputs to the execution linked at level ℓ, where $\ell' \sqsubset \ell$. Messages transmitted on these channels have type (*FilePath*, *String*), i.e., pairs of a filename and its contents. Function *broadcast* c l *file* x broadcasts the pair (*file*, x) on the channels linked to executions at higher security levels, i.e., channels $c_{l,\ell}$ such that $l \sqsubset \ell$. Function *reuseInput* c l *file* matches the filename *file* as the first component of the pairs in channel $c_{level\ file,l}$ and returns the second component, i.e., the contents of the file.

```
sme :: ME a → IO ()
sme t = do
    c ← newChanMatrix
    l ← newEmptyMVar
    h ← newEmptyMVar

    forkIO (do run L c t; putMVar l ())
    forkIO (do run H c t; putMVar h ())

    takeMVar l; takeMVar h
```

Fig. 5. Secure multi-execution

Multithreaded secure multi-execution is orchestrated by the function *sme*. This function is responsible for creating communication channels to implement the reuse of inputs, creating synchronization variables to wait for the different threads to finish, and, for each security level, forking a new thread that runs the interpreter at that level. Fig. 5 shows a specialized version of *sme* for the two-point security lattice. However, in the library implementation, the function *sme* works for an arbitrary finite lattice. Function *newChanMatrix* creates the communication channels. Synchronization variables are just simple empty *MVars*. When a thread tries to read (*takeMVar*) from an empty *MVar* it will block until another thread writes to it (*putMVar*) [21]. Function *forkIO* spawns threads that respectively execute the interpreter *run* at levels *L* and *H*, and then signal termination by writing (*putMVar l* (); *putMVar h* ()) to the thread's synchronization variable. The main thread locks on these variables by trying to read from them (*takeMVar l*; *takeMVar h*).

Unlike [7], function *sme* does not require the scheduler to keep the execution at level *L* ahead of the execution at level *H*. In [7], this requirement helps to avoid timing leaks at the price of probably modifying the runtime system (i.e, the scheduler). As mainstream information-flow compilers, monad *ME* also ignores timing leaks.

5   A Motivating Example

We present a small example of how to build programs using monad *ME*. We consider the scenario of a financial company who wants to preserve the confidentiality

```
data CreditTerms = CT { discount :: Rational, ddays :: Rational, net :: Rational }
calculator :: ME ()
calculator = do loanStr   ← readFile "Client"
                termsStr  ← readFile "Client-Terms"
                let loan      = read loanStr
                    terms     = read termsStr
                    interest  = loan − loan * (1 − discount terms / 100)
                    disct     = discount terms / (100 − discount terms)
                    ccost     = disct * 360 / (net terms − ddays terms)
                writeFile "Client-Interest" (show interest)
                writeFile "Client-Statistics" (show ccost)
                -- writeFile "Client-Statistics" (show ccost ++ loanStr)
```

Fig. 6. Financial calculator

of their clients but, at the same time, compute statistics by hiring a third-party consultant company. Given certain loan, the company wants to write code to compute the *cost of credit* [5] and the total amount of interest that it will receive as income. When taking a loan, credit terms usually indicate a due date as well as a cash discount if the credit is canceled before an expiration date. We consider credit terms of the form "*discount / discount period* net / *credit period*", which indicates that if payment is made within *discount period* days, a *discount* percent cash discount is allowed. Otherwise, the entire amount is due in *credit period* days. Given a credit term, the amount of money paid when the credit is due is $loan − loan \times (1 − discount/100)$. The yearly cost of credit, i.e., the cost of borrowing money under certain terms is $\frac{discount}{100−discount} \times \frac{360}{credit\ period−discount\ period}$. For instance, in an invoice of $1000 with terms 2 /10 net 30, the total interest payed at the due date is $1000 − $1000 \times (1 − .2) = 20, and the cost of credit becomes $\frac{2}{98} \times \frac{360}{20} = .3673$, i.e., 37%.

In this setting, we consider the amount of every loan to be confidential (secret) information, while cost of credit is public and thus available for statistics. By writing our program using monad *ME*, we can be certain that confidential information is never given for statistics. In other words, the third-party consultant company does not learn anything about the amount in the loans provided by the financial company. Figure 6 shows one possible implementation of the program to compute interests and cost of credit. Files "Client" and "Client-Interest" are considered secret (level H), while "Client-Terms" and "Client-Statistics" are considered public (level L). The code is self-explanatory.

If a programmer writes, by mistake or malice, *show ccost ++ loanStr* as the information to be written into the public file (see commented line), then secure multi-execution avoids leaking the sensitive information in *loanStr* by given the empty string to the execution linked to security level L.

6   Related Work

Previous work addresses non-interference and functional languages [11, 33, 24, 29]. The seminal work by Li and Zdancewic [14] shows that information-flow security can also be provided as a library for real programming languages. Morgenstern et al. [18]

encode a programming language aware of authorization and information-flow policies in Agda. Devriese and Piessens [8] enforce non-interference, either dynamically or statically, using monad transformers in Haskell. Different from that work, the monad ME does not encode static checks in the Haskell's type-system or monitor every step of programs' executions. Moreover, Devriese and Piessens' work requires to encode programs as values of a certain data type, while our approach only models I/O operations.

Russo et al. [26] outline the ground idea for secure multi-execution as a naive transformation. A transformed program runs twice: one execution computes the public results, where secret inputs were removed, and the second execution computes the secret outputs of the program. Devriese and Piessens [7] propose secure multi-execution as a novel approach to enforce non-interference. Devriese and Piessens implement secure multi-execution for the Spider-monkey JavaScript engine. The implementation presented in this work is clean and short (approximately 130 lines of code), and thus making it easy to understand how multi-execution works concretely. Unlike [7], our approach does not consider termination and timing covert channels. We argue that dealing with termination and timing covert channels in a complex language, without being too conservative, is a difficult task. In this light, it is not surprising that the main information-flow compilers (Jif [20] –based on Java–, and FlowCaml [30] –based on Caml–) ignore those channels.

Close to the notion of secure multi-execution, Jif/split [34] automatically partitions a program to run securely on heterogenously trusted hosts. Different from secure multi-execution, the partition of the code is done to guarantee that if host h is subverted, hosts trusting h are the only ones being compromised. Swift [2] uses Jif/split technology to partition the program into JavaScript code running on the browser, and JavaScript code running on the web server.

7   Concluding Remarks

We propose a monad and an interpreter for secure multi-execution. To the best of our knowledge, we are the first ones to describe secure multi-execution in a functional language. We implement our core ideas in a small Haskell library of around 130 lines of code and present a running example. The implementation is compact and clear, which makes it easy to understand how secure multi-execution works concretely. Broadcasting input values to executions at higher levels is a novelty of our implementation if compared with Devriese and Piessens' work. This design decision is not tied to the Haskell implementation, and the idea can be used to implement the reuse of inputs in any secure multi-execution approach for any given language. The library is publicly available [13].

Future work. Our long-term goal is to provide a fully-fledged library for secure multi-execution in Haskell. The IO monad can perform a wide range of input and output operations. It is then interesting to design a mechanism capable to lift, as automatically as possible, IO operations into the monad ME [12]. Another direction for future work is related with declassification, or deliberate release of confidential information [28]. Declassification in secure multi-execution is still an open challenge. Due to the structure of monadic programs, we believe that it is possible to identify, and restrict, possible synchronization points where declassification might occur. Then, declassification cannot happen arbitrarily inside programs but only on those places where we can give some guarantees about the security of programs. To evaluate the capabilities of our library, we plan to use it to implement a medium-size web application. Web applications are good candidates for case studies due to their demand on confidentiality as well as frequent input and output operations (i.e. server requests and responses). It is also our intention to perform benchmarks to determine the overhead introduced by our library. The library seems to multiply execution time by the number of levels, but since file operations are only done once, the reality could be better if the broadcast mechanism is not expensive.

Acknowledgments. Alejandro Russo was partially funded by the Swedish research agency VR. We would like to thank Arnar Birgisson, Andrei Sabelfeld, Dante Zanarini and the anonymous reviewers for their helpful comments.

References

[1] Andrews, M.: Guest Editor's Introduction: The State of Web Security. IEEE Security and Privacy 4(4), 14–15 (2006)

[2] Chong, S., Liu, J., Myers, A.C., Qi, X., Vikram, K., Zheng, L., Zheng, X.: Secure web applications via automatic partitioning. In: Proc. ACM Symp. on Operating System Principles, pp. 31–44 (October 2007)

[3] Cohen, E.S.: Information transmission in computational systems. ACM SIGOPS Operating Systems Review 11(5), 133–139 (1977)

[4] Conti, J.J., Russo, A.: A taint mode for Python via a library. In: NordSec 2010. Selected paper by OWASP AppSec Research 2010 (2010)

[5] Credit Research Foundation. Ratios and formulas in customer financial analysis (1999), http://www.crfonline.org/orc/cro/cro-16.html

[6] Del Tedesco, F., Russo, A., Sands, D.: Implementing erasure policies using taint analysis. In: Aura, T. (ed.) The 15th Nordic Conf. in Secure IT Systems. Springer, Heidelberg (2010)

[7] Devriese, D., Piessens, F.: Noninterference through secure multi-execution. In: Proc. of the 2010 IEEE Symposium on Security and Privacy, SP 2010, pp. 109–124. IEEE Computer Society, Washington, DC (2010)

[8] Devriese, D., Piessens, F.: Information flow enforcement in monadic libraries. In: Proc. of the 7th ACM SIGPLAN Workshop on Types in Language Design and Implementation, TLDI 2011, pp. 59–72. ACM, New York (2011)

[9] Federal Aviation Administration (US). Review of Web Applications Security and Intrusion Detection in Air Traffic Control Systems. Note: thousands of vulnerabilities were discovered (June 2009), http://www.oig.dot.gov/sites/dot/files/pdfdocs/ATC_Web_Report.pdf

[10] Goguen, J.A., Meseguer, J.: Security policies and security models. In: Proc. IEEE Symp. on Security and Privacy, pp. 11–20 (April 1982)

[11] Heintze, N., Riecke, J.G.: The SLam calculus: programming with secrecy and integrity. In: Proc. ACM Symp. on Principles of Programming Languages, pp. 365–377 (January 1998)

[12] Jaskelioff, M.: Lifting of Operations in Modular Monadic Semantics. PhD thesis, University of Nottingham (2009)

[13] Jaskelioff, M., Russo, A.: Secure multi-execution in Haskell. software release (2011), http://www.cse.chalmers.se/~russo/sme/

[14] Li, P., Zdancewic, S.: Encoding Information Flow in Haskell. In: CSFW 2006: Proc. of the 19th IEEE Workshop on Computer Security Foundations. IEEE Computer Society (2006)

[15] Magazinius, J., Phung, P.H., Sands, D.: Safe wrappers and sane policies for self protecting JavaScript. In: Aura, T. (ed.) The 15th Nordic Conf. in Secure IT Systems. Springer, Heidelberg (2010)

[16] Moggi, E.: An abstract view of programming languages. Technical Report ECS-LFCS-90-113, Edinburgh University, Edinburgh, Scotland (1989)

[17] Moggi, E.: Computational lambda-calculus and monads. In: Proc., Fourth Annual Symposium on Logic in Computer Science, pp. 14–23. IEEE Computer Society (1989)

[18] Morgenstern, J., Licata, D.R.: Security-typed programming within dependently typed programming. In: Proc. of the 15th ACM SIGPLAN Int. Conf. on Funct. Prog., ICFP 2010, pp. 169–180. ACM, New York (2010)

[19] Myers, A.C.: JFlow: Practical mostly-static information flow control. In: Proc. ACM Symp. on Principles of Programming Languages, pp. 228–241 (January 1999)

[20] Myers, A.C., Zheng, L., Zdancewic, S., Chong, S., Nystrom, N.: Jif: Java information flow. Software release (July 2001), Located at http://www.cs.cornell.edu/jif

[21] Peyton Jones, S., Gordon, A., Finne, S.: Concurrent haskell. In: POPL 1996: Proc. of the 23rd ACM SIGPLAN-SIGACT Symposium on Principles of Programming Languages, pp. 295–308. ACM, New York (1996)

[22] Peyton Jones, S.L., Wadler, P.: Imperative functional programming. In: Proc. of the ACM Conf. on Principles of Programming, pp. 71–84 (1993)

[23] Phung, P.H., Sands, D., Chudnov, A.: Lightweight self-protecting javascript. In: Safavi-Naini, R., Varadharajan, V. (eds.) ACM Symposium on Information, Computer and Communications Security (ASIACCS 2009). ACM Press, Sydney (2009)

[24] Pottier, F., Simonet, V.: Information flow inference for ML. In: Proc. ACM Symp. on Principles of Programming Languages, pp. 319–330 (January 2002)

[25] Russo, A., Claessen, K., Hughes, J.: A library for light-weight information-flow security in Haskell. In: Haskell 2008: Proc. of the 1st ACM SIGPLAN Symp. on Haskell. ACM (2008)

[26] Russo, A., Hughes, J., Naumann, J.D.A., Sabelfeld, A.: Closing Internal Timing Channels by Transformation. In: Okada, M., Satoh, I. (eds.) ASIAN 2006. LNCS, vol. 4435, pp. 120–135. Springer, Heidelberg (2008)

[27] Sabelfeld, A., Myers, A.C.: Language-based information-flow security. IEEE J. Selected Areas in Communications 21(1), 5–19 (2003)

[28] Sabelfeld, A., Sands, D.: Dimensions and principles of declassification. In: Proc. IEEE Computer Security Foundations Workshop, pp. 255–269 (June 2005)

[29] Simonet, V.: Flow caml in a nutshell. In: Hutton, G. (ed.) Proc. of the First APPSEM-II Workshop, pp. 152–165 (March 2003)

[30] Simonet, V.: The Flow Caml system. Software release (July 2003), http://cristal.inria.fr/~simonet/soft/flowcaml

[31] Swierstra, W., Altenkirch, T.: Beauty in the beast. In: Proc. of the ACM SIGPLAN Workshop on Haskell, Haskell 2007, pp. 25–36. ACM, New York (2007)

[32] Tsai, T.C., Russo, A., Hughes, J.: A library for secure multi-threaded information flow in Haskell. In: Proc. of the 20th IEEE Computer Security Foundations Symposium (July 2007)

[33] Zdancewic, S.: Programming Languages for Information Security. PhD thesis, Cornell University (July 2002)

[34] Zdancewic, S., Zheng, L., Nystrom, N., Myers, A.C.: Untrusted hosts and confidentiality: Secure program partitioning. In: Proc. ACM Symp. on Operating System Principles (2001)

Towards an Open Framework for C Verification Tools Benchmarking

Alexey Khoroshilov, Vadim Mutilin, Eugene Novikov,
Pavel Shved, and Alexander Strakh

Institute for System Programming of the Russian Academy of Sciences
{khoroshilov,mutilin,joker,shved,strakh}@ispras.ru

Abstract. The paper presents a twofold verification system that aimes to be an open platform for experimentation with various verification techniques as well as an industrial-ready domain specific verification tool for Linux device drivers. We describe the architecture of the verification system and discuss a perspective to build an open benchmarking suite on top of it.

Keywords: verification tools benchmarking, static analysis, device driver verification, domain specific verification, reachability verification, aspect-oriented programming.

1 Introduction

Static source code analysis is a means of checking if certain properties hold for a program by analyzing a formal representation of the program without executing it. Its primary benefits are omission of test data and test environment, which are to be specifically developed for testing, and capability of exploring all possible program paths, including those rare and badly reproducible when the program is tested dynamically.

However, application of static source code analysis has a number of limitations in practice. The primary limitation is its runtime. Modern programs are quite large and complicated, which leads to implausibility of a complete static analysis of industrially-large applications in any sensible timeframe, exhaustive dynamic testing still being implausible as well though. In practice, this forces static analysis tools to deploy various simplifications and heuristics of the program models analyzed, thus decreasing the quality of the analysis. The key characteristics of the quality are frequencies of false positives and of false negatives. Based on anticipated runtime and degree of simplification, we can separate "lightweight" and "heavyweight" approaches to static verification.

Lightweight approaches aim at getting the result fast, with runtime comparable to that of compilation of the application being analyzed. Such speed is achieved by applying various heuristics to dataflow analyses. It eventually leads to reducing quality of the analysis by increasing both rate of false positives, and number of the errors overlooked. The increased rate of false positives is the

E. Clarke, I. Virbitskaite, and A. Voronkov (Eds.): PSI 2011, LNCS 7162, pp. 179–192, 2012.

primary drawback, since the experience of practical application of static analysis tools demonstrates that a high rate of false positive makes such tools dramatically less effective. Nevertheless, lightweight approaches are well-developed nowadays, and are employed by a lot of tools, which are involved in software development throughout the industry. The most successful commercial tools include Coverity [1] and Klocwork Insight [2], academic ones include Svace [3], Saturn [4], FindBugs [5], Splint [6] et. al.

Heavyweight approaches do not make runtime its primary objective, while they should keep it reasonably small. This allows to utilize less heuristics during program interpretation, which leads to decreasing rate of false positives, and to increasing the number of actual errors found. However, heavyweight approaches are barely used today in analysis of non-academic applications. A lot of projects propose various implementations of different heavyweight approaches, namely SLAM [7], BLAST [8], CPAchecker [9], CBMC [10], ARMC [11] et al. Still, only one project, Microsoft SDV [12], has made its way to industrial use. SDV provides a comprehensive toolset for heavyweight analysis of source code of device drivers of Microsoft Windows OS. These tools are used in the process of device driver certification, and have been included in Microsoft Windows Driver Developer Kit since 2006. Microsoft SDV proves heavyweight approaches capable of being employed in industrial projects. However, Microsoft SDV is specifically tailored for analysis of device drivers of Microsoft Windows. Moreover, it is a proprietary software, which prohibits its application to other domains or to experiments with different static analysis algorithms outside Microsoft.

The other heavyweight static analysis tools are just used spottily, in very specific domains. No wonder that there is no uniform domain for comparison of performance of various verification tools, let alone a domain based on actively-developed industrial code base. The Linux Driver Verification (LDV) project [13,14,15] attempts to build such a platform for the verification tools – primarily, heavyweight – that can verify C programs; the source code to analyze being based on real Linux device drivers. This article analyzes the requirements for the architecture of such a platform, which should also serve as a verification system of industrial quality.

The article is organized like this. Section 2 devises the requirements for an open verification framework for Linux device drivers, and is followed by comparison of existing heavyweight static analysis tools for Windows and Linux OS in section 3. Section 4 contains an elaboration of the architecture proposed of LDV framework and its components. Section 5 discusses a perspective to build an open benchmarking framework on top of the LDV.

2   Requirements for an Open Verification Framework

One of the main goals of the LDV project is creating an open platform for experimenting with applications of various methods (primarily, heavyweight) of static source code analysis to actively used programs. To achieve this goal, the verification framework should provide convenient ways for integrating new tools and for comparison of their efficiency under various settings. Target sources to verify are currently Linux device drivers; however, the architecture should be capable to expand beyond this domain.

Linux device drivers is a promising target for heavyweight static analysis because:

- there is a lot of Linux device drivers, and the pace of development of the new ones only grows;
- most drivers are published as a source code, which is necessary for the majority of static analysis tools;
- the errors in drivers are critical, because the drivers run with the same privileges as the rest of the Linux kernel;
- almost no use of floating point arithmetcs;
- rare use of recursive functions;
- source code of each particular driver is quite small.

At the same time, some of the facts about Linux kernel should be taken into account during the development of the verification framework. First, Linux kernel is one of the most fast-paced software projects. Beginning with kernel 2.6.30, which was released in the middle of 2009, about 9000 lines are added, 4500 lines are removed, and 2000 lines are modified on average every day [16]. Up to 70% of Linux kernel source code belong to device drivers, and more than 85% errors, which lead to hangs and crashes of the whole operating system (OS), are also in the drivers' sources [17,18]. Nowadays it is not easy to maintain the safety of all the drivers manually, despite quite a number of active developers (more than a thousand of people today [16]). The reason is that a lot of source code lines (more than 13 million [16]) should satisfy a large set of correctness rules, which include generic rules for C programs, and domain-specific rules that describe the correct way of interaction between the drivers and the kernel interfaces. An important difference between Linux and the other OS is an explicitly declared instability of interface between drivers and the kernel core, which is constantly improved and expanded. Thus, new correctness rules appear, and the old are modified. As a result, Linux device drivers verification framework, and particularly, its correction rules, should be capable to improve with the pace that fits that of the kernel development.

The second goal of the LDV project is to develop a verification framework, which is ready for industrial use, i.e. provides convenient interface, and requires a minimal involvement of users into the verification process. To minimize the involvement the tools should automatically extract information on the structure of the drivers to verify and on its compilation options out of the typical shipment of a driver's source code. The tools should also balance the number of dependencies of a driver and the amount of the source code to analyze, as it should not be very high.

Another issue of decreasing human involvement is the absence of a conventional entry point (i.e. of a "main" function) in device driver sources. Most heavyweight approaches require an entry point, as their task is to explore all paths that start at it. So driver verification requires generation of an artificial entry point. We name it "driver environment", as it contains invocations of handlers (driver initialization, reading from a device file handler, etc.), which are defined in the sources of drivers, and calls them the same way they are called during interaction of the driver with its environment: the kernel core and devices.

By convenient interface we understand the convenience both of launching verification and analysis of its results; the latter being even more important, as the analysis whether the errors found are real ones may require considerable time of an experienced developer.

3   Related Work

The most comprehensive tool is implemented in the aforementioned Microsoft SDV toolset [12]. The properties of this framework include:

- For driver environment to be generated user is to annotate each handler function in the source code of the driver with its role.
- The correctness rules to verify are formalized with SLIC [19], which defines the binding with the source code with aid of aspect-oriented clauses that intercept kernel core function calls. As of today, about 200 rules are formalized, and the research version of the toolset even supports adding new rules. Windows kernel, unlike Linux, has a more stable interface, so the problem of ever-changing core interface is not of current concern.
- Two static source code verifiers are known to be supported by Microsoft SDV in research activities: SLAM and Yogi [20]. There is no infrastructure to plug third-party verifiers in.
- Statistical data and thorough error traces are generated after verification results.

As for the Linux, there are several existing toolsets that use heavyweight static approach for Linux device drivers verification: Avinux [21] and DDVerify [22].

The Avinux toolset's features are:

- Driver's sources are extracted by patching kernel's build process. However, Avinux supports only work with a single preprocessed source, and those drivers that consist of several files may only be verified after they are assembled manually.
- To create driver environment, manual creation of a main function simulating the operating system's use of the driver and selection of relevant source code files are required. Based on this, however, the code to initialize input parameters is generated automatically.
- Correctness rules are defined by aspect-oriented clauses similar to those of SLIC.
- An only static verifier, CBMC [10], is integrated into Avinux.

The DDVerify toolset's features are as follows:

- The tool ignores kernel's native makefiles, and uses its own instead. Therefore, it can not take into account all the nuances of how kernel sources are built.

– Only three (out of several dozens) of environment patterns are implemented for automatic environment generation.
– There is no infrastructure to separate definition of correctness rules and the implementation of the kernel core infrastructure. Therefore the rules are imposed by severe modifications of kernel headers.
– Only two static verifiers are supported: CBMC [10] and SATABS [23].

This demonstrates that no toolset among those we have overviewed above fulfills all the goals we formulated. Microsoft SDV is a proprietary tool that is applicable to Windows drivers verification; and it does not support third-party verifiers. Avinux and DDVerify do not meet the requirements of large-scale industrial use: Avinux requires manual annotation and manual merge of several .c files, and DDVerify requires severe manual modifications to kernel's build process, headers and model of the kernel core for each new kernel version. Figure 1 summarizes the comparison of compliance of the tools with the requirements we formulated.

Requirement	Microsoft SDV	Avinux	DDVerify
External rules	+	+	±
External verifiers	–	–	–
Environment generation	By annotations	Manual	For 3 types of drivers only
Native build process support	+	Single-file drivers	–
Tolerance to changes of the kernel	Inapplicable	+	–
Automation of error trace analysis	+	–	–
Automation of comparative results analysis	–	–	–

Fig. 1. Compliance of the tools with the requirements to the open architecture

4   LDV Architecture

The architecture of LDV was developed to meet the goals described above: provide a highly-automated infrastructure for verification of Linux device drivers, with capability of plugging in various heavyweight static verification tools.

You can see the sketch of the architecture on the figure 2. The components of the LDV toolset are shown in the middle. The arrows describe the data flow. On the left there are data supplied by user; they may also supply additional verification engines by writing proper wrappers to them. The developers of LDV framework ship a dozen of rule models and wrappers for two static verification tools. On the right the process of generation of the final report is depicted.

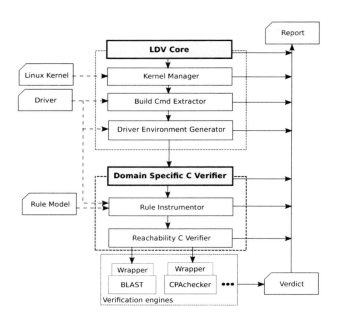

Fig. 2. Components of the LDV architecture, input data and data flow

4.1   Key Components

Verification process begins with launching *LDV Core*; at first it calls *Kernel Manager* that creates an instance of a kernel supplied by user as an archive or as a git repository, and patches its build process. The kernels may both be a source of driver sources themselves, or be used for external drivers to be compiled against.

Then drivers are compiled and *Build Cmd Extractor* reads the stream of compile and link commands, sources and dependencies between source files yielded by the modified build process, and to select those relevant to the drivers to verify. After extraction of the full command stream it is divided into several small parts, each being relevant to one kernel module only. This is particularly important for analysis of drivers shipped with kernel, as the kernel's build subsystem does not separate them on its own.

Linux device driver usually consists of one or several kernel modules. They are not executed as usual programs, but rather they register in kernel core a set of event handlers and the kernel core calls them when appropriate userspace or hardware requests occur. The purpose of *Driver Environment Generator* is to generate one or more models for driver's environment for each type of driver encountered: how the module's loaded and unloaded, and how the kernel core invokes its handlers. The model generated is printed as C's main function, which allocates the proper structures and calls the driver's handlers.

Currently *Driver Environment Generator* can generate the following models:

1. A fixed sequence of handlers invocations.
2. A limited sequence of invocations of handlers in an arbitrary order.
3. Potentially infinite sequence of invocations of handlers in an arbitrary order.

Each model may include initialization of handler parameters and checking of preconditions and return values of handler calls. Initialization of out-of-scope pointers and data structures in the environment is not supported now, but may be done with external tools like DEC[24].

The *Domain Specific C Verifier* component provides an interface for verification of a C program against a set of rules, which does not depend on how rules are formulated. Input of *Domain Specific C Verifier* is a set of build commands with entry points of interest specified, and a set of rule model identifiers to verify against.

Rule Instrumentor is a component that weaves the formalized models of correctness rules into the source code of a program, the resultant program being then verified by a static verification tool. Aside from build commands and sources, *Rule Instrumentor* takes rule model identifier as an input. The interpretation of each of these identifiers is stored in the rule database, which, basically, contains aspect files to apply to the source code for certain models, and additional information for verification engines to interpret. The language of aspect files resembles an aspect-oriented extension of C.

For example, consider the rule about using mutex-type objects in Linux kernel. These objects provide exclusive access to sections of executable code. Thus retrying to acquire the current mutex will inevitably lead to a deadlock-situation. Deadlocks should be avoided, hence the rule says that the mutex should not be locked twice by the same process. To formalize it, in Aspect 1 we introduce the mutex state variable *islocked* and the model function *model_mutex_lock*. The function checks the mutex state and if it is already locked then the *ERROR* label indicates that the rule is violated. Otherwise, the function updates the mutex state. We omit definition of *model_mutex_unlock*, which is similar to *model_mutex_lock*.

Aspect 1 – the model state and functions:
```
int islocked = UNLOCKED;  // Initialization of model state
void model_mutex_lock() { // Definition of model function
  if (islocked == LOCKED) // Checking the rule
    ERROR: abort();       // Error state
  islocked = LOCKED;      // Modeling the behaviour
}
```

The second aspect defines points where we want to insert calls to model functions defined in Aspect 1.

Aspect 2 – connection of Aspect 1 with a source code:
```
before: call($ mutex_lock(..)) { // Before each call to mutex_lock
 model_mutex_lock();                // Insert a call to the model function
}
```
The source code (drivers/pcmcia/cs.c):
```
...
// The call to extern void mutex_lock(struct mutex *)
mutex_lock(&socket_mutex);
...
```

As the result of instrumentation for the above original source code we get the source code where calls to model functions are inserted before calls to original ones.

The instrumented source code:
```
...
// Calling auxiliary function
ldv_mutex_lock(&socket_mutex);
...
// The definition of auxiliary function
void ldv_mutex_lock(struct mutex *arg) {
 model_mutex_lock(); // Calling the model function
 mutex_lock(arg); // Calling original mutex_lock
}
```

Note, that information that is specific to Linux device drivers verification is hidden inside model descriptions in aspect files, while *Domain Specific C Verifier* component only operates with abstract identifiers of these descriptions. Therefore, it is applicable to domains other than Linux drivers. For example, currently the rule database contains a model suitable for usual C programs: no assertion should be failed. So *Domain Specific C Verifier* may be run directly, without any wrapping *LDV Core* functionality, to verify a program against that rule.

Reachability C Verifier component transforms the concrete verification task from internal LDV framework format to the format specific to each verification tool. The component receives instrumented sources with entry points specified and correctness rules instrumented, and invokes a user-defined wrapper around a verifier, which should contain the following:

1. Invocation of the verifier itself (command line).
2. Invocation of preprocessors that simplify, or link input files together, or make another user-defined transformations.
3. Interpretation of information about entry points and error labels for the verifier to understand.
4. Interpretation of hints from the model database, and of user-defined options.
5. Translation of analysis results (error trace, verdict) to a common notation.

Currently we implemented wrappers for BLAST and CPAchecker, which serve the aim of feature demonstration and testing.

Reachability C Verifier component receives C source code which can be compiled by GCC compiler, but a wrapper may intentionally simplify the input source code for the verifier. For example, CPAchecker requires that the input source code should be transformed with a special tool CIL[25].

A verifier reports one of the three verdicts: *safe, unsafe* or *unknown.* The verdict is *safe* if the verifier is convinced that the rule is not violated. The verdict *unsafe* means that the rule is violated and in this case the verifier provides the error trace which shows a path to an error label. The verdict *unknown* means that for some reasons the verifier cannot decide whether the rule is violated.

The verdict reported by verifier is processed by all the components in the reverse order, each component adding information about its own work to the report, finally forming the report about the whole verification task originally launched.

Components communicate with a special command stream structure. In the beginning it is just a representation of build commands (currently in XML notation), but as the work progresses it is modified by the components. They can alter preprocessor options, add meta-information to commands, and even create modified copies of sources and substitute paths in the XML. All components have an established interface, and may be substituted or reimplemented independently.

The inherent separation of major tasks, such as "verify all drivers for this kernel" into independent subtasks ("verify one driver") renders the parallelization of the work quite natural. The tools already support concurrent work on a single machine, which is useful to occupy all the resources of a multi-core CPU, and the parallelization in a cloud is currently being implemented.

4.2   User Interface

The user interacts with the LDV framework via the high-level command-line interface, which allows launching verification of a set of drivers (either internal or external) against a set of kernels and rules. Unless an abnormal exception occurred, it produces an archive that contains verification results, some information about the work of underlying components, error traces, and the source code required to demonstrate the errors found, if any. After that, the archive can be uploaded to a database and used for further analysis.

Statistics Server is a component that implements a web interface on top of the database that facilitates analysis of verification results. It provides statistics on:

- verification verdicts for all drivers verified;
- time spent for verification by each component;
- internal errors occured in verification tools and clusterized using a configurable knowledge base.

Another important feature of the *Statistics Server* is a comparison report for different verification tasks. In particular, it is very useful as a convenient way for comparison of different verification tools and/or their configurations. For instance, when we run an experiment with CPAchecker [9] to compare Single-Block Encoding and Large-Block Encoding [26], *Statistics Server* allows us to immediately see all the differencies in details. On the screenshot (figure 3) we may see that LBE configuration, otherwise superior (see improvements in the two rightmost columns), demonstrated regressions on certain inputs (see circled regression for rule model nr. 68_1).

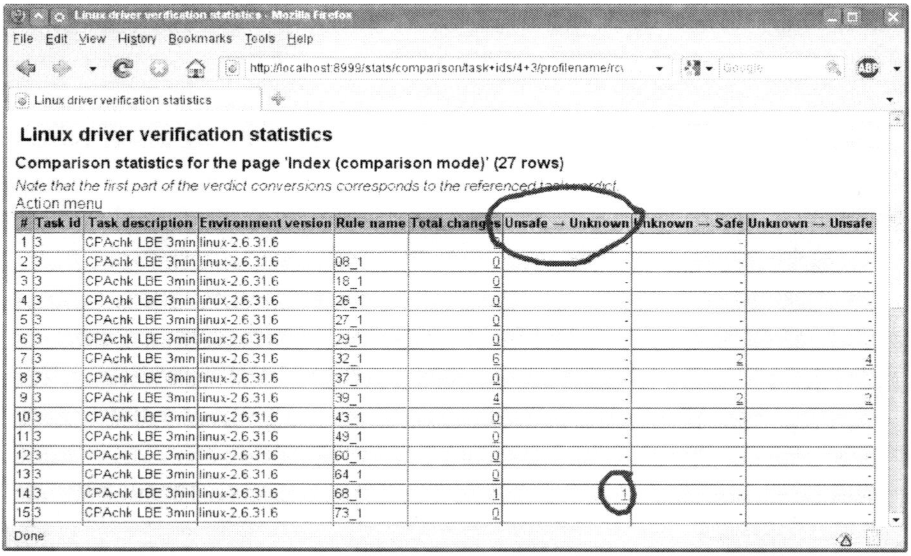

Fig. 3. Comparison of CPAchecker configurations with LDV analytical tools

Statistics Server is integrated with *Error Trace Visualizer* component that automates analysis of unsafe verdicts helping either to find real errors in drivers or to identify a source of false positives. *Error Trace Visualizer* gets error trace in common notation from a wrapper of a verification tool and presents it in convenient web interface.

Error Trace Visualizer tries to bind the error trace description to the source code created by drivers developers and to Linux kernel core sources. So the component also displays source code files traversed in an error trace, and establishes links from trace to them. To simplify the view *Error Trace Visualizer* removes auxiliary constructions from error trace, hides most of the part of error trace that is not interesting for error analysis. For visual purposes *Error Trace Visualizer* also uses different styles and colors for error trace constructions, source code syntax highlighting. Almost all elements in error trace can be hidden and shown, either individually or as a group.

The visualization components do not assume that the input programs are drivers and may be used for the other domains as well.

4.3   Summary

In this section we presented an open framework which supports plugging in external verifiers by providing wrappers. New verification rules may be added with the help of aspect-oriented language. Environment generation is fully automatic, so we can easily verify any number of drivers. To track changes in the kernel interface we have a test suite which detects the changes, but the aspects which connect model functions with a source code should be changed manually. The framework is integrated with kernel build process, so all necessary information is extracted during the build. Special components are developed for error trace analysis and comparison of the results.

5   Verification Tools Benchmarking

Seeking to build an open platform for experimentation with various verification techniques, LDV framework provides a solid platform for benchmarking C verifiers as well.

- LDV defines an explicit and simple interface to plug in new verification tools.
- LDV provides convenient ways for comparison of different verification tools and/or their configurations.
- LDV enables verification of massive volume of uniform real-life industrial software code base.
- LDV contains a set of safety rules for Linux device drivers that are automatically transformed in conventional reachability problem.
- LDV provides a tool to define and automatically apply new reachability and nonreachability rules to source code of C programs.

At the same time, benchmarking assumes a permanent and representative set of data to be used for comparison of various C verification tools. At the moment, we do not have such set of data and careful selection of the data is a topic for future work.

To demonstrate typical characteristics of C programs prepared by LDV framework for C verification tools, let us consider an example of application a rule specifying correctness of locking and unlocking of mutexes to all device drivers shipped as a module within the kernel of version 2.6.31.6. There are 2158 such drivers, but only 712 of them use mutexes. Below we consider nondegenerate drivers only in the driver environment: potentially infinite sequence of invocations of handlers in an arbitrary order.

The drivers sources were analyzed with static verifier BLAST [8]. The tool tracked how many abstraction refinements it performed, and how many predicates it devised from analyses of these traces with an interpolating prover (analysis of one trace may contribute several predicates to the abstraction). We turned off all the heuristics that could omit the refinement procedures that would otherwise be traversed during a cannonical CEGAR [27] analysis. Each BLAST run was forcibly terminated after 10 minutes, and the results obtained are thus only a lower-bound assessment of the actual driver attributes.

LOC bounds	N	CFG edges	Trace length		Refinements		Predicates	
from – to		average	avg	max	avg	max	avg	max
0 – 1999	340	1356	853	6102	19	224	14	123
2000 – 3999	129	3073	1750	10997	36	372	26	215
4000 – 5999	57	4855	1993	7326	18	226	15	95
6000 – 7999	61	7396	5873	30531	16	95	17	143
8000 – 9999	29	8349	4708	13518	29	99	16	67
10000– 11999	35	14038	4161	8082	10	93	10	62
12000– 13999	11	10588	8365	12103	10	58	6	23
14000– 25208	50	18054	9396	18949	6	47	6	75

Fig. 4. Characteristics of C programs prepared by LDV framework for C verification tools (bucketed by Lines of Code)

You may see the attributes on figure 4. The drivers were separated into buckets, based on Lines of Code in their .c files. For all drivers of each bucket, the following characteristics is obtained: total amount of verifier launches (N); size of Control-Flow Graph (particularly, a number of edges in it); average and maximum of maximal error trace size for each driver, the "size" being the number of minterms in the path formula; the number of abstraction refinements (each refinement follows an error trace analysis); and the number of predicates discovered before the verifier finished its work or was terminated.

The data above demonstrates that even a simple correctness rule requires a considerable amount of refinement passes and supplies CEGAR with noticeable payload. However, the more careful selection of a smaller set of the more complex drivers is yet to be made.

There are other approaches for preparing benchmarks, for example, there are collections of small programs addressing some verification challenges (like aliasing, side effects, control transfer etc.)[28]. LDV framework is ready to verify programs which are not drivers, so the programs especially constructed to expose some problematic features may also be included into the resulting benchmark. The purpose of using using drivers as benchmark programs is to check whether a C verification tool is applicable for real-life industrial software code base.

6   Conclusion

The paper presents an architecture of an open verification framework for Linux device drivers. The framework is already useful for quality assurance of in-kernel device drivers. It has helped us find 25 unsafes in latest Linux kernels, which were recognized as errors by kernel developers [29]. Besides being capable of finding errors the framework could be used as a ground for experiments with application of various methods of static analysis to actively developed industrial codebase. For that purpose the third-party verifiers may be plugged in and the framework supply the users with analytical interfaces that ease the comparison of different verifiers and their different configurations.

Primarily for benchmarking C verifiers we use drivers shipped within Linux kernel that allows to run verifiers on millions lines of code in total. Thus the framework is useful to investigate characteristics of C verifiers on the industrial workload. Also it can be used as a basis for creation targeted benchmarks covering selected sets of C programs.

References

1. Web-site: Coverity, http://www.coverity.com/products/static-analysis.html
2. Web-site: Klocwork insight, http://www.klocwork.com/products/insight/
3. Nesov, V.: Automatically finding bugs in open source programs. In: Third International Workshop on Foundations and Techniques for Open Source Software Certification. OpenCert 2009, vol. 20, pp. 19–29 (2009)
4. Dillig, I., Dillig, T., Aiken, A.: Sound, complete and scalable path-sensitive analysis. SIGPLAN Not. 43, 270–280 (2008)
5. Hovemeyer, D., Pugh, W.: Finding bugs is easy. SIGPLAN Not. 39, 92–106 (2004)
6. Evans, D., Larochelle, D.: Improving security using extensible lightweight static analysis. IEEE Softw. 19, 42–51 (2002)
7. Ball, T., Bounimova, E., Kumar, R., Levin, V.: SLAM2: Static driver verification with under 4% false alarms. In: Formal Methods in Computer Aided Design (2010)
8. Beyer, D., Henzinger, T.A., Jhala, R., Majumdar, R.: The software model checker Blast: Applications to software engineering. Int. J. Softw. Tools Technol. Transf. 9(5), 505–525 (2007)
9. Beyer, D., Keremoglu, M.E.: CPAchecker: A tool for configurable software verification. Technical report, School of Computing Science, Simon Fraser University (2009)
10. Clarke, E., Kroning, D., Lerda, F.: A Tool for Checking ANSI-C Programs. In: Jensen, K., Podelski, A. (eds.) TACAS 2004. LNCS, vol. 2988, pp. 168–176. Springer, Heidelberg (2004)
11. Podelski, A., Rybalchenko, A.: ARMC: The Logical Choice for Software Model Checking with Abstraction Refinement. In: Hanus, M. (ed.) PADL 2007. LNCS, vol. 4354, pp. 245–259. Springer, Heidelberg (2006)
12. Ball, T., Bounimova, E., Levin, V., Kumar, R., Lichtenberg, J.: The Static Driver Verifier Research Platform. In: Touili, T., Cook, B., Jackson, P. (eds.) CAV 2010. LNCS, vol. 6174, pp. 119–122. Springer, Heidelberg (2010)
13. Khoroshilov, A., Mutilin, V.: Formal methods for open source components certification. In: 2nd International Workshop on Foundations and Techniques for Open Source Software Certification. OpenCert 2008, pp. 52–63 (2008)
14. Khoroshilov, A., Mutilin, V., Shcherbina, V., Strikov, O., Vinogradov, S., Zakharov, V.: How to cook an automated system for Linux driver verification. In: 2nd Spring Young Researchers' Colloquium on Software Engineering. SYRCoSE 2008, vol. 2, pp. 11–14 (2008)
15. Khoroshilov, A., Mutilin, V., Petrenko, A., Zakharov, V.: Establishing Linux Driver Verification Process. In: Pnueli, A., Virbitskaite, I., Voronkov, A. (eds.) PSI 2009. LNCS, vol. 5947, pp. 165–176. Springer, Heidelberg (2010)
16. Kroah-Hartman, G., Corbet, J., McPherson, A.: Linux kernel development: How fast it is going, who is doing it, what they are doing, and who is sponsoring it (2010), http://www.linuxfoundation.org/docs/lf_linux_kernel_development_2010.pdf

17. Chou, A., Yang, J., Chelf, B., Hallem, S., Engler, D.: An empirical study of operating systems errors. In: SOSP 2001: Proceedings of the Eighteenth ACM Symposium on Operating Systems Principles, pp. 73–88. ACM, New York (2001)

18. Swift, M.M., Bershad, B.N., Levy, H.M.: Improving the reliability of commodity operating systems. In: SOSP 2003: Proceedings of the Nineteenth ACM Symposium on Operating Systems Principles, pp. 207–222. ACM, New York (2003)

19. Ball, T., Rajamani, S.K.: SLIC: A specification language for interface checking. Technical report, Microsoft Research (2001)

20. Beckman, N.E., Nori, A.V., Rajamani, S.K., Simmons, R.J.: Proofs from tests. In: Proceedings of the 2008 International Symposium on Software Testing and Analysis, ISSTA 2008, pp. 3–14. ACM, New York (2008)

21. Post, H., Küchlin, W.: Integrated Static Analysis for Linux Device Driver Verification. In: Davies, J., Gibbons, J. (eds.) IFM 2007. LNCS, vol. 4591, pp. 518–537. Springer, Heidelberg (2007)

22. Witkowski, T., Blanc, N., Kroening, D., Weissenbacher, G.: Model checking concurrent Linux device drivers. In: ASE 2007: Proceedings of the Twenty-Second IEEE/ACM International Conference on Automated Software Engineering, pp. 501–504. ACM, New York (2007)

23. Clarke, E., Kroning, D., Sharygina, N., Yorav, K.: SATABS: SAT-Based Predicate Abstraction for ANSI-C. In: Halbwachs, N., Zuck, L.D. (eds.) TACAS 2005. LNCS, vol. 3440, pp. 570–574. Springer, Heidelberg (2005)

24. Post, H., Küchlin, W.: Automatic data environment construction for static device drivers analysis. In: Proceedings of the 2006 Conference on Specification and Verification of Component-Based Systems, SAVCBS 2006, pp. 89–92. ACM, New York (2006)

25. Necula, G.C., McPeak, S., Rahul, S.P., Weimer, W.: CIL: Intermediate Language and Tools for Analysis and Transformation of C Programs. In: CC 2002. LNCS, vol. 2304, pp. 213–228. Springer, Heidelberg (2002)

26. Beyer, D., Cimatti, A., Griggio, A., Keremoglu, M.E., Sebastiani, R.: Software model checking via large-block encoding. In: Formal Methods in Computer-Aided Design, FMCAD 2009, pp. 25–32 (November 2009)

27. Clarke, E., Grumberg, O., Jha, S., Lu, Y., Veith, H.: Counterexample-guided Abstraction Refinement. In: Emerson, E.A., Sistla, A.P. (eds.) CAV 2000. LNCS, vol. 1855, pp. 154–169. Springer, Heidelberg (2000)

28. Weide, B.W., Sitaraman, M., Harton, H.K., Adcock, B., Bucci, P., Bronish, D., Heym, W.D., Kirschenbaum, J., Frazier, D.: Incremental Benchmarks for Software Verification Tools and Techniques. In: Shankar, N., Woodcock, J. (eds.) VSTTE 2008. LNCS, vol. 5295, pp. 84–98. Springer, Heidelberg (2008)

29. Web-site: Problems found in Linux kernels,
http://linuxtesting.org/results/ldv

Solving Coverability Problem for Monotonic Counter Systems by Supercompilation

Andrei V. Klimov[*]

Keldysh Institute of Applied Mathematics
Russian Academy of Sciences
4 Miusskaya sq., Moscow, 125047, Russia
klimov@keldysh.ru

Abstract. We put the program transformation method known as *super-compilation* in the context of works on counter systems, well-structured transition systems, Petri nets, etc. Two classic versions of the supercompilation algorithm are formulated for counter systems, using notions and notation adopted from the literature on transition systems.

A procedure to solve the coverability problem for a counter system by iterative application of a supercompiler to the system along with initial and target sets of states, is presented. Its correctness for monotonic counter systems provided the target set is upward-closed and the initial set has a certain form, is proved.

The fact that a supercompiler can solve the coverability problem for a lot of practically interesting counter systems has been discovered by A. Nemytykh and A. Lisitsa when they performed experiments on verification of cache-coherence protocols and other models by means of the Refal supercompiler SCP4, and since then theoretical explanation why this was so successful has been an open problem. Here the solution for the monotonic counter systems is given.

Keywords: supercompilation, verification, reachability, coverability, well-structured transition systems, counter systems.

1 Introduction

In this paper we formally explain why *supercompilers* (program transformers based on *supercompilation* by Valentin Turchin [27] and its further development) are capable of solving the *reachability and coverability problems* for *monotonic counter systems* where a set of target states is upward-closed and a set of initial states has a certain form.

The idea of verification by supercompilation stems from the pioneering work by V. Turchin [26]. In case of solving the *reachability problem* it sounds as follows. Let a program S encode a transition system $\mathcal{S}$ under study in the source language of a supercompiler: in Refal for the Refal Supercompiler SCP4 [24] and in Java for the Java Supercompiler JScp [10,12]. To simulate a non-deterministic

---

[*] Supported by Russian Foundation for Basic Research project No. 09-01-00834-a.

E. Clarke, I. Virbitskaite, and A. Voronkov (Eds.): PSI 2011, LNCS 7162, pp. 193–209, 2012.

system the program S takes an additional argument a, 'actions', a sequence (array) of integers used to select non-deterministic choices: each time a choice is encountered the next integer i from a is used to select the i-th alternative. Given an initial state s, program $S(s, a)$ returns the final state s' reachable by the transition system $\mathcal{S}$ with the use of 'actions' a. We want to decide whether a set of target states U is reachable or not from a set of initial states I:

$$\exists s \in I,\ a \in \mathbb{N}^*\colon\ S(s, a) \in U.$$

Let the sets of initial and target states I and U be given by programs I and U respectively, returning **true** or **false**. Define a program P that tells whether the set U is unreachable[1] from a state s belonging to the initial set I with the use of actions a:

$$P(s, a) = \textbf{if}\ I(s)\ \textbf{then}\ \neg U(S(s, a))\ \textbf{else}\ \textbf{true}.$$

A supercompiler Scp given a program P transforms it to an equivalent program P' referred to as a *residual* one.

1. If P' has the form where the result **false** is found on one of the **if** branches from the top, e.g.,

   $$P(s, a) = \textbf{if}\ C_1(s, a)\ \textbf{then if}\ C_2(s, a)\ \textbf{then false else}\ \ldots\ \textbf{else}\ \ldots$$

   then we conclude U is reachable from I (provided the conditionals C_i are simple enough to evaluate whether their conjunctions are inhabited or not). A counter-example, the values of s and a, can be found by analyzing the sequence of tests C_i leading to **false**, e.g., $C_1(s, a) \wedge C_2(s, a)$ in this example.
2. Alternatively, the code of the residual program P' contains no word **false**, only words **true** occur in the places were the result is returned. Then we conclude that $P(s, a)$ always returns **true** (when it terminates), i.e., U is unreachable from I by the transition system.
3. In the general case, the code of P' contains both constants **true** and **false**, and we conclude nothing by its inspection.

We have applied this approach to a specific class of programs that encode counter transition systems. To explain the results, in this paper two classic versions of supercompilation algorithms are formulated directly for counter systems, using notions and notation adopted from the literature on transition systems.

We have proved that for monotonic counter systems the case 3 can be avoided by the following iterative procedure. Let Scp_l be a supercompiler with a parameter l that prohibits generalization of non-negative integers $i < l$. Apply Scp_0 to a program that encodes a transition system. If the residual program is of the third form, apply Scp_1, and so on for $l = 2, 3, \ldots$, until the residual program has the first or second form. In the first case we conclude the transition system is 'unsafe' w.r.t. the sets I and U, and 'safe' in the second case.

---

[1] By tradition of applications a target set U is considered as 'bad', 'unsafe' and the answer 'Unreachable' as positive.

The fact that this procedure terminates in practice was discovered by A. Nemytykh and A. Lisitsa when they performed experiments on verification of cache-coherence protocols and other models by means of the Refal supercompiler SCP4 [19,20,21,22]. It was a non-trivial guess by A. Nemytykh and A. Lisitsa that such a restriction on generalization should be tried. To reproduce the results with the Java supercompiler JScp, the integer option l to restrict generalization of integers has been added to JScp [12]. For our experiments [11,12] the values $l = 0$ (no restriction on generalization of integers) and $l = 1$ (values 0 is never generalized) were sufficient. However, the theoretical study presented below shows that in general case an arbitrary l may be needed.

The paper is organized as follows. In Section 2 we recall some known notions from the theory of transition systems as well as give specific notions from supercompilation theory used in the algorithm presented in Section 3. Section 4 contains an outline of a correctness proof. In Section 5 we discuss related work, and in Section 6 conclude.

2   Basic Notions

2.1   Transition Systems

We use the common notions of *transition system, monotonic transition system, well-structured transition system, counter system* and related ones.

A *transition system* $\mathcal{S}$ is a tuple $\langle S, \Rightarrow \rangle$ such that S is a possibly infinite set of states, $\Rightarrow \subseteq S \times S$ a transition relation.

A *transition function* $\mathsf{Post}(\mathcal{S}, s)$ is used to denote the set $\{s' \mid s \Rightarrow s'\}$ of one-step successors of s.[2]

$\mathsf{Post}^*(\mathcal{S}, s)$ denotes the set $\{s' \mid s \stackrel{*}{\Rightarrow} s'\}$ of successors of s.

$\mathsf{Reach}(\mathcal{S}, I)$ denotes the set $\bigcup_{s \in I} \mathsf{Post}^*(\mathcal{S}, s)$ of states *reachable* from a set of states I.

We say a transition system $\langle S, \Rightarrow \rangle$ is (*quasi-, partially*) *ordered* if some (quasi-,[3] partial[4]) order $\preccurlyeq$ is defined on its set of states S.

For a quasi-ordered set X, $\downarrow X$ denotes $\{x \mid \exists y \in X \colon x \preccurlyeq y\}$, the downward closure of X. $\uparrow X$ denotes $\{x \mid \exists y \in X \colon x \succcurlyeq y\}$, the upward closure of X.

Definition 1 (Covering set). *The* covering set *of $\mathcal{S}$ w.r.t. an initial set I, noted* $\mathsf{Cover}(\mathcal{S}, I)$, *is the set* $\downarrow \mathsf{Reach}(\mathcal{S}, I)$, *the downward closure of the set of states reachable from I.*

Definition 2 (Coverability problem). *The* coverability problem *for a transition system $\mathcal{S}$, an initial set of states I and an upward-closed target set of states U asks a question whether U is reachable from I:* $\exists s \in I, s' \in U \colon s \stackrel{*}{\Rightarrow} s'$.[5]

---

[2] For effectiveness, we assume the set of one-step successors is finite.

[3] A *quasi-order* (*preorder*) is a reflexive and transitive relation.

[4] A *partial order* is an antisymmetric quasi-order.

[5] In other words, the coverability problem asks a question whether such a state r is reachable from I that $\downarrow\{r\} \cap U \neq \emptyset$, where there is no requirement that the target set U is upward-closed.

A quasi-order $\preccurlyeq$ is a *well-quasi-order* iff for every infinite sequence $\{x_i\}$ there are two positions $i < j$ such that $x_i \preccurlyeq x_j$.

A transition system $\langle S, \Rightarrow \rangle$ equipped with a quasi-order $\preccurlyeq \subseteq S \times S$ is said to be *monotonic* if for every $s_1, s_2, s_3 \in S$ such that $s_1 \Rightarrow s_2$ and $s_1 \preccurlyeq s_3$ there exists $s_4 \in S$ such that $s_3 \overset{*}{\Rightarrow} s_4$ and $s_2 \preccurlyeq s_4$.

A transition system is called *well-structured (WSTS)* if it is equipped with a well-quasi-order $\preccurlyeq \subseteq S \times S$ and is monotonic w.r.t. this order.

Definition 3 (Counter system). *A k-dimensional counter system $\mathcal{S}$ is a transition system $\langle S, \Rightarrow \rangle$ with states $S = \mathbb{N}^k$, k-tuples of non-negative integers. It is equipped with the component-wise partial order $\preccurlyeq$ on k-tuples of integers:*

$$s_1 \preccurlyeq s_2 \quad \text{iff} \quad \forall i \in [1, k]: \ s_1(i) \le s_2(i),$$
$$s_1 \prec s_2 \quad \text{iff} \quad s_1 \preccurlyeq s_2 \wedge s_1 \ne s_2.$$

Proposition 1. *The component-wise order $\preccurlyeq$ of k-tuples of non-negative integers is a well-quasi order. A counter system equipped with this order $\preccurlyeq$ is a well-structured transitions system.*

2.2   Configurations

In supercompilation the term *configuration* denotes a representation of a set of states, while in Petri net and transition system theories the same term stands for a ground state. In this paper the supercompilation terminology is used. Our term *configuration* is equivalent to ω-*configuration* and ω-*marking* in Petri net theory.

The general rule of construction of the notion of a configuration in a supercompiler from that of the program state in an interpreter is as follows: add configuration variables to the data domain and allow these to occur anywhere where a ground value can occur. A configuration represents the set of states that can be obtained by replacing configuration variables with all possible values. Thus the notion of a configuration implies a set represented by some constructive means rather than an arbitrary set.

A state of a counter system is a k-tuple of integers. According to the above rule, a configuration should be a tuple of integers and configuration variables. For the purpose of this paper we use a single symbol ω for all occurrences of variables and consider each occurrence of ω a distinct configuration variable.

Thus, in supercompilation of k-dimensional counter systems *configurations* are k-tuples over $\mathbb{N} \cup \{\omega\}$, and we have the set of all configurations $\mathcal{C} = (\mathbb{N} \cup \{\omega\})^k$.

A configuration $c \in \mathcal{C}$ represents a set of states noted $[\![c]\!]$:

$$[\![c]\!] = \{\langle x_1, \ldots, x_k \rangle \mid x_i \in \mathbb{N} \text{ if } c(i) = \omega, \ x_i = c(i) \text{ otherwise}, \ 1 \le i \le k\}.$$

These notations agree with that used in Petri net and counter system theories. Notice that by using one symbol ω we cannot capture information about equal unknown values represented by repeated occurrences of a variable. However, when supercompiling counter systems, repeated variables do not occur in practice, and such simplified representation satisfies our needs.

We also use an extension of $[\![\cdot]\!]$ to sets of configurations to denote all states represented by the configurations from a set C: $[\![C]\!] = \bigcup_{c \in C} [\![c]\!]$.

Definition 4 (Coverability set). *A coverability set is a finite set of configurations C that represents the covering set in the following way: $\downarrow[\![C]\!] = \mathsf{Cover}(\mathcal{S}, I)$.*

Notice that if we could find a coverability set, we could solve the coverability problem by checking its intersection with the target set U.

2.3   Residual Graph, Tree and Set

Definition 5 (Residual graph and residual set). *Given a transition system $\mathcal{S} = \langle S, \Rightarrow \rangle$ along with an initial set $I \subseteq S$ and a set $\mathcal{C}$ of configurations, a residual graph is a tuple $\mathcal{T} = \langle N, B, n_0, C \rangle$, where N is a set of nodes, $B \subseteq N \times N$ a set of edges, $n_0 \in N$ a root node, $C \colon N \to \mathcal{C}$ a labeling function of the nodes by configurations, and*

1. *$[\![I]\!] \subseteq [\![C(n_0)]\!]$, and for every state $s \in S$ reachable from I there exists a node $n \in N$ such that $s \in [\![C(n)]\!]$, and*
2. *for every node $n \in N$ and states s, s' such that $s \in [\![C(n)]\!]$ and $s \Rightarrow s'$ there exists an edge $\langle n, n' \rangle \in B$ such that $s' \in [\![C(n')]\!]$.*

We call the set $\{C(n) \mid n \in N\}$ of all configurations in the graph a residual set.

Notice that a residual set is a representation of an over-approximation of the set of reachable states: $\downarrow[\![\{C(n) \mid n \in N\}]\!] \supseteq \mathsf{Reach}(\mathcal{S}, I)$.

The term *residual* is borrowed from the supercompilation terminology, where the output of a supercompiler is referred to as a *residual graph* and a *residual program*. In the literature on transition systems, the term *coverability set* is used for a specific case of a residual set, where it is a precise representation of the covering set $\mathsf{Cover}(\mathcal{S}, I) = \downarrow\mathsf{Reach}(\mathcal{S}, I)$.

The value of these notions for our purpose is as follows. To solve the coverability problem it is sufficient to find a coverability set among the residual sets: then we check whether all configurations in the coverability set are disjoint with the target set or not. Unfortunately, computing a coverability set is undecidable for counter systems of our interest. Fortunately, this is not necessary. It is sufficient to build a sequence of residual sets that contains a coverability set. We may not know which one among the residual sets is a coverability set (this is incomputable), it is sufficient to know it exists in the sequence. This is the main idea of our algorithm and the 'Expand, Enlarge and Check' (EEC) algorithmic schema of [6].

Notice that such procedure of solving the coverability problem does not use the edges of the residual graph, and we can keep in B only those edges that are needed for the work of our versions of supercompilation algorithms. Hence the definition of a residual tree:

Definition 6 (Residual tree). *A residual tree is a spanning tree of a residual graph. The root of the tree is the root node n_0 of the graph.*

2.4   Operations on Configurations

To define a supercompiler we need the transition function Post on states to be extended to the corresponding function Drive on configurations. It is referred to as (one-step) *driving* in supercompilation and must meet the following properties (where $s \in S$, $c \in C$):

1. $\mathsf{Drive}(\mathcal{S}, s) = \mathsf{Post}(\mathcal{S}, s)$ — a configuration with ground values represents a singleton and its successor configurations are respective singletons;
2. $[\![\mathsf{Drive}(\mathcal{S}, c)]\!] \supseteq \bigcup \{\mathsf{Post}(\mathcal{S}, s) \mid s \in [\![c]\!]\}$ — the configurations returned by Drive over-approximate the set of one-step successors. This is the *soundness* property of driving. The over-approximation suits well for applications to program optimization, but for verification the result of Drive must be more precise. Hence the next property:
3. $[\![\mathsf{Drive}(\mathcal{S}, c)]\!] \subseteq {\downarrow}\bigcup \{\mathsf{Post}(\mathcal{S}, s) \mid s \in [\![c]\!]\}$ — for solving the coverability problem it is sufficient to require that configurations returned by Drive are subsets of the downward closure of the set of the successors.

For the practical counter systems we experimented with, the transition function Post is defined in form of a finite set of partial functions taking the coordinates v_i of the current state to the coordinates v_i' of the next state:

$$v_i' = \text{ if } G_i(v_1, \ldots, v_k) \text{ then } E_i(v_1, \ldots, v_k), i \in [1, k],$$

where the 'guards' G_i are conjunctions of elementary predicates $v_j \geq a$ and $v_j = a$, and the arithmetic expressions E_i consist of operations $x + y$, $x + a$ and $x - a$, where x and y are variables or expressions, $a \in \mathbb{N}$ a constant.

The same partial functions define the transition function Drive on configurations, the operations on ground data being generalized to the extended domain $\mathbb{N} \cup \{\omega\}$: $\forall a \in \mathbb{N}$: $a < \omega$ and $\omega + a = \omega - a = \omega + \omega = \omega$.

2.5   Restricted Ordering of Configurations of Counter Systems

To control termination of supercompilers we use a restricted partial order on integers $\preccurlyeq_l$ parameterized by $l \in \mathbb{N}$. For $a, b \in \mathbb{N} \cup \{\omega\}$, we have:

$$a \preccurlyeq_l b \quad \text{iff} \quad l \leq a \leq b < \omega.$$

This partial order makes two integers incompatible when one of them is less than l.[6] The order is a well-quasi-order.

---

[6] Alternatively, for supercompiler ScpL (Algorithm 1), the following partial order can be used, where two integers are incompatible when both are less than l:

$$a \preccurlyeq_l b \quad \text{iff} \quad a \leq b \wedge l \leq b < \omega$$

Then the partial order on states and configurations of counter systems is the respective component-wise comparison: for $c_1, c_2 \in \mathcal{C} = (\mathbb{N} \cup \{\omega\})^k$,

$$c_1 \preccurlyeq_l c_2 \quad \text{iff} \quad \forall i \in [1, k]: \ c_1(i) \preccurlyeq_l c_2(i).$$

This order is also a well-quasi-order. It may be regarded as a specific case of the homeomorphic embedding of terms used in supercompilation to force termination. As we will see in the supercompilation algorithms below, when two configurations c_1 and c_2 are met on a path such that $c_1 \preccurlyeq_l c_2$, 'a whistle blows' and generalization of c_1 and c_2 is performed. Increasing parameter l prohibits generalization of small non-negative integers and makes 'whistle' to 'blow' later. When $l = 0$, the order is the standard component-wise well-quasi-order on tuples of integers. When $l = 1$, value 0 does not compare with other positive integers and generalization of 0 is prohibited. And so on.

2.6   Generalization

When the set of states represented by a configuration c is a subset of the set represented by a configuration g, $[\![c]\!] \subseteq [\![g]\!]$, we say the configuration g is *more general* than the configuration c, or g is a *generalization* of c.[7] Let $\sqsubseteq$ denote a *generalization relation* $\sqsubseteq \in \mathcal{C} \times \mathcal{C}$: $c \sqsubseteq g$ iff $[\![c]\!] \subseteq [\![g]\!]$, $c \sqsubset g$ iff $[\![c]\!] \subsetneq [\![g]\!]$.

We use a function $\mathsf{Generalize}: \mathcal{C} \times \mathcal{C} \to \mathcal{C}$ to find a configuration g that is more general than two given ones. Usually $\mathsf{Generalize}(c_1, c_2)$ returns the least general configuration, however this is not formally required for the soundness and termination of supercompilation, as well as for the results of this paper, although it is usually desirable for obtaining 'better' residual programs.

A natural requirement of generalization is its soundness: A generalization function $\mathsf{Generalize}$ is *sound* iff [8]

$$\forall c_1, c_2 \in \mathcal{C}: c_i \sqsubseteq \mathsf{Generalize}(c_1, c_2), \ i = 1, 2.$$

For termination of supercompilation generalization must meet additional requirements, the most important being the *upward well-foundness* of the generalization relation.[9]

The next question is how the generalization relation and the well-quasi-order that is used to catch the moment when to force generalization, relate to each other. For simplification of the code and the termination proof of the supercompiler ScpL with lower-node generalization (Algorithm 1 below), we require that the relations '*disagree*':

Definition 7 (Disagreement). *We say two relations* $\prec$ *and* $\sqsubset$ *disagree if*

$$a \prec b \ \text{implies} \ a \not\sqsubset b.$$

---

[7] In Petri net and counter system theories generalization is referred to as *acceleration*.

[8] Actually, the soundness may be relaxed: for Algorithm 1 the generalization function must be sound w.r.t. the second argument, and for Algorithm 2 w.r.t. the first one.

[9] A relation $\sqsubset$ is *upward well-founded* iff each increasing chain $a \sqsubset b \sqsubset c \sqsubset \ldots$ has a finite number of elements.

Now let us define a specific generalization function for configurations of counter systems. Function $\mathsf{Generalize}(c_1, c_2)$ sets to ω those coordinates where configurations c_1 and c_2 differ:

$\mathsf{Generalize}(c_1, c_2) = c$ s.t. $\forall i \in [1, k]$: $c(i) = c_1(i)$ if $c_1(i) = c_2(i)$, ω otherwise.

It is easy to see that the so defined $\mathsf{Generalize}$ is sound, well-founded and disagree with the well-quasi-orders $\preccurlyeq_l$ on $(\mathbb{N} \cup \{\omega\})^k$.

Notice that the function $\mathsf{Generalize}$ has no parameter l. However in the supercompilation algorithms below it is called in cases where $c_1 \prec_l c_2$. Hence generalization is not performed when one of the integers is less than l.

3   Algorithms

In this section we define two supercompilation algorithms for well-structured transition systems (WSTS) and an algorithm for deciding the coverability problem for counter systems, a particular case of WSTS.

3.1   Supercompilation of Well-Structured Transitions Systems

Supercompilation is usually understood as an equivalence transformation of programs, transition systems, etc., from a *source* one to a *residual* one. However, for the purpose of this paper the supercompilation algorithms presented here returns a part of information sufficient to extract the residual set of configurations rather than a full representation of a residual transition system.

Two algorithms, Algorithm 1 ScpL and Algorithm 2 ScpU, have very much in common. They take a transition system $\mathcal{S}$, a quasi-order $\prec$ on the set of configurations and an initial configuration I, and return a residual tree, which represents an over-approximation of the set of states reachable from the initial configuration I. The order $\prec$ is a parameter that controls the execution of the algorithms, their termination and influences resulting residual trees. If the order is a well-quasi-order the algorithms terminates for sure. Otherwise, in general, the algorithms sometimes terminate and sometimes do not.

The residual trees are gradually constructed from the root node n_0.

The nodes are labeled with configurations by a labeling function $C : N \to \mathcal{C}$, initially $C(n_0) = I$.

Untreated leaves are kept in a set T ('to treat') in Algorithm 1 and in a stack T in Algorithm 2. The first algorithm is non-deterministic and takes leaves from set T in arbitrary order. The second algorithm is deterministic and takes leaves from stack T in FIFO order. The algorithms terminate when $T = \emptyset$ and $T = \epsilon$ (the empty sequence) respectively.

At each step, one of three branches is executed, marked in comments as (1), (2) and (3). Branches (1) and (3) are almost identical in the two algorithms.

Branches (1): if a configuration $C(\bar{n})$ more general than the current one $C(n)$ exists in the already constructed tree, the current path is terminated and nothing is done.

Algorithm 1. ScpL: Supercompilation of a quasi-ordered transition system with lower-node generalization.

Data: S a transition system
Data: I an initial configuration
Data: $\prec$ a quasi-order on configurations, a 'whistle'
Result: $\mathcal{T}$ a residual tree

$\mathsf{ScpL}(S, I, \prec)$

    $\mathcal{T} \leftarrow \langle N, B, n_0, C \rangle$ where $N = \{n_0\}$, $B = \emptyset$, $C(n_0) = I$, n_0 a new node
    $T \leftarrow \{n_0\}$
    while $T \neq \emptyset$ **do**
        select some node $n \in T$
        $T \leftarrow T \setminus \{n\}$
        if $\exists \bar{n} \in N : C(\bar{n}) \sqsupseteq C(n)$ **then**   — terminate the current path (1)
         | do nothing
        else if $\exists \bar{n} : B^+(\bar{n}, n) \wedge C(\bar{n}) \prec C(n)$ **then** — generalize on whistle (2)
            $\bar{n} \leftarrow$ some node such that $B^+(\bar{n}, n) \wedge C(\bar{n}) \prec C(n)$
            $C(n) \leftarrow \mathsf{Generalize}(C(\bar{n}), C(n))$
            mark n as generalized
            $T \leftarrow T \cup \{n\}$
        else   — unfold (drive) otherwise (3)
            foreach $c \in \mathsf{Drive}(S, C(n))$ **do**
                $n' \leftarrow$ a new node
                $C(n') \leftarrow c$
                $N \leftarrow N \cup \{n'\}$
                $B \leftarrow B \cup \{\langle n, n' \rangle\}$
                $T \leftarrow T \cup \{n'\}$
    return $\mathcal{T}$

Branches (3): if the conditions on branches (1) and (2) do not hold, a *driving step* is performed: the successors of the current configuration $C(n)$ are evaluated by the function Drive; for each new configuration c a new node n' is created; edges from the current node n to the new ones are added to the tree and the new nodes are added to set (or respectively, stack) T of untreated nodes.

Branches (2) check whether on the path to the current node n (call it *lower*) there exists a node $\bar{n}$ (call it *upper*) with the configuration $C(\bar{n})$ which is less than the current one $C(n)$, generalize the two configurations and assign the generalized configuration to the lower node in Algorithm 1 ScpL and to the upper node in Algorithm 2 ScpU. In the latter case the nodes below $\bar{n}$ are deleted from the residual tree and from stack T of untreated nodes. The nodes where generalization has been performed are marked as 'generalized'. These marks are used in the Algorithm 3.

Algorithm 2. ScpU: Supercompilation of a quasi-ordered transition system with upper-node generalization.

Data: $\mathcal{S}$ a transition system
Data: I an initial configuration
Data: $\prec$ a quasi-order on configurations, a 'whistle'
Result: $\mathcal{T}$ a residual tree

ScpU$(\mathcal{S}, I, \prec)$
    $\mathcal{T} \leftarrow \langle N, B, n_0, C \rangle$ where $N = [n_0]$, $B = \emptyset$, $C(n_0) = I$, n_0 a new node
    $T \leftarrow [n_0]$
    while $T \neq \epsilon$ **do**
        $n \leftarrow \mathsf{Last}(T)$
        $T \leftarrow T \setminus \{n\}$
        if $\exists \bar{n} \in N \colon C(\bar{n}) \sqsupseteq C(n)$ **then**   — terminate the current path (1)
        | do nothing
        else if $\exists \bar{n} \colon B^+(\bar{n}, n) \wedge C(\bar{n}) \prec C(n)$ **then** — generalize on whistle (2)
            $\bar{n} \leftarrow$ the highest node such that $B^+(\bar{n}, n) \wedge C(\bar{n}) \prec C(n)$
            $C(\bar{n}) \leftarrow \mathsf{Generalize}(C(\bar{n}), C(n))$
            mark $\bar{n}$ as generalized
            $\mathcal{T} \leftarrow \mathsf{RemoveSubtreeExceptRoot}(\bar{n}, \mathcal{T})$
            $T \leftarrow T \setminus \{n \mid B^+(\bar{n}, n)\}$ — drop nodes lower than $\bar{n}$
            $T \leftarrow \mathsf{Append}(T, \bar{n})$
        else   — unfold (drive) otherwise (3)
            foreach $c \in \mathsf{Drive}(\mathcal{S}, C(n))$ **do**
                $n' \leftarrow$ a new node
                $C(n') \leftarrow c$
                $N \leftarrow N \cup \{n'\}$
                $B \leftarrow B \cup \{\langle n, n' \rangle\}$
                $T \leftarrow \mathsf{Append}(T, n')$
    return $\mathcal{T}$

3.2 Deciding the Coverability Problem for Counter Systems

Algorithm 3 Reachable$(\mathcal{S}, I, U)$ takes a counter system $\mathcal{S}$, an initial configuration I and a target upward-closed set U and iteratively applies supercompiler ScpL or ScpU with the well-quasi-order $\prec_l$ of counter configurations with integer parameter $l = 0, 1, 2, \ldots$

At each step the residual set is extracted form the residual tree produced by Scp$(\mathcal{S}, I, \prec_l)$ and assigned to a variable *Over*. It is used as a representation of an over-approximation of the covering set: $\downarrow[\![Over]\!] \supseteq \mathsf{Cover}(\mathcal{S}, I)$. Its part *Under* comprised of the configurations developed from the initial configuration without generalization (where all nodes on the path are not marked as 'generalized') represents an under-approximation: $\downarrow[\![Under]\!] \subseteq \mathsf{Cover}(\mathcal{S}, I)$.

The approximations are used to check for reachability of the downward-closed target set U. If the over-approximation $[\![Over]\!]$ is disjoint with U, it is unreachable. If the under-approximation $[\![Under]\!]$ intersects with U, it is reachable. For monotonic counter systems one of the cases eventually happens.

Algorithm 3. A supercompilation-based algorithm to decide the coverability problem for monotonic counter systems.

Data: $\mathcal{S}$ a counter system with the component-wise partial order $\preccurlyeq_l$
Data: I an initial configuration
Data: U an upward-closed target set
Result: Is U reachable from I?

Reachable($\mathcal{S}, I, U$)
  for $l = 0, 1, 2, \ldots$ **do**
    $\langle N, B, n_0, C \rangle \leftarrow \mathsf{Scp}(\mathcal{S}, I, \preccurlyeq_l)$ — $\mathsf{Scp} = \mathsf{ScpL}$ or ScpU
    $Over \leftarrow \{C(n) \mid n \in N\}$
    $Under \leftarrow \{C(n) \mid n \in N \wedge \forall \bar{n} \text{ s.t. } B^*(\bar{n}, n) \colon \bar{n} \text{ is not marked as generalized}\}$
    if $[\![\,Under\,]\!] \cap U \neq \emptyset$ **then**
      return 'Reachable'
    else if $[\![\,Over\,]\!] \cap U = \emptyset$ **then**
      return 'Unreachable'

---

4 Correctness

It this section we give an outline of a proof of the algorithm correctness with more detail on evaluation of an upper estimate of parameter l.

We omit the proofs of soundness and termination of Algorithms 1 ScpL and 2 ScpU as they follow the traditional supercompilation algorithms that can be found in the literature [14,25,27,28]. Let us just state the result:

Theorem 1 (Termination of supercompilation). *Given a well-quasi-ordered transition system $\langle \mathcal{S}, \prec \rangle$ and an initial configuration $I \in \mathcal{C}$, Algorithms 1 ScpL and 2 ScpU terminate provided the generalization relation is upward well-founded and, for Algorithm 1, the well-quasi-order and the generalization relation disagree.*

For the purpose of solving the coverability problem, the soundness of supercompilation algorithms means the covering set is covered by the residual set *Over* and under-approximated by its subset *Under* (see Algorithm 3):

$$\downarrow[\![\,Under\,]\!] \subseteq \mathsf{Cover}(\mathcal{S}, I) \subseteq \downarrow[\![\,Over\,]\!].$$

Termination of Algorithm Reachable($\mathcal{S}, I, U$) is to be proved for two cases.

Case 1 (Reachable). If a finite path from the initial set I to the target set U exists, it will be eventually unrolled without generalization with some value of parameter l. Hence,

Theorem 2 (Deciding reachability). *For every counter system $\mathcal{S}$ equipped with the component-wise partial order $\preccurlyeq$, for every initial configuration I and target set of states U such that $\mathsf{Reach}(\mathcal{S}, I) \cap U \neq \emptyset$, there exists $l \in \mathbb{N}$ such that Algorithm 3 Reachable terminates and returns 'Reachable' with each of the supercompilation algorithms 1 ScpL and 2 ScpU.*

Case 2 (Unreachable). The case $U = \emptyset$ is trivial. Hence, $U \neq \emptyset$ is assumed below.

We are to prove there exists an integer $l \in \mathbb{N}$ such that the over-approximation *Over* produced by $\mathsf{Scp}(\mathcal{S}, I, \preccurlyeq_l)$ represents a proper coverability set: $\downarrow[\![Over]\!] = \mathsf{Cover}(\mathcal{S}, I)$.

An upper estimate of l is a function of the covering set, based on the following lemma about generalization of counter configurations: given a downward-closed set $D \subseteq \mathbb{N}^k$, a 'cover', if a configuration belongs to the cover then its generalizations also belong to the cover provided coordinates less than some integer l are not generalized. (l depends on D.)

Lemma 1 (Restricted generalization preserves a cover). *Given a set $S = \mathbb{N}^k$ with the component-wise partial order $\preccurlyeq$, for every downward-closed set $D = \downarrow D \subseteq S$, there exists $l \in \mathbb{N}$ such that for all $c, g \in \mathcal{C} = (\mathbb{N} \cup \{\omega\})^k$:*

$$[\![c]\!] \subseteq D \quad and \quad c \sqsubseteq_l g \quad implies \quad [\![g]\!] \subseteq D.$$

Proof. Consider the non-trivial case where $c \neq g$, $c \sqsubseteq_l g$.

Let $U = \overline{D}$, the complement of the downward-closed set D. Set U is upward-closed. As the order $\preccurlyeq$ is a well-quasi-order, there exists a finite set $\min(U)$ of minimal elements of U (a *generator* of U) such that $\uparrow \min(U) = U$.

Let m be the maximum of the coordinates of the elements of $\min(U)$:

$$m = \max_{s \in \min(U)} \max_{i \in [1,k]} s(i).$$

It can be proved that each $l \geq m$ satisfies the condition of the Lemma.   □

Corollary 1 (Restricted generalization preserves the covering set). *For every counter system $\mathcal{S}$ and initial configuration I, there exists $l \in \mathbb{N}$ such that for all configurations $c, g \in \mathcal{C} = (\mathbb{N} \cup \{\omega\})^k$:*

$$[\![c]\!] \subseteq \mathsf{Cover}(\mathcal{S}, I) \quad and \quad c \sqsubseteq_l g \quad implies \quad [\![g]\!] \subseteq \mathsf{Cover}(\mathcal{S}, I).$$

Proof. Follows from Lemma 1 as $\mathsf{Cover}(\mathcal{S}, I)$ is downward-closed.   □

Notice that the monotonicity of the counter system has not been used yet. The next step is to prove that all states reachable from configurations covered by the set of reachable states are covered by $\mathsf{Cover}(\mathcal{S}, I)$ as well. This time the monotonicity comes into play.

Lemma 2 (The covering set is closed under coverability). *For every monotonic transition system $\mathcal{S}$ and initial configuration I, for every configuration $c \in \mathcal{C} = (\mathbb{N} \cup \{\omega\})^k$:*

$$[\![c]\!] \subseteq \mathsf{Cover}(\mathcal{S}, I) \quad implies \quad \mathsf{Cover}(\mathcal{S}, c) \subseteq \mathsf{Cover}(\mathcal{S}, I).$$

Proof. A consequence of monotonicity. This proposition is known in the literature, e.g., Lemma 2.2 in [5, page 182]. □

Corollary 2 (Restricted generalization preserves coverability). *For every monotonic counter system $\mathcal{S}$ and initial configuration I, there exists $l \in \mathbb{N}$ such that for all configurations $c, g \in \mathcal{C}$:*

$$[\![c]\!] \subseteq \mathsf{Cover}(\mathcal{S}, I) \ \ and \ \ c \sqsubseteq_l g \ \ implies \ \ \mathsf{Cover}(\mathcal{S}, g) \subseteq \mathsf{Cover}(\mathcal{S}, I).$$

Proof. Follows from Corollary 1 and Lemma 2. □

Lemma 3 (Existence of a coverability set among residual sets). *For every monotonic counter system $\mathcal{S}$ and initial configuration I, there exists $l \in \mathbb{N}$ such that the residual set Over produced by $\mathsf{Scp}(\mathcal{S}, I, \prec_l)$ is a coverability set, i.e.,*

$$\downarrow[\![Over]\!] = \mathsf{Cover}(\mathcal{S}, I).$$

Proof. Consider the value of l satisfying the condition of Lemma 1 and hence that of Corollaries 1 and 2. In Algorithms 1 ScpL and 2 ScpU, each generalization restricted with this l extends the downward closure of the set of the states reachable form the configurations collected so far, up to not more than the covering set. Hence, the residual set obtained with this l is (representation of) a proper coverability set. □

Theorem 3 (Deciding unreachability). *For every monotonic counter system $\mathcal{S}$ equipped with the component-wise partial order $\preccurlyeq$, for every initial configuration I and upward-closed target set of states U such that $\mathsf{Reach}(\mathcal{S}, I) \cap U = \emptyset$, there exists $l \in \mathbb{N}$ such that Algorithm 3 Reachable terminates and returns 'Unreachable' with each of the supercompilation algorithms 1 ScpL and 2 ScpU satisfying the conditions of Theorem 1.*

By conjunction of Theorems 2 and 3 we obtain the correctness of Algorithm 3 Reachable that solves the coverability problem.

Remark that we don't know in advance the value of generalization parameter l where the supercompiler solves the coverability problem. Even we cannot compute its upper estimate m, because the problem of finding a coverability set for a monotonic counter system is undecidable (this follows from the results of [3]). Nevertheless, we know that such l exists for any monotonic counter system with non-empty set of unreachable states. Only when we are given an unreachable upward-closed set U, we can compute l, a lower estimate of m. That is why the decidability of the coverability problem [1] does not contradict to the incomputability of a coverability set.

5   Related Work

Supercompilation. This research originated from the experimental work by A. Nemytykh and A. Lisitsa on verification of cache-coherence protocols and other models by means of the Refal supercompiler SCP4 [19,20,21,22]. It came as a surprise that all of the considered correct models had been successfully verified rather than some of the models had been verified while others had not, as is a common situation with supercompiler applications. It was also unclear whether the evaluation of the heuristic parameter to control generalization of integers discovered by A. Nemytykh could be automated. Since then the theoretical explanation of these facts was an open problem.

In invited talk [18] A. Lisitsa and A. Nemytykh reported that supercompilation with upper-node generalization and without the restriction of generalization (i.e., with $l = 0$) was capable of solving the coverability problem for ordinary Petri nets, based on the model of supercompilation presented in their paper [22].

In this paper the problem has been solved for a larger class, and the sense of the generalization parameter has been uncovered. However the problem to formally characterize some class of non-monotonic counter systems verifiable by supercompilation, which the other part of the successful examples belongs to, remains open.

Partial Deduction. Similar work to establish a link between algorithms in Petri net theory and program specialization has been done in [8,16,17]. Especially close is the work [17] where a simplified version of partial deduction is put into one-to-one correspondence with the Karp&Miller algorithm [9] to compute a coverability tree of a Petri net. Here a Petri net is implemented as a (non-deterministic) logic program and partial deduction is applied to produce a specialized program from which a coverability set can be directly obtained.

(Online) partial deduction and supercompilation has many things in common. The method of [17] can be transferred from partial deduction to supercompilation, and our work is a step forward in the same direction after [17].

Petri Nets and Transition Systems. Transition systems and their subclasses—Petri nets and counter systems—have been under intensive study during last decades: [1,2,4,5,6,7,9], just to name a few. Supercompilation resembles forward analysis algorithms proposed in the literature.

A recent achievement is an algorithmic schema referred to as 'Expand, Enlarge and Check' (EEC). In paper [6] and in the PhD thesis by G. Geeraerts [5] a proof is given that any algorithm that fits EEC terminates on a well-structured transition systems (WSTS) and an upper-closed target set and solves the coverability problem.

The presented algorithm fits the EEC schema, and could be proved correct by reduction to EEC. Nevertheless, the direct proof is much simpler and makes it easier to reveal particular conditions and dependencies that are violated when one applies such an algorithm beyond its domain of correctness, e.g., for non-monotonic counter systems.

Algorithm 1 ScpL can be seen as a further development of the classic Karp&Miller algorithm [9] to compute a coverability set of a Petri net, and Algorithm 2

ScpU resembles the *minimal coverability tree* (MCT) algorithm by A. Finkel [4] (in which an error has been found [7]) and later attempts to fix it [7,23].[10]

6   Conclusion

Two supercompilation-based algorithms to solve the coverability problem for monotonic counter systems are presented and proved correct.

Although the algorithms are rather short they present the main notions of supercompilation: configurations, driving as well as configuration analysis of two kinds—with lower-node and upper-node generalization. To construct complete supercompilers for counter systems from these ones, one have to add the production of residual transitions on edges from respective source transition rules and the generation of a residual counter system from the residual tree. However, this is unneeded for our purpose.

The correctness proof has refuted the hypothesis (expressed in [12]) that the use of the 'whistle' (a rule when to stop driving and generalize) based on homeomorphic embedding and propagation of restrictions on integer variables of form $x \geq a$ were essential for solving the coverability problem. In fact, this problem can be solved by a supercompiler with a weaker whistle: 'generalize non-negative integers greater or equal than a given value l'. Based on this observation, an even simpler supercompilation-based algorithm to solve the coverability problem can be constructed. We elaborate on this in another paper [13].

Our main contribution into supercompilation theory and practice is presentation of the largest known to date class of problems provably solvable by supercompilers—the coverability problem for programs that mimics monotonic counter systems as well as well-structured transition systems.

The presented supercompilation-based algorithm may be considered an instance of *multi-result supercompilation*, the idea suggested by I. Klyuchnikov and S. Romanenko in [15]. They have shown the usefulness of multi-result supercompilation for proving the equivalence of expressions and in two-level supercompilation, while here a problem unsolvable by plain supercompilation, but solvable by enumerating a potentially infinite set of supercompilation results parameterized by an integer parameter of generalization, has been demonstrated.

Acknowledgements. I am very grateful to Sergei Abramov, Robert Glück, Arkady Klimov, Yuri Klimov, Ilya Klyuchnikov, Alexei Lisitsa, Andrei Nemytykh, Anton Orlov, Sergei Romanenko, Artem Shvorin and other participants of the Moscow Refal seminar for the pleasure to collaborate with them and exchange ideas on supercompilation and its applications. My work and life have been greatly influenced by Valentin Turchin whom we remember forever.

---

[10] The master thesis by K. Luttge [23] is beyond my reach. But its essence is explained in the PhD thesis by G. Geeraerts [5, pages 172–174].

References

1. Abdulla, P.A., Cerans, K., Jonsson, B., Tsay, Y.-K.: General decidability theorems for infinite-state systems. In: Proceedings of the 11th Annual IEEE Symposium on Logic in Computer Science, New Brunswick, New Jersey, July 27-30, pp. 313–321. IEEE Computer Society (1996)
2. Bardin, S., Finkel, A., Leroux, J., Petrucci, L.: FAST: acceleration from theory to practice. International Journal on Software Tools for Technology Transfer 10(5), 401–424 (2008)
3. Dufourd, C., Finkel, A., Schnoebelen, P.: Reset Nets Between Decidability and Undecidability. In: Larsen, K.G., Skyum, S., Winskel, G. (eds.) ICALP 1998. LNCS, vol. 1443, pp. 103–115. Springer, Heidelberg (1998)
4. Finkel, A.: The Minimal Coverability Graph for Petri Nets. In: Rozenberg, G. (ed.) APN 1993. LNCS, vol. 674, pp. 210–243. Springer, Heidelberg (1993)
5. Geeraerts, G.: Coverability and Expressiveness Properties of Well-Structured Transition Systems. PhD thesis, Université Libre de Bruxelles, Belgique (May 2007), http://www.ulb.ac.be/di/verif/ggeeraer/thesis.pdf
6. Geeraerts, G., Raskin, J.-F., Van Begin, L.: Expand, Enlarge and Check: New algorithms for the coverability problem of WSTS. Journal of Computer and System Sciences 72(1), 180–203 (2006)
7. Geeraerts, G., Raskin, J.-F., Van Begin, L.: On the Efficient Computation of the Minimal Coverability Set for Petri Nets. In: Namjoshi, K.S., Yoneda, T., Higashino, T., Okamura, Y. (eds.) ATVA 2007. LNCS, vol. 4762, pp. 98–113. Springer, Heidelberg (2007)
8. Glück, R., Leuschel, M.: Abstraction-Based Partial Deduction for Solving Inverse Problems - A Transformational Approach to Software Verification. In: Bjorner, D., Broy, M., Zamulin, A.V. (eds.) PSI 1999. LNCS, vol. 1755, pp. 93–100. Springer, Heidelberg (2000)
9. Karp, R.M., Miller, R.E.: Parallel program schemata. J. Comput. Syst. Sci. 3(2), 147–195 (1969)
10. Klimov, And.V.: An approach to supercompilation for object-oriented languages: the Java Supercompiler case study. In: Nemytykh, A.P. (ed.) Proceedings of the First International Workshop on Metacomputation in Russia, Pereslavl-Zalessky, Russia, July 2-5, pp. 43–53. Ailamazyan University of Pereslavl, Pereslavl-Zalessky (2008)
11. Klimov, And.V.: JVer Project: Verification of Java programs by Java Supercompiler (2008), http://pat.keldysh.ru/jver/
12. Klimov, And.V.: A Java Supercompiler and Its Application to Verification of Cache-Coherence Protocols. In: Pnueli, A., Virbitskaite, I., Voronkov, A. (eds.) PSI 2009. LNCS, vol. 5947, pp. 185–192. Springer, Heidelberg (2010)
13. Klimov, And.V.: Yet another algorithm for solving coverability problem for monotonic counter systems. In: Nepomnyaschy, V., Sokolov, V. (eds.) Second Workshop on Program Semantics, Specification and Verification: Theory and Applications, PSSV 2011, St. Petersburg, Russia, June 12-13, pp. 59–67. Yaroslavl State University (2011)
14. Klyuchnikov, I.: Supercompiler HOSC 1.1: proof of termination. Preprint 21, Keldysh Institute of Applied Mathematics, Moscow (2010)
15. Klyuchnikov, I., Romanenko, S.: Multi-result Supercompilation as Branching Growth of the Penultimate Level in Metasystem Transitions. In: Clarke, E., Virbitskaite, I., Voronkov, A. (eds.) PSI 2011. LNCS, vol. 7162, pp. 210–226. Springer, Heidelberg (2012)

16. Leuschel, M., Lehmann, H.: Coverability of Reset Petri Nets and Other Well-Structured Transition Systems by Partial Deduction. In: Palamidessi, C., Moniz Pereira, L., Lloyd, J.W., Dahl, V., Furbach, U., Kerber, M., Lau, K.-K., Sagiv, Y., Stuckey, P.J. (eds.) CL 2000. LNCS (LNAI), vol. 1861, pp. 101–115. Springer, Heidelberg (2000)

17. Leuschel, M., Lehmann, H.: Solving coverability problems of Petri nets by partial deduction. In: Proceedings of the 2nd International ACM SIGPLAN Conference on Principles and Practice of Declarative Programming, Montreal, Canada, September 20-23, pp. 268–279. ACM (2000)

18. Lisitsa, A.P., Nemytykh, A.P.: Solving coverability problems by supercompilation. Invited talk. In: The Second Workshop on Reachability Problems in Computational Models (RP 2008), Liverpool, UK, September 15-17 (2008)

19. Lisitsa, A.P., Nemytykh, A.P.: Towards verification via supercompilation. In: COMPSAC (2), pp. 9–10. IEEE Computer Society (2005)

20. Lisitsa, A.P., Nemytykh, A.P.: Experiments on verification via supercompilation (2007), http://refal.botik.ru/protocols/

21. Lisitsa, A.P., Nemytykh, A.P.: Verification as a parameterized testing (experiments with the SCP4 supercompiler). Programming and Computer Software 33(1), 14–23 (2007)

22. Lisitsa, A.P., Nemytykh, A.P.: Reachability analysis in verification via supercompilation. Int. J. Found. Comput. Sci. 19(4), 953–969 (2008)

23. Luttge, K.: Zustandsgraphen von Petri-Netzen. Master's thesis, Humboldt-Universität zu Berlin, Germany (1995)

24. Nemytykh, A.P.: The Supercompiler SCP4: General Structure. In: Broy, M., Zamulin, A.V. (eds.) PSI 2003. LNCS, vol. 2890, pp. 162–170. Springer, Heidelberg (2004)

25. Sørensen, M.H., Glück, R.: An algorithm of generalization in positive supercompilation. In: Lloyd, J.W. (ed.) International Logic Programming Symposium, Portland, Oregon, December 4-7, pp. 465–479. MIT Press (1995)

26. Turchin, V.F.: The Use of Metasystem Transition in Theorem Proving and Program Optimization. In: de Bakker, J.W., van Leeuwen, J. (eds.) ICALP 1980. LNCS, vol. 85, pp. 645–657. Springer, Heidelberg (1980)

27. Turchin, V.F.: The concept of a supercompiler. Transactions on Programming Languages and Systems 8(3), 292–325 (1986)

28. Turchin, V.F.: The algorithm of generalization in the supercompiler. In: Bjørner, D., Ershov, A.P., Jones, N.D. (eds.) Partial Evaluation and Mixed Computation, pp. 531–549. North-Holland (1988)

Multi-result Supercompilation as Branching Growth of the Penultimate Level in Metasystem Transitions[*]

Ilya Klyuchnikov and Sergei A. Romanenko

Keldysh Institute of Applied Mathematics
Russian Academy of Sciences

Abstract. The paper deals with some aspects of metasystem transitions in the context of supercompilation. We consider the manifestations of the law of *branching growth of the penultimate level* in the case of higher-level supercompilation and argue that this law provides some useful hints regarding the ways of constructing metasystems by combining supercompilers. In particular we show the usefulness of multi-result supercompilation for proving the equivalence of expressions and in two-level supercompilation.

1 Introduction

A *supercompiler* is a source-to-source program transformer SC based on *supercompilation* techniques [26,27,29], which, given an input program p, generates a *residual program* $p' = SC[\![p]\!]$. Supercompilation is often seen as a method of program optimization but also may be used for program analysis. Since our area of research is program analysis by supercompilation, we assume all the supercompilers we deal with to strictly preserve the semantics of programs.

The general concept of *metasystem transition* was put forward by V.F. Turchin in 1970-s [25, Chapter 3, Section "The Metasystem Transition"]:

> We shall call the system made up of control subsystem X and the many homogeneous subsystems A_1, A_2, A_3 ... controlled by it a metasystem in relation to systems A_1, A_2, A_3 ... Therefore we shall call the transition from one stage to the next the *metasystem transition*.

In particular, by treating supercompilation as an elementary operation, we can use supercompilers as building blocks for constructing more complex systems [28,29], which may be considered as an instance of metasystem transition.

There is no generally accepted term for systems built from supercompilers by metasystem transitions. Thus, for lack of something better, we use the term "higher-level supercompilation"[1].

---

[*] Supported by Russian Foundation for Basic Research project No. 09-01-00834-a.
[1] A possible alternative could be "meta-supercompilation" or "metacomputation" (suggested by V.F. Turchin [29]).

E. Clarke, I. Virbitskaite, and A. Voronkov (Eds.): PSI 2011, LNCS 7162, pp. 210–226, 2012.

Higher-level supercompilation is a new area of research whose potential is not fully realized, some aspects being still poorly understood. The *law of branching growth of the penultimate level* is one of such aspects. Of course, laws are called "laws", because they manifest itself regardless of whether we are aware of them or not. However, if a law is well understood, its intentional use often enables us to find more elegant and (conceptually) simple solutions, as compared to those obtained by blind trial and error.

In the subsequent sections we consider how the law of branching growth of the penultimate level manifests itself in higher-level supercompilation and how it can be used when constructing metasystems composed of a number of super-compilers.

2   Diversity of Higher-Level Supercompilation

In the following, higher-level supercompilation is assumed to mean the construction of systems that use SC, the operation of supercompilation, as a primitive. Here are some examples of higher-level supercompilation:

- Self-application of a supercompiler [20], or, more generally, an application of supercompilers to supercompilers [3] (also known as Futamura projections [2]). In this case an instance of a supercompiler, essentially, controls the execution of another instance of the same supercompiler.
- Proving the equivalence of expressions by supercompilation [17,15]. In this case supercompilation is used as a means of normalizing programs for further check for syntactic isomorphism.
- Two-level supercompilation [16], in which the "upper" supercompiler uses improvement lemmas proved by the "lower" supercompiler.
- Distillation [4,6,5], which involves comparing recursive (supercompiled) representations of configurations, instead of configurations (although the separation of the ground level and the metalevel is not as clear as in the case of two-level supercompilation).

This list, which is certainly incomplete, shows that constructing metasystems by combining supercompilers may be done in a variety of ways. However, until recently, the idea of *self-application* (in the form of Futamura projections) has enjoyed the most popularity. The point is that this form is not the only possible form of higher-level supercompilation[2].

3   Branching Growth of the Penultimate Level in Metasystem Transitions

What is the concrete mechanics of a metasystem transition? Some light on this is shed in "The phenomenon of science" by V.F. Turchin [25, Chapter 3, Section "The Metasystem Transition"]:

---

[2] Note, that the emergence of various forms of higher-level supercompilation can also be seen as the growth of the penultimate level leading to a metasystem transition.

In general we must note that the integration of subsystems is by no means the end of their evolutionary development. We must not imagine that systems A_1, A_2, A_3, ... are reproduced in large numbers after which the control device X suddenly arises "above them". On the contrary, the rudiments of the control system form when the number of subsystems A_i is still quite small. As we saw above, this is the only way the trial and error method can operate. But after control subsystem X has formed, there is a massive replication of subsystems A_i and during this process both A_i and X are refined. The appearance of the structure for control of subsystems A_i does not conclude rapid growth in the number of subsystems A_i; rather, it precedes and causes this growth because it makes multiplication of A_i useful to the organism. The carrier of a definite level of organization branches out only after the new, higher level begins to form. This characteristic can be called the law of *branching growth of the penultimate level*. In the phenomenological functional description, therefore, the metasystem transition does not appear immediately after the establishment of a new level; it appears somewhat later, after the penultimate level has branched out.

This can be summed up by the "formula":

$$Control + Branching\ Growth \implies Metasystem\ Transition \quad (1)$$

In some cases of higher-level supercompilation, such as self-application [2,20] and the simplest two-level supercompilation [15,16], there is a single (and fixed) supercompiler under control. However, this straightforward approach is unable to take advantage of the real potential of metasystem transition, because any real control implies the possibility of choice, which does not exist without some variety and/or multiplicity at the lower level.

A multiplicity of choice may exist *in time* (if there is a single unit at the lower level, whose state may be controlled or modified) or *in space* (if there is a number of controllable units). In general, there may be a combination of multiplicity in time and in space. However, in computer science, the division into space and time may be rather arbitrary. For example, we may run a program several times with different options, in which case the variants will be separated "in time". But, given a supercomputer, we may run the program with different options on multiple nodes, in which case the variants will be separated "in space".

The emergence of multiplicity of choice brings about the need for improvements and refinements in the control system, and often leads to a metasystem transition, which was formulated by V.F. Turchin as the law of branching growth of the penultimate level.

The next section considers some forms of branching growth in the context of supercompilation.

4 Multi-result Supercompilation and Program Analysis

At a high level of abstraction, supercompilation can be seen as a *transformation relation SC* [8,11], such that, given two programs p and p', p SC p' means that p' is a residual program with respect to the source program p.

From this viewpoint, there may exist several residual programs for a given input program, and we may construct a supercompiler producing a set of residual programs, rather than a single program. In such cases we will speak about *multi-result supercompilation*, to distinguish it from traditional (single-result) supercompilation.

Until recently, multi-result supercompilation was not paid sufficient attention. This situation was probably because supercompilation was primarily considered as a tool for program *optimization*. And, when seen as an optimizer, a supercompiler is usually expected to produce a single program $p' = SC[\![p]\!]$.

Indeed, the word "optimization" implies that we are interested in obtaining the best result[3]. Hence, an optimizing supercompiler is expected to return a single result, "the best" one, even if it could produce several residual programs. The suboptimal results are not exposed explicitly – there is some logic under the hood that chooses "the best" variant [4].

Optimizing supercompilers usually are implemented in the form of deterministic algorithms. If a deterministic supercompiler faces a choice, it only considers a single variant, which it believes to result into "the best" residual program.

In the case of optimization, the concepts of "better" and "worse" are relatively easy to formalize. A program p' is usually assumed to be better than p if it is faster and/or smaller. The execution speed and code size are measurable and can be expressed numerically. So the criteria used by optimizing supercompiler in order to choose "the best" (or at least not the worst) variant, when non-determinism appears during supercompilation, are formalizable.

But, if supercompilation is used for program analysis by transformation, things get more complicated. In this case a residual program p' is better than p'' if p' is easier to analyze than p''. This criteria is less formalizable than the notions of execution speed and code size. Besides, some choices that appeared to be obvious or natural in the case of an optimizing supercompiler may not be good if residual programs are meant for subsequent analysis, rather than execution. Moreover, the influence of the choices made during supercompilation on the "analyzability" of residual programs are rather difficult to foresee.

On the other hand, the results of transformation are much easier to estimate post factum. So multi-result supercompilation seems to be a natural solution for program analysis, since the results of choices made during supercompilation can be evaluated by examining the final results.

It is interesting that some choices which look unnatural during supercompilation may lead to interesting and useful final results (see Section 5.4).

---

[3] In Latin "optimus" means "the best".

[4] Note that multiplicity is internally used by some optimizers [24].

5 The Synergy of Two-Level and Multi-result Supercompilation

In the context of supercompilation the formula from Section 3

Control + Branching Growth ⇒ Metasystem Transition

can be instantiated in the following way:

Two-Level Supercompilation + Multi-Result Supercompilation ⇒ Metasystem Transition

In other words: combining two-level supercompilation (control) with multi-result supercompilation (growth of the penultimate level) leads to a metasystem transition, thereby increasing the power of two-level supercompilation.

The evolution history of HOSC [9] – a supercompiler for a subset of Haskell – seems to be a good illustration for the quotation in Section 3. The initial goal of the project was to study the applicability of supercompilation to program analysis by transformation, the previous studies in the field of optimizing supercompilation serving as the starting point. The stages the project HOSC has passed through are considered in the following subsections.

5.1 Stage 0. Proving the Equivalence of Expressions: Rudiments of Control

The development of HOSC started with the simple motto: transformed programs are to be analyzed, rather than executed. So we made a few minor modifications, which could be unacceptable in the context of program optimization, but are quite natural in the case of program analysis:

1. A supercompiler is allowed to duplicate code.
2. A supercompiler is allowed to generate a non-modular flat program.

These modifications enabled the internals of the supercompiler to be considerably simplified. In addition, it was found that these simplifications enhanced the ability of the supercompiler to transform equivalent programs to the same syntactic form. That is, the supercompiler HOSC proved to be more powerful at "normalizing" programs, than optimizing compilers.

The mechanism of program normalization can be metaphorically explained in this way: it is easier to transform two programs to the same bad form, than to the same good form (where "goodness" is measured in terms of size and execution speed).

The details of this approach are described in [15]. HOSC turned out to be quite good at normalizing modular programs with heavy use of higher-order functions (especially, various forms of combinators).

Let us consider a quite spectacular example. A Haskell program defining fragments of Peano and Church arithmetics is shown in Fig. 1. A conjecture in Fig. 2

```
data Peano = Z | S Peano;
type Church x = (x → x) → (x → x);

foldn :: (t → t) → t → Peano → t;
foldn = λs z n → case n of { Z → z; S n1 → s (foldn s z n1); };

add :: Peano → Peano → Peano;
add = λx y → foldn S y x;

mult :: Peano → Peano → Peano;
mult = λx y → foldn (add y) Z x;

mult' :: Church x → Church x → Church x;
mult' = λm n f → m (n f);

peano2church :: Peano → Church x;
peano2church = λp → foldn (λm f x → f (m f x)) (λf x → x) p;

church2peano :: Church Peano → Peano;
church2peano = λn → n S Z;
```

Fig. 1. Fragments of Peano and Church arithmetics: definitions in Haskell

∀x y. mult x y ≅ church2peano (mult' (peano2church x) (peano2church y))

Fig. 2. A conjecture about the equivalence of expressions

```
letrec f = λm n → case m of {
  Z → Z;
  S p → letrec g = λz → case z of { S v → S (g v); Z → f p n; } in g n;
} in f x y
```

Fig. 3. Proof by supercompilation: both parts of the conjecture are transformed to the same residual expression (shown in the Figure)

states the operational equivalence of two expressions with universally quantified variables. HOSC transforms both expressions to the same residual expression depicted in Fig. 3 and thus deduces that the conjecture holds.

Certainly, launching two instances of the same supercompiler, followed by comparing the results, can be regarded as a form of control, but as a very primitive one.

5.2   Stage 1. Two-Level Supercompilation: Shaping of Control

Simply put, supercompilation is based on the following simple operations on *configurations* (expressions with free variables):

```
data Bool = True | False;
data Peano = Z | S Peano;
even = λx → case x of { Z → True; S x1 → odd x1; };
odd = λx → case x of { Z → False; S x1 → even x1; };
or = λx y → case x of { True → True; False → y; };
```

Fig. 4. Numeric operations

```
letrec f = λw →
  case w of { Z → True; S x → case x of { Z → True; S z → f z; };}
in f m
```

Fig. 5. or (even m) (odd m): the result of two-level supercompilation

1. Driving: rewriting a configuration into an *equivalent* one, in order to *simplify* it.
2. Case analysis: splitting a configuration into a finite number of subconfigurations.
3. Folding: comparing two configurations for syntactic isomorphism, in order to reduce the current configuration to a previously encountered one.
4. Generalization: replacing a configuration with a more general one, in order to guarantee termination.

Generalization often leads to redundancy in residual programs, so that supercompilers should try to avoid it.

The main idea of two-level supercompilation [16,12] consists in avoiding generalization as much as possible. When a two-level supercompiler encounters a configuration A that has to be generalized according to the rules of ordinary supercompilation, it tries to replace A with an equivalent configuration B that does not have to be generalized. The equivalence of A and B is proven by invoking two instances of a lower-level supercompiler.

For example, let us consider the expression or (even m) (odd m) in the context of the program shown in Fig. 4. The single-level HOSC is unable to transform this expression into a program that is certain not to return False. During supercompilation the following expressions are checked for syntactic isomorphism:

1. case (even m) of { True → True; False → odd m; }
2. case (even n) of { True → True; False → odd (S (S n)); }

Since these expressions are not syntactically isomorphic, the single-level HOSC has to perform a generalization. However, the two-level HOSC is able to prove (by calling the single-level HOSC twice) that the following configuration (3)

3. case (even n) of { True → True; False → odd n; }

is equivalent to the configuration (2). Now the configuration (3) is syntactically isomorphic to the configuration (1). Hence, we can fold (3) to (1), thereby avoiding generalization. The corresponding residual program is shown in Fig. 5. This program is certain not to return `False` (just because `False` does not appear in the program).

5.3   Stage 2. Multi-result Supercompilation: Branching Growth of the Penultimate Level

The two-level supercompiler described in [16] calls an instance of itself [5]. Moreover, there exists a "recipe" of turning *some* classical single-level supercompilers into two-level ones. This procedure can be schematically represented by the following formula (which may seem a bit obscure for now, but it will be explained in Section 6 in detail):

$$L2(Sc) = Sc_{mod}(Sc)$$

where Sc_{mod} is a modification of a classical supercompiler Sc. Thus a modified instance of a classical supercompiler uses an unmodified instance of the *same* supercompiler.

In the paper [12] this formula is generalized as follows:

$$L2'(Sc', Sc'') = Sc'_{mod}(Sc'')$$

The point is that a two-level supercompiler can be produced from two *different* supercompilers[6]. And $L2(Sc) = L2'(Sc, Sc)$ is just a special case, where $Sc' = Sc''$.

The fruitfulness of this generalization is illustrated in [12] by the following example. Let us express two BNF-grammars by means of combinators:

```
doubleA1 = ε | A doubleA1 A
doubleA2 = ε | A A doubleA2
```

Although these grammars are equivalent, the corresponding parsers are different, the complexity of the first parser being $O(n^2)$, while the complexity of the second one being $O(n)$. The paper [12] shows that there is no two-level supercompiler $L2(Sc_i)$ produced from supercompilers $\overline{Sc_i}$ from [10] that can transform the first grammar into the second one. The problem is that each time when the upper supercompiler makes a conjecture (about the equivalence of expressions), the lower supercompiler is unable to prove this conjecture.

However, we can combine supercompilers described in [10] by means of the formula $L2'(Sc_i, Sc_j)$, in which case it is possible to find two supercompilers Sc_i and Sc_j, such that $L2'(Sc_i, Sc_j)$ transforms the first parser into the second one[7].

In a sense, $L2$ and $L2'$ can be regarded as devices for breeding and multiplying supercompilers, $L2'$ being more "productive". Indeed, for 8 different single-level

---

[5] So, it can be regarded as a special case of self-application.

[6] In the context of Futamura projections, the idea of combining *different* versions of a partial evaluator was considered by R. Glück [3].

[7] As was shown by Sørensen [23], a classical single-level supercompiler for a lazy functional language can not improve the runtime complexity of a program.

```
data List a = Nil | Cons a (List a);

app = λxs ys →
  case xs of { Nil → ys; Cons z zs → Cons z (app zs ys); };
rev = λxs →
  case xs of { Nil → Nil; Cons y ys → app (rev ys) (Cons y Nil); };
```

Fig. 6. Naive list reversal

```
letrec f = λx y → case x of { Nil → y; Cons v w → f w (Cons v y); }
in f xs Nil
```

Fig. 7. rev xs: a result of multi-result two-level supercompilation

supercompilers described in [10], the formula $L2$ may produce only 8 different two-level supercompilers, while $L2'$ may produce 64 different supercompilers.

Now suppose that Sc'' in $L2'$ is a multi-result supercompiler. Again, we get one single-result two-level supercompiler. Applying $L2'$ to 8 different single-level supercompilers from [10], we get 8 different single-result two-level supercompilers.

And finally, combining these two-level supercompilers we can get one multi-result two-level supercompiler.

As was shown in [12] the construction of a two-level supercompiler by combining two single-result supercompilers is unable to reveal many opportunities for two-level supercompilation. However, using multi-result supercompiler as the lower supercompiler produces new results.

So using a multi-result supercompiler as the lower supercompiler in a two-level supercompiler increases the potential of two-level supercompilation and may be regarded as branching growth of the penultimate level according to V.F. Turchin.

5.4   Stage 3. Multi-generalization: Refinement of Control

Supercompilation can be described as a non-deterministic algorithm [11], which has a set of choices at almost every step. But a deterministic implementation of supercompilation has to choose a single variant at each step.

The previous section shows how to build a multi-result supercompiler by combining several single-result supercompilers (treated as black-boxes). Multi-result supercompilers thus produced will be said to be of the first kind.

Is it possible to derive a multi-result supercompiler from a single-result one? Yes, by turning a deterministic supercompiler into a non-deterministic one and then turning it into a multi-result one. The subtle point is that a non-deterministic supercompiler, in principle, may produce an infinite number of residual programs or even not terminate, while a multi-result supercompiler, for practical reasons, should always terminate and produce a finite set of residual programs. Hence, we need some reasonable finite non-determinism.

Multi-generalization is a technique that enables a single-result supercompiler to be turned into a multi-result supercompiler that always terminates and produces a finite number of residual programs.

The main idea of multi-generalization is that when a supercompiler has to generalize a configuration, it should consider *all* possible generalizations of the configuration, rather than a most specific generalization only. If the set of possible generalizations is always finite (which is true of the HOSC supercompilation relation), the set of possible residual programs is also finite. A multi-result supercompiler thus produced will be said to be of the second kind.

If Sc' is a multi-result single-level supercompiler of the second kind and Sc'' a multi-result single-level supercompiler of the first kind, $L2'(Sc', Sc'')$ turns out to be a powerful multi-result two-level supercompiler, which is capable of finding non-trivial generalizations by means of multi-generalization, thereby coming to non-trivial results.

Let us consider the configuration `rev xs` for the program in Fig. 6. During supercompilation the following configuration:

```
case case v5 of {Cons p q → app (rev q) (Cons p Nil); Nil → Nil;} of {
    Cons r s → Cons r (app s (Cons v4 Nil));
    Nil → Cons v4 Nil;
}
```

is compared with a bit complicated configuration:

```
case
case (case v2 of {Cons p q → app (rev q) (Cons p Nil); Nil → Nil;}) of {
    Cons t u → Cons t (app u (Cons v1 Nil));
    Nil → Cons v1 Nil;
} of {
    Cons r s → Cons r (app s (Cons v4 Nil));
    Nil → Cons v4 Nil;
}
```

After this comparison a classic single-level deterministic supercompiler would perform the following generalization of the first configuration:

```
let g = case v5 of {Cons p q → app (rev q) (Cons p Nil); Nil → Nil;}
in
case g of {
    Cons r s → Cons r (app s (Cons v4 Nil));
    Nil → Cons v4 Nil;
}
```

which would not produce non-trivial results. However, by using multi-generalization, it is possible to find the following generalization:

```
let g = Cons v4 Nil in
case case v5 of {Cons p q → app (rev q) (Cons p Nil); Nil → Nil;} of {
    Cons r v21 → Cons r (app s g);
    Nil → g;
}
```

This allows the upper supercompiler to make a conjecture that is provable by the lower supercompiler, which gives the residual program shown in Fig. 7.

A yet another interesting point is that, in the case of two-level supercompilation, given an input program, we can introduce a "measure of non-triviality" on the set of corresponding residual programs. Namely, the "non-triviality" can be defined as the number of lemmas used during supercompilation. Note that in the case of single-level supercompilation there seems to be no simple measure of "non-triviality".

So, we see that multi-result supercompilation provides numerous opportunities for refining control.

6   MRSC: A Multi-result Supercompilation Framework

For the first time, the described examples were obtained and tested when working with an experimental version of the supercompiler HOSC[8] for the language Haskell. Later we created an experimental version of the supercompiler SPSC[9] dealing with a first-order functional language, and were able to reproduce similar examples in the first-order setting. These results led us to the idea of the framework MRSC.

Before going into the details of MRSC, let us classify the ways of implementing a supercompiler. Basically, there are two main approaches. The first one is based on constructing a graph of configurations and, after the graph is completed, transforming it into a residual program [27,22,14,9]. (Let us call it "the graph-based approach".) Obviously, this graph of configurations is an intermediate data structure that has to be constructed and deconstructed, which slows down the supercompiler. For this reason, in order to be fast, some optimizing supercompilers [1,19,7], avoid the construction of graphs of configurations. (Let us call it "the direct approach".)

We have found that multi-result supercompilers are easier to implement using the graph-based approach rather than the direct approach. Also, when a supercompiler is used as a prover, a graph of configurations can be used to extract a proof readable by humans. Moreover, some additional transformations, which cannot be easily performed in a direct-style supercompiler, can be applied to a completed graph. For example, some parts of the graph can be re-arranged in order to simplify it. (However, for the lack of space, we will not discuss such transformations here.)

MRSC[10] is a multi-result supercompilation framework that is agnostic to the object language it deals with. The base abstractions MRSC is based upon are sketched (in pseudo-Haskell) in Fig. 8. At the heart of MRSC is a mini-framework for manipulating graphs of configurations, the core concept being `SCGraph e`, representing a supercompilation graph, parameterized by `e`, the type of expressions used as configurations. The logic of a supercompiler `SC e` is represented

---

[8] http://code.google.com/p/hosc/, [9].

[9] http://code.google.com/p/spsc/, [14].

[10] http://github.com/ilya-klyuchnikov/mrsc

```
data DriveStep e = DriveStep e
type Driver e = e → DriveStep e
type Whistle e = [e] → e → Maybe e
type Rebuilder e = e → e → e
type MRebuilder e = e → e → [e]

data SC e = SC {drive :: Driver e, whistle :: Whistle e,
                rebuild :: Rebuilder e}
data MSC e = MSC {mdrive :: Driver e, mwhistle :: Whistle e,
                  mrebuild :: MRebuilder e}

data SCGraph e = SCGraph e

runSC :: SC e → e → e
runMSC :: MSC e → e → [e]
```

Fig. 8. MRSC: base abstractions

in MRSC as a set of functions for driving, identifying dangerous configurations (that might cause nontermination), and rebuilding of configurations.

drive evaluates an expression with free variables, whistle checks an expression in the history for being dangerous (i.e. a possible cause of non-termination of the transformation), and rebuild e1 e2 rebuilds a current expression[11] e2 with respect to a dangerous expression e1[12]. If we encode a classical positive supercompiler [23,22] in terms of MRSC, then the whistle will be implemented as the homeomorphic embedding relation, and the rebuilder of configurations as a most specific generalization.

However, in MRSC a supercompiler SC e does not perform transformations: it just represents the logic of a supercompiler. All dirty work of constructing supercompilation graphs and transforming them into residual programs is done by runSC, "applying" a supercompiler to an expression.

The logic of a multi-result supercompiler MSC e differs from that of a single-result supercompiler in a single detail: it may rebuild a current expression in several different ways. As in the case of SC e, MSC e does not perform transformations: all transformations are done by runMSC. The peculiarity of runMSC is that when multiple rebuildings are encountered, runMSC applies all of them "in parallel" by multiplying the current graph of configuration and applying each rebuilding to the corresponding copy[13].

---

[11] Historically, the are two approaches to rebuilding: rebuilding of the current expression and rebuilding of the dangerous expression. In the latter case we need to prune a subtree with a root labeled by a dangerous expression. Here we consider the rebuilding of the current expression only (for the sake of brevity and simplicity).

[12] In order to ensure the correctness of transformations, we require e1 to be an improvement of e2 [21].

[13] No real copying is performed here: the pieces of the "old" graph are just shared by new graphs.

The main feature of MRSC is that, by design, `runMSC` always produces a finite set of residual expressions.

6.1   Constructing Two-Level Supercompilers

A supercompiler written in functional style usually is represented as a composition of functions [1,19,13]. The subtle problem with such representation is that it is almost impossible to extract the ingredients of this composition in order to modify and rearrange them in a new way. This is why a supercompiler in MRSC is represented as a decomposable structure: we can disassemble a supercompiler, modify some of its ingredients, and re-assemble the modified parts back.

Now let us consider some ways of constructing new supercompilers from existing ones by means of MRSC. A few recipes described in previous sections are, more formally, presented in Fig. 9.

First, we have to define what is a substitution `Subst e` for expressions of type `e` and to implement the operation `//`, applying a substitution to an expression, and the function `test`, discovering whether there is a correspondence via substitution between two expressions. Then we can use three constructors of two-level supercompilers provided by MRSC: `l2`, `l2'` and `l2''`.

`l2` replaces the rebuilder `rb` of the given supercompiler `sc` with a new rebuilder `rb'`: when there is a request to rebuild an expression `e2` with respect to a dangerous expression `e1`, the new rebuilder `rb'` tries to find a substitution

```
type Subst e = e → e
(//) :: e → Subst e → e
test :: e → e → Maybe (Subst e)

-- makes a two-level single-result supercompiler
-- from a single-result supercompiler
l2 :: SC e → SC e
l2 sc@(SC d w rb) = SC d w rb' where
    rb' e1 e2 =
        maybe (rb e1 e2) (e1 //) (test (runSC sc e1) (runSC sc e2))
-- makes a two-level single-result supercompiler by combining
-- two different single-result supercompilers
l2' :: SC e → SC e → SC e
l2' (SC d w rb) sc = SC d w rb' where
    rb' e1 e2 =
        maybe (rb e1 e2) (e1 //) (test (runSC sc e1) (runSC sc e2))
-- makes a two-level single-result supercompiler by combining
-- a single-result supercompiler and multi-result supercompiler
l2'' :: SC e → MSC e → SC e
l2'' (SC d w rb) msc = SC d w rb' where
    rb' e1 e2 = maybe (rb e1 e2) (e1 //) res where
        res = msum [test x y | x <- es1, y <- es2]
        (es1, es2) = (runMSC msc e1, runMSC msc e1)
```

Fig. 9. MRSC: recipes for constructing single-result two-level supercompilers

between the supercompiled (by the unmodified supercompiler `sc`) expressions, and if there is any, it applies this substitution to the dangerous expression and returns the result. Otherwise, it delegates the rebuilding to the original `rb`. `l2'` is defined in a similar way, but tries to find a substitution by means of the second supercompiler `sc`.

The constructor `l2''` checks all combinations of the residual expressions produced by a lower multi-result supercompiler `msc`. In the next section we will see how to construct a multi-result supercompiler from a single-result one.

6.2 Working with Multi-result Supercompilers

Although the framework MRSC allows multi-result supercompilers to be implemented "by bare hands", it also provides a few ready-to-use constructors for turning ordinary supercompilers into multi-result ones.

The constructor `multi`, shown in Fig. 10, is the simplest one. It just replaces the ordinary rebuilding of a current expression with respect to a dangerous expression by a multi-generalization of the current expression. A surprising fact is that `multi` builds a supercompiler that always produces a finite set of residual programs, regardless of how `runMSC` is implemented.

The constructor `multi'` combines a multi-result supercompiler with a single-result one to produce a new multi-result supercompiler. The main trick here is that the new rebuilder `rb'` does not throw away the old rebuildings, but merges them with the *single* rebuilding (if any) returned by the lower supercompiler `sc`. This trick is further strengthened in the constructor `multi''`, where the set of old rebuildings is merged with the *set* of new rebuildings.

6.3 The Current State and Directions of Future Work

MRSC is a work in progress and is under active development now. So far we have finalized and tuned the core part of the framework operating, in a generic way, with graphs of configurations. Also we have reimplemented SPSC, a classical supercompiler for a simple first-order functional language SLL [23,22,14], by means of MRSC, and then automatically transformed SPSC into its multi-result and two-level versions (producing the same results as the corresponding hand-crafted versions).

We have carried out only "proof-of-concept" experiments with MRSC so far. Our plans are the following:

- To continue experiments with MRSC in the context of program analysis.
- To compare how various whistles affect the size and properties of the sets of residual programs generated by multi-result supercompilation. Until now, we have tried only whistles based on the homeomorphic embedding relation. However, in the context of optimizing supercompilation, there have appeared new approaches to constructing whistles, such as based on tag-bags [18,1].
- To compare how in the context of multi-result supercompilation rebuilding of the dangerous expression differs from rebuilding of the current expression.
- To reimplement HOSC, a higher-order supercompiler, in terms of MRSC.

```
type MGeneralizer e = e → [e]
-- makes a multi-result one-level supercompiler by combining
-- a single-result supercompiler and multi-generalization
multi :: SC e → MGeneralizer e → MSC e
multi (SC d w _) g = MSC d w rb where
    rb _ e2 = g e2
-- makes a multi-result two-level supercompiler by combining
-- an upper multi-result supercompiler and
-- a lower single-result supercompiler
multi' :: MSC e → SC e → MSC e
multi' (MSC d w rb) sc = (MSC d w rb') where
    rb' e1 e2 = ex ++ (rb e1 e2) where
        ex = map (e1 //) $ maybeToList (test (runSC sc e1) (runSC sc e2))
-- makes a multi-result two-level supercompiler by combining
-- two multi-result supercompiler
multi'' :: MSC e → MSC e → MSC e
multi'' (MSC d w rb) msc = (MSC d w rb') where
    rb' e1 e2 = extra ++ (rb e1 e2) where
        extra = map (e1 //) $ catMaybes $ [test x y | x <- es1, y <- es2]
        (es1, es2) = (runMSC msc e1, runMSC msc e1)
```

Fig. 10. MRSC: recipes for constructing multi-result supercompilers

7 Conclusion

When supercompilation is used for the purposes of program optimization, the usual practice is to consider only deterministic algorithms (involving some heuristics), which, given an input program, produce a single residual program.

However, if we reformulate supercompilation in more abstract terms, in form of a *transformation relation* [8,11], we naturally come to the idea of *multi-result supercompilation*. Namely, given an input program p, a multi-result supercompiler may produce several output programs p', such that $p\ SC\ p'$, where SC is a supercompilation relation.

Note that we differentiate the terms *non-deterministic* supercompilation and *multi-result* supercompilation. A non-deterministic supercompiler, in principle, may produce an infinite number of residual programs, or even not terminate, while a multi-result supercompiler, for practical reasons, should always terminate and produce a finite set of residual programs.

We have demonstrated that, when used for program analysis, multi-result supercompilation produces more nontrivial and stable results, as compared to single-result supercompilation.

The fact that multi-result supercompilation naturally arises in the context of two-level supercompilation, can be regarded as a manifestation of the general law of branching growth of the penultimate level in a metasystem transition [25]. It would be interesting to consider other manifestations of this law in the field of computer science.

Acknowledgements. The authors express their gratitude to all participants of Refal seminar at Keldysh Institute for useful comments and fruitful discussions of this work. Extra special thanks are to Sergei Abramov for his attention and support of this work.

References

1. Bolingbroke, M., Peyton Jones, S.L.: Improving supercompilation: tag-bags, rollback, speculation, normalisation, and generalisation (2011) (Submitted to ICFP 2011)
2. Futamura, Y.: Partial evaluation of computation process – an approach to a compiler-compiler. Systems, Computers, Controls 2(5), 45–50 (1971)
3. Glück, R.: Is there a fourth Futamura projection? In: Proceedings of the 2009 ACM SIGPLAN Workshop on Partial Evaluation and Program Manipulation, PEPM 2009, pp. 51–60. ACM, New York (2009)
4. Hamilton, G.W.: Distillation: extracting the essence of programs. In: Proceedings of the 2007 ACM SIGPLAN Symposium on Partial Evaluation and Semantics-Based Program Manipulation, pp. 61–70. ACM Press, New York (2007)
5. Hamilton, G.W.: A graph-based definition of distillation. In: Second International Workshop on Metacomputation in Russia (2010)
6. Hamilton, G.W., Kabir, M.H.: Constructing programs from metasystem transition proofs. In: Proceedings of the First International Workshop on Metacomputation in Russia (2008)
7. Jonsson, P.A.: Positive supercompilation for a higher-order call-by-value language. Luleå University of Technology (2008)
8. Klimov, A.V.: A program specialization relation based on supercompilation and its properties. In: Proceedings of the First International Workshop on Metacomputation in Russia, pp. 54–78. Ailamazyan University of Pereslavl (2008)
9. Klyuchnikov, I.: Supercompiler HOSC 1.0: under the hood. Preprint 63, Keldysh Institute of Applied Mathematics, Moscow (2009)
10. Klyuchnikov, I.: Supercompiler HOSC 1.5: homeomorphic embedding and generalization in a higher-order setting. Preprint 62, Keldysh Institute of Applied Mathematics (2010)
11. Klyuchnikov, I.: Supercompiler HOSC: proof of correctness. Preprint 31, Keldysh Institute of Applied Mathematics, Moscow (2010)
12. Klyuchnikov, I.: Towards effective two-level supercompilation. Preprint 81, Keldysh Institute of Applied Mathematics (2010)
13. Klyuchnikov, I.: The ideas and methods of supercompilation. Practice of Functional Programming 7 (2011) (in Russian)
14. Klyuchnikov, I., Romanenko, S.: SPSC: a simple supercompiler in Scala. In: PU 2009 (International Workshop on Program Understanding) (2009)
15. Klyuchnikov, I., Romanenko, S.: Proving the Equivalence of Higher-Order Terms by Means of Supercompilation. In: Pnueli, A., Virbitskaite, I., Voronkov, A. (eds.) PSI 2009. LNCS, vol. 5947, pp. 193–205. Springer, Heidelberg (2010)
16. Klyuchnikov, I., Romanenko, S.: Towards higher-level supercompilation. In: Second International Workshop on Metacomputation in Russia (2010)
17. Lisitsa, A.P., Webster, M.: Supercompilation for equivalence testing in metamorphic computer viruses detection. In: Proceedings of the First International Workshop on Metacomputation in Russia (2008)

18. Mitchell, N.: Rethinking supercompilation. In: ICFP 2010 (2010)
19. Mitchell, N., Runciman, C.: A Supercompiler for Core Haskell. In: Chitil, O., Horváth, Z., Zsók, V. (eds.) IFL 2007. LNCS, vol. 5083, pp. 147–164. Springer, Heidelberg (2008)
20. Nemytykh, A.P., Pinchuk, V.A., Turchin, V.F.: A Self-Applicable Supercompiler. In: Danvy, O., Thiemann, P., Glück, R. (eds.) Dagstuhl Seminar 1996. LNCS, vol. 1110, pp. 322–337. Springer, Heidelberg (1996)
21. Sands, D.: Total correctness by local improvement in the transformation of functional programs. ACM Trans. Program. Lang. Syst. 18(2), 175–234 (1996)
22. Sørensen, M.H., Glück, R., Jones, N.D.: A positive supercompiler. Journal of Functional Programming 6(6), 811–838 (1993)
23. Sørensen, M.H.: Turchin's supercompiler revisited: an operational theory of positive information propagation. Master's thesis, Københavns Universitet, Datalogisk Institute (1994)
24. Tate, R., Stepp, M., Tatlock, Z., Lerner, S.: Equality saturation: a new approach to optimization. SIGPLAN Not. 44, 264–276 (2009)
25. Turchin, V.F.: The phenomenon of science. A cybernetic approach to human evolution. Columbia University Press, New York (1977)
26. Turchin, V.: The Language Refal: The Theory of Compilation and Metasystem Analysis. Department of Computer Science, Courant Institute of Mathematical Sciences, New York University (1980)
27. Turchin, V.F.: The concept of a supercompiler. ACM Transactions on Programming Languages and Systems (TOPLAS) 8(3), 292–325 (1986)
28. Turchin, V.F.: Program transformation with metasystem transitions. Journal of Functional Programming 3(03), 283–313 (1993)
29. Turchin, V.: Metacomputation: Metasystem Transitions Plus Supercompilation. In: Danvy, O., Thiemann, P., Glück, R. (eds.) Dagstuhl Seminar 1996. LNCS, vol. 1110, pp. 481–509. Springer, Heidelberg (1996)

Symbolic Loop Bound Computation for WCET Analysis

Jens Knoop, Laura Kovács, and Jakob Zwirchmayr[*]

Vienna University of Technology

Abstract. We present an automatic method for computing tight upper bounds on the iteration number of special classes of program loops. These upper bounds are further used in the WCET analysis of programs. To do so, we refine program flows using SMT reasoning and rewrite multi-path loops into single-path ones. Single-path loops are further translated into a set of recurrence relations over program variables. Recurrence relations are solved and iteration bounds of program loops are derived from the computed closed forms. For solving recurrences we deploy a pattern-based recurrence solving algorithm and compute closed forms only for a restricted class of recurrence equations. However, in practice, these recurrences describe the behavior of a large set of program loops. Our technique is implemented in the r-TuBound tool and was successfully tried out on a number of challenging WCET benchmarks.

1 Introduction

The *worst case execution time (WCET)* analysis of programs aims at deriving an accurate time limit, called the WCET of the program, ensuring that all possible program executions terminate within the computed time limit. One of the main difficulties in WCET analysis comes with the presence of loops and/or recursive procedures, as the WCET crucially depends on the number of loop iterations and/or recursion depth.

To overcome this limitation, state-of-the-art WCET analysis tools, see e.g. [8,20,12], rely on user-given program assertions describing loop and/or recursion bounds.

Manual annotations are however a source for imprecision and errors. The effectiveness of WCET analysis thus crucially depends on whether bounds on loop iterations and/or recursion depth can be deduced automatically.

In this paper we address the problem of *automatically inferring iteration bounds* of imperative program loops. For doing so, we identified special classes of loops with assignments and conditionals, where updates over program variables are linear expressions (Sections 5.1-5.3). For such loops, we deploy recurrence solving and theorem proving techniques and automatically derive tight iteration bounds, as follows.

(i) A loop with multiple paths arising from conditionals is first transformed into a loop with only one path (Section 5.3). We call a loop with multiple paths, respectively with a single path, a multi-path loop, respectively a simple loop. To this end, the control flow of the multi-path loop is analyzed and refined using *satisfiability modulo theory (SMT) reasoning over arithmetical expressions* [13,4]. The resulting simple loop

---

[*] This research is supported by the CeTAT project of TU Vienna. The second author is supported by an FWF Hertha Firnberg Research grant (T425-N23). This research was partly supported by Dassault Aviation and by the FWF National Research Network RiSE (S11410-N23).

E. Clarke, I. Virbitskaite, and A. Voronkov (Eds.): PSI 2011, LNCS 7162, pp. 227–242, 2012.

soundly over-approximates the multi-path loop. Iteration bounds of the simple loop are thus safe iteration bounds of the multi-path loop.

(ii) A simple loop is next rewritten into a set of *recurrence equations* over those scalar variables that are changed at each loop iteration (Section 5.1). To this end, a new variable denoting the loop counter is introduced and used as the summation variable. The recurrence equation of the loop iteration variable captures thus the dependency between various iterations of the loop.

(iii) Recurrence equations of loop variables are next solved and the values of loop variables at arbitrary loop iterations are computed as functions of the loop counter and the initial values of loop variables (Section 5.1). In other words, the *closed forms of loop variables* are derived. Our framework overcomes the limitations of missing initial values by a simple *over-approximation of non-deterministic assignments* (Section 5.2).

We note that solving arbitrary recurrence equations is undecidable. However, in our approach we only consider loops with linear updates. Such loops yield linear recurrences with constant coefficients, called C-finite recurrences [5]. As C-finite recurrences can always be solved, our method succeeds in computing the closed forms of loop variables.

For solving C-finite recurrences we deploy a *pattern-based recurrence solving algorithm*. In other words, we instantiate unknowns in the closed form pattern of C-finite recurrences by the symbolic constant coefficients of the recurrence to be solved. Unlike powerful algorithmic combinatorics techniques that can solve complex recurrences, our framework hence only solves a particular class of recurrence equations. However, it turned out that in WCET analysis the recurrences describing the iteration behavior of program loops are not arbitrarily complex and can be solved by our approach (Section 6).

(iv) Closed forms of loop variables together with the loop condition are used to express the value of the loop counter as a function of loop variables (Section 5.1). The upper bound on the number of loop iterations is finally derived by computing the *smallest value of the loop counter* such that the loop is terminated. To this end, we deploy SMT reasoning over arithmetical formulas. The inferred iteration bound is further used to infer an accurate WCET of the program loop.

Experiments. Our approach is implemented as an extension to the TuBound tool [20], denoted r-TuBound, and successfully evaluated on WCET benchmarks (Section 6). Our experimental results give practical evidence for the applicability of our method for the WCET analysis of programs.

Contributions. In this paper, we make the following contributions:

- we introduce a pattern-based recurrence solving approach for WCET analysis of imperative program loops;
- we describe a flow refinement approach for translating multi-path loops into simple loops, by proving arithmetical properties using SMT technology;
- we present the summary of an experimental evaluation of our approach on challenging WCET benchmarks.

Our work advances the state-of-the-art in WCET analysis by a conceptually new and fully automated approach to loop bound computation. Moreover, our approach extends the application of program analysis methods by integrating WCET techniques with recurrence solving and SMT reasoning.

2 Related Work

Our work is closely related to the WCET analysis of software and invariant generation of program loops.

WCET Analysis. WCET analysis is usually two-tiered. A low-level analysis estimates the execution times of program instructions on the underlying hardware and computes a concrete time value of the WCET. On the other hand, a high-level analysis is, in general, platform-independent and is concerned, for example, with loop bound computation. In [14] a framework for parametric WCET analysis is introduced, and symbolic expressions as iteration bounds are derived. Instantiating the symbolic expressions with specific inputs yields then the WCET of programs. The approach presented in [15] automatically identifies induction variables and recurrence relations of loops using abstract interpretation [2]. Recurrence relations are further solved using precomputed closed form templates, and iteration bounds are hence derived. In [20] iteration bounds are obtained using data flow analysis and interval based abstract interpretation. However, state-of-the-art WCET analysis tools, including [8,15,20], compute loop bounds automatically only for loops with relatively simple flow and arithmetic [10]. For more complex loops iteration bounds are supplied manually in the form of auxiliary program annotations. Unlike the aforementioned approaches, we require no user guidance but automatically infer iteration bounds for special classes of loops with non-trivial arithmetic and flow.

Invariant Generation and Cost Analysis. Loop invariants describe loop properties that are valid at any, and thus also at the last loop iteration. Invariant generation techniques therefore can be used to infer bounds on program resources, such as time and memory – see e.g. [6,7,1,3,9].

The work described in [6] instruments loops with various counters at different program locations. Then an abstract interpretation based linear invariant generation method is used to derive linear bounds over each counter variable. Bounds on counters are composed using a proof-rule-based algorithm, and non-linear disjunctive bounds of multipath loops are finally inferred. The approach is further extended in [7] to derive more complex loop bounds. For doing so, disjunctive invariants are inferred using abstract interpretation and flow refinement. Next, proof-rules using max, sum, and product operations on bound patterns are deployed in conjunction with SMT reasoning in the theory of linear arithmetic and arrays. As a result, non-linear symbolic bounds of multi-path loops are obtained. Abstract interpretation based invariant generation is also used in [1] in conjunction with so-called cost relations. Cost relations extend recurrence relations and can express recurrence relations with non-deterministic behavior which arise from multi-path loops. Iteration bounds of loops are inferred by constructing evaluation trees of cost relations and computing bounds on the height of the trees. For doing so, linear invariants and ranking functions for each tree node are inferred. Unlike the aforementioned techniques, we do not use abstract interpretation but deploy a recurrence solving approach to generate bounds on simple loops. Contrarily to [6,7,1], our method is limited to multi-path loops that can be translated into simple loops by SMT queries over arithmetic.

Recurrence solving is also used in [3,9]. The work presented in [9] derives loop bounds by solving arbitrary C-finite recurrences and deploying quantifier elimination over integers and real closed fields. To this end, [9] uses some algebraic algorithms as black-boxes built upon the computer algebra system Mathematica [23]. Contrarily to [9], we only solve C-finite recurrences of order 1, but, unlike [9], we do not rely on computer algebra systems and handle more complex multi-path loops. Symbolic loop bounds in [3] are inferred over arbitrarily nested loops with polynomial dependencies among loop iteration variables. To this end, C-finite and hypergeometric recurrence solving is used. Unlike [3], we only handle C-finite recurrences of order 1. Contrarily to [3], we however design flow refinement techniques to make our approach scalable to the WCET analysis of programs.

3   Motivating Example

Consider the C program in Figure 1. Between lines 5-21, the method func iterates over a two-dimensional array a row-by-row[1], and updates the elements of a, as follows: In each visited row k, the array elements in columns 1, 4, 13, and 53 are set to 1 according to the C-finite update of the simple loop from lines 6-9. Note that the number of visited rows in a is conditionalized by the non-deterministic assignment from line 2. Depending on the updates made between lines 6-9, the multi-path loop from lines 10-14 conditionally updates the elements of a by -1. Finally, the abrupt termination of the multi-path loop from lines 15-18 depends on the updates made throughout lines 6-14.

```
1   void func() {
2     int i = nondet();
3     int j, k = 0;
4     int a[32][100];
5     for (; i > 0; i = i ≫ 1) {
6       for (j = 1; j < 100; j = j * 3 + 1) {
7         a[k][j] = 1;
8         ♯pragma wcet_loopbound(4)
9       }
10      for (j = 0; j < 100; j++) {
11        if (a[k][j] == 1) j++;
12        else a[k][j] = -1;
13        ♯pragma wcet_loopbound(100)
14      }
15      for (j = 0; j < 100; j++) {
16        if (a[k][j] != -1 && a[k][j] != 1) break;
17        ♯pragma wcet_loopbound(100)
18      }
19      k++;
20      ♯pragma wcet_loopbound(32)
21    }
22  }
```

Fig. 1. C program annotated with the result of loop bound computation

Computing an accurate WCET of the func method requires thus tight iteration bounds of the four loops between lines 5-21. The difficulty in computing the number of loop iterations comes with the presence of the non-deterministic initialization and shift updates of the loop from lines 5-21; the use of C-finite updates in the simple loop from lines 6-9; the conditional updates of the multi-path loop from lines 10-14; and the presence of abrupt termination in the multi-path loop from lines 15-18.

We overcome these difficulties as follows.

---

[1] We denote by a[k][j] the array element from the kth row and jth column of a.

- We design a pattern-based recurrence solving algorithm (Section 5.1). Using this algorithm, the iteration bound of the loop from lines 6-9 is inferred to be precisely 4.
- We deploy SMT reasoning to translate multi-path loops into simple ones (Section 5.3). Using our flow refinement approach, the iteration bounds of the loops from lines 10-14, respectively lines 15-18, are both over-approximated to 100.
- We over-approximate non-deterministic initializations (Section 5.2). As a result, the upper bound of the loop from lines 5-21 is derived to be 31.

The iteration bounds inferred automatically by our approach are listed in Figure 1, using the program annotations ♯pragma wcet_loopbound(...).

The rest of the paper discusses in detail how we automatically compute iteration bounds for simple and multi-path loops.

4   Theoretical Considerations

This section contains a brief overview of algebraic techniques and WCET analysis as required for the development of this paper. For more details, we refer to [5,17].

Algebraic Considerations. Throughout this paper, $\mathbb{N}$ and $\mathbb{R}$ denote the set of natural and real numbers, respectively.

Let $\mathbb{K}$ be a field of characteristic zero (e.g. $\mathbb{R}$) and $f : \mathbb{N} \to \mathbb{K}$ a *univariate sequence* in $\mathbb{K}$. Consider a rational function $R : \mathbb{K}^{r+1} \to \mathbb{K}$. A *recurrence equation* for the sequence $f(n)$ is of the form $f(n+r) = R(f(n), f(n+1), ..., f(n+r-1), n)$, where $r \in \mathbb{N}$ is the *order* of the recurrence.

Given a recurrence equation of $f(n)$, one is interested to compute the value of $f(n)$ as a function depending *only* on the summation variable n and some given initial vales $f(0), \ldots, f(n-1)$. In other words, a *closed form* solution of $f(n)$ is sought. Although solving arbitrary recurrence equations is an undecidable problem, special classes of recurrence equations can be effectively decided using algorithmic combinatorics techniques.

We are interested in solving one particular class of recurrence equations, called *C-finite recurrences*. An *inhomogeneous* C-finite recurrence equation is of the form $f(n+r) = a_0 f(n) + a_1 f(n+1) + ... + a_{r-1} f(n+r-1) + h(n)$, where $a_0, \ldots, a_{r-1} \in \mathbb{K}$, $a_0 \neq 0$, and $h(n)$ is a linear combination over $\mathbb{K}$ of exponential sequences in n with polynomial coefficients in n. The C-finite recurrence is *homogeneous* if $h(n) = 0$. C-finite recurrences fall in the class of decidable recurrences. In other words, closed forms of C-finite recurrences can always be computed [5].

Example 1. Consider the C-finite recurrence $f(n+1) = 3f(n) + 1$ with initial values $f(0) = 1$. By solving $f(n)$, we obtain the closed form $f(n) = \frac{3}{2} * 3^n - \frac{1}{2}$.

WCET Analysis. Efficient and precise WCET analysis relies on program analysis and optimization techniques. We overview below four methods on which our WCET analysis framework crucially depends on. Throughout this paper, we call a loop *simple* if it has a single path (i.e. the loop body is a sequence of assignment statements). A loop is called *multi-path* if it has multiple paths (i.e. the loop body contains conditionals and/or loops). We also assume that integers are represented using 32-bits.

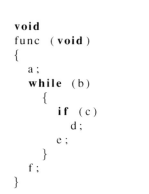

```
void
func  ( void )
{
    a ;
    while  ( b )
    {
        if  ( c )
            d ;
        e ;
    }
    f ;
}
```

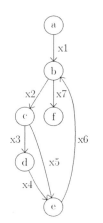

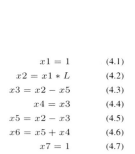

$$x1 = 1 \qquad (4.1)$$
$$x2 = x1 * L \qquad (4.2)$$
$$x3 = x2 - x5 \qquad (4.3)$$
$$x4 = x3 \qquad (4.4)$$
$$x5 = x2 - x3 \qquad (4.5)$$
$$x6 = x5 + x4 \qquad (4.6)$$
$$x7 = 1 \qquad (4.7)$$

Fig. 2. Abstracted C program, where b and c are boolean expressions and a, d, e, and f denote program statements

Fig. 3. Graph representation of program flow. The execution frequencies are listed on edges

Fig. 4. Execution frequencies of program expressions. Equations (4.1) and (4.7) state that the program is entered and exited once. Equation (4.2) states that the loop body is executed L times, where L denotes the number of loop iterations.

(1) Interval and points-to analysis implements a forward directed data flow interval analysis, yielding variable values and aliasing information for all program locations.

(2) Counter-based loop analysis derives bounds for simple loops with incremented/decremented updates, by constructing symbolic equations that are solved using pattern matching and term rewriting. If no values are available for variables in the loop initialization, condition, and increment expression, then the analysis fails in deriving loop bounds. Note that in certain cases variables with unknown values can be discarded, and thus loop bounds can be derived.

(3) Constraint-based loop analysis models and enumerates the iteration space of nested loops. To this end, a system of constraints is constructed that reflects dependencies between iteration variables and thus yields better results than just multiplying the bounds of nested loops. The solution to the constraint system is computed by a constraint logic programming solver over finite domains.

(4) Implicit path enumeration technique (IPET) first maps the program flow to a set of graph flow constraints describing relationships between execution frequencies of program blocks. Execution times for expressions are evaluated by a low-level WCET-analysis. The execution times are then summed up to get execution times for program blocks. Finally, the longest execution path (exposing the WCET) of the program is found by maximizing the solution to the constraint system. We illustrate the IPET in Example 2.

Example 2. Consider the program given in Figure 2. Its program flow is given in Figure 3. The dependency relations between execution frequencies of program blocks are extracted from Figure 3 and are listed in Figure 4. For simplicity, we assume that all expressions take one time unit to execute. Therefore, execution of one loop iteration takes at most 4 time units: 1 unit to check each boolean condition b and c, and 1 unit to execute each statement d and e. The longest path through the loop is the node sequence $b \rightarrow c \rightarrow d \rightarrow e$. We consider[2] the loop bound L to be 10. The WCET for func is further derived by maximizing the sum of block costs in the process of satisfying the dependency relations of Figure 4. As a result, the WCET of func is computed to be 42 time units.

The accuracy of a WCET limit crucially depends on the precision of the available loop bounds. The difficulty of inferring precise upper bounds on loop iterations comes from the presence of complex loop arithmetic and control flow. In what follows, we describe an approach for inferring precise upper bounds on the number of loop iterations by using recurrence solving and SMT reasoning in a unified framework. For simplicity, we sometimes say *loop upper bounds* or *loop bound* to mean upper bounds on the number of loop iterations.

5   Symbolic WCET Analysis

In our approach to derive tight loop bounds, we identify special classes of loops and infer upper bounds on loop iterations, as follows. We apply a pattern-based recurrence solving algorithm to get bounds for simple loops with linear arithmetic updates (Section 5.1) and over-approximate non-deterministic initializations (Section 5.2). We translate multi-path loops with abrupt termination and monotonic conditional updates into simple loops (Section 5.3). The computed loop bounds are further used to obtain accurate WCET of programs.

5.1   Recurrence Solving in Simple Loops

We identified a special class of loops with linear updates and conditions, as below.

$$
\textbf{for } (i = a; \ i < b; \ i = c * i + d) ;
$$
$$
\text{where } a, b, c, d \in \mathbb{K} \text{ do not depend on } i, \text{ and } c \neq 0. \tag{5.1}
$$

Hence, in loops matching (5.1), loop iteration variables (i.e. i) are bounded by symbolic constants and updated by linear expressions over iteration variables.

For a loop like (5.1), we derive an *exact* upper bound on the number of loop iterations. In more detail, we proceed as follows.
(i) We first model the loop iteration update as a recurrence equation over a new variable $n \in \mathbb{N}$ denoting the loop counter. To do so, we write $i(n)$ to denote the value of variable i at the nth loop iteration. The recurrence equation of i corresponding to (5.1) is given below.

$$
i(n + 1) = c * i(n) + d \quad \text{with the initial value} \quad i(0) = a. \tag{5.2}
$$

Note that (5.2) is a C-finite recurrence of order 1 as variable updates of (5.1) are linear.
(ii) Next, recurrence (5.2) is solved (cf. Section 4) and the closed form of i as a function

---

[2] L can be either inferred by a loop analysis step or given as a manual annotation.

over n is derived. More precisely, depending on the value of c, the closed form of $i(n)$ is given below.

$$i(n) = \alpha * c^n + \beta, \text{ if } c \neq 1$$

where

$$\begin{cases} \alpha + \beta = a \\ \alpha * c + \beta = a * c + d \end{cases}$$

and

$$i(n) = \alpha + \beta * n, \text{ if } c = 1$$

where

$$\begin{cases} \alpha = a \\ \alpha + \beta = a + d \end{cases}$$

(5.3)

(iii) The closed form of $i(n)$ is further used to derive a tight upper integer bound on the number of loop iterations of (5.1). To this end, we are interested in finding the value of n such that the loop condition holds at the nth iteration and is violated at the $n + 1$th iteration. We are thus left with computing the (smallest) positive integer value of n such that the below formula is satisfied:

$$n \in \mathbb{N} \land i(n) < b \land i(n+1) \geq b. \tag{5.4}$$

```
for (j=1; j<100; j = j*3+1);
```

Fig. 5. Loop with C-finite update

```
for (i=nondet(); i>0; i≫=1);
```

Fig. 6. Loop with non-deterministic initialization

The smallest n derived yields a tight upper bound on the number of loop iterations. This upper bound is further used in the WCET analysis of programs containing a loop matching (5.1).

Example 3. Consider Figure 5. Updates over j describe a C-finite recurrence, whereas the loop condition is expressed as a linear inequality over j. Let $n \in \mathbb{N}$ denote the loop counter. Based on (5.3), the value of j at arbitrary loop iteration n is $j(n) = \frac{3}{2} * 3^n - \frac{1}{2}$. Using (5.4), the upper bound on loop iterations is further derived to be 4 – we consider 0 to be the starting iteration of a loop.

Solving the recurrence equation (5.2) can be done using powerful symbolic computation packages, such as [16,11]. These packages are implemented on top of the computer algebra system (CAS) Mathematica [23]. Integrating a CAS with program analysis tools is however problematic due to the complexity and closed-source nature of CAS. Moreover, the full computational power of CAS algorithms is hardly needed in applications of program analysis and verification. Therefore, for automatically inferring exact loop bounds for (5.1) we designed a *pattern-based recurrence solving* algorithm which is not based on CAS. Our method relies on the crucial observation that in our approach to WCET analysis we do not handle arbitrary C-finite recurrences. We only consider loops matching the pattern of (5.1), where updates describe C-finite recurrences of order 1. Closed forms of such recurrences are given in (5.3). Therefore, to compute upper bounds on the number of loop iterations of (5.1) we do not deploy the general C-finite recurrence solving algorithm given in [5], but instantiate the closed form pattern (5.3). In other words, whenever we encounter a loop of the form (5.1), the closed form of the iteration variable is derived by instantiating the symbolic constants $a, b, c, d, \alpha, \beta$ of (5.3) with the concrete values of the loop under study. Hence, we do not make use of general purpose C-finite recurrence solving algorithms, but handle loops (5.1) by pattern-matching C-finite recurrences of order 1. However, our approach can be further extended to handle loops with more complex linear updates than those in (5.1).

Finally let us make the observation that while reasoning about (5.1), we consider the iteration variable i and the symbolic constants $a, b, c, d, \alpha, \beta$ to have values in $\mathbb{K}$. That is, when solving recurrences of (5.1) the integer variables and constants of (5.1) are safely approximated over $\mathbb{K}$. However, when deriving upper bounds of (5.1), we restrict the satisfiability problem (5.4) over integers. If formulas in (5.4) are linear, we obtain a tight loop bound satisfying (5.4) by using SMT reasoning over linear arithmetic. Otherwise, a loop bound satisfying (5.4) is computed using SMT reasoning over non-linear arithmetic (with bounded integers).

5.2   Non-deterministic Analysis in Shift-Loops

We call a loop a *shift-loop* if updates over the loop iteration variables are made using the bit-shift operators $\ll$ (left shift) or $\gg$ (right shift). Let us recall that the operation $i \ll m$ (respectively, $i \gg m$) shifts the value of i left (respectively, right) by m bits.

Consider a shift-loop with iteration variable i, where i is shifted by m bits. Hence, updates over i describe a C-finite recurrence of order 1. Upper bounds on the number of loop iterations can thus be derived as described in Section 5.1, whenever the initial value of i is specified as a symbolic constant. However, the initial value of i might not always be given or derived by interval analysis. A possible source of such a limitation can, for example, be that the initialization of i uses non-deterministic assignments, as given in (5.5)(a) and (b).

```
for (i = nondet(); i > d;  i >>= m) ;        for (i = nondet(); i < d;  i <<= m) ;
```

$$\text{(a)} \qquad\qquad\qquad\qquad\qquad\qquad \text{(b)} \qquad\qquad\qquad\qquad (5.5)$$

where $d \in \mathbb{K}$ does not depend on i and $m \in \mathbb{N}$.

For shift-loops matching pattern (5.5), the method presented in Section 5.1 would thus fail in deriving loop upper bounds. To overcome this limitation, we proceed as below.

(i) We soundly approximate the non-deterministic initial assignment to i by setting the initial value of i to be the integer value that allows the maximum number of shift operations within the loop (i.e. the maximum number of loop iterations). To this end, we distinguish between left and right shifts as follows.

If i is updated using a right-shift operation (i.e. (5.5)(a)), the initial value of i is set to be the maximal integer value, yielding a maximum number of shifts within the loop. The initial value of i is hence assumed to have the value 2147483647, that is $010\ldots0$ in a 32-bit binary representation (the most significant, non-sign, bit of i is set).

If i is updated using a left-shift operation (i.e. (5.5)(b)), we assume the initial value of i to be the integer value resulting in the maximum number of shift operations possible: i is set to have the value 1, that is $0\ldots01$ in a 32-bit binary representation (the least significant bit of i is set).

(ii) The upper bound on the number of loop iterations is then obtained by first computing the difference between the positions of the highest bits set in the initial value of i and d, and then dividing this difference by m. If no value information is available for m, we assume m to be 1.

Example 4. Consider the shift-loop of Figure 6 with right shift updates. The initial value of i is set to INT_MAX. The upper bound on the number of loop iteration is then derived to be 31.

Let us note that the treatment of non-deterministic initial assignments as described above is not only restricted to shift-loops, but can be also extended to (5.1). For doing so, one would however need to investigate the monotonic behavior of C-finite recurrences in order to soundly approximate the initial value of loop iteration variables. We leave this study for future research.

5.3 Flow Analysis on Multi-path Loops

Paths of multi-path loops can interleave in a non-trivial manner. Deriving tight loop upper bounds, and thus accurate WCET, for programs containing multi-path loops is therefore a challenging task.

In our approach to WCET analysis, we identified special classes of *multi-path loops with only conditionals* which can be translated into simple loops by refining the control flow of the multi-path loops. Loop bounds for the obtained simple loops are further derived as described in Sections 5.1 and 5.2, yielding thus loop bounds of the original multi-path loops. In what follows, we describe in more detail what type of multi-path loops our approach can automatically handle and overview the flow analysis techniques deployed in our work. For simplicity reasons, in the rest of the paper we consider multi-path loops (arising from conditionals) with only 2 paths.

Loops with abrupt termination. One class of multi-path loops that can automatically be analyzed by our framework is the class of linearly iterating loops with abrupt termination arising from non-deterministic conditionals, as given in (5.6) (a)–(c).

```
int i = a;                int i = nondet();         int i = nondet();
for (; i < b; i = c * i + d)   for (; i > e; i >>= m)     for (; i < e; i <<= m)
  if (nondet()) break;       if (nondet()) break;      if (nondet()) break;
        (a)                       (b)                       (c)
```

$$(5.6)$$

where $a, b, c, d, e \in \mathbb{K}$ do not depend on i, $c \neq 0$, and $m \in \mathbb{N}$.

We are interested in computing the *worst case* execution time of a loop from (5.6). Therefore, we safely over-approximate the number of loop iterations of (5.6) by assuming that the abruptly terminating loop path is not taken. In other words, the non-deterministic conditional statement causing the abrupt termination of (5.6) is ignored, and we are left with a simple loop as in (5.1) or (5.5). Upper bounds on the resulting loops are then computed as described in Sections 5.1 and 5.2, from which an over-approximation of the WCET of (5.6) is derived.

Example 5. Consider Figure 7. Assuming that the abruptly terminating loop path is not taken, we obtain a simple loop as in (5.1). We thus get the loop bound 100.

```
for (j = 0; j < 100; j++)          for (j = 0; j < 100; j++)
  if (nondet())  break ;             if (nondet()) j++;
```

Fig. 7. Loop with abrupt termination   Fig. 8. Loop with monotonic conditional update

Loops with monotonic conditional updates. By analyzing the effect of conditional statements on the number of loop iterations, we identified the class of multi-path loops as listed in (5.7).

```
for (i = a; i < b; i = c * i + d)
  if (B) i = f₁(i);                                                    (5.7)
  else   i = f₂(i);
```

where $a, b, c, d \in \mathbb{K}$ do not depend on i, $c \neq 0$, B is a boolean condition over loop variables,

and: $\begin{cases} f_1, f_2 : \mathbb{K} \to \mathbb{K} \text{ are monotonically increasing functions, if } c > 0 \\ f_1, f_2 : \mathbb{K} \to \mathbb{K} \text{ are monotonically decreasing functions, if } c < 0 \end{cases}$.

We refer to the assignment $i = f_1(i)$ as a *conditional monotonic assignment (or update)*, as its execution depends on the truth value of B.

Let $g : \mathbb{K} \to \mathbb{K}$ denote the function $i \mapsto c * i + d$ describing the linear updates over i made at *every* iteration of a loop matching (5.7). Note that the monotonic behavior of g depends on c and coincides with the monotonic properties of f_1 and f_2. To infer loop upper bounds for (5.7), we aim at computing the *worst case* iteration time of (5.7). To do so, we ignore B and transform (5.7) into a single-path loop by *safely over-approximating* the multi-path behavior of (5.7), as given below. In what follows, let $\Delta = |g(i+1) - g(i)|$, $\Delta_1 = |f_1(i+1) - f_1(i)|$, and $\Delta_2 = |f_2(i+1) - f_2(i)|$, where $|x|$ denotes the absolute value of $x \in \mathbb{K}$.

(i) If c is positive, let $m = \min\{\Delta + \Delta_1, \Delta + \Delta_2\}$. That is, m captures the minimal value by which i can be increased during an arbitrary iteration of (5.7). Alternatively, if c is negative, we take $m = \max\{\Delta + \Delta_1, \Delta + \Delta_2\}$. That is, m captures the maximal value by which i can be decreased during an arbitrary iteration of (5.7).
(ii) Loop (5.7) is then over-approximated by the simple loop (5.8) capturing the worst case iteration time of (5.7).

$$\begin{cases} \textbf{for } (i = a; i < b; \{i = c * i + d; i = f_1(i)\}), & \text{if } c > 0 \text{ and } m = \Delta + \Delta_1 \\ \textbf{for } (i = a; i < b; \{i = c * i + d; i = f_2(i)\}), & \text{if } c > 0 \text{ and } m = \Delta + \Delta_2 \\ \textbf{for } (i = a; i < b; \{i = c * i + d; i = f_1(i)\}), & \text{if } c < 0 \text{ and } m = \Delta + \Delta_1 \\ \textbf{for } (i = a; i < b; \{i = c * i + d; i = f_2(i)\}), & \text{if } c < 0 \text{ and } m = \Delta + \Delta_2 \end{cases} \quad (5.8)$$

Hence, the control flow refinement of (5.7) requires checking the arithmetical monotonicity constraints of f_1 and f_2. We automatically decide this requirement using arithmetical SMT queries.
(iii) We are finally left with computing loop upper bounds of (5.8). To this end, we need to make additional constraints on the monotonic functions f_1 and f_2 of (5.7) so that the approach of Section 5.1 can be applied. Namely, we restrict f_1 (respectively, f_2) to be a linear monotonic function $i \mapsto u * i + v$, where $u, v \in \mathbb{K}$ do not depend on i and $u \neq 0$. As linear monotonic functions are closed under composition, updates over the iteration variable i in (5.8) correspond to C-finite recurrences of order 1. Upper bounds on loop iterations of (5.8) can thus be derived as presented in Section 5.1.

```for (i = x; i < 65536; i *= 2) ;```	```int s = x; while (s) s >>= 1;```	```while (i > 0) if (i >= c) i = -c; else i- = 1;```	```M = 12; for (i = 0; i < M; i++) A[i] = malloc(N) if (!A[i]) break;```
(a) Loop with C-finite update. Iteration bound is 12.	(b) Shift-loop. Iteration bound is 31.	(c) Loop with conditional updates. With no initial value information on i, the bound is INT_MAX.	(d) Abruptly terminating loop. Iteration bound is 12.

Fig. 9. Examples from[10]

Note that the additional constraints imposed over f_1 and f_2 restrict our approach to the multi-path loops (5.9) with linear conditional updates.

$$
\begin{aligned}
&\textbf{for } (i = a; i < b; i = c * i + d)\\
&\{\\
&\quad \textbf{if } (B)\ i = u_1 * i + v_1;\\
&\quad \textbf{else }\ i = u_2 * i + v_2;\\
&\}
\end{aligned}
\tag{5.9}
$$

where $a, b, c, d, u_1, u_2, v_1, v_2 \in \mathbb{K}$ do not depend on i, and $c, u_1, u_2 \neq 0$,

B is a boolean condition over loop variables, and $\begin{cases} u_1 > 0 \text{ and } u_2 > 0, \text{ if } c > 0 \\ u_1 < 0 \text{ and } u_2 < 0, \text{ if } c < 0 \end{cases}$

Loops (5.9) form a special case of (5.7). Let us however note, that extending the approach of Section 5.1 to handle general (or not) C-finite recurrences with monotonic behavior would enable our framework to compute upper bounds for arbitrary (5.7). We leave the study of such extensions for future work.

Example 6. Consider Figure 8. The conditional update over j is linear, and hence the multi-path loop is transformed into the simple loop **for** $(j = 0; j < 100; j++)$. The loop bound of Figure 8 is therefore derived to be 100.

6   Experimental Evaluation

We implemented our approach to loop bound computation in the TuBound tool [19]. TuBound is a static analysis tool with focus on program optimization and WCET analysis of the optimized program. TuBound is based on the Static Analysis Tool Integration Engine (SATIrE) framework and developed at VUT. Given a C program, the work flow of TuBound consists of a forward-directed flow-sensitive interval analysis and a unification based flow-insensitive points-to analysis, followed by a loop bound analysis. The analysis results are weaved back into the program source as compiler-pragmas (i.e. annotations). A WCET-aware GNU C compiler translates then the source to annotated assembler code. Finally, a WCET bound of the input C program is calculated using the IPET approach. For more details about TuBound we refer to [19,17].

   We extended TuBound's loop bound inference engine by our approach to infer iteration bounds of loops with non-trivial linear updates and refinable control flow. However, to make our approach applicable to real world examples, we also extended TuBound's

Table 1. Experimental results and comparisons with r-TuBound and TuBound

Benchmark Suite	# Loops	TuBound	r-TuBound	Types
Mälardalen	152	120	121	CF
Debie-1d	75	58	59	SH, CU
Scimark	34	24	26	AT, CF
Dassault	77	39	46	AT, CF-CU-AT (3), CU(4)
Total	338	241	252	AT (2), SH, CU (5), CF (2), CF-CU-AT (3)

loop preprocessing step. The preprocessing step transforms arbitrary loop constructs into `for`-loops, and applies simple loop rewriting techniques.

The new version of TuBound implementing our approach to loop bound computation is called *r-TuBound*.

WCET Benchmarks. We investigated two benchmark suites that originate from the WCET community: the Mälardalen Real Time and the Debie-1d benchmark suites [10]. The Mälardalen suite consists of 152 loops. r-TuBound was able to infer loop bounds for 121 loops from the Mälardalen examples. By analyzing our results, we observed that 120 out of these 121 loops involved only incrementing/decrementing updates over iteration variables, and 1 loop required more complex C-finite recurrence solving as described in Section 5.1. When compared to TuBound [19], we noted that TuBound also computed bounds for the 120 Mälardalen loops with increment/decrement updates. However, unlike r-TuBound, TuBound failed on analyzing the loop with more complex C-finite behavior.

The Debie benchmark suite contains 75 loops. r-TuBound successfully analyzed 59 loops. These 59 loops can be classified as follows: 57 simple loops with increment/decrement updates, 1 shift-loop with non-deterministic initialization, and 1 multi-path loop with conditional update. When compared to TuBound, we observed that TuBound could analyze the 58 simple loops and failed on the multi-path loop. Moreover, r-TuBound derived a tighter loop bound for the shift-loop than TuBound.

Scientific Benchmarks. We ran r-TuBound on the SciMark2 benchmark suite containing 34 loops. Among other arithmetic operations, SciMark2 makes use of fast Fourier transformations and matrix operations. r-TuBound derived loop bounds for 26 loops, whereas TuBound could analyze 24 loops. The 2 loops which could only be handled by r-TuBound required reasoning about abrupt-termination and C-finite updates.

Industrial Benchmarks. We also evaluated r-TuBound on 77 loops sent by Dassault Aviation. r-TuBound inferred loop bounds for 46 loops, whereas TuBound analyzed only 39 loops. When compared to TuBound, the success of r-TuBound lies in its power to handle abrupt termination, conditional updates, and C-finite behavior.

Experimental Results. Altogether, we ran r-TuBound on 4 different benchmark suites, on a total of 338 loops and derived loop bounds for 253 loops. Out of these 253 loops, 243 loops were simple and involved only C-finite reasoning, and 10 loops were multi-path and required the treatment of abrupt termination and conditional updates. Unlike r-TuBound, TuBound could only handle 241 simple loops. Figure 9 shows example of loops that could be analyzed by r-TuBound, but not also by TuBound.

We summarize our results in Table 1. Column 1 of Table 1 lists the name of the benchmark suite, whereas column 2 gives the number of loops contained in the benchmarks. Columns 3 and 4 list respectively how many loops were successfully analyzed by TuBound and r-TuBound. Column 5 describes the reasons why some loops, when compared to TuBound, could only be analyzed by r-TuBound. To this end, we distinguish between simple loops with C-finite updates (CF), shift-loops with non-deterministic initializations (SH), multi-path loops with abrupt termination (AT), and multi-path loops with monotonic conditional updates (CU). Column 5 of Table 1 also lists, in parenthesis, how many of such loops were encountered and could only be analyzed by r-TuBound. For example, among the loops sent by Dassault Aviation 4 multi-path loops with monotonic conditional update, denoted as CU(4), could only be analyzed by r-TuBound. Some loops on which only r-TuBound succeeds are, for example, multi-path loops with C-finite conditional updates and abrupt termination; such loops are listed in Table 1 as CF-CU-AT.

Analysis of Results. Table 1 shows that 74.55% of the 338 loops were successfully analyzed by r-TuBound, whereas TuBound succeeded on 71.30% of the 338 loops. That is, when compared to TuBound, the overall quality of loop bound analysis within r-TuBound has increased by 3.25%. This relatively low performance increase of r-TuBound might thus not be considered significant, when compared to TuBound.

Let us however note that the performance of r-TuBound, compared to TUBound, on the WCET and scientific benchmarks was predictable in some sense. These benchmarks are used to test and evaluate WCET tools already since 2006. In other words, it is expected that state-of-the-art WCET tools are fine tuned with various heuristics so that they yield good performance results on loops occurring in "classical" WCET benchmarks, including Debie-1D, Mälarden, or even Scimark.

The benefit of r-TuBound wrt TuBound can be however evidenced when considering new benchmarks, where loops have more complicated arithmetic and/or control flow. Namely, on the 77 examples coming from Dassault Aviation, r-TuBound derives loop bounds for 46 programs. That is, 60% of new benchmarks can be successfully analysed by r-TuBound. When compared to TuBound, we note that r-TuBound outperforms TuBound on these new examples by a performance increase of 9%. The programs which can only be handled by r-TuBound require reasoning about multi-path loops where updates to scalars yield linear recurrences of program variables (in many cases, with $c \neq 1$ in (5.1)) . These recurrences cannot be solved by the simple variable increment/decrement handling of TuBound. Moreover, TuBound fails in handling multi-path loops. Based on the results obtained on these new benchmark suite, we believe that our pattern-based recurrence solving approach in conjunction with SMT reasoning for flow refinement provides good results for computing bounds for complex loops with r-TuBound.

Let us also note that in WCET analysis, loops, even simple ones, are in general manually annotated with additional information on loop bounds. Automated generation of loop bounds would significantly increase the applicability of WCET tools in embedded software. The techniques presented in this paper can automatically deal with loops

```
while (abs(diff) >= 1.0e-05)        while (k < j)
{                                    {                        while (((int)p[i]) != 0)
   diff = diff * −rad * rad/            j -= k;                  i++;
       (2.0 * inc) * (2.0 * inc + 1.0);  k /= 2;
   inc++;                            }
}
```

(a)   (b)   (c)

Fig. 10. Limitations of r-TuBound

which often occur real-time systems, and therefore can be successfully applied for automated WCET analysis of programs.

Limitations. We investigated examples on which r-TuBound failed to derive loop bounds. We list some of the failing loops in Figure 10. Note that the arithmetic used in the simple loop Figure 10(a) requires extending our framework with more complex recurrence solving techniques, such as [22,11], and deploy SMT solving over various numeric functions, such as the absolute value computations over floats or integers. On the other hand, Figure 10(b) suggests a simple extension of our method to solving blocks of C-finite recurrences. Finally we note that Figure 10(c) illustrates the need of combining our approach with reasoning about array contents, which can be done either using SMT solvers [13,4] or first-order theorem provers [21]. We leave this research challenges for future work.

7 Conclusion

We describe an automatic approach for deriving iteration bounds for loops with linear updates and refinable control flow. Our method implements a pattern-based recurrence solving algorithm, uses SMT reasoning to refine program flow, and over-approximates non-deterministic initializations. The inferred loop bounds are further used in the WCET analysis of programs. When applied to challenging benchmarks, our approach succeeded in generating tight iteration bounds for large number of loops.

In the line of [18], we plan to extend the recurrence solving algorithm in r-TuBound to analyze loops with more complex arithmetic. We also intend to integrate our approach with flow refinement techniques based on invariant generation, such as in [7]. Moreover, we plan to compete in the WCET-Challenge 2011.

References

1. Albert, E., Arenas, P., Genaim, S., Puebla, G.: Closed-Form Upper Bounds in Static Cost Analysis. J. Automated Reasoning 46(2), 161–203 (2011)
2. Ammarguellat, Z., Harrison III., W.L.: Automatic Recognition of Induction Variables and Recurrence Relations by Abstract Interpretation. In: Proc. of PLDI, pp. 283–295 (1990)
3. Blanc, R., Henzinger, T.A., Hottelier, T., Kovács, L.: ABC: Algebraic Bound Computation for Loops. In: Clarke, E.M., Voronkov, A. (eds.) LPAR-16 2010. LNCS, vol. 6355, pp. 103–118. Springer, Heidelberg (2010)
4. Brummayer, R., Biere, A.: Boolector: An Efficient SMT Solver for Bit-Vectors and Arrays. In: Kowalewski, S., Philippou, A. (eds.) TACAS 2009. LNCS, vol. 5505, pp. 174–177. Springer, Heidelberg (2009)

5. Everest, G., van der Poorten, A., Shparlinski, I., Ward, T.: Recurrence Sequences. Mathematical Surveys and Monographs, vol. 104. American Mathematical Society (2003)
6. Gulwani, S., Mehra, K.K., Chilimbi, T.M.: SPEED: Precise and Efficient Static Estimation of Program Computational Complexity. In: Proc. of POPL, pp. 127–139 (2009)
7. Gulwani, S., Zuleger, F.: The Reachability-Bound Problem. In: Proc. of PLDI, pp. 292–304 (2010)
8. Gustafsson, J., Ermedahl, A., Sandberg, C., Lisper, B.: Automatic Derivation of Loop Bounds and Infeasible Paths for WCET Analysis Using Abstract Execution. In: Proc. of RTSS, pp. 57–66 (2006)
9. Henzinger, T., Hottelier, T., Kovács, L.: Valigator: A Verification Tool with Bound and Invariant Generation. In: Proc. of LPAR-15, pp. 333–342 (2008)
10. Holsti, N., Gustafsson, J., Bernat, G., Ballabriga, C., Bonenfant, A., Bourgade, R., Cassé, H., Cordes, D., Kadlec, A., Kirner, R., Knoop, J., Lokuciejewski, P., Merriam, N., de Michiel, M., Prantl, A., Rieder, B., Rochange, C., Sainrat, P., Schordan, M.: WCET 2008 - Report from the Tool Challenge 2008 - 8th Intl. Workshop on Worst-Case Execution Time (WCET) Analysis. In: Proc. of WCET (2008)
11. Kauers, M.: SumCracker: A Package for Manipulating Symbolic Sums and Related Objects. J. of Symbolic Computation 41(9), 1039–1057 (2006)
12. Kirner, R., Knoop, J., Prantl, A., Schordan, M., Kadlec, A.: Beyond Loop Bounds: Comparing Annotation Languages for Worst-Case Execution Time Analysis. J. of Software and System Modeling (2010); Online edition
13. de Moura, L., Bjørner, N.: Z3: An Efficient SMT Solver. In: Ramakrishnan, C.R., Rehof, J. (eds.) TACAS 2008. LNCS, vol. 4963, pp. 337–340. Springer, Heidelberg (2008)
14. Lisper, B.: Fully Automatic, Parametric Worst-Case Execution Time Analysis. In: Proc. of WCET, pp. 99–102 (2003)
15. Michiel, M.D., Bonenfant, A., Cassé, H., Sainrat, P.: Static Loop Bound Analysis of C Programs Based on Flow Analysis and Abstract Interpretation. In: Proc. of RTCSA, pp. 161–166 (2008)
16. Paule, P., Schorn, M.: A Mathematica Version of Zeilberger's Algorithm for Proving Binomial Coefficient Identities. J. of Symbolic Computation 20(5-6), 673–698 (1995)
17. Prantl, A.: High-level Compiler Support for Timing-Analysis. PhD thesis, Vienna University of Technology (2010)
18. Prantl, A., Knoop, J., Kirner, R., Kadlec, A., Schordan, M.: From Trusted Annotations to Verified Knowledge. In: Proc. of WCET, pp. 39–49 (2009)
19. Prantl, A., Knoop, J., Schordan, M., Triska, M.: Constraint Solving for High-Level WCET Analysis. In: Proc. of WLPE, pp. 77–89 (2008)
20. Prantl, A., Schordan, M., Knoop, J.: TuBound - A Conceptually New Tool for WCET Analysis. In: Proc. of WCET, pp. 141–148 (2008)
21. Riazanov, A., Voronkov, A.: The Design and Implementation of Vampire. AI Communications 15(2-3), 91–110 (2002)
22. Schneider, C.: Symbolic Summation with Single-Nested Sum Extensions. In: Proc. of ISSAC, pp. 282–289 (2004)
23. Wolfram, S.: The Mathematica Book. Version 5.0. Wolfram Media (2003)

GoRRiLA and Hard Reality

Konstantin Korovin[*] and Andrei Voronkov[**]

The University of Manchester
{korovin,voronkov}@cs.man.ac.uk

Abstract. We call a *theory problem* a conjunction of theory literals and a *theory solver* any system that solves theory problems. For implementing efficient theory solvers one needs benchmark problems, and especially hard ones. Unfortunately, hard benchmarks for theory solvers are notoriously difficult to obtain. In this paper we present two tools: *Hard Reality* for generating theory problems from real-life problems with non-trivial boolean structure and *GoRRiLA* for generating random theory problems for linear arithmetic. Using GoRRiLA one can generate problems containing only a few variables, which however are difficult for all state-of-the-art solvers we tried. Such problems can be useful for debugging and evaluating solvers on small but hard problems. Using Hard Reality one can generate hard theory problems which are similar to problems found in real-life applications, for example, those taken from SMT-LIB [2].

1 Introduction

All modern satisfiability modulo theories (SMT) solvers contain two major parts: the boolean reasoning part and the theory reasoning part. Both boolean and theory reasoning are important for an efficient solver and both are highly optimised. Usually, a theory solver can be seen as a standalone procedure solving satisfiability of sets of theory literals (e.g., if we consider linear real arithmetic then the theory solver is required to solve systems of equations and inequalities). The development of theory solvers is on its own right a highly non-trivial problem. Unfortunately, currently there are no available benchmarks for debugging and evaluating theory solvers. Indeed, almost all problems in the standard SMT benchmark library SMT-LIB are problems with a non-trivial boolean structure and cannot be used for evaluating dedicated theory solvers. Moreover, when evaluating an SMT solver it is usually not clear where the performance bottleneck is: in the theory or the boolean part. In addition to the evaluation problem, one needs a good set of benchmarks for debugging and checking consistency of theory solvers. There are three common ways of generating theory problems: (i) randomly, (ii) based on proof obligations coming from applications, and (iii) based on logging benchmarks generated by running solvers on real-life problems [10].

In this paper we present two tools: GoRRiLA for randomly generating small yet hard theory problems for linear (integer and rational) arithmetic and Hard Reality for generating theory problems from real-life problems with non-trivial boolean structure. The advantage of randomly generated problems is that we can generate many diverse

---

[*] Supported by a Royal Society University Research Fellowship.
[**] Partially supported by an EPSRC grant.

E. Clarke, I. Virbitskaite, and A. Voronkov (Eds.): PSI 2011, LNCS 7162, pp. 243–250, 2012.

problems, and therefore such problems are well-suited for testing correctness especially of newly developing solvers. We observed that there are a number of randomly generated problems with only few variables that are hard for all SMT solvers we tried. For example in the case of linear integer arithmetic already problems with 4 variables can be hard for many state-of-the-art SMT solvers. Therefore, we believe randomly generated problems can also be used for exploring efficiency issues with theory solvers. Moreover, using our tool we found small linear integer arithmetic problems on which some state-of-the-art SMT solvers return inconsistent results. In Section 2 we present our tool, called GoRRiLA, for randomly generating hard linear arithmetic problems and evaluating solvers on such problems.

Randomly generated problems have one major disadvantage: usually they are very different from the problems occurring in practice. On the other hand, problems coming from applications are not easy to find. In fact, this work appeared as a side-effect of our work on evaluating solvers for linear arithmetic, since we were unable to find good collections of systems of linear inequalities over rationals for testing and benchmarking our system. In Section 3 we present our tool, called Hard Reality, for generating theory problems from real-life quantifier-free SMT problems. Using Hard Reality we have been able to generate a variety of theory problems that at the same time are representative of the problems that the theory parts of SMT solvers are dealing with.

The intended applications of the obtained theory benchmarks by GoRRiLA and Hard Reality are the following:

- testing correctness and efficiency of theory reasoners on both randomly generated and realistic benchmarks.
- evaluating and comparing dedicated theory reasoners and theory reasoners within SMT solvers.

In this paper we leave out evaluation of incrementality of theory solvers. Although incrementality is crucial for theory solvers within the SMT framework (see, e.g., [7]), we believe it is an orthogonal issue to the main goal of this paper: generation of hard theory problems. Hard theory problems can also be used to evaluate incrementality of theory solvers, but this goes beyond the scope of this paper.

2 GoRRiLA

It is well-known how to generate random propositional SAT problems and in particular hard SAT problems (see, e.g., [9]). In this section we present a method for randomly generating hard linear arithmetic problems which is inspired by methods used in the propositional case. First we consider the case of linear integer arithmetic and later show that our method is also suitable for linear rational arithmetic. For each integer $n \geq 1$, let X_n denote a set of n variables $\{x_1, \ldots, x_n\}$.

A *linear constraint with integer coefficients over the set of variables* X_n, (or simply a *linear constraint over* X_n), is an expression of the form $a_1 x_1 + \ldots + a_n x_n + a_0 \diamond 0$ where $\diamond \in \{\geq, >, =, \neq\}$ and $a_i \in \mathbb{Z}$ for $1 \leq i \leq n$. A *linear problem with integer coefficients over the set of variables* X_n (or simply a *linear problem*) is a set of linear constraints.

Suppose we would like to generate a random linear inequality $a_1 x_1 + \ldots + a_n x_n + a_0 \geq 0$. To this end, we fix the following parameters:

- the number n of variables;
- the lower and the upper integer bounds on coefficients;
- the number k of variables that can have non-zero coefficients in the constraint.

Let $\mathscr{C}$ denote the set of all integers between the lower and the upper bound on the coefficients. Then we generate:

1. a random subset $i_1, \ldots, i_k$ of X_n of cardinality k, each subset is selected with an equal probability;
2. uniformly and randomly k integers $a_1, \ldots, a_k$ in $\mathscr{C} \setminus \{0\}$;
3. uniformly and randomly an integer $a_0 \in \mathscr{C}$.

After that we use $a_1 x_{i_1} + \ldots + a_k x_{i_k} + a_0 \geq 0$ as the random inequality. In the same way we can select random constraints of other kinds, for example, strict inequalities.

In order to generate a random system of linear constraints we also fix, $N_\geq$, $N_>$, $N_=$ and $N_{\neq}$ – the numbers of constraints of each kind respectively. When all problem parameters are fixed a *random linear problem* is generated as a set containing $N_\diamond$ random constraints of each type $\diamond \in \{\geq, >, =, \neq\}$. Below we assume that $\diamond$ ranges over all constraint types $\{\geq, >, =, \neq\}$. For simplicity, we assume that the set of coefficients $\mathscr{C}$ and the number of variables k in the constraints are uniformly fixed. Similar to the propositional case, we can observe a transition from almost always satisfiable problems to almost always unsatisfiable ones when we increase the number of constraints relative to the number of variables. As in the propositional case, it turned out that problems hard for modern solvers occur in the region where approximately 50% of generated problems are satisfiable. In order to generate a sequence of *hard random problems* we take the number of variables n as the leading parameter and the numbers of constraints of each type as $N_\diamond = q_\diamond * n$, where $q_\diamond$ is a rational number. Generally, since we have different types of constraints, hard problems can occur with different combinations of parameters $q_\diamond$, for our purposes we can take any such combination or introduce a bias towards some types of constraints.

Let us remark that any constraint with rational coefficients can be normalised into an equivalent constraint with integer coefficients. Therefore we can use the procedure for generating linear integer problems to generate linear rational problems.

We implemented our random generation procedure in GoRRiLA, where the user can specify problem parameters and number of problems to be generated. Each randomly generated problem is submitted to a specified theory solver for evaluation. As a result of a GoRRiLA run we obtain a file, each line of which encodes: a random problem, name of the theory solver used for the evaluation of this problem, the result of the evaluation and the time used by the solver. Using GoRRiLA, we also can evaluate and compare results with other solvers. GoRRiLA has an option to choose between storing either the generated problems or their codes. Using codes is motivated by the fact that we can generate hundreds of thousands of problems out of which only a small fraction is of interest to be generated explicitly.

Using GoRRiLA we found that many state-of-the-art SMT solvers return inconsistent results already on problems with 3 variables. For example: SMT-COMP'08 versions of MathSAT and Z3 both return incorrect results and the SMT-COMP'09 version of SatEEn returns segmentation fault on small problems generated by GoRRiLA within

$random\_set(L)$ $\quad\quad\quad\quad \Rightarrow$ add L to $\mathscr{L}$;

$random\_set(F_1 \wedge \ldots \wedge F_n) \Rightarrow random\_set(F_1); \ldots ; random\_set(F_n);$

$random\_set(F_1 \vee \ldots \vee F_n) \Rightarrow random\_set(F_i)$, where i is a random integer between 1 and n.

Fig. 1. Naive algorithm for formulas in negation normal form

a few seconds. Although these bugs (at least for MathSAT and Z3) seems to be fixed in the current versions of these solvers we believe that if the designers of the systems used GoRRiLA, they would have found these bugs quickly and easily.

Using GoRRiLA we can easily generate linear integer problems with only 4 variables hard for all SMT solvers we tried. For linear rational arithmetic we evaluated SMT solvers over 10^5 easy problems with 3 to 9 variables. All solvers returned consistent results on these problems. Using GoRRiLA we can generate hard linear rational arithmetic problems for all SMT solvers we tried, starting from 30 variables. Below we show the number of problems which turned out to be hard for various SMT solvers, out of generated 1000 linear integer problems (LIA) with 4 variables and 100 linear rational problems (LRA) with 40 variables. All experiments were run on a 2GHz Linux machine with 4GB RAM.

	Barcelogic	CVC3	MathSAT	Z3
LIA (4 vars) $> 10s$	11	2	16	25
LRA (40 vars) $> 10s$	75	100	26	100

3   Hard Reality

We will work with a family $\mathscr{A}$ of randomised algorithms which, given a formula F as an input, produce a theory problem G. This formula G will be relevant to F, in the sense described below.

We will use the notion of a *path through (the matrix) of F*, defined in [1,4]. Essentially a path is a conjunction of literals occurring in F, that is, a theory problem built from literals occurring in F. In the simplest case when F is in CNF, every path contains one literal from every clause in F. In general, the set of all paths $G_1, \ldots, G_n$ through F has the property that F is equivalent to $G_1 \vee \ldots \vee G_n$. One can argue that each path through the matrix of F is *relevant* to SMT solving for F since an SMT solver can generate this path as a theory problem. In the rest of this section we will describe several randomized algorithms for generating relevant theory problems as paths through formulas.

Naive algorithm. We start with a naive algorithm shown in Figure 1. In the algorithm L ranges over literals. It uses a set of theory literals $\mathscr{L}$ which initially is empty. When the algorithm terminates, the conjunction of literals in $\mathscr{L}$ is the output theory problem. It is not hard to argue that the algorithm computes a random path through F, moreover, each path is computed with an equal probability.

$$random\_set(L) \qquad\qquad \Rightarrow \textbf{if } \widetilde{L} \in \mathscr{L} \textbf{ then } \text{fail;}$$
$$\qquad\qquad\qquad\qquad\qquad \text{add } L \text{ to } \mathscr{L};$$
$$random\_set(F_1 \wedge \ldots \wedge F_n) \Rightarrow \textbf{if } \text{for some } F_i \text{ we have } \widetilde{F}_i \in \mathscr{L} \textbf{ then } \text{fail;}$$
$$\qquad\qquad\qquad\qquad\qquad \text{let } G_1, \ldots, G_m \text{ be all formulas among the } F_i\text{'s not belonging to } \mathscr{L};$$
$$\qquad\qquad\qquad\qquad\qquad \text{add } G_1, \ldots, G_m \text{ to } \mathscr{L};$$
$$\qquad\qquad\qquad\qquad\qquad random\_set(G_1); \ \ldots \ ; random\_set(G_m);$$
$$random\_set(F_1 \vee \ldots \vee F_n) \Rightarrow \textbf{if } \text{some } F_i \text{ belongs to } \mathscr{L} \textbf{ then return};$$
$$\qquad\qquad\qquad\qquad\qquad \text{let } G_1, \ldots, G_m \text{ be all formulas among the } F_i\text{'s}$$
$$\qquad\qquad\qquad\qquad\qquad\qquad \text{such that } \widetilde{F}_i \text{ does not belong to } \mathscr{L};$$
$$\qquad\qquad\qquad\qquad\qquad \textbf{if } m = 0, \textbf{ then } \text{fail;}$$
$$\qquad\qquad\qquad\qquad\qquad \text{let } i \text{ be a random integer between 1 and } m;$$
$$\qquad\qquad\qquad\qquad\qquad \text{add } G_i \text{ to } \mathscr{L}; random\_set(G_i)$$

Fig. 2. Improved algorithm

Improved Algorithm. The naive algorithm *random_set* has a major deficiency that the probability of producing trivially unsatisfiable theory set is very high. For example, if we consider a conjunction consisting of n repetitions of a tautology $(L \vee \neg L)$ then the probability of generating a trivially unsatisfiable theory set containing both L and $\neg L$ is $1 - 1/2^{n-1}$. It is worth noting that unit propagation in SMT solvers guarantees that such sets are never passed to theory solvers. There is an easy fix to address this problem by restricting the random choice of the formula F_i in a disjunction to avoid having complementary literals to $\mathscr{L}$. If we change the algorithm in this way, it may be the case that the disjunctive case may fail: this happens when every F_i in the disjunction is a literal whose complement is in $\mathscr{L}$. In this case we restart the algorithm.

Algorithms of this kind still have a very high probability of generating a trivially unsatisfiable set in some cases, especially when we have to deal with formulas containing equivalence or if-then-else. The problem occurs when the algorithm is first applied to a non-literal F and later to the negation of F. In addition, it may generate problems that we call *unrealistic*: these are problems that would be avoided by SMT solvers. For example, consider the case when we apply it to a formula $F \wedge F$. Then it will process both copies of F and may select different sets of literals from these copies.

Therefore, we modify the algorithm to avoid both kinds of problem. The modified algorithm stores arbitrary formulas in $\mathscr{L}$. We assume that the input formula contains no occurrences of subformulas of the form $\neg\neg F$ (such occurrences of double negation can be trivially eliminated). Similarly to literals, we call formulas F and $\neg F$ *complementary*. The formula complementary to F will be denoted by $\widetilde{F}$. The improved algorithm is shown in Figure 2. This algorithm stores in $\mathscr{L}$ formulas to which it has previously been applied. It returns the conjunction of all literals in $\mathscr{L}$. Upon failure, it restarts from scratch. Next we consider connectives that often occur in the SMT problems and have to be handled with care to avoid generating both trivial and unrealistic problems. These are if-then-else, $\leftrightarrow$ and *xor*. In addition, the SMT-LIB language has if-then-else terms that create extra problems for the algorithm. The rule for handling the if-then-else connective is given below, other rules are omitted due to lack of space.

random_set(if F then F_1 else F_2) $\Rightarrow$
   case $F \in \mathcal{L}$ or $\widetilde{F_2} \in \mathcal{L}$: call *random_set*($F \wedge F_1$);
   case $\widetilde{F} \in \mathcal{L}$ or $\widetilde{F_1} \in \mathcal{L}$: call *random_set*($\widetilde{F} \wedge F_2$);
   otherwise: call randomly either *random_set*($F \wedge F_1$) or *random_set*($\widetilde{F} \wedge F_2$)

Implementation, Options and Experimental Results. We implemented the improved algorithm (Figure 2) in the Hard Reality tool, which uses an SMT parser provided by the SMT-LIB initiative [8]. A simple way to use Hard Reality is by providing:

- a path to the directory with SMT problems,
- a path to an SMT solver,
- complexity of the resulting theory problem (this is done by specifying lower time limit required by the SMT solver to solve the problem),
- search time limit for the output theory problem.

Given these options, for each file in the input directory Hard Reality will search for randomly generated problems based on the improved algorithm, until a sufficiently hard problem is found (for the given SMT solver), or the search time reaches the specified limit. Hard Reality has also options for generating a maximal satisfiable subset/minimal unsatisfiable subset of the generated theory set (based on the SMT solver). We find that (attempting) generating maximal satisfiable sets can produce hard problems. Generating minimal unsatisfiable problems also gives us an insight to the theory problems occurring in applications.

   Let us note that since an SMT solver typically needs to solve thousands of theory problems during the proof search, even theory problems requiring tenths of a second to be solved can be considered as non-trivial. Hard Reality has successfully generated problems using different solvers such as Barcelogic [11], CVC3 [3] and Z3 [6]. The following table summarises the numbers of generated hard theory problems in different theories with the times based on the Z3 solver. It is easier to generate problems hard for other solvers. The theory problems are generated from problems in the SMT-LIB.

Theory	QF_LRA	QF_LIA	QF_BV	QF_AUFBV
Timeout after 120s	79	1	2	14
Solved in $0.1s \leq t \leq 120s$	30	72	79	87

4   Conclusion

We presented two tools: GoRRiLA for random generation of small yet hard problems for linear arithmetic and Hard Reality for randomly extracting hard and realistic theory problems.

   GoRRiLA is well-suited for generating diverse problems for linear arithmetic which can be used for debugging and exploring efficiency issues with theory solvers. We have shown that using GoRRiLA it is easy to find bugs in theory solvers. We observe that generated problems with only few variables are already hard for theory reasoners within state-of-the-art SMT solvers. As a future work it would be useful to extend GoRRiLA to other theory domains and combination of theories.

Using Hard Reality we have been able to generate a number of theory problems which are closely related to problems coming from applications and non-trivial for state-of-the-art SMT solvers. One of the issues we considered is how to avoid generating trivially unsatisfiable problems. Other approaches to this problem can be investigated, in particular one can first apply the definitional transformation to the original formula F to obtain a CNF equisatisfiable with F and delegate the problem of choosing relevant theory literals to a SAT solver. Another approach to theory problem generation can be based on logging problems generated on different branches during proof search of an SMT solver, but this would require modifications to a specific SMT solver, whereas in our approach we can use any SMT solver as an input to Hard Reality (or use no SMT solver at all). With our approach we were able to generate theory problems which were even harder for solvers than the original problem used in the generation process. We observed that only when we used most efficient SMT solvers we were able to generate theory problems hard for all solvers. A further application of Hard Reality can be in using generated hard theory problems to evaluate incrementality of the theory solvers.

Our benchmarking and testing of various versions of SMT solvers gave remarkable results: we have found a number of problems on which these solvers were unsound and also many problems on which some versions of solvers were running very long times as compared to other solvers. Although some of these bugs and performance problems have been fixed in the following versions of the solvers these problems could have been fixed much earlier if the designers of the solvers used our tools.

In a related work [5] random problems with non-trivial boolean structure are used for debugging solvers for theories of bitvectors and arrays (the tool was later extended to other theories). The main differences with our work is that we are focusing on generating: (i) theory problems, (ii) which are hard and (iii) related to problems coming from applications. GoRRiLA and Hard Reality with examples of generated problems are freely available at http://www.cs.man.ac.uk/~korovink/.

We thank Leonardo de Moura and Nikolaj Bjørner with whom we exchanged many letters during this work.

References

1. Andrews, P.B.: Theorem proving via general matings. Journal of the ACM 28(2), 193–214 (1981)
2. Barrett, C., Ranise, S., Stump, A., Tinelli, C.: The Satisfiability Modulo Theories Library, SMT-LIB (2008), www.SMT-LIB.org
3. Barrett, C., Tinelli, C.: CVC3. In: Damm, W., Hermanns, H. (eds.) CAV 2007. LNCS, vol. 4590, pp. 298–302. Springer, Heidelberg (2007)
4. Bibel, W.: On matrices with connections. Journal of the ACM 28(4), 633–645 (1981)
5. Brummayer, R., Biere, A.: Fuzzing and delta-debugging SMT solvers. In: 7th Intl. Workshop on on Satisfiability Modulo Theories, SMT 2009 (2009)
6. de Moura, L.M., Bjørner, N.: Z3: An Efficient SMT Solver. In: Ramakrishnan, C.R., Rehof, J. (eds.) TACAS 2008. LNCS, vol. 4963, pp. 337–340. Springer, Heidelberg (2008)
7. Faure, G., Nieuwenhuis, R., Oliveras, A., Rodríguez-Carbonell, E.: SAT Modulo the Theory of Linear Arithmetic: Exact, Inexact and Commercial Solvers. In: Kleine Büning, H., Zhao, X. (eds.) SAT 2008. LNCS, vol. 4996, pp. 77–90. Springer, Heidelberg (2008)
8. Hagen, G., Zucchelli, D., Tinelli, C.: SMT parser v3.0, http://combination.cs.uiowa.edu/smtlib/

9. Mitchell, D.G., Selman, B., Levesque, H.J.: Hard and easy distributions of SAT problems. In: AAAI 1992, pp. 459–465. AAAI Press/MIT Press (1992)

10. Nieuwenhuis, R., Hillenbrand, T., Riazanov, A., Voronkov, A.: On the Evaluation of Indexing Techniques for Theorem Proving. In: Goré, R.P., Leitsch, A., Nipkow, T. (eds.) IJCAR 2001. LNCS (LNAI), vol. 2083, pp. 257–271. Springer, Heidelberg (2001)

11. Nieuwenhuis, R., Oliveras, A.: Decision Procedures for SAT, SAT Modulo Theories and Beyond. The Barcelogic Tools. (Invited Paper). In: Sutcliffe, G., Voronkov, A. (eds.) LPAR 2005. LNCS (LNAI), vol. 3835, pp. 23–46. Springer, Heidelberg (2005)

Reachability in One-Dimensional Controlled Polynomial Dynamical Systems[*]

Margarita Korovina[1] and Nicolai Vorobjov[2]

[1] The University of Manchester and IIS SB RAS Novosibirsk,
Margarita.Korovina@manchester.ac.uk
[2] University of Bath, UK
nnv@cs.bath.ac.uk

Abstract. In this paper we investigate a case of the reachability problem in controlled o-minimal dynamical systems. This problem can be formulated as follows. Given a controlled o-minimal dynamical system initial and target sets, find a finite choice of time points and control parameters applied at these points such that the target set is reachable from the initial set. We prove that the existence of a finite control strategy is decidable and construct a polynomial complexity algorithm which generates finite control strategies for one-dimensional controlled polynomial dynamical systems. For this algorithm we also show an upper bound on the numbers of switches in finite control strategies.

1 Introduction

A fundamental problem in the design of biological, chemical or physical processes is to automatically synthesise models from performance specifications. In general, by practical and theoretical reasons, it is highly nontrivial to achieve. However, in some cases, given by partial designs, it could be possible to automatically complete modelling in order to get desired properties.

In this paper we consider synthesis of finite control strategies to meet reachability and time requirements for partial designs given by controlled polynomial dynamical systems (CPDS).

A controlled polynomial dynamical system is defined by a polynomial depending on control parameters. The choice of a parameter determines a certain motion. In general case, in order to achieve reachability or time requirements it is necessary to switch between motions corresponding to various control parameters at certain points of time. We focus on the following problem.

Problem of finite control synthesis. For a partial design, given by CPDS, determine whether there exist finite sequences of time points and control parameters that guide the system from an initial state to a desired state. If the answer is positive then a finite control strategy is automatically synthesised.

---

[*] This research was partially supported by EPSRC grant EP/E050441/1, DFG-RFBR 09-01-91334-NNIO-a.

E. Clarke, I. Virbitskaite, and A. Voronkov (Eds.): PSI 2011, LNCS 7162, pp. 251–261, 2012.

In the general class of o-minimal dynamical systems this problem is undecidable as demonstrated in [1,2,6]. Indeed, it has been shown that the reachability problem is already undecidable for three-dimensional piecewise constant
derivative systems and two-dimensional o-minimal dynamical systems with non-
determinism. Moreover, for one-dimensional o-minimal dynamical systems with
non-determinism, the problem remains open. In this paper we show that it is possible to find finite control strategies for the certain broad class of one-dimensional
controlled polynomial dynamical systems.

The key results of the paper are summarised next. Firstly, we prove that
for this class of one-dimensional controlled polynomial dynamical systems the
existence of a finite control strategy is decidable and construct an polynomial
complexity algorithm which synthesises finite control strategies. Secondary, for
the algorithm we show an upper bound on the numbers of switches in finite
control strategies. Finally, we prove that finite control strategies generated by
the algorithm are time-optimal.

The paper is organised as follows. In Section 2 we define the problem of finite
control strategy synthesis for controlled polynomial dynamical systems. Section 3
contains essential relative properties of the integral curves of a given dynamics.
In Section 4 the main results are proven. We conclude with future and related
work.

2   Problem Description

In this section we formalise the problem of finite control strategy synthesis for
controlled polynomial dynamical systems. Let

$$\gamma : Y \times T \to X$$

$$(y, t) \mapsto x,$$

be a polynomial function, where $Y \subseteq \mathbb{R}^m$, $T \subseteq \mathbb{R}$ and $X \subseteq \mathbb{R}^n$. We consider
γ as a controlled dynamical system with control parameters from Y. For every
fixed control value $y_0 \in Y$ the function $\gamma(y_0, t) : T \to X$ describes the motion of
a point in the state space X. In what follows we will use the notation $x^{y_0}(t)$ for
$\gamma(y_0, t)$, and call the function $x^{y_0}(t)$ *integral curve*.

We are considering the following problem of reachability: given a point and
a subset in X, decide whether or not the subset can be reached from the point
using a combination of motions corresponding to various controls.

Definition 1. *Let* $t_0, t_1, \ldots, t_k \in T$ *be points of time and* $y_0, y_1, \ldots, y_k \in Y$ *be
controls. Assume also that* $x^{y_j}(t_{j+1}) = x^{y_{j+1}}(t_{j+1})$ *for every* $j \in \{0, \ldots, k-1\}$.
Then

$$C = \bigcup_{0 \le j \le k-1} \{(t, x) \in T \times X \mid t \in [t_j, t_{j+1}], \ x = x^{y_j}(t)\}$$

is called piecewise integral *curve and the tuple* $< (t_0, y_0), \ldots, (t_k, y_k) >$ *is called*
finite control strategy.

Now we can reformulate the reachability problem formally as follows. Given a polynomial function γ, *initial conditions* $(t_0, x_0) \in T \times X$ and a definable *target subset* $\Omega \subset X$ decide whether there exists a piecewise integral curve C reaching Ω, i.e., such that $\Omega \cap x^{y_k}(t) \neq \emptyset$.

If the polynomial in γ has integer coefficients while Y, T and X are "simple" enough (e.g., open intervals on the straight line) then the reachability problem can be considered as computational, and one can ask the natural questions about decidability and computational complexity. An interesting weaker question is to bound from above the number k in a reaching piecewise integral curve C in the case when an instance of the computational problem has the positive output.

Remark 1. It is worth noting that in this case, by quantifier elimination for the first order theory of the reals, the finite control strategy problem is semi-decidable.

Remark 2. If we fix an upper bound on the number of switches k then the finite control strategy problem become to be decidable.

Now we assume that Y, T, $X \subset \mathbb{R}$ are open intervals, and

$$\Gamma := \{(y, t, x) | x = \gamma(y, t)\} \subset Y \times T \times X \subset \mathbb{R}^3$$

is the graph of the function γ. Denote by $\pi : \Gamma \to T \times X$ the projection map, and let U be one of the connected open sets into which the set of all critical values of π divides $\pi(\Gamma)$. Then all fibres $\pi^{-1}(x, t)$ for $(x, t) \in U$ are finite and have the same cardinality ℓ. Moreover, by the implicit function theorem, $\pi^{-1}(U)$ is a union of ℓ smooth surfaces (graphs of smooth functions) $\Gamma^1, \dots, \Gamma^\ell$ such that the restriction of π on each Γ^i is a diffeomorphism.

Observe that for any Γ^i and $y_1 \neq y_2$, the projections $x^{y_1}(t)$ and $x^{y_2}(t)$ of the two non-empty intersections $\Gamma^i \cap \{y = y_1\}$ and $\Gamma^i \cap \{y = y_2\}$ respectively on $T \times X$, have the empty intersection, $x^{y_1}(t) \cap x^{y_2}(t) = \emptyset$, because $\Gamma^i \cap \{y = y_1\}$, $\Gamma^i \cap \{y = y_2\}$ are two different level sets of a function. On the other hand, for Γ^{i_1}, Γ^{i_2}, where $i \neq j$, the projections $x^{y_1}(t)$, $x^{y_2}(t)$ of non-empty intersections $\Gamma^{i_1} \cap \{y = y_1\}$, $\Gamma^{i_2} \cap \{y = y_2\}$, being smooth real algebraic curves may intersect, either by coinciding or at a finite number of points.

It follows, that in any piecewise integral curve C, restricted on U, any two subsequent integral curves $x^{y_j}(t)$, $x^{y_{j+1}}(t)$ are projections on $T \times X$ of intersections $\Gamma^{i_1} \cap \{y = y_j\}$, $\Gamma^{i_2} \cap \{y = y_{j+1}\}$ with $i_1 \neq i_2$. In particular, at any point $(x, t) \in U$ there is a finite number of possible choices of the control.

It seems unavoidable to consider, as a part of the general reachability problem, its following restriction. Given γ, an open connected subset U of regular values of the projection π, initial conditions $(t_0, x_0) \in U$ and the target point $w \in X$ decide whether there exists a piecewise integral curve $C \subset U$ such that $w \in x^{y_k}(t)$. In this paper we consider, in essence, this restricted version of reachability.

Let U be the square $(-1, 1) \times (0, 1)$ with coordinates (t, x). Consider ℓ families $x^i_\alpha(t)$ of disjoint graphs of functions in U, where $i \in \{1, \dots, \ell\}$ enumerates families and $\alpha \in \mathbb{R}$ parametrises continuously functions within the family.

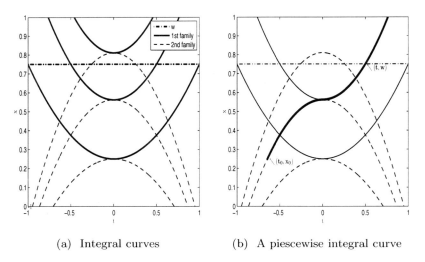

(a) Integral curves   (b) A piescewise integral curve

Fig. 1. The pictures illustrate Example 1. In Picture 1a the first family of integral curves corresponds to $y \in (0,1)$, and the second family of integral curves correspons to $y \in (-1,0)$. The piescewise integral curve in Picture 1b correspons to the strategy $< (t_0,y_0),(t_1,y_1) >=< (-\frac{3}{5}, -\frac{3}{4}),(0,\frac{3}{4}) >$ which solves the reachability problem for $(t_0,x_0) = (-\frac{3}{5}, \frac{117}{400})$ and $\Omega = \{x | 1 > x \geq \omega\}$.

More precisely, there are ℓ surjective Nash functions $\Gamma^i : U \to \mathbb{R}$, $1 \leq i \leq \ell$ (i.e., real analytic functions such that $P(t,x,\Gamma^i(t,x)) = 0$ for some polynomial $P \in \mathbb{R}[z_1, z_2, z_3]$ and every $(t,x) \in U$, see [3]). Assume that for every i and for every $\alpha \in \mathbb{R}$ the level set $x_\alpha^i(t) := \{(t,x) \in U | \Gamma^i(t,x) = \alpha\}$ is either empty or a graph of a smooth function on a subinterval of $(-1,1)$ of the t-axis. It follows that for each point $(t_0,x_0) \in U$ and every $i \in \{1, \ldots, \ell\}$ there is $\alpha \in \mathbb{R}$ such that $x_\alpha^i(t_0) = x_0$.

The aim is, having the initial point $(t_0,x_0) \in U$ to find the points of time $t_1, \ldots, t_k \in (-1,1)$ and the corresponding controls $i_1, \ldots, i_k$ such that the piecewise integral curve

$$C = \bigcup_{0 \leq j \leq k-1} \{(t,x) \in U | t \in [t_j, t_{j+1}], x = x_j^{i_j}(t)\}$$

reaches the set $\Omega \subseteq X$. (Here the notation $x_r^i(t)$ is used for the integral curve belonging to the family i and passing through the point (x_r, t_r) under the control $i \in \{1, \ldots, \ell\}$.) Of course, if $x_0 \in \Omega$ then the problem solves trivially.

Example 1. Let a polynomial function $\gamma := y^2 + yt^2$ be defined on $(-1,1) \times (-1,1)$ and $\Omega = \{x | x \geq \omega\}$. The set of all critical values, $\{(t,x) | x = -t^4/4\}$, of the projection map $\pi : \{(y,t,x) \in \mathbb{R}^3 | x = y^2 + yt^2\} \to \mathbb{R}^2$ lies outside U, and $\ell = 2$.

Let $\Gamma^1(U) = (0,1)$ and $\Gamma^2(U) = (-1,0)$. Observe that for every $y \in (0,1)$ (respectively, $y \in (-1,0)$) the integral curve $x_y^1(t)$ (respectively, $x_y^2(t)$) is a parabola having a minimum (respectively, maximum) at $t = 0$.

Assume that $x_0 < \omega$. It is easy to see that there is a piecewise integral curve reaching $\omega \in (0,1)$ if and only if the initial point (t_0, x_0) satisfies either the conjunction of inequalities $x_0 \geq \alpha^2 - \alpha t_0^2$, $t_0 \leq 0$ or of inequalities $x_0 \geq \alpha^2 + \alpha t_0^2$, $t_0 \geq 0$, where $\alpha := (-1 + \sqrt{1 + 4\omega})/2$.

Suppose that $x_0 \geq \alpha^2 - \alpha t_0^2$ and $t_0 \leq 0$, and let $\beta \geq \alpha$ be such that $x_{-\beta}^2(t)$ passes through (t_0, x_0). If $\omega > \beta^2$ then the target ω is reached by the piecewise integral curve

$$\{(t,x) \in U \,|\, t \in [t_0, 0], \; x = x_{-\beta}^2(t)\} \cup \{(t,x) \in U \,|\, t \in [0, t_2], \; x = x_\beta^1(t)\},$$

where $x_\beta^1(t_2) = \omega$. If $\omega \leq \beta^2$ then ω is reached by the piecewise integral curve

$$\{(t,x) \in U \,|\, t \in [t_0, t_1], \; x = x_{-\beta}^2(t),$$

where $x_{-\beta}^2(t_1) = \omega$.

Suppose that $x_0 \geq \alpha^2 + \alpha t_0^2$ and $t_0 \geq 0$, and let $\delta \geq \alpha$ be such that $x_\delta^1(t)$ passes through (t_0, x_0). If $\omega > \delta^2$ then ω is reached by

$$\{(t,x) \in U \,|\, t \in [t_0, t_1], \; x = x_\delta^1(t)\},$$

where $x_\delta^1(t_1) = \omega$. Otherwise, x_0 is already in Ω.

Note that under any of these suppositions there may be other piecewise integral curves reaching the target. On the other hand, it is easy to prove that the described above motion is the fastest one.

3   Relative Properties of Integral Curves

In this section we prove basic properties of integral curves of CPDS which we use later in the synthesis of finite control strategies.

Observe that any integral curve $x_\alpha^i(t)$, being a graph of a continuous function, divides U into two disjoint subsets, $U_+(i, \alpha)$ which contains a point $(t', x') \in U$ such that $x' > x_\alpha^i(t')$, and $U_-(i, \alpha)$ which contains a point $(t'', x'') \in U$ such that $x'' < x_\alpha^i(t'')$.

Definition 2.   *1. A point $(t', x') \in U$ is called* above *an integral curve $x_\alpha^i(t)$ if $(t', x') \in U_+(i, \alpha)$.*

2. For two integral curves $x_\alpha^i(t)$ and $x_\beta^i(t)$ from the same family i, $x_\beta^i(t)$ is called above *$x_\alpha^i(t)$ if $x_\beta^i(t) \subset U_+(i, \alpha)$.*

3. For two integral curves $x_\alpha^i(t)$ and $x_\beta^j(t)$ from two different families $i \neq j$, $x_\beta^j(t)$ is called locally above *$x_\alpha^i(t)$ at $(t_0, x_0) \in U$ if there is a neighbourhood U_0 of (t_0, x_0) in U such that $x_\beta^j(t) \cap U_0 \subset U_+(i, \alpha) \cap U_0$.*

4. We say that (t_0, x_0) is a local minimum *point of $x_\beta^j(t)$ relative to $x_\alpha^i(t)$ if $x_\alpha^i(t)$ and $x_\beta^j(t)$ are tangent at (t_0, x_0), and $x_\beta^j(t)$ is locally above $x_\alpha^i(t)$.*

Lemma 1. *Let (t_0, x_0) be a local minimum point of $x^j_\beta(t)$ relative to $x^i_\alpha(t)$. There are no other local minimum points of $x^j_\lambda(t)$ relative to $x^i_\alpha(t)$ in a neighbourhood of (t_0, x_0) on $x^i_\alpha(t)$ for any λ. In particular, there is a finite number of local minima relative to $x^i_\alpha(t)$.*

Proof. If the claim is not true then there is a point $(t', x') \in x^i_\alpha(t)$ and an integral curve $x^j_\lambda(t)$, having a local minimum at (t', x') relative to $x^i_\alpha(t)$, such that $x^j_\beta(t) \cap x^j_\lambda(t) \neq \emptyset$. This contradicts to the condition that integral curves in the same family do not intersect.

Definition 3. *Let $G_{i,j}$ denote the set of all points $(t, x) \in U$ such that (t, x) is a point of local minimum of $x^j_\beta(t)$ relative to $x^i_\alpha(t)$ for some i, j.*

Corollary 1.   *1. $G_{i,j}$ is a curve in U.*
2. $G_{i,j} \cap G_{j,i} = \emptyset$.

Proof. (1)   According to Lemma 1, for every fixed α there is a finite number of minima relative to $x^i_\alpha(t)$. Considering α as a parameter, we obtain a semialgebraic curve.
(2)   Obvious from the definition of $G_{i,j}$.

Lemma 2. *Each connected component of the curve $G_{i,j}$ is homeomorphic to the interval $(0, 1)$ and is intersected by each curve $x^i_\alpha(t)$ at most once, and by each curve $x^j_\beta(t)$ at most once.*

Proof. Suppose that a connected component G of $G_{i,j}$ is intersected by a certain integral curve $x^i_\alpha(t)$ at more than one point. Let A and B be some two neighbouring among them. Then there will be curves $x^i_\lambda(t)$ in the family i each having at least two intersection points with G between A and B, say A_λ, B_λ, as close to one another as needed. By the definition of $G_{i,j}$, at points A_λ, B_λ, some curves $x^j_\mu(t)$ and $x^j_\eta(t)$ have local minima relative to $x^i_\lambda(t)$. We get a contradiction with the fact that curves in the same family j do not intersect.

Suppose that $G_{i,j}$ is not homeomorphic to $(0, 1)$. Then one can find a curve $x^i_\alpha(t)$ intersecting $G_{i,j}$ more than twice which we proved to be impossible.

4   An Algorithm Synthesising Finite Control Strategies

Without loss of generality let us assume $\ell = 2$. Consider the following piecewise integral curve C passing through $(t_0, x_0) \in U$. Choose at (t_0, x_0) a control $i \in \{1, 2\}$ realising the maximal possible speed $\dot{x}^i_0(t_0)$. There are two possible cases.

1. $\dot{x}^1_0(t_0) \neq \dot{x}^2_0(t_0)$ (assume for definiteness that $\dot{x}^1_0(t_0) > \dot{x}^2_0(t_0)$);
2. $\dot{x}^1_0(t_0) = \dot{x}^2_0(t_0)$.

In case (1), for every point (t', x') on the curve $x^1_0(t)$ sufficiently close to (t_0, x_0), the inequality $\dot{x}^1_0(t') > \dot{x}^2_\alpha(t')$ holds true for any $x^2_\alpha(t)$ such that

$$x^1_0(t') \cap x^2_\alpha(t') = (t', x').$$

This follows from the transversely of $x_0^1(t)$ and $x_0^2(t)$ at (t_0, x_0). Therefore, in case (1), at any such point (t', x') there is no reason to switch from 1 to 2.

In case (2), there are the following possibilities.

(i) (t_0, x_0) is an inflection point of $x_0^2(t)$ relative to $x_0^1(t)$. In this case $x_0^2(t)$ starts above $x_0^1(t)$ (see Definition 2, (1)), is tangent to $x_0^1(t)$ at (t_0, x_0) and then goes below $x_0^1(t)$. For any point (t', x') on $x_0^1(t)$ sufficiently close to (t_0, x_0) there is no reason to switch from 1 to 2.

(ii) (t_0, x_0) is an inflection point of $x_0^1(t)$ relative to $x_0^2(t)$. This case is analogous to (i).

(iii) (t_0, x_0) is a local minimum point of $x_0^2(t)$ relative to $x_0^1(t)$ (see Definition 2, (3)). We choose the control $i = 2$ in this case.

(iv) (t_0, x_0) is a local minimum point of $x_0^1(t)$ relative to $x_0^2(t)$. We choose the control $i = 1$ in this case.

Assume, for definiteness, that we have either case (1), or (2, i), or (2, iii). According to Lemma 1, in case (iii) (t_0, x_0) is an isolated local minimum point on $x_0^1(t)$. It follows that the nearest point to (t_0, x_0) on $x_0^1(t)$ at which there may be a reason to switch to the family 2 is the nearest point at which some curve $x_\alpha^2(t)$ has a local minimum relative to $x_0^1(t)$. According to Lemma 1, there is a finite number of such points on $x_0^1(t)$. Moreover, since these points are definable in the first order theory of the reals, we can bound their number from above via the format of γ.

Algorithm

1. If at (t_0, x_0) the integral curves $x_0^i(t_0)$, $i = 1, 2$ intersect transversely then choose at (t_0, x_0) a control $i \in \{1, 2\}$ realising the maximal possible slope $\dot{x}_0^i(t_0)$. Let it be for definiteness $i = 1$.

    If (t_0, x_0) is an inflection point of the integral curves (for definiteness, let (t_0, x_0) be an inflection point of $x_0^2(t)$ relative to $x_0^1(t)$) choose the control $i = 1$.

    If (t_0, x_0) is a local minimum of one integral curve relative another (for definiteness, let $x_0^1(t)$ have local minimum relative to $x_0^2(t)$) then choose the control $i = 1$.

2. The curve $x_0^1(t)$ has the finite number of local minima relative to it of curves of the type $x_\alpha^2(t)$. Choose the right-closest to (t_0, x_0) on $x_0^1(t)$ such minimum, and let it correspond to $\alpha = 1$. Denote the minimum point by (t_1, x_1). Observe that for the smallest $j > 0$ for which the jth derivative $x_1^{2,j}(t_1)$ of $x_1^2(t_1)$ is larger than $\dot{x}_0^1(t_1) = \dot{x}_1^2(t_1)$ we have $x_1^{2,j}(t_1) > x_0^{1,j}(t_1)$.

3. The curve $x_1^2(t)$ has the finite number of local minima relative to it of curves of the type $x_\beta^1(t)$. Choose the right-closest to (t_1, x_1) on $x_1^2(t)$ such minimum, and let it correspond to $\beta = 2$. Denote the minimum point by (t_2, x_2). Observe that for the smallest $j > 0$ for which the jth derivative $x_2^{1,j}(t_2)$ of $x_2^1(t_2)$ is larger than $\dot{x}_1^2(t_2) = \dot{x}_2^1(t_2)$ we have $x_2^{1,j}(t_2) > x_1^{2,j}(t_2)$.

4. Continue recursively until at a point (t_k, x_k) a control $i_k \in \{1, 2\}$ will be chosen realising the local minimum of some $x_k^{i_k}(t)$ relative $x_{k-1}^{i_{k-1}}(t)$, and there

will be no right-closest tangent points of curves from the complement family. If $x_k^{i_k}(t) = \omega$ for some $t_k < t \le 1$ then ω is reachable, otherwise not.

Theorem 1. *The number of steps in the Algorithm is finite, moreover, in algebraic case it is bounded from above via the format of γ.*

Proof. Let (t_ℓ, x_ℓ) be a switching point of the piecewise integral curve C constructed in the Algorithm, for definiteness from $i_{\ell-1} = 1$ to $i_\ell = 2$. Let G be a connected component of $G_{1,2}$ such that $(t_\ell, x_\ell) \in G$. According to Lemma 2, (t_ℓ, x_ℓ) is the unique point of intersection of G and $x_\ell^{i_\ell}(t)$. Recall from the beginning of Section 3 that the integral curve $x_\ell^{i_\ell}(t)$ divides U into the upper part $U_+(i_\ell, \ell)$ and the lower part $U_-(i_\ell, \ell)$.

If $G \cap U_+(i_\ell, \ell) = \emptyset$ then there will be no point $(t_m, x_m) \in C$ with $\ell < m$ such that $(t_m, x_m) \in G$. So, suppose that $G_+ := G \cap U_+(i_\ell, \ell)$ is non-empty. Since, by Lemma 2, G is homeomorphic to $(0,1)$, so is G_+. One endpoint of G_+ is (t_ℓ, x_ℓ), while for the other endpoint, denoted by A, we have three possibilities:

(i) $A \in \{t = -1, x < 1\}$, i.e., A belongs to the left-hand vertical side of the square U;
(ii) $A \in \{x = 1\}$, i.e., A belongs to the upper side of U;
(iii) $A \in \{t = 1\}$, i.e., A belongs to the right-hand vertical side of the U.

In any case G_+ divides $U_+(i_\ell, \ell)$ into two domains. In case (i) the *left* domain is the one which is adjacent to $\{t = -1\}$ and not adjacent to $\{x = 1\}$, the other is the *right* domain. In case (ii) the *left* domain is adjacent to the left interval into which A divides $\{x = 1\}$, the other is the *right* domain. In case (iii) the *right* domain is the one which is adjacent to $\{t = 1\}$ and not adjacent to $\{x = 1\}$, the other is the *left* domain.

Note that the point $(t_{\ell+1}, x_{\ell+1}) \in C$ belongs to the right domain otherwise $x_\ell^{i_\ell}(t)$ would have at least two intersection points with G which is impossible by Lemma 2.

Suppose there is a switching point $(t_m, x_m) \in C$ with $\ell < m$ such that $(t_m, x_m) \in G_+$, and let this be the first such point between ℓ and m. The curve $x_{m-1}^{i_{m-1}}(t)$ "approaches G_+ from the right" (this means that $x_{m-1}^{i_{m-1}}(t)$, restricted to $[t_{m-1}, t_m]$, lies in the right domain). There are two possibilities: either $x_{m-1}^{i_{m-1}}(t)$ is "tangent" to G_+ (i.e., after passing (t_m, x_m) remains in the right domain) or enters the left domain. In case the first possibility realises, G_+ remains under the graph $x_{m-1}^{i_{m-1}}(t)$ and never appears again.

Consider the second possibility. Suppose we have case (i) (see above). If the origin of the integral curve $x_{m-1}^{i_{m-1}}(t)$ belongs to the right domain, then after entering the left domain at (t_m, x_m) it has to leave the left domain at some time point $t' > t_m$ in order to reach either $\{t = 1\}$ or $\{x = 1\}$. This contradicts to the uniqueness of the intersection point $G \cap x_{m-1}^{i_{m-1}}(t)$. If the origin of $x_{m-1}^{i_{m-1}}(t)$ belongs to the left domain, then $x_{m-1}^{i_{m-1}}(t)$ already intersected G at some time point $t'' < t_m$ in order to reach the right domain, and we have a contradiction again.

In cases (ii) or (iii), the curve $x_{m-1}^{i_{m-1}}(t)$ always enters the right domain by crossing G_+ (rather than $x_\ell^{i_\ell}(t)$). Indeed, $x_{\ell+1}^{i_{\ell+1}}(t)$ has a local minimum at the point $(x_{\ell+1}, t_{\ell+1})$ and is the closest to (t_ℓ, x_ℓ) with this property, and therefore $x_{\ell+1}^{i_{\ell+1}}(t)$ enters the right domain by crossing G_+. But $x_{m-1}^{i_{m-1}}(t)$ is either above $x_\ell^{i_\ell}(t)$ or above $x_{\ell+1}^{i_{\ell+1}}(t)$. So we get the same contradiction as before.

We conclude that G is intersected by C at most twice. Since the switching points of C belong to the connected components G the number of these points does not exceed twice the number of the connected components. The latter is finite, and in algebraic case estimated from above via the format of γ.

Theorem 2. *Let the polynomials P defining Nash functions Γ^i have degrees not exceeding d. Then for the piecewise integral curve C, constructed in the Algorithm, $k = d^{O(1)}$.*

Proof. It follows from the proof of Theorem 1 that it is sufficient to estimate the number of connected components of the curve $G_{1,2}$. This curve is definable by a formula (with quantifiers) of the first order theory of the reals with some fixed finite number of variables. According to [4], the number of connected components of $G_{1,2}$ does not exceed $k = d^{O(1)}$.

Definition 4. *A piecewise integral curve C_{opt} reaching Ω from (x_0, t_0) at the time point t_{opt} is called* time-optimal *if $t_k^{\text{opt}} \leq t_k$ for any C reaching Ω from (x_0, t_0) at some time point t_k. If $t_k^{\text{opt}} < t_k$, we say that C_{opt} is* faster *than C.*

Theorem 3. *The piecewise integral curve C, constructed in the Algorithm, is time-optimal. In particular, the Algorithm is correct.*

Proof. Let

$$C = \bigcup_{0 \leq j \leq k-1} \{(t, x) \in U \mid t \in [t_j, t_{j+1}], \; x = x_j^{i_j}(t)\}.$$

We prove the theorem by induction on k.

If $k = 1$ (the base of the induction), then C is the integral curve $x_0^i(t)$ restricted on $[t_0, t_1]$, i.e., $C = \{(t, x) \in U \mid [t_0, t_1], \; x = x_0^i(t)\}$, and there are no other integral curve $x_\alpha^j(t)$ and a point $(t', x') \in C$, such that $j \neq i$ and $x_\alpha^j(t)$ has a local minimum relative to $x_0^i(t)$ at (t', x'). If C was not time-optimal then there would be at least one integral curve $x_\beta^j(t)$ whose restriction on a subinterval $[t', t'']$ of $[t_0, t_1]$ included in a faster piecewise integral curve. Then there would be an integral curve $x_\alpha^i(t)$ in the family j (possibly, with $\alpha = \beta$) having a local minimum relative to $x_0^i(t)$ at some $(t', x') \in C$. We got a contradiction.

Let $k > 1$. Suppose there is a faster than C piecewise integral curve C'. Let $x_1 := x_1^{i_1}(t_1)$. The line $\{(t, x) \mid x = x_1\}$ is reached by C' at some time point t'. If $t' < t_1$ then we get the case as in the base of the induction (replacing ω by x_1) which we led to a contradiction.

If $t' = t$ then by the inductive hypothesis the piecewise integral curve C restricted on $[t_1, t_k]$ is time-optimal for the initial point (t_1, x_1), hence C' is not faster than C and we get a contradiction.

If $t' > t$ then, since C' is faster than C, there exists a point $(t'', x'') \in C \cap C'$, where $t'' > t'$, and by the inductive hypothesis C restricted on $[t'', t_k]$ is time-optimal for the initial point (t'', x''). It follows that C' is not faster than C and we get a contradiction.

Remark 3. The number t_k in the piecewise integral curve, computed by the Algorithm, is the minimal time required to reach Ω from the initial point (t_0, x_0). Thus, the Algorithm solves the optimal control problem of finding a time minimization strategy.

5   Conclusion, Related, and Future Work

O-minimality is an fruitful theoretical concept for formal verification of dynamical and hybrid systems. It has been successfully used for proving that certain classes of dynamical and hybrid systems admit finite-state bisimilar models [10,5,8]; for computing combinatorial types of trajectories [9]; for mode switching synthesis [7], etc. In this paper we investigated synthesis of finite control strategy for one-dimentional controlled polynomial dynamical systems while setting up the framework for synthesis of finite control strategies for wider classes of controlled dynamical systems and studying related problems.

The main interesting future development would be to consider the domains of integral curves to be more general than a rectangle, and possibly to include critical values of the projection π. Of course, generalizations of the problem to higher dimensions are of great interest.

Finally, let us mention a two-person zero-sum game version of our problem. In a game the right of the first move is prescribed. When it's a player's turn to move, at a time point t_i, it chooses a control $y_{i+1} \in \gamma^{-1}(x) \cap \{t = t_i\}$ and a stopping time t_{i+1}. At the time point t_{i+1} the other player makes a move. The player 1 wins (player 2 looses) if and only if Ω is reached. In the Example 1, let $\omega > \alpha^2$. The player 1 always looses, independently of who is prescribed to make the first move if $x_0 < \alpha^2 + \alpha t_0^2$. If $x_0 \geq \alpha^2 + \alpha t_0^2$ then the player 1 wins if and only if it has the first move, or it has the second move but $x_0 \geq \omega - \sqrt{\omega} t_0^2$ and $t_0 < 0$. It would be interesting to construct a general efficient algorithm for computing optimal strategies in dynamical games from this class.

References

1. Asarin, E., Maler, O., Pnueli, A.: Reachability analysis of dynamical systems having piecewise-constant derivatives. Theoret. Comput. Sci. 138(1), 35–65 (1995)
2. Asarin, E., Mysore, V., Pnueli, A., Schneider, G.: Low dimensional Hybrid Systems - Decidable, Undecidable, Don't Know. Accepted for publication in Information and Computation (2010)
3. Bochnak, J., Coste, M., Roy, M.-F.: Real Algebraic Geometry. Results in Mathematics and Related Areas (3), vol. 36. Springer, Berlin (1998)
4. Basu, S., Pollack, R., Roy, M.-F.: Algorithms in real algebraic geometry, 2nd edn. Algorithms and Computation in Mathematics, vol. 10, p. x+662. Springer, Berlin (2006)

5. Brihaye, T., Michaux, C.: On the expressiveness and decidability of o-minimal hybrid systems. Journal of Complexity 21(4), 447–478 (2005)

6. Brihaye, T.: A note on the undecidability of the reachability problem for o-minimal dynamical systems. Math. Log. Q. 52(2), 165–170 (2006)

7. Bouyer, P., Brihaye, T., Chevalier, F.: Control in o-minimal Hybrid Systems. In: Proc. LICS 2006, pp. 367–378 (2006)

8. Korovina, M., Vorobjov, N.: Pfaffian Hybrid Systems. In: Marcinkowski, J., Tarlecki, A. (eds.) CSL 2004. LNCS, vol. 3210, pp. 430–441. Springer, Heidelberg (2004)

9. Korovina, M., Vorobjov, N.: Computing combinatorial types of trajectories in Pfaffian Dynamics. Journal of Logic and Algebraic Programming 79(1), 32–37 (2010)

10. Lafferriere, G., Pappas, G.J., Sastry, S.: O-minimal hybrid systems. Math. Control Signals Systems 13(1), 1–21 (2000)

Insertion Modeling System

Alexander A. Letichevsky[1], Olexandr A. Letychevskyi[1],
and Vladimir S. Peschanenko[2]

[1] Glushkov Institute of Cybernetics,
Academy of Sciences of Ukraine,
let@cyfra.net, lit@iss.org.ua
[2] Kherson State University,
vladimirius@gmail.com

Abstract. The paper relates to practical aspects of insertion modeling. Insertion modeling system is an environment for the development of insertion machines, used to represent insertion models of distributed systems. The architecture of insertion machines and insertion modeling system IMS is presented. Insertion machine for program verification is specified as an example, and as a starting point of 'verifiable programming' project.

1 Introduction

Insertion modeling is the approach to modeling complex distributed systems based on the theory of interaction of agents and environments [1,2,3]. Mathematical foundation of this theory was presented in [4]. During the last decade insertion modeling was applied to the verification of requirements for software systems [5,6,7,8,9].

First time the theory of interaction of agents and environments was proposed as an alternative to well known theories of interaction such as Milner's CCS [10] and pi-calculus [11], Hoare's CSP [12], Cardelli's mobile ambients [13] and so on. The idea of representing a system as a composition of environment and agents inserted into this environment implicitly exists in all theories of interaction and for some special case it appears explicitly in the model of mobile ambients.

Another source of ideas for insertion modeling is the search of universal programming paradigms such as Gurevich's ASM [14], Hoare's unified theories of programming [15], rewriting logic of Meseguer [16]. These ideas were taken as a basis for the system of insertion programming [17] developed as the extension of algebraic programming system APS [18]. Now this system initiated the development of insertion modeling system IMS which started in Glushkov Institute of Cybernetics. The development of this system is based on the version of APS enhanced by V. Peschanenko. The first version of IMS and some simple examples of its use are available from [19].

To implement the insertion model in IMS one must develop insertion machine with easily extensible input language, the rules to compute insertion functions and a program of interpretation and analysis of insertion models. IMS is considered as an environment for the development of insertion machines. Presentation

E. Clarke, I. Virbitskaite, and A. Voronkov (Eds.): PSI 2011, LNCS 7162, pp. 262–273, 2012.

of the architecture of insertion machines, input languages and examples of insertion machines is the main goal of the paper. The second section presents the architecture of insertion modeling system and the general architecture of insertion machines with examples. The third section presents the main properties of input languages of insertion machines, and typical restrictions for insertion machines that can be met in practice. The verification insertion machine for the class of imperative programming languages is considered in the fourth section This machine does not depend on the syntax of input language and can be easily extended to the parallel programs over shared and distributed memory (message pasing), and spatial mobile agents.

2   The Architecture of Insertion Modeling System

Insertion modeling system is an environment for the development of insertion machines and performing experiments with them. The notion of insertion machine was first introduced in [17] and it was used as a tool for programming with some special class of insertion functions. Later this notion was extended for more wide area of applications, different levels of abstraction, and multilevel structures.

Insertion model of a system represents this system as a composition of environment and agents inserted into it. Contrariwise the whole system as an agent can be inserted into another environment. In this case we speak about internal and external environment of a system. Agents inserted into the internal environment of a system themselves can be environments with respect to their internal agents. In this case we speak about multilevel structure of agent or environment and about high level and low level environments.

Usually, insertion function is denoted as $E[u]$ were E is the state of environment and u is the state of an agent (agent in a given state). $E[u]$ is a new environment state after insertion an agent u. So, the expression $E[u[v], F[x, y, z]]$ denotes the state of a two level environment with two agents inserted into it. At the same time E is an external environment of a system $F[x, y, z]$ and F is an internal environment of it. All agents and environments are labeled or attributed transition systems (labeled systems with states labeled by attribute labels [9]). The states of transition systems are considered up to bisimilarity denoted as $\sim_B$. This means that we should adhere to the following restriction in the definition of states: if $E \sim_B E'$ and $u \sim_B u'$ then $E[u] \sim_B E'[u']$ ($\sim_B$ denotes bisimilarity).

The main invariant of bisimilarity is the behavior beh(E) of transition system in the state E (an oriented tree with edges labeled by actions and nodes labeled by attribute labels,for exact definition see [4]). Therefore the restriction above can be written as follows:

$$\text{beh}(E) = \text{beh}(E') \wedge \text{beh}(u) = \text{beh}(u') \Rightarrow \text{beh}(E[u]) = \text{beh}(E'[u'])$$

Behaviors themselves can be considered as states of transition systems. If the states are behaviors then the relation above is valid automatically, because in this case beh(E) = E, beh(u) = u. Otherwise the correctness of insertion function must be proved in addition to its definition. In any case we shall identify the states with the corresponding behaviors independently from their representation.

To define finite behaviors we use the language of behavior algebra (a kind of process algebra defined in [4]). This algebra has operation of prefixing, nondeterministic choice, termination constants $(\Delta, 0, \perp)$ and approximation relation. For attributed transition systems we introduce the labeling operator for behaviors. To define infinite behaviors we use equations in behavior algebra. Usually these equations have the form of recursive definitions $u_i = F_i(u), i \in I$. Left hand sides of these definitions can depend on parameters $u_i(x_i) = F_i(u, x), i \in I$. To define the attribute labels we use the set of attributes, symbols taking their values in corresponding data domains. These attributes constitute a part of a state of a system and change their values in time. All attributes are devided to external (observable) and internal (nonobservable). By default the attribute label of a state is the set of values of all observable attributes for this state.

The general architecture of insertion machine is represented on the Figure 1. The main component of insertion machine is model driver, the component which

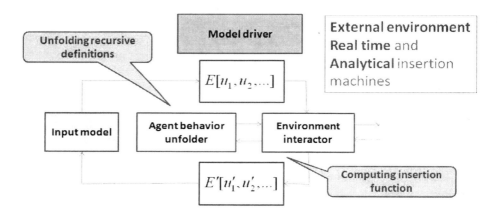

Fig. 1. Architecture of Insertion Machine

controls the machine movement along the behavior tree of a model. The state of a model is represented as a text in the input language of insertion machine and is considered as an algebraic expression. The input language includes the recursive definitions of agent behaviors, the notation for insertion function, and possibly some compositions for environment states. Before computing insertion function the state of a system must be reduced to the form $E[u_1, u_2, \ldots]$. This functionality is performed by the module called agent behavior unfolder. To make the movement, the state of environment must be reduced to the normal form

$$\sum_{i \in I} a_i.E_i + \varepsilon$$

where a_i are actions, E_i are environment states, ε is a termination constant. This functionality is performed by the module environment interactor. It computes the insertion function calling if it is necessary the agent behavior unfolder. If the infinite set I of indices in the normal form is allowed, then the weak normal form $a.F + G$ is used, where G is arbitrary expression of input language.

Two kinds of insertion machines are considered: *real time* or *interactive* and *analytical* insertion machines. The first ones exist in the real or virtual environment, interacting with it in the real or virtual time. Analytical machines intended for model analyses, investigation of its properties, solving problems etc. The drivers for two kinds of machines correspondingly are also divided into *interactive* and *analytical drivers*.

Interactive driver after normalizing the state of environment must select exactly one alternative and perform the action specified as a prefix of this alternative. Insertion machine with interactive driver operates as an agent inserted into external environment with insertion function defining the laws of functioning of this environment. External environment, for example, can change a behavior prefix of insertion machine according to their insertion function. Interactive driver can be organized in a rather complex way. If it has criteria of successful functioning in external environment intellectual driver can accumulate the information about its past, develop the models of external environment, improve the algorithms of selecting actions to increase the level of successful functioning. In addition it can have specialized tools for exchange the signals with external environment (for example, perception of visual or acoustical information, space movement etc.).

Analytical insertion machine as opposed to interactive one can consider different variants of making decision about performed actions, returning to choice points (as in logic programming) and consider different paths in the behavior tree of a model. The model of a system can include the model of external environment of this system, and the driver performance depends on the goals of insertion machine. In the general case analytical machine solves the problems by search of states, having the corresponding properties(goal states) or states in which given safety properties are violated. The external environment for insertion machine can be represented by a user who interacts with insertion machine, sets problems, and controls the activity of insertion machine.

Analytical machine enriched by logic and deductive tools are used for generating traces of symbolic models of systems. The state of symbolic model is represented by means of properties of the values of attributes rather then their concrete values.

General architecture of insertion modeling system is represented on Figure 2. High level model driver provides the interface between the system and external environment including the users of the system. Design tools based on algebraic programming system APS are used for the development of insertion machines and model drivers for different application domains and modeling technologies. Verification tools are used for the verification of insertion machines, proving their properties statically or dynamically. Dynamic verification uses generating symbolic model traces by means of special kinds of analytical model drivers and deductive components.

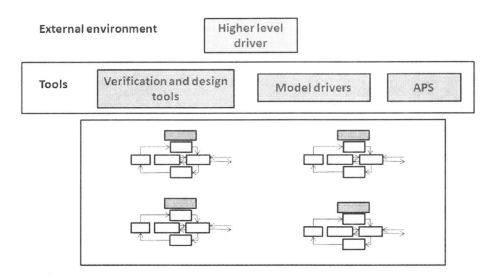

Fig. 2. Architecture of Insertion Modeling System IMS

The repository of insertion machines collects already developed machines and their components which can be used for the development of new machines as their components or templates for starting. Special library of APLAN functions supports the development and design in new projects. The C++ library for IMS supports APLAN compilers and efficient implementation of insertion machines. Deductive system provides the possibility of verification of insertion models.

3   Input Languages of Insertion Machines

Input language of insertion machine is used to describe the properties of a model and its behavior. This description consists of the following parts: environment description, behavior description (including the behavior of environment and the behaviors of agents), and insertion function. The behavior description has the following very simple syntax:

<behavior>::= Delta | bot | 0 | < action > | <action> . <behavior> |
    <behavior> + <behavior>|
    <environment state>[<list of named agent behaviors separated by ,>]|
    <functional expression>
  <named agent behavior>::=<agent name>:<behavior>

Therefore, the language of behavior algebra (termination constants, prefixing and nondeterministic choice) is extended by functional expressions and explicit representation of insertion function. The syntax and semantics of actions, environment states, and functional expressions are defined in the environment description. We shall not consider all possibilities and details of environment description language restricting ourselves by making only some necessary comments.

First of all note, that all main components of behavior algebra language (actions, environment states, and functional expressions) are algebraic or logic expressions of base language (terms and formulas). This language is a multisorted (multitype) first order logic language. The signature of this language is defined in the environment description. Functional and predicate symbols can be interpreted and uninterpreted. Interpreted symbols have fixed domains and interpretations given by algorithms of computing values or reducing to canonical forms. All uninterpreted symbols have types and their possible interpretations are restricted by definite domains and ranges. Uninterpreted functional symbols are called *attributes*. They represent the changing part of the environment. Attributes of arity 0 are called simple attributes, others are called *functional* ones. Predicates are considered as functions ranging in Boolean type $\{0, 1\}$. If an attribute f has functional type $(\tau_1, \tau_2, \ldots) \to \tau$ then *attribute expressions* $f(t_1, t_2, \ldots)$ are available for all other expressions.

3.1   Examples of Insertion Machines

The simplest insertion machines are machines for parallel and sequential insertion. Insertion function is called *sequential* if $E[u, v] = E[u; v]$ where ";" means sequential composition of behaviors. Special case of sequential insertion is a *strong sequential composition*: $E[u] = (E; u)$. This definition assumes that actions of agents and environment are the same and environment is defined by its behaviors. The sequentiality of this composition follows from associativity of sequential composition of behaviors.

Example of insertion machine with strong sequential insertion is represented on Figure 3.1.

```
Model Sequential
    interactor rs(P,Q,a)(
        Delta[P+Q]=Delta[P]+Delta[Q],
        Delta[a.P]=a.Delta[P],
        Delta[P]=Delta[unfold P],
        Q[P]=(Q;P)
    );
    unfolder rs(x,y)(
        (x;y)=seq(x,y),
        A=a.A+Delta,
        C=c.C+Delta
    );
    initial(C[A]);
    terminal(Delta[Delta])
)
```

Fig. 3. Example of Strong Sequential Insertion

The function **seq** is a function from IMS library that defines the sequential composition of behaviors:

$$(u; v) = \sum_{u \xrightarrow{a} u'} a.(u'; v) + \sum_{u=u+\varepsilon} (\varepsilon; v), (0; v) = 0, (\Delta; v) = v, (\bot; v) = \bot$$

The function **unfold** reduces the behavior expression to normal form $\sum a_i.u_i + \varepsilon$. This insertion machine generates a word $c^n a^m$ with nondeterministically chosen $m, n \geq 0$ and successfully terminates. We can define as the condition for the goal state the equality $m = n$ and the driver for this machine will terminate on traces $c^n a^n$.

An example of sequential (not strong) insertion is shown on Figure 4.

```
Model Imperative(
    insertion rs(P,Q,H,a,x,y,u,v)(
        E[P+Q]=Delta[P]+Delta[Q],
        E[define_env H.P]=H[P],
        E[(x:=y).P]=assign_proc(E,x,y,P),
        E[check(u,x,y).P]=if(compute_obj(E,u),E[x;P],E[y;P]),
        E[a.P]=a.Delta[P],
        E[P]=E[unfold P]
    )where(
        assign_proc:=proc(E,x,y,P)(E.x⟶compute_obj(E,y);return E[P])
    );
    behaviors rs(P,Q,x,y,z,u)(
        (x;y)=seq(x,y),
        (u→ else Q)=check(u,P,Q),
        while(u,P)=check(u,(P;while(u,P)),Delta),
        for(x,y,z,P)=(x;while(y,(P;z)))
    );
    initial(
        define_env obj(i:Nil,x:10,y:Nil,fact:Nil);
        y:=1;for(i:=1,i ≤ x,i:=i+1,y:=y*i);
        fact:=y
    );
    terminal rs(E)(E[Delta]=1,E=0)
)
```

Fig. 4. Model of Simple Imperative Language

This example is a model of simple imperative language and can be considered as insertion representation of its operational semantics.

Insertion function is called a *parallel* insertion function if $E[u, v] = E[u \parallel v]$. Special case of parallel composition is a *strong parallel insertion*: $E[u] = E \parallel u$. As in the case of strong sequential composition this definition assumes that actions of environment and agents are the same. Example of a model with strong parallel insertion is presented on the Figure 5. Functions **synchr**, **lmrg**, and

Model Parallel
    interactor rs(P,Q,a)(
        Delta[P+Q]=Delta[P]+Delta[Q],
        Delta[a.P]=a.Delta[P],
        Delta[P]=Delta[unfold P],
        Q[P]=(Q || P)
    );
    unfolder rs(x,y,n)(
        (x;y)=seq(x,y),
        x || y = synchr(x,y)+lmrg(x,y)+lmrg(y,x)+delta(x,y),
        x |^ 1=x,
        x |^ 2=synchr(x,x)+lmrg(x,x)+delta(x,x),
        x |^ n= x || (x |^(n-1))),
    );
    initial (Delta[((a;b) || (a;b));a+b]);
    terminal (Delta[Delta])
)

Fig. 5. Example of Strong Parallel Insertion

delta from IMS library are used for definition of parallel composition. Their meaning can be defined by the following formulas:

$$\mathbf{synchr}(x, y) = \sum_{\substack{x \xrightarrow{a} x' \\ y \xrightarrow{b} y'}} (a \times b).(x', y'),$$

$$\mathbf{lmrg}(x, y) = \sum_{x \xrightarrow{a} a'} a. (x' || y), \mathbf{delta}(x, y) = \sum_{\substack{x=x+\varepsilon \\ y=y+\mu}} \varepsilon || \mu$$

Function $a \times b$ defined on the set of actions is called a *combination of actions* and must be defined by user in terms of basic programming language as an associative commutative operation.

Note that the most of traditional algebras of interacting (communicating) processes can be modeled by means of strong parallel insertion plus recursively defined functions (compositions). For example, CCS can be modeled by strong sequential composition using the function $a \times b$ for defined so that $a \times b = \tau$ if $a = \bar{b}$ and $a \times b = 0$ otherwise where $0.u = 0$. Similarly CSP can be modeled using for combination a function defined so that $a \times b = a$ if $a = b$ and $a \times b = 0$ otherwise. Other compositions for these calculations can be defined by simple recursive definitions.

3.2   Restrictions on Insertion Functions

The most typical restriction is additivity. Insertion function is called additive if $E[u+v] = E[u]+E[v], (E+F)[u] = E[u]+F[u]$. Another restriction, which allows to reduce the number of considered alternatives when behaviors are analyzed is the commutativity of insertion function: $E[u, v] = E[v, u]$. Especially the parallel insertion is a commutative one. Some additional equations: $0[u] = 0, \Delta[u] = u, \bot[u] = \bot$.

The state of environment is called indecomposable if from $E = F[u]$ it follows that $E = F$ and $u = \Delta$. Equality means bisimilarity. The set of all indecomposable states constitutes the kernel of a system. Indecomposable states (if they exist) can be considered as states of environment without inserted agents. For indecomposable states usually the following equations hold: $E[0] = 0, E[\Delta] = E, E[\bot] = \bot$.

In [3] the classification of insertion functions was presented: one-step insertion, head insertion, and look-ahead insertion. Later we shall use insertion functions with the following main rule:

$$\frac{E \xrightarrow{a} E', \alpha : u \xrightarrow{b} \beta : u'}{E[\alpha : u] \xrightarrow{c} E'[\beta : u']}, P(E, a, \alpha, b, \beta, c),$$

where P is a continuous predicate. Continuous means that the value of this predicate depends only on some part of behavior tree in the environment state E, which has a finite height (prefix of the tree E of finite height). Hereby, this rule refers to a head insertion. The rules for indecomposable environment states and for termination constants should be added to the main rule.

The next rule

$$\frac{E \xrightarrow{a} E', u \xrightarrow{b} \beta : u'}{E[u] \xrightarrow{c} E'[u']}, P(E, a, c),$$

is the particular case for the head insertion rule in combination with additivity and parallel insertion or commutativity requirements. Such rule is called *permitted rule*. It could be interpreted as follows: agent can perform the action a, and environment permits to perform this action. Predicate E for permitted rule is called *permitting predicate*.

4   Verification Machine for Programming Languages

Research of program verification has a big history, which is started from works of Hoare [21] and Floyd [22]. The specification of programs looks like $\alpha \rightarrow< P > \beta$ or $\alpha \rightarrow [P] \beta$. Formulae α and β (pre- and postcondition) are formulae in specification language, which is assumed to be the first order predicate calculus, P - specification program (it is supposed that an initial state of memory is given). The first formula means that if condition α is valid and program P terminates, then condition β is valid on a final memory state. The second one expresses complete correctness and means that if condition α is valid then the program is terminating and condition β is valid.

The first program for verification of partial correctness was developed by D. King at 1969. It was considered as the first step for developing of verifying compiler. However, as per T. Hoare at 2006, a 'verifying compiler' is still a Grand Challenge for Computing research.

In present work we consider the reduced variant of analytical insertion machine of Floyd's method (Floyd's machine). Input is annotated program, which is based on assignments, conditional, go to statements and *stop* statement. Annotations in program as usual are of two kinds - assumptions and assertions. The example of annotated program is presented in Figure 6. The first assumption

L0: **assumption**:$x \geq 0$
    y:=x;
    z:=1;
L1:y:=y-1;
L2:**assertion**: $-1 \leq y < x \wedge x! = z * (y+1)!$;
    if $y \geq 0$
    then $z := z * (y+1)$
    else go to L3;
    go to L1
L3:**assertion**: $z = x!$
    stop

Fig. 6. Example of Annotated Program

defines the precondition of program's specification and the last one - its postcondition. Hereby, the program is purposed for computation of factorial function in accordance with its specification. The third annotation is required for loop's breaking by control points and presents itself the main invariant of the loop. Control points are states of the system, which are marked by annotations. The program itself is considered as the attributed transition system. The set of actions of that system consists of assignment statements, *stop* statement and *ask u* statement, where u is a condition. Attribute labels are labels of the program, which mark some of its states. It decomposes into units while inserting into environment. Each unit begins from a labeled statement. There are no labeled statements inside a unit, and its final statements go to statements. Units are collected into data structure named *model*, and the access to a unit, labeled by L, is defined by expression $(model.L)$.

The symbol of the factorial is not the symbol of the language and information about that function should be somewhere in a library (knowledge base) of APLAN language in order to prove auxiliary statements. E.g., it could be the formula, which gives the recursive definition of factorial:

$$(0! = 1) \wedge \forall (x \geq 0) ((x+1)! = x * (x+1))$$

The insertion function of Floyd's insertion machine is the permitting function for sequential or parallel insertion. Formulae of predicate calculus are environment state. The transition relation of system is presented in Figure 7.

Here p is a parallel assignment or Δ. Function *Sat u*, which checks satisfiability of formula u, is used for permitting conditions. Conditional operator

$$\varphi\,[p] \xrightarrow{ask\ u} (\varphi \wedge [p]\,u)\,[p]\,, Sat(\varphi \wedge [p]\,u)$$
$$\varphi\,[p] \xrightarrow{x:=y} \varphi\,[p * (x := y)]$$
$$\varphi\,[p] \xrightarrow{go\ to\ L} \varphi\,[p, model.L]$$
$$\varphi\,[p] \xrightarrow{assumption\ \psi} (\varphi \wedge [p]\,\psi)\,[p]$$
$$\varphi\,[p] \xrightarrow{assertion\ \psi} \psi\,[empty]\,, \neg Sat(\neg(\varphi \rightarrow [p]\,\psi))$$
$$\varphi\,[p] \xrightarrow{assertion\ \psi} 0, Sat(\neg(\varphi \rightarrow [p]\,\psi))$$
$$\varphi\,[p] \xrightarrow{stop} \psi\,[Delta]$$

Fig. 7. Relations of System's Transitions

if u **then** P **else** Q is considered as functional expression and is translated by unfolder by means of the rule:

$$\textbf{if } u \textbf{ then } P \textbf{ else } Q = \textbf{ask } u.P + (\textbf{ask } \neg u).Q$$

Loops operators and other programming constructions could be introduced in a similar way. The Floyd's machine could prove the partial correctness of nondeterministic program, because nondeterministic choice is an initial operation of an input language of the system. If unfolding for parallel composition is defined, then Floyd's machine could prove a partial correctness of parallel programs over shared memory.

Floyd's machine was realized in insertion modeling system IMS and is used for teaching of proving programming in Ukrainian Taras Shevchenko National University of Kyiv.

5   Conclusion

The main concepts of insertion modeling system has been considered in the paper. The system was successfully used for the development of prototypes of the tools for industrial VRS (Verification of Requirement Specifications) system and research projects in Glushkov Institute of Cybernetics. Now it is used for the development of program verification tool and 'verifiable programming' project. The system continues its enhancement and new features are added while developing new projects.

The far goal in the developing IMS consists in getting on its basis sufficiently rich cognitive architecture, which could be used in the artificial intelligence research.

The results presented in the paper were obtained under financial support of the State Agency for Science, Innovation and Informatization of Ukraine (project F40.1/004).

References

1. Gilbert, D.R., Letichevsky, A.A.: A universal interpreter for nondeterministic concurrent programming languages. In: Gabbrielli, M. (ed.) Fifth Compulog Network Area Meeting on Language Design and Semantic Analysis Methods (September 1996)

2. Letichevsky, A., Gilbert, D.: A general theory of action languages. Cybernetics and System Analyses 1 (1998)
3. Letichevsky, A., Gilbert, D.: A Model for Interaction of Agents and Environments. In: Bert, D., Choppy, C., Mosses, P.D. (eds.) WADT 1999. LNCS, vol. 1827, pp. 311–328. Springer, Heidelberg (2000)
4. Letichevsky, A.: Algebra of behavior transformations and its applications. In: Kudryavtsev, V.B., Rosenberg, I.G. (eds.) Structural Theory of Automata, Semigroups, and Universal Algebra. NATO Science Series II. Mathematics, Physics and Chemistry, vol. 207, pp. 241–272. Springer, Heidelberg (2005)
5. Baranov, S., Jervis, C., Kotlyarov, V., Letichevsky, A., Weigert, T.: Leveraging UML to Deliver Correct Telecom Applications. In: Lavagno, L., Martin, G., Selic, B. (eds.) UML for Real: Design of Embedded Real-Time Systems. Kluwer Academic Publishers, Amsterdam (2003)
6. Letichevsky, A., Kapitonova, J., Letichevsky Jr., A., Volkov, V., Baranov, S., Kotlyarov, V., Weigert, T.: Basic Protocols, Message Sequence Charts, and the Verification of Requirements Specifications. Computer Networks 47, 662–675 (2005)
7. Kapitonova, J., Letichevsky, A., Volkov, V., Weigert, T.: Validation of Embedded Systems. In: Zurawski, R. (ed.) The Embedded Systems Handbook. CRC Press, Miami (2005)
8. Letichevsky, A., Kapitonova, J., Volkov, V., Letichevsky Jr., A., Baranov, S., Kotlyarov, V., Weigert, T.: System Specification with Basic Protocols. Cybernetics and System Analyses 4 (2005)
9. Letichevsky, A., Kapitonova, J., Kotlyarov, V., Letichevsky Jr, A., Nikitchenko, N., Volkov, V., Weigert, T.: Insertion modeling in distributed system design. Problems of Programming 4, 13–39 (2008) ISSN 1727-4907
10. Milner, R.: Communication and Concurrency. Prentice Hall (1989)
11. Milner, R.: Communicating and Mobile Systems: the Pi Calculus. Cambridge University Press (1999)
12. Hoare, C.A.R.: Communicating Sequential Processes. Prentice Hall (1985)
13. Cardelli, L., Gordon, A.D.: Mobile Ambients. In: Nivat, M. (ed.) FOSSACS 1998. LNCS, vol. 1378, pp. 140–155. Springer, Heidelberg (1998)
14. Gurevich, Y.: Evolving Algebras 1993: Lipari Guide. In: Borger, E. (ed.) Specification and Validation Methods, pp. 9–36. Oxford University Press (1995) ISBN 0-19-853854-5
15. Hoare, C.A.R., He, J.: Unifying Theories of Programming. Prentice Hall International Series in Computer Science (1998) ISBN 0-13-458761-8. OCLC 38199961
16. Meseguer, J.: Conditional rewriting logic as a unified model of concurrency. Theoretical Computer Science 96, 73–155 (1992)
17. Letichevsky, A., Kapitonova, J., Volkov, V., Vyshemirsky, V., Letichevsky Jr., A.: Insertion programming. Cybernetics and System Analyses 1 (2003)
18. Kapitonova, J.V., Letichevsky, A.A., Konozenko, S.V.: Computations in APS. Theoretical Computer Science 119, 145–171 (1993)
19. http://apsystem.org.ua/
20. Kozen, D., Harel, D., Tiuryn, J.: Dynamic Logic, p. 400 (2000)
21. Hoare, C.A.R.: An axiomatic basis for computer programming. Communications of the ACM 12(10), 576–580, 583 (1969)
22. Floyd, R.W.: Assigning meanings to programs. In: Proceedings of the American Mathematical Society Symposia on Applied Mathematics, vol. 19, pp. 19–31 (1967)

Decidability of Modular Logics for Concurrency

Radu Mardare*

Aalborg University, Denmark

Abstract. The modular logics we approach in this paper are logics for concurrent systems that reflect both behavioral and structural properties of systems. They combine dynamic modalities that express behavioural properties of a system with polyadic modalities that join properties of subsystems. Spatial and Separation Logics are examples of modular logics. Being the complex algebraic-coalgebraic semantics, these logics have interesting decidability properties. In this paper we provide a taxonomy of the decision problems for a class of modular logics with semantics based on CCS processes.

1 Introduction

The success of Process Algebras [2] in modelling a wide class of concurrent and distributed systems from Computer Science and Artificial Intelligence to Systems Biology and Biochemistry, raises the necessity to develop analysis techniques for studying and predicting the behaviour of modelled systems. This is the origin of the idea of defining complex query languages specifically designed to express temporal and structural properties of the systems. The dual nature of these calculi—algebraic/equational syntax versus coalgebraic operational semantics, makes them particularly appropriate for a modal logic-based approach.

The process semantics for modal logics are special cases of Kripke semantics: they involve structuring the classes of processes as Kripke models with accessibility relations based on the syntax and the semantics of processes. On one hand, the accessibility relations induced by transition systems have been considered with Hennessy-Milner logic [14] and temporal logics [24]. In addition, mobile, concurrent [12,22] and dynamic-epistemic [16,19,15] features have been added to express more complex semantics. On the other hand, the *spatial logics* [7,3] use accessibility relations that reflect syntactic properties of processes. They are *intensional logics* [23] able to differentiate bisimilar processes with different structures by using *modular operators* – the logical counterparts of the program constructors of process calculi. Thus, the *parallel operator* specifies properties of complementary (parallel) modules of a program; its adjoint, the *guarantee operator*, quantifies on possible interactive contexts of a program. Some spatial logics consider also operators for specifying the space of computation, such as ambient logic [7], or operators for name passing and name restrictions in process calculi [3], but these are outside the scope of this paper.

By combining the dynamic and the modular operators, one gets an interesting polyadic modal logic. The parallel operator, for instance, is a modal operator of

---

* Research supported by Sapere Aude: DFF-Young Researchers Grant 10-085054 of the Danish Council for Independent Research.

E. Clarke, I. Virbitskaite, and A. Voronkov (Eds.): PSI 2011, LNCS 7162, pp. 274–288, 2012.

arity 2 that satisfies the axioms of associativity, commutativity, and modal distribution [20,17,18]. Similar operators have been studied, e.g., in the context of *Arrow Logic* [1,13], of *Relevant* and *Substructural Logics* [25], of linear and intensional logics – see [7] for a detailed discussion.

In spite of the similarities with other logics, the combination of dynamic and modular operators raises genuinely new problems concerning decidability and complexity for satisfiability, validity, and model checking against the semantics based on process algebras. In this paper we study and classify by decidability the modular logics for a fragment of CCS [21]. In spite of the restrictive semantics, these logics are already showing interesting behaviours. In this paper we survey the results of [4,11] (the cases PML_4 and SOL_4) and complete them with new results which improve the state of art and allow us to organize the taxonomy presented in Table 1. We also present some proof methods for process logics that can be further used in various contexts.

Table 1. The decidability problems for modular logics

Name	Signature	Model checking	Satisfiability
PML_1	$\phi := 0, 1 \mid \neg\phi \mid \phi \wedge \phi \mid \phi\mid\phi \mid \diamond \phi$	decidable	unknown
PML_2	$\phi := 0, 1 \mid \neg\phi \mid \phi \wedge \phi \mid \phi\mid\phi \mid \langle\alpha\rangle\phi \mid \phi \triangleright \phi$	decidable	decidable
PML_3	$\phi := 0, 1 \mid \neg\phi \mid \phi \wedge \phi \mid \phi\mid\phi \mid \langle\alpha,\overline{\alpha}\rangle\phi \mid \phi \triangleright \phi$	decidable	decidable
PML_4	$\phi := 0, 1 \mid \neg\phi \mid \phi \wedge \phi \mid \phi\mid\phi \mid \diamond \phi \mid \phi \triangleright \phi$	undecidable	undecidable
SOL_0	$\phi := 0, 1 \mid \neg\phi \mid \phi \wedge \phi \mid \exists x.\phi \mid \langle x\rangle\phi$	decidable	unknown
SOL_1	$\phi := 0, 1 \mid \neg\phi \mid \phi \wedge \phi \mid \top\mid\phi \mid \exists x.\phi \mid \langle x\rangle\phi$	decidable	undecidable
SOL_2	$\phi := 0, 1 \mid \neg\phi \mid \phi \wedge \phi \mid \phi\mid\phi \mid \exists x.\phi \mid \langle x\rangle\phi$	decidable	undecidable
SOL_3	$\phi := 0, 1 \mid \neg\phi \mid \phi \wedge \phi \mid \phi\mid\phi \mid \exists x.\phi \mid \langle x\rangle\phi \mid \top \triangleright \phi$	undecidable	undecidable
SOL_4	$\phi := 0, 1 \mid \neg\phi \mid \phi \wedge \phi \mid \phi\mid\phi \mid \exists x.\phi \mid \langle x\rangle\phi \mid \langle\overline{x}\rangle\phi \mid \diamond \phi \mid \phi \triangleright \phi$	undecidable	undecidable

In [4] it is proved that validity/satisfiability and model checking are undecidable for the logic combining the modular operators with a modality $\diamond$ that encodes the τ-transitions (PML_4) and with second order modalities of type $\exists x.\langle x\rangle\phi$ (SOL_4). We improve these results by showing that the undecidability of satisfiability for modular logics with second order quantifiers derives from the undecidability of a more basic logic that contains second order quantifiers but does not contain the guarantee or the parallel operators. The expressive power of $\top\mid\phi$ is sufficient to generate, in this context, undecidability for satisfiability ($\top$ is "true"). Moreover, the model-checking problem remains undecidable for any similar logic that can express at least $\top \triangleright \phi$ (which is less expressive than the guarantee operator). On the other hand, we prove that the absence of guarantee operator makes the model checking decidable. For the logics without second order operators, we prove that by replacing $\diamond$ (studied in [4]) with a class of operators of type $\langle\alpha,\overline{\alpha}\rangle$, that expresses a synchronization of the action α and its co-action, we obtain a decidable logic even in the presence of parallel and guarantee operators. The same result is obtained by replacing $\diamond$ with the class of dynamic operators $\langle\alpha\rangle$ which encode atomic actions. We also show that the model-checking problem is decidable for the logic combining parallel and $\diamond$ operators, in the absence of guarantee operator.

2 Preliminaries on Process Algebra

In this section we recall basic notions of process algebra and establish the terminology and the notations. We introduce a finite fragment of CCS [21] which will be used later as the semantics for modular logics. In spite of its simplicity, this fragment is already sufficient to rise important decidability problems for the modular logics.

Definition 1 (CCS processes). *Let Σ be a countable set of actions and $0 \notin \Sigma$ a constant called null process. The class $\mathbb{P}$ of CCS processes is introduced, for arbitrary $\alpha \in \Sigma$, by*
$$P := 0 \mid \alpha.P \mid P|P.$$

Definition 2 (Structural congruence). *The structural congruence is the smallest equivalence relation on $\mathbb{P}$ such that*

1. $(P|Q)|R \equiv P|(Q|R)$ 2. $P|0 \equiv P$ 3. $P|Q \equiv Q|P$
4. *If $P \equiv P'$, then for any $\alpha \in \Sigma$ and $Q \in \mathbb{P}$, $\alpha.P \equiv \alpha.P'$ and $P|Q \equiv P'|Q$.*

Definition 3 (Operational semantics). *Let $\tau \notin \Sigma \cup \mathbb{P}$ and consider an involution on Σ that associates to each action $\alpha \in \Sigma$ its co-action $\overline{\alpha}$, such that $\overline{\overline{\alpha}} = \alpha$ and $\overline{\alpha} \neq \alpha$. The operational semantics presented bellow defines a labeled transition system $\mathbb{T} : \mathbb{P} \to (\Sigma \cup \{\tau\}) \times \mathbb{P}$, where $\mathbb{T}(P) = (\mu, Q)$ is denoted by $P \xrightarrow{\mu} Q$ for any $\mu \in \Sigma \cup \{\tau\}$.*

$$\frac{}{\alpha.P \xrightarrow{\alpha} P}, \alpha \in \Sigma \qquad\qquad \frac{}{\alpha.P|\overline{\alpha}.Q \xrightarrow{\tau} P|Q}, \alpha \in \Sigma$$

$$\frac{P \equiv Q \qquad P \xrightarrow{\mu} P'}{Q \xrightarrow{\mu} P'}, \mu \in \Sigma \cup \{\tau\} \qquad\qquad \frac{P \xrightarrow{\mu} P'}{P|Q \xrightarrow{\mu} P'|Q}, \mu \in \Sigma \cup \{\tau\}$$

In this paper we consider, in addition, the transitions labeled by pairs of complementary actions $(\alpha, \overline{\alpha})$ defined by $\alpha.P'|\overline{\alpha}.P''|P''' \xrightarrow{\alpha,\overline{\alpha}} P'|P''|P'''$. We call a process P *guarded* if $P \equiv \alpha.Q$ for some $\alpha \in \Sigma$ and we use the notation $P^k \stackrel{def}{=} \underbrace{P|...|P}_{k}$ for $k \geq 1$.

Definition 4. *For an arbitrary process $P \in \mathbb{P}$, let $Act(P) \subset \Sigma$ be defined by*
1. $Act(0) \stackrel{def}{=} \emptyset$ 2. $Act(\alpha.P) \stackrel{def}{=} \{\alpha\} \cup Act(P)$ 3. $Act(P|Q) \stackrel{def}{=} Act(P) \cup Act(Q)$.

For $\Omega \subseteq \Sigma$ and h, w nonnegative integers we define the class $\mathbb{P}^{\Omega}_{(h,w)}$ of processes with actions from Ω and syntactic trees bound by two dimensions: the *depth* h of the tree and the *width* w (this represents the maximum number of structural congruent processes that can be found in a node of the tree). $\mathbb{P}^{\Omega}_{(h,w)}$ is introduced inductively on h.

$\mathbb{P}^{\Omega}_{(0,w)} = \{0\}$;
$\mathbb{P}^{\Omega}_{(h+1,w)} = \{(\alpha_1.P_1)^{k_1}|...|(\alpha_i.P_i)^{k_i}, \text{ for } k_j \leq w, \alpha_j \in \Omega, P_j \in \mathbb{P}^{\Omega}_{(h,w)}, \forall j = 1..i\}$.

Observe that if $\Omega \subseteq \Sigma$ is a finite set, then $\mathbb{P}^{\Omega}_{(h,w)}$ is a finite set of processes.

In what follows, we introduce *structural bisimulation*, a relation on processes similar to the *pruning relation* proposed for trees (static ambient processes) in [5]. This relation will play an essential role in establishing the bounded model property for some modular logics. The structural bisimulation is indexed by a set $\Omega \subseteq \Sigma$ of actions and by two nonnegative integers h, w. Intuitively, two processes are Ω-*structural bisimilar* on size (h, w) if they look indistinguishable for an external observer that sees only the actions in Ω, does not follow a process for more than h transition steps, and cannot distinguish more than w cloned parallel subprocesses of an observed process.

Definition 5 (Ω-Structural Bisimulation). *Let $\Omega \subseteq \Sigma$ and h, w two nonnegative integers. The Ω-structural bisimulation on $\mathbb{P}$, $\approx_{(h,w)}^{\Omega}$, is defined inductively as follows.*

If $P \equiv Q \equiv 0$, then $P \approx_{(h,w)}^{\Omega} Q$;
If $P \not\equiv 0$ and $Q \not\equiv 0$, then
   $P \approx_{(0,w)}^{\Omega} Q$ *always.*
   $P \approx_{(h+1,w)}^{\Omega} Q$ *iff for any $i \in 1..w$ and any $\alpha \in \Omega$:*

- $P \equiv \alpha.P_1|...|\alpha.P_i|P'$ *implies* $Q \equiv \alpha.Q_1|...|\alpha.Q_i|Q'$, $P_j \approx_{(h,w)}^{\Omega} Q_j$, $j = 1..i$;
- $Q \equiv \alpha.Q_1|...|\alpha.Q_i|Q'$ *implies* $P \equiv \alpha.P_1|...|\alpha.P_i|P'$, $Q_j \approx_{(h,w)}^{\Omega} P_j$, $j = 1..i$.

We emphasize further some properties of Ω-structural bisimulation. The proofs of these results can be found in Appendix.

Lemma 1 (Equivalence). $\approx_{(h,w)}^{\Omega}$ *is an equivalence relations on $\mathbb{P}$.*

Lemma 2 (Congruence). *Let $\Omega \subseteq \Sigma$ be a set of actions.*
1. If $P \approx_{(h,w)}^{\Omega} Q$, then $\alpha.P \approx_{(h+1,w)}^{\Omega} \alpha.Q$.
2. If $P \approx_{(h,w)}^{\Omega} P'$ and $Q \approx_{(h,w)}^{\Omega} Q'$, then $P|Q \approx_{(h,w)}^{\Omega} P'|Q'$.

For nonnegative integers h, h', w, w' we convey to write $(h', w') \leq (h, w)$ iff $h' \leq h$ and $w' \leq w$.

Lemma 3 (Restriction). *Let $\Omega' \subseteq \Omega \subseteq \Sigma$ and $(h', w') \leq (h, w)$. If $P \approx_{(h,w)}^{\Omega} Q$, then $P \approx_{(h',w')}^{\Omega'} Q$.*

Lemma 4 (Split). *If $P'|P'' \approx_{(h,w_1+w_2)}^{\Omega} Q$ for some $\Omega \subseteq \Sigma$, then there exist $Q', Q'' \in \mathbb{P}$ such that $Q \equiv Q'|Q''$ and $P' \approx_{(h,w_1)}^{\Omega} Q'$, $P'' \approx_{(h,w_2)}^{\Omega} Q''$.*

Lemma 5 (Step-wise propagation). *If $P \approx_{(h,w)}^{\Omega} Q$ and $P \xrightarrow{\alpha} P'$ for some $\alpha \in \Omega \subseteq \Sigma$, then there exists a transition $Q \xrightarrow{\alpha} Q'$ such that $P' \approx_{(h-1,w-1)}^{\Omega} Q'$; if $P \xrightarrow{\alpha,\overline{\alpha}} P'$, then there exists a transition $Q \xrightarrow{\alpha,\overline{\alpha}} Q'$ such that $P' \approx_{(h-2,w-2)}^{\Omega} Q'$.*

As Σ is a denumerable set, assume a lexicographic order $\ll \subseteq \Sigma \times \Sigma$ on it. Then, any element $\alpha \in \Sigma$ has a successor denoted by $succ(\alpha)$ and any finite subset $\Omega \subset \Sigma$ has a maximum element denoted by $sup(\Omega)$. We define $\Omega^+ = \Omega \cup \{succ(sup(\Omega))\}$.

The next lemma states that for any finite set Ω and any nonnegative integers h, w, the equivalence relation $\approx_{(h,w)}^{\Omega}$ partitions the class $\mathbb{P}$ of processes in equivalence classes such that each equivalence class has a representative in the finite set $\mathbb{P}_{(h,w)}^{\Omega^+}$.

Lemma 6 (Representation Theorem). *For any finite set $\Omega \subseteq \Sigma$, any nonnegative integers h, w and any process $P \in \mathbb{P}$, there exists a process $Q \in \mathbb{P}_{(h,w)}^{\Omega^+}$ such that $P \approx_{(h,w)}^{\Omega} Q$.*

3 Modular Logic

In this section we introduce the modular logics. One class contains the *propositional modular logics* (PMLs) that extend the classic propositional logic with modular and dynamic operators. The other class consists of *second order modular logics* (SOLs) that are equipped with variables and quantifiers over modalities.

Definition 6 (Syntax). *Let Σ and X be two disjoint countable sets. Consider the logics defined for arbitrary $\alpha \in \Sigma$ and $x, y \in X$ as follows.*

$$
\begin{aligned}
PML_1 \quad & \phi := 0, 1 \mid \neg\phi \mid \phi \wedge \phi \mid \phi|\phi \mid \quad \diamond\phi \\
PML_2 \quad & \phi := 0, 1 \mid \neg\phi \mid \phi \wedge \phi \mid \phi|\phi \mid \langle\alpha\rangle\phi \mid \phi \triangleright \phi \\
PML_3 \quad & \phi := 0, 1 \mid \neg\phi \mid \phi \wedge \phi \mid \phi|\phi \mid \langle\alpha, \overline{\alpha}\rangle\phi \mid \phi \triangleright \phi \\
PML_4 \quad & \phi := 0, 1 \mid \neg\phi \mid \phi \wedge \phi \mid \phi|\phi \mid \quad \diamond\phi \mid \phi \triangleright \phi
\end{aligned}
$$

$$
\begin{aligned}
SOL_0 \quad & \phi := 0, 1 \mid \neg\phi \mid \phi \wedge \phi \mid \qquad \exists x.\phi \mid \langle x \rangle\phi \\
SOL_1 \quad & \phi := 0, 1 \mid \neg\phi \mid \phi \wedge \phi \mid \top|\phi \mid \exists x.\phi \mid \langle x \rangle\phi \\
SOL_2 \quad & \phi := 0, 1 \mid \neg\phi \mid \phi \wedge \phi \mid \phi|\phi \mid \exists x.\phi \mid \langle x \rangle\phi \\
SOL_3 \quad & \phi := 0, 1 \mid \neg\phi \mid \phi \wedge \phi \mid \phi|\phi \mid \exists x.\phi \mid \langle x \rangle\phi \mid \top \triangleright \phi \\
SOL_4 \quad & \phi := 0, 1 \mid \neg\phi \mid \phi \wedge \phi \mid \phi|\phi \mid \exists x.\phi \mid \langle x \rangle\phi \mid \langle\overline{x}\rangle\phi \mid \diamond\phi \mid \phi \triangleright \phi
\end{aligned}
$$

Here 0 and 1 are modal operators of arity 0 that characterize the null process and the guarded processes respectively.

The semantics is given for the class $\mathbb{P}$ of CCS processes as frames. In particular, a definition of the satisfiability operator, $P \models \phi$ that relates a process $P \in \mathbb{P}$ with the property ϕ written in the syntax of *PMLs*, is given.

Definition 7 (Semantics of PMLs). *Let $P \in \mathbb{P}$ and ϕ a formula of PML_i, $i = 1..4$. The relation $P \models \phi$ is defined inductively as follows.*

$P \models 0$ *iff* $P \equiv 0$.
$P \models 1$ *iff there exist $\alpha \in \Sigma$ and $Q \in \mathbb{P}$ such that $P \equiv \alpha.Q$.*
$P \models \neg\phi$ *iff* $P \not\models \phi$.
$P \models \phi \wedge \psi$ *iff* $P \models \phi$ *and* $P \models \psi$.
$P \models \phi|\psi$ *iff* $P \equiv Q|R$, $Q \models \phi$ *and* $R \models \psi$.
$P \models \top|\phi$ *iff* $P \equiv Q|R$ *and* $R \models \phi$.
$P \models \diamond\phi$ *iff there exists a transition* $P \xrightarrow{\tau} P'$ *and* $P' \models \phi$.
$P \models \langle\alpha\rangle\phi$ *iff there exists a transition* $P \xrightarrow{\alpha} P'$ *and* $P' \models \phi$.
$P \models \langle\alpha, \overline{\alpha}\rangle\phi$ *iff there exists a transition* $P \xrightarrow{\alpha, \overline{\alpha}} P'$ *and* $P' \models \phi$.
$P \models \phi \triangleright \psi$ *iff for any $Q \in \mathbb{P}$, $Q \models \phi$ implies $P|Q \models \psi$.*
$P \models \top \triangleright \phi$ *iff for any Q, $P|Q \models \phi$.*

Observe that, equivalently, we can introduce the semantics in the modal logic fashion by defining a frame for PMLs as the structure

$\mathcal{M} = (\mathbb{P}, i, \mathcal{R}_0, \mathcal{R}_1, (\mathcal{R}_\alpha)_{\alpha \in \Sigma}, (\mathcal{R}_{(\alpha, \overline{\alpha})})_{\alpha \in \Sigma}, \mathcal{R}_\tau, \mathcal{R}_|, \mathcal{R}_\triangleright)$ where
$i : \mathbb{P} \to 2^{\{0\}}$ is the interpretation function defined by $i(P) = \{0\}$ for $P \equiv 0$ and $i(P) = \emptyset$ else;

$\mathcal{R}_0 = \{0\}$ and $\mathcal{R}_1 = \{\alpha.P : \alpha \in \Sigma, P \in \mathbb{P}\}$ are accesibility relations of arity 1;
$(\mathcal{R}_\alpha)_{\alpha \in \Sigma}$ is a class of accessibility relations $\mathcal{R}_\alpha \subseteq \mathbb{P} \times \mathbb{P}$ indexed by actions and defined
by $(P, Q) \in \mathcal{R}_\alpha$ iff $P \xrightarrow{\alpha} Q$.
$(\mathcal{R}_{(\alpha,\overline{\alpha})})_{\alpha \in \Sigma}$ is a class of accessibility relations indexed by pairs of complementary actions
and defined by $(P, Q) \in \mathcal{R}_{(\alpha,\overline{\alpha})}$ iff $P \xrightarrow{\alpha,\overline{\alpha}} Q$.
$\mathcal{R}_\tau$ is an accessibility relations $\mathcal{R}_\tau$ defined by $(P, Q) \in \mathcal{R}_\alpha$ iff $P \xrightarrow{\tau} Q$.
$\mathcal{R}_| \subseteq \mathbb{P} \times \mathbb{P} \times \mathbb{P}$ is a relation defined by $(P, Q, R) \in \mathcal{R}_|$ iff $P \equiv Q|R$
$\mathcal{R}_\triangleright \subseteq \mathbb{P} \times \mathbb{P} \times \mathbb{P}$ is a relation defined by $(P, Q, R) \in \mathcal{R}_\triangleright$ iff $R \equiv P|Q$.

In this presentation $0, 1$ are modal operators of arity 0, $\langle \alpha \rangle$, $\langle \alpha, \overline{\alpha} \rangle$ and $\diamond$ are modal
operators of arity 1, while $|$ and $\triangleright$ are modal operators of arity 2.

Before introducing the semantics of second order modular logics (SOLs), we should
stress the fact that in our syntax X is a set of variables that will be interpreted over Σ.
As usual, we call an occurrence of a variable $x \in X$ in a formula ϕ (written in the syntax
of SOL_i, $i = 0, \ldots, 4$) a *free occurrence* if it is not in the scope of a quantifier $\exists x$. We
call a variable x a *free variable* in a formula if it has at least one free occurrence[1]. A
formula ϕ is *closed* if it contains no free variables; else, we call it *open*. A valuation
$v : X \hookrightarrow \Sigma$ is a partial function that associates values in Σ to some variables in X. If v
is a valuation, $x \in X$ is a variable that is not in the domain of v, and $\alpha \in \Sigma$, we denote
by $v_{\{x \to \alpha\}}$ the valuation v' that extends v with $v'(x) = \alpha$.

The semantics of second order modular logics (SOLs) is given by the satisfiability
operator, $P, v \models \phi$ that relates a process $P \in \mathbb{P}$ and valuation $v : X \to \Sigma$ interpreting the
free variable of ϕ, to a well formed formula ϕ of SOL_i, $i = 0, \ldots, 4$.

Definition 8 (Semantics of SOLs). *The relation $P, v \models \phi$ is defined as follows.*

$P, v \models 0$ *iff* $P \equiv 0$.
$P, v \models 1$ *iff there exists* $\alpha.Q \in \mathbb{P}$ *such that* $P \equiv \alpha.Q$.
$P, v \models \neg\phi$ *iff* $P, v \not\models \phi$.
$P, v \models \phi \wedge \psi$ *iff* $P, v \models \phi$ *and* $P, v \models \psi$.
$P, v \models \phi|\psi$ *iff* $P \equiv Q|R$, $Q, v \models \phi$ *and* $R, v \models \psi$.
$P, v \models \top|\phi$ *iff* $P \equiv Q|R$, $Q, v \models \phi$.
$P, v \models \diamond\phi$ *iff* $P \xrightarrow{\tau} P'$ *and* $P', v \models \phi$.
$P, v \models \langle x \rangle\phi$ *iff* $P \xrightarrow{v(x)} P'$ *and* $P', v \models \phi$.
$P, v \models \langle \overline{x} \rangle\phi$ *iff* $P \xrightarrow{\overline{v(x)}} P'$ *and* $P', v \models \phi$.
$P, v \models \phi \triangleright \psi$ *iff for any process* $P' \in \mathbb{P}$, $P', v \models \phi$ *implies* $P'|P, v \models \psi$.
$P, v \models \top \triangleright \phi$ *iff for any process* P', $P'|P, v \models \phi$.
$P, v \models \exists x.\phi$ *iff there exists* $\alpha \in \Sigma$ *such that* $P, v_{\{\alpha \to x\}} \models \phi$.

In addition to the boolean operators we also introduce the next derived operators that
will be used both with PMLs and SOLs.

$$\top \stackrel{def}{=} 0 \vee \neg 0 \qquad \perp \stackrel{def}{=} \neg\top \qquad \phi \parallel \psi \stackrel{def}{=} \neg(\neg\phi|\neg\psi)$$
$$\diamond\phi \stackrel{def}{=} (\neg\phi) \triangleright \perp \qquad \phi^\vee \stackrel{def}{=} \phi \parallel \top \qquad \alpha.\phi \stackrel{def}{=} 1 \wedge \langle \alpha \rangle\phi$$

---

[1] As usual, we assume that variables occurring under different boundaries or both bound and
free do not clash, even if the same (meta-)symbol $x \in X$ is used to name them.

⊤ and ⊥ are boolean constants, hence ⊤|φ and ⊤ ▷ φ are particular instances of ψ|φ and ψ ▷ φ respectively. Notice that in the logics where φ|ψ is a legal construction, 1 can be defined from 0 by $1 \stackrel{def}{=} \neg 0 \wedge (0 \parallel 0)$. Observe also that the operator ∘, that can be defined in a logic where φ ▷ ψ is legal, is a universal modality and ∘φ encodes the validity of φ over $\mathbb{P}$.

Definition 9. *A formula φ of PMLs is* satisfiable *if there exists a process $P \in \mathbb{P}$ such that $P \models \phi$; it is* valid *(a* validity*) if for any process $P \in \mathbb{P}$, $P \models \phi$. A closed formula φ of SOLs is* satisfiable *if there exists a process $P \in \mathbb{P}$ such that $P, \emptyset \models \phi$, where $\emptyset$ is the empty valuation; it is* valid *(a* validity*) if for any process $P \in \mathbb{P}$ $P, \emptyset \models \phi$.*

We denote the fact that φ is a validity by $\models \phi$. Hereafter, we call the **satisfiability problem (validity problem)** for a logic against a given semantics the problem of deciding if an arbitrary formula is satisfiable (valid). The **model checking problem** for PMLs consists in deciding, for an arbitrary formula φ and an arbitrary process P, if $P \models \phi$. The same problem for SOLs consists in deciding, for an arbitrary closed formula φ and an arbitrary process P, if $P, \emptyset \models \phi$.

   Observe that Definition 9 implies that φ is a validity iff ¬φ is not satisfiable and reverse, φ is satisfiable iff ¬φ is not valid. Consequently, satisfiability and validity are dual problems implying that once one has been proved decidable/undecidable, the other shares the same property.

4   Decision Problems for Second Order Modular Logics

In [4] it is proved that SOL_4 is undecidable. The proof is based on the method proposed previously in [11] where it is shown that the second order quantifiers (over ambient names) in ambient logic, in combination with the parallel operator, can induce undecidability for satisfiability. A corollary of this result is the undecidability of SOL_2. In what follows, we use the same method for proving a stronger result, i.e. that satisfiability for SOL_1 is undecidable. This result shows that even in absence of the parallel operator (in SOL_1, the parallel operator can only appear in constructions of type ⊤|φ) second order quantification implies the undecidability of satisfiability for SOL_2, SOL_3 and SOL_4.

   In the second part of this section we approach the model checking problem. For SOL_2 model checking is decidable (implying decidability of model checking for both SOL_1 and SOL_0), while for SOL_3 model checking is undecidable (implying the undecidability of model checking for SOL_4). This shows that the expressivity of guarantee operator is not the one responsable of the undecidability of model checking, but the expressivity of ⊤ ▷ φ. Notice that $P, v \models \top \triangleright \phi$ implies that all processes having P as subprocess have the property φ under the evaluation v, i.e. we face a universal quantification over the class of upper processes of P. The satisfiability of SOL_0 is open.

4.1   The Satisfiability Problem

In what follows, we prove that the satisfiability problem of SOL_1 is equivalent with the satisfiability problem of a fragment of first order logic known to be undecidable for finite domains[2]. This fragment is FOL introduced inductively, for a single binary predicate $p(x, y)$ and for $x, y \in X$, by:

$$f := p(x, y) \mid \neg f \mid f \wedge f \mid \exists x.f.$$

The semantics of FOL is defined for a finite domain $D \subseteq \Sigma$, for an interpretation $I \subseteq D \times D$ of the predicate and for a valuation $v : X \rightarrow D$ as follows.

$(D, I), v \models p(x, y)$ iff $(v(x), v(y)) \in I$
$(D, I), v \models \neg f$ iff $(D, I), v \not\models f$
$(D, I), v \models f \wedge g$ iff $(D, I), v \models f$ and $(D, I), v \models g$
$(D, I), v \models \exists x.f$ iff there exists $\alpha \in D$ and $(D, I), v_{\{x \rightarrow \alpha\}} \models f$.

It is known that satisfiability for FOL is undecidable. We will prove further that satisfiability of FOL is equivalent with satisfiability for SOL_1.

We begin by describing a special class $\mathcal{P} \subseteq \mathbb{P}$ of processes that can be characterized by the formulas of SOL_1.

Consider the following derived operators in SOL_1:

$D(x) = \langle x \rangle 0$, $R(x, y) = 1 \wedge \langle x \rangle \langle y \rangle 0$ and
$Model = [(1 \rightarrow (\exists x D(x) \vee \exists x \exists y R(x, y))) | \top] \wedge [\forall x \forall y ((R(x, y) | \top) \rightarrow (D(x) | \top \wedge D(y) | \top))]$.

We prove that $Model$ characterizes the class $\mathcal{P}$ of process containing 0 and all processes of type $\alpha_1.0|...|\alpha_k.0 \mid \alpha_{i_1}.\alpha_{j_1}.0|...|\alpha_{i_l}.\alpha_{j_l}.0$ for $i_1, ..., i_l, j_1, .., j_l \in \{1, ..k\}$.

Lemma 7. $P, v \models Model$ iff either $P \in \mathcal{P}$.

Proof. $P, v \models (1 \rightarrow (\exists x D(x) \vee \exists x \exists y R(x, y))) | \top$ iff for any Q s.t. $P \equiv Q|R$ we have that if $Q \models 1$ (i.e. $Q \equiv \alpha.Q'$ for some α), then $Q' \equiv 0$ or $Q' \equiv \beta.0$. Hence, $Q \models 1$ implies $Q \equiv \alpha.0$ or $Q \equiv \alpha.\beta.0$ for some $\alpha, \beta \in \Sigma$. Moreover, $P, v \models \forall x \forall y ((R(x, y) | \top) \rightarrow (D(x) | \top \wedge D(y) | \top))$ iff $P \equiv \alpha.\beta.0|Q$ implies $P \equiv \alpha.0|\beta.0|P'$.

Now, we describe a method for associating to each pair (D, I) used in the semantics of FOL, a process $P_D^I \in \mathcal{P}$.

Let $D \subseteq \Sigma$ be a finite set and $I \subset D \times D$ a relation on D. Suppose that $D = \{\alpha_1, ...\alpha_k\}$ with $k \geq 1$, and $I = \{(\alpha_{i_1}, \alpha_{j_1}), (\alpha_{i_2}, \alpha_{j_2}), ..., (\alpha_{i_l}, \alpha_{j_l})\}$, with $i_1, ..., i_l, j_1, .., j_l \in \{1, ..k\}$. We denote by $Dom(\Sigma)$ the class of these pairs (D, I). We associate to each pair $(D, I) \in Dom(\Sigma)$ the process $P_D^I \in \mathcal{P}$ defined by $P_D^I \equiv \alpha_1.0|...|\alpha_k.0 \mid \alpha_{i_1}.\alpha_{j_1}.0|...|\alpha_{i_l}.\alpha_{j_l}.0$.

Reverse, consider a process $P \in \mathcal{P}$ for which there exists $\alpha_1, ...\alpha_k \in \Sigma$, not necessarily distinct, and $i_1, ..., i_l, j_1, .., j_l \in \{1, ..k\}$ s.t. $P \equiv \alpha_1.0|...|\alpha_k.0 \mid \alpha_{i_1}.\alpha_{j_1}.0|...|\alpha_{i_l}.\alpha_{j_l}.0$.

We take $D = \{\alpha_1, ...\alpha_k\}$ and $I = \{(\alpha_{i_1}, \alpha_{j_1}), (\alpha_{i_2}, \alpha_{j_2}), ..., (\alpha_{i_l}, \alpha_{j_l})\}$ and this is the pair we associate to P. Notice that, by construction, if $\alpha_i = \alpha_j$ then it appears in D only once and similarly, if $(\alpha_{i_s}, \alpha_{j_s}) = (\alpha_{i_t}, \alpha_{j_t})$ for some $s \neq t$, then it is taken only once in I.

For proving the equivalence between the two decidability problems, we define the encoding [ ] that associates each formula of FOL to a formula of SOL_1 by

$[p(x, y)] = R(x, y) | \top$; $[\neg f] = \neg [f]$; $[f \wedge g] = [f] \wedge [g]$; $[\exists x.f] = \exists x.((D(x) | \top) \wedge [f])$.

Lemma 8. $(D, I), v \models f$ iff $P_I^D, v \models [f]$.

---

[2] The same fragment of first order logic is used in [4] for proving the undecidability of SOL_4.

Proof. We prove it by induction on $f \in FOL$. The non-trivial cases are:

The case $f = \exists x.g$: $(D, I), v \models \exists x.g$ iff there exists $\alpha \in D$ s.t. $(D, I), v_{\{x \to \alpha\}} \models g$. Further, the inductive hypothesis gives $P_I^D, v_{\{x \to \alpha\}} \models [g]$. But because $P_I^D \equiv \alpha.0|P'$, we obtain that $P_I^D, v_{\{x \to \alpha\}} \models D(x)|\top$. Hence $P_I^D, v_{\{x \to \alpha\}} \models D(x)|\top \wedge [g]$ that implies $P_I^D, v \models \exists x.(D(x)|\top \wedge [g])$ that is equivalent with $P_I^D, v \models [f]$.

The case $f = p(x, y)$: $(D, I), v \models p(x, y)$ iff $(v(x), v(y)) \in I$. But this is equivalent with $P_I^D \equiv v(x).v(y).0|P'$ that implies $P_I^D, v \models (1 \wedge \langle x \rangle \langle y \rangle.0)|\top$, i.e. $P_I^D, v \models [f]$.

Lemma 9. *Let f be a closed formula of FOL. Then f is satisfiable in FOL iff Model $\wedge$ $[f]$ is satisfiable in SOL_1.*

Proof. *Model* characterizes the class $\mathcal{P}$ of processes. So, if there exists a model $(D, I) \in Dom(\Sigma)$ such that $(D, I), \emptyset \models f$, then $P_I^D, \emptyset \models Model \wedge [f]$, where $\emptyset$ is the empty valuation. Reverse, if there is a process $P \in \mathbb{P}$ that satisfies $Model \wedge [f]$, then $P, \emptyset \models Model$, i.e. $P \in \mathcal{P}$ meaning that there exists $(D, I) \in Dom(\Sigma)$ such that $P \equiv P_I^D$. Then $P_I^D, \emptyset \models [f]$ that implies $(D, I), \emptyset \models f$.

Theorem 1. *For SOL_1 validity and satisfiability are undecidable.*

This result implies the undecidability of satisfiability for the more expressive logics.

Corollary 1. *The satisfiability is undecidable for SOL_2 and SOL_3.*

4.2 The Model-Checking Problem

With model checking the situation is different. The simple presence of second order quantification does not imply undecidability, as for the case of satisfiability.

Theorem 2. *For SOL_2 model checking is decidable.*

Proof. Observe that for arbitrary P, ϕ, v' and $\alpha, \beta \notin Act(P) \cup dom(v')$, we have $P, v'_{\{x \to \alpha\}} \models \phi$ iff $P, v'_{\{x \to \beta\}} \models \phi$. Due to this property, for deciding $P, v \models \phi$ it is sufficient to only consider the valuations assigning values from $Act(P) \cup \{\alpha_1, ..., \alpha_k\}$ to the free variables of ϕ, where $\alpha_i \notin Act(P)$ for $i = 1..k$ and k is the number of distinct variables that appear in ϕ. Further, one can prove that the operators can be eliminated inductively, and the model-checking problem can be reduced, at each step, to a finite number of model-checking problems involving the subprocesses of P (which are finitely many, modulo structural congruence) and the subformulas of ϕ.

Corollary 2. *The model-checking problems for SOL_1 and SOL_0 are decidable.*

The presence in a logic of the operator $\top \triangleright \phi$ is sufficient to make the model-checking problem undecidable. Notice that $P, v \models \top \triangleright \phi$ involves a universal quantification over the class of upper processes of P.

Theorem 3. *For SOL_3 model checking is undecidable.*

Proof. The proof is based on the observation, emphasized also in [11], that in any logic which can express $\top \triangleright \phi$, the decidability of model-checking problem implies the decidability of satisfiability. Hence, the undecidability of satisfiability implies undecidability of model checking. Indeed, for an arbitrary formula ϕ in SOL_3, it is trivial to verify that $\models \phi$ iff $0, \emptyset \models \top \triangleright \phi$. As for SOL_3 validity is undecidable, we obtain undecidability for model checking.

5   Decision Problems for Propositional Modular Logics

In this section we focus on propositional modular logics. In [4] it has been proved that for PML_4 satisfiability, validity and model checking are undecidable against the semantics presented in Section 3. The proof is based on the equivalence between the satisfiability problems for SOL_4 and PML_4. The result reveals that the combination of the modality $\diamond$ based on τ-transition with the modular operators | and $\triangleright$, generates undecidability.

In this section we show that the combination of the two modular operators and a transition-based modality does not always produce undecidability. We will show that for PML_2 and PML_3 both the satisfiability/validity and model-checking problems are decidable. PML_2 contains dynamic operators indexed by actions $\langle \alpha \rangle$ that reflect the interleaving semantics of CCS. PML_3 is closer to PML_4 as it expresses communications by the dynamic operators $\langle \alpha, \overline{\alpha} \rangle$. But while the communications reflected by $\diamond$ have an anonymous status, the communications expressible in PML_3 can also specify the pairs of actions involved. Observe that $\diamond$ can be seen as an existential quantifier over the class of $\langle \alpha, \overline{\alpha} \rangle$ and in this sense PML_4 has a second-order nature that might explain its undecidability.

In the second part of the section we consider the logic PML_1 which combines $\diamond$ with the parallel operator. We prove that for this logic model checking is decidable. However, the satisfiability for PML_1 is an open problem.

5.1   Decidability of PML_2 and PML_3

We prove that for PML_2 and PML_3 satisfiability/validity problems are decidable. The proofs are based on the *bounded model property* technique which consists in showing that, given a formula ϕ of PML_2 or PML_3, we can identify a finite class of processes $\mathbb{P}_\phi$, bound by the dimension of ϕ, such that if ϕ has a model in $\mathbb{P}$, then it has a model in $\mathbb{P}_\phi$. Thus, the satisfiability problem in $\mathbb{P}$ is equivalent with the satisfiability in $\mathbb{P}_\phi$. This result can be further used to prove the decidability of satisfiability for the two logics. Indeed, as $\mathbb{P}_\phi$ is finite, checking the satisfiability of a formula can be done by exhaustively verifying it for all the processes in $\mathbb{P}_\phi$.

The method adapted for modular logics was first proposed in [6] and reused in [5] for the case of static ambient logic. It consists in identifying a structural equivalence on processes, sensitive to the dimension of the logical formulas, that relates two processes whenever they satisfy the same formulas of a given size. In our case this relation is the structural bisimulation defined in Section 2.

Definition 10 (Size of a formula). *The sizes of a formula of PML_3, denoted by $(\!|\phi|\!) = (h, w)$, is defined inductively assuming that $(\!|\phi|\!) = (h, w)$ and $(\!|\psi|\!) = (h', w')$, as follows.*

1. $(\!|0|\!) \overset{def}{=} (1, 1)$.

2. $(\!|\neg\phi|\!) \overset{def}{=} (\!|\phi|\!)$.

3. $(\!|\phi \wedge \psi|\!) \overset{def}{=} (max(h, h'), max(w, w'))$.

4. $(\!|\langle \alpha \rangle \phi|\!) \overset{def}{=} (h + 1, w + 1)$.

5. $(\!|\phi \triangleright \psi|\!) \overset{def}{=} (max(h, h'), w + w')$.

6. $(\!|\phi|\psi|\!) \overset{def}{=} (max(h, h'), w + w')$.

7. $(\!|\langle \alpha, \overline{\alpha} \rangle \phi|\!) \overset{def}{=} (h + 2, w + 2)$.

Definition 11. *The set of actions of a formula* ϕ, $act(\phi) \subseteq \Sigma$ *is given by:*

1. $act(0) \overset{def}{=} \emptyset$ 2. $act(\neg\phi) = act(\phi)$

3. $act(\phi \wedge \psi) \overset{def}{=} act(\phi) \cup act(\psi)$ 4. $act(\langle\alpha\rangle\phi) \overset{def}{=} \{\alpha\} \cup act(\phi)$

5. $act(\phi \triangleright \psi) \overset{def}{=} act(\phi) \cup act(\psi)$ 6. $act(\phi|\psi) \overset{def}{=} act(\phi) \cup act(\psi)$

7. $act(\langle\alpha, \overline{\alpha}\rangle\phi) \overset{def}{=} \{\alpha, \overline{\alpha}\} \cup act(\phi)$.

The next Lemma states that a formula ϕ of PML_2 or PML_3 expresses a property of a process P up to $\approx_{(\!|\phi|\!)}^{act(\phi)}$. A sketch of its proof can be found in Appendix.

Lemma 10. *The next assertion is true for PML_2 and PML_3.*
If $P \approx_{(\!|\phi|\!)}^{act(\phi)} Q$, *then* $[P \models \phi$ *iff* $Q \models \phi]$.

This result guarantees the bounded model property for both PML_2 and PML_3.

Theorem 4 (Bounded model property). *For PML_2 and PML_3,*
if $P \models \phi$, *then there exists* $Q \in \mathbb{P}_{(\!|\phi|\!)}^{act(\phi)^+}$ *such that* $Q \models \phi$.

Theorem 5 (Decidability). *For PML_2 and PML_3 validity and satisfiability are decidable against process semantics.*

Proof. The decidability of satisfiability derives, for both logics, from the bounded model property. Indeed, if ϕ has a model, by Lemma 4, it has a model in $\mathbb{P}_{(\!|\phi|\!)}^{act(\phi)^+}$. As $act(\phi)$ is finite, $\mathbb{P}_{(\!|\phi|\!)}^{act(\phi)^+}$ is finite. Hence, checking for membership is decidable.

5.2   The Model-Checking Problems

We focus now on the model-checking problems. We start by stating the decidability of model checking for PML_2 and PML_3.

Theorem 6. *For PML_2 and PML_3 model checking is decidable.*

Proof. Given the process P and the formula ϕ, we show inductively on the structure of ϕ that $P \models \phi$ is decidable, by showing that the problem can be reduced, step by step, to a finite number of model checking problems involving subformulas of ϕ. The only interesting case is $\phi = \phi_1 \triangleright \phi_2$. Due to the bounded model property, $P \models \phi_1 \triangleright \phi_2$ iff for any $Q \in \mathbb{P}_{(\!|\phi_1|\!)}^{act(\phi_1)^+}$ we have that $Q \models \phi_1$ implies $P|Q \models \phi_2$. As there are only a finite number of processes $Q \in \mathbb{P}_{(\!|\phi_1|\!)}^{act(\phi_1)^+}$, we are done.

Theorem 7. *For PML_1 model checking is decidable.*

Proof. As before, we reduce the problem $P \models \phi$ to a finite number of model checking problems involving subprocesses of P (we do not have $\triangleright$) and subformulas of ϕ. The only difference w.r.t. PML_2 or PML_3 is case $\phi = \diamond\psi$. We have $P \models \diamond\psi$ iff there exists a transition $P \overset{\tau}{\longrightarrow} P'$ such that $P' \models \psi$. But the number of processes P' such that $P \overset{\tau}{\longrightarrow} P'$ is finite modulo structural congruence. Hence, also in this case, the problem can be reduced to a finite number of model checking problems that refers to ψ.

6   Conclusive Remarks

The goal of this paper was to present the taxonomy in Table 1. The results improve the state of the arts: the undecidability of satisfiability of SOL_1 explains the undecidability of SOL_4 reported in [4] and the undecidability of model checking of SOL_3 is linked to the undecidability of model checking for SOL_4. The results on propositional modular logics are, to the best of our knowledge, original. The decidability of PML_3 shows that the communication in combination with the modular operators is not necessarily undecidable. The decidability of SOL_2 is useful for applications in which interleaving semantics is relevant. Notice that, in light of Table 1, the undecidability of satisfiability seems generated either by the combination of second order quantifiers with $\top|\phi$, or by the combination of $\diamond$ and $\triangleright$. Undecidability of model checking seems generated by the presence of $\top \triangleright \phi$ in the context of undecidable satisfiability.

For future work we intend to extend these results for more complex frameworks, especially for the case of stochastic and probabilistic systems. We are interested in studying the decision problems for the case of Markovian Logics [8,9]. These are complex logics for stochastic/probabilistic systems with modular properties. They can be used to specify properties of, e.g., stochastic-CCS processes [10] and they enjoy most of the properties established for modular logics.

References

1. van Benthem, J.: Language in action. Categories, Lambdas and Dynamic Logic. Elsevier Science Publisher (1991)
2. Bergstra, J.A., Ponse, A., Smolka, S.A. (eds.): Handbook of Process Algebra. Elsevier (2001)
3. Caires, L., Cardelli, L.: A Spatial Logic for Concurrency (Part I). Inf. and Comp. 186/2 (2003)
4. Caires, L., Lozes, É.: Elimination of Quantifiers and Undecidability in Spatial Logics for Concurrency. In: Gardner, P., Yoshida, N. (eds.) CONCUR 2004. LNCS, vol. 3170, pp. 240–257. Springer, Heidelberg (2004)
5. Calcagno, C., Cardelli, L., Gordon, A.D.: Deciding validity in a spatial logic for trees. Journal of Functional Programming 15 (2005)
6. Calcagno, C., Yang, H., O'Hearn, P.W.: Computability and Complexity Results for a Spatial Assertion Language for Data Structures. In: Hariharan, R., Mukund, M., Vinay, V. (eds.) FSTTCS 2001. LNCS, vol. 2245, pp. 108–119. Springer, Heidelberg (2001)
7. Cardelli, L., Gordon, A.D.: Anytime, Anywhere: Modal Logics for Mobile Ambients. In: Proc. of 27th ACM Symposium on Principles of Programming Languages (2000)
8. Cardelli, L., Larsen, K.G., Mardare, R.: Continuous Markovian Logics - From Complete Axiomatization to the Metric Space of Formulas. In: Proc. of Computer Science Logic CSL 2011 (2011)
9. Cardelli, L., Larsen, K.G., Mardare, R.: Modular Markovian Logic. In: Aceto, L., Henzinger, M., Sgall, J. (eds.) ICALP 2011, Part II. LNCS, vol. 6756, pp. 380–391. Springer, Heidelberg (2011)
10. Cardelli, L., Mardare, R.: The Measurable Space of Stochastic Processes. In: QEST 2010. IEEE Press (2010)
11. Charatonik, W., Talbot, J.-M.: The Decidability of Model Checking Mobile Ambients. In: Fribourg, L. (ed.) CSL 2001 and EACSL 2001. LNCS, vol. 2142, pp. 339–354. Springer, Heidelberg (2001)

12. Dam, M.: Model checking mobile processes. Inf. and Comp. 129(1) (1996)
13. Gyuris, V.: Associativity does not imply undecidability without the axiom of Modal Distribution. In: Marx, M., et al. (eds.) Arrow Logic and Multi-Modal Logic, CSLI and FOLLI (1996)
14. Hennessy, M., Milner, R.: Algebraic laws for Nondeterminism and Concurrency. JACM 32(1) (1985)
15. Mardare, R.: Logical analysis of Complex Systems. Dynamic Epistemic Spatial Logics. PhD thesis, DIT, University of Trento (2006)
16. Mardare, R.: Observing Distributed Computation. A Dynamic-Epistemic Approach. In: Mossakowski, T., Montanari, U., Haveraaen, M. (eds.) CALCO 2007. LNCS, vol. 4624, pp. 379–393. Springer, Heidelberg (2007)
17. Mardare, R., Priami, C.: A logical approach to security in the context of Ambient Calculus. Electronic Notes in Theoretical Computer Science 99, 3–29 (2004)
18. Mardare, R., Priami, C.: A Propositional Branching Temporal Logic for the Ambient Calculus. Tech.Rep. DIT-03-053, University of Trento, Italy (2003)
19. Mardare, R., Priami, C.: Decidable Extensions of Hennessy-Milner Logic. In: Najm, E., Pradat-Peyre, J.-F., Donzeau-Gouge, V.V. (eds.) FORTE 2006. LNCS, vol. 4229, pp. 196–211. Springer, Heidelberg (2006)
20. Mardare, R., Policriti, A.: A Complete Axiomatic System for a Process-Based Spatial Logic. In: Ochmański, E., Tyszkiewicz, J. (eds.) MFCS 2008. LNCS, vol. 5162, pp. 491–502. Springer, Heidelberg (2008)
21. Milner, R.: A Calculus of Communicating Systems. Springer-Verlag New York, Inc. (1982)
22. Milner, R., Parrow, J., Walker, D.: Modal logics for mobile processes. TCS 114 (1993)
23. Sangiorgi, D.: Extensionality and Intensionality of the Ambient Logics. In: Proc. of the 28th ACM Annual Symposium on Principles of Programming Languages (2001)
24. Stirling, C.: Modal and temporal properties of processes. Springer-Verlag New York, Inc. (2001)
25. Urquhart, A.: Semantics for Relevant Logics. Journal of Symbolic Logic 37(1) (1972)

Appendix

In this appendix we present some of the proofs of the main lemmas presented in the paper.

*Proof (**Proof of Lemma 2**).*

2. We prove it by induction on h. The case $h = 0$ is immediate.

For the case $h + 1$, suppose that $P \approx^{\Omega}_{(h+1,w)} P'$ and $Q \approx^{\Omega}_{(h+1,w)} Q'$.

Consider any $i = 1..w$, and any $\alpha \in \Omega$ such that $P|Q \equiv \alpha.R_1|...|\alpha.R_i|R_{i+1}$. Suppose, without loss of generality, that R_j are ordered in such a way that there exist $k \in 1..i$, P'', Q'' such that $P \equiv \alpha.R_1|...|\alpha.R_k|P''$, $Q \equiv \alpha.R_{k+1}|...|\alpha.R_i|Q''$ and $R_{i+1} \equiv P''|Q''$. Because $k \in 1..w$, from $P \approx^{\Omega}_{(h+1,w)} P'$ we have $P' \equiv \alpha.P'_1|...|\alpha.P'_k|P_0$ such that $R_j \approx^{\Omega}_{(h,w)} P'_j$ for $j = 1..k$. Similarly, from $Q \approx^{\Omega}_{(h+1,w)} Q'$ we have $Q' \equiv \alpha.Q'_{k+1}|...|\alpha.Q'_i|Q_0$ such that $R_j \approx^{\Omega}_{(h,w)} Q'_j$ for $j = (k+1)..i$. Hence, $P'|Q' \equiv \alpha.P'_1|...|\alpha.P'_k|\alpha.Q'_{k+1}|...|\alpha.Q'_i|P_0|Q_0$ with $R_j \approx^{\Omega}_{(h,w)} P'_j$ for $j = 1..k$ and $R_j \approx^{\Omega}_{(h,w)} Q'_j$ for $j = (k+1)..i$.

*Proof (**Proof of Lemma 4**).*

We prove it by induction on h. The case $h = 0$ is trivial.

The case $h + 1$: Suppose that $P'|P'' \approx^{\Omega}_{(h+1,w)} Q$. Let $w = w_1 + w_2$.

Following an idea proposed in [5], we say that a process P is in $\Omega_{(h,w)}$-*normal form* if whenever $P \equiv \alpha_1.P_1 | \alpha_2.P_2 | P_3$ for $\alpha_1, \alpha_2 \in \Omega$ and $P_1 \approx^{\Omega}_{(h,w)} P_2$ then $P_1 \equiv P_2$. Note that $P \approx^{\Omega}_{(h+1,w)} \alpha_1.P_1 | \alpha_2.P_1 | P_3$. This shows that for any P, any Ω and any (h,w) we can find a P_0 such that P_0 is in (h,w)-normal form and $P \approx^{\Omega}_{(h+1,w)} P_0$.

We can suppose, without loosing generality, that the canonical representations of P', P'' and Q are[3]: $P' \equiv (\alpha_1.P_1)^{k'_1} | ... | (\alpha_n.P_n)^{k'_n} | P_1$, $P'' \equiv (\alpha_1.P_1)^{k''_1} | ... | (\alpha_n.P_n)^{k''_n} | P_2$ and $Q \equiv (\alpha_1.P_1)^{l_1} | ... | (\alpha_n.P_n)^{l_n} | Q_1$, where P_1, P_2, Q_1 have all the guarded subprocesses prefixed by actions that are not in Ω. For each $i \in 1..n$, we split $l_i = l'_i + l''_i$ in order to obtain a splitting of Q. We define the splitting of l_i such that $(\alpha_i.P_i)^{k'_i} \approx^{\Omega}_{h+1,w_1} (\alpha_i.P_i)^{l'_i}$ and $(\alpha_i.P_i)^{k''_i} \approx^{\Omega}_{h+1,w_2} (\alpha_i.P_i)^{l''_i}$. We do this as follows:

If $k'_i + k''_i < w_1 + w_2$ then $P' | P'' \approx^{\Omega}_{h+1,w} Q$ implies $l_i = k'_i + k''_i$, so we can choose $l'_i = k'_i$ and $l''_i = k''_i$.

If $k'_i + k''_i \geq w_1 + w_2$ then $P' | P'' \approx^{\Omega}_{h+1,w} Q$ implies $l_i \geq w_1 + w_2$. We meet the following subcases:

- $k'_i \geq w_1$ and $k''_i \geq w_2$. We choose $l'_i = w_1$ and $l''_i = l_i - w_1$ (note that as $l_i \geq w_1 + w_2$, we have $l''_i \geq w_2$).
- $k'_i < w_1$, then we must have $k''_i \geq w_2$. We choose $l'_i = k'_i$ and $l''_i = l_i - k'_i$. So $l''_i \geq w_2$ as $l_i \geq w_1 + w_2$ and $l'_i < w_1$.
- $k''_i < w_2$ is similar with the previous one. We choose $l''_i = k''_i$ and $l'_i = l_i - k''_i$.

Now, for $Q' \equiv (\alpha_1.P_1)^{l'_1} | ... | (\alpha_n.P_n)^{l'_n}$ and $Q'' \equiv (\alpha_1.P_1)^{l''_1} | ... | (\alpha_n.P_n)^{l''_n}$, the result is verified.

Proof (**Proof of Lemma 5**).

Because $P \approx^{\Omega}_{(h,w)} Q$, $\alpha \in \Omega$ and $P \equiv \alpha.P' | P''$, we obtain that $Q \equiv \alpha.Q' | Q''$ with $P' \approx^{\Omega}_{(h-1,w)} Q'$. We prove that $P' | P'' \approx^{\Omega}_{(h-1,w-1)} Q' | Q''$.

Consider $\beta \in \Omega$ and $i = 1..w - 1$ such that: $P' | P'' \equiv \beta.P_1 | ... | \beta.P_i | P^\star$. We can suppose that, for some $k \leq i$, we have $P' \equiv \beta.P_1 | ... | \beta.P_k | P^+$, $P'' \equiv \beta.P_{k+1} | ... | \beta.P_i | P^-$ and $P^\star \equiv P^+ | P^-$. Because $P' \approx^{\Omega}_{(h-1,w)} Q'$ and $k \leq i \leq w - 1$, we obtain that $Q' \equiv \beta.Q_1 | ... | \beta.Q_k | Q^+$ with $P_j \approx^{\Omega}_{(h-2,w)} Q_j$ for $j = 1..k$. Further we distinguish two cases.

1. If $\alpha \neq \beta$, then we have $P \equiv \beta.P_{k+1} | ... | \beta.P_i | (P^- | \alpha.P')$ and because $P \approx^{\Omega}_{(h,w)} Q$, we obtain $Q \equiv \beta.R_{k+1} | ... | \beta.R_i | R^\star$ with $R_j \approx^{\Omega}_{(h-1,w)} P_j$ for $j = k + 1..i$. But $Q \equiv \alpha.Q' | Q''$ and because $\alpha \neq \beta$, we obtain $Q'' \equiv \beta.R_{k+1} | ... | \beta.R_i | R^+$ that gives us in the end $Q' | Q'' \equiv \beta.Q_1 | ... | \beta.Q_k | \beta.R_{k+1} | ... | \beta.R_i | (R^+ | Q^+)$, with $P_j \approx^{\Omega}_{(h-2,w)} Q_j$ for $j = 1..k$ (hence, $P_j \approx^{\Omega}_{(h-2,w-1)} Q_j$) and $P_j \approx^{\Omega}_{(h-1,w)} R_j$ for $j = k + 1..i$ (hence, $P_j \approx^{\Omega}_{(h-2,w-1)} R_j$).

2. If $\alpha = \beta$, then we have $P \equiv \alpha.P_{k+1} | ... | \alpha.P_i | \alpha.P' | P^-$ and as $P \approx^{\Omega}_{(h,w)} Q$ and $i \leq w - 1$, we obtain $Q \equiv \alpha.R_{k+1} | ... | \alpha.R_i | \alpha.R' | R^\star$, with $R_j \approx^{\Omega}_{(h-1,w)} P_j$ for $j = k + 1..i$ and $R' \approx^{\Omega}_{(h-1,w)} P'$. Because $P' \approx^{\Omega}_{(h-1,w)} Q'$ and $\approx^{\Omega}_{(h,w)}$ is an equivalence relation, we can suppose that[4]

---

[3] Else we can replace P', P'' with $(h + 1, w)$-related processes having the same (h,w)-normal forms.

[4] Indeed, if $\alpha.Q'$ is a subprocess of $R^\star$ then we can just substitute R' with Q'; if $\alpha.Q' \equiv \alpha.R_s$, then $Q' \approx^{\Omega}_{(h-1,w)} P_s$ and as $Q' \approx^{\Omega}_{(h-1,w)} P'$ and $P' \approx^{\Omega}_{(h-1,w)} R'$ we derive $R' \approx^{\Omega}_{(h-1,w)} P_s$ and $Q' \approx^{\Omega}_{(h-1,w)} P'$, so we can consider this correspondence.

$R' \equiv Q'$. Consequently, $Q \equiv \alpha.R_{k+1}|...|\alpha.R_i|\alpha.Q'|R^\star$ that gives $Q'' \equiv \alpha.R_{k+1}|...|\alpha.R_i|R^\star$, which entails further $Q'|Q'' \equiv \alpha.Q_1|...|\alpha.Q_k|\alpha.R_{k+1}|...|\alpha.R_i|(R^\star|Q^+)$ with $P_j \approx^{\Omega}_{(h-2,w)} Q_j$ for $j = 1..k$ (hence, $P_j \approx^{\Omega}_{(h-2,w-1)} Q_j$) and $P_j \approx^{\Omega}_{(h-1,w)} R_j$ for $j = k + 1..i$ (hence, $P_j \approx^{\Omega}_{(h-2,w-1)} R_j$).

All these prove that $P'|P'' \approx^{\Omega}_{(h-1,w-1)} Q'|Q''$.

The communication case goes similarly.

Proof (**Proof of Lemma 6**). We construct Q inductively on h. For the case $P \equiv 0$ we take $Q \equiv P$, as $0 \in \mathbb{P}^{\Omega^+}_{(h,w)}$.

Suppose $P \not\equiv 0$. Let $\beta = succ(sup(\Omega))$. In the case $h = 0$ we just take $Q \equiv \beta.0$.

The case $h + 1$. Suppose, without loss of generality, that

$$P \equiv (\alpha_1.P_1)^{k_1}|...|(\alpha_n.P_n)^{k_n}|(\gamma_{n+1}.P_{n+1})^{k_{n+1}}|...|(\gamma_{n+m}.P_{n+m})^{k_{n+m}}$$

where $\alpha_1,..\alpha_n \in \Omega$ with $\alpha_i.P_i \not\equiv \alpha_j.P_j$ for $i \neq j$, and $\gamma_{n+1},..\gamma_{n+m} \in \Sigma \setminus \Omega$ with $\gamma_i.P_i \not\equiv \gamma_j.P_j$ for $i \neq j$.

Let P'_j for $j = 1..n$ be the processes constructed at the previous inductive step such that $P_j \approx^{\Omega}_{(h,w)} P'_j$ with $P'_j \in \mathbb{P}^{\Omega^+}_{(h,w)}$ - their existence is guaranteed by the inductive hypothesis. Let $l_i = min(k_i, w)$ and consider the process $P' \equiv (\alpha_1.P'_1)^{l_1}|...|(\alpha_n.P'_n)^{l_n}|\beta.0$. It is trivial to verify that P' is a process that fulfills the requirements of the lemma, i.e. $P \approx^{\Omega}_{(h,w)} P'$ and $P' \in \mathbb{P}^{\Omega^+}_{(h,w)}$.

Proof (**Proof of Lemma 10**). Induction on the structure of ϕ. We show here only the nontrivial cases.

The case $\phi = \langle\alpha\rangle\psi$: $P \models \langle\alpha\rangle\psi$ iff $P \xrightarrow{\alpha} P'$ and $P' \models \psi$. Suppose that $(|\psi|) = (h, w)$. Then $(|\phi|) = (h + 1, w + 1)$. Because $\alpha \in act(\phi)$ and $P \approx^{act(\phi)}_{(h+1,w+1)} Q$, we obtain applying Lemma 5 that $Q \xrightarrow{\alpha} Q'$ and $P' \approx^{act(\phi)}_{(h,w)} Q'$. We can apply the inductive hypothesis, as $P' \models \psi$ and we obtain $Q' \models \psi$. Then $Q \models \phi$.

The case $\phi = \langle\alpha, \overline{\alpha}\rangle\psi$: can be prove as the previous one using the second part of Lemma 5.

The case $\phi = \psi_1|\psi_2$: $P \models \psi_1|\psi_2$ iff $P \equiv S|R$, $S \models \phi_1$ and $R \models \psi_2$. Suppose that $(|\psi_1|) = (h_1, w_1)$ and $(|\psi_2|) = (h_2, w_2)$. Then $(|\phi|) = (max(h_1, h_2), w_1 + w_2)$. Applying Lemma 4 for $P \approx^{act(\phi)}_{(max(h_1,h_2),w_1+w_2)} Q$, we obtain that $Q \equiv S'|R'$ such that $S \approx^{act(\phi)}_{(max(h_1,h_2),w_1)} S'$ and $R \approx^{act(\phi)}_{(max(h_1,h_2),w_2)} R'$. Further Lemma 3 gives $S \approx^{act(\psi_1)}_{(h_1,w_1)} S'$ and $R \approx^{act(\psi_2)}_{(h_2,w_2)} R'$. Further, the inductive hypothesis gives $S' \models \psi_1$ and $R' \models \psi_2$, i.e. $Q \models \psi_1|\psi_2$.

The case $\phi = \psi_1 \triangleright \psi_2$: $P \models \psi_1 \triangleright \psi_2$ iff any $R \models \psi_1$ implies $P|R \models \psi_2$. But $P \approx^{act(\phi)}_{(|\phi|)} Q$ and $R \approx^{act(\phi)}_{(|\phi|)} R$ implies, by Lemma 2, that $P|R \approx^{act(\phi)}_{(|\phi|)} Q|R$. Further $P|R \approx^{act(\psi_2)}_{(|\psi_2|)} Q|R$ and because $P|R \models \psi_2$, we can apply the inductive hypothesis deriving $Q|R \models \psi_2$. Hence, $R \models \psi_1$ implies $Q|R \models \psi_2$, i.e., $Q \models \psi_1 \triangleright \psi_2$.

Partial Evaluation of Janus
Part 2: Assertions and Procedures

Torben Ægidius Mogensen

DIKU, University of Copenhagen,
Universitetsparken 1, DK-2100 Copenhagen O, Denmark
`torbenm@diku.dk`

Abstract. We continue earlier work on partial evaluation of the reversible language Janus. In this paper, we improve the handling of assertions and extend the partial evaluation method to handle procedure calls, which were omitted in the previous work. The partial evaluator now handles the full Janus language.

1   Introduction

Reversible computation [2–4, 7, 12] can theoretically be done using less energy than irreversible computation [7], since irreversible operations increase entropy. Most studies of reversible computation use low-level computational models such as reversible Turing machines [2, 11], but some studies use structured reversible programming languages[1, 9, 13–15].

Partial evaluation [5, 6] is a technique for generating specialised programs by fixing to constants the values of some of the inputs of more general programs. The intent is to make the specialised programs more efficient than the originals, and this has often been observed in practice. Specialised programs may perform fewer computations (and, hence, use less energy), so they can be of interest to further reduce energy comsumption.

In [10], we worked towards partial evaluation of Janus, but did not achieve partial evaluation of the full language, because procedure calls were not handled. In this paper, we will remedy this limitation and add a number of refinements to the way assertions are handled by the method described in [10]. These refinements improve the quality of residual programs and extend the set of programs that can be effectively specialised.

2   The Reversible Language Janus

Janus is a structured, imperative reversible programming language originally designed for a class at Caltech [9].

Variables in Janus are global. A Janus program starts with a declaration of variables divided into inputs, outputs and other variables. Variables are either integer variables or arrays of integers. The size of an array is either a constant number or given by a previously declared input variable. The main part of a Janus program is a list of procedure declarations and a sequence of reversible statements that can use conditionals, loops and procedure calls. A special feature is that procedures can be run backwards by calling them with the keyword uncall instead of call. A grammar for Janus is shown in Figure 1 and Figure 2 shows a few examples of Janus programs:

E. Clarke, I. Virbitskaite, and A. Voronkov (Eds.): PSI 2011, LNCS 7162, pp. 289–301, 2012.

$$Prog \rightarrow Dec^* \text{ -> } Dec^* \text{ (with } Dec^*)^? \text{ ; } Stat \, Proc^*$$

$$Dec \rightarrow \textbf{id}$$
$$Dec \rightarrow \textbf{id} \, [\, \textbf{size} \,]$$

$$Stat \rightarrow Lval \mathrel{+}= Exp$$
$$Stat \rightarrow Lval \mathrel{-}= Exp$$
$$Stat \rightarrow Lval \mathrel{<=>} Lval$$
$$Stat \rightarrow Stat \text{ ; } Stat$$
$$Stat \rightarrow \texttt{skip}$$
$$Stat \rightarrow \texttt{assert} \, Cond$$
$$Stat \rightarrow \texttt{if} \, Cond \, \texttt{then} \, Stat \, \texttt{else} \, Stat \, \texttt{fi} \, Cond$$
$$Stat \rightarrow \texttt{from} \, Cond \, \texttt{do} \, Stat \, \texttt{loop} \, Stat \, \texttt{until} \, Cond$$
$$Stat \rightarrow \texttt{call} \, \textbf{id}$$
$$Stat \rightarrow \texttt{uncall} \, \textbf{id}$$

$$Lval \rightarrow \textbf{id}$$
$$Lval \rightarrow \textbf{id} \, [\, Exp \,]$$

$$Exp \rightarrow \textbf{num}$$
$$Exp \rightarrow Lval$$
$$Exp \rightarrow Exp + Exp$$
$$Exp \rightarrow Exp - Exp$$
$$Exp \rightarrow Exp \mathbin{/} 2$$
$$Exp \rightarrow (\, Exp \,)$$

$$Cond \rightarrow Exp < Exp$$
$$Cond \rightarrow Exp == Exp$$
$$Cond \rightarrow \texttt{odd}(Exp)$$
$$Cond \rightarrow \texttt{!} \, Cond$$
$$Cond \rightarrow Cond \mathrel{\&\&} Cond$$
$$Cond \rightarrow Cond \mathbin{||} Cond$$
$$Cond \rightarrow (\, Cond \,)$$

$$Proc \rightarrow \texttt{procedure} \, \textbf{id} \, Stat$$

Fig. 1. Syntax of Janus

(a) Encryption. This is a rather naive encryption program shown mostly to illustrate the use of procedure calls.

(b) DFA interpreter. This program will read a reversible DFA (with both to and from transitions) and a bitstring represented as an array of integers. If the DFA matches the string, it returns the input unchanged, otherwise an assertion will fail. We have included this program to show the improved handling of assertions.

(c) Two-register machine. This program interprets a simple reversible language using two variables x and y. The inverse counterparts of instructions (represented by negative numbers) are handled by uncalling the op procedure with i set to the "positive" version of the instruction. This example illustrates the use of uncall to run procedures backwards and shows multiple specialisations of the same procedure.

2.1 Informal Semantics of Janus

We will in this paper only describe Janus informally and refer to [15] for a formal semantics of the language.

When the program starts, variables and array elements that are not inputs are initialised to 0. When the program ends, variables and array elements that are not outputs are verified to be 0. If the verification fails, the program stops with a failed assertion. A variable or array can be both input and output.

A Janus program can either end normally and produce output, it can be nonterminating or it can fail due to a failed assertion. Semantically, we treat all fail assertions as equivalent.

Statements in Janus can take the following forms:

Update. The left-hand side of an update is either an integer variable or an element of an array. The update can either add or subtract the value of the right-hand side to this. The right-hand side can be any expression that does *not* contain the variable

```
                                              size pgm[size] x
                                               -> size pgm[size] y
                                              with pc i;
                st to0[st] to1[st] from0[st]
key x -> key x  from1[st] n input[n]          from y==0 do
with j t;       ->                              from pc==0 do
                st to0[st] to1[st] from0[st]      if pgm[pc]<0 then
  from j==0 do  from1[st] n input[n]               i -= pgm[pc];
    call step;                                     uncall op;
    j += 1      with i s t v;                      i += pgm[pc]
  loop skip                                      else
  until j==19;  from i==0 do                       i += pgm[pc];
  j -= 19         if input[i]==1 then              call op;
                    t += to1[s];                   i -= pgm[pc]
procedure step      s -= from1[t];              fi pgm[pc]<0;
  t += x/2;         s <=> t                      pc += 1
  if odd(x) then  else                          loop
    x -= t+1;        t += to0[s];                  skip
    t -= x;          s -= from0[t];              until pc==size;
    x += key         s <=> t                     pc -= size
  else            fi input[i]==1;               loop
    x -= t;         i += 1                        skip
    t -= x        loop                          until x==0
  fi !x<key         skip
                  until i==n;                   procedure op
                  i -= n                          if i==0 then x <=> y
                                                else
                                                  if i==1 then x += y
                                                  else x += i-1
                                                  fi i==1
                                                fi i==0
```

(a) Encryption   (b) DFA interpreter   (c) Two-register machine

Fig. 2. Janus programs

or array used on the left-hand side, and if the left-hand side is an array element, the array can not be used in the expression specifying the index into the array. For example, the update a[a[0]] += 1 is illegal. These restrictions ensure that the update can be reversed.

Swap. A statement of the form lv_1 <=> lv_2 swaps the contents of lv_1 and lv_2, which can be integer variables or array elements. It is possible to swap two elements of the same array, but the index expression of an array element can not contain any of the array or integer variables used anywhere in the swap statement. Again, these restrictions are required for reversibility.

Sequence. Two statements separated by a semicolon are executed in sequence.

Skip. No effect.

Assertion. A statement of the form assert c verifies that the condition c is true. If it is not, the program stops and reports a failed assertion.

Conditional. A statement of the form if c_1 then s_1 else s_2 fi c_2 is executed by first evaluating the condition c_1. If this is true, the statement s_1 is executed and it is verified that the condition c_2 is true. If c_1 is false, s_2 is executed and it is verified that the condition c_2 is false. If the exit-assertion c_2 does not have the expected value, the program stops and reports a failed assertion. The construction can be illustrated by the flowchart in Figure 3(a), where a two-entry assertion is shown as a circle with two entry arrows marked with the expected truth value.

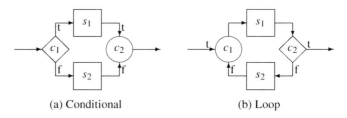

(a) Conditional   (b) Loop

Fig. 3. Flowchart diagrams for conditional and loop

Loop. A statement of the form from c_1 do s_1 loop s_2 until c_2 is executed by first evaluating the assertion condition c_1. If this is false, the program stops and reports a failed assertion, otherwise s_1 is executed and the condition c_2 is evaluated. If this is true, the loop terminates. Otherwise, s_2 is executed and c_1 is evaluated (again). If c_1 is true, the program stops with an error message, otherwise the loop repeats from s_1. The construction can be illustrated with the flowchart in Figure 3(b).

Procedure call. A procedure call is either of the form call p or uncall p, where p is a procedure name. call p executes the body statement of p and afterwards returns to the place of the call. uncall p executes the body of p *in reverse* and then returns to the place of the call. Hence, if call p completes without an error or failed assertion, uncall p undoes the effects, so the combined sequence call p; uncall p has no net effect on the state. Procedures are mutually recursive.

2.2   Reverse Execution

Statements can be executed both forwards and backwards (e.g, when a procedure is called with uncall). Backwards execution can be realised by syntactically reversing the statement and then executing the resulting statement forwards. A whole program can be reversed by swapping input and output variables and reversing the body statement. Procedure declarations are kept unchanged. The function R below shows how statements are reversed.

$$R(lv \mathrel{+}= e) = lv \mathrel{-}= e \qquad\qquad R(lv \mathrel{-}= e) = lv \mathrel{+}= e$$
$$R(lv_1 \mathrel{<=>} lv_2) = lv_1 \mathrel{<=>} lv_2 \qquad R(s_1; s_2) = R(s_2); R(s_1)$$
$$R(\text{skip}) = \text{skip} \qquad\qquad R(\text{assert } c) = \text{assert } c$$
$$R(\text{call } p) = \text{uncall } p \qquad\qquad R(\text{uncall } p) = \text{call } p$$
$$R(\text{if } c_1 \text{ then } s_1 \text{ else } s_2 \text{ fi } c_2) = \text{if } c_2 \text{ then } R(s_1) \text{ else } R(s_2) \text{ fi } c_1$$
$$R(\text{from } c_1 \text{ do } s_1 \text{ loop } s_2 \text{ until } c_2) = \text{from } c_2 \text{ do } R(s_1) \text{ loop } R(s_2) \text{ until } c_1$$

In all cases, if a statement s completes without errors or failed assertions, the sequence $s; R(s)$ has no net effect on the state.

3   Partial Evaluation

Partial evaluation is a process where a program is specialised by fixing some inputs to constant values. Good overviews of partial evaluation can be found in [6] and [5]. We will in this paper focus on *offline* partial evaluation, i.e., where a binding-time analysis first determines which parts of the program depend only on the known (static) inputs, so they can be eliminated during partial evaluation, and which must be postponed to when the specialised program (called *the residual program*) is executed with the remaining (dynamic) inputs.

3.1   Summary of Previous Work

The partial evaluator described in [10] uses the following steps:

1. Translation into flowchart form.
2. Binding-time analysis.
3. Polyvariant program-point specialisation of the flowchart form.
4. Translation of residual programs from flowchart form to structured Janus programs.

A reversible flowchart language similar to Janus is described in [13]. This is used as the intermediate form for the partial evaluator. We briefly describe the flowchart form below:

The body of a Janus program or procedure is converted into a list of basic blocks. Each basic block consists of three parts: An entry point, a body and a jump. An entry point can be one of the following:

- The keyword start that indicates the block where execution starts.
- A named label.
- A two-entry assertion consisting of a condition c and two named labels l_1 and l_2. This is written as if c from l_1 l_2. The condition c must be true if the basic block is entered by a jump to l_1 and false if the basic block is entered by a jump to l_2.

The body of a basic block is either empty or any statement that does not contain structured control statements (conditionals and loops). The jump can be:

- The keyword return that indicates the end of the program or procedure.
- An unconditional jump to a named label l. This is written as goto l.
- A conditional jump consisting of a condition c and two named labels l_1 and l_2. This is written as if c goto l_1 l_2. If c is true, the jump goes to l_1, otherwise to l_2.

Jumps can not cross procedure borders.

To ensure reversibility, there must be exactly one occurrence of start and return and each label must occur in exactly one entry point and one jump. A basic block $e : s; j$, where e is an entry point, s a statement and j a jump is reversed into $R(j) : R(s); R(e)$, where R from section 2.2 is extended to handle entry points and jumps as shown below:

$$R(\text{start}) = \text{return} \qquad\qquad R(\text{return}) = \text{start}$$
$$R(l) = \text{goto } l \qquad\qquad R(\text{goto } l) = l$$
$$R(\text{if } c \text{ from } l_1\ l_2) = \text{if } c \text{ goto } l_1\ l_2 \qquad R(\text{if } c \text{ goto } l_1\ l_2) = \text{if } c \text{ from } l_1\ l_2$$

Translation from Janus (sans procedures) into the flowchart form, binding-time analysis, specialisation and translation back to structured code is shown in [10]. Procedures are translated by translating their body statements into flowcharts.

We note a detail relevant to the work described below: To ensure that there is a unique exit-point from the residual program produced by partial evaluation, we require that static output variables are not modified inside the program. Hence, any output variable that is modified inside the program will be classified as dynamic.

4   Improved Handling of Assertions

During partial evaluation, assertions on static variables may occur. These come in three forms:

- Statements of the form `assert` c, where c is static.
- Entry-points of the form `if` c `from` l_1 l_2 where c is static.
- The requirement that static non-output variables must be zero at the end of execution (i.e., at a `return` jump that is not inside a procedure).

The partial evaluator in [10] handles these in a trivial manner: If a static assertion fails during specialisation, the entire specialisation process is aborted with an error message.

While failed static assertions can be a sign that the residual program (if it was produced) would always fail, this is not always the case: The partial evaluator explores all execution paths, so even if it encounters a failing static assertion, this does not imply that *all* executions of the original program with the given static inputs will fail. In fact, the path leading to the failing assertion might be unrealisable.

Hence, we want to treat static failed assertions more intelligently: Instead of failing the whole partial evaluation process, we want to produce a residual program that only fails if the failing assertion is reached. This can sometimes be realised simply by producing an always-failing residual assertion in place of a static failed assertion, but care has to be taken to ensure that the resulting program is well formed:

- A static `assert` c statement where c fails can be made into residual `assert false` statement.
- A static jump to l_1, where the block for l_1 is headed by `if` c `from` l_1 l_2 and c is false, can be unfolded to `assert false` followed by the specialised body of the block.
- A non-zero non-output static variable at a `return` can not just be specialised to `assert false` followed by `return`, as the possibility of non-zero static non-output variables at the end of the program can cause multiple `return` jumps in the residual program. Hence, the failed assertion must be followed by a residual jump that is not a `return` jump. We can do this by replacing the `return` jump with a jump `goto` l_1 to a block of the form `if false from` l_1 l_2: `goto` l_2 where l_1 and l_2 are new labels. Note that each of the new labels occur in exactly one jump and one entry.

While the above specialisation is correct, we don't really exploit the static nature of the failed assertion: We have just made it dynamic. And in the two first cases, we continue producing residual code after the failed assertion, even though this code is not reachable. So there is clearly room for improvement.

Since execution of a residual basic block containing a static failed assertion *will* lead to the failed assertion, the residual basic block can be completely eliminated and the jump to the eliminated basic block can be replaced by a failed assertion. How this is done depends on the type of jump:

If the jump to the eliminated basic block is an unconditional jump, the basic block that contains this jump will also lead to certain failure, so we can eliminate this too, propagating the failure back to the previous jump. This is illustrated in Figure 4(a).

If the jump is a conditional jump of the form if c goto l_1 l_2 and l_2 is the label of the eliminated block, we rewrite this into assert c; goto l_1. Hence, any jump to the failing basic block will instead immediately cause a failed assertion. This is illustrated in Figure 4(b). In the symmetric case (l_1 is the label of the eliminated block), we instead rewrite into assert $!c$; goto l_2. If both branches of a conditional jump lead to failing assertions, the conditional jump is replaced by a failing assertion, which is propagated further backwards, as illustrated in Figure 4(c).

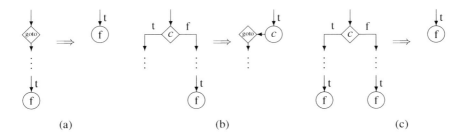

(a)   (b)   (c)

Fig. 4. Cutting away failing paths

In summary, we move from a failed static assertion backwards through the residual program to the closest dynamic branch that determines if the program will definitely reach the failed assertion. We then replace this dynamic branch with an assertion that the non-failing branch is taken and an unconditional jump to this.

The modified residual program will now fail if and only if the unmodified residual program will, but it might fail earlier. Since all failures are treated as equivalent and no sid effects are visible until the program ends, this preserves semantics.

This treatment of failed assertions is similar to the treatment of failure when specialising logic programs [8]: Any eventually failing branch is cut away completely.

The modification to the partial evaluator is surprisingly simple:

Specialisation of basic blocks is done in a depth-first manner: When a dynamic conditional jump is specialised, the residual basic blocks that are jumped to are immediately constructed (unless they already have been). If the specialiser finds a failed static assertion when specialising one of the target blocks, it raises an exception, which is caught at the place where the dynamic conditional jump is specialised. Because of the depth-first order of specialisation, this will be the closest conditional dynamic jump prior to the failed assertion and, hence, the place where we can cut the failing branch away.

If no exceptions happen when specialising the target basic blocks, a normal residual conditional jump is produced. If specialisation of one target basic block raises an exception, the jump to the other block is made unconditional and preceded by the (possibly negated) condition as a dynamic assertion. If specialisation of both target blocks raise exceptions, a new exception is raised to signal that the current basic block (that ended with the conditional jump) will always lead to static failure. This way, the exception is propagated back to the earliest point where the certain failure can be detected.

If an exception is not caught at any dynamic conditional jump, the residual program will always fail, so an error message to this effect is produced and no residual program is produced.

Another refinement to the handling of assertions is that two adjacent dynamic assertions are combined into one: assert c_1; assert c_2 is rewritten to assert c_1 && c_2. Such combinations occur fairly frequently when specialising Janus programs.

5   Procedure Calls

There are basically two ways we can specialise a procedure call:

- We may *unfold* the procedure call by replacing the call with the body of the called procedure and then specialising the body.
- We may *residualise* the call by replacing it with a call to a specialised procedure. The specialised procedure is at some point (now or later) added to the residual program.

5.1   Unfolding

Let us assume we put all procedure calls in separate basic blocks of the form l_1: call p; goto l_2. We can then unfold the call by replacing this basic block by the basic blocks from the body of p where start is replaced by l_1, return is replaced by goto l_2 and all labels from p are given new names to avoid name clashes. After this, we specialise in the usual way. uncall is handled by syntactically reversing the body of p before unfolding.

However, if we unfold all procedure calls, we can not specialise recursive procedures and we risk code explosion as several calls to the same procedure are unfolded to separate copies of its body.

So while it can be useful to unfold a call, it can not be the only treatment of procedure calls during specialisation.

5.2   Residualising

Residualising procedure calls can handle recursion and avoid code explosion, as separate calls to the same original procedure can be made into separate residual calls to the same residual procedure (if the static state is identical). In partial evaluators for functional languages, residual calls are typically handled in the following way:

1. When a dynamic call to a function f is encountered, it is residualised to a call to a residual function whose name is a combination of f and the values of its static parameters – much like we residualise a jump to a dynamic label by replacing it with a jump to a residual label constructed from the original label name and the static state.

2. The definition of the residual function is later added to the residual program.

This works fine because there are no side effects in a functional language, so we can postpone specialising the function until later knowing it can not change the current static state. All this requires is that the result of the function is classified as dynamic. In an imperative language, however, procedures can have side effects on global variables, and we need to know the static state at the procedure return before we can continue specialisation after the call.

C-mix, as described in section 11.3.3 of [6], requires that no static global variables are modified, so procedure calls can be specialised in the same way as it is done in functional languages. As mentioned in section 3.1 we use a similar restriction to avoid multiple exit points to a program: Any modified output variable is classified as dynamic by the binding-time analysis. It is easy to extend this principle to classify any variable modified by a procedure as dynamic, hence ensuring that no procedure call can modify static state. The restriction has the added benefit that the specialised procedure body will only have one basic block ending in a return jump. In fact, no basic block in the procedure will yield more than one residual basic block.

Thie means we can just insert a residual call and continue specialisation after this call with unchanged static state, just as for functional languages.

So we specialise a call or uncall to a residual call or uncall to a procedure with a name that is created by combining the original name and the values of static global variables, just like a residual label name is made by combining the original label name and the static state.

At some later time, we must make a definition of the residual procedure: We first set the static variables to the values they had at the call and then specialise the procedure body like we specialise the program body, as described in 3.1. This may lead to further residual procedure calls, which need to be specialised later. Since no static state is modified during specialisation of procedures, this will eventually terminate.

5.3   Implementation

We have implemented residual procedure calls as described in section 5.2. To illustrate specialisation of procedures, we have specialised the program in Figure 2(a) to key=5555555. The result is shown in Figure 5. The step procedure is specialised in 19 versions (not all shown), because the static variable j takes 19 different values at the call sites. However, since step doesn't actually use j, the 19 specialised procedures are identical (except for their names).

Avoiding code duplication. To avoid generating a large number of identical specialisations, we have modified the partial evaluator to specialise a procedure only to variables that are used in the procedure and in any procedures called by this. With this modification, we get only one specialised version of step, as shown in Figure 6.

6   Experiments and Results

One of the experiments in [10] was specialising an interpreter for reversible DFAs similar to the one shown in Figure 2(b). The DFA interpreter in Figure 2(b) signals failure

```
x  -> x with t ;

call step_140478;
call step_203981;          procedure step_203981
call step_57771;           t += x/2;
call step_121274;          if odd(x) then
call step_184777;          x -= t+1;
call step_38567;           t -= x;
call step_102070;          x += 5555555
call step_165573;          else
call step_19363;           x -= t;
call step_82866;           t -= x
call step_18412;           fi !(x<5555555)
call step_81915;
call step_145418;              :
call step_208921;              :
call step_62711;               :
call step_126214;              :
call step_189717;
call step_43507;           procedure step_107010
call step_107010           t += x/2;
                           if odd(x) then
procedure step_140478      x -= t+1;
t += x/2;                  t -= x;
if odd(x) then             x += 5555555
x -= t+1;                  else
t -= x;                    x -= t;
x += 5555555               t -= x
else                       fi !(x<5555555)
x -= t;
t -= x
fi !(x<5555555)
```

Fig. 5. Specialised encryption program

```
x  -> x with t ;

call step_140478;
call step_140478;
call step_140478;
call step_140478;
call step_140478;
call step_140478;          procedure step_140478
call step_140478;          t += x/2;
call step_140478;          if odd(x) then
call step_140478;          x -= t+1;
call step_140478;          t -= x;
call step_140478;          x += 5555555
call step_140478;          else
call step_140478;          x -= t;
call step_140478;          t -= x
call step_140478;          fi !(x<5555555)
call step_140478;
call step_140478;
call step_140478;
call step_140478
```

Fig. 6. Improved specialised encryption program

```
x   -> y ;

from y==0 do                        procedure op_38887
call op_203781;                     x += y
call op_38887;
call op_83706;                      procedure op_203781
call op_203781;                     x<=>y
uncall op_83706
loop                                procedure op_83706
skip                                x += 1
until x==0
```

Fig. 7. Residual two-register machine

	Dynamic assertion	Static assertion
DFA interpreter lines	34	25
Residual interpreter lines	112	62
Residual steps (success)	216	211
Residual steps (failure)	184	162

Fig. 8. Improved handling of assertions

	Original program	Residual program
Encryption lines	18	30
Encryption steps	225	173
Two-register machine lines	29	16
Two-register machine steps	2799	639

Fig. 9. Specialising procedures

of recognition by the DFA by failing an assertion. Since the partial evaluator reported in [10] fails when it reaches a static failing assertion, code was added to the DFA interpreter to change this assertion to a dynamic assertion. Hence the residual program produced by the partial evaluator reported i [10]n was littered with dynamic, but definitely failing assertions.

With the better treatment of static failing assertion, the assertion in the DFA interpreter can be kept static. The result is that any transition in the DFA that will lead to certain failure will be eliminated during specialisation, which greatly reduces the size of the residual programs compared to what is reported in [10]. For example, specialising the DFA interpreter to a DFA that recognizes bitstrings of numbers divisible by 5, the residual program produced by the new specialiser is roughly half the size of the residual program produced by the old specialiser and also about 10% faster in th ecases where a failed assertion occurs, as the failure is detected earlier. The numbers are shown in Figure 8. Only non-blank lines of programs are counted.

The other two programs are not affected by the improved handling of assertions, and they use procedures not handled by the previous specialiser, so we can't compare these results with similar results using the previous specialiser. The table in Figure 9 shows sizes and steps for the original and residual versions of the programs in Figures 2(a) and 2(c).

The residual programs are shown in Figures 6 and 7. The interpreter for the two-register machine is specialised to a five-instruction program encoded by the number sequence 0 1 2 0 -2. Note that the residual program calls the procedure op_83706 with both call and uncall, as the interpreted program contains the instructions 2 and -2 that are inverses of each other. If we specialised op with respect to all static variables, we would have generated two different procedures forthe instructions 2 and -2 as well as for the two different occurences of the 0 instruction. This, again, illustrates the advantage of specialising a procedure only to variables that are used by the procedure.

The residual encryption program is larger than the original since the loop is unrolled. Most of the speedup is also due to the unrolling, as the residual step procedures are identical to the original step procedure. The interpreter for the two-register machine is more interesting. The residual program is a bit shorter than the original, but that is mainly because the interpreted program is small – a longer instruction sequence would yield a longer residual program. The residual program is about 4 times faster than the original because the overhead of fetching and decoding instructions is eliminated by the partial evaluator. This is quite common when specialising interpreters.

7 Conclusion and Future Work

The refined treatment of static assertions works well and can greatly reduce the size of residual programs with potentially failing assertions and also somwehat reduce the time taken when an assertion fails, as the failure is detected earlier. There may also be a small speedup for non-failing computations, as some conditional jumps are reduced to simple assertions (which are slightly cheaper).

Specialising a procedure only to variables that are used in the procedure is similar to specialising a basic block to only live variables, which in [6] was noted to have a great effect on the size of residual programs when specialising flowchart programs. In Janus, variables never die (as this would violate reversibility), so this particular trick can not be used for basic-block specialisation in Janus, but, as evidenced, the same basic idea is useful for procedures.

Procedures in Janus have no local variables. This means that the restriction that no global static variable can be modified in a procedure means that *no* static variable can be modified in a procedure. This means that a procedure, for example, can not have a statically controlled loop, which limits the usefulness of specialising procedures.

The residual program for the two-register machine interpreter has some very small residual procedures. If these were inlined, the speedup would have been higher.

We will investigate better approaches to procedure specialisation in the future. In addition to inlining/unfolding, a possibility is allowing modifications to static variables inside procedures if these updates are not control-dependent on dynamic variables, so there is only one possible sequence of updates to the static variables. This preserves the property that there is only one possible static state at the end of the procedure, so a well-formed residual procedure can be made. The static state is now modified by a residual call, so a procedure must be specialised immediately when called to find the modified static state, where the current specialiser postpones specialisation of a called procedure until specialisation of the current procedure (or main program) is finished.

Some extensions of Janus [14] include local variables and parameters to procedures. Adding such would make specialisation of procedures more useful even if no static global variables can be updated by procedures. C-mix [6], for example, does quite well with this restriction, as C procedures usually use local variables for loop counters and similar control-flow.

References

1. Abramsky, S.: A structural approach to reversible computation. Oxford University Computing Laboratory (2001) (manuscript)
2. Bennett, C.H.: Time/space trade-offs for reversible computation. SIAM Journal on Computing 18(4), 766–776 (1989)
3. Buhrman, H., Tromp, J., Vitányi, P.: Time and Space Bounds for Reversible Simulation. In: Orejas, F., Spirakis, P.G., van Leeuwen, J. (eds.) ICALP 2001. LNCS, vol. 2076, pp. 1017–1027. Springer, Heidelberg (2001)
4. Feynman, R.P.: Reversible computation and the thermodynamics of computing. Feynman Lectures on Computation, ch. 5, pp. 137–184. Addison-Wesley (1996)
5. Hatcliff, J., Mogensen, T.Æ., Thiemann, P. (eds.): Partial Evaluation. Practice and Theory. DIKU 1998 International Summer School. LNCS, vol. 1706. Springer, Heidelberg (1999)
6. Jones, N.D., Gomard, C.K., Sestoft, P.: Partial Evaluation and Automatic Program Generation. Prentice-Hall (1993)
7. Landauer, R.: Irreversibility and heat generation in the computing process. IBM Journal of Research and Development 5(3), 183–191 (1961)
8. Leuschel, M.: Logic Program Specialisation. In: Hatcliff, J., Mogensen, T.Æ., Thiemann, P. (eds.) Partial Evaluation. Practice and Theory. DIKU 1998 International Summer School. LNCS, vol. 1706, pp. 155–188. Springer, Heidelberg (1999)
9. Lutz, C.: Janus: a time-reversible language. A letter to Landauer (1986), http://www.cise.ufl.edu/~mpf/rc/janus.html
10. Mogensen, T.Æ.: Partial evaluation of the reversible language janus. In: submitted to PEPM 2010. ACM Press (2010)
11. Morita, K., Shirasaki, A., Gono, Y.: A 1-tape 2-symbol reversible turing machine. IEICE Transactions E72(3), 223–228 (1989)
12. Toffoli, T.: Reversible Computing. In: de Bakker, J.W., van Leeuwen, J. (eds.) ICALP 1980. LNCS, vol. 85, pp. 632–644. Springer, Heidelberg (1980)
13. Yokoyama, T., Axelsen, H.B., Glück, R.: Reversible Flowchart Languages and the Structured Reversible Program Theorem. In: Aceto, L., Damgård, I., Goldberg, L.A., Halldórsson, M.M., Ingólfsdóttir, A., Walukiewicz, I. (eds.) ICALP 2008, Part II. LNCS, vol. 5126, pp. 258–270. Springer, Heidelberg (2008)
14. Yokoyama, T., Axelsen, H.B., Glück, R.: Principles of a reversible programming language. In: Proceedings of the 5th Conference on Computing Frontiers, CF 2008, pp. 43–54. ACM, New York (2008)
15. Yokoyama, T., Glück, R.: A reversible programming language and its invertible self-interpreter. In: PEPM 2007: Proceedings of the 2007 ACM SIGPLAN Symposium on Partial Evaluation and Semantics-Based Program Manipulation, pp. 144–153. ACM, New York (2007)

Scalable Parallel Interval Propagation
for Sparse Constraint Satisfaction Problems

Evgueni Petrov

Intel
evgueni.s.petrov@gmail.com

Abstract. Multi-core processors have been broadly available to the public in the last five years. Parallelism has become a common design feature for computational intensive algorithms. In this paper we present a parallel implementation of an algorithm called interval constraint propagation for solution of constraint satisfaction problems over real numbers. Unlike existing implementations of this algorithm, our implementation scales well to many CPU cores with shared memory for sparse constraint satisfaction problems. We present scalability data for a quad-core processor on a number of benchmarks for non-linear constraint solvers.

1   Introduction

Constraint programming is a technique for solving constraint satisfaction problems. Many leaders in the areas of ecommerce, transport, energy, consumer electronics, automotive industry, information & computer technology, aerospace-defense-security, food & nutrition industry use constraint programming toolkits for scheduling, staff allocation, assignment, routing, and design [1].

Interval constraint propagation was introduced in [9]. It is a data-driven algorithm that contains a large amount of parallelism. Existing parallel implementations of constraint propagation scale well to many CPU cores with shared memory only if the constraint satisfaction problem is *dense*, that is, when each constraint involves a large number of variables. In such cases, the time required to process the constraints outweighs the time needed to update the set of constraints waiting to be processed, and scalability factor is limited only by the number of processors [2, 10, 12]. However large dense constraint satisfaction problems are rare. For this reason, recent papers on parallel constraint solvers over integral and real numbers focus on parallel exhaustive search in combination with sequential constraint propagation [11, 13, 14] rather than on pure parallel constraint propagation.

In this paper we present a parallel implementation of interval constraint propagation that scales well to many CPU cores with shared memory for dense and *sparse* constraint satisfaction problems, which has been a challenge for some time. In experiments with a quad-core processor, our implementation scales linearly with the number of processors on a number of benchmarks for constraint solvers over real numbers.

E. Clarke, I. Virbitskaite, and A. Voronkov (Eds.): PSI 2011, LNCS 7162, pp. 302–312, 2012.
© Springer-Verlag Berlin Heidelberg 2012

The paper is organized as follows. Sections 2 and 3 provide an overview of existing techniques in software parallelization and outline the general principles of interval constraint propagation. In Section 4, we describe our parallel implementation of interval constraint propagation. Section 5 reports scalability data that we obtained with our parallel implementation on a set of benchmarks on a quad-core processor.

2   Software Parallelization Techniques

Support for multi-core processors and multi-processor machines becomes a de facto standard for computation-intensive applications, which makes software manufacturers develop libraries and language extensions that automate parallelization. In this section we briefly review these means of parallelization from lower to higher level of the software stack: POSIX threads [4] and Windows threads libraries [5], Intel Threading Building Blocks library [6], OpenMP [7] and Cilk [8] language extensions. Concurrent programming languages such as SISAL [16] and distributed memory parallelism are out of our scope.

Ultimately, the libraries and extensions discussed in this section are functionally equivalent, that is we can program any parallel behavior using any of them. Below we point out the main differences between these libraries and language extensions.

POSIX threads and Windows threads provide threading and synchronization primitives that are very close to the level of the operating system and hence are the fastest. The application that uses such libraries is fully responsible for thread workload balance, thread data locality, and other higher level aspects of parallelization.

Intel (R) Threading Building Blocks (Intel TBB) library consists of a runtime resource manager and a C++ template library that provide higher level parallel constructs, such as parallel reduction, parallel for, blocked range, etc. The Intel TBB runtime resource manager takes some care of balancing thread workloads by transferring workload from overloaded CPU cores to idle CPU cores. The overhead introduced by the Intel TBB runtime resource manager is moderate for all available implementations.

The OpenMP and Cilk language extensions minimize the amount of changes in the source code that are needed to parallelize an existing sequential application. The OpenMP extension adds to the C and FORTRAN languages a number of pragmas that describe the parallelism existing in the source code. Similarly the Cilk extension describes parallelism by special keywords.

Overall, Cilk is more sophisticated than OpenMP. In addition to parallel sections, parallel for-loops, and parallel reduction that are supported by both OpenMP and Cilk, Cilk provides more mechanisms to balance thread workloads and to support nested parallelism. However the OpenMP extension is more mature than the Cilk extension that only starts to be supported by commercial compilers. For this reason, we use the OpenMP extension to C to present parallel interval constraint propagation.

3   Interval Constraint Propagation

Interval constraint propagation [9] was invented in the late 1980s. It was one of the first constraint programming algorithms for solving constraint satisfaction problems over real numbers. Given a set of constraints and a bounding box for the set of solutions to the constraints, interval constraint propagation reduces this bounding box without losing solutions. Below we give pseudocode for interval constraint propagation.

Let V be a set of variables that take values from the set $\mathbf{R}$ of real numbers. Let C be a set of constraints over V. Let proj(c, v) be the convex hull of projection of a constraint c (as a subset of some $\mathbf{R}^k$) to the variable v (as an axis of the same $\mathbf{R}^k$). We denote by dependent(v) $\subseteq C$ the set of all constraints that contain v. We denote by $c(v_1, v_2, ..., v_k)$ the fact that the constraint c contains only variables $v_1, v_2, ..., v_k$. We denote the empty set by { } and element selection (which can be non-deterministic) by select(). Finally, we denote the Cartesian product by ×.

Sequential interval constraint propagation is shown in Fig.1. Notice that we overload notation and use the variables V to denote the projections of the bounding box to the axes of the solution space (lines 6, 7, 9 in Fig.1). A useful optimization for inconsistent constraint satisfaction problems is to exit the while-loop as soon as *newvi* is empty (line 6 in Fig.1).

```
 1 Q = C;
 2 while (Q != {}) {
 3     c(v[1], v[2], ..., v[k]) = select(Q);
 4     Q = Q \ { c };
 5     for (i = 1; i <= k; k++) {
 6         newvi = proj(c ∩ v[1] × v[2] × ... × v[k], v[i]);
 7         if (v[i] != newvi) {
 8             Q = Q ∪ dependent(v[i]);
 9             v[i] = newvi;
10 }}}
```

Fig. 1. Sequential interval constraint propagation

A correctly rounded floating point implementation of interval constraint propagation terminates in finite time, preserves the set of solutions to C, and is deterministic despite a non-deterministic operation select (after the while-loop is exited, the bounding box for the set of solutions is the same regardless of the specific sequence of constraints returned by select in line 3 that can change from run to run).

Accurately computing the projections proj(c, v) for an arbitrary constraint c is computationally infeasible [15]. For this reason, most implementations of interval constraint propagation decompose c into simple constraints that involve one operation/function and two or three variables [9], and in most cases interval constraint propagation is applied to sparse constraint satisfaction problems. For example, since computing $x \cdot (1 - x)$ means first computing $r = 1 - x$ and then $y = x \cdot r$, the constraint $x \cdot (1 - x) < 1$ is replaced by constraints $r = 1 - x$, $y = x \cdot r$, and $y < 1$.

4   Parallel Interval Constraint Propagation

Interval constraint propagation is parallel by nature, because the bounding box for the set of solutions can be updated in parallel without damaging the correctness of the algorithm (line 6 in Fig.1).

Since parallelization applies mostly to loops, the first candidate for parallelization is the while-loop (line 2 in Fig.2). To ensure correctness, we need to protect the set of constraints by either an OpenMP critical section or by an OpenMP lock (similar to critical sections, not shown). A similar implementation with additional pre-processing of the constraint satisfaction problem is described in [10].

```
 1 Q = C;
 2 while (Q != {}) {
 3     #pragma omp parallel shared(Q, v[])
 4     {
 5         #pragma omp critical
 6         {
 7             c(v[1], v[2], ..., v[k]) = select(Q);
 8             Q = Q \ { c };
 9         }
10         for (i = 1; i <= k; k++) {
11             newvi = proj(c ∩ v[1] × v[2] × ... × v[k], v[i]);
12             if (v[i] != newvi) {
13                 #pragma omp critical
14                 {
15                     Q = Q ∪ dependent(v[i]);
16                     v[i] = newvi;
17                 }
18 }}}}
```

Fig. 2. Parallel interval constraint propagation with limited scalability

Notice that we do not need to serialize updates to the bounding box (line 11 in Fig.2), because they are monotonic with respect to the set inclusion. Though a thread may ignore some updates to the bounding box made by the other threads, this fact does not lead to a loss in precision since all threads share the same set of constraints. The worst consequence might be a minor loss in performance.

The problem with the algorithm in Fig.2 is that it serializes the updates to the set of constraints (lines 8 and 15 in Fig.2). This fact limits the gain from additional CPU cores for large constraint satisfaction problems, especially large sparse constraint satisfaction problems that consist of simple constraints. Under such conditions, updates to the bounding box are faster than updates to the set Q and, by the Amdahl's law, the scalability factor is limited by 2x for any number of CPU cores. This fact agrees well with the scalability data reported in [10] – 1.25x on a machine with 64 processors.

To avoid synchronization on the set Q in the algorithm in Fig.2, we give to each thread its own copy of Q and let the threads share the bounding box. The downside of this design is that updates to these copies do not propagate across threads and some thread may exit the constraint propagation loop too early. Such an event would decrease the scalability factor, because the constraint satisfaction problem C would be solved by one fewer CPU core. To preserve the scalability factor, each thread needs to restart constraint propagation while there is a chance to update the bounding box.

The resulting algorithm is shown in Fig.3a. Each thread tracks the size of the bounding box without synchronization with the other threads (line 14 in Fig.3a; the function width returns the width of intervals) and restarts constraint propagation until the bounding box is small enough   (line 15 in Fig.3a).

```
1  #pragma omp parallel shared(v[])
2  {
3       do {
4           Q = C; solved = 1;
5           while (Q != {}) {
6               c(v[1], v[2], ..., v[k]) = select(Q);
7               Q = Q \ { c };
8               for (i = 1; i <= k; k++) {
9                   newvi = proj(c ∩ v[1] × v[2] × ... × v[k], v[i]);
10                  if (v[i] != newvi) {
11                      Q = Q ∪ dependent(v[i]);
12                      v[i] = newvi;
13                  }
14                  solved *= width(v[i]) < ε;
15       }}} while (!solved);
16 }
```

Fig. 3a. Scalable parallel interval constraint propagation (convergent case)

The algorithm in Fig.3a has a serious problem: it enters an infinite loop (lines 3-15 in Fig.3a), if interval constraint propagation "stagnates" and cannot solve the constraint satisfaction problem C to the desired accuracy ε. In the ideal world, we would quickly recognize such constraint satisfaction problem by their syntax and would apply a different parallelization technique. In the real world, such syntactic checks are not invented yet and we have to recognize "stagnation" at runtime by tracking the number of the threads that execute the while-loop (lines 5-15 in Fig.3a). As soon as there are no such threads, the thread can exit the parallel section without loss in scalability and accuracy.

The algorithm that avoids the infinite loop is shown in Fig.3b. If interval constraint propagation converges to a small bounding box, the algorithms in Fig.3a and Fig.3b have the same scalability because the while-loop (lines 8-18 in Fig.3b) overweighs the serialized increments and decrements to the counter *alive* (lines 6-7 and 19-20 in Fig.3b). In case of "stagnation", the scalability factor for the implementation in Fig.3b is limited unless the "stagnation" happens after a long computation. In the next section, we show the scalability data for the algorithm shown in Fig.3b.

```
1  alive = 0;
2  #pragma omp parallel shared(v[], alive)
3  {
4      do {
5          Q = C; reduced = 0;
6          #pragma omp atomic
7              alive += 1;
8          while (Q != {}) {
9              c(v[1], v[2], …, v[k]) = select(Q);
10             Q = Q \ { c };
11             for (i = 1; i <= k; k++) {
12                 newvi = proj(c ∩ v[1] × v[2] × … × v[k], v[i]);
13                 if (v[i] != newvi) {
14                     Q = Q ∪ dependent(v[i]);
15                     v[i] = newvi;
16                     reduced = 1;
17                 }
18         }}
19         #pragma omp atomic
20             alive -= 1;
21     } while (reduced && alive);
22 }
```

Fig. 3b. Scalable parallel interval constraint propagation (general case)

5 Scalability of Parallel Interval Constraint Propagation

We experimented with benchmarks for constraint solvers over real numbers from the public AMPL repository [3]. Each problem involves 50-5000 variables and constraints. See the Appendix for sample problems used in the paper or visit the AMPL repository for more details.

We benchmarked our parallel implementation of interval constraint propagation on a quad-core machine at 3GHz and with 8G RAM. The best of 8 experimental runs was recorded for each problem and a given number of threads. Each OpenMP thread was pinned to a unique CPU core.

The table in Figure 4 shows the time (in seconds) spent by our parallel implementation of interval constraint propagation to solve each constraint satisfaction problem to accuracy of 10^{-4} or higher. The chart displays the speedup compared to one CPU core. The second column in the table in Fig.4 shows how sparse is each constraint satisfaction problem: the number of variables in the biggest constraint and the total number of variables in the constraint satisfaction problem. We see that our implementation scales linearly to many CPU cores for sparse and dense constraint satisfaction problems.

	#var (constr. / total)	1 core	2 cores	3 cores	4 cores
artif	3/5000	0.281	0.203	0.172	0.141
bdvalue	3/100	17.61	8.000	5.437	4.156
broydn3d	3/1000	2.625	0.641	0.422	0.297
cbratu2d	6/529	8.375	3.813	2.734	2.063
cbratu3d	9/2000	2.500	1.031	0.766	0.609
chandheq	64/64	0.188	0.078	0.063	0.047
chemrcta	5/200	47.38	20.06	13.72	9.547
chemrctb	2/100	9.671	5.203	3.078	2.391
integreq	127/127	3.969	1.984	1.469	1.203

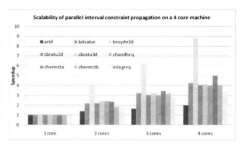

Fig. 4. Scalability data for parallel interval constraint propagation

6   Concluding Remarks

This paper presented a scalable parallel implementation of interval constraint propagation.

The value and the novelty of our implementation is that it scales well to many processors with shared memory for large sparse and dense constraint satisfaction problems. Our experiments showed that interval constraint propagation can be highly scalable even if the constraint satisfaction problem is sparse and each constraint involves very few variables. The key feature of our implementation that unlocks scalability for sparse constraint satisfaction problems is the very small amount of synchronization across the threads.

We plan to benchmark and tune our implementation of interval constraint propagation for machines with a large number of CPU cores. Another direction for our future research is to achieve scalability to many processors with shared memory in the case where interval constraint propagation stagnates.

References

1. van Beek, P., Walsh, T.: Principles of Constraint Programming and Constraint Processing: A Review. AI Magazine 25(4) (2004)
2. Rolf, C.C., Kuchcinski, K.: Parallel Consistency in Constraint Programming. In: Proc. Int. Conf. on Parallel and Distributed Processing Techniques and Applications (PDPTA), pp. 638–644. CSREA Press (2009)
3. Vanderbei, R.: Cute AMPL models,
    http://www.orfe.princeton.edu/~rvdb/ampl/nlmodels/cute/

4. The Open Group and IEEE. POSIX Threads // IEEE Standard 1003.1. – The Open Group and IEEE (2004)
5. Richter, J., Nasarre, C.: Windows (R) via C/C++, 5th edn. Microsoft Press (2007) ISBN 9780735624245
6. Reinders, J.: Intel Threading Building Blocks, p. 336. O'Reilly Print (2007) ISBN 9780596514808
7. The OpenMP API specification for parallel programming, http://openmp.org
8. Blumofe, R.D., Joerg, C.F., Kuszmaul, B.C., Leiserson, C.E., Randall, K.H., Zhou, Y.: Cilk: An Efficient Multithreaded Runtime System. In: Proc. 5th ACM SIGPLAN Symp. on Principles and Practice of Parallel Programming (PPoPP), pp. 207–216 (1995)
9. Davis, E.: Constraint propagation with interval labels. J. Artificial Intelligence 32(3) (1987)
10. Granvilliers, L., Hains, G.: A conservative scheme for parallel interval narrowing. J. Inf. Process. Lett. 74(3-4), 141–146 (2000)
11. Beelitz, T., Bischof, C.H., Lang, B., Althoff, K.S.: Result-Verifying Solution of Nonlinear Systems in the Analysis of Chemical Processes. In: Alt, R., Frommer, A., Kearfott, R.B., Luther, W. (eds.) Dagstuhl Seminar 2003. LNCS, vol. 2991, pp. 198–205. Springer, Heidelberg (2004) ISBN 3540212604
12. Kasif, S.: On the parallel complexity of discrete relaxation in constraint satisfaction networks. J. Artif. Intel. 45(3), 99–118 (1990)
13. Bordeaux, L., Hamadi, Y., Samulowitz, H.: Experiments with Massively Parallel Constraint Solving. In: Proc. Int. Joint Conf. on Artif. Intel., pp. 443–448 (2009)
14. Kalinnik, N., Schubert, T., Ábrahám, E., Wimmer, R., Becker, B.: Picoso - A Parallel Interval Constraint Solver. In: Proc. Int. Conf. on Parallel and Distributed Processing Techniques and Applications (PDPTA), pp. 473–479. CSREA Press (2009)
15. Rohn, J., Kreinovich, V.: Computing exact componentwise bounds on solutions of linear systems with interval data is NP-hard. SIAM J. Matr. Anal. Appl. 16, 415–420 (1995)
16. Cann, D.: Retire Fortran?: a debate rekindled. Communications of the ACM 35(8) (1992)

Appendix

For convenience, this section lists the constraint satisfaction problems from the public AMPL repository [3] that we used to benchmark our parallel implementation of interval constraint propagation.

artif
```
const int N = 5000;
all (i = 2, 1, N+1; x[i] >= 0.00001;
(-0.05*(x[i] + x[i+1] + x[i-1]) + atg( sin( i*x[i] ) )) = 0);
x[1] = 0.0; x[N+2] = 0.0;
```

Mathematical notation for the same constraints is $N = 5000$, $x_1 = x_{N+2} = 0$, $x_i \geq 0.00001$, and $-0.05 \cdot (x_i + x_{i+1} + x_{i-1}) + \arctg \sin(i \cdot x_i) = 0$ for $i = 2, \ldots, N+1$.

bdvalue
```
const int ndp = 100;
h=1/(ndp-1);
all(i = 2, 1, ndp-1; x[i] > -1;
( -x[i-1]+2*x[i]-x[i+1]+0.5*h^2*(x[i]+i*h+1)^3 ) = 0);
x[1] = 0.0; x[ndp] = 0.0;
```

broydn3d
```
const int N = 1000;
kappa1 = 2.0, kappa2 = 1.0;
all(i = 1, 1, N; x[i] = [-1,1]);
(-2*x[2]+kappa2+(3-kappa1*x[1])*x[1]) = 0;
all(i = 2, 1, N-1; (-x[i-1]-2*x[i+1]+kappa2+(3-kappa1*x[i])*x[i]) = 0);
(-x[N-1]+kappa2+(3-kappa1*x[N])*x[N]) = 0;
```

cbratu2d
```
const int p = 23;
lambda = 5.0; h = 1/(p-1); c = h^2/lambda;
all(i = 2, 1, p-1; all(j = 2, 1, p-1;
      (4*u[i,j]-u[i+1,j]-u[i-1,j]-u[i,j+1]-u[i,j-1]-
      c*exp(u[i,j])*cos(x[i,j])) = 0));
all(i = 2, 1, p-1; all(j = 2, 1, p-1;
      (4*x[i,j]-x[i+1,j]-x[i-1,j]-x[i,j+1]-x[i,j-1]-
              c*exp(u[i,j])*sin(x[i,j])) = 0));
all(j = 1, 1, p; all(i = 1, 1, p; u[i,j] = [-1,1]; x[i,j] = [-1,1]));
all(j = 1, 1, p; u[1,j] = 0.0; u[p,j] = 0.0; x[1,j] = 0.0; x[p,j] = 0.0);
all(i = 2, 1, p-1; u[i,p] = 0.0; u[i,1] = 0.0; x[i,p] = 0.0; x[i,1] = 0.0);
```

cbratu3d
```
const int p = 10;
lambda = 6.80812; h = 1/(p-1); c = h^2/lambda;
all(i = 2, 1, p-1; all( j = 2, 1, p-1; all(k = 2, 1, p-1;
      u[i,j,k] = [-1, 1]; x[i,j,k] = [-1, 1];
      (6*u[i,j,k]-u[i+1,j,k]-u[i-1,j,k]-u[i,j+1,k]-u[i,j-1,k]-
      u[i,j,k-1]-u[i,j,k+1]-c*exp(u[i,j,k])*cos(x[i,j,k])) = 0;
      (6*x[i,j,k]-x[i+1,j,k]-x[i-1,j,k]-x[i,j+1,k]-x[i,j-1,k]-
      u[i,j,k-1]-u[i,j,k+1]-c*exp(u[i,j,k])*sin(x[i,j,k])) = 0
)));
all(j = 1, 1, p; all(k = 1, 1, p;
      u[1,j,k] = 0.0; u[p,j,k] = 0.0; x[1,j,k] = 0.0; x[p,j,k] = 0.0
));
all(i = 2, 1, p-1; all( k = 1, 1, p;
      u[i,p,k] = 0.0; u[i,1,k] = 0.0; x[i,p,k] = 0.0; x[i,1,k] = 0.0
));
```

```
all(i = 2, 1, p-1; all(j = 2, 1, p-1;
      u[i,j,1] = 0.0; u[i,j,p] = 0.0; x[i,j,1] = 0.0; x[i,j,p] = 0.0
));
```

chandheq
```
const int n = 64;
c = 1;
all(i = 1, 1, n; x[i] = i/n; w[i] = 1/n; h[i] = [0, 1]);
all(i = 1, 1, n;
      sum (j = 1, 1, n; -0.5*c*w[j]/(x[i]+x[j])*h[j]*x[i]*h[i]
      + h[i]) = 1.0
);
```

chemrcta
```
const int n = 100;
pem = 1.0; peh = 5.0; d = 0.135; b = 0.5;
beta = 2.0; gamma = 25.0; h = 1/(n-1);
cu1 = -h*pem; cui1 = 1/(h^2*pem)+1/h; cui = -1/h - 2/(h^2*pem);
ct1 = -h*peh; cti1 = 1/(h^2*peh)+1/h; cti = -beta -1/h -
2/(h^2*peh);
all(i=1,1,n; t[i] = [0,1]; u[i] = [0,1]);
(cu1*u[2]-u[1]+h*pem) = 0; (ct1*t[2]-t[1]+h*peh) = 0;
all(i=2,1,n-1;
      (-d*u[i]*exp(gamma-gamma/t[i])+(cui1)*u[i-1] + cui*u[i] +
      u[i+1]/(h^2*pem)) = 0;
      (b*d*u[i]*exp(gamma-gamma/t[i])+(cti1)*t[i-1] + cti*t[i]
      + t[i+1]/(h^2*peh)) = 0
);
(u[n]-u[n-1]) = 0; (t[n]-t[n-1]) = 0;
```

chemctrb
```
const int n = 100;
pe = 5.0; d = 0.135; b = 0.5; gamma = 25.0;
h = 1/(n-1); ct1 = -h*pe; cti1 = 1/h + 1/(h^2*pe); cti = -1/h-
2/(h^2*pe);
all(i = 1, 1, n; t[i] <= 1);
(ct1*t[2]-t[1]+h*pe) = 0; (t[n]-t[n-1]) = 0;
all(i = 2, 1, n-1;
      d*(b+1-t[i])*exp(gamma-gamma/t[i])+cti1*t[i-
1]+cti*t[i]+t[i+1]/(h^2*pe)=0
);
```

```
integreq
const int N=127;
h = 1/(N+1); x[1] = 0; x[N+2] = 0;
all(i = 1, 1, N; t[i+1] = i*h; x[i+1] < 1);
all(i = 1, 1, N;
        (   x[i+1]+h*(    (1-t[i+1])*sum    (j    =    1,    1,    i;
        t[j+1]*(x[j+1]+t[j+1]+1)^3)  +  t[i+1]*sum(j  =  i+1,  1,  N;
        (1-t[j+1])*(x[j+1]+t[j+1]+1)^3)/2)  )  = 0
);
```

A Combined Technique for Automatic Detection of Backward Binary Compatibility Problems

Andrey Ponomarenko and Vladimir Rubanov

ROSA Lab, Russia
{andrey.ponomarenko,rubanov}@rosalab.ru

Abstract. This paper discusses the problem of ensuring backward compatibility between new and old versions of software components (e.g., libraries). Linux environment is considered as the main example. Breakage of the compatibility in a new version of a software component may result in crashing or incorrect behavior (at binary level) or inability to build (at source level) of applications targeted at a previous version of the component when the applications are used with the new version of the component. The paper describes typical issues that cause backward compatibility problems at binary level and presents a new method for automatic detection of such issues during component development (focusing on changes in structure of interfaces). C/C++ language is used as the main example. Unlike the existing means, the suggested method can verify a broad spectrum of backward compatibility problems by comparing function signatures and type definitions obtained from the component's header files in addition to analyzing symbols in the component's binaries. Also, this paper describes an automated checker tool that implements the suggested method with some results of its practical usage.

Keywords: backward compatibility, software interfaces (API and ABI), software components, libraries, static checking.

1 Introduction

Software components that provide application programming interfaces (API) to other software components play an important role in the architecture of computing systems. Such components can be combined together to form whole *software platforms*. Usually, one may distinguish three main layers in the software stack of a computing system - operating system kernel, system libraries and applications. System libraries rely on the kernel and each other to provide higher level functionality API to applications.

In the modern operating systems and especially in Linux, there are a lot of system libraries and other software components that are rapidly evolving with new versions appearing quite frequently, every few months in average. Applications are developed in parallel with this evolution. As a result, different versions of applications rely on different versions of system components. And it is typical that a system library has to be updated in the system to meet the needs of a new application being installed into

E. Clarke, I. Virbitskaite, and A. Voronkov (Eds.): PSI 2011, LNCS 7162, pp. 313–321, 2012.

the system. But it is crucially important to ensure that the new version of the library keeps binary compatibility with the previous version so that old applications continue working together with the new library version successfully.

Backward binary compatibility is a characteristic of a new version of a software component against an old version of the same component to guarantee that applications (and other components) working with the old version keep working correctly with the new version without recompilation.

Source level backward compatibility means that applications and other dependent components need to be rebuilt in order to work with the new version of the base component. But no changes in source code are necessary – only recompilation and rebuild.

There are *intentional and unintentional changes* that can break backward compatibility. Intentional changes may occur when developers of the library decide that breaking compatibility is paid off by some significant additional value that is impossible without applying the change. Unintentional changes occur when developers do not realize that some changes in the code can result in breaking backward compatibility (at binary or source level or both) because they are focused on solving functional problems at the moment of the change.

There are well-known public stories when developers of libraries came to know about breaking backward compatibility from user complaints after releasing new versions of their libraries. For example, in October 2007 developers of the popular C++ standard library libstdc++ occasionally changed the order of declaring methods in a class, which resulted in changing the structure of the corresponding virtual table and loosing backward binary compatibility with the previous versions. This was a bright example of an unintentional compatibility break. In 2009 FreeType2 developers changed the structure of PS_FontInfoRec_ data type, but this resulted in many complaints from users so that FreeType2 had to revert the change in the next version of the library. One of the recent cases (Nov 2010) that created high user resonance was removing symbol versions from the 2.7.8 release of libxml2 library.

This paper discusses the problem of easy automated verification of backward compatibility for software components. The first step towards this goal is *static analysis of the structural changes in the component interfaces* at the binary level and it is this step that is the focus of the article. The main advantage of this step is that it can be easily applied to any component without significant efforts while allowing to detect quite a number of practical issues (see statistics in Section 4). C/C++ programming languages and Linux are used as the target environment in this article. Meanwhile, the static analysis of the structure of binary interfaces cannot detect changes that affect backward compatibility through changing function's semantics (behavior). That's why we suggest the further steps if this level of changes needs to be checked. Generally, for detecting backward compatibility problems related with changes in semantics, it is recommended to use *run-time testing techniques* (e.g., see [1]-[7] for Linux domain specific run-time testing frameworks).

The paper contains three main sections. The first section presents classification of the most popular problems in backward binary compatibility and their root causes. The second section overviews existing approaches to mitigate the backward binary compatibility issues. The third section contains the description of the presented approach for the "first step" and the corresponding tool with some results of its practical usage. Steps to further improve automatic means for backward compatibility verification are discussed in the conclusion.

2   Types of Backward Binary Compatibility Problems and Their Root Causes

We have identified 8 main types of changes in C/C++ source code of library implementations that can cause various backward binary compatibility problems. This analysis was performed based on available papers describing rules for developing libraries for Linux [8]-[10] and based on studying C/C++ function calling conventions in Application Binary Interface (ABI) specifications of the most popular microprocessor architectures such as x86, x86-64, PowerPC, Itanium, S390 and ARM.

The main types of backward binary compatibility problems identified are:

1. Removing Functions from the Library
2. Changing Virtual Table Structure
3. Changing the Number or Order of Function Parameters
4. Changing "static" Specifier of Class Methods
5. Changing Types of Function Parameters
6. Changing Type of Function Return Value
7. Changing Values in Enumeration Types or Macros
8. Overriding Virtual Functions.

The research on identifying other types of dangerous changes is still in progress (now we are performing systematic analysis of the C and C++ language standards). Meanwhile, the identified 8 types cover the major part of the changes that we have seen in our practice (also see statistics in Section 4).

3   Existing Approaches to Address Backward Compatibility

There are a number of methods used by library and application developers to mitigate risks associated with breaking backward binary compatibility in new versions of software components. These methods include both technical and organizational means.

There are tools that can automatically check for missing symbols in the new library version against some old library version (**checker tools for symbol presence**). Examples include dpkg-gensymbols [11], chkshlib [12], cmpdylib [13], cmpshlib [14]. These tools extract lists of public symbols from two versions of the library and compare them. The tools use only binary versions of libraries to perform this analysis. Unfortunately, this allows detecting only the first type of issues (Excluding Functions from the Library) and not all the types described in Section 2.

Creating **run-time tests** that can be run against new library versions and detect all dangerous changes both in ABI structure and semantics is the most powerful technical method to prevent backward compatibility regressions. There are frameworks for automated development of run-time tests (e.g., [1]-[7]). But the main problem is that run-time tests have to be specifically developed for every API in the target software component. This means huge amount of effort for creating a run-time testing suite for each target component. In real world, only few developers can afford creating good run-time testing suites for their components.

There are a number of approaches based on creating **compatibility layers** on top of the new library version that can simulate binary interface of the old library version [15]-[17]. Such compatibility layers seem to applications as if they are the old library and they translate all old ABI calls to proper ABI calls of the new library. Construction of a compatibility layer can be usually automated based on some formal description/specification of the mapping between the old and the new ABI. However, such mappings must be created manually and thus cover only *known* (intentional) changes of ABI and may miss occasional changes that break ABI unintentionally. ReBA approach [17] suggests fully automated solution for constructing compatibility layers based on analyzing the log of specific refactoring code changes that were applied to the old library version to get the new one. Such logs can be retrieved from an IDE like Eclipse that automatically logs all refactorings and deletions. However, full change logs are not always available. One more common drawback of compatibility layers that should be mentioned is performance and memory overhead.

The main method for indicating the degree of changes in backward binary compatibility of a new library version is **explicit version numbering (versioning)**. At the library level, each library has a name (soname) that reflects the major version of the library ABI. Applications are built against particular version of library (soname) and will fail to load if the library with the same soname is missing in the system. Changing soname of a library means significant incompatible changes in ABI. Meanwhile, library versioning is just the means of communicating intentional ABI changes from library developers to library users. Unfortunately, there are cases when unintentional ABI changes occur even when just micro version of the component is changed (for example, see the cases mentioned in the Introduction).

GNU development environment allows **versioning of binary symbols** in libraries. This enables existence of several implementations of the same function in a library. The scenario for using this is adding a new function implementation version each time any incompatible changes in function behavior or ABI occur. Applications can be built to use specific versions of necessary functions. So, for example, the same library can provide old function version to one application and the new function version to another. This approach helps to maintain backward binary compatibility for the cost of increasing library size and complexity of maintaining the number of different function implementations. Of course this method works only for intentional changes in binary compatibility and cannot prevent problems due to unintentional effects.

It is possible for application developers to **statically link** a specific version of necessary library with the application code. In this case, there is no external dependency on system library and thus no problem of backward binary compatibility arises at all. However, this way has two significant drawbacks - increasing the size of application binary and inability to update the library without application recompilation. The latter issue is best seen when some security updates are released for the library. Static linking will prevent using the updated library version and will expose the application to the security problems. In the normal scenario of using shared library the problem would be automatically fixed during regular system update.

4   Suggested Method and Tool

Our approach is targeted at enabling an automated tool that can check all the kinds of changes that cause backward binary compatibility problems described in Section 2. In order to achieve this, we suggest not just analyzing binaries of the target library versions but also parsing library header files and comparing type definitions and function signatures in the corresponding intermediate representations of the syntax tree structures. We have implemented this approach in a tool called abi-compliance-checker. Some interesting details of internal architecture and design findings are presented below.

At the first stage, the abi-compliance-checker tool uses readelf utility to extract the lists of symbols (including different symbol versions) from the old and new library binaries (.so files). This allows understanding which functions are exposed as public for the library and detect added/removed functions.

At the second stage, we take two sets of library headers and feed them to gcc parser with the additional fdump-translation-unit and fdump-class-hierarchy options, which allows dumping intermediate representation of the syntax trees and consequently allows structured understanding of signatures of all functions and corresponding data type definitions as well as the layout of class v-tables.

Based on this information it is possible to analyze the two dumps of information and automatically detect all the changes that can cause problems presented in the Section 2. The analysis is done using "function by function" comparison of function signatures in the two syntax trees. Corresponding subtrees for each function are recursively traversed and corresponding nodes (parameters, return values, their types and constituent subtypes, etc.) are compared to analyze if their differences are "dangerous" or not (e.g., if the size of the type is changed or not).

We divide found issues into three categories by their "severity level" - high, medium or low. High severity issues include missing entire binary symbols, medium severity issues cover possible data corruption or misreads and, finally, low severity issues indicate changes that can be reflections of possibly incompatible semantic changes. Detailed mapping between different code changes and their severity levels is given in Table 1.

Table 1. Severity of Code Changes that Affect Backward Binary Compatibility

Kind of Changes		Language	Severity
Removing functions from the library		C/C++	High
Changing virtual table structure		C++	High
Changing the number or order of parameters		C++	High
		C	Medium
Removing the last parameter with non-important semantics		C	Low
Changing type of a parameter	destructive	C/C++	Medium
	non-destructive	C++	Medium
	non-destructive	C	Low
Changing type of return value	struct <-> intrinsic	C/C++	Medium
	destructive	C/C++	Medium
	non-destructive	C/C++	Low
Adding/removing "static" specifier of a method		C++	Medium
Changing values in Enumeration types or macros		C/C++	Low
Overriding virtual functions		C++	Low

Sometimes, it is not obvious what the specific library consists of in terms of particular files in the system. To "define" each library version we support so called "library descriptor" as an additional input to the abi-compliance checker tool that identifies the necessary library version to analyze. Such descriptor is created separately for each library version as an XML-file with three main sections - <version>, <headers> and <libs>. <version> section sets the library version id to use in the reports. <headers> section defines paths to directories or individual files that contain library header files. <libs> section defines paths to directories or individual files with binary .so files for the library. Please note that a library may contain more than one .so file and we support this scenario by allowing analyzing the set of files as a whole.

Also, there are a number of optional sections in the library descriptor that can specify additional data necessary to correctly parse the header files, resolve external undefined symbols, skip some headers, individual functions or opaque types because some of them can be internal and should not be included in ABI compatibility analysis to prevent false positives in the reports.

An HTML report is generated as output of the abi-compliance-checker tool, which visualizes the results of comparing ABI of two versions of the input library. All issues are divided by category (issues with functions and issues with data types) and by severity. For all data type issues, lists of particular functions they affect are presented.

Results in the abi-compliance-checker report can be filtered in the context of a specific application. There is an optional parameter that specifies an application binary. If this parameter is provided then abi-compliance-checker will automatically detect all external functions (binary symbols) that are required by this application from the examined library and will report only those backward binary compatibility issues that affect this particular application (i.e., problems in the functions or corresponding data types that are actually used by the application).

Table 2. Detected ABI Changes in Practical Study

Kind of ABI Change Detected		Severity	Count	%
Removing functions from the library		High	10040	51.72%
Changing virtual table structure		High	300	1.55%
Changing the number or order of parameters		Medium	445	2.29%
Changing type of a parameter	destructive	Medium	1971	10.15%
	non-destructive	Low	3923	20.21%
Changing type of return value	destructive	Medium	23	0.12%
	non-destructive	Low	633	3.26%
Adding/removing "static" specifier		Medium	26	0.13%
Changing values in Enumeration types or macros		Low	1291	6.65%
Overriding Virtual Functions		Low	760	3.92%

The abi-compliance-checker has been tested on 255 Linux libraries (78 C++ and 177 C) (as of 15.02.2011). When selecting the libraries we tried to cover the most popular ones - we used information about the usage frequency of various libraries available in the LSB Navigator [18] and we preferred libraries included in the Linux Standard Base (LSB) [19].

Over 4943 different versions have been processed of the 255 libraries (usually, there were many different versions of the same library, which were analyzed sequentially). 19412 issues with backward binary compatibility have been detected. Distinction between intentional and unintentional changes has not been inspected. Statistics for the detected change kinds are given in Table 2. Detailed data on particular changes detected in this analysis have been published in [20]. Please note that Table 2 contains fewer lines than Table 1. This is because Table I is for source code changes while Table 2 is for the consequences of these changes at the binary level. So some kinds of source code changes merge to the same kind of binary compatibility problem, for example, changing the number or order of parameters in a C++ method leads to excluding the old binary symbol at all.

The tool has been accepted in the Alt Linux, Debian, FreeBSD, Gentoo, Haiku, Maemo, Mandriva and Ubuntu repositories and has been included as an additional checking step into the installation procedure managed by apt and rpm5 tools.

Developers of libssh and Barry library have acknowledged the tool and included it in the main development cycle as mandatory QA step. Also, to the authors' knowledge, Juniper Routers, Nokia, MStar and Samsung companies have been using the tool as part of their internal QA cycle.

5   Conclusion

In this paper, we have discussed the problem of backward binary compatibility between evolving versions of shared software components. C/C++ and Linux environment were used as the main example. Meanwhile, the approach and the findings are applicable to other operating systems, specific ABI conventions and programming languages. We have identified 8 different types of possible changes in component source code that can cause breakage of binary interface structure. We have suggested a method based on combined binary and header source code static analysis and developed a corresponding `abi-compliance-checker` tool for automatic detection of all the identified types of issues, which is not available in the existing tools of the kind. The tool can help component developers to automatically catch *unintended* changes in the ABI structure in new versions of their components and thus maintain backward binary compatibility guarantee for their users. Using the modern mechanisms described in Section 3 for communicating *intended* ABI changes can leverage the tool and help component developers to deliver consistent policy in changing component ABI as it evolves. The `abi-compliance-checker` is a free open-source tool published in [21] and is available in a number of major Linux repositories. Also, the tool has been adopted by a number of industrial companies.

Finally, we believe that the presented method and the tool represent implementation of just the first step (though self-sufficient step) towards automatic verification of backward compatibility at various levels. The main advantage of this approach is that it is easy and cheap to use without regard to the target component's size and the number of its interfaces. Also it does not require a working run-time environment in order to do the analysis. Meanwhile, if necessary, the next steps can employ actual execution of the target component in a working environment and should be based on run-time testing to be able to check semantic changes in the component's interfaces.

In future work, we plan to do systematic analysis of C and C++ reference standards in order to identify more types of possible "dangerous" changes that can cause breakage of backward compatibility separately for binary and source levels. We will implement detection of these changes in the new versions of the `abi-compliance-checker` tool (to be renamed to `backward-compatibility-checker` to reflect capability of detecting both source and binary level issues). Analysis of backward compatibility problems for other programming languages (first of all C# and Java) and developing checker tools for other development platforms (first of all Windows) is also the topic of future work.

References

1. Kuliamin, V., Petrenko, A., Kossatchev, A., Bourdonov, I.: UniTesK: Model Based Testing in Industrial Practice. In: Proc. of 1st European Conference on Model-Driven Software Engineering, Nurnberg, Germany, pp. 55–63 (December 2003)
2. Kuliamin, V.: Model Based Testing of Large-scale Software: How Can Simple Models Help to Test Complex System. In: Proc. of 1st International Symposium on Leveraging Applications of Formal Methods, Cyprus, pp. 311–316 (October 2004)
3. Grinevich, A., Khoroshilov, A., Kuliamin, V.V., Markovtsev, D., Petrenko, A.K., Rubanov, V.: Formal Methods in Industrial Software Standards Enforcement. In: Virbitskaite, I., Voronkov, A. (eds.) PSI 2006. LNCS, vol. 4378, pp. 456–466. Springer, Heidelberg (2007) ISBN 978-3-540-70880-3

4. Zybin, R.S., Kuliamin, V.V., Ponomarenko, A.V., Rubanov, V.V., Chernov, E.S.: Automation of broad sanity test generation. In: Programming and Computer Software, vol. 34(6), pp. 351–363. Springer, Heidelberg (2008); ISSN 0361-7688 (Print), ISSN 1608-3261 (Online), doi: 10.1134/S0361768808060066

5. Khoroshilov, A., Rubanov, V., Shatokhin, E.: Automated Formal Testing of C API Using T2C Framework. In: Leveraging Applications of Formal Methods, Verification and Validation: Proceedings of 3rd Intl. Symposium, ISoLA 2008, Porto Sani, Greece, October 13-15. CCIS, vol. 17, part 3, pp. 56–70. Springer, Heidelberg (2009), ISSN 1865-0929, ISBN 978-3-540-88478-1, doi: 10.1007/978-3-540-88479-8_5

6. Ponomarenko, A., Rubanov, V.: Header-Driven Generation of Sanity API Tests for Shared Libraries. In: Proceedings of the Sixth International Conference on Software Engineering (CEE-SECR 2010), Moscow, October 11-15, pp. 92–95 (2010) (in Russian)

7. Drepper, U.: How to write shared libraries (December 2010), `http://www.akkadia.org/drepper/dsohowto.pdf` (link checked on April 30, 2011)

8. KDE TechBase. Policies/Binary Compatibility Issues With C++, `http://developer.kde.org/documentation/other/binarycompatibility.html` (link checked on April 30, 2011)

9. Wheeler, D.A.: Program Library HOWTO.V. 1.36 (May 15, 2010), `http://www.dwheeler.com/program-library/Program-Library-HOWTO.pdf` (link checked on April 30, 2011)

10. dpkg-gensymbols, `http://man.he.net/man1/dpkg-gensymbols` (link checked on April 30, 2011)

11. chkshlib, `http://osr507doc.sco.com/en/man/html.CP/chkshlib.CP.html` (link checked on April 30, 2011)

12. cmpdylib, `http://developer.apple.com/documentation/Darwin/Reference/ManPages/man1/cmpdylib.1.html` (link checked on April 30, 2011)

13. cmpshlib, `http://www.myths.com/pub/doc/oh_really/unix_bookshelf_3.0/mac/ch07_01.htm` (link checked on April 30, 2011)

14. Savga, I., Rudolf, M.: Refactoring-based support for binary compatibility in evolving frameworks. In: GPCE 2007: Proc. of Generative Programming and Component Engineering, pp. 175–184 (2007)

15. Savga, I., Rudolf, M., Sliwerski, J., Lehmann, J., Wendel, H.: API Changes - How FarWould You Go? In: Proc. of 11th European Conference on Software Maintenance and Reengineering (CSMR 2007), pp. 329–330 (2007)

16. Dig, D., Negara, S., Johnson, R., Mohindra, V.: ReBA: refactoring-aware binary adaptation of evolving libraries. In: Proceedings of the 30th International Conference on Software Engineering, pp. 441–450 (2008)

17. LSB Navigator, `http://dev.linuxfoundation.org/navigator/browse/app_stats.php` (link checked on April 30, 2011)

18. Linux Standard Base, `http://www.linuxbase.org` (link checked on April 30, 2011)

19. Linux Upstream Tracker Demo, `http://linuxtesting.org/upstream-tracker/index.html` (link checked on April 30, 2011)

20. ABI Compliance Checker Home Page, `http://ispras.linuxfoundation.org/index.php/ABI_compliance_checker` (link checked on April 30, 2011)

Weighted Lumpability on Markov Chains

Arpit Sharma [*] and Joost-Pieter Katoen [**]

RWTH Aachen University, Software Modeling and Verification Group, Germany
{arpit.sharma,katoen}@cs.rwth-aachen.de

Abstract. This paper reconsiders Bernardo's T-lumpability on continuous-time Markov chains (CTMCs). This notion allows for a more aggressive state-level aggregation than ordinary lumpability. We provide a novel structural definition of (what we refer to as) weighted lumpability, prove some elementary properties, and investigate its compatibility with linear real-time objectives. The main result is that the probability of satisfying a deterministic timed automaton specification coincides for a CTMC and its weigthed lumped analogue. The same holds for metric temporal logic formulas.

Keywords: continuous-time Markov chain, bisimulation, weighted lumpability, deterministic timed automaton, metric temporal logic.

1 Introduction

Continuous-time Markov chains (CTMCs) have a wide applicability ranging from classical performance evaluation to systems biology. Various branching-time relations on CTMCs have been defined such as weak and strong variants of bisimulation equivalence and simulation pre-orders. Strong bisimulation coincides with ordinary lumping equivalence [11]. Their compatibility to (fragments of) stochastic variants of CTL has been thoroughly investigated, cf. [4]. These relations allow for a state-space reduction prior to model checking; in particular, bisimulation minimisation yields considerable reductions and time savings [15] thanks to an efficient minimisation algorithm [13,19].

This paper focuses on a notion of lumpability that allows for a more aggressive state-space aggregation than ordinary lumpability. It originates by Bernardo [6] who considered Markovian testing equivalence over sequential Markovian process calculus (SMPC), and coined the term T-lumpability for the induced state-level aggregation where T stands for testing. His testing equivalence coincides with ready trace equivalence on CTMCs [20], it is a congruence w.r.t. parallel composition, and preserves transient as well as steady-state probabilities [6]. A logical characterisation via a variant of Hennessy-Milner logic has been given in [9,8] establishing the preservation of expected delays. Bernardo defines T-lumpability using four process-algebraic axioms, and alternatively, calls two states T-lumpable if their expected delays w.r.t. any testing process coincide. In this paper, we take a different route and start from a structural definition using first Markov chain principles. As so-called weighted rates are the key to this definition we baptize it weighted lumpability.

---

[*] Supported by the European Commission under the India4EU project.
[**] Supported by the European Commission under the MoVeS project, FP7-ICT-2009-257005.

E. Clarke, I. Virbitskaite, and A. Voronkov (Eds.): PSI 2011, LNCS 7162, pp. 322–339, 2012.
© Springer-Verlag Berlin Heidelberg 2012

Whereas ordinary lumpability compares states on the basis of their direct successors —the cumulative probability to directly move to any equivalence class must be equal— weighted lumpability (WL, for short) considers a *two-step* perspective. Before explaining the main principle of WL, let us recall that every transition of a CTMC is labeled with a positive real number λ. This parameter indicates the rate of the exponential distribution, i.e., the probability of a λ-labeled transition to be enabled within t time units equals $1 - e^{-\lambda \cdot t}$. In fact, the average residence time in a state is determined as the reciprocal of the sum of the rates of its outgoing transitions. Roughly speaking, two states s and s' are weighted lumpable if for each pair of their direct predecessors the weighted rate to directly move to any equivalence class via the equivalence class $[s] = [s']$ coincides. The main principle is captured in Fig. 1 where $\lambda_{1,1} + \lambda_{1,2} = \lambda_{2,1} + \lambda_{2,2}$, and $\lambda_{C_1} = p_1 \cdot \lambda_{1,1}$, $\lambda_{C_2} = p_1 \cdot \lambda_{1,2} + p_2 \cdot \lambda_{2,1}$, $\lambda_{C_3} = p_2 \cdot \lambda_{2,2}$ with $p_1 = \frac{\lambda_1}{\lambda_1 + \lambda_2}$ and $p_2 = \frac{\lambda_2}{\lambda_1 + \lambda_2}$. Here states s_1 and s_2 are weighted lumpable, as the probability to move from s_0 to all the states in the equivalence class C_i (for $i=1, 2, 3$) via all the states in $[s_1]$ is equal. This allows for the aggregation of s_1 and s_2, cf. the right CTMC in Fig. 1.

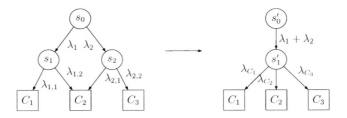

Fig. 1. CTMC aggregation under weighted lumpability

In this paper we define WL as a *structural* notion on CTMCs. We define the quotient under WL, and show that any CTMC is equivalent to its quotient under WL. Our structural definition allows for a simple proof that WL is (strictly) coarser than bisimulation, i.e., ordinary lumpability. Our main focus and motivation, however, is to investigate the preservation of *linear real-time objectives* under WL. We first show that the probability of satisfying a deterministic timed automaton (DTA) [1] specification for any CTMC coincides with that probability for its quotient. This allows for an a priori state-space reduction in linear real-time CTMC model checking [12,5], and implies the preservation of "flat" (i.e., unnested) timed reachability properties and CSL^{TA} formulas [14]. In addition, we study metric temporal logic (MTL) [16], a real-time variant of LTL that is typically used for timed automata (and not for CTMCs). DTA and MTL have incomparable expressiveness [17,3,10]. It is shown that WL-quotienting of CTMCs preserves the probability to satisfy any MTL formula. As a prerequisite result, we show that MTL formulas (interpreted on CTMCs) are measurable.

Organisation of the paper. Section 2 briefly recalls the main concepts of CTMCs. Section 3 defines weighted lumpability and treats some basic properties. Sections 4 and 5 discuss the preservation of DTA properties and MTL-formulas, respectively. Finally, Section 6 concludes the paper. All the proofs are contained in the appendix.

2   Continuous-Time Markov Chains

This section presents the necessary definitions and basic concepts related to continuous-time Markov chains that are needed for the understanding of the rest of this paper.

Definition 1 (CTMC). *A (labeled) continuous-time Markov chain (CTMC) is a tuple* $\mathcal{M} = (S, R, AP, L, s_0)$ *where:*

- *S is a non-empty finite set of states,*
- $R : S \times S \rightarrow \mathbb{R}_{\geq 0}$ *is a rate function,*
- *AP is a finite set of atomic propositions,*
- $L : S \rightarrow 2^{AP}$ *is a labeling function,*
- $s_0 \in S$ *is the initial state.*

The *exit rate* $E(s)$ for state $s \in S$ is defined by $E(s) = \sum_{s' \in S} R(s, s')$. A state s is called *absorbing* iff $E(s) = 0$. The semantics of a CTMC is defined as follows. The probability of moving from s to s' in a single step is defined by $P(s, s') = \frac{R(s,s')}{E(s)}$, if s is non-absorbing and $P(s, s') = 0$ otherwise. The probability to exit state s within t time units is given by $1 - e^{-E(s) \cdot t}$. The probability to move from a non-absorbing state s to s' within t time units equals $P(s, s') \cdot (1 - e^{-E(s) \cdot t})$.

Definition 2 (CTMC timed paths). *Let* $\mathcal{M} = (S, R, AP, L, s_0)$ *be a CTMC. An infinite path* π *in* $\mathcal{M}$ *is an alternating sequence of states* $s_i \in S$ *and time instants* $t_i \in \mathbb{R}_{>0}$, *i.e.,* $s_0 \xrightarrow{t_0} s_1 \xrightarrow{t_1} s_2 \cdots s_{n-1} \xrightarrow{t_{n-1}} s_n \cdots$ *s.t.* $R(s_i, s_{i+1}) > 0$ *for all* $i \in \mathbb{N}$. *A finite path* π *is an alternating sequence of states* $s_i \in S$ *and time instants* $t_i \in \mathbb{R}_{>0}$, *i.e.,* $s_0 \xrightarrow{t_0} s_1 \xrightarrow{t_1} s_2 \cdots s_{n-1} \xrightarrow{t_{n-1}} s_n$ *s.t.* $R(s_i, s_{i+1}) > 0$ *for all* $i < n$.

Let $Paths^{\mathcal{M}} = Paths_{fin}^{\mathcal{M}} \cup Paths_{\omega}^{\mathcal{M}}$ denote the set of all paths in $\mathcal{M}$, where $Paths_{fin}^{\mathcal{M}} = \bigcup_{n \in \mathbb{N}} Paths_n^{\mathcal{M}}$ is the set of all finite paths in $\mathcal{M}$ and $Paths_{\omega}^{\mathcal{M}}$ is the set of all infinite paths in $\mathcal{M}$. For infinite path $\pi = s_0 \xrightarrow{t_0} s_1 \xrightarrow{t_1} s_2 \cdots s_{n-1} \xrightarrow{t_{n-1}} s_n \cdots$ and any $i \in \mathbb{N}$, let $\pi[i] = s_i$, the $(i + 1)$st state of π. Let $\delta(\pi, i) = t_i$ be the time spent in state s_i. For any $t \in \mathbb{R}_{\geq 0}$ and i, the smallest index s.t. $t \leq \sum_{j=0}^{i} t_j$, let $\pi@t = \pi[i]$, the state occupied at time t. For finite path $s_0 \xrightarrow{t_0} s_1 \xrightarrow{t_1} s_2 \cdots s_{n-1} \xrightarrow{t_{n-1}} s_n$, which is either a finite prefix of an infinite path or s_n is absorbing, $\pi[i]$, $\delta(\pi, i)$ are only defined for $i \leq n$, and for $i < n$ defined as in the case of infinite paths. For all $t > \sum_{j=0}^{n-1} t_j$, let $\pi@t = s_n$; otherwise $\pi@t$ is defined as in the case of infinite paths. Let $\delta(\pi, n) = \infty$. Let $\alpha : S \rightarrow [0, 1]$, be the intial probability distribution s.t. $\sum_{s \in S} \alpha(s) = 1$. Since $\mathcal{M}$ has a single initial state s_0, $\alpha(s_0) = 1$, and $\forall s \in S$ s.t. $s \neq s_0$, $\alpha(s) = 0$. Let $Paths(s_0)$ denote the set of all paths that start in s_0.

Example 1. Consider the CTMC $\mathcal{M}$ in Fig. 2(a), where $S = \{s_0, s_1, s_2, s_3, s_4, s_5, s_6, s_7\}$, $AP = \{a, b\}$ and s_0 is the initial state. The transition rates are associated with the transitions. An example timed path π is $s_0 \xrightarrow{1.3} s_1 \xrightarrow{1.5} s_3 \xrightarrow{2} s_6$. Here $\pi[3] = s_6$ and $\pi@3 = s_3$.

Definition 3 (Cylinder set). *Let* $s_0, \ldots, s_k \in S$ *with* $P(s_i, s_{i+1}) > 0$ *for* $0 \leq i < k$ *and* $I_0, \ldots, I_{k-1}$ *be nonempty intervals in* $\mathbb{R}_{\geq 0}$. $Cyl(s_0, I_0, \ldots, I_{k-1}, s_k)$ *denotes the cylinder set consisting of all paths* $\pi \in Paths(s_0)$ *s.t.* $\pi[i] = s_i$ *for* $i \leq k$, *and* $\delta(\pi, i) \in I_i$ *for* $(i < k)$.

The definition of a Borel space on paths of a CTMC follows [2]. Let $\mathcal{F}(Paths(s_0))$ be the smallest σ-algebra on $Paths(s_0)$ which contains all sets $Cyl(s_0, I_0, \ldots, I_{k-1}s_k)$ s.t. $s_0, \ldots, s_k$ is a state sequence with $P(s_i, s_{i+1}) > 0$ $(0 \leq i < k)$ and $I_0, \ldots, I_{k-1}$ ranges over all sequences of nonempty intervals in $\mathbb{R}_{\geq 0}$.

Definition 4. *The probability measure* $\Pr_\alpha$ *on* $\mathcal{F}(Path(s_0))$ *is the unique measure defined by induction on* k *in the following way. Let* $\Pr_\alpha(Cyl(s_0)) = \alpha(s_0)$ *and for* $k > 0$:

$$\Pr_\alpha(Cyl(s_0, I_0, \ldots, s_k, I', s')) = \Pr_\alpha(Cyl(s_0, I_0, \ldots, s_k)) \cdot P(s_k, s', I')$$

where $P(s_k, s', I') = P(s_k, s') \cdot \left(e^{E(s_k) \cdot a} - e^{E(s_k) \cdot b}\right)$ *with* $a = \inf I'$ *and* $b = \sup I'$.

Assumptions. Throughout this paper we assume that every state of CTMC $\mathcal{M}$ has at least one predecessor, i.e., $pred(s) = \{s' \in S \mid P(s', s) > 0\} \neq \varnothing$ for any $s \in S$. This is not a restriction, as any CTMC (S, R, AP, L, s_0) can be transformed into an equivalent CTMC (S', R', AP', L', s_0') which fulfills this condition. This is done by adding a new state $\hat{s}$ to S equipped with a self-loop and which has a transition to each state in S without predecessors. The transition rates for $\hat{s}$ are set to some arbitrary value, e.g., $R(\hat{s}, \hat{s}) = 1$ and $R(\hat{s}, s) = 1$ if $pred(s) = \varnothing$ and 0 otherwise. To distinguish this state from the others we set $L'(\hat{s}) = \bot$ with $\bot \notin AP$. (All other labels, states and transitions remain unaffected.) Let $s_0' = s_0$. It follows that all states in $S' = S \cup \{\hat{s}\}$ have at least one predecessor. Moreover, the reachable state space of both CTMCs coincides. We also assume that the initial state s_0 of a CTMC is distinguished from all other states by a unique label, say $\$$. This assumption implies that for any equivalence that groups equally labeled states, $\{s_0\}$ constitutes a seperate equivalence class. Both assumptions do not affect the basic properties of the CTMC such as transient or steady-state distributions. For convenience, we neither show the state $\hat{s}$ nor the label $\$$ in figures.

3 Weighted Lumpability

Before defining weighted lumpability, we first define two auxiliary concepts. All definitions in this section are relative to a CTMC $\mathcal{M} = (S, R, AP, L, s_0)$. For $C \subseteq S$ and $s \in S$, let $P(s, C) = \sum_{s' \in C} P(s, s')$ be the cumulative probability to directly move from state s to some state in $C \subseteq S$.

Definition 5. *For* $s, s' \in S$ *and* $C \subseteq S$, *the function* $P : S \times S \times 2^S \to \mathbb{R}_{\geq 0}$ *is defined by:*

$$P(s, s', C) = \begin{cases} \frac{P(s,s')}{P(s,C)} & \text{if } s' \in C \text{ and } P(s, C) > 0 \\ 0 & \text{otherwise.} \end{cases}$$

Intuitively, $P(s, s', C)$ is the probability to move from state s to s' under the condition that s moves to some state in C.

Example 2. Consider the example in Fig. 2(a). Let $C = \{s_3, s_4, s_5\}$. Then $P(s_1, s_3, C) = 1/4$, $P(s_1, s_4, C) = 3/4$, $P(s_2, s_4, C) = 3/4$, and $P(s_2, s_5, C) = 1/4$.

Definition 6 (Weighted rate). *For $s \in S$, and $C, D \subseteq S$, the function $wr : S \times 2^S \times 2^S \to \mathbb{R}_{\geq 0}$ is defined by:*

$$wr(s, C, D) = \sum_{s' \in C} P(s, s', C) \cdot R(s', D)$$

where $R(s', D) = \sum_{s'' \in D} R(s', s'')$.

Intuitively, $wr(s, C, D)$ is the (weighted) rate to move from s to some state in D in two steps via any state $s' \in C$. Since $P(s', D) = \frac{R(s', D)}{E(s')}$, $wr(s, C, D)$ equals $\sum_{s' \in C} P(s, s', C) \cdot P(s', D) \cdot E(s')$.

Example 3. Consider the example in Fig. 2(a). Let $D = \{s_6\}$. Then $wr(s_1, C, D) = P(s_1, s_3, C) \cdot R(s_3, D) + P(s_1, s_4, C) \cdot R(s_4, D) = \frac{1}{2}$, $wr(s_2, C, D) = P(s_2, s_4, C) \cdot R(s_4, D) + P(s_2, s_5, C) \cdot R(s_5, D) = \frac{1}{2}$. Similarly, for $D = \{s_7\}$, we get $wr(s_1, C, D) = P(s_1, s_3, C) \cdot R(s_3, D) + P(s_1, s_4, C) \cdot R(s_4, D) = \frac{3}{2}$, $wr(s_2, C, D) = P(s_2, s_4, C) \cdot R(s_4, D) + P(s_2, s_5, C) \cdot R(s_5, D) = \frac{3}{2}$.

The above ingredients allow for the following definition of weighted lumpability, the central notion in this paper. For $C \subseteq S$, let $pred(C) = \bigcup_{s \in C} pred(s)$.

Definition 7 (WL). *Equivalence $\mathcal{R}$ on S is a* weighted lumping *(WL) if we have:*

1. $\forall (s_1, s_2) \in \mathcal{R}$ *it holds:* $L(s_1) = L(s_2)$ *and* $E(s_1) = E(s_2)$, *and*
2. $\forall C, D \in S/_\mathcal{R}$ *and* $\forall s', s'' \in pred(C)$ *it holds:* $wr(s', C, D) = wr(s'', C, D)$.

States s_1, s_2 are weighted lumpable, *denoted by $s_1 \cong s_2$, if $(s_1, s_2) \in \mathcal{R}$ for some WL $\mathcal{R}$.*

The first condition asserts that s_1 and s_2 are equally labeled and have identical exit rates. The second condition requires that for any two equivalence classes $C, D \in S/_\mathcal{R}$, where $S/_\mathcal{R}$ denotes the set consisting of all $\mathcal{R}$-equivalence classes, the weighted rate of going from any two predecessors of C to D via any state in C must be equal. Note that, by definition, any WL is an equivalence relation. Weighted lumpability coincides with Bernardo's notion of T-lumpability [6,7] that is defined in an axiomatic manner for action-labeled CTMCs. Roughly speaking, two states are T-lumpable if their expected delays w.r.t. to any test process, put in parallel to the CTMC, coincide for both the states.

Example 4. For the CTMC in Fig. 2(a), the equivalence relation induced by the partitioning $\{\{s_0\}, \{s_1\}, \{s_2\}, \{s_3, s_4, s_5\}, \{s_6\}, \{s_7\}\}$ is a WL relation.

Definition 8 (Quotient CTMC). *For WL relation $\mathcal{R}$ on $\mathcal{M}$, the quotient CTMC $\mathcal{M}/_\mathcal{R}$ is defined by $\mathcal{M}/_\mathcal{R} = (S/_\mathcal{R}, R', AP, L', s_0')$ where:*

- *$S/_\mathcal{R}$ is the set of all equivalence classes under $\mathcal{R}$,*
- *$R'(C, D) = wr(s', C, D)$ where $C, D \in S/_\mathcal{R}$ and $s' \in pred(C)$,*
- *$L'(C) = L(s)$, where $s \in C$ and*
- *$s_0' = C$ where $s_0 \in C$.*

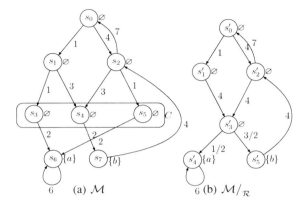

Fig. 2. (a) A CTMC and (b) its quotient under weighted lumpability

Note that $R'(C, D)$ is well-defined as for any predecessors s', s'' of C it follows $wr(s', C, D) = wr(s'', C, D)$. Similarly, L' is well-defined as states in any equivalence class C are equally labeled.

Example 5. The quotient CTMC for the Fig. 2(a) under the WL relation with partition $\{\{s_0\}, \{s_1\}, \{s_2\}, \{s_3, s_4, s_5\}, \{s_6\}, \{s_7\}\}$ is shown in Fig. 2(b).

Next, we show that any CTMC $\mathcal{M}$ and its quotient under WL relation are $\cong$-equivalent.

Definition 9. *For WL $\mathcal{R}$ on $\mathcal{M}$, let $\mathcal{M} \cong \mathcal{M}/_{\mathcal{R}}$ iff $\forall C \in S/_{\mathcal{R}}, s \in C$ it holds $s \cong C$.*

Theorem 1. *Let $\mathcal{M}$ be a CTMC and $\mathcal{R}$ be a WL on $\mathcal{M}$. Then $\mathcal{M} \cong \mathcal{M}/_{\mathcal{R}}$.*

Remark 1. The notion of WL-equivalent states cannot be lifted to WL equivalent time-abstract paths. That is to say, in general, $s \cong s'$ does not imply that for every path π_1 of s, there exists a statewise $\cong$-equivalent path π_2 in s', i.e., $\pi_1 \cong \pi_2$ iff $s_{i,1} \cong s_{i,2}$ for all $i \geq 0$. Consider, e.g., Fig. 2(a). Here $s_3 \cong s_4$, but the time-abstract paths from s_3, s_4 are not $\cong$-equivalent, as s_3 can move to s_6 but there is no direct successor s of s_4 with $s \cong s_6$. (Note that $L(s_6) \neq L(s_7)$.) As a consequence, $\cong$ is not finer than probabilistic trace equivalence [20].

To conclude this section, we investigate the relationship of WL to bisimulation, i.e., ordinary lumping [4,11]. This relationship is not novel; it is also given for T-lumpability in [6], but its proof is now quite simple thanks to the simplicity of the definition of WL.

Definition 10 (Bisimulation [4]). *Equivalence $\mathcal{R}$ on S is a bisimulation on $\mathcal{M}$ if for any $(s_1, s_2) \in \mathcal{R}$ we have: $L(s_1) = L(s_2)$, and $R(s_1, C) = R(s_2, C)$ for all C in $S/_{\mathcal{R}}$. s_1 and s_2 are bisimilar, denoted $s_1 \sim s_2$, if $(s_1, s_2) \in \mathcal{R}$ for some bisimulation $\mathcal{R}$.*

These conditions require that any two bisimilar states are equally labeled and have identical cumulative rates to move to any equivalence class C. Note that as $R(s, C) = P(s, C) \cdot E(s)$, the condition on the cumulative rates can be reformulated as $P(s_1, C) = P(s_2, C)$ for all $C \in S/_{\mathcal{R}}$ and $E(s_1) = E(s_2)$.

Lemma 1. $\sim$ *is strictly finer than* $\cong$.

The proof that $\sim$ is finer than $\cong$ is in the appendix. It follows from Fig. 2 that $s_1 \cong s_2 \not\sim s_1 \sim s_2$. Consider the equivalence class $C = \{s_3, s_4, s_5\}$ in Fig. 2(a). Here $s_3 \not\sim s_4$ since s_3 can reach an a-state while s_4 cannot.

4 Preservation of DTA Specifications

Bisimulation equivalence coincides with the logical equivalence of the branching-time logic CSL [4], a probabilistic real-time variant of CTL [2]. This implies that bisimilar states satisfy the same CSL formulas, a property that—thanks to efficient minimisation algorithms [13]— is exploited by model checkers to minimise the state space prior to verification. In order to investigate the kind of real-time properties for CTMCs that are preserved by WL, we study in this section *linear* real-time objectives that are given by Deterministic Timed Automata (DTA) [1]. These include, e.g., properties of the form: what is the probability to reach a given target state within the deadline, while avoiding "forbidden" states and not staying too long in any of the "dangerous" states on the way. Such properties can neither be expressed in CSL nor in dialects thereof [14]. A model-checking algorithm that verifies a CTMC against a DTA specification has recently been developed [12]; first experimental results are provided in [5]. The key issue is to compute the probability of all CTMC paths that are accepted by a DTA. In this section, we will deal with finite acceptance conditions, i.e., a DTA accepts the timed path if one of its final locations is reached. The results, however, also carry over to Muller acceptance conditions.

Deterministic timed automata. A DTA is a finite-state automaton equipped with a finite set of real-valued variables, called *clocks*. Clocks increase implicitly, all at the same pace, they can be inspected (in guards) and can be reset to the value zero. Let $\mathcal{X}$ be a finite set of clocks ranged over by x and y. A *clock constraint* g over set $\mathcal{X}$ is either of the form $x \bowtie c$ with $c \in \mathbb{N}$ and $\bowtie \in \{<, \leq, >, \geq\}$, or of the form $x - y \bowtie c$, or a conjunction of clock constraints. Let $\mathcal{CC}(\mathcal{X})$ denote the set of clock constraints over $\mathcal{X}$.

Definition 11 (DTA). *A deterministic timed automaton (DTA) is a tuple* $\mathcal{A} = (\Sigma, \mathcal{X}, Q, q_0, F, \rightarrow)$ *where:*

- Σ *is a finite alphabet,*
- $\mathcal{X}$ *is a finite set of clocks,*
- Q *is a nonempty finite set of locations with the initial location* $q_0 \in Q$,
- $F \subseteq Q$ *is a set of accepting (or final) locations,*
- $\rightarrow \subseteq Q \times \Sigma \times \mathcal{CC}(\mathcal{X}) \times 2^{\mathcal{X}} \times Q$ *is the edge relation satisfying:*

$$\left(q \xrightarrow{a,g,X} q' \text{ and } q \xrightarrow{a,g',X'} q'' \text{ with } g \neq g'\right) \quad \text{implies} \quad g \cap g' = \varnothing.$$

Intuitively, the edge $q \xrightarrow{a,g,X} q'$ asserts that the DTA $\mathcal{A}$ can move from location q to q' when the input symbol is a and the guard g holds, while the clocks in X should be reset when entering q' (all other clocks keep their value). DTA are deterministic as they have a single initial location, and outgoing edges of a location labeled with the same input symbol are required to have disjoint guards. In this way, the next location is uniquely determined for a given location and a given set of clock values. In case no guard is satisfied in a location for a given clock valuation, time can progress. If the advance of time will never reach a situation in which a guard holds, the DTA will stay in that location *ad infinitum*. Note that DTA do not have location invariants.

The semantics of a DTA is given by an infinite-state transition system. We do not provide the full semantics, cf. [1], but we define the notion of paths, i.e., runs or executions of a DTA. This is done using some auxiliary notions. A *clock valuation* η for a set $\mathcal{X}$ of clocks is a function $\eta : \mathcal{X} \to \mathbb{R}_{\geq 0}$, assigning to each clock $x \in \mathcal{X}$ its current value $\eta(x)$. The clock valuation η over $\mathcal{X}$ satisfies the clock constraint g, denoted $\eta \models g$, iff the values of the clocks under η fulfill g. For instance, $\eta \models x - y > c$ iff $\eta(x) - \eta(y) > c$. Other cases are defined analogously. For $d \in \mathbb{R}_{\geq 0}$, $\eta + d$ denotes the clock valuation where all clocks of η are increased by d. That is, $(\eta + d)(x) = \eta(x) + d$ for all clocks $x \in \mathcal{X}$. Clock *reset* for a subset $X \subseteq \mathcal{X}$, denoted by $\eta[X := 0]$, is the valuation η' defined by: $\forall x \in X.\eta'(x) := 0$ and $\forall x \notin X.\eta'(x) := \eta(x)$. We denote the valuation that assigns 0 to all the clocks by $\mathbf{0}$. An (infinite) path of DTA $\mathcal{A}$ has the form $\rho = q_0 \xrightarrow{a_0, t_0} q_1 \xrightarrow{a_1, t_1} \cdots$ such that $\eta_0 = \mathbf{0}$, and for all $j \geq 0$, it holds $t_j > 0$, $\eta_j + t_j \models g_j$, $\eta_{j+1} = (\eta_j + t_j)[X_j := 0]$, where η_j is the clock evaluation on entering q_j. Here, g_j is the guard of the j-th edge taken in the DTA and X_j the set of clock to be reset on that edge. A path ρ is accepted by $\mathcal{A}$ if $q_i \in F$ for some $i \geq 0$. Since the DTA is deterministic, the successor location is uniquely determined; for convenience we write $q' = succ(q, a, g)$. A path in a CTMC $\mathcal{M}$ can be "matched" by a path through DTA $\mathcal{A}$ by regarding sets of atomic propositions in $\mathcal{M}$ as input symbols of $\mathcal{A}$. Such path is accepted, if at some point an accepting location in the DTA is reached:

Definition 12 (CTMC paths accepted by a DTA). *Let CTMC $\mathcal{M} = (S, R, AP, L, s_0)$ and DTA $\mathcal{A} = (2^{AP}, \mathcal{X}, Q, q_0, F, \to)$. The CTMC path $\pi = s_0 \xrightarrow{t_0} s_1 \xrightarrow{t_1} s_2 \cdots$ is accepted by $\mathcal{A}$ if there exists a corresponding DTA path*

$$q_0 \xrightarrow{L(s_0), t_0} \underbrace{succ\big(q_0, L(s_0), g_0\big)}_{= q_1} \xrightarrow{L(s_1), t_1} \underbrace{succ\big(q_1, L(s_1), g_1\big)}_{= q_2} \cdots$$

such that $q_j \in F$ for some $j \geq 0$. Here, $\eta_0 = \mathbf{0}$, g_i is the (unique) guard in q_i such that $\eta_i + t_i \models g_i$ and $\eta_{i+1} = (\eta_i + t_i)[X_i := 0]$, and η_i is the clock evaluation on entering q_i, for $i \geq 0$. Let $Paths^{\mathcal{M}}(\mathcal{A}) = \{\pi \in Paths^{\mathcal{M}} \mid \pi \text{ is accepted by DTA } \mathcal{A}\}$.

Theorem 2 ([12]). *For any CTMC $\mathcal{M}$ and DTA $\mathcal{A}$, the set $Paths^{\mathcal{M}}(\mathcal{A})$ is measurable.*

The main result of this theorem is that $Paths^{\mathcal{M}}(\mathcal{A})$ can be rewritten as the combination of cylinder sets of the form $Cyl = (s_0, I_0, \ldots, I_{n-1}, s_n)$ (Cyl for short) which are all accepted by DTA $\mathcal{A}$. A cylinder set (Cyl) is accepted by DTA $\mathcal{A}$ if all its paths are accepted by $\mathcal{A}$. That is

$$Paths^{\mathcal{M}}(\mathcal{A}) = \bigcup_{n \in \mathbb{N}} \bigcup_{\pi \in Paths_n^{\mathcal{M}}(\mathcal{A})} Cyl_\pi, \tag{1}$$

where $Paths_n^{\mathcal{M}}(\mathcal{A})$ is the set of accepting paths by $\mathcal{A}$ of length n and Cyl_π is the cylinder set that contains π.

Definition 13 (WL equivalent cylinder sets). *Cylinder sets* $Cyl = (s_0, I_0, \ldots, I_{n-1}, s_n)$ *and* $Cyl' = (s'_0, I_0, \ldots, I_{n-1}, s'_n)$ *are WL equivalent, denoted* $Cyl \cong Cyl'$, *if they are statewise WL equivalent:* $Cyl \cong Cyl'$ *iff* $s_i \cong s'_i$ *for all* $0 \leqslant i \leqslant n$.

Definition 14 (WL-closed set). *The set* Π *of cylinder sets is WL-closed if* $\forall Cyl \in \Pi$, *and* Cyl' *with* $Cyl' \cong Cyl$ *implies* $Cyl' \in \Pi$.

A finite path π in the CTMC $\mathcal{M}$ is compatible with Π if the cylinder set for this path $Cyl_\pi \in \Pi$. Since the cylinder sets contained in Π are disjoint, we have $\mathrm{Pr}_s(\Pi) = \mathrm{Pr}_s(\bigcup_{Cyl \in \Pi} Cyl) = \sum_{Cyl \in \Pi} \mathrm{Pr}_s(Cyl)$, where $\mathrm{Pr}_s(\Pi)$ is the probability of all the paths starting in s which are compatible with Π. For paths compatible with Π but not starting from s, the probability equals 0. We denote WL-closed set of cylinder sets of length n by Π_n. If $n = 0$, Π_n is the set of states and $\mathrm{Pr}_s(\Pi_n) = \alpha(s)$ if $s \in \Pi_n$, 0 otherwise, where $\alpha(s)$ is the probability of s being the initial state of CTMC $\mathcal{M}$.

Example 6. Consider the example given in Fig. 3, where we have the CTMC $\mathcal{M}$ (left) and its quotient $\mathcal{M}/_\mathcal{R}$ (right). If $\Pi = \{Cyl(s_0, I_0, s_1, I_1, s_3), Cyl(s'_0, I_0, s'_1, I_1, s'_2)\}$ is a WL closed set of cylinder sets in $\mathcal{M}$, and $\mathcal{M}/_\mathcal{R}$ that are accepted by DTA $\mathcal{A}$, then:

$$\mathrm{Pr}_{s_0}(\Pi) = \mathrm{Pr}_{s_0}(Cyl(s_0, I_0, s_1, I_1, s_3)) + \mathrm{Pr}_{s_0}(Cyl(s'_0, I_0, s'_1, I_1, s'_2))$$

$$= 1/2 \cdot (e^{-E(s_0)\cdot \inf I_0} - e^{-E(s_0)\cdot \sup I_0}) \cdot (e^{-E(s_1)\cdot \inf I_1} - e^{-E(s_1)\cdot \sup I_1}) + 0.$$

The second term is 0 as the cylinder set does not start from s_0. Similarly,

$$\mathrm{Pr}_{s'_0}(\Pi) = \mathrm{Pr}_{s'_0}(Cyl(s_0, I_0, s_1, I_1, s_3)) + \mathrm{Pr}_{s'_0}(Cyl(s'_0, I_0, s'_1, I_1, s'_2))$$

$$= 0 + (e^{-E(s'_0)\cdot \inf I_0} - e^{-E(s'_0)\cdot \sup I_0}) \cdot 1/2 \cdot (e^{-E(s'_1)\cdot \inf I_1} - e^{-E(s'_1)\cdot \sup I_1}).$$

Definition 15. *For CTMC $\mathcal{M}$ and DTA $\mathcal{A}$, let* $\mathrm{Pr}(\mathcal{M} \models \mathcal{A}) = \mathrm{Pr}\left(Paths^{\mathcal{M}}(\mathcal{A})\right)$.

Stated in words, $\mathrm{Pr}(\mathcal{M} \models \mathcal{A})$ denotes the probability of all the paths in CTMC $\mathcal{M}$ that are accepted by DTA $\mathcal{A}$. Note that we slightly abuse notation, since Pr on the right-hand side is the probability measure on the Borel space of infinite paths in the CTMC. This brings us to one of the main results of this paper:

Theorem 3 (Preservation of DTA specifications). *For any CTMC $\mathcal{M}$, a WL $\mathcal{R}$ on $\mathcal{M}$ and DTA $\mathcal{A}$:*

$$\mathrm{Pr}(\mathcal{M} \models \mathcal{A}) = \mathrm{Pr}(\mathcal{M}/_\mathcal{R} \models \mathcal{A}).$$

The detailed proof is in the appendix and consists of two main steps:

1. We prove that for any cylinder set Cyl in the quotient CTMC $\mathcal{M}/_\mathcal{R}$ which is accepted by the DTA $\mathcal{A}$, there is a corresponding *set* of cylinder sets in the CTMC $\mathcal{M}$ that are accepted by the DTA $\mathcal{A}$ and that jointly have the same probability as Cyl, cf. Lemma 2 below.

2. We show that the sum of probabilities of all the cylinder sets in $\mathcal{M}/_{\mathcal{R}}$ that are accepted by DTA $\mathcal{A}$ equals the sum of probabilities of all the corresponding sets of cylinder sets in $\mathcal{M}$.

Lemma 2. *Let $\mathcal{M} = (S, R, AP, L, s_0)$ be a CTMC and $\mathcal{R}$ be a WL on $\mathcal{M}$. If Π is a WL-closed set of cylinder sets which are accepted by DTA $\mathcal{A}$, then for any $D \in S/_{\mathcal{R}}$ and $s_0' \in pred(D)$:*

$$\sum_{s_1 \in D} P(s_0', s_1, D) \cdot \Pr_{s_1}(\Pi) = \Pr_D(\Pi).$$

From Lemma 2 we conclude

$$\sum_{D \in S/_{\mathcal{R}}} \sum_{s_1 \in D} P(s_0', s_1, D) \cdot \Pr_{s_1}(\Pi) = \sum_{D \in S/_{\mathcal{R}}} \Pr_D(\Pi). \qquad (2)$$

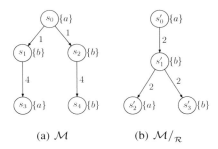

(a) $\mathcal{M}$ (b) $\mathcal{M}/_{\mathcal{R}}$

Fig. 3. WL equivalent cylinder sets

Corollary 1. *WL preserves transient state probabilities.*

5   Preservation of MTL Specifications

In this section we show that the quotient CTMC obtained under WL can be used for verifying Metric Temporal Logic (MTL) formulae [16,18,10]. It is interesting to note that the expressive power of MTL is different from that of DTA. Temporal properties like $(\lozenge \square a)$ cannot be expressed using deterministic timed automata, since nondeterminism is needed to compensate for the non causality [17]. On the other hand, DTA expressible languages that involve counting [3], e.g., a should only occur at even positions, cannot be expressed using MTL. We now recall the syntax and semantics of Metric Temporal Logic [18,10].

Definition 16 (Syntax of MTL). *Let AP be a set of atomic propositions, then the formulas of MTL are built from AP using Boolean connectives, and time-constrained versions of the* until *operator* U *as follows:*

$$\varphi ::= tt \mid a \mid \neg\varphi \mid \varphi \wedge \varphi \mid \varphi \, U^I \, \varphi$$

where $I \subseteq \mathbb{R}_{\geq 0}$ is a nonempty interval with rational bounds, and $a \in AP$.

Whereas, typically, the semantics of MTL is defined over timed paths of timed automata, we take a similar approach by interpreting MTL formulas over CTMC paths.

Definition 17 (Semantics of MTL formulas). *The meaning of MTL formulas is defined by means of a satisfaction relation, denoted by $\models$, between a CTMC $\mathcal{M}$, one of its paths π, MTL formula φ, and time $t \in \mathbb{R}_{\geq 0}$. Let $\pi = s_0 \xrightarrow{t_0} s_1 \cdots s_{n-1} \xrightarrow{t_{n-1}} s_n \cdots$ be a finite or infinite path of $\mathcal{M}$, then $(\pi, t) \models \varphi$ is defined inductively by:*

$$
\begin{array}{ll}
(\pi, t) \models tt & \\
(\pi, t) \models a & \text{iff } a \in L(\pi@t) \\
(\pi, t) \models \neg\varphi & \text{iff } not \ (\pi, t) \models \varphi \\
(\pi, t) \models \varphi_1 \wedge \varphi_2 & \text{iff } (\pi, t) \models \varphi_1 \ and \ (\pi, t) \models \varphi_2 \\
(\pi, t) \models \varphi_1 \, \mathrm{U}^I \, \varphi_2 & \text{iff } \exists t' \in t+I. \ ((\pi, t') \models \varphi_2 \wedge \forall t \leq t'' < t'. (\pi, t'') \models \varphi_1) .
\end{array}
$$

The semantics for the propositional fragment is straightforward. Recall that $\pi@t$ denotes the state occupied along path π at time t. Path π at time t satisfies $\varphi_1 \, \mathrm{U}^I \, \varphi_2$ whenever for some time point t' in the interval $I+t$, defined as $[a, b]+t = [a+t, b+t]$ (and similarly for open intervals), φ_2 holds, and at all time points between t and t', path π satisfies φ_1. Let $\pi \models \varphi$ if and only if $(\pi, 0) \models \varphi$. The standard temporal operators like $\Diamond$ ("eventually") and its timed variant $\Diamond^I$ are derived in the following way: $\Diamond^I \varphi = tt \, \mathrm{U}^I \, \varphi$ and $\Diamond\varphi = tt \, \mathrm{U} \, \varphi$. Similarly, $\Box$ ("globally") and its timed variant are derived as follows:

$$
\Box^I \varphi = \neg(\Diamond^I \neg\varphi) \text{ and } \Box\varphi = \neg(\Diamond\neg\varphi).
$$

Example 7. Using MTL, various interesting properties can be specified such as:

- $\Box(down \rightarrow \Diamond^{[0,5]} up)$, which asserts that whenever the system is down, it should be up again within 5 time units.
- $\Box(down \rightarrow alarm \, \mathrm{U}^{[0,10]} \, up)$, which states that whenever the system is down, an alarm should ring until it is up again within 10 time units.

More complex properties can be specified by nesting of until path formulas.

Theorem 4 ([2]). *The probability measure of the set of converging paths is zero.*

As a next result, we address the measurability of a set of CTMC paths satisfying an MTL formula φ.

Theorem 5. *For each MTL formula φ and state s of CTMC $\mathcal{M}$, the set $\{\pi \in Paths(s) \mid \pi \models \varphi\}$ is measurable.*

Definition 18 (Probability of MTL formulas). *The probability that state s satisfies MTL formula φ refers to the probability for the sets of paths for which that formula holds as follows:*

$$
\Pr(s \models \varphi) = \Pr_s(\pi \in Paths(s) \mid \pi \models \varphi).
$$

Since $\mathcal{M}$ has a single initial state, i.e., s_0, the probability of all the paths in $\mathcal{M}$ that satisfy MTL formula φ is given by $\Pr(\mathcal{M} \models \varphi) = \Pr(s_0 \models \varphi)$.

Theorem 6. *Let $\mathcal{M}$ be a CTMC and $\mathcal{R}$ be a WL on $\mathcal{M}$. Then for any MTL formula φ:*

$$
\Pr(\mathcal{M} \models \varphi) = \Pr(\mathcal{M}/_{\mathcal{R}} \models \varphi).
$$

6 Conclusions

This paper considered weighted lumpability (WL), a structural notion that coincides with Bernardo's T-lumpability [6] defined in a process-algebraic setting. Whereas Bernardo defines T-lumpability in an axiomatic manner, our starting point is a structural definition using first CTMC principles. The main contribution of this paper is the preservation of DTA and MTL specifications under WL quotienting. We note that this implies the preservation of transient probabilities as well as timed reachability probabilities. Future work is to develop an efficient quotienting algorithm for WL; we hope that our structural definition facilitates a reduction algorithm along the partition-refinement paradigm.

Acknowledgements. We thank Marco Bernardo for his constructive comments on a draft version of this paper.

References

1. Alur, R., Dill, D.L.: A theory of timed automata. Theor. Comput. Sci. 126(2), 183–235 (1994)
2. Baier, C., Haverkort, B.R., Hermanns, H., Katoen, J.-P.: Model-checking algorithms for continuous-time Markov chains. IEEE Trans. Software Eng. 29(6), 524–541 (2003)
3. Baier, C., Katoen, J.-P.: Principles of Model Checking. MIT Press (2008)
4. Baier, C., Katoen, J.-P., Hermanns, H., Wolf, V.: Comparative branching-time semantics for Markov chains. Inf. Comput. 200(2), 149–214 (2005)
5. Barbot, B., Chen, T., Han, T., Katoen, J.-P., Mereacre, A.: Efficient CTMC Model Checking of Linear Real-Time Objectives. In: Abdulla, P.A., Leino, K.R.M. (eds.) TACAS 2011. LNCS, vol. 6605, pp. 128–142. Springer, Heidelberg (2011)
6. Bernardo, M.: Non-bisimulation-based Markovian behavioral equivalences. J. Log. Algebr. Program. 72(1), 3–49 (2007)
7. Bernardo, M.: Towards State Space Reduction Based on T-Lumpability-Consistent Relations. In: Thomas, N., Juiz, C. (eds.) EPEW 2008. LNCS, vol. 5261, pp. 64–78. Springer, Heidelberg (2008)
8. Bernardo, M.: Uniform logical characterizations of testing equivalences for nondeterministic, probabilistic and Markovian processes. ENTCS 253(3), 3–23 (2009)
9. Bernardo, M., Botta, S.: A survey of modal logics characterising behavioural equivalences for non-deterministic and stochastic systems. Math. Structures in Comp. Sci. 18(1), 29–55 (2008)
10. Bouyer, P.: From Qualitative to Quantitative Analysis of Timed Systems. Mémoire d'habilitation, Université Paris 7, Paris, France (January 2009)
11. Buchholz, P.: Exact and ordinary lumpability in finite Markov chains. J. of Appl. Prob. 31(1), 59–75 (1994)
12. Chen, T., Han, T., Katoen, J.-P., Mereacre, A.: Quantitative model checking of continuous-time Markov chains against timed automata specifications. In: LICS, pp. 309–318. IEEE Computer Society (2009)
13. Derisavi, S., Hermanns, H., Sanders, W.H.: Optimal state-space lumping in Markov chains. Inf. Process. Lett. 87(6), 309–315 (2003)
14. Donatelli, S., Haddad, S., Sproston, J.: Model checking timed and stochastic properties with CSL^{TA}. IEEE Trans. Software Eng. 35(2), 224–240 (2009)

15. Katoen, J.-P., Kemna, T., Zapreev, I.S., Jansen, D.N.: Bisimulation Minimisation Mostly Speeds Up Probabilistic Model Checking. In: Grumberg, O., Huth, M. (eds.) TACAS 2007. LNCS, vol. 4424, pp. 87–101. Springer, Heidelberg (2007)
16. Koymans, R.: Specifying real-time properties with metric temporal logic. Real-Time Systems 2(4), 255–299 (1990)
17. Maler, O., Nickovic, D., Pnueli, A.: Checking Temporal Properties of Discrete, Timed and Continuous Behaviors. In: Avron, A., Dershowitz, N., Rabinovich, A. (eds.) Trakhtenbrot/Festschrift. LNCS, vol. 4800, pp. 475–505. Springer, Heidelberg (2008)
18. Ouaknine, J., Worrell, J.: Some Recent Results in Metric Temporal Logic. In: Cassez, F., Jard, C. (eds.) FORMATS 2008. LNCS, vol. 5215, pp. 1–13. Springer, Heidelberg (2008)
19. Valmari, A., Franceschinis, G.: Simple $O(m \log n)$ Time Markov Chain Lumping. In: Esparza, J., Majumdar, R. (eds.) TACAS 2010. LNCS, vol. 6015, pp. 38–52. Springer, Heidelberg (2010)
20. Wolf, V., Baier, C., Majster-Cederbaum, M.E.: Trace machines for observing continuous-time Markov chains. ENTCS 153(2), 259–277 (2006)

Appendix

Proof of Theorem 1

Proof. Let $\mathcal{M} = (S, R, AP, L, s_0)$ be a CTMC and $\mathcal{M}/_{\mathcal{R}} = (S/_{\mathcal{R}}, R', AP, L', s_0')$ be its quotient under WL. Since we have defined the WL relation on a single state space, to prove this theorem we take the disjoint union $S \cup S/_{\mathcal{R}}$. Let us define an equivalence relation $\mathcal{R}^* \subseteq (S \cup S/_{\mathcal{R}}) \times (S \cup S/_{\mathcal{R}})$ with $\{(s, C) | s \in C\} \subseteq \mathcal{R}^*$. The exit rate $E'(C)$ for $C \in S/_{\mathcal{R}}$ is defined by $\sum_{x \in (S \cup S/_{\mathcal{R}})} R'(C, x)$.

Now we prove that $\mathcal{R}^*$ is a WL relation. This is done by checking both conditions of Def. 7. Let $(s, C) \in \mathcal{R}^*$. The proofs for pairs (s, s'), (C, s), and (C, C) are similar and omitted.

1. $L'(C) = L(s)$ by definition of $\mathcal{M}/_{\mathcal{R}}$. We prove that $E'(C) = E(s)$ as follows:

$$
\begin{aligned}
E'(C) &= \sum_{x \in (S \cup S/_{\mathcal{R}})} R'(C, x) = \sum_{D \in S/_{\mathcal{R}}} R'(C, D) \\
&= \sum_{D \in S/_{\mathcal{R}}} wr(s_0', C, D) \text{ for some } s_0' \in pred(C) \\
&= \sum_{D \in S/_{\mathcal{R}}} \sum_{s \in C} P(s_0', s, C) \cdot R(s, D) \\
&= \sum_{s \in C} \left(P(s_0', s, C) \cdot \sum_{D \in S/_{\mathcal{R}}} R(s, D) \right) \\
&= \sum_{s \in C} \left(P(s_0', s, C) \cdot \sum_{D \in S/_{\mathcal{R}}} \sum_{s' \in D} R(s, s') \right) \\
&= \sum_{s \in C} \left(P(s_0', s, C) \cdot \sum_{s' \in S} R(s, s') \right)
\end{aligned}
$$

$$= \sum_{s \in C} (P(s_0', s, C) \cdot E(s))$$

$$= \left(\sum_{s \in C} P(s_0', s, C) \right) \cdot E(s), \text{ since for all } s' \in C, E(s') = E(s)$$

$$= E(s).$$

2. Finally we prove that $\forall E, F \in (S \cup S/\mathcal{R})/\mathcal{R}^*$ and $\forall x_0', x_0'' \in pred(E)$ it holds $wr(x_0', E, F) = wr(x_0'', E, F)$. Let $x_0', x_0'' \in pred(E)$. Consider the following three cases based on the successors of x_0', x_0'' such that these successors are in E.

   a) The successors of both x_0', x_0'' belong to S. Since we know that $\mathcal{R}$ is a WL, it follows $wr(x_0', E, F) = wr(x_0'', E, F)$.
   b) The successors of both x_0', x_0'' belong to $S/\mathcal{R}$. In this case, $wr(x_0', E, F) = wr(x_0', \{E_1\}, F)$ where $E_1 \in E \cap S/\mathcal{R}$, which equals

$$\sum_{x' \in \{E_1\}} \frac{P(x_0', x')}{P(x_0', E_1)} \cdot R'(x', F) = R'(E_1, F).$$

   Similarly $wr(x_0'', E, F) = wr(x_0'', \{E_1\}, F) = R'(E_1, F)$.
   c) The successors of x_0', x_0'' belong to S and $S/\mathcal{R}$ respectively. In this case we get, $wr(x_0'', E, F) = wr(x_0'', \{E_1\}, F) = R'(E_1, F)$.
   We know that the successors of $E_1 \in S/\mathcal{R}$, hence using Def. 8 we conclude:

$$R'(E_1, F) = wr(x_0', E_1, F) = wr(x_0', E, F).$$

Since all the conditions of Def. 7 are satisfied by the relation $\mathcal{R}^*$, it is a WL relation.   □

Proof of Lemma 1

Proof. Let $s_1 \sim s_2$. We prove that both conditions for $\cong$ are satisfied.

 - $L(s_1) = L(s_2)$, follows directly from $s_1 \sim s_2$.
 - $E(s_1) = E(s_2)$, since we know that

$$E(s_1) = \sum_{s \in S} R(s_1, s) = \sum_{C \in S/\sim} \sum_{s \in C} R(s_1, s) = \sum_{C \in S/\sim} R(s_1, C).$$

If $s_1 \sim s_2$, then $R(s_1, C) = R(s_2, C)$. Therefore:

$$E(s_1) = \sum_{C \in S/\sim} R(s_1, C) = \sum_{C \in S/\sim} R(s_2, C) = E(s_2).$$

- Let $C, D \in S/_\sim$ and $s_0', s_0'' \in pred(C)$. Since $R(s_1, D) = R(s_2, D)$ for all $s_1, s_2 \in C$, then for all $s^* \in C$:

$$
\begin{aligned}
wr(s_0', C, D) &= \sum_{s \in C} \frac{P(s_0', s)}{P(s_0', C)} \cdot R(s, D) \\
&= R(s^*, D) \cdot \sum_{s \in C} \frac{P(s_0', s)}{P(s_0', C)} \\
&= R(s^*, D) \\
&= R(s^*, D) \cdot \sum_{s \in C} \frac{P(s_0'', s)}{P(s_0'', C)} \\
&= \sum_{s \in C} \frac{P(s_0'', s)}{P(s_0'', C)} \cdot R(s, D) \\
&= wr(s_0'', C, D).
\end{aligned}
$$

Thus $s_1 \cong s_2$.   □

Proof of Lemma 2

Proof. We will prove this lemma by induction over the length of the cylinder set $Cyl \in \Pi$. That is, we will prove for any $n \in \mathbb{N}$:

$$
\sum_{s_1 \in D} P(s_0', s_1, D) \cdot \Pr_{s_1}(\Pi_n) = \Pr_D(\Pi_n).
$$

- **Base Case**: In this case, $n = 0$ and

$$
\sum_{s_1 \in D} P(s_0', s_1, D) \cdot \Pr_{s_1}(\Pi_0) = 1 = \Pr_D(\Pi_0),
$$

if $s_0 \in D, \Pi_0$, and 0, otherwise.
- **Induction Hypothesis**: Assume that for cylinder sets of length $n \in \mathbb{N}$, it holds:

$$
\sum_{s_1 \in D} P(s_0', s_1, D) \cdot \Pr_{s_1}(\Pi_n) = \Pr_D(\Pi_n).
$$

- **Induction Step**: Consider the case $n + 1$:

$$
\begin{aligned}
&\sum_{s_1 \in D} P(s_0', s_1, D) \cdot \Pr_{s_1}(\Pi_{n+1}) \\
&= \sum_{s_1 \in D} P(s_0', s_1, D) \cdot \sum_{s_2 \in S} P(s_1, s_2) \cdot (e^{-E(s_1) \cdot \inf I_0} - e^{-E(s_1) \cdot \sup I_0}) \cdot \Pr_{s_2}(\Pi_n)
\end{aligned}
$$

Let $(e^{-E(s_1)\cdot\inf I_0} - e^{-E(s_1)\cdot\sup I_0}) = \delta(s_1, I_0)$, then the above expression is equal to:

$$\sum_{s_1 \in D} P(s_0', s_1, D) \cdot \sum_{s_2 \in S} P(s_1, s_2) \cdot \delta(s_1, I_0) \cdot \Pr_{s_2}(\Pi_n)$$

$$= \sum_{s_1 \in D} P(s_0', s_1, D) \cdot \sum_{C \in S/\mathcal{R}} \sum_{s_2 \in C} P(s_1, s_2) \cdot \delta(s_1, I_0) \cdot \Pr_{s_2}(\Pi_n)$$

$$= \sum_{C \in S/\mathcal{R}} \sum_{s_1 \in D} P(s_0', s_1, D) \cdot \sum_{s_2 \in C} P(s_1, s_2) \cdot \delta(s_1, I_0) \cdot \Pr_{s_2}(\Pi_n).$$

Multiplying the above expression by $\dfrac{R(s_1, C)}{R(s_1, C)}$ and using $P(s_1, s_2) = \dfrac{R(s_1, s_2)}{E(s_1)}$ yields:

$$\sum_{C \in S/\mathcal{R}} \sum_{s_1 \in D} P(s_0', s_1, D) \cdot \sum_{s_2 \in D} \frac{R(s_1, C)}{R(s_1, C)} \cdot \frac{R(s_1, s_2)}{E(s_1)} \cdot \delta(s_1, I_0) \cdot \Pr_{s_2}(\Pi_n).$$

Since $\forall s_1, s_1' \in D$, $E(s_1) = E(s_1')$, we have $\delta(s_1, I_0) = \delta(s_1', I_0)$. We get:

$$\frac{\delta(s_1, I_0)}{E(s_1)} \sum_{C \in S/\mathcal{R}} \sum_{s_1 \in D} P(s_0', s_1, D) \cdot R(s_1, C) \cdot \sum_{s_2 \in C} \frac{R(s_1, s_2)}{R(s_1, C)} \cdot \Pr_{s_2}(\Pi_n)$$

$$= \frac{\delta(s_1, I_0)}{E(s_1)} \sum_{C \in S/\mathcal{R}} \sum_{s_1 \in D} P(s_0', s_1, D) \cdot R(s_1, C) \cdot \sum_{s_2 \in C} P(s_1, s_2, C) \cdot \Pr_{s_2}(\Pi_n).$$

We have already proved that $\forall s \in D$, $E(s) = E(D)$, cf. Theorem 1. From the induction hypothesis we have:

$$\sum_{s_2 \in C} P(s_1, s_2, C) \cdot \Pr_{s_2}(\Pi_n) = \Pr_{C}(\Pi_n).$$

Also from Def. 6 and Def. 8 we know that:

$$\sum_{C \in S/\mathcal{R}} \sum_{s_1 \in D} P(s_0', s_1, D) \cdot R(s_1, C) = \sum_{C \in S/\mathcal{R}} R'(D, C),$$

since $\sum_{s_1 \in D} P(s_0', s_1, D) \cdot R(s_1, C) = wr(s_0', D, C) = R'(D, C)$. Therefore we get:

$$\frac{\delta(D, I_0)}{E(D)} \sum_{C \in S/\mathcal{R}} R'(D, C) \cdot \Pr_{C}(\Pi_n) = \Pr_{D}(\Pi_{n+1}).$$

$\square$

Proof of Theorem 3

Proof. Let C_n be the set of all the cylinder sets in $\mathcal{M}$, and $\mathcal{M}/_\mathcal{R}$ of length n that are accepted by DTA $\mathcal{A}$ and $C_{n/\Pi}$ be the set of subsets of C_n grouped according to WL-closed set of cylinder sets. Let Cyl_π be the cylinder set that contains π. Since the cylinder sets in Eq. (1) are disjoint, we have:

$$\Pr(\mathcal{M} \models \mathcal{A}) = \Pr\left(\bigcup_{n \in \mathbb{N}} \bigcup_{\pi \in Paths_n^\mathcal{M}(\mathcal{A})} Cyl_\pi\right)$$

$$= \sum_{n \in \mathbb{N}} \sum_{Cyl \in C_n} \Pr(Cyl)$$

$$= \sum_{n \in \mathbb{N}} \sum_{\Pi \in C_{n/\Pi}} \sum_{D \in S/_\mathcal{R}} \sum_{s_1 \in D} P(s_0', s_1, D) \cdot \Pr_{s_1}(\Pi).$$

Then we get using Eq. (2):

$$\Pr(\mathcal{M} \models \mathcal{A}) = \sum_{n \in \mathbb{N}} \sum_{\Pi \in C_{n/\Pi}} \sum_{D \in S/_\mathcal{R}} \sum_{s_1 \in D} P(s_0', s_1, D) \cdot \Pr_{s_1}(\Pi)$$

$$= \sum_{n \in \mathbb{N}} \sum_{\Pi \in C_{n/\Pi}} \sum_{D \in S/_\mathcal{R}} \Pr_D(\Pi)$$

$$= \Pr(\mathcal{M}/_\mathcal{R} \models \mathcal{A}).$$

$\square$

Proof of Theorem 5

Proof. We prove the measurability by showing that for any path $\pi = s_0 \xrightarrow{t_0} s_1 \xrightarrow{t_1} s_2 \cdots s_{n-1} \xrightarrow{t_{n-1}} s_n \in Paths_n^\mathcal{M}(s_0 \models \varphi)$ where $Paths_n^\mathcal{M}(s_0 \models \varphi)$ is the set of paths of length n starting from s_0 that satisfy φ, there exists a cylinder set $Cyl(s_0, I_0, \ldots, I_{n-1}, s_n)$ (Cyl for short) s.t. $\pi \in Cyl$ and $Cyl \subseteq Paths_n^\mathcal{M}(s_0 \models \varphi)$. Since the only interesting case is time-bounded "until", we consider $\varphi = \varphi_1 U^{[a,b]} \varphi_2$, where $a, b \in \mathbb{Q}$. Let $\sum_{i=0}^{n-1} t_i - \Delta > a$ and $\sum_{i=0}^{n-2} t_i + \Delta < b$, where $\Delta = \dfrac{2n}{10^k}$, and k is large enough. We construct Cyl by considering intervals I_i with rational bounds that are based on t_i. Let $I_i = [t_i^-, t_i^+]$ s.t. $t_i^- = t_i = t_i^+$ if $t_i \in \mathbb{Q}$, and otherwise:

$$t_i^- < t_i < t_i^+, \; t_i^- > t_i - \frac{\Delta}{2n} \text{ and } t_i^+ < t_i + \frac{\Delta}{2n}.$$

We have to show for $t_i \notin \mathbb{Q}$, Eq. (3) and Eq. (4) hold:

$$\sum_{i=0}^{n-1} t_i^- > a. \tag{3}$$

Proof. We know that $\displaystyle\sum_{i=0}^{n-1} t_i - \Delta > a \implies \sum_{i=0}^{n-1} t_i^- + n \cdot \frac{\Delta}{2n} - \Delta > a$

$$\implies \sum_{i=0}^{n-1} t_i^- + \frac{\Delta}{2} - \Delta > a \implies \sum_{i=0}^{n-1} t_i^- - \frac{\Delta}{2} > a \implies \sum_{i=0}^{n-1} t_i^- > a.$$

$$\sum_{i=0}^{n-2} t_i^+ < b. \tag{4}$$

Proof. We know that $\sum_{i=0}^{n-2} t_i + \Delta < b \implies \sum_{i=0}^{n-2} t_i^+ - (n-1) \cdot \dfrac{\Delta}{2n} + \Delta < b$

$$\implies \sum_{i=0}^{n-2} t_i^+ + \dfrac{(n+1) \cdot \Delta}{2n} < b \implies \sum_{i=0}^{n-2} t_i^+ < b.$$

One way is to pick t_i^-, t_i^+ as follows:

$$t_i^- = \lfloor t_i \rfloor + \dfrac{\lfloor \{t_i\} \cdot 10^k \rfloor}{10^k},$$

$$t_i^+ = \lfloor t_i \rfloor + \dfrac{\lfloor \{t_i\} \cdot 10^k \rfloor + 1}{10^k},$$

where $\{t_i\}$ represents the fractional part of the irrational number t_i. It can be checked that picking t_i^-, t_i^+ this way satisfies the above mentioned constraints.

From this derivation we conclude that $\{\pi \in Paths(s_0) | \pi \models \varphi\}$ can be rewritten as the combination of cylinder sets of the form $Cyl = (s_0, I_0, \ldots, I_{n-1}, s_n)$. That is,

$$\{\pi \in Paths(s_0) | \pi \models \varphi\} = \bigcup_{n \in \mathbb{N}} \bigcup_{\pi \in Paths_n^{\mathcal{M}}(s_0 \models \varphi)} Cyl_\pi, \tag{5}$$

where $Paths_n^{\mathcal{M}}(s_0 \models \varphi)$ is the set of paths of length n starting from s_0 which satisfy φ. $\qquad \square$

Proof of Theorem 6

Proof. The proof is similar to that of Theorem 3. We consider the WL-closed set of cylinder sets of length n in $\mathcal{M}$, $\mathcal{M}/_\mathcal{R}$ such that this set satisfies φ. The rest of the proof remains the same. $\qquad \square$

Development of the Computer Language Classification Knowledge Portal*

Nikolay V. Shilov[1], Alexander A. Akinin[2],
Alexey V. Zubkov[2], and Renat I. Idrisov[2]

[1] A.P. Ershov Institute of Informatics Systems,
Lavrent'ev av., 6, Novosibirsk 630090, Russia,
`shilov@iis.nsk.su`
[2] Novosibirsk State University
Koptyug Av., 2, Novosibirsk 630090, Russia,
{`akinin3113,ortoslon`}`@gmail.com`, `ren@ngs.ru`

Abstract. During the semicentennial history of Computer Science and Information Technologies, several thousands of computer languages have been created. The computer language universe includes languages for different purposes: programming languages, specification languages, modeling languages, languages for knowledge representation, etc. In each of these branches of computer languages it is possible to track several approaches (imperative, declarative, object-oriented, etc.), disciplines of processing (sequential, non-deterministic, parallel, distributed, etc.), and formalized models, such as Turing machines or logic inference machines. Computer language paradigms are the basis for classification of the computer languages. They are based on joint attributes which allow us to differentiate branches in the computer language universe. Currently the number of essentially different paradigms is close to several dozens. The study and precise specification of computer language paradigms (including new ones) are called to improve the choice of appropriate computer languages for new Software projects and information technologies. This position paper presents an approach to computer languages paradigmatization (i. e. paradigm specification) and classification that is based on a unified approach to formal semantics, and an open wiki-like ontology for pragmatics, formal syntax and informal "style".

1 The Problem of Computer Language Classification

We understand by a computer language any language that is designed or used for automatic information processing, i.e. data and process representation, handling and management. A classification of some universe (the universe of computer languages in particular) consists in means of identification and separation of items/entities/objects, classes and their roles, and navigation between them.

---

* Research is supported by Integration Research Program 2/12 of Russian Academy of Science.

E. Clarke, I. Virbitskaite, and A. Voronkov (Eds.): PSI 2011, LNCS 7162, pp. 340–348, 2012.

The *History of Programming Languages* poster by O'REILLY is well known (http://www.oreilly.com/news/graphics/prog_lang_poster.pdf). It represents chronological and influence relations between 2500 programming languages. Due to the number of existing computer languages alone, there is a necessity for their systematization or, more precisely, for their classification. At the same time, classification of already developed and new computer languages is a very important problem for Computer Science, since software engineers and information technology experts could benefit by a sound framework for computer language choice of components for new program and information systems.

At the initial stage of the history of programming and information technology (1950-65), it was possible to classify computer languages chronologically with annotations like in Herodotus' "History", i.e. including lists of authors, their intentions, personal stories, etc. The matter is that at the first stage almost all computer languages were imperative languages for von Neumann's computers. But since the late 60s this approach has become unacceptable. Since then, the variety of computer languages included not only programming languages, but also specification languages, data representation languages, etc. Some of these branches included declarative languages (functional in particular). In the late 70s and the early 80s, new approaches to computer language design appeared (e.g., logical and object-oriented). Drawing an analogy between Computer Science and other sciences, we could say that classification of computer languages could be done in the style of Linnaeus (i.e., a taxonomy like: Kingdom - Phylum - Class - Order - Family - Subfamily - Genus - Species). For example, look at *Taxonomic system for computer languages* at http://hopl.murdoch.edu.au/taxonomy.html.

However, the 90s and the beginning of the new millennium became the time of rapid growth of existing and new branches of computer languages such as knowledge representation languages, languages for parallel/concurrent computing, languages for distributed and multi-agent systems, etc. Each of these new computer languages has its own, sometimes very particular syntax, a certain model of information processing (i.e., semantics or a virtual machine), and its pragmatics (i.e., the sphere of its application and distribution). And though there were rather small groups of computer languages (e.g., Hardware Description Languages), many groups had already been crowded (e.g., Specification Languages) and some of them went through the period of explosion and migration (e.g., Markup Languages). Sometimes computer language experts have difficulties in putting some languages into one definite group[1]. Rapid generation of new computer languages will continue while new spheres of human activities will be computerized. Thereby the situation in computer languages radically differs from that of the natural sciences: in biology or chemistry the situation is much more static, while in computer languages it is rather dynamic. Due to these

---

[1] For example, programming language Ruby. "Its creator, Yukihiro "matz", blended parts of his favorite languages (Perl, Smalltalk, Eiffel, Ada, and Lisp) to form a new language that balanced functional programming with imperative programming" (http://www.ruby-lang.org/en/about/ – visited January 20, 2011).

arguments alone, the natural sciences analogies cannot be adequately adopted to the classification of computer languages.

We think that a modern classification of the computer languages universe can be built upon the flexible notion of *computer language paradigms*. In the general methodology of science, *paradigm* is an approach to the formulation of problems and their solutions. The term comes from Greek and means "pattern", "example" (noun), "exhibit", "represent" (verb). The contemporary meaning of the term is due to the well-known book [7] by Tomas Kuhn. Robert Floyd was the first who had explicitly used the term "paradigm" in the Computer Science context. In particular, he addressed "Paradigms of Programming" in his Turing Award Lecture [5]. Unfortunately, R. Floyd did not define this concept explicitly.

Recently Peter van Roy has published the taxonomy *The principal programming paradigms* (http://www.info.ucl.ac.be/~pvr/paradigms.html) with 27 different paradigms and advocated it in the paper [10]. Surprisingly, the cited paper does not provide a convincing and concise definition of the notion *Programming Paradigm*. We can refer to the following quotation only: "A programming paradigm is an approach to programming a computer based on a mathematical theory or a coherent set of principles. Each paradigm supports a set of concepts that makes it the best for a certain kind of problem." [10]

We would not like to say that the above definition is irrelevant but it is restricted to programming languages, and we are afraid that references to the general concept of paradigm as well as the phrase "programming a computer" are too vague. So we would like to provide our own definition that is more general, more precise and descriptive, but (we believe) is coherent with the general concept.

Definition 1

1. *Computer paradigms are alternative approaches (patterns) to formalization of information problem formulation, presentation, handling and processing.*
2. *They are fixed in the form of formal (mathematical) theory and accumulated in computer languages.*
3. *Every natural class of computer languages is the extent of some paradigm, and vice versa, every computer paradigm is the intent of some class of computer languages.*
4. *A paradigm can be characterized by a set of problems/application areas that the paradigm fits better than the other ones.*
5. *The educational value of paradigms is to teach to think different about information problems and to choose the best paradigm to solve them.*

Preliminary formulations of the first three clauses have been published in [1,2]. The fourth clause follows from the above definition by Peter van Roy. The last clause has been suggested and motivated in [3].

2   The Syntactic-Semantic-Pragmatic Approach

For natural and artificial languages (including computer languages), the terms *syntax*, *semantics* and *pragmatics* are used to categorize descriptions of language characteristics. The syntax is the orthography of the language. The meaning of syntactically-correct constructs is provided through the language semantics. Pragmatics is the practice of use of meaningful syntactically-correct constructs. Therefore the approach that is based on the features of syntax, semantics and pragmatics could be natural for the specification of paradigms and the classification of computer languages.

The syntactic aspect of computer language classification should reflect both the formal syntax and the human perspective. Certainly, it is very important for the compiler implementation whether a particular language has regular, context-free or context-sensitive syntax. Thus, syntactic properties of computer languages could be attributes in the classification. These attributes can be brought from formal language theory (e.g., the Chomsky hierarchy) or any other formal classification of formal languages. But informal annotations (attributes) like *flexibility*, *naturalness*, *style* (supported by a library of good-style examples), *clarity* from a human standpoint (including a portion of *syntactic sugar*) become much more important.

The role of formal semantics for the classification of computer languages is well known. The major problem with semantics of computer languages is that different formalisms and different level of formalization are adopted for different computer languages. This difference makes it extremely hard to compare semantics of different computer languages. Nevertheless, we think that the problem can be solved by development of multidimensional stratification of paradigmatic[2] computer languages. For example, educational semantics and formal semantics are two particular semantic dimensions. They can be stratified into *levels* and *layers* as follows.

- The layer hierarchy is an educational, human-centric semantic representation. It should comprise 2-3 layers that could be called *elementary*, *basic*, and *full*. The elementary layer would be an educational dialect of the language for the first-time study of primary concepts and features. The basic layer would be a subset for regular users of the language which requires skills and experience. The full layer is the language itself, it is for advanced and experienced users.
- The level hierarchy is a formal-oriented semantic representation. It should comprise several levels for the basic layer of the language and optionally for some other layers. The levels of the basic layer could be called *kernel*, *intermediate*, and *complete*. The kernel level would have executable semantics and provide tools for the implementation of the intermediate level; the intermediate level in turn should provide implementation tools for the complete level. Implementation of intermediate level should be of semantics-preserving transformation. Please refer [9] for example of 3-level hierarchy for programming language C#.

In contrast to syntax and semantics, pragmatics relies upon highly informal expertise and experience of people that are involved in the computer language

---

[2] We discuss what is *paradigmatic computer language* in the next section. To be short, paradigmatic languages are the most typical ones for a particular paradigm (class).

life cycle (i. e. design, implementation, promotion, usage and evolution). In other words, we need to formalize expert knowledge (views) about computer languages, related concepts, and relations between computer languages. It naturally leads to the idea of representing this knowledge with an ontology.

"Ontology is the theory of objects and their ties. Ontology provides criteria for distinguishing various types of objects (concrete and abstract, existent and non-existent, real and ideal, independent and dependent) and their ties (relations, dependencies and predication)" [4]. Roughly speaking, an ontology is a partial formalization of knowledge about a particular problem domain (computer languages for instance). This knowledge could include empirical facts, mathematical theorems, personal beliefs, expert resolutions, shared viewpoints, etc.

3   Towards an Open Temporal Evolving Ontology for the Classification of Computer Languages

Expert knowledge for pragmatics of computer languages should be formalized in an open versioned temporal ontology that includes syntactic and semantic (both formal and informal) knowledge in the form of annotations and attributes. Openness means that the ontology is open for access and editing. Temporality means that the ontology changes in time, admits temporal queries and assertions, and that all entries in the ontology are timestamped. Versioning means that the ontology tracks all its changes. Wikipedia, the free encyclopedia, is a good example an of open, temporal and versioned ontology.

Let us remark that the *History of Programming Languages* poster by O'REL-LY already defines an ontology of programming languages where the class differentiation and navigation method is explicit enumeration of languages, *influence lines* and *chronology*. The same holds for *History of Programming Languages* at http://hopl.murdoch.edu.au/ (HOPL). HOPL represents historical and implementation information about an impressive number (>8500) of programming languages. Unfortunately, HOPL is not open for editing, hasn't been updated since 2006, and does not deal with any inter-language relations other than *language-dialect-variant-implementation*. The situation is different with *Progopedia* (http://progopedia.ru/), a wiki-like encyclopedia of programming languages. It is open for editing and is tracing its history. But Progopedia has poor temporal navigation means. While HOPL provides some taxonomy instruments, Progopedia only has a trivial one (language-dialect-variant-implementation). In comparison with HOPL and the O'REILLY poster, Progopedia is relatively small. At present it contains information about ~50 languages, ~80 dialects, ~190 implementations, and ~500 versions. All these "ontologies" do not have means for constructing classes by users or deriving classes, and only manual navigation among the classes is supported. We believe that a more comprehensive ontology could solve the problem of computer languages classification, i.e. identification and differentiation of classes of computer languages and navigation among them.

In the proposed ontology for computer languages, objects should be computer languages (also their levels and layers), concepts/classes (in terms of DL/OWL)

– collections of computer languages that can be specified by concept terms (in DL), ties (DL-roles or OWL-properties) - relations between computer languages. For example, Pascal, LISP, PROLOG, SDL, LOTOS, UMLT, as well as C, C-light and C-kernel, OWL-Lite, OWL-DL and OWL-full should be objects of the ontology. Since we understand computer language paradigms as specifications of classes of computer languages, and we consider classes of computer languages DL-concepts/OWL-classes, then we have to adopt DL concept terms as paradigms of computer languages. In this setting, computer language paradigms and classification will not be taxonomic trees based on property inheritance from sup-class to sub-class. Objects (i.e. computer languages) of the proposed ontology could be described with different formal attributes (e.g., formal syntax properties) and informal annotations (e.g., libraries of samples of good style).

Let us remark that the list of formal attributes and informal annotations is not fixed but instead open for modifications and extensions. Nevertheless, it makes sense to provide certain attributes and annotations for all objects (e.g., an attribute "date of birth" with various time granularity, or an annotation "URL of an external link" for references) but allow to assign an indefinite value for them. In contrast, some other attributes and annotations will be very specific to objects. For example, "try-version" annotation with a link to an easy to install or web-based small implementation (that can be freeware or shareware) makes sense for elementary levels or kernel layers.

We have already discussed a number of examples of concepts/classes in the proposed ontology: "has context-free syntax", "functional languages", "specification languages", "executable languages", "static typing", "dynamic binding", etc. (More examples can be found at [13].) All listed examples should be elementary DL-concepts/OWL-classes. All elementary DL-concepts/OWL-classes should be explicitly annotated by appropriate attributes ("has a context-free syntax", "is a functional language", "is a specification language", etc.). Non-elementary concepts/classes could be specified by means that are supported by OWL and DL (by standard set-theoretic operations *union* and *intersection* in particular). For example, "executable specification languages" is the intersection of "executable languages" and "specification languages". We have some doubts about *complement*, since the proposed ontology will always be an open-world ontology with incomplete information. For example, if a language has no explicitly attached attribute "has a context-free syntax", it does not mean that the language has no CF-syntax. At present we adopt a temporary solution to use explicit positive (e.g., "has context-free syntax", "is a functional language", "is a specification language", etc.) and negative attributes (that are counterparts of positive one, e.g., "DOES NOT have a context-free syntax", "is NOT a functional language", "is NOT a specification language", etc.) and to use positive DL concept terms for paradigm specification (i.e. concept terms without complement).

But the proposed ontology should have a special elementary concept/class for *paradigmatic computer languages* that comprises few (but one at least) representatives for every elementary concept/class. Of course, all elementary concepts/classes (including paradigmatic languages) should be created on the basis of expert knowledge and be open for editing. A special requirement for the proposed ontology should be the following constraint: every legal (i.e. *well-formed*) non-empty concept/class must contain a paradigmatic language. This is common sense: if experts can not point out a representative example of a paradigm, then it should be empty.

Roles/properties in the proposed ontology could also be natural: "is a dialect of", "is a layer of", "uses the syntax of", etc. For example: "REAL is a dialect of SDL", "C-light is a layer of C", "OWL uses the syntax of XML". All listed examples are elementary DL-roles/OWL-properties. Standard (positive) relational algebra operations *union, intersection, composition*, and *transitive closure* can be used and are meaningful for construction of new roles/properties. For example, "uses the syntax of a dialect of" is the composition of "uses the syntax of" and "is a dialect of": REAL [8] executional[3] specifications "uses syntax of dialect of" SDL [12]. Again we have some doubts about usage of *complement* and *inverse* and, maybe, we will adopt the use of explicit complement and inverse for elementary DL-roles/OWL-properties.

Let us remark that the computer language domain has four domain-specific ties between languages: *is a dialect of, is a variant of, is a version of*, and *is an implementation of*. Of course these ties must be present in the proposed ontology as elementary DL-roles/OWL-properties. But, unfortunately, there is no consensus about definition of these ties. For example, *Progopedia* considers that an implementation can have a version, while [13] promotes an opposite view that a version can have an implementation. Detailed discussion of this issue is a topic for further research, but currently we adopt the following definition. *Dialects* are languages with joint elementary level. *Variants* are languages with joint basic level. A *version "series"* is a partially ordered "collection" of variants such that every smaller *version* is a compatible subset of all "later" versions[4]. An *implementation* is a platform-dependent variant of a language.

Universal and *existential quantifier restrictions* that are used in OWL and DL for construction of new classes/concepts also could get a natural and useful meaning. An example of existential restriction (in DL notation): a concept $(markup\_language) \sqcap \exists uses\_syntaxof : (\neg\{XML\})$ consists of all computer languages that are markup languages but do not use the syntax of the Extensible Markup Language XML; an example of a language of this kind is LaTeX. An example of a universal restriction and a terminological sentence (in DL notation also) follows: the sentence $\{XML\} \sqsubseteq is\_dialect\_of : (\neg\{ML\})$ expresses that XML is a dialect of any computer language but the functional programming "Meta Language" ML.

We would like to emphasize that the proposed ontology for pragmatics of computer languages should be an open versioned (evolving) temporal ontology. *Openness* of the ontology will be supported by the wiki technology for editing.

---

[3] Exactly *executional*, not *executable*.

[4] Several incompatible versions can coexists. For example, Object C and C++ are object-oriented variants of C, but for sure these two languages are incompatible.

Versioning will be supported by automatic timestamping and history of all edits. *Temporality* will be supported by temporal extensions of Description Logic for paradigm specification.

4   Current State of the Project

Recently we have started implementation of a prototype of a computer languages classification knowledge portal that eventually (we hope) will evolve into an Open Temporal Evolving Ontology for Classification of Computer Languages. We believe that it will provide Computer Language researchers with a sound and easy to maintain and update framework for new language design and language choice/selection tools for new Software engineers and Information Technology managers.

The prototype is designed for small-scale experimentation aims, and at present does not support full functionality. The prototype is implemented as a web application, so "experts" (i.e. members of the laboratory) can enter it with a web browser. The interface allows users to view and edit information contained in the portal, which is formed as an ontology.

The main elements of the prototype ontology are computer languages (objects of the ontology), elementary classes of languages (arbitrary, explicitly user-specified subsets of the set of objects), relations between the languages (binary relations over the set of objects), attributes (mappings from the set of languages to some external data types, e.g. text strings, URL's) and the Knowledge Base (Description Logic statements that represent laws of the problem domain of Computer Languages). The data is represented internally as an RDF-repository. All these entities can be viewed and modified directly by the user.

Two main services (that are already provided) are the ontology model checker and visualization. The model checker is used for computing classes of objects and ties from specifications (concept and role terms), and for checking consistency of the ontology (data and the Knowledge Base). Visualization is used for displaying classes and ties graphically.

The model checker is an explicit-state model checker for description logic ALBO/FCA [11]. This logic is expressively equivalent to ALBO, but has two special constructs for concept terms borrowed from Formal Concept Analysis (FCA) [6]. These constructs are upper and lower derivatives. (The lower derivative is the same as the *window operator*.)

Why do we use a model checker as a reasoning tool instead of any available DL inference machine (like Fact++, Kaon2, etc.)? Because our ontology is for empirical expert knowledge about rapidly developing and changing domain of Computer Languages, not a domain with a set of predefined domain-specific laws. We use an explicit-state model checker (not a symbolic one) since the domain numbers thousands of objects, i.e. it fits explicit state representation well.

Why are we developing a self-contained tool for the ontology instead of using some other ontology tool (Protege for instance)? Since we developing a tool for a small community-oriented ontology for Computer Language experts, where people would like to use a simple interface instead of studying a manual or a tutorial before using the tool.

References

1. Akinin, A.A., Shilov, N.V., Zubkov, A.V.: Towards Ontology for Classification of Computer Languages. In: Proceedings of the Knowledge and Ontology *ELSE-WHERE* Workshop, pp. 1–12. University High School of Economics, Moscow (2009), http://www.iis.nsk.su/files/ELSEWHERE.pdf (visited January 20, 2011)
2. Anureev, I.S., Bodin, E.V., Gorodnyay, L.V., Marchuk, A.G., Murzin, F.A., Shilov, N.V.: On the Problem of Computer Language Classification. Joint NCC&IIS Bulletin, Series Computer Science, vol. 27, pp. 1–20 (2008)
3. Andreeva, T.A., Anureev, I.S., Bodin, E.V., Gorodnyay, L.V., Marchuk, A.G., Murzin, F.A., Shilov, N.V.: Obrazovatelnoe znachenie klassifikacii komp'uternyh yazykov (Educational value of Computer Languages classification). Market DS publisher, Prikladnaya Informatika (Applied Informatics) 4(6-24), 18–28 (2009)
4. Corazzon, R.: Ontology. A Resource Guide for Philosophers, http://www.formalontology.it/ (visited January 20, 2011)
5. Floyd, R.W.: The paradigms of Programming. Communications of ACM 22, 455–460 (1979)
6. Ganter, B., Wille, R.: Formal Concept Analysis. Mathematical Foundations. Springer, Heidelberg (1996)
7. Kuhn, T.S.: The structure of Scientific Revolutions. Univ. of Chicago Press (1970); 3rd edn. (1996)
8. Nepomniaschy, V.A., Shilov, N.V., Bodin, E.V., Kozura, V.E.: Basic-REAL: Integrated Approach for Design, Specification and Verification of Distributed Systems. In: Butler, M., Petre, L., Sere, K. (eds.) IFM 2002. LNCS, vol. 2335, pp. 69–88. Springer, Heidelberg (2002)
9. Nepomniaschy, V.A., Anureev, I.S., Dubranovskii, I.V., Promsky, A.V.: Towards verification of C# programs: A three-level approach. Programming and Computer Software 32(4), 190–202 (2006)
10. van Roy, P.: Programming Paradigms for Dummies: What Every Programmer Should Know. In: Assayag, G., Gerzso, A. (eds.) New Computational Paradigms for Computer Music, IRCAM/Delatour, France, pp. 9–38 (2009)
11. Shilov, N.V.: Realization Problem for Formal Concept Analysis. In: Proceedings of the 21st International Workshop on Description Logics (DL 2008). CEUR Workshop Proceedings, vol. 353 (2008)
12. Turner, K.J. (ed.): Using Formal Description Techniques: An Introduction to Estelle, LOTOS and SDL. John Wiley and Sons (1993)
13. Kinnersley, W.: The Language List, http://people.ku.edu/~nkinners/LangList/Extras/langlist.htm (visited January 20, 2011)

Justified Terminological Reasoning

Thomas Studer

Institut für Informatik und angewandte Mathematik
Universität Bern, Swizerland
tstuder@iam.unibe.ch
http://www.iam.unibe.ch/~tstuder

Abstract. Justification logics are epistemic logics that include explicit justifications for an agent's knowledge. In the present paper, we introduce a justification logic $\mathcal{JALC}$ over the description logic $\mathcal{ALC}$. We provide a deductive system and a semantics for our logic and we establish soundness and completeness results. Moreover, we show that our logic satisfies the so-called internalization property stating that it internalizes its own notion of proof. We then sketch two applications of $\mathcal{JALC}$: (i) the justification terms can be used to generate natural language explanations why an $\mathcal{ALC}$ statement holds and (ii) the terms can be used to study data privacy issues for description logic knowledge bases.

Keywords: Justification logic, description logic, inference tracking, explanations, data privacy.

1 Introduction

Description logics [7] are a variant of modal logic that is used in knowledge representation to model the universe of discourse of an application domain and to reason about it. In the present paper we study the basic logic $\mathcal{ALC}$ which is the minimal description logic that is closed under boolean connectives. Our aim is to extend $\mathcal{ALC}$ with so-called justification terms yielding a justification logic over $\mathcal{ALC}$.

Justification logics [4] are epistemic logics that feature explicit justifications for an agent's knowledge and they allow to reason with and about these justifications. The first logic of this kind, the *logic of proofs* LP, has been developed by Artemov [2,3] to solve the problem of a provability semantics for S4. Since then many applications of justification logics have been studied. For instance, these logics have been used to create a new approach to the logical omniscience problem [6], to explore self-referential proofs [18], to study evidence tracking [5], and to investigate the role of the announcement as a justification in public announcement logics [10,11].

Instead of the simple statement A *is known*, denoted $\Box A$, justification logics reason about justifications for knowledge by using the construct $[t]A$ to formalize t *is a justification for* A, where the evidence term t can be viewed as an informal justification or a formal mathematical proof depending on the application.

E. Clarke, I. Virbitskaite, and A. Voronkov (Eds.): PSI 2011, LNCS 7162, pp. 349–361, 2012.

S4 axioms	**LP axioms**	
$\Box(\phi \to \psi) \to (\Box\phi \to \Box\psi)$	$[t](\phi \to \psi) \to ([s]\phi \to [t \cdot s]\psi)$	(application)
$\Box\phi \to \phi$	$[t]\phi \to \phi$	(reflexivity)
$\Box\phi \to \Box\Box\phi$	$[t]\phi \to [!t][t]\phi$	(inspection)
	$[t]\phi \vee [s]\phi \to [t+s]\phi$	(sum)

Fig. 1. Axioms of S4 and LP

Evidence terms are built by means of operations that correspond to the axioms of S4 as Fig. 1 shows.

Internalization is a key property for any justification logic. It states that for each derivation $\mathcal{D}$ of a theorem A of the logic in question, there is a step-by-step construction that transforms $\mathcal{D}$ into a term $t_{\mathcal{D}}$ such that $[t_{\mathcal{D}}]A$ is also a theorem of the logic. Therefore, the term $t_{\mathcal{D}}$ describes why, according to the logic, A must hold.

In this paper, we introduce a new logic $\mathcal{JALC}$ of justified $\mathcal{ALC}$ - that is we extend $\mathcal{ALC}$ by justification terms - and study its main features. We start with a brief introduction to the description logic $\mathcal{ALC}$. In Section 3, we introduce the language of $\mathcal{JALC}$ and present a deductive system for it. We then prove the so-called Lifting lemma saying that $\mathcal{JALC}$ internalizes its own notion of proof. We define a semantics for $\mathcal{JALC}$ and establish soundness and completeness of the deductive system in Section 4. Then a section about applications follows where we give a detailed example of internalization. We make use of this example to illustrate how internalization can be applied to

1. the problem of generating natural language explanations and
2. the problem of data privacy for $\mathcal{ALC}$ knowledge bases.

In Section 6, we present related work. Finally we conclude the paper and mention some further research directions.

2   The Description Logic $\mathcal{ALC}$

In this section, we briefly recall the main definitions concerning $\mathcal{ALC}$. We will not only study subsumption but also introduce formulas for $\mathcal{ALC}$, which will be useful when we add justification terms. Also compactness of $\mathcal{ALC}$ will play an important role later.

Definition 1 (Concept). *We start with* countably many *concept names and role names. The set of* concepts *is then defined inductively as follows:*

1. *Every concept name is a concept.*
2. *If C and D are concepts, R is a role name, then the following expressions are concepts:*
$$\neg C, \quad C \sqcap D, \quad \forall R.C.$$

As usual, we define $C \sqcup D := \neg(\neg C \sqcap \neg D)$, $\exists R.C := \neg\forall R.\neg C$, and $\top := A \sqcup \neg A$ for some fixed concept name A.

Definition 2 ($\mathcal{L}_A$ formula)

1. If C and D are concepts, then $C \sqsubseteq D$ is an (atomic) $\mathcal{L}_A$ formula.
2. If ϕ and ψ are $\mathcal{L}_A$ formulas, then the following expressions are $\mathcal{L}_A$ formulas:

$$\neg\phi, \quad \phi \wedge \psi.$$

Definition 3 ($\mathcal{ALC}$ interpretation). An $\mathcal{ALC}$ interpretation is a pair $\mathcal{I} = (\Delta_\mathcal{I}, \cdot^\mathcal{I})$ where $\Delta_\mathcal{I}$ is a non-empty set called the domain of $\mathcal{I}$ and $\cdot^\mathcal{I}$ maps each concept name A to a subset $A^\mathcal{I} \subseteq \Delta_\mathcal{I}$ and each role name R to a binary relation $R^\mathcal{I}$ on $\Delta_\mathcal{I}$. An interpretation is extended to non-atomic concepts as follows.

1. $(\neg C)^\mathcal{I} = \Delta_I \setminus C^\mathcal{I}$
2. $(C \sqcap D)^\mathcal{I} = C^\mathcal{I} \cap D^\mathcal{I}$
3. $(\forall R.C)^\mathcal{I} = \{d \in \Delta_I \; : \; \forall d' \in \Delta_I(R^\mathcal{I}(d, d') \to C^\mathcal{I}(d'))\}$.

Definition 4 ($\mathcal{ALC}$ satisfiability). We inductively define when an $\mathcal{L}_A$ formula is satisfied in an $\mathcal{ALC}$ interpretation $\mathcal{I}$.

1. $\mathcal{I} \models C \sqsubseteq D$ iff $C^\mathcal{I} \subseteq D^\mathcal{I}$
2. $\mathcal{I} \models \neg\phi$ iff not $\mathcal{I} \models \phi$
3. $\mathcal{I} \models \phi \wedge \psi$ iff $\mathcal{I} \models \phi$ and $\mathcal{I} \models \psi$

We say an $\mathcal{L}_A$ formula ϕ is $\mathcal{ALC}$ valid (and write $\models_{\mathcal{ALC}} \phi$) if for all interpretations $\mathcal{I}$ we have $\mathcal{I} \models \phi$. For a set of $\mathcal{L}_A$ formulas Φ, we write $\models_{\mathcal{ALC}} \Phi$ if for all $\phi \in \Phi$ we have $\models_{\mathcal{ALC}} \phi$.

By the work of Schild [22], we know that $\mathcal{ALC}$ can be seen as a notational variant of the multi-modal logic K_n. Thus we can transfer results from K_n to $\mathcal{ALC}$. In particular, we immediately get the following lemma about compactness of $\mathcal{ALC}$ from compactness of K_n.

Lemma 1 ($\mathcal{ALC}$ compactness). $\mathcal{ALC}$ is compact: for any set Φ of $\mathcal{L}_A$ formulas we have

$$\models_{\mathcal{ALC}} \Phi \text{ if and only if for all finite subsets } \Phi' \subseteq \Phi \text{ we have } \models_{\mathcal{ALC}} \Phi'.$$

3   Syntax of $\mathcal{JALC}$

The aim of this section is to introduce the language of $\mathcal{JALC}$, the logic of justified $\mathcal{ALC}$. Then we present a deductive system for $\mathcal{JALC}$ and show that it satisfies internalization.

Definition 5 (Terms). We fix countable sets of constants Con and variables Var, respectively. Terms t are now built according to the following grammar

$$t ::= x \mid c \mid t \cdot t \mid t + t \mid \,!t$$

where x is a variable and c is a constant. Tm denotes the set of terms.

Definition 6 ($\mathcal{L}_J$ Formula)

1. *If C and D are concepts, then $C \sqsubseteq D$ is an (atomic) $\mathcal{L}_J$ formula.*
2. *If ϕ and ψ are $\mathcal{L}_J$ formulas and t is a term, then the following expressions are $\mathcal{L}_J$ formulas:*

$$\neg\phi, \quad \phi \wedge \psi, \quad [t]\phi.$$

We denote the set of $\mathcal{L}_J$ formulas by Fml_J. As usual, we define

$$\phi \vee \psi := \neg(\neg\phi \wedge \neg\psi) \quad \text{and} \quad \phi \to \psi := \neg\phi \vee \psi.$$

Note that every $\mathcal{L}_A$ formula also is an $\mathcal{L}_J$ formula.

Definition 7 ($\mathcal{JALC}$ deductive system). *The axioms of $\mathcal{JALC}$ consist of all Fml_J instances of the following schemes:*

1. *All valid $\mathcal{L}_A$ formulas ϕ, i.e. for which $\models_{\mathcal{ALC}} \phi$ holds*
2. *$[t](\phi \to \psi) \to ([s]\phi \to [t \cdot s]\psi)$*   *(application)*
3. *$[t]\phi \vee [s]\phi \to [t + s]\phi$*   *(sum)*
4. *$[t]\phi \to \phi$*   *(reflexivity)*
5. *$[t]\phi \to [!t][t]\phi$*   *(introspection)*

A constant specification $\mathcal{CS}$ is any subset

$$\mathcal{CS} \subseteq \{[c]\phi \ : \ c \text{ is a constant and } \phi \text{ is an axiom of } \mathcal{JALC}\}.$$

A constant specification $\mathcal{CS}$ is called axiomatically appropriate *if for every axiom ϕ of $\mathcal{JALC}$, there is a constant c such $[c]\phi \in \mathcal{CS}$.*

The deductive system $\mathcal{JALC}(\mathcal{CS})$ *is the Hilbert system that consists of the above axioms of $\mathcal{JALC}$ and the following rules of* modus ponens *and* axiom necessitation*:*

$$\frac{\phi \quad \phi \to \psi}{\psi} \quad , \qquad \frac{}{[c]\phi} \quad \text{where } [c]\phi \in \mathcal{CS}.$$

For a set of $\mathcal{L}_J$ formulas Φ we write $\Phi \vdash_{\mathcal{CS}} \phi$ to state that ϕ is derivable from Φ in $\mathcal{JALC}(\mathcal{CS})$. When the constant specification $\mathcal{CS}$ is clear from the context we will write only $\vdash$ instead of $\vdash_{\mathcal{CS}}$.

We say a set Φ of $\mathcal{L}_J$ formulas is $\mathcal{CS}$ consistent if there exists a formula ϕ such that $\Phi \nvdash_{\mathcal{CS}} \phi$. The set Φ is called *maximal $\mathcal{CS}$ consistent* if it is $\mathcal{CS}$ consistent but has no proper extension that is $\mathcal{CS}$ consistent.

The Lifting Lemma states the $\mathcal{JALC}$ internalizes its own notion of proof. This is a standard property that any justification logic should have.

Lemma 2 (Lifting lemma). *Let $\mathcal{CS}$ be an axiomatically appropriate constant specification. If*

$$[x_1]\phi_1, \ldots, [x_n]\phi_n, \psi_1, \ldots \psi_m \vdash_{\mathcal{CS}} \chi,$$

then there is a term $t(x_1, \ldots, x_n, y_1, \ldots, y_m)$ such that

$$[x_1]\phi_1, \ldots, [x_n]\phi_n, [y_1]\psi_1, \ldots, [y_m]\psi_m \vdash_{\mathcal{CS}} [t(x_1, \ldots, x_n, y_1, \ldots, y_m)]\chi.$$

Proof. Let Φ be the set $\{[x_1]\phi_1, \ldots, [x_n]\phi_n, [y_1]\psi_1, \ldots, [y_m]\psi_m\}$. We proceed by induction on the length of the derivation of χ and distinguish the following cases.

1. χ is an axiom of $\mathcal{JALC}$. Since $\mathcal{CS}$ is axiomatically appropriate, there is a constant c such that $[c]\chi \in \mathcal{CS}$. Thus $\vdash [c]\chi$ follows by axiom necessitation.
2. χ is $[x_i]\phi_i$ for some i. We find $[x_i]\phi_i \vdash [!x_i][x_i]\phi_i$ by *(introspection)* and modus ponens.
3. χ is ψ_i for some i. We immediately have $[y_i]\psi_i \vdash [y_i]\psi_i$.
4. χ follows from $\psi \to \chi$ and ψ by modus ponens. By the induction hypothesis there are terms $t_1(x_1, \ldots, x_n, y_1, \ldots, y_m)$ and $t_2(x_1, \ldots, x_n, y_1, \ldots, y_m)$ such that

$$\Phi \vdash [t_1(x_1, \ldots, x_n, y_1, \ldots, y_m)](\psi \to \chi)$$

and

$$\Phi \vdash [t_2(x_1, \ldots, x_n, y_1, \ldots, y_m)]\psi.$$

Thus

$$\Phi \vdash [t_1(x_1, \ldots, x_n, y_1, \ldots, y_m) \cdot t_2(x_1, \ldots, x_n, y_1, \ldots, y_m)]\chi$$

follows from *(application)* and applying modus ponens twice.
5. χ is the conclusion of axiom necessitation. Then χ has the form $[c]\chi'$. Thus we find $\vdash [!c][c]\chi'$ by *(introspection)* and modus ponens. $\square$

4   Semantics of $\mathcal{JALC}$

The semantics of $\mathcal{JALC}$ is based on so-called F-models [16] for justification logics. These models consist of a Kripke frame and an evidence function specifying for each state which terms are admissible evidence for which formulas. This evidence function has to satisfy certain closure conditions matching the axioms of $\mathcal{JALC}$. Finally, we assign to each state an $\mathcal{ALC}$ interpretation that gives meaning to concept and role names.

Definition 8 ($\mathcal{JALC}$ model). *A $\mathcal{JALC}$ model meeting a constant specification $\mathcal{CS}$ is a tuple $\mathcal{M} = (W, \lhd, \mathcal{E}, I)$ where*

1. *W is a non-empty set (of states)*
2. *$\lhd$ is a binary relation on W that is transitive and reflexive*
3. *$\mathcal{E}$ is an evidence function $\mathcal{E} : W \times \mathsf{Tm} \to \mathcal{P}(\mathsf{Fml}_J)$ that satisfies the following closure conditions for any states $w, v \in W$:*
   (a) if $[c]\phi \in \mathcal{CS}$, then $\phi \in \mathcal{E}(w, c)$
   (b) if $\lhd(w, v)$, then $\mathcal{E}(w, t) \subseteq \mathcal{E}(v, t)$
   (c) if $(\phi \to \psi) \in \mathcal{E}(w, t)$ and $\phi \in \mathcal{E}(w, s)$, then $\psi \in \mathcal{E}(w, t \cdot s)$
   (d) $\mathcal{E}(w, s) \cup \mathcal{E}(w, t) \subseteq \mathcal{E}(w, s + t)$
   (e) if $\phi \in \mathcal{E}(w, t)$, then $[t]\phi \in \mathcal{E}(w, !t)$
4. *I associates with each $w \in W$ an $\mathcal{ALC}$ interpretation $I(w) = (\Delta_w, \cdot^{\mathcal{I}(w)})$.*

We use the standard notion of satisfiability for F-models. A formula $[t]\phi$ holds at a state w if ϕ holds at all states reachable from w and the term t is admissible evidence for ϕ at w.

Definition 9 (Satisfiability). *We inductively define when a formula is satisfied in a model $\mathcal{M} = (W, \lhd, \mathcal{E}, I)$ at a world $w \in W$.*

1. *$\mathcal{M}, w \models C \sqsubseteq D$ iff $C^{\mathcal{I}(w)} \subseteq D^{\mathcal{I}(w)}$*
2. *$\mathcal{M}, w \models \neg\phi$ iff not $\mathcal{M}, w \models \phi$*
3. *$\mathcal{M}, w \models \phi \wedge \psi$ iff $\mathcal{M}, w \models \phi$ and $\mathcal{M}, w \models \psi$*
4. *$\mathcal{M}, w \models [t]\phi$ iff $\mathcal{M}, w' \models \phi$ for all $w' \in W$ such that $w \lhd w'$ and $\phi \in \mathcal{E}(w, t)$.*

We write $\models_{\mathcal{CS}} \phi$ and say that the formula ϕ is *valid with respect to the constant specification $\mathcal{CS}$* if for all models $\mathcal{M} = (W, \lhd, \mathcal{E}, I)$ that meet $\mathcal{CS}$ and all $w \in W$ we have $\mathcal{M}, w \models \phi$.

As usual, soundness follows by a straightforward induction on the length of $\mathcal{JALC}(\mathcal{CS})$ derivations.

Theorem 1 (Soundness). *Let ϕ be an $\mathcal{L}_J$ formula and $\mathcal{CS}$ a constant specification. We have*

$$\vdash_{\mathcal{CS}} \phi \quad implies \quad \models_{\mathcal{CS}} \phi.$$

In the remainder of this section, we will establish completeness of the deductive system $\mathcal{JALC}(\mathcal{CS})$. Our aim is to construct a canonical model. To do so, we first need to show that certain $\mathcal{ALC}$ interpretations exist.

Definition 10. *Let Φ be a set of $\mathcal{L}_J$ formulas. We set*

$$G_\Phi := \{\phi \in \Phi \ : \ \phi \text{ is an } \mathcal{L}_A \text{ formula}\}.$$

Lemma 3 (Existence of $\mathcal{ALC}$ interpretations). *There exists a function I_G that maps any consistent set of formulas Φ to an $\mathcal{ALC}$ interpretation $I_G(\Phi)$ such that $I_G(\Phi) \models G_\Phi$.*

Proof. We show that there exists an $\mathcal{ALC}$ interpretation $\mathcal{I}$ such that $\mathcal{I} \models G_\Phi$. We suppose G_Φ is not $\mathcal{ALC}$ satisfiable and aim at a contradiction. By compactness of $\mathcal{ALC}$ there exists a finite subset $\Phi'_G \subseteq \Phi_G$ that is not $\mathcal{ALC}$ satisfiable. That means $\bigwedge \Phi'_G$ is not satisfiable which implies $\models_{\mathcal{ALC}} \neg \bigwedge \Phi'_G$. Therefore, $\neg \bigwedge \Phi'_G$ is an axiom of $\mathcal{JALC}$ and thus

$$\vdash \neg \bigwedge \Phi'_G. \tag{1}$$

Since $\Phi'_G \subseteq \Phi_G$, we also obtain

$$\Phi \vdash \bigwedge \Phi'_G. \tag{2}$$

From (1) and (2) we conclude $\Phi \vdash A$ for any formula A, which contradicts the assumption that Φ is consistent.

Thus for any $\mathcal{JALC}$ consistent set of formulas Φ there exists an $\mathcal{ALC}$ interpretation $\mathcal{I}$ with $\mathcal{I} \models G_\Phi$. We let I_G be a function that chooses for each consistent Φ such an interpretation $\mathcal{I}$. □

Definition 11 (Canonical model). *We define the* canonical model $\mathcal{M} = (W, \lhd, \mathcal{E}, I)$ *meeting a constant specification* $\mathcal{CS}$ *as follows.*

1. *W is the set of all maximal $\mathcal{CS}$ consistent subsets of Fml_J*
2. *$w \lhd v$ if and only if for all $t \in \mathsf{Tm}$, we have $[t]A \in w$ implies $A \in v$*
3. *$\mathcal{E}(w, t) := \{A \in \mathsf{Fml}_J \; : \; [t]A \in w\}$*
4. *$I := I_G$.*

It is standard to show that the canonical model is indeed a $\mathcal{J\!ALC}$ model, meaning that $\lhd$ satisfies the frame conditions and $\mathcal{E}$ satisfies the closure conditions of evidence functions. For details we refer to Fitting [16]. Thus we have the following lemma.

Lemma 4. *The canonical model meeting a constant specification $\mathcal{CS}$ is a $\mathcal{J\!ALC}$ model meeting $\mathcal{CS}$.*

Lemma 5 (Truth lemma). *Let $\mathcal{M}$ be the canonical model meeting a constant specification $\mathcal{CS}$. For all $\mathcal{L}_J$ formulas ϕ and all states w in $\mathcal{M}$, we have*

$$\phi \in w \text{ if and only if } \mathcal{M}, w \models_{\mathcal{CS}} \phi.$$

Proof. Proof by induction on the structure of ϕ. If ϕ is atomic, then we have by Lemma 3

$$\phi \in w \text{ iff } \phi \in G_w \text{ iff } I_G(w) \models \phi \text{ iff } \mathcal{M}, w \models_{\mathcal{CS}} \phi.$$

The cases where ϕ is not atomic are standard and follow easily from the closure conditions on the evidence function, again see [16]. □

As usual, the Truth lemma implies completeness of the corresponding deductive system.

Theorem 2 (Completeness). *Let ϕ be an $\mathcal{L}_J$ formula and $\mathcal{CS}$ be a constant specification. We have*

$$\models_{\mathcal{CS}} \phi \quad \text{implies} \quad \vdash_{\mathcal{CS}} \phi.$$

5   Applications

Inference tracking. One distinguished feature of justification terms is that they keep track of the inferences made in a logical derivation. Let us illustrate this with the following example about a business information system storing information about managers and their salaries.

Let Φ be a knowledge base containing the three statements:

1. If a person gets a high salary, then she handles key accounts only

$$\texttt{high} \sqsubseteq \forall\texttt{handles.keyAcc} \quad . \tag{ϕ_1}$$

2. Everyone who handles something gets a high or a low salary

$$\exists \mathtt{handles}.\top \sqsubseteq \mathtt{high} \sqcup \mathtt{low} \quad . \tag{ϕ_2}$$

3. Person 1 handles something that is not a key account

$$\mathtt{P1} \sqsubseteq \exists \mathtt{handles}.\neg \mathtt{keyAcc} \quad . \tag{ϕ_3}$$

From this knowledge base we can derive that Person 1 gets a low salary. That is we have

$$\phi_1, \phi_2, \phi_3 \vdash \mathtt{P1} \sqsubseteq \mathtt{low}. \tag{3}$$

However, this does not give us any information on how the derivation looks like. We can change this situation by applying the Lifting lemma to (3) which results in

$$[v]\phi_1, [w]\phi_2, [x]\phi_3 \vdash_{\mathcal{CS}} [t]\mathtt{P1} \sqsubseteq \mathtt{low}.$$

Now the term t will provide explicit information about a derivation of $\mathtt{P1} \sqsubseteq \mathtt{low}$.

To apply the Lifting lemma we need an axiomatically appropriate constant specification $\mathcal{CS}$. We assume $\mathcal{CS}$ is such that for all concepts A, B, C and role names R, the following are elements of $\mathcal{CS}$:

$$[a](A \sqsubseteq B \to \exists R.A \sqsubseteq \exists R.B),$$
$$[b](A \sqsubseteq B \to (C \sqsubseteq A \to C \sqsubseteq B)),$$
$$[c](A \sqsubseteq B \to \neg B \sqsubseteq \neg A),$$
$$[d](A \sqsubseteq B \sqcup C \to (A \sqsubseteq \neg B \to A \sqsubseteq C)),$$
$$[e]\neg \mathtt{keyAcc} \sqsubseteq \top.$$

We now find that from $[v]\phi_1, [w]\phi_2, [x]\phi_3$ the following statements are derivable in $\mathcal{JALC}(\mathcal{CS})$:

$$[a \cdot e]\exists \mathtt{handles}.\neg \mathtt{keyAcc} \sqsubseteq \exists \mathtt{handles}.\top$$
$$[b \cdot (a \cdot e)](\mathtt{P1} \sqsubseteq \exists \mathtt{handles}.\neg \mathtt{keyAcc} \to \mathtt{P1} \sqsubseteq \exists \mathtt{handles}.\top)$$
$$[(b \cdot (a \cdot e)) \cdot x]\mathtt{P1} \sqsubseteq \exists \mathtt{handles}.\top$$
$$[b \cdot w](\mathtt{P1} \sqsubseteq \exists \mathtt{handles}.\top \to \mathtt{P1} \sqsubseteq \mathtt{high} \sqcup \mathtt{low})$$
$$[(b \cdot w) \cdot ((b \cdot (a \cdot e)) \cdot x)](\mathtt{P1} \sqsubseteq \mathtt{high} \sqcup \mathtt{low})$$
$$[c \cdot v]\exists \mathtt{handles}.\neg \mathtt{keyAcc} \sqsubseteq \neg \mathtt{high}$$
$$[(b \cdot (c \cdot v)) \cdot x]\mathtt{P1} \sqsubseteq \neg \mathtt{high}$$
$$[(d \cdot ((b \cdot w) \cdot ((b \cdot (a \cdot e)) \cdot x))) \cdot ((b \cdot (c \cdot v)) \cdot x)]\mathtt{P1} \sqsubseteq \mathtt{low}$$

In the last line, the justification term

$$(d \cdot ((b \cdot w) \cdot ((b \cdot (a \cdot e)) \cdot x))) \cdot ((b \cdot (c \cdot v)) \cdot x) \tag{4}$$

represents the logical steps that led to the conclusion $\mathtt{P1} \sqsubseteq \mathtt{low}$. We can now use this justification term for two purposes: to give explanations and to study data privacy.

Explanations. The justification terms can be employed to give a natural language description of the reasoning steps performed in the proof. For instance, since the term c justifies $A \sqsubseteq B \rightarrow \neg B \sqsubseteq \neg A$, we can translate, for instance, $[c \cdot v]\psi$ into

> taking the contrapositive of the statement justified by v results in ψ.

Using v from our example, we get

> taking the contrapositive of $\text{high} \sqsubseteq \forall \text{handles.keyAcc}$
> gives us $\exists \text{handles.}\neg\text{keyAcc} \sqsubseteq \neg\text{high}$.

Of course, for practical applications it is important to find the right level of abstraction. In a long proof, we do not want to mention every single axiom and every single application of an inference rule that is used. That means we do not give an explanation for every single proof constant and every single application occurring in a proof term. Instead, terms of a certain complexity should be regarded as one unit representing one step in the proof. For example, because the variable x justifies $\text{P1} \sqsubseteq \exists \text{handles.}\neg\text{keyAcc}$ and a, b, e are constants and thus justify logical axioms, we can read

$$[(b \cdot (a \cdot e)) \cdot x]\text{P1} \sqsubseteq \exists\text{handles.}\top$$

in a more abstract way as

> $\text{P1} \sqsubseteq \exists\text{handles.}\neg\text{keyAcc}$ implies
> $\text{P1} \sqsubseteq \exists\text{handles.}\top$ by simple logical reasoning in $\mathcal{ALC}$.

Data Privacy. Inference tracking is also important for applications in the area of data privacy. In privacy aware applications only a part of a given knowledge base is publicly accessible (say via views or via aggregation) and other parts (say containing personally identifiable information) should be kept secret. A violation of privacy occurs if it is possible for an agent to infer some secret information from the public part of the knowledge base.

There are basically two possibilities to prevent such privacy violations: (i) to refuse an answer to a query, that is make the public part of the knowledge base smaller, or (ii) to lie about the answer, that is distort the knowledge base. In both cases it is important to understand what led to the privacy breach. That means to understand how it was possible a secret could be inferred from the public knowledge. Again, if we model this situation in a justification logic, then we can apply the Lifting lemma to obtain a term that tracks the inferences leading to the leaked secret. This term is essentially a blueprint of a derivation of the secret. Thus it contains information about which elements of the published part of the knowledge base are responsible for the privacy violation and this information can be used to alter the knowledge base such that it does no longer leak private data.

Consider our example above about the knowledge base Φ. We assume that P1 $\sqsubseteq$ low should be kept secret since it contains information that is related to a specific person. As we have seen before, there is a violation of privacy since we have $\Phi \vdash$ P1 $\sqsubseteq$ low and now the question is what part of Φ is responsible for this. The justification term (4) constructed by the Lifting lemma contains the variables v, w, x. This tells us that $\{\phi_1, \phi_2, \phi_3\}$ is a subset of Φ from which the secret can be inferred. Thus to prevent this privacy breach it is a good strategy to restrict access to at least on these three elements. Of course, this does not guarantee privacy since there may be other derivations of the secret that start from a different subset of Φ. Still the justification term provides valuable information for a heuristic to construct a privacy preserving knowledge base.

6   Related Work

Modalized description logics. The study of multi-agent epistemic description logics started with the investigations by Laux, Gräber, and Bürckert [19,17]. In those papers, like in $\mathcal{JALC}$, the modal operators apply only to axioms, but not to concepts. A similar approach for temporalizing (instead of modalizing) logics had earlier been provided by Finger and Gabbay [15]. Baader and Laux [8] present a description logic in which modal operators can be applied to both axioms and concepts. Modalized description logics of this kind have then been investigated in detail, see for example [20].

Explanations. For some reasoning services offered by an ontological information system, users will not only be interested in the result but also in an explanation of it. That is, users will need to understand how deductions were made and what manipulations were done. There are many studies on how to generate explanations. We confine ourselves to mentioning two of them. McGuiness and Pinheiro da Silva [21] give an overview about requirements for answer explanation components of such a system. A very promising approach to provide explanations is based on meta-inferencing [1]. While processing a query, the reasoning engine produces a proof tree for any given answer. This proof tree acts then as input for a second inference run which returns answers that are explaining the proof tree in natural language. In $\mathcal{JALC}$ we can employ the justification terms as input to this second inference run.

Data privacy. Although knowledge base systems enter more and more application domains, privacy issues in the context of description logics are not yet well studied. Notable exceptions are the following: Calvanese et al. [12] address the problem of privacy aware access to ontologies. They show how view based query answering is able to conceal from the user information that are not logical consequences of the associated authorization views. Grau and Horrocks [13] study different notions of privacy for logic based information systems. They look at privacy preserving query answering as reasoning problem and establish a connection between such reasoning problems and probabilistic privacy guarantees such as perfect privacy. Safe reasoning strategies for very expressive description logics and for hierarchical ontologies are studied in [9,24]. The approach used there is based on the principles of locality and conservative extensions for description logics. A decision procedure for provable data privacy in the context of $\mathcal{ALC}$ as well as a sufficient condition for $\mathcal{ALC}$ data privacy that can be checked efficiently is presented in [23].

7   Conclusion

We extended the description logic $\mathcal{ALC}$ with justifications. This results in an epistemic logic $\mathcal{JALC}$ over $\mathcal{ALC}$ where not only an agent's knowledge can be expressed but one also has explicit justifications for that knowledge. We presented a deductive system as well as a semantics for $\mathcal{JALC}$ and proved soundness and completeness. Moreover, we showed that the justification terms of $\mathcal{JALC}$ reflect its provability notion and allow thus to internalize proofs of $\mathcal{JALC}$. We finally explored two applications of this property: generating explanations and data privacy.

It is worth noticing that our approach for adding justifications is very general and does not rely on the particular choice of $\mathcal{ALC}$. This is due to the fact that there is no deep interaction between the justification logic part and the description logic part of $\mathcal{JALC}$ (this is very similar to Finger and Gabbay's [15] way of temporalizing logics). Basically, we only needed the compactness property of $\mathcal{ALC}$ to establish completeness. Thus we could add justifications also to other description logics in the same way as presented here for $\mathcal{ALC}$ and our applications would still be possible.

Further work starts with investigating more deeply the basic properties of $\mathcal{JALC}$. We need decision procedures for it and their complexities have to be determined. On a more practical level, we have to elaborate on the applications of $\mathcal{JALC}$. In particular, we would like to fully develop the *justification terms as explanations* approach and we think it is also worthwhile to further investigate justification terms in the context of data privacy.

There is also a second direction of future work: namely, to combine justifications and terminological reasoning by integrating justification terms in concept descriptions. The definition of a concept then includes a clause of the form

if t is a term and C is a concept, then $[t]C$ is a concept.

On the semantic side, the concept $[t]C$ includes all individuals a for which t justifies that a belongs to C. A similar approach was explored for pure modal logic where concepts of the form $\Box C$ were included into the language of description logic, see for instance [8]. Concepts of this modalized form turned out to be important for several applications including procedural extension of description logics [14]. We believe that considering justifications in concept descriptions also is very promising.

References

1. Angele, J., Moench, E., Oppermann, H., Staab, S., Wenke, D.: Ontology-based query and answering in chemistry: OntoNova @ project halo. In: Proc. of the 2nd Int. Semantic Web Conference ISWC (1993)
2. Artemov, S.N.: Operational modal logic. Technical Report MSI 95–29, Cornell University (December 1995)
3. Artemov, S.N.: Explicit provability and constructive semantics. Bulletin of Symbolic Logic 7(1), 1–36 (2001)
4. Artemov, S.N.: The logic of justification. The Review of Symbolic Logic 1(4), 477–513 (2008)
5. Artemov, S.: Tracking Evidence. In: Blass, A., Dershowitz, N., Reisig, W. (eds.) Fields of Logic and Computation. LNCS, vol. 6300, pp. 61–74. Springer, Heidelberg (2010)
6. Artemov, S.N., Kuznets, R.: Logical omniscience as a computational complexity problem. In: Heifetz, A. (ed.) Theoretical Aspects of Rationality and Knowledge, Proceedings of the Twelfth Conference (TARK 2009), Stanford University, California, July 6-8, pp. 14–23. ACM (2009)
7. Baader, F., Calvanese, D., McGuinness, D.L., Nardi, D., Patel-Schneider, P.F. (eds.): The Description Logic Handbook, 2nd edn. Cambridge University Press (2007)
8. Baader, F., Laux, A.: Terminological logics with modal operators. In: Proc. of IJCAI 1995, pp. 808–814. Morgan Kaufmann (1995)
9. Bao, J., Slutzki, G., Honavar, V.: Privacy-preserving reasoning on the semantic web. In: Web Intelligence 2007, pp. 791–797 (2007)
10. Bucheli, S., Kuznets, R., Renne, B., Sack, J., Studer, T.: Justified belief change. In: Arrazola, X., Ponte, M. (eds.) LogKCA 2010, Proceedings of the Second ILCLI International Workshop on Logic and Philosophy of Knowledge, Communication and Action, pp. 135–155. University of the Basque Country Press (2010)
11. Bucheli, S., Kuznets, R., Studer, T.: Partial Realization in Dynamic Justification Logic. In: Beklemishev, L.D., de Queiroz, R. (eds.) WoLLIC 2011. LNCS, vol. 6642, pp. 35–51. Springer, Heidelberg (2011)
12. Calvanese, D., De Giacomo, G., Lenzerini, M., Rosati, R.: View-based query answering over description logic ontologies. In: Principles of Knowledge Representation and Reasoning, pp. 242–251 (2008)
13. Cuenca Grau, B., Horrocks, I.: Privacy-preserving query answering in logic-based information systems. In: ECAI 2008 (2008)
14. Donini, F., Lenzerini, M., Nardi, D., Nutt, W., Schaerf, A.: An epistemic operator for escription logics. Artificial Intelligence 100(1-2), 225–274 (1998)
15. Finger, M., Gabbay, D.: Adding a temporal dimension to a logic system. Journal of Logic Language and Information 1, 203–233 (1992)
16. Fitting, M.: The logic of proofs, semantically. Annals of Pure and Applied Logic 132(1), 1–25 (2005)
17. Gräber, A., Bürckert, H., Laux, A.: Terminological reasoning with knowledge and belief. In: Knowledge and Belief in Philosophy and Artificial Intelligence, pp. 29–61. Akademie Verlag (1995)
18. Kuznets, R.: Self-referential justifications in epistemic logic. Theory of Computing Systems 46(4), 636–661 (2010)
19. Laux, A.: Beliefs in multi-agent worlds: a terminological approach. In: Proc. of ECAI 1994, pp. 299–303 (1994)

20. Lutz, C., Sturm, H., Wolter, F., Zakharyaschev, M.: A tableau decision algorithm for modalized ALC with constant domains. Studia Logica 72, 199–232 (2002)
21. McGuiness, D., Pinheiro da Silva, P.: Inference web: Portable and shareable explanations for question answering. In: Proc. of AAAI Workshop on New Directions for Question Answering (1993)
22. Schild, K.: A correspondence theory for terminological logics: Preliminary report. In: Proc. of IJCAI, pp. 466–471 (1991)
23. Stouppa, P., Studer, T.: Data Privacy for $\mathcal{ALC}$ Knowledge Bases. In: Artemov, S., Nerode, A. (eds.) LFCS 2009. LNCS, vol. 5407, pp. 409–421. Springer, Heidelberg (2008)
24. Studer, T.: Privacy Preserving Modules for Ontologies. In: Pnueli, A., Virbitskaite, I., Voronkov, A. (eds.) PSI 2009. LNCS, vol. 5947, pp. 380–387. Springer, Heidelberg (2010)

Implementing Conflict Resolution

Konstantin Korovin *, Nestan Tsiskaridze, and Andrei Voronkov **

The University of Manchester
{korovin,tsiskarn,voronkov}@cs.man.ac.uk

Abstract. The *conflict resolution* method, introduced by the authors in [4] is a new method for solving systems of linear inequalities over the rational and real numbers. This paper investigates various heuristics for optimisation of the method and presents experimental evaluation. The method and heuristics are evaluated against various benchmarks and compared to other methods, such as the Fourier-Motzkin elimination method and the simplex method.

1 Introduction

In this paper we present an evaluation of our *conflict resolution* method [4] for checking solvability of systems of linear inequalities.

Conflict resolution is a solution driven method. Given a system of linear inequalities and an arbitrary initial assignment on variables, the method iteratively modifies the assignment aiming at obtaining a solution. During this process a conflict can arise when the current assignment cannot be directly modified to satisfy the system of inequalities. In this case there exists at least one pair of conflicting inequalities which impedes the refinement. Such a conflict is resolved by deriving a new inequality from the conflicting pair and adding it to the current system of inequalities. The process continues until either the assignment is refined into a solution, or a trivially unsatisfiable inequality is derived, showing unstaisfiability of the initial system of inequalities. In [4] the conflict resolution method is shown to be sound, complete and terminating.

The performance of the method can be improved by using various strategies for selecting conflicting pairs, refinement of assignments, and choosing the order on variables. In this paper we introduce a number of heuristics and strategies for the conflict resolution method. We evaluate them on various benchmarks and compare to other methods for solving systems of linear inequalities such as the Fourier-Motzkin elimination method and the simplex method.

This paper is structured as follows. In Section 2 we give some preliminary notations. Section 3 briefly overviews the conflict resolution method. In Section 4 we present heuristics whose performance is studied in the paper. Section 5 describes the set of benchmarks used for the experimental evaluation. In Section 6 we describe preprocessing methods used in the evaluation. . The results of experiments are discussed in Section 7. In Section 8 we summarise the presented work and discuss further research directions.

* Supported by a Royal Society University Research Fellowship.
** Partially supported by an EPSRC grant.

E. Clarke, I. Virbitskaite, and A. Voronkov (Eds.): PSI 2011, LNCS 7162, pp. 362–376, 2012.

2   Preliminaries

Let $\mathbb{Q}$ denote the set of rationals, and X be a finite set of variables $\{x_1, \ldots, x_n\}$ where n is a positive integer. We call a *rational linear constraint over* X either a formula $a_n x_n + \ldots + a_1 x_1 + b \diamond 0$, where $\diamond \in \{\geq, >, =\}$ and $a_i \in \mathbb{Q}$ for $1 \leq i \leq n$, or one of the formulas $\bot, \top$. The formula $\bot$ is always false and $\top$ is always true. The constraints $\bot$ and $\top$ are called *trivial*.

We introduce an order on variables, without loss of generality we can assume: $x_n \succ x_{n-1} \succ \ldots \succ x_1$. For simplicity, we consider all constraints throughout the paper to be *normalised*, i.e. be of one of the forms: $\bot, \top, x_k + q \diamond 0$ or $-x_k + q \diamond 0$, where $\diamond \in \{\geq, >, =\}$, x_k is the maximal variable in the respective constraint, and q does not contain x_k. Evidently, every constraint can be effectively changed to an equivalent normalised constraint. We introduce a notion of the *level* of a constraint as follows: if the maximal variable in a constraint c is x_k, then we say that k is the *level* of c. If c contains no variables, then we define the level of c to be the 0. Note that, since all constraints are assumed to be normalised, a constraint written in the form $x_k + p \geq 0$ or $-x_k + q \geq 0$ is of the level k.

We define an *assignment* σ over the set of variables X as a mapping from X to $\mathbb{Q}$, i.e. $\sigma : X \to \mathbb{Q}$. Given an assignment σ, a variable $x \in X$ and a value $v \in \mathbb{Q}$, we call the *update of* σ *at* x *by* v, denoted by σ_x^v, the assignment obtained from σ by changing the value of x by v and leaving the values of all other variables unchanged.

For a linear form q over X, denote by $q\sigma$ the value of q after replacing all variables $x \in X$ by the corresponding values $\sigma(x)$. An assignment σ is called a *solution of a linear constraint* $q \diamond 0$ if $q\sigma \diamond 0$ is true; it is a *solution of a system* of linear constraints if it is a solution of every constraint in the system. If σ is a solution of a linear constraint c (or a system S of such constraints), we also say that σ *satisfies* c (respectively, S), denoted by $\sigma \models c$ (respectively, $\sigma \models S$), otherwise we say that σ *violates* c (respectively, S). A system of linear constraints is said to be *satisfiable* if it has a solution.

For simplicity, we consider only algorithms for solving systems of linear constraints of the form $q \geq 0$, $\bot$ and $\top$.

We define a *state* as a pair (S, σ), where S is a system of linear constraints and σ an assignment. Let $\mathbb{S} = (S, \sigma)$ be a state and k a positive integer. We say that $\mathbb{S}$ *contains a k-conflict* $(x_k + p \geq 0, -x_k + q \geq 0)$ if (i) both $x_k + p \geq 0$ and $-x_k + q \geq 0$ are linear constraints in S and (ii) $p\sigma + q\sigma < 0$. Instead of "k-conflict" we will sometimes simple say "conflict". Note that if σ is a solution of S, then $\mathbb{S}$ contains no conflicts.

3   The Conflict Resolution Algorithm

We will now formulate our method. Given a system S of linear constraints, it starts with an initial state (S, σ), where σ is an arbitrary assignment, and repeatedly transforms the current state by either adding a new linear constraint to S or updating the assignment. We will formulate these rules below as transformation rules on states $\mathbb{S} \Rightarrow \mathbb{S}'$, meaning that $\mathbb{S}$ can be transformed into $\mathbb{S}'$. Let k be an integer such that $1 \leq k \leq n$.

Algorithm 1. The Conflict Resolution Algorithm CRA

Input: A set S of linear constraints.
Output: A solution of S or "unsatisfiable".

1: **if** $\bot \in S$ **then return** "unsatisfiable"
2: $\sigma :=$ arbitrary assignment;
3: $k := 1$
4: **while** $k \leq n$ **do**
5:     **if** $\sigma \not\models S_{=k}$ **then**
6:         **while** (S, σ) contains a k-conflict $(x_k + p \geq 0, -x_k + q \geq 0)$ **do**
7:             $S := S \cup \{p + q \geq 0\}$;   ▷ application of **CR**
8:             $k :=$ the level of $(p + q \geq 0)$;
9:             **if** $k = 0$ **then return** "unsatisfiable"
10:         **end while**
11:         $\sigma := \sigma_{x_k}^v$, where v is an arbitrary value in $I(S, \sigma, k)$ ▷ application of **AR**
12:     **end if**
13:     $k := k + 1$
14: **end while**
15: **return** σ

The conflict resolution rule (CR) (at the level k) is the following rule:

$$(S, \sigma) \Rightarrow (S \cup \{p + q \geq 0\}, \sigma),$$

where (S, σ) contains a k-conflict $(x_k + p \geq 0, -x_k + q \geq 0)$.
The assignment refinement rule (AR) (at the level k) is the following rule:

$$(S, \sigma) \Rightarrow (S, \sigma_{x_k}^v),$$

where

1. σ satisfies all constraints in S of the levels $0, \ldots, k - 1$.
2. σ violates at least one constraint in S of the level k.
3. $\sigma_{x_k}^v$ satisfies all constraints in S of the level k.

We will call any instance of an inference rule an *inference*. Thus, our algorithm will perform CR-inferences and AR-inferences. Note that the conflict resolution rule derives a linear constraint violated by σ.

In the description of the conflict resolution algorithm we use the following notation. For every set S of linear constraints and a positive integer k, denote by $S_{=k}$ (respectively, $S_{<k}$) the subset of S consisting of all constraints of the level k (respectively, of all levels strictly less than k). For any system S of linear constraints, a non-negative integer k and an assignment σ denote

$$L(S, \sigma, k) \stackrel{\text{def}}{=} \max\{-p\sigma \mid (x_k + p \geq 0) \in S\};$$
$$U(S, \sigma, k) \stackrel{\text{def}}{=} \min\{q\sigma \mid (-x_k + q \geq 0) \in S\};$$
$$I(S, \sigma, k) \stackrel{\text{def}}{=} [L(S, \sigma, k), U(S, \sigma, k)].$$

Informally, the interval $I(S, \sigma, k)$ will be used in our main algorithm to define the range of admissible values of the variable x_k for the assignment refinement rule.

The *Conflict Resolution Algorithm CRA* is given as Algorithm 1. CRA is shown to be sound, complete and terminating in [4].

The CRA algorithm can be parametrised by various strategies for (i) selection of conflicting pairs: we can choose any conflicting pair (at line: 6); (ii) refinement of assignments: we can choose any value v inside the interval $I(S, \sigma, k)$ (at line: 11); and (iii) selection of the order on variables $\succ$. We consider these strategies in the next section.

4   Strategies for Conflict Resolution

In this section we discuss strategies and heuristics used for fine-tuning the conflict resolution method. First we consider strategies based on the main parameters of the CRA algorithm:

1. strategies for selecting conflicts,
2. strategies for selecting values in the assignment refinement rule,
3. strategies for selecting the order on variables.

Then we discuss optimization-related strategies for: i) reducing the number of derived constraints, ii) dealing with half-bounded levels and iii) reducing coefficients in the constraints.

For each of the heuristics we introduce short namings and then combine them to address particular set of heuristics in our experiments and discussions.

4.1   Strategies for Selecting Conflicts

The issue of selecting a conflicting pair of constraints arises naturally when more than one conflicting pairs occur on a level. We implemented a number of various strategies. To illustrate these strategies, we will use the following example:

$$
\begin{array}{llll}
x_4 - 2x_3 & + & x_1 + 5 \geq 0 & (1) \\
x_4 - x_3 + x_2 & & + 2 \geq 0 & (2) \\
-x_4 + x_3 & + 2x_1 - 4 \geq 0 & & (3) \\
-x_4 - x_3 + & + x_1 + 1 \geq 0 & & (4) \\
x_3 & + x_1 - 1 \geq 0 & & (5) \\
- x_3 + x_2 - 2x_1 + 5 \geq 0 & & & (6)
\end{array}
$$

We consider order on variables $x_4 \succ x_3 \succ x_2 \succ x_1$ and initial assignment $\sigma : \{x_4 \mapsto 0; x_3 \mapsto 0; x_2 \mapsto 0; x_1 \mapsto 0\}$. To illustrate the algorithm, we will split all inequalities into subsets corresponding to their levels. This initially gives two non-empty levels as shown bellow:

Level 4

$$\begin{array}{lllll}
(1) & 2x_3 & -\ x_1 - 5 \leq x_4 & x_4 \leq\ \ x_3 & +\ 2x_1 - 4 & (3) \\
(2) & x_3 - x_2 & -\ 2 \leq x_4 & x_4 \leq -x_3 + & +\ x_1 + 1 & (4)
\end{array}$$

Level 3

$$\begin{array}{llll}
(5) & -\ x_1 + 1 \leq x_3 & x_3 \leq & x_2 - 2x_1 + 5 & (6)
\end{array}$$

CRA starts with level 3. At this level $\sigma \not\models S_{=k}$ and the interval $I(S, \sigma, 3) = [1; 5]$ is non-empty, thus AR rule is applicable. AR refines the assignment $\sigma := \sigma^v_{x_3}$, updating the value of the variable x_3 by v, where v is an arbitrary value in $I(S, \sigma, 3)$. Let $v = 4$. CRA moves to level 4 with $\sigma : \{x_4 \mapsto 0; x_3 \mapsto 4; x_2 \mapsto 0; x_1 \mapsto 0\}$ and $\sigma \models S_{<4}$. At level 4 the interval $I(S, \sigma, 4)$ is empty $[3; -3]$ and CRA detects 4 conflicts (all pairs of constraints at level 4, with complementary signs on x_4 are conflicting). To proceed, CRA selects one of the conflicts.

In the following we discuss our strategies for selecting conflicts.

Algebraic or Maximal Overlap approach (MO). One of the strategies we tried is based on maximal overlaps, defined as follows. We select a k-conflict $x_k + p \geq 0$ and $-x_k + q \geq 0$ in S (i.e., $p\sigma + q\sigma < 0$), such that $p\sigma = L(S, \sigma, k)$ and $q\sigma = U(S, \sigma, k)$. To explain the rationale behind this strategy we refer to the notion of 'almost' non-redundant constraints, defined in [4]. For readers' convenience we recall this notion here.

Lemma 1. *Consider the set S^+ of all constraints at a level k having the form $x_k + p \geq 0$. Consider its subset S' consisting of all constraints $x_k + p \geq 0$ such that $-p\sigma = L(S, \sigma, k)$. Then S' is not implied by $S_{<k} \cup (S^+ - S')$.* ❑

Based on this definition, choice of a conflict with maximal overlap guaranties that the constraints $x_k + p \geq 0$ and $-x_k + q \geq 0$ are 'almost' non-redundant in the above sense. In our example the maximal overlap $[3; -3]$ is obtained for the conflict: $((1), (4))$. Resolvent of the conflict $x_3 \leq \frac{2}{3}x_1 + 2$ is added to level 3. New bounds on the variable x_3 define a non-empty interval $I(S, \sigma, 3) = [1; 2]$ which does not contain the current value of $x_3 = 4$. The assignment refinement rule is applied. Let the new value of x_3 be 1. Moving to level 4, the algorithm detects the only conflict $((2), (3))$ giving the empty interval $I(S, \sigma, 4) = [-1; -3]$. This time resolvent of the conflict $-2x_1 + 2 \leq x_2$ is added to level 2. Having the only constraint at level 2 the interval $I(S, \sigma, 2)$ is half-bounded $[2; +\infty)$ and the current value of $x_2 = 0$ lies outside it. Again, the assignment refinement rule updates σ by assigning x_2 a new value from the interval, suppose this value is 2. One can easily check that following up to level 3 and level 4 no more conflicts are formed and no assignment refinement is needed. Thus, the system is satisfiable and $\sigma : \{x_4 \mapsto 0, x_3 \mapsto 1, x_2 \mapsto 2, x_1 \mapsto 0\}$ is a solution.

Geometric or Relaxation Method approach (RM). Another strategy for selecting a conflict comes from the geometrical ideas behind the *relaxation method*, (see, e.g., [8]). As we know, an assignment σ represents a point M in the n-dimensional space and the system of linear inequalities S defines a polyhedron in this space. The relaxation method iteratively changes the assignment trying to get inside the polyhedron defined by S. New assignment is chosen by reflecting M over a hyperplane that (i) is defined by a constraint in S that is violated by M, i.e., M is outside the feasible area defined by a hyperplane of one of the facets of the polyhedron and (ii) is on the maximal distance from M. A constraint defining such a hyperplane is called *the most violated* constraint. The original relaxation method has a substantial drawback – each iteration leads to solving of a new problem. Moreover the relaxation method does not always terminate, producing approximations converging to a solution but never achieving it.

However, the idea of reflection over the hyperplane of the most violated constraint is itself geometrically attractive. We integrated this idea into our algorithm as a conflict selection criterion: choose a conflicting pair of constraints with the most violated resolvent. In contrast to the relaxation method our algorithm with the same conflict selection criterion does not require solving a new problem after each iteration, and moreover guarantees termination.

Let us show how CRA selects a conflict using the geometric approach. Let us return to level 4 with the refined assignment $\sigma : \{x_4 \mapsto 0; x_3 \mapsto 4; x_2 \mapsto 0; x_1 \mapsto 0\}$. As mentioned above, all pairs are conflicting at this stage. Assignment σ corresponds to the point $M(0, 4, 0, 0)$ which is outside the solution space. To use the geometric approach, CRA searches for the hyperplane which is defined by one of the resolvents of these conflicts and is the furthermost to M. The distance from a point $P = (p_n, \ldots, p_1)$ to a hyperplane corresponding to the constraint $a_n x_n + \ldots a_1 x_1 + b \geq 0$ is calculated using the formula:

$$\frac{|a_n p_n + \ldots a_1 p_1 + b|}{\sqrt{a_n^2 + \ldots + a_1^2}}$$

Since we need the maximal distance we compared squares of the distances to avoid calculations with roots. It is easy to see, that the furthermost hyperplane to M is defined by the resolvent of the conflict $((2), (4)) : x_3 \leq \frac{1}{2}x_2 + \frac{1}{2}x_1 + \frac{3}{2}$. This constraint is of level 3. The interval $I(S, \sigma, 3)$ becomes $[1; \frac{3}{2}]$ and the assignment can be refined by updating the value of x_3. Let $\sigma := \sigma_{x_3}^1$. Moving to level 4, we find that the interval is empty $I(S, \sigma, 4) = [-1; -3]$ and the only conflicting pair of constraints is $((2), (3))$. The resolvent of this conflict $-2x_1 + 2 \leq x_2$ is added to level 2. This constraint defines a half-bounded interval for the values of $I(S, \sigma, 2) = [2; +\infty)$ which does not contain the current value of x_2. Let us update the assignment by setting $x_2 := 2$. Following the algorithm it is easy to check that all constraints at level 3 and level 4 are satisfied, thus the system is also satisfied and $\sigma : \{x_4 \mapsto 0; x_3 \mapsto 1; x_2 \mapsto 2; x_1 \mapsto 0\}$ is a solution.

Take the first conflict (FC). The next strategy we tried simply takes the first detected conflict. It saves the calculation time needed for computing all conflicts at a level. The first conflict detected in our example is $((1), (3))$. Its resolvent $x_3 \leq 3x_1 + 1$ is of level 3 and narrows the interval $I(S, \sigma, 3)$ to $[1; 1]$. Thus $x_3 := 1$. Moving to level 4 with a refined assignment $\sigma : \{x_4 \mapsto 0, x_3 \mapsto 1, x_2 \mapsto 0, x_1 \mapsto 0\}$ CRA detects the only conflict $((2), (3))$. Obtained resolvent $-2x_1 + 2 \leq x_2$ sets bounds on the variable x_2 at level 2: $I(S, \sigma, 2) = [1; +\infty)$. By setting $x_2 := 2$ one can check that CRA passes all remaining levels without any conflicts and changes in the assignment.

Random choice of conflict (RC). The last conflict selection heuristics we implemented is randomly choosing a conflict with an equal probability. Assume that the randomly selected conflict is $((2),(3))$. The derived constraint $-2x_1+2 \le x_2$ is of level 2 and the bound on x_2 forms a half-bounded interval $I(S,\sigma,2) = [2;+\infty)$. If the value of x_2 is set to 2, we move to level 3 and pass it without refining an assignment. At level 4 CRA detects that only the selected conflict $((2),(3))$ is resolved, and three other conflicts are remained. Let us select the conflict randomly again, and assume it is $((1),(4))$. Its resolvent $x_3 \le \frac{2}{3}x_1 + 2$ narrows the interval for x_3 to $[1;2]$ and forces the value of x_3 to be updated. Let $x_3 := 2$. One can check that all constraints at level 4, and thus in the initial system, became satisfied.

As we see each of the conflict selection strategies results in a different behaviour of the algorithm. The running time of the algorithm depends significantly on the choice of values for the variables in the assignment refinement rule. In the following, we discuss the strategies for assignment refinement used in our experiments.

4.2 Strategies for Assignment Refinement

We tried several strategies for selecting values in the assignment refinement rule, we list them bellow.

Minimal (Maximal) point (MIN/MAX). Select always the minimal (or always the maximal) endpoint of the interval $I(S,\sigma,k)$. As we saw from the examples of using strategies for selecting conflicts, the course of the algorithm and its performance can be significantly affected by the choice of the values of variables. For instance, if the value of the variable x_3 selected from the interval $[1;5]$ for the first time is 1 and not 4 the algorithm avoids derivation of a conflict needed to adjust the value of x_3.

Interleaved (swapped minimal and maximal) points (SW). A natural extension of the previous strategy is to interleave the selection of the maximal and the minimal endpoints of the interval $I(S,\sigma,k)$ each time the interval is updated.

Random assignment value choice (RA). Another strategy is a random choice of the assignment value within the interval $I(S,\sigma,k)$.

Middle point. Select the middle point of the interval $I(S,\sigma,k)$.

Our experiments show that these strategies can result in a rapid growth of the sizes of numerators and denominators of rational values in the assignment, which in turn leads to heavy calculations. The next strategy is aimed at reducing sizes of rational numbers used in the assignment values.

Closest binary to the middle point (BMP). If the endpoints of $I(S,\sigma,k)$ coincide, we select this point. Otherwise, we select a rational number n/m in $I(S,\sigma,k)$ such that (i) m is the least power of 2 among denominators of all rationals in $I(S,\sigma,k)$, and (ii) n is such that, n/m is the closest rational to the middle point of the interval, among all rationals satisfying (i). It can be shown that a rational satisfying both (i) and (ii) always exists. In particular, if $I(S,\sigma,k)$ contains integer points, then our strategy will select an integer in $I(S,\sigma,k)$ closest to the middle point. As our experiments show, such choice of values considerably simplifies the assignment values and constraint evaluation.

4.3   Strategies for Selecting the Order on Variables

We implemented the following strategies for selecting the order on variables.

Random order (RO). The first strategy we tried sets the order on variables randomly before running the CRA algorithm.

Length-based order (LO). The second strategy orders variables giving preference to variables occurring in short constraints. For simplicity, we formalise the second strategy as follows. To each variable x we associate a pair of integers $(l(x), t(x))$, where $l(x)$ is the length of the shortest constraint containing variable x and $t(x)$ is a number of such constraints. We define the ordering on variables $\succ$ as follows: for two variables x, y we have $x \succ y$ if (i) $l(x) > l(y)$ or (ii) $l(x) = l(y)$ and $t(y) > t(x)$. That is, we try to put variables occurring in shortest constraints on lower levels.

4.4   Optimization-Related Strategies

There are also other heuristics that we considered interesting to study. One of them concerns adding resolvents to the current system at run-time.

Adding resolvents. In general, adding a derived constraint to its level may result in new conflicts at this level. Thus resolving one conflict may result in a cascade of conflicts in lower levels. Adding all such consecutive resolvents may result in a quick expansion of the system. Based on this we studied the following heuristics:

1. add all resolvents derived during the run-time of the algorithm;
2. do not add a resolvent if it results in a new conflict at its level, rather keep resolving conflicts without adding them until a resolvent is derived which results in no conflicts (backjumping – **BJ**).

The latter heuristic describes a process of 'backjumping' to the lowest level (the first non-conflicting level) and adding only the last resolvent to the system.

Two other heuristics we considered are: (i) dealing with half-bounded intervals in the AR rule, and (ii) reducing constraints by the greatest common divisor of their coefficients.

Dealing with half-bounded intervals in the AR rule. In our experiments half-bounded intervals in the assignment refinement rule occur very frequently. We deal with such cases by introducing an artificial bound on the intervals. If during the run-time CRA returns to a level with a half-bounded interval considerably often, we considered increasing the size of the interval consecutively. We tried two heuristics for dealing with half-bounded intervals:

1. increase the size of an artificial interval exponentially each time CRA returns to the corresponding level; in the experiments we tried this strategy with increments of powers of 2 (**pow2**);
2. keep the size of artificial intervals constant, in the experiments fixed to 10 (**const10**).

Reducing constraints by gcd. The last implemented heuristic corresponds to the problem of decreasing size of numerators and denominators of rational numbers during the calculations. Namely, if all coefficients in a constraint have the greatest common divisor different from 1 than the constraint can be reduced by dividing its coefficients by their greatest common divisor. This simple idea yields the heuristics:

1. always reduce constraints by gcd (**gcd**);
2. never reduce constraints by gcd.

We studied various combinations of all presented heuristics and integrated them into the CRA algorithm. We call *major heuristics* the ones (i) for selecting conflicts, and (ii) for selecting assignment values. The heuristics (a) for dealing with half-bounded intervals in the assignment refinement rule and (b) for reducing constraints by gcd of their coefficients are *general* in their nature and can be combined with any major heuristic mentioned above.

5 Benchmarks

This section describes the benchmarks used in our experiments. We evaluated our solver on two types of benchmarks: randomly generated benchmarks and benchmarks extracted from real-life problems. The real-life benchmarks consist of systems of linear constraints extracted from SMT-LIB problems [1].

Real-life problems are substantially different from randomly generated ones. They differ not only by their size but also by their structure. In real-life problems the number of variables and constraints is considerably higher and most of the problems contain hundreds of variables and constraints. In addition, real-life problems often have sparse matrices and relatively simple coefficients.

Benchmarks with randomly generated problems. We used random benchmarks with integer coefficients generated by the GoRRiLA tool [5]. GoRRiLA is a generator of random problems for propositional logic and for systems of linear constraints over the rational and integer numbers. GoRRiLA can generate random problems of a given number of variables, so that each constraint has the number of variables in a certain range (for example, between 3 and 5 variables).

We evaluated CRA on two sets of random benchmarks.

1. The first set consists of 1600 problems with a number of variables ranging from 11 to 18;
2. The second set consists of 400 problems with a number of variables ranging from 19 to 26.

Benchmarks extracted from SMT-LIB. In order to study the performance of our solver on real-life problems we ran a series of experiments with real-life benchmarks extracted from the SMT-LIB library. We used the benchmarks from the QF_LRA division of the SMT-LIB: these benchmarks contain quantifier-free SMT problems in the theory of linear real arithmetic.

We obtained real-life benchmarks using the Hard Reality Tool (HRT) [5]. HRT allows randomly extracting hard and realistic theory problems from SMT problems. The extracted theory problems are given as a conjunction of constraints from this theory.

We used two sets of real-life benchmarks generated by us with the Hard Reality Tool (HRT) [5]. The difference between these sets is in their difficulty levels which reflect the time needed to solve the problem by the best solver. The sets contain both satisfiable and unsatisfiable problems.

1. The first set consists of 305 problems with a number of variables ranging from 37 to 1416.
2. The second set consists of 128 problems of considerable higher difficulty level with a number of variables ranging between 251 and 1067.

6 Preprocessing

Our real-life benchmarks contained several hundreds of variables and constraints. On many instances we observed that our solver was continuously passing a considerable number of levels, adding new constraints to them and expanding the system without any contribution to the solving process. We used the following preprocessing of the input system which considerably improved the performance on such problems.

Eliminating half-bounded variables. We call a variable x *half-bounded* in a system of constraints S if all occurrences of x in S are of the same sign. It is easy to see that we can remove all constraints containing half-bounded variables without affecting satisfiability. Indeed, let x be a half-bounded variable in S and S' the system obtained from S by removing all constraints containing x. Then, any solution of S' can be extended to a solution of S by taking the value of x to be any value in the half-bounded intervals obtained by substituting the solution values of the other variables in S. Consecutively eliminating all half-bounded variables from the system reduces the number of constraints without affecting its satisfiability.

Eliminating unit-half-bounded variables. We extend the above preprocessing by considering *unit-half-bounded variables*. The difference between unit-half-bounded variables and half-bounded variables is in allowing unit constraints to bound the variable. A constraint is called *unit constraint*, if it contains only one variable. First note that if the system contains two unit inequalities on the same variable with the same sign then one of them can be eliminated. Assume that our system of constraints contains a unit constraint u. We consider three cases.

Case (i): u is of the form $x = a$ (where $a \in \mathbb{Q}$). This constraint explicitly assigns a value to the variable x. We can directly eliminate x from the system by simply substituting all occurrences of x by a. This brings us to an equivalent system with one variable less. If the modified system has a solution, the solution of the initial system can be easily obtained by extending the assignment with the value a for the variable x.

Case (ii): u is of the form $x \geq a$. Further, assume that the coefficients of x in the rest of the constraints are negative. Then, one can eliminate the variable x from the system by substituting all occurrences of x by a. If the derived system has no solutions, the initial system has no solutions either. Otherwise, similar to the half-bounded case, we can extend a solution of the derived system to a solution of the initial system by taking the value of x to be any number within the intervals defined by substituting the values of the other variables.

Case (iii): u is of the form $-x \geq a$. This case is analogues to Case (ii).

Note, that we can eliminate from the system all such variables one after another, thus reduce the dimension of the system without affecting satisfiability. Let us note that after eliminating a variable new variables may become eligible for the preprocessing, We apply this preprocessing exhaustively, i.e., until no eligible variables remains.

7   Experimental Evaluation

We run our experiments on Intel Xeon Quad Core machines with 2.33 GHz and 12 GB of memory. We set a 20 second timeout for each problem. In the following we say a problem was solved if it was solved within this timeout.

For readers' convenience we name heuristics based on the abbreviation of major strategies for selecting conflicts (see Section 4.1), assignment refinements (see Section 4.2), and other general heuristics (see Section 4.4). For example in a heuristic MO_MAX_pow2 we use the maximal overlap strategy for conflict selection, the maximal point strategy for assignment refinement and increase half bounded intervals by powers of two. We present a full list of abbreviations used throughout the paper in Table 1.

Table 1. Abbreviation of Strategies

List of Strategies					
Selecting Conflict		**Selecting Assignment**		**Optimisation-related**	
Abbrev.	**Strategy**	**Abbrev.**	**Strategy**	**Abbrev.**	**Strategy**
FC	First Conflict	BMP	Binary Middle Point	BJ	Back Jumping
MO	Maximal Overlap	MAX	Maximal Endpoint	RO	Random Order
RC	Random Conflict	MIN	Minimal Endpoint	LO	Length-based Order
RM	Relaxation Method	SW	Swap Endpoints	pow2	Exp. Half-bounded
		RA	Random Assignment	const10	Const. Half-bounded
				gcd	Reduction by gcd
				prep	Preprocessing

We determine the best choice of combination of heuristics for both random and real-life benchmarks. First we select the best set of general heuristics for each major heuristic. Then we compare selected combinations of heuristics between each other.

7.1   Randomly Generated Benchmarks

On randomly generated problems all implemented strategies had certain similarities in performance and behaviour.

- In the problems with the number of variables ranging between 11 and 18 all heuristics showed an insignificant difference in the number of problems solved and in performance.

– The difference in the number of solved problems became more significant as the number of variables in the problems increased ranging between 19 and 26.

Experiments showed that the reduction of constraints by gcd is almost always beneficial. A better performance was also observed when we increased half-bounded intervals by powers of two.

On Fig. 1 we plotted all major heuristics combined with the best choices of general heuristics for them. A point (x, y) on the chart indicates that x problems were solved in y time or less.

As wee see, the best heuristic appeared to be MO_BMP_BJ_pow2, followed by MO_BMP_pow2 and then by RM_BMP_pow2, all close to each other. This chart shows that our non-random heuristics considerably outperform the random ones.

7.2 Real-Life Benchmarks

For real-life benchmarks we added preprocessing to our solver, as discussed in Section 6. The results of our experiments for the most representative combinations of heuristics are shown on Fig. 2. The top performances were shown by MO_BMP_pow2, FC_pow2, and RM_BMP_pow2.

Our experiments showed that performance of various bundles of heuristics of the CRA algorithm differs on randomly generated benchmarks and real-life benchmarks. On both types of problems different heuristics substantially affected the performance. This indicates that the good choice of heuristics is crucial for the performance of CRA.

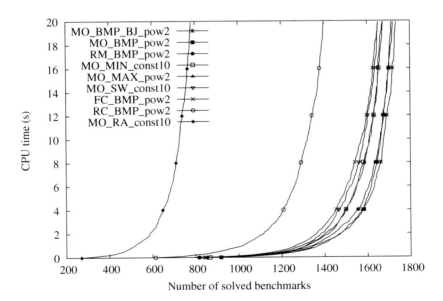

Fig. 1. CRA: major heuristics on randomly generated problems (all using reduction by gcd). On the left hand-side, heuristics are ordered by the number of solved problems.

For both randomly generated and real-life problems, the top performances were achieved by the combinations of the following major heuristics: the maximal overlap (MO) and the relaxation method (RM) strategies for conflict selection, combined with the binary middle point strategy (BMP) for the assignment refinement and with the back jumping (BJ) strategy.

For most of the major heuristics combination with the strategies of reduction by gcd and exponential increase of half-bounded intervals was effective for many problems, but with some had insignificant improvement. Overall, the use of reduction by gcd and exponential increase of half-bounded intervals were almost always beneficial.

7.3   CRA vs. State-of-the-Art SMT Solvers

For further experiments we used the implementation of the CRA algorithm that uses one of the best combinations of the heuristics listed in the previous sections, and incorporates the preprocessing discussed earlier in Section 6 and the length-based variable ordering. Namely, we used a strategy MO_BMP_pow2_gcd_LO_prep which incorporates preprocessing, the length-based order on variables and the following strategies: the maximal overlap strategy for selecting the conflict, the closest binary middle point strategy for the assignment refinement, reduction of constraints by gcd and exponential increase of half-bounded intervals.

In the following we present results of comparison of this implementation of CRA to other linear arithmetic solvers incorporated in the state-of-the-art SMT solvers. On Fig. 3 we compared on real-life problems different solvers: Barcelogic, CVC3, Z3, and CRA incorporating preprocessing and the length-based order on variables.

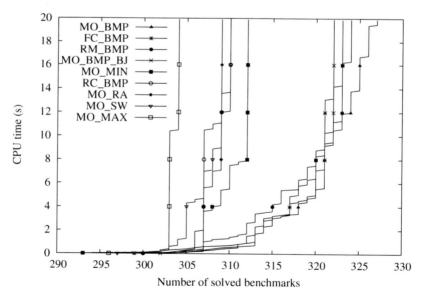

Fig. 2. CRA: major heuristics on real-life problems (all using preprocessing and gcd_pow2 strategy). On the left hand-side, heuristics are ordered by the number of solved problems.

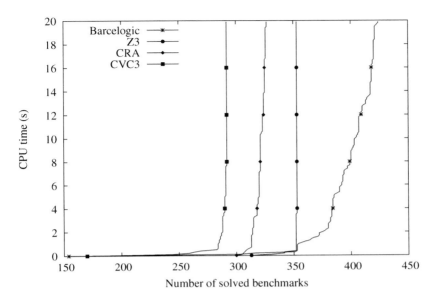

Fig. 3. CRA (MO_BMP_pow2_gcd_LO_prep) vs CVC3, Z3 and Barcelogic on real-life problems. On the left hand-side, solvers are ordered by the number of solved problems.

Table 2. CRA (MO_BMP_pow2_LO_prep) vs Barcelogic, CVC3, Z3 on real-life benchmarks

CRA	Faster	Same	Slower
Barcelogic	165	119	148
CVC3	157	274	1
Z3	18	48	366

On studied real-life benchmarks CRA considerably outperforms the Fourier-Motzkin elimination based CVC3 solver, and shows a competitive behaviour compared to the simplex based Barcelogic and Z3. In our experiments with random problems CRA outperforms CVC3 on almost all problems and in some cases CRA is about twice as faster as Barcelogic and Z3.

The results of the experiments with real-life benchmarks are presented in the Table 2.

CRA with implemented preprocessing is faster than CVC3 on about one third of the problems and has the same performance for almost all other problems. Compared to Barcelogic, CRA performs better again on about one third of the problems, has the same performance on the second third, and Barcelogic is faster than CRA on the other third of the problems. As for Z3, on both sets of real-life problems CRA showed a competitive performance – on about 85% of the problems it showed similar performance, outperformed Z3 on about 4% of the problems, and was slower than Z3 on about 11%. As we see, the CRA algorithm not only outperforms the Fourier-Motzkin algorithm but is also highly competitive with the simplex method.

8   Summary

Our experiments showed that choosing various parameters has a significant impact on the performance of the CRA solver. Also, depending on the nature of the problem different heuristics may appear preferable. Let us outline the strategies behaving the best in general.

In selecting a conflicting pair the best two choices turned out to be the maximal overlap strategy and the relaxation approach. For selecting the assignment one could overall recommend taking the middle point (based on the binary approximation). Interestingly, using the boundary value assignments may also appear successful in some special cases.

Among the general heuristics, the reduction by gcd and exponential increase in the case of of half-bounded intervals turned out to improve the performance nearly in all cases.

The algorithm appeared to be sensitive to the implemented combination of heuristics and preprocessing. Integrating effective preprocessing to the CRA algorithm and more strategies for selecting appropriate ordering on variables may also result in a significant benefit. This problem needs further detailed studies.

On the whole, considering that we used some of the best SMT solvers for comparison, conflict resolution showed itself to be potentially competitive with the simplex method, and definitely outperforms the Fourier-Motzkin method with modifications.

References

1. Barrett, C., Ranise, S., Stump, A., Tinelli, C.: The Satisfiability Modulo Theories Library, SMT-LIB (2008), http://www.SMT-LIB.org
2. Barrett, C., Tinelli, C.: CVC3. In: Damm, W., Hermanns, H. (eds.) CAV 2007. LNCS, vol. 4590, pp. 298–302. Springer, Heidelberg (2007)
3. Chandru, V.: Variable elimination in linear constraints. Comput. J. 36(5), 463–472 (1993)
4. Korovin, K., Tsiskaridze, N., Voronkov, A.: Conflict Resolution. In: Gent, I.P. (ed.) CP 2009. LNCS, vol. 5732, pp. 509–523. Springer, Heidelberg (2009)
5. Korovin, K., Voronkov, A.: GoRRiLA and Hard Reality. In: Clarke, E., Virbitskaite, I., Voronkov, A. (eds.) PSI 2011. LNCS, vol. 7162, pp. 243–250. Springer, Heidelberg (2012)
6. de Moura, L., Bjørner, N.: Z3: An Efficient SMT Solver. In: Ramakrishnan, C.R., Rehof, J. (eds.) TACAS 2008. LNCS, vol. 4963, pp. 337–340. Springer, Heidelberg (2008)
7. Nieuwenhuis, R., Oliveras, A.: Decision Procedures for SAT, SAT Modulo Theories and Beyond. The Barcelogic Tools. (Invited Paper). In: Sutcliffe, G., Voronkov, A. (eds.) LPAR 2005. LNCS (LNAI), vol. 3835, pp. 23–46. Springer, Heidelberg (2005)
8. Schrijver, A.: Theory of Linear and Integer Programming. John Wiley and Sons (1998)

Symbolic Tree Transducers

Margus Veanes and Nikolaj Bjørner

Microsoft Research,
Redmond, WA, USA
{margus,nbjorner}@microsoft.com

Abstract. Symbolic transducers are useful in the context of web security as they form the foundation for sanitization of potentially malicious data. We define Symbolic Tree Transducers as a generalization of Regular Transducers as finite state input-output tree automata with logical constraints over a parametric background theory. We examine key closure properties of Symbolic Tree Transducers and we develop a composition algorithm and an equivalence decision procedure for linear single-valued transducers.

1   Introduction

Several applications, ranging from web-sanitizers, XML transformations to generic functional programs, rely on finite state machines that transform strings or trees into strings or trees. Such state machines can conveniently be captured by tree transducers. This work develops symbolic tree transducers (STTs) that are defined modulo a background theory. STTs are easily seen more expressive than tree transducers defined over finite alphabets, yet our main results establish that composition of STTs and equivalence checking for linear single valued STTs is computable, modulo the background theory. Symbolic transducers are also practically useful for exploiting efficient symbolic solvers when performing basic automata-theoretic transformations. Prior work [35,19] on symbolic string recognizers and transducers takes advantage of this observation. We here investigate the case of the more expressive class of *tree* transducers. The complexity of decision problems are highly sensitive to the expressive power given to tree transducers and we here identify a class of top-down transducers that admit decidable equivalence checking modulo decidability of the symbolic background component.

2   Preliminaries

We use basic notions from classical automata theory [20], classical logic, and model theory [18]. Our notions regarding tree transducers are consistent with [15]. For finite state (string) transducers a brief introduction is given in [36].

E. Clarke, I. Virbitskaite, and A. Voronkov (Eds.): PSI 2011, LNCS 7162, pp. 377–393, 2012.

2.1   Background Structure

We work modulo a *background* structure $\mathcal{U}$ over a language that is multi-sorted. We also write $\mathcal{U}$ for the universe (domain) of $\mathcal{U}$. For each sort σ, $\mathcal{U}^{\sigma}$ denotes a nonempty sub-domain of $\mathcal{U}$. There is a Boolean sort BOOL, $\mathcal{U}^{\text{BOOL}} = \{\textbf{true}, \textbf{false}\}$, and the standard logical connectives are assumed to be part of the background. *Terms* are defined by induction as usual and are assumed to be well-sorted. Function symbols with range sort BOOL are called relation symbols. Boolean terms are called formulas or predicates. A term without free variables is *ground*.

We use *parameterized algebraic* sorts to represent labeled trees. An algebraic sort is associated with a finite collection of *constructors* and *accessors*. In particular, we use the sort $\text{T}^k\langle\sigma\rangle$ to denote the set of σ-labeled k-ary trees, for $k \geq 1$, that is associated with the constructors

$$f : \sigma \times \text{T}^k\langle\sigma\rangle \times \cdots \times \text{T}^k\langle\sigma\rangle \to \text{T}^k\langle\sigma\rangle, \quad \epsilon : \text{T}^k\langle\sigma\rangle,$$

for constructing a nonempty tree and an empty tree respectively. The accessors of $\text{T}^k\langle\sigma\rangle$ are the subtree accessors $\boldsymbol{1}, \ldots, \boldsymbol{k} : \text{T}^k\langle\sigma\rangle \to \text{T}^k\langle\sigma\rangle$ and the label accessor $\boldsymbol{0} : \text{T}^k\langle\sigma\rangle \to \sigma$. For all $t_0 : \sigma$, $t_i : \text{T}^k\langle\sigma\rangle$, $1 \leq i \leq k$, $\boldsymbol{i}(f(t_0, t_1, \ldots, t_k)) = t_i$. Note that constructors have term interpretation, thus, for all $t, u : \text{T}\langle\sigma\rangle$,

$$t = u \quad \Leftrightarrow \quad t = u = \epsilon \lor t \neq \epsilon \land u \neq \epsilon \land \bigwedge_{i=0}^{k} \boldsymbol{i}(t) = \boldsymbol{i}(u).$$

A *position* is a sequence of accessors. We write $t|_{\pi}$ for the subterm of t at position π, e.g., $f(a, f(b, t, u), v)|_{12} = u$. We write $t[\pi \leftarrow v]$ for replacing the occurrence of the subterm at position π in t by v, e.g.,

$$f(a, \epsilon, f(b, \epsilon, \epsilon))[\boldsymbol{22} \leftarrow v] = f(a, \epsilon, f(b, \epsilon, v))$$

We often omit k from $\text{T}^k\langle\sigma\rangle$. We write $\text{L}\langle\sigma\rangle$ for the σ-*list* sort $\text{T}^1\langle\sigma\rangle$. We use the notation $[e_1, e_2, \ldots, e_n | t]$ for the list $f(e_1, f(e_2, \ldots f(e_n, t)))$ and we write $[e_1, e_2, \ldots, e_n]$ when $t = \epsilon$.

The *trace ending in tree position* π of a tree t or a π-*trace of* t is the list of labels from the root of t up to π, e.g., if $t = f(a, \epsilon, f(b, f(c, \epsilon, \epsilon), \epsilon))$ then the $\boldsymbol{22}$-trace of t is $[a, b]$, the $\boldsymbol{211}$-trace of t is $[a, b, c]$, the ε-trace of t is ϵ.

2.2   Top-Down Tree Transducers

A top-down tree transducer describes a transformation function from trees in a given input domain into trees in a given output domain. Several equivalent formal definitions are possible. Typically, the rules specify how an input tree is transformed through a recursive descent over the structure of the input domain. Here, trees are terms of sort $\text{T}\langle\sigma\rangle$ of a given label sort σ. The following definition is tailored to a generalization for symbolic tree transducers introduced below. We write $t[x_1, \ldots, x_k]$ to indicate that all free variables in t are among $x_1, \ldots, x_k$ distinct variables, and we write $t[t_1, \ldots, t_k]$ for substituting x_i in t by t_i for $1 \leq i \leq k$. The term t is *linear* if each x_i occurs at most once in t.

Definition 1. A *(top-down) tree transducer from* $\mathrm{T}\langle \iota \rangle$ *to* $\mathrm{T}\langle o \rangle$ is a tuple (Q, q^0, R) where Q is a finite set of unary constructors $q : \mathrm{T}\langle \iota \rangle \to \mathrm{T}\langle o \rangle$, called *states*, $q^0 \in Q$ is the *initial state*, R is a set of *rules* of the form

$$q(\epsilon) \to e, \quad q(f(a, y_1, \ldots, y_k)) \to u[q_1(y_1), \ldots, q_k(y_k)]$$

where $e : \mathrm{T}\langle o \rangle$ and $a : \iota$ are ground terms, $y_i : \mathrm{T}\langle \iota \rangle$ are distinct variables, $u[x_1, \ldots, x_k] : \mathrm{T}\langle o \rangle$ is a term that does not contain states, and $q, q_1, \ldots, q_k \in Q$. Given a rule $l \to r$, l is the *left-hand side* and r the *right-hand side* of the rule.

Tree transducers do not have explicit *final* states, since using a rule $q(\epsilon) \to \epsilon$ is effectively equivalent to declaring the state q as a final state. We write $A^{\mathrm{T}\langle \iota \rangle / \mathrm{T}\langle o \rangle}$ for a tree transducer from $\mathrm{T}\langle \iota \rangle$ to $\mathrm{T}\langle o \rangle$. A tree transducer *with epsilon moves* may additionally have rules of the form $p(x) \to q(x)$ where p and q are states and x is a variable. A rule is *linear* if its right-hand side is linear and A is *linear* if all of its rules are linear. A is *deterministic* if it has no epsilon moves and no two rules with overlapping left-hand sides.

Although Definition 1 is specialized for labeled trees with fixed arity and a single nonempty constructor, this does not cause any loss of generality and simplifies the presentation technically. For example, a term $f(n, t_1, t_2)$ of sort $\mathrm{T}^2\langle \mathrm{INT} \rangle$, where n is a fixed integer value, can be seen as a representation for $f_n(t_1, t_2)$ for some binary constructor f_n. A key distinction from a standard definition of tree transducers is that the universes of input labels ($\mathcal{U}^\iota$) and output labels ($\mathcal{U}^o$) may be infinite.

The definition allows *nondeterminism* and does not require the rules to be *total*. While for certain purposes it is sufficient that tree transducers are deterministic and total by definition [15], both nondeterminism and partiality of the rules in Definition 1 play an important role in the context of *symbolic* tree transducers, as discussed below.

We say that a ground term or a tree t is *basic* (with respect to a tree transducer A) if it does not contain any states from A. The *transformation* or *transduction* induced by a tree transducer $A^{\mathrm{T}\langle \iota \rangle / \mathrm{T}\langle o \rangle}$ is a function $\mathbf{T}_A$ from basic trees of sort $\mathrm{T}\langle \iota \rangle$ to sets of basic trees of sort $\mathrm{T}\langle o \rangle$. The definition of $\mathbf{T}_A$ is a direct generalization of the standard definition: $\mathbf{T}_A(t)$ is the set of all basic trees modulo $\mathcal{U}$ in the closure of $\{q^0(t)\}$ under the rules of A.

Definition 2. A tree transducer A is *single-valued* if $|\mathbf{T}_A(t)| \leq 1$ for all t.

3   Symbolic Tree Transducers

In this section we introduce an extension of tree transducers through a symbolic encoding of labels by predicates. The main advantage of the extension is succinctness and modularity with respect to the background theory of labels.

Definition 3. A *symbolic tree transducer (STT) from* $\mathrm{T}\langle \iota \rangle$ *to* $\mathrm{T}\langle o \rangle$ is a tuple (Q, q^0, R) with Q as a finite set of states, $q^0 \in Q$ as the initial state, and R as a finite set of *(guarded) rules*

$$q(\epsilon) \to e, \quad q(f(x, y_1, \ldots, y_k)) \xrightarrow{\varphi[x]} u[x, q_1(y_1), \ldots, q_k(y_k)]$$

where e is a basic ground term, x is a variable, y_i, for $1 \le i \le k$, are distinct variables, $u[x, x_1, \ldots, x_k]$ is a basic term, $q, q_1, \ldots, q_k \in Q$, and $\varphi[x]$ is a predicate called the *guard* of the rule.

A guarded rule $\rho = q(f(x, y_1, \ldots, y_k)) \xrightarrow{\varphi[x]} u[x, q_1(y_1), \ldots, q_k(y_k)]$ denotes the set of rules

$$[\![\rho]\!] \stackrel{\text{def}}{=} \{q(f(a, y_1, \ldots, y_k)) \to u[a, q_1(y_1), \ldots, q_k(y_k)] \mid a \in \mathcal{U}^\iota, \varphi[a] \text{ holds}\}$$

Thus $[\![\rho]\!]$ may be infinite when $\mathcal{U}^\iota$ is infinite. Given an STT $A = (Q, q_0, R)$ we write $[\![A]\!]$ for the tree transducer $(Q, q_0, \cup\{[\![\rho]\!] \mid \rho \in R\})$ and $\mathbf{T}_A$ for $\mathbf{T}_{[\![A]\!]}$. An STT A is *linear* (resp. *single-valued, deterministic*) if $[\![A]\!]$ is linear (resp. single-valued, deterministic). Note that the right-hand sides of rules of a linear STT are allowed to contain multiple occurrences of the input label variable x. In particular, all STTs over lists are linear.

In the following examples, all STTs are single-valued and linear. The first example illustrates some simple STTs over $\mathrm{T}^2\langle\mathrm{INT}\rangle$. The point is to illustrate how global STT properties depend on the theory of labels.

Example 1. Let the input and the output domains be $\mathrm{T}^2\langle\mathrm{INT}\rangle$. *Swap* is an STT that swaps the left and the right subtrees if the label is non-zero. *Neg* is an STT that multiplies all labels by -1, *Double* multiplies labels by 2. *Cut* is an STT that cuts the left subtree y_1 of $f(x, y_1, y_2)$ when $x > 0$ and cuts the right subtree y_2 when $x < 0$.

$$Swap = (\{q\}, q, \{q(\epsilon) \to \epsilon, q(f(x, y_1, y_2)) \xrightarrow{x \ne 0} f(x, q(y_2), q(y_1)),$$
$$q(f(x, y_1, y_2)) \xrightarrow{x = 0} f(x, q(y_1), q(y_2))\})$$
$$Neg = (\{q\}, q, \{q(\epsilon) \to \epsilon, q(f(x, y_1, y_2)) \xrightarrow{true} f(-x, q(y_1), q(y_2))\})$$
$$Double = (\{q\}, q, \{q(\epsilon) \to \epsilon, q(f(x, y_1, y_2)) \xrightarrow{true} f(2x, q(y_1), q(y_2))\})$$
$$Cut = (\{q\}, q, \{q(\epsilon) \to \epsilon, q(f(x, y_1, y_2)) \xrightarrow{x > 0} f(x, \epsilon, q(y_2)),$$
$$q(f(x, y_1, y_2)) \xrightarrow{x < 0} f(x, q(y_1), \epsilon)$$
$$q(f(x, y_1, y_2)) \xrightarrow{x = 0} f(x, q(y_1), q(y_2))\})$$

Note that global properties such as commutativity and idempotence of the STTs clearly depend on the theory of labels, e.g., that multiplication by a positive number preserves polarity, implying in this case for example that *Swap* and *Neg* commute, *Cut* and *Double* commute, and *Cut* is idempotent. Note also that none of the examples can be expressed as a finite tree transducer. Our results about composition and equivalence checking for STTs, that are discussed in the below sections, allow to establish equivalences, such as *Cut* is equivalent to *Swap* followed by *Neg*, *Cut*, then finally *Swap*. The equivalence is modulo the theory of arithmetic that establishes logical equivalences, such as $-x < 0 \equiv x > 0$. ⊠

The following example illustrates a nontrivial use of the label theory. The STT *Encode* in the example represents the string sanitizer `AntiXSS.EncodeHtml` from version 2.0 of the Microsoft AntiXSS library. The sanitizer transforms an input string into an Html friendly format. For each character x in the input string, either x is kept verbatim or encoded through numeric Html escaping. The example can be extended to be part of a tree transducer over abstract syntax trees of Html where certain parts of the tree (corresponding to strings) are encoded using *Encode*.

Example 2. The example illustrates a single-state INT-list STT $Encode^{\text{L}\langle\text{INT}\rangle/\text{L}\langle\text{INT}\rangle}$ that transforms an input list of characters represented by positive integers, into an encoded, possibly longer, list of characters. We assume that '...' below represents the integer encoding of the given fixed (ASCII) character, e.g. 'a' = 97 and 'z' = 122. Let $\varphi[x]$ be the following linear arithmetic formula:

$$('a' \leq x \leq 'z') \vee ('A' \leq x \leq 'Z') \vee$$
$$('0' \leq x \leq '9') \vee x = '\ ' \vee x = '.' \vee x = ',' \vee x = '-' \vee x = '\_'$$

Encode contains the following seven rules ($Q_{Encode} = \{q\}$):

$$q(\epsilon) \quad \longrightarrow \qquad\qquad \epsilon$$
$$q([x|y]) \xrightarrow{\varphi[x]} \qquad\qquad [x|q(y)]$$
$$q([x|y]) \xrightarrow{\neg\varphi[x]\wedge 0\leq x<10} \qquad ['\&', '\#', \mathbf{d}_0(x), ';'|q(y)]$$
$$q([x|y]) \xrightarrow{\neg\varphi[x]\wedge 10''\leq x<10^{n+1}} ['\&', '\#', \mathbf{d}_n(x), \ldots, \mathbf{d}_0(x), ';'|q(y)] \quad \text{(for } 1 \leq n \leq 4)$$

where
$$\mathbf{d}_i(x) \overset{\text{def}}{=} ((x \div 10^i)\%10) + 48$$

is a term in linear arithmetic representing the (ASCII) character value of the i'th decimal position of x, where $\div$ is integer division, $+$ is integer addition, and $\%$ computes the integer remainder after dividing its first operand by its second. By using that '&' = 38 (i.e., $\mathbf{d}_1('\&') = '3'$ and $\mathbf{d}_0('\&') = '8'$) and that $\varphi['\&']$ does not hold, it follows for example that

$$\mathbf{T}_{Encode}(['\&', 'a']) = \{['\&', '\#', '3', '8', ';', 'a']\}.$$

Note that *Encode* is deterministic because all the guards are mutually exclusive and therefore $[\![Encode]\!]$ contains no two rules whose left-hand sides are equal but whose right-hand sides are different. From determinism follows also that *Encode* is single-valued. ⊠

The following example illustrates another class of common single-valued list-transductions over an *infinite* label domain that are captured by a nondeterministic STT but not by any deterministic STT. While it is well-known that nondeterministic tree transducers are more expressive than deterministic tree transducers, the following example illustrates a case where a deterministic tree transducer would exist if the label domain was *finite*.

Example 3. The example illustrates an INT-list STT *Extract* that extracts from a given input list all subsequences of elements of the form $['<', x, '>']$, where $x \neq '<'$. For example

$$\mathbf{T}_{Extract}(['<', '<', 'a', '>', '<', '<', '>', '<', 'b', '>']) = ['<', 'a', '>', '<', 'b', '>']$$

Extract has states $\{q_0, q_1, q_2, q_3\}$ where q_0 is the initial state. *Extract* can be visualized as follows, where a rule $q(\epsilon) \to \epsilon$ is depicted by marking q as a final state, and a rule $q([x|y]) \xrightarrow{\varphi[x]} [t_1, \ldots, t_n | p(y)]$, for $n \geq 0$, is depicted as a transition from q to p having label $\varphi[x]/[t_1, \ldots, t_n]$:

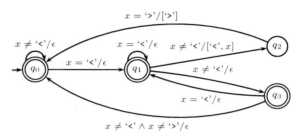

A deterministic version would need a state to remember each element $x \neq '<'$ from q_1 in order to later decide whether to output or to delete the elements, which depends on whether x is followed by '>' or not.   ⊠

4   Composition and Equivalence of STTs

In this section we investigate feasibility of *composition* and *equivalence* of STTs. First, we prove that STTs are closed under composition and we provide a practical algorithm for composing STTs. The composition algorithm preserves linearity. Second, we show that equivalence of linear single-valued STTs is decidable modulo a decidable theory over labels and we provide a practical algorithm for this case. The immediate applications of these two algorithms are decision procedures for *commutativity* and *idempotence* of linear single-valued STTs.

4.1   Composition of STTs

The composition of two transductions $\mathbf{T}_1$ and $\mathbf{T}_2$ is the transduction

$$\mathbf{T}_1 \circ \mathbf{T}_2(t) \overset{\text{def}}{=} \bigcup_{u \in \mathbf{T}_1(t)} \mathbf{T}_2(u)$$

Notice that $\circ$ applies first $\mathbf{T}_1$, then $\mathbf{T}_2$, contrary to how $\circ$ is used for standard function composition. (The definition follows the convention used in [15].)

Note that if $\mathbf{T}_1$ and $\mathbf{T}_2$ are single-valued then so is $\mathbf{T}_1 \circ \mathbf{T}_2$. Given two STTs $A^{\iota/\sigma}$ and $B^{\sigma/o}$ we provide an algorithm for constructing an STT $A \circ B^{\iota/o}$ such that $\mathbf{T}_{A \circ B} = \mathbf{T}_A \circ \mathbf{T}_B$. The algorithm is a symbolic generalization of the classical composition algorithm for (top-down) tree transducers (cf. [15, Theorem 3.39]).

In the following let A and B be fixed STTs. The description of the algorithm assumes absence of epsilon moves.[1] We assume, for ease of presentation, that the input and the output trees have the same sort.

As a convention, rules without an explicit guard have an implicit guard that is *true*. Given a set of guarded rewrite rules R and a pair (φ, t) where φ is a formula and t a term, an R-*derivation step* is of the form:

$$(\varphi, t) \Rightarrow_R (\varphi \wedge \psi[t_0], t[\pi \leftarrow r[t_0, \bar{s}]]) \quad \text{if} \quad \begin{cases} l[x, \bar{y}] \xrightarrow{\psi[x]}_R r[x, \bar{y}] \\ t|_\pi = l[t_0, \bar{s}] \end{cases}$$

That is, in the context of condition φ, a subterm of t at position π can be rewritten using a rule from R while accumulating the side-condition for the rule. We write $(\varphi, t) \downarrow_R$ for the set of all (φ', t') such that $(\varphi, t) \Rightarrow_R^* (\varphi', t')$ and there exists no R-derivation step from t'. We use a pairing function $\langle p, q \rangle$ for $p \in Q_A, q \in Q_B$ to denote states in the composed transducer. The states come from a composition $q(p(y))$ and to give us access to the pair we augment R_B to

$$R'_B = R_B \cup \{q(p(y)) \rightarrow \langle p, q \rangle(y) \mid p \in Q_A, q \in Q_B\}$$

We can now define the composition of two transducers by $(Q, \langle q_A^0, q_B^0 \rangle, R)$, where R and Q are given by a least fixed point with respect to the following conditions:

1. $\langle q_A^0, q_B^0 \rangle \in Q$
2. If $\langle p, q \rangle \in Q, p(v) \xrightarrow{\varphi} u \in R_A, (\psi, t) \in (\varphi, q(u)) \downarrow_{R'_B}$ then $\langle p, q \rangle(v) \xrightarrow{\psi} t \in R$
3. If $\langle p, q \rangle(v) \xrightarrow{\varphi} t[\langle p', q' \rangle(y)] \in R$ then $\langle p', q' \rangle \in Q$

The least fixed-point can be computed using a DFS traversal over the states reachable from $\langle q_A^0, q_B^0 \rangle$. The algorithm for computing $(\varphi, q(u)) \downarrow_{R'_B}$ can be implemented using backtracking search. A practically important optimization of the algorithm, is *satisfiability checking* of the induced guard formulas. If a formula φ' in a derivation $(\varphi, t) \Rightarrow_R^* (\varphi', t')$ is unsatisfiable, the continued search from that point on is aborted.

Example 4. Consider the self-composition of *Encode* from Example 2. For the sake of clarity let $A = Encode$ but rename q_A^0 to p. Let $B = Encode$. Thus $Q_A \times Q_B = \{\langle p, q \rangle\}$.

1. Case $p(\epsilon) \rightarrow_A \epsilon$. Then $(true, q(\epsilon)) \downarrow_R = \{(true, \epsilon)\}$, so $\langle p, q \rangle(\epsilon) \rightarrow \epsilon$.
2. Case $p([x|y]) \xrightarrow{\varphi[x]}_A [x|p(y)]$. We get that (formulas are simplified):

$$(\varphi[x], q([x|p(y)])) \Rightarrow_{R'_B} (\varphi[x], [x|q(p(y))]) \Rightarrow_{R'_B} (\varphi[x], [x|\langle p, q \rangle(y)]) \not\Rightarrow_{R'_B}$$

while any other derivation causes a conflict, e.g.

$$(\varphi[x], q([x|p(y)])) \Rightarrow_{R'_B} (\varphi[x] \wedge \neg\varphi[x] \wedge \ldots, ['\&', \ldots])\star$$

---

[1] Epsilon moves can be handled similarly, first *epsilon-loops*, that are circular paths of epsilon moves $p(y) \rightarrow \cdots \rightarrow p(y)$, are eliminated in order to avoid nonterminating derivations.

It follows that $\langle p, q\rangle([x|y]) \xrightarrow{\varphi[x]} [x|\langle p, q\rangle(y)]$.

3. Case $p([x|y]) \xrightarrow{\neg\varphi[x] \wedge 0 \leq x < 10}_A ['\&', '\#', \mathbf{d}_0(x), ';'|p(y)]$. Then

$$
\begin{aligned}
&(\varphi[x] \wedge 0 \leq x < 10, q(['\&', '\#', \mathbf{d}_0(x), ';'|p(y)])) \Rightarrow^*_{R'_B} \\
&\quad (\varphi[x] \wedge 0 \leq x < 10 \wedge \varphi[\mathbf{d}_0(x)], \\
&\quad ['\&', '\#', \mathbf{d}_1('\&'), \mathbf{d}_0('\&'), ';', '\&', '\#', \mathbf{d}_1('\#'), \mathbf{d}_0('\#'), ';', \\
&\quad \mathbf{d}_0(x), '\&', '\#', \mathbf{d}_1(';'), \mathbf{d}_0(';'), ';'|\langle p, q\rangle(y)]) \not\Rightarrow_{R'_B}
\end{aligned}
$$

The remaining cases are similar. Note that, for all x and i, $\varphi[\mathbf{d}_i(x)]$ holds because '0' $\leq \mathbf{d}_i(x) \leq$ '9', while for $x \in \{'\&', '\#', ';'\}$, $\neg\varphi[x] \wedge 10 \leq x \leq 100$ holds, and thus double-encoding occurs for these characters in $A \circ B$.

The importance of early pruning of the search space using satisfiability checks is obvious in this example. Brute force exploration would cause a combinatorial explosion of the different paths, while most of them are infeasible.   ⊠

The following result characterizes compositionality of STTs.

Theorem 1 (Composition). *STTs are effectively closed under composition. Moreover, linear STTs are effectively closed under composition.*

Proof. The first statement can be shown along the lines of the proof of compositionality of TOP [15, Theorem 3.39]. While the second statement can be shown similarly to compositionality of l-TOP [15, Corollary 3.41], a simpler argument, using the definition of R'_B, shows that linearity is preserved by $\Rightarrow_{R'_B}$.

Suppose A and B are linear and consider the definition of $(\varphi, t)\downarrow_{R'_B}$. Suppose t is $\bar{y}$-linear (linear with respect to $\bar{y} = (y_1, \ldots, y_k)$ assuming that the tree sort is $\mathrm{T}^k\langle\sigma\rangle$, recall that nonlinearity is allowed with respect to the label variable x). Then, $t|_\pi = l[t_0, \bar{s}]$, where $\bar{s} = (s_1, \ldots, s_k)$, is also $\bar{y}$-linear and

$$
\begin{aligned}
y_i \in FV(\bar{s}) &\implies y_i \notin FV(t[\pi \leftarrow \epsilon]) \\
y_i \in FV(s_j) &\implies y_i \notin FV(s_{j'}) \qquad \text{(for } j \neq j')
\end{aligned}
$$

Since the rule $l[x, \bar{y}] \xrightarrow{\psi[x]}_{R'_B} r[x, \bar{y}]$ is $\bar{y}$-linear, it follows that $r[t_0, \bar{s}]$ is also $\bar{y}$-linear and consequently $t[\pi \leftarrow r[t_0, \bar{s}]]$ is $\bar{y}$-linear. Therefore, by linearity of A and by induction on the length of R'_B-derivations, all terms in $(\varphi, t)\downarrow_{R'_B}$, are $\bar{y}$-linear. It follows that each rule added to R is $\bar{y}$-linear, ∴ $A \circ B$ is linear.   ⊠

4.2   Equivalence of Linear Single-Valued STTs

Equivalence checking of finite transducers is undecidable when the possible number of outputs for a given input is unbounded [17,21]. The case that is practically more directly relevant for us is when transducers are single-valued, since this case corresponds closely to functional transformations computed by concrete programs over structured data (possibly over a restricted input domain). For (top-down) tree transducers it is known that equivalence is decidable for the single-valued case [8,13], or more generally, for the *finite-valued* case [31] (when there exists k such that, for all t, $|\mathbf{T}_A(t)| \leq k$). Here we investigate the more restricted equivalence problem for *linear single-valued* STTs as the practically most common case, while the generalization to either nonlinear or finite-valued STTs is left as a future research topic.

STTs A and B are *equivalent* if $\mathbf{T}_A = \mathbf{T}_B$. Let $Dom(A) \stackrel{\text{def}}{=} \{t \mid \mathbf{T}_A(t) \neq \emptyset\}$. For a single-valued STT A and $t \in Dom(A)$ we write $A(t) = u$ for $\mathbf{T}_A(t) = \{u\}$. In the following let $A^{\mathrm{T}\langle \iota \rangle / \mathrm{T}\langle o \rangle}$ and $B^{\mathrm{T}\langle \iota \rangle / \mathrm{T}\langle o \rangle}$ be fixed linear single-valued STTs. Equivalence of A and B reduces to two separate decision problems:

1. *Domain equivalence*: $Dom(A) = Dom(B)$.
2. *Partial equivalence* $A \cong B$: for all $t \in Dom(A) \cap Dom(B)$, $A(t) = B(t)$.

Note that both problems are independent of each other and together imply equivalence. Domain equivalence requires the notion of a *symbolic tree automaton* (*STA*) that is an STT such that each rule is either $q(\epsilon) \rightarrow \epsilon$ or a linear rule $q(f(x, y_1, \dots, y_k)) \xrightarrow{\varphi[x]} f(x, q_1(y_1), \dots, q_k(y_k))$, i.e., the notion of the output tree is obsolete. The STA for $Dom(A)$ can be constructed directly from the STT A. By a *label theory* we mean a quantifier free set of formulas that is closed under substitutions, Boolean operations and equality, and allows free variables of the label sort.

Deciding equivalence of two STAs A and B is a generalization of the equivalence problem of tree automata [16] and is decidable modulo decidability of the label theory. The equivalence algorithm of symbolic tree automata uses the result that symbolic tree automata are closed under intersection and complement [33], that is a generalization of corresponding closure properties of symbolic automata [34]. We use the following proposition below.

Proposition 1. *Equivalence of symbolic tree automata is decidable modulo a decidable label theory.*

For many practical considerations, domain equivalence is not as important as partial equivalence because the transductions of A and B are known to correspond to *total* functions from $\mathcal{U}^{\mathrm{T}\langle \iota \rangle}$ to $\mathcal{U}^{\mathrm{T}\langle o \rangle}$, i.e., $Dom(A) = Dom(B) = \mathcal{U}^{\mathrm{T}\langle \iota \rangle}$, reflecting a *robustness* assumption of the underlying programs.

In the following we develop a practical algorithm for deciding partial equivalence $A \cong B$. First, we adjust the formalism of linear STTs a bit so that it is technically better suited for the purposes here, by separating the acceptance condition of the input term from the construction of the output term. For ease of presentation assume $k = 2$ (i.e., the input domain is $\mathrm{T}^2\langle \iota \rangle$). For each rule

$$p(f(x, y_1, y_2)) \xrightarrow{\varphi[x]} r[x, p_1(y_1), p_2(y_2)],$$

where $r[x, z_1, z_2]$ is basic (z_i is the transformation $p_i(y_i)$), is represented by the following *transition* whose i'th target component is the state that transforms y_i:

$$p \xrightarrow{\varphi[x]/r[x, z_1, z_2]} (p_1, p_2)$$

If z_i does not occur in r we use a special *sink* state $p_i = p^*$ with transition

$$p^* \xrightarrow{true/\epsilon} (p^*, p^*)$$

For each rule $p(\epsilon) \to e$ we say that p is *final* with a *final output* e, denoted by $p\xrightarrow{/e}$. In particular, $p^* \xrightarrow{/\epsilon}$. For example,

$$p(f(x, y_1, y_2)) \xrightarrow{true} f(x, \epsilon, q(y_1)) \quad \text{corresponds to} \quad p \xrightarrow{true/f(x,\epsilon,z_1)} (q, p^*).$$

Note that all input trees are accepted from p^*, e.g., in the above example y_2 can be an arbitrary input tree. Note also that the given transition view is not possible for arbitrary nonlinear STTs.

We assume that A and B are *clean*, i.e., contain no rules with unsatisfiable guards. We also assume that A and B have no *unreachable states* and no *deadends*, where an unreachable state is a state such that no derivation from the initial state can reach it, and a deadend is a state p that is reachable but is not final and, for all transitions $p \to (p_1, p_2)$, either p_1 or p_2 is a deadend. The corresponding decision problems are classical forward and backward reachability algorithms that are linear in the number of states.

The partial equivalence algorithm uses the notion of a *product* $A \times B$ of A and B that is intuitively a *2-output-STT* whose definition is based on the transition view of A and B. $A \times B$ has states $Q_A \times Q_B$ and its transitions are constructed as follows, where $\bar{z}^A$ (resp. $\bar{z}^B$) is a unique renaming of each z_i by z_i^A (resp. z_i^B),

$$\left. \begin{array}{l} p \xrightarrow{\varphi[x]/t[x,\bar{z}]}_A (p_1, p_2) \\ q \xrightarrow{\psi[x]/u[x,\bar{z}]}_B (q_1, q_2) \end{array} \right\} \implies \langle p, q \rangle \xrightarrow{\varphi \wedge \psi[x]/(t[x,\bar{z}^A], u[x,\bar{z}^B])}_{A \times B} (\langle p_1, q_1 \rangle, \langle p_2, q_2 \rangle)$$

$$\left. \begin{array}{l} p \xrightarrow{/a}_A \\ q \xrightarrow{/b}_B \end{array} \right\} \implies \langle p, q \rangle \xrightarrow{/(a,b)}_{A \times B}$$

Unsatisfiable guards, unreachable states, and deadends are eliminated from $A \times B$ (where the first two are by virtue of constructing $A \times B$ by using DFS).

Let $A^{\langle p,q \rangle}(v)$ denote the A-output of $A \times B$ that is produced starting from state $\langle p, q \rangle$ for any v that is accepted from that state. Similarly for B. The following property follows from the definitions.

$$(\forall t \in Dom(A) \cap Dom(B)) \quad A^{\langle q_A^0, q_B^0 \rangle}(t) = B^{\langle q_A^0, q_B^0 \rangle}(t) \Leftrightarrow A(t) = B(t)$$

A *tree context* is a tree term with exactly one occurrence of a special free variable $\bullet$. A *promise* of a state $\langle p, q \rangle$ is a pair $\langle \alpha[\bullet], \beta[\bullet] \rangle$ of tree contexts where $\alpha = \bullet$ or $\beta = \bullet$, such that there exists a derivation in $A \times B$ for some input tree t and position π in t that reaches $\langle p, q \rangle$ at π and, for some output position π', the π'-traces of the outputs from A and B are equal and the remaining outputs from position π' in A and B are $\alpha[A^{\langle p,q \rangle}(t|_\pi)]$ and $\beta[B^{\langle p,q \rangle}(t|_\pi)]$ respectively. Two promises $\langle \alpha_1[\bullet], \beta_1[\bullet] \rangle$ and $\langle \alpha_2[\bullet], \beta_2[\bullet] \rangle$ *conflict* if $\alpha_1[u] \neq \alpha_2[u]$ or $\beta_1[u] \neq \beta_2[u]$ for some tree u. Otherwise, we say that the promises *match*. Note that matching really means that the promises are identical trees (modulo equality of labels).

Example 5. Consider two SFTs A and B over $\text{T}^2\langle\text{INT}\rangle$ where $Q_A = \{p\}$ and $Q_B = \{q\}$ that contain the following transitions:

$$p \xrightarrow{/\epsilon}_A, \quad p \xrightarrow{x\leq2/f(x,f(x,z_1,\epsilon),z_2)}_A (p,p), \quad q \xrightarrow{/\epsilon}_B, \quad q \xrightarrow{x\geq2/f(x,z_1,z_2)}_B (q,q).$$

Then $A \times B$ contains the following transitions

$$\langle p,q\rangle \xrightarrow{/(\epsilon,\epsilon)}_{A\times B}, \quad \langle p,q\rangle \xrightarrow{x=2/(f(x,f(x,z_1^A,\epsilon),z_2^A),f(x,z_1^B,z_2^B))}_{A\times B} (\langle p,q\rangle,\langle p,q\rangle)$$

State $\langle p,q\rangle$ has a promise $\langle\bullet,\bullet\rangle$ for position ε since $\langle p,q\rangle$ is the initial state. It also has a conflicting promise $\langle f(2,\bullet,\epsilon),\bullet\rangle$ due to the following. Consider the input tree $t = f(2,t_1,t_2)$ and position $\pi = \mathbf{1}$ in t. After a single step derivation in $A\times B$ we get that $A(t) = f(2,f(2,A(t_1),\epsilon),A(t_2))$ and $B(t) = f(2,B(t_1),B(t_2))$. Thus, for the output position $\pi' = \mathbf{1}$ we have that, the π'-traces of $A(t)$ and $B(t)$ are equal, $A(t)|_{\pi'} = f(2,A^{\langle p,q\rangle}(t|_\pi),\epsilon)$ and $B(t)|_{\pi'} = B^{\langle p,q\rangle}(t|_\pi)$.   ⊠

A state $\langle p,q\rangle$ is *input dependent for A* if there exist $v_1 \neq v_2$ such that $A^{\langle p,q\rangle}(v_1) \neq A^{\langle p,q\rangle}(v_2)$. Similarly for B. A state $\langle p,q\rangle$ is *input dependent* if it is input dependent for both A and B.

We make use of the following key lemma in the main theorem that provides us with an argument to detect $A \not\cong B$ in $O(|A\times B|)$ number of steps. The lemma is not constructive; it does not provide a witness t such that $A(t) \neq B(t)$.

Lemma 1 (Promise). *If an input dependent state $\langle p,q\rangle$ is reached with two conflicting promises then $A \not\cong B$.*

Proof. Suppose there is a state $\langle p,q\rangle$ with conflicting promises $\langle\alpha_1[\bullet],\beta_1[\bullet]\rangle$ and $\langle\alpha_2[\bullet],\beta_2[\bullet]\rangle$. Since $\langle p,q\rangle$ is reachable and not a deadend, there exist input trees u_1 and u_2 where $u_1|_{\pi_1} = v$ and $u_2|_{\pi_2} = v$ for some positions π_1 and π_2, and v is an input term accepted from $\langle p,q\rangle$, and

- $\langle p,q\rangle \mapsto \langle\alpha_1[\bullet],\beta_1[\bullet]\rangle$ is reached at some position π_1' in the outputs from u_1,
- $\langle p,q\rangle \mapsto \langle\alpha_2[\bullet],\beta_2[\bullet]\rangle$ is reached at some position π_2' in the outputs from u_2.

By single-valuedness of A and B there exist $v^A = A^{\langle p,q\rangle}(v)$ and $v^B = B^{\langle p,q\rangle}(v)$ such that

$$A(u_1)|_{\pi_1'} = \alpha_1[v^A], \ A(u_2)|_{\pi_2'} = \alpha_2[v^A], \ B(u_1)|_{\pi_1'} = \beta_1[v^B], \ B(u_2)|_{\pi_2'} = \beta_2[v^B].$$

Suppose $A \cong B$. Then $\alpha_1[v^A] = \beta_1[v^B]$ and $\alpha_2[v^A] = \beta_2[v^B]$. We reach a contradiction by case analysis. Note that the cases make use of the assumption that in each promise at least one of the terms is a $\bullet$.

- Case $\alpha_1 = \bullet, \beta_1 = \bullet, \alpha_2 = \bullet, \beta_2 \neq \bullet$: Then $v^B = v^A = \beta_2[v^B]$, but $\beta_2 \neq \bullet$.
- Case $\alpha_1 \neq \bullet, \beta_1 = \bullet, \alpha_2 = \bullet, \beta_2 \neq \bullet$: Then $\alpha_1[v^A] = v^B, v^A = \beta_2[v^B]$, but $\alpha_1[\beta_2[v^B]] \neq v^B$.
- Case $\alpha_1 = \bullet, \beta_1 \neq \bullet, \alpha_2 = \bullet, \beta_2 \neq \bullet$: Then $\beta_1[v^B] = v^A = \beta_2[v^B]$. This is only possible if $\beta_1[t] = \beta_2[t]$ for a fixed tree t (e.g. $\beta_1 = f(t_0,\bullet,t)$ and $\beta_2 = f(t_0,t,\bullet)$) or else $\langle\alpha_1,\beta_1\rangle$ and $\langle\alpha_2,\beta_2\rangle$ match. Thus $v^B = t$. By input independence of $\langle p,q\rangle$ for B we can choose v and $v_0 \neq v$ so that $v^B \neq v_0^B = B^{\langle p,q\rangle}(v_0)$. But this contradicts that $v_0^B = t$ must hold.

The remaining cases are symmetrical.   ⊠

We apply the following normalization on $A \times B$ before turning to the main algorithm. First, we effectively decide if a state $\langle p, q \rangle$ is input dependent for A (resp. B) and, otherwise compute a concrete term $t_A^{\langle p,q \rangle}$ (resp. $t_B^{\langle p,q \rangle}$) such that for all v, $A^{\langle p,q \rangle}(v) = t_A^{\langle p,q \rangle}$ (resp. $B^{\langle p,q \rangle}(v) = t_B^{\langle p,q \rangle}$). Next, for each transition

$$\langle p, q \rangle \xrightarrow{\varphi/(t,u)} (\langle p_1, q_1 \rangle, \langle p_2, q_2 \rangle)$$

if $\langle p_i, q_i \rangle$ is not input dependent for A, replace z_i in t by $t_A^{\langle p_i,q_i \rangle}$, similarly for u and B. In the following assume:

(*) *If an output variable z_i occurs in t (resp. u) then $\langle p_i, q_i \rangle$ is input dependent for A (resp. B).*

The main algorithm is a search procedure (that can be implemented using DFS). There is a set Q of reached states annotated with promises. Initially $Q = \{\langle q_A^0, q_B^0 \rangle \mapsto \langle \bullet, \bullet \rangle\}$. Given an unexplored reached state $\langle p, q \rangle \mapsto \langle \alpha[\bullet], \beta[\bullet] \rangle$ the following steps are performed.

Check final outputs: If $\langle p, q \rangle \xrightarrow{/(a,b)}$ and if $\alpha[a] \neq \beta[b]$ then $\mathbf{A} \not\approx \mathbf{B}$.

Check transitions: Perform the following steps for each transition

$$\langle p, q \rangle \xrightarrow{\varphi[x]/(t[x,z_1^A,z_2^A],u[x,z_1^B,z_2^B])} (\langle p_1, q_1 \rangle, \langle p_2, q_2 \rangle)$$

Unify $\alpha[t]$ with $\beta[u]$. If a unifier does not exist then $\mathbf{A} \not\approx \mathbf{B}$. Else, the result is a pair $(C[x], \theta)$ where C is a conjunction of equality constraints on labels and θ is a substitution from those $\bar{z}$ that occur in t or u to tree terms.

Validate labels: If $\varphi \wedge \neg C$ is satisfiable then there exists a label x such that $\alpha[t[x, \bar{z}^A]] \neq \beta[u[x, \bar{z}^B]]$ for all $\bar{z}^A$ and $\bar{z}^B$. Thus $\mathbf{A} \not\approx \mathbf{B}$.

Validate trees: Suppose $z_1^A \mapsto v[x, z_1^B, z_2^B] \in \theta$. (The other cases are symmetrical.) We proceed by case analysis on v.

   Independent term: Assume v does not contain z_1^B. Suppose v' is an arbitrary ground instance of v. By (*), there exist two outputs $a_1 \neq a_2$ for z_1^A and therefore, either $t[\_, a_1, \_] \neq t[\_, v', \_]$ or $t[\_, a_2, \_] \neq t[\_, v', \_]$. Thus $\mathbf{A} \not\approx \mathbf{B}$.

   Mixed dependency: Assume v contains z_1^B and also z_2^B. By using (*), there exist two different outputs for z_2^B independent of z_1^A and x. Thus, there exist two conflicting promises for $\langle p_1, q_1 \rangle$. By the Promise lemma, $\mathbf{A} \not\approx \mathbf{B}$.

   Multiple labels: Assume $v[x, z_1^B]$ contains x and z_1^B but not z_2^B. Check if any possible value for x makes any difference in v. If

$$\varphi[x_1] \wedge \varphi[x_2] \wedge v[x_1, \epsilon] \neq v[x_2, \epsilon]$$

is satisfiable then there exist two conflicting promises for $\langle p_1, q_1 \rangle$. By the Promise lemma, $\mathbf{A} \not\approx \mathbf{B}$.

   Dependent term: Let t_0 be any value such that $\varphi[t_0]$ is true. Note that $v[t_0, \bullet]$ is the same independent of t_0 by the previous step. Let $\alpha_1 = \bullet$, $\beta_1 = v[t_0, \bullet]$:

1. If $\langle p_1, q_1 \rangle \notin Q$ then add $\langle p_1, q_1 \rangle \mapsto \langle \alpha_1, \beta_1 \rangle$ to Q and push $\langle p_1, q_1 \rangle$.
2. else let $\langle \alpha_2, \beta_2 \rangle = Q(\langle p_1, q_1 \rangle)$. If $\langle \alpha_1, \beta_1 \rangle$ and $\langle \alpha_2, \beta_2 \rangle$ conflict (are not identical), then, by the Promise lemma, $\mathbf{A} \not\cong \mathbf{B}$.

Partial equivalence: The search is exhaustive and establishes that $\mathbf{A} \cong \mathbf{B}$.

Recall that a *label theory* is a quantifier free set of formulas that is closed under substitutions, Boolean operations and equality, and allows free variables of the label sort. A typical label theory is quantifier free integer linear arithmetic. Note that decidability of a theory refers to decidability of the problem of checking satisfiability of a given formula in the theory.

Theorem 2 (Equivalence). *Equivalence of linear single-valued STTs is decidable over a decidable label theory.*

Proof. Termination of the partial equivalence checking algorithm follows from finiteness of $Q_{A \times B}$ and decidability of the assumed label theory. Partial correctness of the algorithm and how the Promise lemma is used follows from the description of the core steps of the algorithm. Decidability of domain equivalence follows from Proposition 1.   ⊠

Note that the satisfiability checks that are actually performed during the search require the use of *at most one* free label variable and no other free variables. In particular, the statisfiability check in the **Multiple labels** step above, that is expressed using two variables, can be replaced (given any value a such that $\varphi[a]$ holds) with the satisfiability check of the formula $\varphi[x] \wedge v[x, \epsilon] \neq v[a, \epsilon]$ containing at most one free variable x. This observation is relevant in order to provide a precise complexity bound for the given algorithm, provided that the complexity of the used label theory over at most one free variable is known. The algorithm can be implemented using any SMT solver or constraint solver as an oracle that supports satisfiability checking and model generation, such as the SMT solver Z3 [6].

4.3   Checking Non-equivalence Symbolically

The algorithm produces at most $|Q_A \times Q_B|$ states and requires examining at most $|R_A| \cdot |R_B|$ transitions. This bound obviously does not work when comparing tree transducers whose number of outputs is unbounded. In practice, however, we can use a common symbolic algorithm that unfolds an STT. In the general case it can be used as a semi-decision algorithm for non-equivalence. Given a transducer A, that does not contain ϵ loops, we can encode a predicate $Acc_A(q_A^0, t, s, n)$, such that A takes the term t and produces the term s with at most n transitions along any given branch. Non-equivalence can then be checked by showing that

$$\exists t, s, n \, . \, \left(\begin{array}{l} (Acc_A(q_A^0, t, s, n) \wedge \neg Acc_B(q_B^0, t, s, n)) \\ \vee \, (\neg Acc_A(q_A^0, t, s, n) \wedge Acc_B(q_B^0, t, s, n)) \end{array} \right).$$

The definition is given by:

$$Acc_A(q, f(t_0, t_1, \ldots, t_k), s, n) \equiv \bigvee_{\tau \in R_A} \begin{pmatrix} n > 0 \wedge \ \varphi[t_0] \wedge \\ s = u[t_0, \ell_1(s), \ldots, \ell_k(s)] \wedge \\ \bigwedge_{i=1}^{k} Acc_A(q_i, t_i, \ell_i(s), n-1) \end{pmatrix}$$

$$Acc_A(q, \epsilon, \epsilon, n) \equiv true$$

where, as usual, τ is of the form $q(f(x, y_1, \ldots, y_k)) \xrightarrow{\varphi} u[x, q_1(y_1), \ldots, q_k(y_k)]$, and $\ell_1(s)$ selects the subterm of s corresponding to the path supplied in u. The formulas produced by unfolding Acc_A are always ground, and satisfiability of the formulas can be checked using the background label theory together with the theory of algebraic data-types. For single valued STTs we can fix n to $|Q_A \times Q_B|$ to bound unfolding; for general STTs we can convert the definition into first-order formulas whose instantiations correspond to step-wise unfoldings of the transition relation.

5   Related Work

Tree transducers and various extensions thereof provide a syntax-directed view of studying different formal models of transformations over tree structured data [15]. Top-down tree transducers were originally introduced in [30,32] for studying properties of syntax-directed translations. The handbook [16] provides a uniform treatment of foundational properties of tree transducers and relations to context-free languages. Basic compositionality results of tree transducers were established in [3,7].

Decidability of equivalence of single-valued top-down tree transducers follows from the decidability result of single-valuedness of top-down tree transducers [8,13]. A specialized method for checking equivalence of *deterministic* top-down tree transducers is provided in [5]. Decision problems, e.g. equivalence, for specific classes of tree transducers are often based on establishing unique normal forms and considering deterministic transducers, including string transducers [4], top-down tree transducers [11], and top-down tree-to-string transducers [24].

Several extensions of top-down tree transducers have been studied in the literature (the following list is not exhaustive). Extended top-down tree transducers allow nonflat left-hand sides in rules [2]. Attributed tree-transducers describe parse trees in attribute grammars [14]. Macro tree-transducers incorporate the notion of implicit tree contexts [12] and have been studied in the context of analysis of XML transformation languages, with macro attributed tree-transducers [15], multi-return macro tree transducers [22], and macro forest transducers [29] as further extensions. Pebble tree transducers were introduced for type checking XML query languages [26] and are extended to pebble macro tree transducers in [10]. Formal relationships between monadic second order logic and macro tree transducers is studied in [9]. Extended top-down tree transducers were recently studied in the context of natural language processing, where it is shown that several interesting cases are not closed under composition [25]. Higher-order multi-parameter tree transducers [23] allow possibly infinite trees in the output and can be applied to higher-order recursion schemes. A related notion of pattern-matching recursion schemes is introduced in [28] to model functional programs that manipulate algebraic data-types.

The above generalizations are all proper extensions of the basic top-down tree transducer model. To the best of our knowledge, none of the extensions has considered a symbolic representation of the transducers modulo a given label theory. The work in [27] introduces the first symbolic generalization of a finite state (string) transducer called a *predicate-augmented finite state transducer* in the context of natural language processing. A symbolic representation of finite (string) transducers modulo a given label theory, called *symbolic finite transducers*, is introduced in [19] in order to encode string sanitization operations over large (possibly infinite) alphabets for web security analysis. The results here extend the algorithms of the string case to trees, in order to symbolically represent transductions over tree structured data such as Html or XML documents. *Streaming transducers* [1] provide another recent symbolic extension of finite transducers where the label theories are restricted to be total orders.

6   Conclusions

We intend to investigate several extensions of our main results for STTs. Single-valued deterministic STTs correspond directly to first-order functional programs. One direction is to develop ground decision procedures for first-order functional programs given as STTs. On the other hand, first-order functional programs are of course much more expressive than STTs (and equivalence of first-order functional programs is Π_1^1 complete). For example list-reversal is not expressible as an STT. It is tempting to extend our results to more general functional programs. Recent work on counter-example guided refinement for verification of higher-order functional programs [28], for instance, is based on repeated refinements starting from tree transducers. Using STTs instead could allow using SMT tools for analyzing functional programs. A simpler extension of our results for STTs is to consider equivalence of non-linear STTs. We conjecture that our Theorem 2 can be extended to nonlinear and single-valued STTs, but our proof cannot be used directly for this case: non-linearity creates dependencies across several states from the same transducer that has to be recorded in a product construction. We also conjecture the theorem can be extended to nonlinear and finite-valued STTs. However, a generalization to the finite-valued case is not expected to be straightforward, because the corresponding generalization of decidability of equivalence for finite-valued tree transducers [31] uses results from combinatorics and is mathematically challenging.

References

1. Alur, R., Cerný, P.: Streaming transducers for algorithmic verification of single-pass list-processing programs. In: 38th ACM SIGACT-SIGPLAN Symposium on Princples of Programming Languages (POPL 2011), pp. 599–610. ACM (2011)
2. Arnold, A., Dauchet, M.: Bi-transductions de forêts. In: Proc. 3rd International Colloquium on Automata, Languages and Programming (ICALP 1976), pp. 74–86. Edinburgh University Press, Edinburgh (1976)
3. Baker, B.S.: Composition of top-down and bottom-up tree transductions. Inform. and Control 41, 186–213 (1979)
4. Choffrut, C.: Minimizing subsequential transducers: a survey. Theoretical Computer Science 292(1), 131–143 (2003)
5. Courcelle, B., Franchi-Zannettacchi, P.: Attribute grammars and recursive program schemes. Theoretical Computer Science 17, 163–191 (1982)
6. de Moura, L., Bjørner, N.: Z3: An Efficient SMT Solver. In: Ramakrishnan, C.R., Rehof, J. (eds.) TACAS 2008. LNCS, vol. 4963, pp. 337–340. Springer, Heidelberg (2008)
7. Engelfriet, J.: Bottom-up and top-down tree transformations – a comparison. Math. Systems Theory 9, 198–231 (1975)
8. Engelfriet, J.: Some open questions and recent results on tree transducers and tree languages. In: Book, R.V. (ed.) Formal Language Theory, pp. 241–286. Academic Press, New York (1980)
9. Engelfriet, J., Maneth, S.: Macro tree transducers, attribute grammars, and mso definable tree translations. Information and Computation 154, 34–91 (1999)
10. Engelfriet, J., Maneth, S.: A comparison of pebble tree transducers with macro tree transducers. Acta Informatica 39 (2003)
11. Engelfriet, J., Maneth, S., Seidl, H.: Deciding equivalence of top-down XML transformations in polynomial time. Journal of Computer and System Science 75(5), 271–286 (2009)
12. Engelfriet, J., Vogler, H.: Macro tree transducers. J. Comp. and Syst. Sci. 31, 71–146 (1985)
13. Esik, Z.: Decidability results concerning tree transducers. Acta Cybernetica 5, 1–20 (1980)
14. Fülöp, Z.: On attributed tree transducers. Acta Cybernetica 5, 261–279 (1981)
15. Fülöp, Z., Vogler, H.: Syntax-Directed Semantics: Formal Models Based on Tree Transducers. EATCS. Springer, Heidelberg (1998)
16. Gécseg, F., Steinby, M.: Tree Automata. Akadémiai Kiadó, Budapest (1984)
17. Griffiths, T.: The unsolvability of the equivalence problem for Λ-free nondeterministic generalized machines. J. ACM 15, 409–413 (1968)
18. Hodges, W.: Model theory. Cambridge Univ. Press (1995)
19. Hooimeijer, P., Livshits, B., Molnar, D., Saxena, P., Veanes, M.: Fast and precise sanitizer analysis with BEK. In: 20th USENIX Security Symposium, pp. 1–16. USENIX Association, San Francisco (2011)
20. Hopcroft, J.E., Ullman, J.D.: Introduction to Automata Theory, Languages, and Computation. Addison Wesley (1979)
21. Ibarra, O.: The unsolvability of the equivalence problem for Efree NGSM's with unary input (output) alphabet and applications. SIAM Journal on Computing 4, 524–532 (1978)
22. Inaba, K., Hosoya, H.: Multi-return macro tree transducers. In: Proc. 6th ACM SIGPLAN Workshop on Programming Language Technologies for XML, San Francisco, California (January 2008)

23. Kobayashi, N., Tabuchi, N., Unno, H.: Higher-order multi-parameter tree transducers and recursion schemes for program verification. In: Proceedings of the 37th Annual ACM SIGPLAN-SIGACT Symposium on Principles of Programming Languages, POPL 2010, pp. 495–508. ACM (2010)
24. Laurence, G., Lemay, A., Niehren, J., Staworko, S., Tommasi, M.: Normalization of Sequential Top-Down Tree-to-Word Transducers. In: Dediu, A.-H., Inenaga, S., Martín-Vide, C. (eds.) LATA 2011. LNCS, vol. 6638, pp. 354–365. Springer, Heidelberg (2011)
25. Maletti, A., Graehl, J., Hopkins, M., Knight, K.: The power of extended top-down tree transducers. SIAM J. Comput. 39, 410–430 (2009)
26. Milo, T., Suciu, D., Vianu, V.: Typechecking for XML transformers. In: Proc. 19th ACM Symposium on Principles of Database Systems (PODS 2000), pp. 11–22. ACM (2000)
27. Noord, G.V., Gerdemann, D.: Finite state transducers with predicates and identities. Grammars 4, 263–286 (2001)
28. Ong, C.-H.L., Ramsay, S.J.: Verifying higher-order functional programs with pattern-matching algebraic data types. In: 38th ACM SIGACT-SIGPLAN Symposium on Princples of Programming Languages (POPL 2011), pp. 587–598. ACM (2011)
29. Perst, T., Seidl, H.: Macro forest transducers. Information Processing Letters 89(3), 141–149 (2004)
30. Rounds, W.C.: Context-free grammars on trees. In: Proc. ACM Symp. on Theory of Comput., pp. 143–148. ACM (1969)
31. Seidl, H.: Equivalence of finite-valued tree transducers is decidable. Math. Systems Theory 27, 285–346 (1994)
32. Thatcher, J.W.: Generalized sequential machine maps. J. Comput. Syst. Sci. 4, 339–367 (1970)
33. Veanes, M., Bjørner, N.: Symbolic tree automata. Submitted to Information Processing Letters (2011)
34. Veanes, M., Bjørner, N., de Moura, L.: Symbolic Automata Constraint Solving. In: Fermüller, C.G., Voronkov, A. (eds.) LPAR-17. LNCS, vol. 6397, pp. 640–654. Springer, Heidelberg (2010)
35. Veanes, M., de Halleux, P., Tillmann, N.: Rex: Symbolic regular expression explorer. In: Third International Conference on Software Testing, Verification and Validation (ICST 2010), pp. 498–507. IEEE Computer Society (2010)
36. Yu, S.: Regular languages. In: Rozenberg, G., Salomaa, A. (eds.) Handbook of Formal Languages, vol. 1, pp. 41–110. Springer, Heidelberg (1997)

Probabilistic Concepts in Formal Contexts*

Alexander Demin[1], Denis Ponomaryov[1], and Evgeny Vityaev[2]

[1] Institute of Informatics Systems, Novosibirsk, Russia
[2] Institute of Mathematics, Novosibirsk, Russia
alexandredemin@yandex.ru, ponom@iis.nsk.su, vityaev@math.nsc.ru

Abstract. We generalize the main notions of Formal Concept Analysis with the ideas of the semantic probabilistic inference. We demonstrate that under standard restrictions, our definitions completely correspond to the original notions of Formal Concept Analysis. From the point of view of applications, we propose a method of recovering concepts in formal contexts in presence of noise on data.

1 Introduction

Assume that a scientist needs to classify some finite set of objects with respect to n attributes. The objects are observed in a number of experiments, where each of them is assigned a certain set of attributes. The results of each experiment can be represented as a table, with rows labelled by the object names, columns labelled by the attribute names, and each cell (i, j) filled iff object i has attribute j. Having results of one particular experiment it is reasonable to classify the objects in the following way: put those objects in groups which have a common set of attributes and no object out of this group has these attributes. It is well known that the pairs ⟨object set, attribute set⟩ of this kind can be naturally ordered and represented in a convenient way as studied in Formal Concept Analysis [2, 3] (FCA). Now assume that we know the results of the whole body of the experiments and we would like to build a classification of the objects with respect to the whole collection of data. Typically, an object may have some attribute in a number of experiments and lack this attribute in the remaining number of them. To cope with this ambiguity when building classifications, we employ the method of semantic probabilistic inference introduced in [10–12]. In this paper, we generalize the standard notion of truth of an implication on data by means of a truth valuation based on a probability measure. We define an analog of the classification unit studied in FCA in terms of fixed points of implications which hold on data with respect to this valuation. To the best of our knowledge, there are no published papers describing similar probabilistic approaches. For instance, in [1] the main notions of Formal Concept Analysis are reformulated in terms

---

* This work was funded by the grant of the President of Russian Federation (grant No. MK-2037.2011.9), the Russian Foundation for Basic Research (grant No. 11-07-00560a), and Integration Projects of the Siberian Division of the Russian Academy of Sciences (grant No. 47, 111, 119).

E. Clarke, I. Virbitskaite, and A. Voronkov (Eds.): PSI 2011, LNCS 7162, pp. 394–410, 2012.

of a probability logic, but their definitions are not generalized in the scope of FCA. By this work, we aim at establishing connections between Formal Concept Analysis and the method of semantic probabilistic inference. The contribution of this paper is the generalization of the key notions of FCA in terms of the semantic probabilistic inference.

2   Preliminaries

Let us start with basic definitions and results from Formal Concept Analysis.

Definition 1. *A formal context is a triple* (G, M, I)*, where* G *and* M *are sets and* $I \subseteq G \times M$ *is a relation between the elements of* G *and* M*. The elements of* G *are called objects and the elements of* M *are called attributes of the context. We call a context finite if* G *and* M *are finite sets.*

For brevity, we omit the word "formal" and call *contexts* the triples (G, M, I) from the definition above. Every context can be naturally represented in a tabular form, as noted in the introduction. For a context (G, M, I), we define the operation $'$ on subsets $A \subseteq G$ and $B \subseteq M$ as follows:

$$A' = \{m \in M \;|\forall\; g \in A \;(g, m) \in I\}, \quad B' = \{g \in G \;|\forall\; m \in B \;(g, m) \in I\}.$$

For $g \in G$, the set $\{g\}'$ will be abbreviated by the notation g'.

Definition 2. *A concept in context* (G, M, I) *is a pair* (A, B) *with* $A \subseteq G$*,* $B \subseteq M$*,* $A' = B$*, and* $B' = A$*. The set* A *is called the extent and* B *the intent of the concept* (A, B)*.*

In fact, a *concept* can be viewed as the classification unit which groups objects and attributes of a context.

The following simple fact will be frequently used in proofs of the main claims in this paper:

Lemma 1. *If* (G, M, I) *is a context and* $B_1, B_2 \subseteq M$ *are sets of attributes, then*

1. $B_1 \subseteq B_2 \Longrightarrow B_2' \subseteq B_1'$
2. $B_1 \subseteq B_1''$.

Definition 3. *A (partial) order* $\leqslant$ *on concepts is defined as follows: if* (A_1, B_1) *and* (A_2, B_2) *are concepts of a context then* $(A_1, B_1) \leqslant (A_2, B_2)$ *if* $A_1 \subseteq A_2$ *(or, equivalently by Lemma 1, if* $B_2 \subseteq B_1$*).*

Theorem. *The relation* $\leqslant$ *induces a complete lattice on the set of concepts of a context, with the infimum and supremum of subsets given, respectively, by:*

$$\bigwedge_{j \in J}(A_j, B_j) = (\bigcap_{j \in J} A_j, \; (\bigcup_{j \in J} B_j)'')$$

$$\bigvee_{j \in J} (A_j, B_j) = ((\underset{j \in J}{\cup} A_j)'', \underset{j \in J}{\cap} B_j).$$

The procedures of computing the complete concept lattice for a given finite context [7, 8] are one of the basic algorithms in Formal Concept Analysis. In fact, they provide a classification of objects of a context with respect to their attributes and allow for finding all possible classes.

If $K = (G, M, I)$ is a context, we may speak about the truth of the following statements on K: "all objects having attribute set $B_1 \subseteq M$ also have attributes $B_2 \subseteq M$". As all properties of a context are in some sense symmetric with respect to the sets G and M, we can formulate the similar statements about subsets of G: "all attributes having the set $A_1 \subseteq G$ as their objects also have the set $A_2 \subseteq G$". W.l.o.g. we consider the statements only of the first kind. In fact, they define a monotone operator, an implication, on the boolean algebra of subsets of M. If a context K is finite, then clearly the set of all such statements true on K is also finite. Let us formalize the notion of an implication true on a context by the definitions from Chapter 2.3 in [2].

Definition 4. *An implication on a set M is an ordered pair of subsets $A, B \subseteq M$ denoted as $A \to B$. The set A is called the premise and B the conclusion of the implication $A \to B$. A subset $T \subseteq M$ respects an implication $A \to B$ if $A \not\subseteq T$ or $B \subseteq T$. A family of subsets of M respects an implication $A \to B$ if every set of this family respects $A \to B$.*

An implication $A \to B$ holds on a context $K = (G, M, I)$ (notation $K \models A \to B$) if $A, B \subseteq M$ and the family of sets $\{g' \mid g \in G\}$ respects $A \to B$.

The premise of an implication $A \to B$ is said to be false on a context $K = (G, M, I)$ if there is no element $g \in G$ such that $A \subseteq g'$. An implication $A \to B$ is called a tautology if $B \subseteq A$.

For a context $K = (G, M, I)$, we denote by $Imp(K)$ the set of all implications on M which hold on K. It is easy to verify that the tautologies and the set of implications whose premise is false in K are subsets of $Imp(K)$. When ambiguity does not arise, we will use the same symbol $\models$ to denote that a set or a family of sets respects an implication.

Every family L of implications on a set M defines the monotone operator $f_L : 2^M \to 2^M$ given by

$$f_L(X) = X \cup \{B \mid A \to B \in L, \ A \subseteq X\}.$$

Clearly, for each $X \subseteq M$, it holds $f_L(X) = X \Leftrightarrow X \models L$.

Remark 1. *Let L be a family of implications on a set M. Then for each $X \subseteq M$, there exists a minimal set $Y \subseteq M$ such that $X \subseteq Y$ and $f_L(Y) = Y$.*

Proof. Consider the following straightforward inductive process of building extensions of a set $X \subseteq M$. First, set $X_0 = X$. If a set X_i is constructed then we define $X_{i+1} = f_L(X_i)$. Finally, we take $Y = \bigcup_{i \in \omega} X_i$. $\qquad \square$

Therefore, any family L of implications on a set M defines the operator $\bar{f}_L :$ $2^M \to 2^M$ which for every $X \subseteq M$ gives the minimal subset $Y \subseteq M$ satisfying the conditions of the remark. Clearly, for each $X \subseteq M$, we have $f_L(X) = X \Leftrightarrow \bar{f}_L(X) = X$.

Remark 2. *If $K = (G, M, I)$ is a context and $A \to B$ is an implication on M then $K \models A \to B \Leftrightarrow \forall m \in B \ (K \models A \to \{m\})$.*

In the following, we consider implications only of the form $A \to \{m\}$ and use the notation $A \to m$ for them.

If K is a context, then for every implication $A \to m \in Imp(K)$ there exists a set $\{A_0 \to m \in Imp(K) \mid A_0 \subseteq A$ and for each $A_1 \subseteq A$, if $A_1 \subset A_0$ then $A_1 \to m \notin Imp(K)\}$. For a context K, let us denote by $MinImp(K)$ the set of all implications of the form $A_0 \to m \in Imp(K)$ in which the premise A_0 is minimal in the above mentioned sense. We note that this definition is a variant of the notion of a law in [10–12].

Now we give a proof of a slightly modified Proposition 20 from [2] which is central for results in this paper.

Proposition 1. *Let $K = (G, M, I)$ be a context, $T \subseteq Imp(K)$ be the set of tautologies on M, and $F \subseteq Imp(K)$ be the set of implications whose premise is false on K. Then for every subset $B \subseteq M$, we have:*

1. $f_{MinImp(K) \backslash T}(B) = B \Leftrightarrow B'' = B$;
2. *if $B' \neq \varnothing$ then $f_{MinImp(K) \backslash \{F \cup T\}}(B) = B \Leftrightarrow B'' = B$.*

Proof. Let us first demonstrate that for every subset $B \subseteq M$, we have $f_{Imp(K)}(B) = B$ iff $f_{MinImp(K)}(B) = B$. If $f_{Imp(K)}(B) \supset B$ for some B then (with Remark 2) there is an implication $A \to m \in Imp(K)$ such that $A \subseteq B$, but $m \notin B$. Then there exists $A_0 \to m \in MinImp(K)$ with $A_0 \subseteq A$ and thus, $A_0 \subseteq B$, $m \notin B$, and $f_{MinImp(K)}(B) \supset B$, a contradiction. The reverse direction of the claim is obvious, since $MinImp(K) \subseteq Imp(K)$.

Similarly, it is not hard to verify that $f_{MinImp(K) \backslash L}(B) = B \Leftrightarrow f_{Imp(K) \backslash L}(B) = B$, where $L = T$ or $L = F \cup T$. This follows from the fact that for each implication $A \to m$ on M and every subset $A_0 \subseteq A$, the condition $A \to m \notin T$ yields $A_0 \to m \notin T$. On the other hand, by Lemma 1, it follows from $A' \neq \varnothing$ that $A_0' \neq \varnothing$. Therefore, we will prove the both claims of the proposition with respect to the set $Imp(K)$, instead of $MinImp(K)$.

1.$\Leftarrow$: Assume $B'' = B$, $A_1 \to A_2 \in Imp(K) \backslash T$, and $A_1 \subseteq B$. We demonstrate that $A_2 \subseteq B$. For each $g \in B'$, we have $g' \supseteq A_2$, because $g' \supseteq B'' = B$ by Lemma 1 and implication $A_1 \to A_2$ holds on K. Therefore, $\bigcap\{g' \mid g \in B'\} \supseteq A_2$. On the other hand, $\bigcap\{g' \mid g \in B'\} = B''$ and since $B'' = B$, we obtain $B \supseteq A_2$.

1.$\Rightarrow$: By Lemma 1, in any case we have $B'' \supseteq B$, so let us assume that $f_{Imp(K) \backslash T}(B) = B$, but $B'' \not\subseteq B$. Then $B \not\models B \to B'' \notin T$ and it is sufficient to demonstrate $B \to B'' \in Imp(K)$ to obtain contradiction.

a) If $B' = \varnothing$ then this obviously holds, since there is no $g \in G$ such that $B \subseteq g'$, i.e. the premise of the implication is false on K.

b) Let $B' \neq \varnothing$; we need to show that $\forall g \in G \ (B \subseteq g' \Rightarrow B'' \subseteq g')$. Clearly $\forall g \in G \ (B \subseteq g' \Leftrightarrow g \in B')$ and, by Lemma 1, we have $\forall g \in B' \ (B'' \subseteq g')$. Therefore, if $B \subseteq g'$ for some $g \in G$ then $B'' \subseteq g'$, i.e. $B \to B'' \in Imp(K)$. Moreover, $B \to B'' \in Imp(K) \setminus F$, because $B' \neq \varnothing$.

2. The sufficiency follows from the proof of claim 1, since the condition $f_{MinImp(K) \setminus T}(B) = B$ clearly, yields $f_{MinImp(K) \setminus \{F \cup T\}}(B) = B$. The necessity is proved by item b above. $\square$

It is straightforward by Definition 2 that for each context $K = (G, M, I)$, a subset $B \subseteq M$ is an intent of some concept in context K iff $B'' = B$. Therefore, as soon as a context $K = (G, M, I)$ is given, we have the set $Imp(K)$ of all implications which hold on K and the fixed points of the operator $f_{MinImp(K) \setminus T} : 2^M \to 2^M$ correspond exactly to the intents of the concepts of K. If we omit the set F of implications from $MinImp(K) \setminus T$ whose premise is false on K then the fixed points of $f_{MinImp(K) \setminus \{F \cup T\}} : 2^M \to 2^M$ correspond to the intents of the concepts of K excluding the single concept $(\varnothing, M)$. Because for each $B \subseteq M$, the condition $B'' \neq M$ obviously yields $B' \neq \varnothing$.

3   Probabilistic Concepts on Classes of Contexts

In Section 2, we have defined the notion of truth of an implication on a given context. Let us now demonstrate how this notion can be generalized with a truth valuation wrt a class of contexts. In this section, we proceed to ideas of the method of semantic probabilistic inference in application to FCA. As described in [10–12], the regularities on data (in particular, implications) are formalized in this method as universal formulas of the first order language of a countable signature consisting of predicates and constants. Thus, the standard notion of implication defined in [2] is far more specific than the concept of regularity on data considered in the semantic probabilistic inference (we note that there have been studied implications in papers on FCA which also go far beyond the definitions in [2]). However, in order to show this method useful in the case of FCA, it will be convenient to stay within the standard algebraic definitions. For this reason, we further present some restriction of the method of semantic probabilistic inference in terms common in Formal Concept Analysis.

Definition 5. *A class of contexts over sets G and M is a family $\mathcal{K} = \{(G, M, I_j)\}_{j \in J \neq \varnothing}$, where for each $j \in J$, the triple (G, M, I_j) is a context. We use the notation $\mathcal{K}(G, M)$ for a class $\mathcal{K}$ of contexts over sets G and M. A probability model of type I is a pair $\mathcal{M} = (\mathcal{K}(G, M), \rho)$, where $G \neq \varnothing$ and ρ is a probability measure on the set $\mathcal{K}$ satisfying the condition: $\forall \ S_1, S_2 \subseteq G \times M \ \forall \ (G, M, I) \in \mathcal{K}$*

$$(S_1 \not\subseteq I \text{ or } S_2 \subseteq I) \iff \rho(\{(G, M, I_j) \mid S_1 \cup S_2 \subseteq I_j\}) = \rho(\{(G, M, I_j) \mid S_1 \subseteq I_j\}).$$

For a subset $S \subseteq G \times M$, we call the value of the function $\nu_{\mathcal{M}}(S) = \rho(\{(G, M, I) \in \mathcal{K} \mid S \subseteq I\})$ the probability of the set S on $\mathcal{M}$.

For brevity, in this section we call the pair $(\mathcal{K}(G, M), \rho)$ from the definition above the *probability model* or simply, *model*.

Let $\mathcal{M} = (\mathcal{K}(G, M), \rho)$ be a probability model and $A \to m$ be an implication on the set M. An instantiation of $A \to m$ on the model $\mathcal{M}$ is a pair $\langle g, A \to m \rangle$, where $g \in G$. The value of the function

$$\mu_{\mathcal{M}}(\langle g, A \to m \rangle) = \begin{cases} \frac{\nu_{\mathcal{M}}(S \cup \{<g, m>\})}{\nu_{\mathcal{M}}(S)} & \text{if } \nu_{\mathcal{M}}(S) \neq 0, \text{ where } S = \{< g, a >| a \in A\} \\ \text{undefined}, & \text{otherwise} \end{cases}$$

is called the probability of the instantiation $\langle g, A \to m \rangle$ on the model $\mathcal{M}$.

If $\mathcal{M} = (\mathcal{K}(G, M), \rho)$ is a probability model and $A \to m$ is an implication on the set M then the value of the function

$$\eta_{\mathcal{M}}(A \to m) = \begin{cases} \text{undefined} & \text{if } \forall g \in G \ \mu_{\mathcal{M}}(\langle g, A \to m \rangle) \text{ is undefined} \\ \inf_{g \in G} \mu_{\mathcal{M}}(\langle g, A \to m \rangle), & \text{otherwise} \end{cases}$$

is called the probability of the implication $A \to m$ on the model $\mathcal{M}$.

Remark 3. *Let* $\mathcal{M} = (\mathcal{K}(G, M), \rho)$ *be a probability model and* $A \to m$ *be an implication on the set* M *whose probability is defined on* $\mathcal{M}$. *Then* $\eta_{\mathcal{M}}(A \to m) = 1$ *iff* $\forall K \in \mathcal{K} \ (A \to m \in Imp(K))$.

Proof. $\Rightarrow$: The condition $\eta_{\mathcal{M}}(A \to m) = 1$ means that for each $g \in G$, the value of $\mu_{\mathcal{M}}(\langle g, A \to m \rangle)$ is either undefined, or equals 1. Thus, for each $g \in G$ and every context $K \in \mathcal{K}$, by the definitions of $\mu_{\mathcal{M}}$ and ρ, we have $A \nsubseteq g'$ or $m \in g'$. This means that $\forall K \in \mathcal{K} \ (A \to m \in Imp(K))$.

$\Leftarrow$: Assume that $\eta_{\mathcal{M}}(A \to m) < 1$. Then there is $g \in G$ such that the value of $\mu_{\mathcal{M}}(\langle g, A \to m \rangle)$ is defined and strictly less than 1. Then there exists a context $K \in \mathcal{K}$ in which $A \subseteq g'$ and $m \notin g'$, but this means that $A \to m \notin Imp(K)$. $\square$

Definition 6. *Let* $\mathcal{M} = (\mathcal{K}(G, M), \rho)$ *be a probability model and* $imp(M)$ *be the set of all those implications on* M *whose probability is defined on* $\mathcal{M}$. *We call an implication* $A \to m \in imp(M)$ *a probabilistic law on* $\mathcal{M}$, *if the following conditions hold:*

- $\eta_{\mathcal{M}}(A \to m) \neq 0$;
- *if* $A_0 \to m \in imp(M)$ *and* $A_0 \subset A$ *then* $\eta_{\mathcal{M}}(A_0 \to m) < \eta_{\mathcal{M}}(A \to m)$.

An implication $A \to m \in imp(M)$ *is called a maximally specific probabilistic law on* $\mathcal{M}$ *if it is a probabilistic law on* $\mathcal{M}$, $A \neq \{m\}$, *and there is no probabilistic law* $A_0 \to m$ *on* $\mathcal{M}$ *such that* $A \subset A_0$ *and* $A_0 \to m$ *is not a tautology.*

Remark 4. *If an implication is a maximally specific probabilistic law on* $\mathcal{M}$ *then it is not a tautology.*

Definition 7. *Let* $\mathcal{M} = (\mathcal{K}(G, M), \rho)$ *be a probability model and* $S(\mathcal{M})$ *be the set of all maximally specific probabilistic laws on* $\mathcal{M}$. *An implication* $A \to m \in S(\mathcal{M})$ *is called the strongest probabilistic law on* $\mathcal{M}$ *if its probability value on* $\mathcal{M}$ *is maximal among all implications* $B \to m \in S(\mathcal{M})$.

We use the notation $D(\mathcal{M})$ *for the set of all strongest probabilistic laws on* $\mathcal{M}$.

Due to the the minor restrictions on the function ρ in the definition of the probability model, the existence of the maximum in the sense of Definition 7 is not guaranteed. Thus, the existence of the strongest probabilistic laws is not guaranteed either. However, we describe further in this section a way to define a probability model (based on a finite class of finite contexts), which gives a large class of models guaranteeing the existence of such implications. Note that in general for a given m, there may exist several strongest probabilistic laws of the form $A \to m$.

Informally, every implication with a defined probability on a model $(\mathcal{K}, \rho)$ can be seen as a "prediction" (wrt some measure of truth) of the fact that in a randomly chosen context $K \in \mathcal{K}$, each object having the attributes from the premise will also have the attribute from the conclusion. Similarly to Formal Concept Analysis (recall Proposition 1), implications in the method of semantic probabilistic inference are directly related to the process of grouping objects and attributes into classification units. If data are represented by a class $\mathcal{K}$ of contexts then the choice of implications wrt their probability on a model $(\mathcal{K}, \rho)$ becomes central for generating classes on the basis of the provided data. The definition of a minimal implication (as given by the set $MinImp(K)$), probabilistic law, maximally specific and the strongest probabilistic law are adopted from the corresponding definitions in [10–12, 15] to the case of FCA. Such implications have a number of useful theoretical and practical properties which justify their application:

- The set of all minimal implications which hold on every context from a class $\mathcal{K}$ gives, in some sense, an axiomatization of this class of contexts: the implicational theory of $\mathcal{K}$ (restricted to implications with non-false premises) semantically follows from it [10, 12] (the analogue of the Duquenne-Guigues theorem on implication base [4]);
- A probabilistic law excludes the possibility that an attribute in the conclusion can be "predicted" by a proper subset of the premise with probability greater than the probability of the law itself; together with the requirement of maximal specificity, this leads in practice to grouping attributes into smaller classes, with greater probability [9];
- The strongest probabilistic laws lead to assigning an attribute to a class which "predicts" it with maximal probability; at the same time, this does not rule out situations when the same attribute can belong to different classes [14];
- The **Discovery** software tool is implemented which allows to find the above mentioned types of implications on tabular data and compute the corresponding object-attribute classes; this software has proved successful in a large number of applications [5, 10, 15].

Definition 8. *Let $\mathcal{M} = (\mathcal{K}(G, M), \rho)$ be a probability model of type I. A pair of sets (A, B) is called a probabilistic concept of a context $(G, M, I) \in \mathcal{K}$ in model $\mathcal{M}$ if it satisfies the following conditions:*

- $A \subseteq G,\ B \subseteq M$,
- $f_{D(\mathcal{M})}(B) = B$,

$-\ \exists E \subseteq B\ (\bar{f}_{D(\mathcal{M})}(E) = B\ and\ E \neq \varnothing \neq E'),$

$-\ A = \bigcup\{E' \mid \varnothing \neq E \subseteq B,\ \bar{f}_{D(\mathcal{M})}(E) = B\},$

where ' is the operation in the context (G, M, I). The set A is called the extent and B the intent of the probabilistic concept (A, B).

Therefore, given a probability model $\mathcal{M} = (\mathcal{K}(G, M), \rho)$, the set of the fixed points of the operator $f_{D(\mathcal{M})}$ restricts the set of all possible probabilistic concepts of contexts from the class $\mathcal{K}$ in the model $\mathcal{M}$.

Theorem 1. *Consider a context $K = (\varnothing \neq G, M, I)$ and a probability model $\mathcal{M} = (\{K\}, \rho)$. For all non-empty subsets $A \subseteq G$ and $B \subseteq M$, the pair (A, B) is a concept in context K iff (A, B) is a probabilistic concept of context K in model $\mathcal{M}$.*

Proof. Let $S \subseteq Imp(K)$ be the set of all tautologies on M and all the implications whose premise is false on the context K. We demonstrate that $MinImp(K) \setminus S = D(\mathcal{M})$.

$\subseteq$: Consider an arbitrary implication $A \to m \in MinImp(K) \setminus S$. By the definition of $\mathcal{M}$, for each subset $S \subseteq G \times M$, we have $\rho(S) = 0$ iff $S \nsubseteq I$. As the premise A is not false on K, we conclude that the probability of $A \to m$ is defined on $\mathcal{M}$ and, by Remark 3, we obtain $\eta_{\mathcal{M}}(A \to m) = 1$. Due to minimality of A, every implication $A_0 \to m$ with $A_0 \subset A$ does not hold on K. Besides, A_0 is not false on K, since A is not false on K. It follows from Remark 3 that $\eta_{\mathcal{M}}(A_0 \to m) = 0$ and thus, $A \to m$ is a probabilistic law on $\mathcal{M}$. Since $\eta_{\mathcal{M}}(A \to m) = 1$ and $m \notin A$, we conclude that $A \to m \in D(\mathcal{M})$.

$\supseteq$: By the definition of $\mathcal{M}$, we have $\forall S \subseteq G \times M\ \rho(S) \in \{0, 1\}$, hence, for every implication $A \to m \in D(\mathcal{M})$, by the definition of a probabilistic law, we obtain $\eta_{\mathcal{M}}(A \to m) = 1$. Then, due to the definition of $\mu_{\mathcal{M}}$, the premise A is not false on K and by Remark 3 and 4, we obtain that $A \to m \in Imp(K) \setminus S$. Assume there exists an implication $A_0 \to m \in Imp(K)$ such that $A_0 \subset A$. Then $A_0 \to m \in Imp(K) \setminus S$ and $\eta_{\mathcal{M}}(A_0 \to m) = 1$, but this contradicts the condition that $A \to m$ is a probabilistic law on $\mathcal{M}$; thus, $A \to m \in MinImp(K) \setminus S$.

Let (A, B) be a probabilistic concept of context K in model $\mathcal{M}$. To show that (A, B) is a concept in context K it is sufficient to verify that $A' = B$ and $B' = A$. Consider the set $\mathcal{C} = \{E \subseteq B \mid \bar{f}_{D(\mathcal{M})}(E) = B,\ E \neq \varnothing \neq E'\}$; it is non-empty by the definition of a probabilistic concept. For each $E \in \mathcal{C}$, due to $\bar{f}_{D(\mathcal{M})}(E) = B$ and the proved above, there exists an implication $E \to B \in Imp(K)$. Then $B' \neq \varnothing$ and since $f_{D(\mathcal{M})}(B) = B$, by point 2 of Proposition 1, we obtain $B'' = B$. Moreover, it follows from $E \to B \in Imp(K)$ that for each $g \in E'$ we have $g' \supseteq B$. This means that for every $g \in \bigcup\{E' \mid E \in \mathcal{C}\} = A$, we have $g' \supseteq B$ and thus, $A \subseteq B'$. On the other hand, for each $E \in \mathcal{C}$, the condition $E \subseteq B$ yields $B' \subseteq E'$, hence, $B' \subseteq \bigcup\{E' \mid E \in \mathcal{C}\} = A$. Therefore, we have $A = B'$ which together with the condition $B'' = B$ gives $A' = B$.

Let (A, B) be a concept in context K where A and B are non-empty sets. We show that (A, B) is a probabilistic concept of context K in model $\mathcal{M}$. As

$A \neq \varnothing$, $B' = A$, we have $B' \neq \varnothing$ and since $B'' = B$, by point 2 of Proposition 1 and the proved above, we obtain $f_{D(\mathcal{M})}(B) = B$. It remains to verify that $A = \bigcup\{E' \mid E \in \mathcal{C}\}$, where $\mathcal{C} = \{E \subseteq B \mid E \neq \varnothing, \; \bar{f}_{D(\mathcal{M})}(E) = B\}$, since clearly $B \in \mathcal{C}$. We have $\bigcup\{E' \mid E \in \mathcal{C}\} \supseteq B' = A$. On the other hand, if $g \in \bigcup\{E' \mid E \in \mathcal{C}\}$ then there exists $E \in \mathcal{C}$ such that $g \in E'$ and thus, $g' \supseteq E$. As $\bar{f}_{D(\mathcal{M})}(E) = B$, we have $E \to B \in Imp(K)$, hence $g' \supseteq B$ and $g \in B' = A$. Thus, all the conditions in the definition of a probabilistic concept are fulfilled. □

Let $\mathcal{K} = \{(\varnothing \neq G, M, I_j)\}_{j \in J \neq \varnothing}$ be a finite class consisting of finite contexts. We now describe a natural way to define a probability model $(\mathcal{K}, \rho)$ on the class $\mathcal{K}$. For each context $K \in \mathcal{K}$, we set $\rho(\{K\}) = 1/|J|$ and for a subset $\mathcal{C} \subseteq \mathcal{K}$ define $\rho(\mathcal{C}) = \sum_{K \in \mathcal{C}} \rho(\{K\})$.

Then ρ is a discrete probability measure on $\mathcal{K}$ and for every $S \subseteq G \times M$, we have $\nu_{\mathcal{M}}(S) = |\tilde{J}|/|J|$, where $\tilde{J}$ is the maximal subset of J satisfying the condition $\forall j \in \tilde{J}$ $(S \subseteq I_j)$. It is easy to verify that $(\mathcal{K}, \rho)$ is indeed, a probability model. We call a model defined in this way the *frequency probability model* (of type I).

Let us illustrate the given definitions.

Example 1. *Consider the sets* $G = \{g_1, g_2\}$, $M = \{m_1, m_2, m_3\}$, *and the class* $\mathcal{K} = \{(G, M, I_j)\}_{j \in \{1,2,3\}}$ *consisting of three contexts given in the tabular form below.*

I_1	m_1	m_2	m_3		I_2	m_1	m_2	m_3		I_3	m_1	m_2	m_3
g_1	×		×		g_1		×	×		g_1	×		×
g_2		×			g_2	×	×			g_2	×	×	

Then the pairs $(\{g_1\}, \{m_1, m_2, m_3\})$ *and* $(\{g_1, g_2\}, \{m_1, m_2\})$ *are the only probabilistic concepts of the context* (G, M, I_1) *in the frequency probability model* $\mathcal{M} = (\mathcal{K}, \rho)$.

Proof. The probability measure ρ defines uniquely the value $\eta_{\mathcal{M}}(A \to m)$ for each implication $A \to m$ on the set M. In the tables below, we give the probability of each implication of the form $A \to m$ on $\mathcal{M}$ which is not a tautology.

$A \to m$	$\eta_{\mathcal{M}}(A \to m)$		$A \to m$	$\eta_{\mathcal{M}}(A \to m)$
$\{\varnothing\} \to m_1$	2/3		$m_3 \to m_2$	1/3
$m_2 \to m_1$	0		$m_1, m_3 \to m_2$	0
$m_3 \to m_1$	2/3		$\varnothing \to m_3$	0
$m_2, m_3 \to m_1$	0		$m_1 \to m_3$	0
$\{\varnothing\} \to m_2$	1/3		$m_2 \to m_3$	0
$m_1 \to m_2$	0		$m_1, m_2 \to m_3$	0

The premises of those implications which form the set $D(\mathcal{M})$ of the strongest probabilistic laws on $\mathcal{M}$ are written in parentheses. Let us give an example of computing the probability of one of the implications from the table above:

$\eta_{\mathcal{M}}(m_3 \to m_1) = \inf_{g \in G} \mu_{\mathcal{M}}(\langle g, m_3 \to m_1 \rangle) = \inf_{g \in G} \frac{\nu_{\mathcal{M}}(\{<g,m_3>,<g,m_1>\})}{\nu_{\mathcal{M}}(\{<g,m_3>\})} =$
$\frac{\nu_{\mathcal{M}}(\{<g_1,m_3>,<g_1,m_1>\})}{\nu_{\mathcal{M}}(\{<g_1,m_3>\})} = 2/3$, because the value of $\mu_{\mathcal{M}}(\langle g_2, m_3 \to m_1 \rangle)$ is undefined due to $\nu_{\mathcal{M}}(\{< g_2, m_3 >\}) = 0$. Note that the implication $m_3 \to m_1$ is
not a probabilistic law, because there exists the implication $\varnothing \to m_1$ having the
same probability on $\mathcal{M}$.

Let us give the values of the operator $f_{D(\mathcal{M})}$ on the subsets $B \subseteq M$:

$B \subseteq M$	$f_{D(\mathcal{M})}(B)$	$B \subseteq M$	$f_{D(\mathcal{M})}(B)$
m_1	m_1, m_2	m_1, m_3	m_1, m_2, m_3
m_2	m_1, m_2	m_2, m_3	m_1, m_2, m_3
m_3	m_1, m_2, m_3	m_1, m_2, m_3	m_1, m_2, m_3
m_1, m_2	m_1, m_2	$\varnothing$	m_1, m_2

Exactly two subsets $B \subseteq M$ satisfy the condition $f_{D(\mathcal{M})}(B) = B$, namely the
sets $\{m_1, m_2\}$ and $\{m_1, m_2, m_3\}$. Finally, we have:

$$\bigcup\{E' \mid \varnothing \neq E \subseteq \{m_1, m_2\}, \ \bar{f}_{D(\mathcal{M})}(E) = \{m_1, m_2\}\} = \{g_1, g_2\},$$

$$\bigcup\{E' \mid \varnothing \neq E \subseteq \{m_1, m_2, m_3\}, \ \bar{f}_{D(\mathcal{M})}(E) = \{m_1, m_2, m_3\}\} = \{g_1\}.$$

The single subset $E \subseteq \{m_1, m_2, m_3\}$ satisfying the conditions in the definition
of a probabilistic concept is the set $\{m_3\}$ for which we have $\{m_3\}' = g_1$.

Therefore, we conclude that $(\{g_1\}, \{m_1, m_2, m_3\})$ and $(\{g_1, g_2\}, \{m_1, m_2\})$ are
the only probabilistic concepts of context (G, M, I_1) in model $\mathcal{M}$.   □

4   Probabilistic Concepts on One Context

In Section 3, we have considered the notion of a probability model of type I
defined on a class of contexts. In fact, every class $\mathcal{K}$ of contexts which allows to
define a probability measure, raises a set of probability models and thus defines
possible families of the strongest probabilistic laws. Based on such implications,
we made a "prediction" of the existence of attributes for objects in an arbitrary
chosen context from class $\mathcal{K}$. Similarly to this approach, we may define the
strongest probabilistic laws on the basis of only one given context. For this, we
need only to slightly modify Definition 5 of a probability model.

Definition 9. *A probability model of type II (a probabilistic context) is a pair*
$\mathcal{M} = (K, \rho)$, *where* $K = (G, M, I)$ *is a context and* ρ *is a probability measure on*
the set G *satisfying the condition*

$$\forall \ B, C \subseteq M \ (B' \subseteq C' \Leftrightarrow \rho((B \cup C)') = \rho(B')).$$

If $B \to m$ *is an implication on the set* M *then the value of the function*

$$\eta_{\mathcal{M}}(B \to m) = \begin{cases} \frac{\rho((B \cup \{m\})')}{\rho(B')} & \text{if } \rho(B') \neq 0 \\ \text{undefined,} & \text{otherwise} \end{cases}$$

is called the probability of $B \to m$ *on the model* $\mathcal{M}$.

For brevity, in this section we call the pair (K, ρ) from the definition above the *probability model* or simply, *model* and use the notation $K(G, M)$ for a context K over the set of objects G and the set of attributes M.

For a finite context $K = (\varnothing \neq G, M, I)$, a model $\mathcal{M} = (K, \rho)$ is called a *frequency probability model* (of type II) if the function ρ is defined as $\rho(\{g\}) = 1/|G|$ for every $g \in G$ and $\rho(A) = \sum_{g \in A} \rho(\{g\})$ for each subset $A \subseteq G$. We have $\forall B \subseteq M$ $(\rho(B') = |B'|/|G|)$. Note that $\mathcal{M}$ is indeed, a model, since for all subsets $B, C \subseteq M$ it holds that $B' \subseteq C' \Leftrightarrow (B \cup C)' = B' \Leftrightarrow |(B \cup C)'| = |B'|$.

Remark 5. *If $\mathcal{M} = (K(G, M), \rho)$ is a probability model and $B \rightarrow m$ is an implication on M then $\eta_{\mathcal{M}}(B \rightarrow m) = 1$ iff $B \rightarrow m \in Imp(K)$ and $B' \neq \varnothing$ (where ' is the operation in the context K).*

Proof. If $\eta_{\mathcal{M}}(B \rightarrow m) = 1$ then $\rho(B') \neq \varnothing$ and thus $B' \neq \varnothing$, i.e. the premise B is not false on K. On the other hand, this condition means that $\rho((B \cup \{m\})') = \rho(B')$, hence, $B' \subseteq \{m\}'$ which is equivalent to $B \rightarrow m \in Imp(K)$. The same argument proves the claim in the reverse direction. □

Let us define the notions of a probabilistic law, maximally specific probabilistic law, and the strongest probabilistic law on a model of type II in full accordance with Definitions 6 and 7. In the following, we use the same notation $D(\mathcal{M})$ as in Section 3 for the set of all strongest probabilistic laws on a model $\mathcal{M}$ of type II.

Proposition 2. *Let $\mathcal{M} = (K(G, M), \rho)$ be a probability model and $S \subseteq Imp(K)$ be the set of all tautologies on M and all the implications whose premise is false on K. Then we have $MinImp(K) \setminus S \subseteq D(\mathcal{M})$.*

Proof. For each implication $B \rightarrow m \in MinImp(K) \setminus S$, it holds that $B' \neq \varnothing$, hence, by Remark 5, we obtain $\eta_{\mathcal{M}}(B \rightarrow m) = 1$. The condition of maximal probability for $B \rightarrow m$ is satisfied and obviously, there can not exist a probabilistic law $B_1 \rightarrow m$ on $\mathcal{M}$ with $B \subset B_1$. Besides, the implication $B \rightarrow m$ is itself a probabilistic law, because, by the condition $B \rightarrow m \in MinImp(K) \setminus S$ and Remark 5, for every subset $B_0 \subset B$ we have $\eta_{\mathcal{M}}(B_0 \rightarrow m) < 1$. Thus, all the conditions in the definition of the strongest probabilistic law are satisfied and $B \rightarrow m \in D(\mathcal{M})$. □

Definition 10. *Let $\mathcal{M} = (K(G, M), \rho)$ be a probability model of type II. A pair of sets (A, B) is called a probabilistic concept in model $\mathcal{M}$ (a concept in probabilistic context $\mathcal{M}$) if it satisfies the conditions of Definition 8.*

Let $\mathcal{M} = (K, \rho)$ be a model with $K = (G, M, I)$. Consider the context $\overline{K} = (G, M, \overline{I})$, where $\overline{I} = \{< g, m > \mid g \in G, \ m \in \bar{f}_{D(\mathcal{M})}(g')\}$, ' is the operation in the context K. In other words, we have $I \subseteq \overline{I}$ and the relation $\overline{I}$ is obtained from I by adding the pairs $< g, m >$ "predicted" by the implications in $D(\mathcal{M})$. To clarify the connection between the concepts in context K and probabilistic concepts in model $\mathcal{M}$, we need to note that *the following statement is false in both directions:*

for all non-empty subsets $A \subseteq G$ and $B \subseteq M$, the pair (A, B) is a probabilistic concept in the model $\mathcal{M}$ iff (A, B) is a concept in the context $\overline{K}$.

To prove this, it is sufficient to consider any of the contexts $K_1 = (\{g_1, g_2\}, \{m_1\}, I_1)$, $K_2 = (\{g_1, g_2\}, \{m_1, m_2, m_3\}, I_2)$ given below together with the corresponding frequency probability models $\mathcal{M}_1 = (K_1, \rho_1)$ and $\mathcal{M}_2 = (K_2, \rho_2)$.

I_1	m_1
g_1	$\times$
g_2	

I_2	m_1	m_2	m_3
g_1	$\times$		
g_2		$\times$	$\times$

For these models, we have $D(\mathcal{M}_1) = \{\varnothing \to m_1\}$ and $D(\mathcal{M}_2) = \{\varnothing \to m_1, \{m_2\} \to m_3, \{m_3\} \to m_2\}$. Therefore, the set of all probabilistic concepts in the model $\mathcal{M}_1$ consists of the single concept $(\{g_1\}, \{m_1\})$ and the set $\{ (\{g_1\}, \{m_1\}), (\{g_2\}, \{m_1, m_2, m_3\}) \}$ represents all the probabilistic concepts in the model $\mathcal{M}_2$.

It is easy to check that for every $j = 1, 2$, the context $\overline{K}_j$ is obtained from K_j by setting $\bar{I}_j = I_j \cup \{< g_2, m_1 >\}$. It remains to note that the set of all concepts in the context $\overline{K}_1$ consists of the single pair $(\{g_1, g_2\}, \{m_1\})$ and the set $\{ (\{g_1, g_2\}, \{m_1\}), (\{g_2\}, \{m_1, m_2, m_3\}) \}$ represents all the concepts in the context $\overline{K}_2$.

Nevertheless, the following property is guaranteed which characterizes the connection between concepts in a context K and probabilistic concepts in a model $\mathcal{M} = (K, \rho)$.

Theorem 2. *Every probability model $\mathcal{M} = (K(G, M), \rho)$ has the following properties:*

1. *for each concept (A, B) in context K with $A \neq \varnothing \neq B$, there exists a probabilistic concept (A_1, B_1) in model $\mathcal{M}$ such that $A \subseteq A_1$ and $B \subseteq B_1$;*
2. *if (A_1, B_1) is a probabilistic concept in model $\mathcal{M}$ then there exists a concept (A, B) in context K with $\varnothing \neq A \subseteq A_1$ and $\varnothing \neq B \subseteq B_1$. Moreover, the set A_1 is the union of the extents of some of these concepts.*

Proof. 1. Let $S \subseteq Imp(K)$ be the set of all tautologies on M and all the implications whose premise is false on K. As (A, B) is a concept in context K, we have $B'' = B$, $B' = A \neq \varnothing$ and by Proposition 1, we obtain $f_{MinImp(K) \backslash S}(B) = B$.

By Proposition 2, the following inclusion holds: $MinImp(K) \backslash S \subseteq D(\mathcal{M})$. Besides, for all families L_1 and L_2 of implications on M and any subset $B \subseteq M$, if $L_1 \subseteq L_2$ then $\bar{f}_{L_1}(B) \subseteq \bar{f}_{L_2}(B)$; therefore, we have $B \subseteq \bar{f}_{D(\mathcal{M})}(B)$. Denote $B_1 = \bar{f}_{D(\mathcal{M})}(B)$, $\mathcal{C} = \{E \subseteq B_1 \mid \bar{f}_{D(\mathcal{M})}(E) = B_1, E \neq \varnothing \neq E'\}$, and $A_1 = \cup\{E' \mid E \in \mathcal{C}\}$. Then obviously, $\bar{f}_{D(\mathcal{M})}(B_1) = B_1$. Note that $B \in \mathcal{C}$, $A = B'$, and $B' \subseteq A_1$, thus, we have $A \subseteq A_1$ and (A_1, B_1) is the required probabilistic concept in $\mathcal{M}$.

2. Consider the set $\mathcal{C} = \{E \subseteq B_1 \mid \bar{f}_{D(\mathcal{M})}(E) = B_1, E \neq \varnothing \neq E'\}$ and an arbitrary $E \in \mathcal{C}$. We have $MinImp(K) \backslash S \subseteq D(\mathcal{M})$, so $\bar{f}_{MinImp(K) \backslash S}(E) \subseteq B_1$. Denote $B = \bar{f}_{MinImp(K) \backslash S}(E)$; then clearly, $\bar{f}_{MinImp(K) \backslash S}(B) = B$. Besides,

it follows from $E \neq \varnothing \neq E'$ that $B \neq \varnothing \neq B'$, hence, by Proposition 1, we obtain $B'' = B$. On the other hand, we have $E \subseteq B$, thus, $E' \supseteq B'$ and $A_1 = \cup\{E' \mid E \in \mathcal{C}\} \supseteq B'$. We conclude that (B', B) is the required concept in context K.

Note that the condition $B = \bar{f}_{MinImp(K)\backslash S}(E)$ yields $E \rightarrow B \in Imp(K)$ which is equivalent to $E' \subseteq B'$; therefore, we obtain $E' = B'$. Because of the arbitrary selection of the set $E \in \mathcal{C}$ and the condition $A_1 = \cup\{E' \mid E \in \mathcal{C}\}$, we conclude that A_1 is the union of the extents of some concepts (A, B) in context K with $\varnothing \neq B \subseteq B_1$. $\square$

Below, we give schemas of computation procedures for finding the set of probabilistic laws and probabilistic concepts on a given frequency probability model $\mathcal{M} = (K, \rho)$, where $K = (G, M, I)$ and $\forall m \in M$ $(\{m\}' \neq \varnothing)$.

Let $S \subseteq Imp(K)$ be the set of all tautologies on M and all the implications whose premise is false on the context K. For the given context K, the cardinality of $MinImp(K)\backslash S$ can be exponential in the value of $|G| \times |M|$. This follows from Theorem 1 in [6], where the construction of the corresponding context is given. By Proposition 2, we have $MinImp(K) \setminus S \subseteq D(\mathcal{M})$ and by definition, the set of all probabilistic laws on $\mathcal{M}$ contains $D(\mathcal{M})$. For this reason, the procedure for finding the set of probabilistic laws is based on a heuristic.

Let us introduce some auxiliary definitions. For an implication $A \rightarrow m$ on a set M, the *length* of $A \rightarrow m$ is the cardinality of the set A; we use the notation $len(A \rightarrow m)$. Call an implication $A_2 \rightarrow m$ a *specification* of an implication $A_1 \rightarrow m$ if $A_2 = A_1 \cup \{n\}$, where $n \in M \setminus A_1$. For a family L of implications, $Spec(L)$ will denote the set of all possible specifications of implications from L.

The computation procedure for finding probabilistic laws is based on the concepts of the semantic probabilistic inference. The main idea is to extend stepwise the premises of implications and check the conditions in the definition of a probabilistic law at each step. This implements a directed enumeration of implications which allows to considerably reduce the search space. The reduction is achieved due to the application of the following heuristic: when the length of the generated implications reaches a certain value (called the *base enumeration depth*), the specification is applied only to those implications which are probabilistic laws.

For simplicity, we give a schema of the computation procedure for finding probabilistic laws of the form $A \rightarrow m$ on the model $\mathcal{M}$ for a chosen attribute $m \in M$. Besides the mentioned probability model $\mathcal{M}$ and the element $m \in M$, the additional input parameter of the procedure is the value d of the base enumeration depth, with $1 \leqslant d \leqslant |M|$. The output of the procedure is the set of the probabilistic laws found on the model $\mathcal{M}$ with the element m in the conclusion.

At step $k = 0$, the set $imp(\mathcal{M})_{(k)}$ of implications is generated which consists of the single implication of zero length of the form $R = \varnothing \rightarrow m$. For the implication R, the conditions on a probabilistic law in the Definition 6 are verified. Denote the set of all probabilistic laws computed at step k of the computation procedure by $REG_{\mathcal{M}}^{(k)}(m)$. If R is a probabilistic law then $REG_{\mathcal{M}}^{(0)}(m) = \{R\}$. Else, we have $REG_{\mathcal{M}}^{(0)}(m) = \varnothing$ and the procedure returns the empty set. Indeed, in this case we have $\eta_{\mathcal{M}}(\varnothing \to m) = 0$ and, by the definition of the model $\mathcal{M}$, the probability of each implication of the form $B \to m$ is either undefined, or equals zero on $\mathcal{M}$. This means that no such implication can be a probabilistic law on $\mathcal{M}$.

At step $1 \leqslant k \leqslant d$, the set $imp(\mathcal{M})_{(k)}$ of specifications is computed for all implications obtained at the previous step whose probability is defined and not equal to zero or one: $imp(\mathcal{M})_{(k)} = Spec(\{R \mid R \in imp(\mathcal{M})_{(k-1)}, \ 0 < \eta_{\mathcal{M}}(R) < 1\})$. Each implication in this set is of length k. For every implication from $imp(\mathcal{M})_{(k)}$ the conditions in the definition of a probabilistic law are verified and thus the set $REG_{\mathcal{M}}^{(k)}(m)$ is formed.

At step $d < k \leqslant |M|$, the set $imp(\mathcal{M})_{(k)}$ of specifications is computed for all implications obtained at the previous step having a probability less than 1: $imp(\mathcal{M})_{(k)} = Spec(\{R \mid R \in REG_{\mathcal{M}}^{(k-1)}(m), \ \eta_{\mathcal{M}}(R) < 1\})$. For each of the obtained implications the conditions in the definition of a probabilistic law are verified and thus the set $REG_{\mathcal{M}}^{(k)}(m)$ is formed. The execution of the computation procedure ends either on the step $k = |M|$, or in case at some step $d < k < |M|$ no probabilistic laws are obtained, i.e. when $REG_{\mathcal{M}}^{(k)}(m) = \varnothing$. The resulting set of the probabilistic laws for the attribute m returned by the procedure is the union $\bigcup_k REG_{\mathcal{M}}^{(k)}(m)$.

To select the strongest (wrt the input parameters) probabilistic laws from the set of the computed implications, it suffices to directly verify the conditions of Definition 7.

The steps $k \leqslant d$ of the procedure are called base enumeration steps and those for $k > d$ are called additional enumeration steps. As proved by experiments, the base enumeration depth of value $d \leqslant 3$ suffices in a large number of applications. In practice, the inequalities in Definition 6 are verified with respect to a statistical criterion (e.g., Fisher's exact test for contingency tables) which is applied with a user defined confidence level α.

Let L be a non-empty set of probabilistic laws on the model $\mathcal{M}$. Note that in case L is the output of the above given procedure for base enumeration depth $d = |M|$, we have $L = D(\mathcal{M})$.

Let us describe an iterative procedure for finding probabilistic concepts in model $\mathcal{M}$ with respect to the family L of implications.

At step $k = 1$ the following set is generated: $C^{(1)} = \{\bar{f}_L(A \cup \{m\}) \mid A \to m \in L\}$.

At step $k > 1$, in case $C^{(k-1)} = \varnothing$, the procedure returns the list of all the computed probabilistic concepts. Otherwise, for each $B \in C^{(k-1)}$, having the family of implications $L_B = \{A \to m \in L \mid A \subseteq B\}$, the set $A = \{g \in G \mid g' \cap B \neq \varnothing, \ f_{L_B}(g' \cap B) = B\}$ is computed. If $A \neq \varnothing$ then the pair (A, B) is added to the list of the computed probabilistic concepts. Further, the set

$C^{(k)} = \{\bar{f}_L(B \cup C) \mid B, C \in C^{(k-1)}, \ \bar{f}_L(B \cup C) \notin C^{(k-1)}\}$ is generated and the next iteration is executed. The description of the procedure is complete.

Example 2. Consider the contexts K_1 and K_2 given in Figure 1. The concepts in context K_1 having a non-empty extent and intent are the pairs $(\{g_1, \ldots, g_{20}\}, \{m_1, \ldots, m_5\})$ and $(\{g_{21}, \ldots, g_{40}\}, \{m_6, \ldots, m_{10}\})$. The context K_2 was obtained from K_1 by adding a random noise. The task was to recover the initial concepts in context K_2. With the given algorithms, the set of the strongest probabilistic laws on the frequency model $\mathcal{M} = (K_2, \rho)$ was computed; it consisted of 22 implications. The set of probabilistic concepts in model $\mathcal{M}$ turned out to be equal to the set of concepts in the initial context K_1 with non-empty extents and intents.

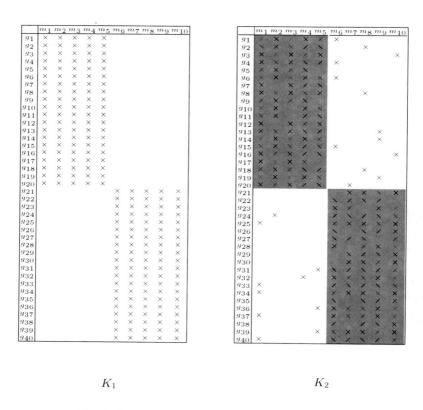

K_1 K_2

Fig. 1. Recovering concepts in the presence of noise

5   Conclusions

It easy to note from Definition 5 and 9 that the distinction between the probability model of type I and II is rather subtle. In particular, for each model $\mathcal{M}_2 = (K, \rho_2)$ of type II with $K = (\varnothing \neq G, M, I)$, it is possible to define a model $\mathcal{M}_1 = (\mathcal{K}, \rho_1)$ of type I such that $D(\mathcal{M}_1) = D(\mathcal{M}_2)$. It suffices to set $\mathcal{K} = \{K_g \mid g \in G,\ K_g = (\{h\}, M, I_g),\ I_g = \{< h, m > \mid < g, m > \in I\}\}$ and define $\forall\ \mathcal{C} \subseteq \mathcal{K}\ \rho_1(\mathcal{C}) = \rho_2(\{g \mid K_g \in \mathcal{C}\})$. Then for every implication $B \to m$ on M, we have $\eta_{\mathcal{M}_1}(B \to m) = \mu_{\mathcal{M}_1}(\langle h, B \to m \rangle) = \frac{\rho_1(\{K_g \mid \{<h,n>\mid n \in B \cup \{m\}\} \subseteq I_g\})}{\rho_1(\{K_g \mid \{<h,n>\mid n \in B\} \subseteq I_g\})} = \frac{\rho_2((B \cup \{m\})')}{\rho_2(B')}$ and thus $\eta_{\mathcal{M}_1}(B \to m) = \eta_{\mathcal{M}_2}(B \to m)$ which clearly, yields $D(\mathcal{M}_1) = D(\mathcal{M}_2)$. However, it is important in practice to make a distinction between the analysis of data represented by a class of contexts and analysis of data on the basis of a single given context. In the first case, we have a problem of classification of objects which are observed in a number of experiments in which every object is assigned a certain set of attributes. In the second case, the classification of objects is based on a single context which represents the whole body of experimental data on these objects. A context uniquely determines whether an object has a particular attribute and Formal Concept Analysis provides tools for building precise classification of objects on the basis of a given context. On the other hand, discovering probabilistic laws on a model over a given context allows to obtain classification units which are stable with respect to noise.

Example 2 demonstrates that the noise of a certain level does not change the set of concepts in a context, i.e. the set of concepts with a non-empty extent and intent in a given context is equal to the set of probabilistic concepts in a new context obtained by adding noise into the initial one. There exist types of noise (a formal definition is given in [10]) such that any level of a noise of this kind does not change the set of concepts in a context; such noise is called *concept preserving* [10]. This raises the problem of characterization of these types of noise.

In the definitions of implications and probabilistic laws in this paper, the notion of negation was not present. Due to this, the formulation of Theorem 2 appeared to be weaker than expected. This is because the negation was not present in the fundamentals of Formal Concept Analysis and we aimed at giving the most simple generalization of the basic notions of this method. The generalization of FCA according to the given ideas will allow to formalize the notions of "natural classification" and "idealization" as defined in [10, 13]. The semantic probabilistic inference which is central in the definitions of probabilistic concepts has been first introduced for first order logic and provides a method for discovering rather complicated regularities on data in comparison to those considered in this paper. Moreover, in the relational approach described in monographs [5, 10], it is argued that the formalization of regularities in the language of first order logic is essential for analyzing the whole body of information contained in data. Some examples of such regularities are given at the Web page [15] at http://math.nsc.ru/AP/ScientificDiscovery/pages/Examples_of_rules.html

References

1. Deogun, J., Jiang, L., Xie, Y., Raghavan, V.: Probability Logic Modeling of Knowledge Discovery in Databases. In: Zhong, N., Raś, Z.W., Tsumoto, S., Suzuki. (eds.) ISMIS 2003. LNCS (LNAI), vol. 2871, pp. 402–407. Springer, Hei (2003)

2. Ganter, B., Wille, R.: Formal Concept Analysis: Mathematical Foundations. Springer, Heidelberg (1999)
3. Ganter, B., Stumme, G., Wille, R. (eds.): Formal Concept Analysis: Foundations and Applications. Springer, Heidelberg (2005)
4. Guigues, J.– L., Duquenne, V.: Families minimales d'implications informatives resultant d'un tableau de données binaires. Math. Sci. Humaines 95, 5–18 (1986)
5. Kovalerchuk, B., Vityaev, E.: Data Mining in Finance: Advances in Relational and Hybrid methods. Kluwer (2000)
6. Kuznetsov, S.: On the intractability of computing the Duquenne–Guigues base. J. UCS 10(8), 927–933 (2004)
7. Kuznetsov, S., Obiedkov, S.: Comparing performance of algorithms for generating concept lattices. J. Exp. Theor. Artif. Intell. 14(2-3), 189–216 (2002)
8. van der Merwe, D., Obiedkov, S., Kourie, D.: AddIntent: A New Incremental Algorithm for Constructing Concept Lattices. In: Eklund, P. (ed.) ICFCA 2004. LNCS (LNAI), vol. 2961, pp. 372–385. Springer, Heidelberg (2004)
9. Smerdov, S., Vityaev, E.: Synthesis of logic, probability, and learning: Formalizing the concept of prediction. Siberian Electronic Mathematical Reports 6, 340–365 (2009) (in Russian, with english abstract)
10. Vityaev, E.: Knowledge Discovery. Computational Cognition. Models of Cognitive Processes, p. 293. Novosibirsk State University (2006) (in Russian)
11. Vityaev, E.: The logic of prediction. In: Proc. 9th Asian Logic Conference, pp. 263–276 (2006)
12. Vityaev, E., Kovalerchuk, B.: Empirical theories discovery based on the Measurement Theory. Mind and Machine 14(4), 551–573 (2005)
13. Vityaev, E., Lapardin, K., Khomicheva, I., Proskura, A.: Transcription factor binding site recognition by regularity matrices based on the natural classification method. Intelligent Data Analysis 12(5), 495–512 (2008); Vityaev, E., Kolchanov, N. (eds.) Special Issue New Methods in Bioinformatics
14. Vityaev, E., Smerdov, S.: New definition of prediction without logical inference. In: Kovalerchuk, B. (ed.) Proc. IASTED Int. Conf. on Computational Intelligence (CI 2009), pp. 48–54 (2009)
15. Scientific Discovery website, http://math.nsc.ru/AP/ScientificDiscovery/

Author Index